The Censorship of British Drama 1900–1968

Volume Two: 1933–1952

The Censorship of British Drama 1900–1968 is based on a systematic exploration of the Lord Chamberlain's correspondence archives, which contain files for every play submitted for a public performance licence in Great Britain. In three volumes, it examines both plays that were banned, and the far greater number that were significantly cut or altered. Steve Nicholson also makes substantial use of the Royal Archives at Windsor to provide new insight into the debates that went on within and beyond the Lord Chamberlain's Office.

This second volume focuses primarily on political and moral censorship, documenting and analysing the control exercised by the Lord Chamberlain. It also reviews the pressures exerted on him and on the theatre by the government, the monarch, the Church, foreign embassies and by influential public figures and organisations.

Among the topics covered are: the ban on criticising the Nazis or portraying Hitler; restrictions on anti-war drama; controlling nudity and strip shows in wartime reviews; comedians and innuendo; youth violence and the shock of realism on the postwar stage; the perceived threat to society from 'sexual perversion'; the campaigns of the Public Morality Council.

Volume Three will cover the period 1953–1968, beginning at the dawn of the Conservative fifties, and will examine how censorship affected the work of Genet, Beckett and the controversial new wave of British playwrights.

Exeter Performance Studies

Exeter Performance Studies aims to publish the best new scholarship from a variety of sources, presenting established authors alongside innovative work from new scholars. The list explores critically the relationship between theatre and history, relating performance studies to broader political, social and cultural contexts. It also includes titles which offer access to previously unavailable material.

Series editors: Peter Thomson, Professor of Drama at the University of Exeter; Graham Ley, Reader in Drama and Theory at the University of Exeter; Steve Nicholson, Reader in Twentieth-Century Drama at the University of Sheffield.

Also published by University of Exeter Press

The Censorship of British Drama
1900–1968

Volume Two: 1933–1952

Steve Nicholson

UNIVERSITY
of
EXETER
PRESS

For Katya and Vikka
Thanks for finding such good uses for all the drafts.

First published in 2005 by
University of Exeter Press
Reed Hall, Streatham Drive
Exeter EX4 4QR
UK
www.exeterpress.co.uk

British Library Cataloguing in Publication Data
A catalogue record for this book is available
from the British Library.

ISBN 0 85989 697 8

Typeset in 10.5pt Aldine
by JCS Publishing Services

Printed in Great Britain by Antony Rowe Ltd, Chippenham

Contents

Acknowledgements

I would like to thank the following for their support, assistance and contributions to the research and the writing of this book: The Arts and Humanities Research Board, whose funding was crucial in allowing me the time to complete this book; the Society for Theatre Research and the University of Huddersfield, both of whom also made generous grants to assist the process of research; Kathryn Johnson, Curator of Modern Drama at the British Library, and an expert at navigating the Lord Chamberlain's archives; staff in the Manuscript Room of the British Library and the Study Room of the Theatre Museum; Queen Elizabeth II for granting me permission to read and make use of material in the Royal Archive at Windsor; staff in the Royal Archive, especially the Registrar, Miss Pamela Clark; Peter Ettridge, Nick Taylor and Clare Walters for transcribing and checking material; University of Exeter Press and its Editorial Board, especially Anna Henderson, Simon Baker, Peter Thomson and Graham Ley; and to all who have continued to offer their support—financial, emotional, intellectual, or any combination of the above. Especially Heather.

'The Most Dispensable of All the Fetters'

If it is unfair to the writers that is not our business
(Lord Chamberlain's Reader, 1934)

After we have finished with it the author would not wish to go on
(Lord Chamberlain's Reader, December 1938)[1]

I suppose it was tempting fate to joke, in my preface to the first volume of this study of the Lord Chamberlain and theatre censorship between 1900 and 1968, that I would need to write six books to tell the story fully. Now I see that my 'six' might have read 'twelve', for this second volume will reach only as far as 1952, and a third volume will be required to take the story through to the final death throes of the system.

One of the factors which has made it necessary to revise and extend the project has been the discovery of a further dimension of material, which is currently contained within the Royal Archive at Windsor Castle. With the probable exception of the former Assistant Comptroller to the Lord Chamberlain, John Johnston, whose book on censorship was an important but hardly an adequate account,[2] no-one else who has written about the subject has had access to this material; just as no-one had previously looked at the fifty thousand or so files on individual plays in the Manuscript Room of the British Library.

Broadly speaking, the Windsor archive contains material which is *not* specifically or primarily related to individual plays. A few more or less randomly chosen file titles give some sense of the range of topics covered: 'Enquiries and Comments by Sir Ian Malcolm Regarding Principles of Censorship to be Observed in Advising the Lord Chamberlain'; . . . 'Press Announcement re Necessity for Giving a Complete Description of a Performance Including Acts in Which there is No Spoken Dialogue, and a Clear Description of the Action, "Business", or Dress'; . . . 'Letter from Public Morality Council, with Reports of their Stage Plays Committee, and Lord Clarendon's Reply, Giving Aspects and Principles of the Censorship'; . . . 'Correspondence with Mr George Black on question of interpolation, in Plays or Revues, of Gags or Business not Previously Approved by the Lord Chamberlain'; . . . 'Mr Cain Complains of Obstruction Caused by playing National Anthem in Theatres and Cinemas'; . . . 'Mr Oteifi Chief Egyptian Censor Interviewed By Assistant Comptroller'; . . . 'Correspondence with Theatrical Managers' Association re. Proposed Production, at Cambridge, of Seventeenth Century Play *'Tis Pity She's A Whore*'; . . . 'Attachment of a Yiddish Playreader'; . . . 'Confidential Correspondence With Public Control Department, LCC, re. Appearance of Max Miller at an Entertainment at Windsor Castle'; . . . 'As to Wearing of Human Bones on the Stage'. Once I had been given permission to consult the archive, such files were plainly not to be ignored. Indeed, information which came to light is integral to almost every paragraph of this book; if the British Library archive of files on individual plays represents a goldmine for the researcher, then these are perhaps the diamonds.

As with the extensive 'Correspondence Files' at the British Library, those in the Royal Archive typically contain letters, minutes of meetings, memoranda, notes, statements, cuttings and other documentation. As some of the titles cited above promise, it is often in these files that the evolving policies and strategies (and the arguments about them) are most clearly made manifest: in the detailed records of conferences called by the Lord Chamberlain to hammer out principles with representatives of government and the theatre industry; or meetings with the licensing wing of the London County Council intended to forge common approaches to dealing with nudity; or of showdowns with individual managers who were not playing the game in the way the Lord Chamberlain wanted it to be played. The issues are also shown in the notes made by the Lord Chamberlain's secretary for his annual lecture on theatre censorship to trainees in the Scottish Police College in West Lothian ('Censorship before production from MSS and largely based on impression . . . Individual and changing interpretation of text possible at every performance', he observed; 'Considerable possibility of evasion of rulings');[3] or in the courteous and detailed response to a senior law lecturer at Manchester University carrying out research into licensing practices ('I am naturally anxious to give anyone in your high position in the academic world as full an answer as I can . . . You will understand, however, that to an ordinary enquirer I should feel unable to answer many of the questions so fully, or indeed at all');[4] or in the bulging files which document the two occasions in 1946 and 1951— occasions about which we previously knew nothing—when the Lord Chamberlain sought the advice of a number of 'wise and responsible men and women' as to whether he should relax his policy in relation to one of the most contentious issues of all:

I am under heavy pressure from some shades of public opinion to lift the ban upon plays in which reference to homosexuality and Lesbianism occur ... it would be a great help to me if you could give me briefly and in confidence the answer to the following question: In your view, am I any longer justified in withholding permission for these two subjects to be mentioned on the stage?[5]

Not only the Lord Chamberlain's letter but all of the replies are preserved, and a revealing and enthralling set of documents they make.[6]

Yet not for a minute should it be thought that the significance of the material in the Royal Archive in any way lessens the importance of the 900 or so files per year which centred on individual plays. It is here that we see the Lord Chamberlain and his staff at the coalface, cutting words or lines or gestures or costumes, negotiating with managers and playwrights, disagreeing with each other. Moreover, the distinction between the content of the two archives is far from absolute; on the one hand it frequently occurs that a report or a letter which begins by responding to a specific text broadens rapidly into matters of general principle. And on the other, what may begin as a general discussion of principle necessarily finds itself citing specific texts as exemplars. Did I say twelve volumes? Actually, one could very easily write a volume for every year.

One of the possible objections to tracking the practice of theatre censorship in the relative detail I have mapped is that it might tell us more than we need to know. In other words, I may simply be piling up examples which duplicate each other, and a more effective approach would content itself with fewer examples from which firm and general policies could be easily and succinctly extrapolated. Maybe the reader of this work will be able to do that better than I have. But it is not for want of trying that I have found myself generally struggling to identify and articulate sets of rules or consistent practices—or that when I have done so they are invariably tentative and hedged with exceptions, reservations and doubts. Every individual play, to a greater or lesser extent, challenged or stretched the censorship because of the gap between the actual and the theoretical—between a specific text and a (more or less) agreed but usually unwritten policy. Nor were the Lord Chamberlain and his staff always of one mind; and though in the end decisions were the responsibility of the Lord Chamberlain alone, he was not expert or certain or devoted enough to be impervious to arguments and claims put to him by his Readers or advisers. In my reading of the evidence, then, it is extremely hard—and becomes a futile exercise—to discover anything approximating to absolute consistency, or, to be more accurate, to find consistency in relation to scripts that were actually written and submitted for licence. There certainly were rigid and fixed principles which could never have been violated, but these operate at the level of unseen ideology, undiscussed and invisible. It is surely unthinkable, for example, that during the period covered by this book one might find the Office having to deal with a play that advocated equal rights for homosexuals, or attacked institutions such as the Church or the monarchy. These were absolute taboos, and no playwright or manager would have wasted time trying to breach them. But the interest lies in the gaps and the hints and the subtexts.

It is only rarely that a play is submitted which is unequivocally seen by the Lord Chamberlain and his Readers as utterly and irredeemably beyond the pale, incapable of ever achieving a licence. Where we have to look is in the constant clash between principles (which were themselves constantly shifting) and individual texts. No two plays or characters or lines could ever be the same as each other—even if they had been, then the political or moral or aesthetic or historical or even geographical context was different. To be sure, the Office was forever endeavouring to compare texts with each other and to think in terms of precedents, but the links were never firm and the situation and pressures never precisely the same. In any case, rather than replicating a decision made last year or last month or last week on a 'similar' play, the Office might be trying to learn from experience and do the opposite. Moreover, even to say that the Office might choose to treat two similar plays quite differently begs the enormous issue of what we might mean—or what the Office might have meant—by 'similar plays'; are we talking about plot and content? Language? Form? Characters? 'Message'? In practice, then, even what might appear—and might sometimes have been claimed—as absolute bans, never really were. Homosexuality could be listed but it couldn't be so easily defined or its presence agreed upon. Certainly you could prevent anyone called 'God' or 'Queen Victoria' or 'Hitler' from appearing on the stage, but that does not necessarily prevent audiences from seeing them there. Much oil was burnt in the Lord Chamberlain's Office (and elsewhere) trying to agree even on a definition of nudity: something which one might have thought would have been relatively unambiguous and stable. What chance, then, that more obviously nebulous concepts could be tied down firmly even within (let alone beyond) St James's Palace? As we well know, theatrical communication is so fundamentally elusive, and the interpretations which occur to audiences derive from so much more than a bare text (even if one includes stage and costume and gestural directions as part of that text) that a system which carries out its censorship before a single performance occurs could never know what was going to be visible in the theatre. The Lord Chamberlain and his staff were not fools—they knew this. Performances— even texts—leaked meanings, and however hard they tried to anticipate them and patch them up, new holes were always appearing. Back in 1918, one of the Lord Chamberlain's advisers had noted: 'I have heard of a comic actor who said he could recite Mary had a Little Lamb in such a way as to make it a monument of obscenity . . . I do not doubt it'.[7]

The Office itself frequently espoused the fact that 'every play is judged according to its merits', and that the Lord Chamberlain 'avoids as far as possible any predetermined code of hard and fast rules'. And this was almost inevitably true. As they told Mr Street, the Manchester law lecturer, in 1952, the key criteria were 'method of treatment and sincerity of object, rather than choice of subject'. This effectively acknowledged that censorship was primarily a matter of interpretation rather than absolutes. The Comptroller went on to inform Mr Street that although the Lord Chamberlain would never 'prejudge' a play, there were four 'themes' on which he had 'not known him pass one'; these were 'The physical appearance of the Deity on the Stage', 'Representation of the Royal Family' (which by this time meant that 'No Member of the Royal Family living after the death of Queen Victoria is permitted to be depicted'); 'Unnatural Vice', here defined—perhaps strangely—as 'pederasty and Lesbianism'; and 'Representations of Living Persons, or those recently dead'. He then concluded: 'None of these prohibitions is necessarily immutable, and they will probably be modified if contemporary conditions ever make this desirable'.[8] I make no apologies, then, for three volumes and the wealth of examples; that is where the riches and the story lie, and that is where we have to go.

In September 1939—a date not insignificant in British and European history of the twentieth century—an article in *New Theatre* described the Lord Chamberlain as 'the most dispensable of all the fetters on theatre art'.[9] He was not dispensed with, however. In three sections covering the pre-war period, the war years themselves, and the immediate post-war period, this book explores the continuing struggles to redefine or remove his absolute authority, and, by detailed reference to extensive examples, to look at the effect of censorship on the development of British theatre over twenty years. We begin with the last third of Lord Cromer's reign as the incumbent of St James's Palace, with Britain and Europe increasingly threatened with destruction and meltdown, and end on the eve of the coronation which ushered in a new Elizabethan England, as Cromer's successor, the Earl of Clarendon, completes his own fourteen-year reign.

Following the general pattern of Volume One, the three chronological sections are divided into eleven thematically based chapters. In practice, however, it is impossible to be either chronologically or thematically tight, since incidents and debates related to individual plays may recur and extend over years and decades. Within each of the three sections I have attempted to divide the focus of separate chapters into broadly political and broadly moral issues, but these are never discrete; in a world familiar with both the concept of sexual politics and immoral politicians, it goes without saying that these are somewhat spurious divisions. Yet they are ones that the Lord Chamberlain's Office and the period recognised, largely without question, and it therefore seems a more appropriate framework than any other I have been able to construct. In Section One, then, the first chapter is devoted entirely to issues surrounding the portrayal of the Nazis and fascism on the British stage in the thirties. The second chapter focuses on moral and sexual issues, but matters relating to what was habitually labelled 'perversion'—which in the parlance of St James's Palace (and, doubtless, beyond) meant homosexuality and incest—are looked at separately in Chapter Three. The final chapter dealing with the pre-war years concentrates on plays engaging with political issues other than the Nazis. In the second section, the heart of Chapter Five is wartime censorship on political grounds, while Chapter Six deals specifically with issues of nudity and the body, and Chapter Seven with other moral concerns. In the final section, Chapter Eight traces the campaigns and the battles fought over censorship in the changing cultural and historical climate of the post-war years, with the 1949 cross-party parliamentary bill which aimed to repeal the Theatres Act as the focal point. Chapter Nine returns to issues of morality in the changing(?) and 'brave new world' established after 1945, Chapter Ten centres on the arguments over whether to lift the ban on the depiction of homosexuality, and Chapter Eleven on dramas engaging with national and international political events.

The fact that the structures within the three sections are broadly similar without being completely formulaic reflects the need to follow where the most important and fiercely contested sites of struggle seemed to occur at different times. Yet I have doubtless excluded material which is deserving of future attention, and which others might see as more significant than some of what I have chosen to include. On another day, I might, like the Lord Chamberlain, have called it differently myself.

SECTION ONE
1933–1939

CHAPTER ONE

'Verboten'

The Nazis Onstage

It is not easy to go on shielding the Germans from their misdeeds being
depicted on the stage in this country.
(The Lord Chamberlain to the Foreign Office, November 1934)[1]

In April 1934, *New Statesman and Nation* published an article by the critic
and playwright Hubert Griffith, provocatively entitled 'The Censor as Nazi
Apologist?'[2] It centred on the recent refusal to license an English translation
of *Die Rassen*, a drama written by the Austrian playwright Theodor Tagger
under his pseudonym of Ferdinand Brückner, and first performed in
Zurich the previous November. Griffith refers to the English version
under the title *Races*, though, possibly to disguise its political content, it had
been submitted to the Lord Chamberlain with what his Reader described as
the 'ironical' title of *Heroes*.[3] The story centred on a female Jewish student
forced to flee the country and abandon her Aryan lover, who is himself
attacked by his Nazi friends for associating with her. Griffith insisted that
the tone was 'moderate' and that any propaganda was 'unspoken and only
implied'. Indeed, he claimed that a Nazi official witnessing a performance
in Switzerland had admitted that 'there was nothing untrue about it, and
that it represented what Jews in German universities had got to expect'.
Griffith told his readers that the official reason given for refusing to license
Heroes was that two other anti-Nazi plays had already been turned down
and that the censorship was bound to be consistent, and he accused Lord
Cromer of being 'more sensitive to the susceptibilities of the German
Embassy than he has any reasonable right to be'.[4] In this instance, however,
the Lord Chamberlain and the British theatre were not standing alone;
productions planned for Prague and Buenos Aires had already been
suppressed, after German representations, while a proposed production in
New York had also been cancelled.

Until—and even after—the day war was declared on Germany in 1939,
the Lord Chamberlain and his Readers were repeatedly embroiled in

negotiations and disagreements as to the stage portrayal of political events in Germany and Europe. Such discussions were partly internal within St James's Palace, but frequently involved the Foreign Office and the German Embassy, as the theatre was required to accommodate itself to national and international political strategies. The Lord Chamberlain's staff were by no means always happy with what was required of them. Reporting on Brückner's play, George Street pointedly observed that 'to those who take the theatre seriously it must seem a pity that matters which have stirred public feeling should be excluded from it'; he commented that it 'does not include attacks on individuals', and, pre-empting another possible ground for objection, expressed his 'doubt if any disturbance would result' from staging it.[5] But Street knew that his personal view as Reader counted for little and would be over-ruled.

Griffith ended his article by announcing that the English translation of *Heroes* was about to be published, and that 'Literature is still (at the moment) freer than the stage'. Although the promised translation never appeared, the general point remains true, and the primary reason for this was that licensing for the stage was in the gift of the head of the royal household. It followed that any play staged in public had been effectively sanctioned and endorsed by the monarch, and that its 'message' could be seen as carrying his support. As a result, the Lord Chamberlain was effectively obliged to ensure that the British stage did not upset the German authorities. In February 1934, Cromer wrote: 'I have no wish to deter people from showing up the brutality of the Nazi regime, but this can perfectly well be done in books and novels, and even published plays, but not by plays acted on the English stage.' As an internal memorandum made explicit, it was not even a question of whether a play was 'fair':

> The brutality of the Nazi regime is, I imagine, beyond question. Books are published on this theme & also plays, but much as my personal sympathies are with those who wish to enlighten the world as to doings in Germany, it would be very mistaken policy to allow such plays to be acted on the English stage.[6]

As early as August 1933, Cromer had insisted on removing a scene called 'The Dictators' from a Lupino Lane revue, even though it had been previously broadcast on radio: 'We cannot have Mussolini or Hitler impersonated on the stage without objections being raised, so this had better come out'.[7] Almost certainly, he was thinking of objections made by the German Embassy rather than by members of the public. The following month a reference to Hitler was cut from a revue at the Prince of Wales's Theatre—even though one to the British prime minister was allowed to remain[8]—and in reading the script for the October *Revudeville* at the Windmill Theatre, Street drew attention to an anti-war song: 'I mark some lines on Hitler; the "straws amongst his hair" I should think can hardly be passed—it is certainly insulting and it is not the moment for exacerbating remarks on the stage'. Cromer agreed, and the lines were removed.[9]

Yet a complete ban on references to contemporary Germany would have been impracticable and probably self-defeating. Whether by coincidence or not, the first serious play about the Nazis was approved for public performance two days after Griffith's article had appeared. *Whither Liberty*, written by Alan Peters, a Leeds doctor, was licensed for Bradford Civic Theatre on 16 April 1934; its cause was probably helped by the fact that it was not to be staged in London, but, more importantly, the script had been substantially rewritten since its first submission nine months earlier under the title *Who Made the Iron Grow*, when Street had described it as 'a strong indictment of the atrocities and excesses committed by the Nazis'.[10] Both the narrative and the form of Peters's play proved to be early models for a succession of scripts to emerge over the next few years, which struggled to fit the horrors of contemporary events into a formulaic straitjacket of 'realistic' characters, setting and dialogue. In this instance, the head of the Bergheim family is a medical professor interested only in science, who has never revealed to his wife—an aristocratic woman of anti-Semitic tendencies—that he is of Jewish origins. One of their sons is drawn to the political right, the other to the left, while their apolitical daughter turns down the sexual advances of a Nazi storm trooper in favour of a Jewish scientist. The playwright attempts to project into this domestic world the increasing violence and prejudices of German society, as one son is killed and the rest of the family flee into exile. Bergheim's wife is officially informed that her husband is a Jew and has lost his post at the university, and she is given the opportunity to annul the marriage. But in the final moments of the play, she recants her prejudices and decides to remain with him, holding up to the audience a crumpled piece of yellow paper with the word 'Jew' on it, which she will stick back on the door from which she had previously torn it down. 'The play is not a good one', wrote Street in July 1933, 'the author is in too great a hurry'; yet in its way it was an important one. More to the point, the Reader realised that it would create 'political difficulties'. Street urged against wholesale rejection, and tentatively questioned the logic of the very particular limitations placed on the stage:

> Since it avoids indictments of policy—except for a few passages which may be excised—and is aimed at atrocities denounced by every English newspaper, by many public men, by the overwhelming majority of English people in private, it would be in my opinion a great mistake to ban it.

He marked specific references likely to inspire objections—'The burning of the Reichstag . . . The denunciation of Hitler . . . The professor's forecast of policy'—but pointedly observed that 'so violent a Revolution ought not to be squeamish about criticism in a foreign play. It is effectually stifled at home'.

Cromer sent the script to the Foreign Office: 'It is a very anti-Hitler piece', he warned them, 'and, although it is only to be produced at Bradford and is unlikely to come to London, there is always the possibility of this'. The Foreign Office responded by strongly recommending that, at the very least, the issues to which Street had drawn specific attention must be amended:

> Even so I expect that we should have a protest from the German Embassy if the play were put on in London; and in view of your complete authority over plays we might not be able to give a very convincing reply.
>
> Whatever one's personal views, the play is a violent attack on a government with which we have friendly relations, and so far as the Foreign Office is concerned the hope of reciprocity in similar circumstances would incline me to deprecate the appearance of the play in London.

It is hard to know whether the Foreign Office was really concerned about how the German stage would represent Britain or the King or whether this was largely an excuse, but it was a point frequently raised over the next few years. In any case, the Lord Chamberlain took the advice of the Foreign Office and refused a licence; when someone from Bradford Civic Playhouse queried the reason, he was invited to attend St James's Palace to obtain further information. 'These people live in Bradford', wrote one of the Lord Chamberlain's staff, 'we can't very well ask them to call'; but Cromer was astutely reluctant to commit himself in writing:

> Care must be taken in the wording of the reply to give no handle for raising a controversy in the Press over 'political censorship'.
>
> The best course really would be to invite Mr Webster—in spite of his living in Bradford—to take an opportunity of calling at St James's. It could then be explained to him verbally that a propaganda play of this nature, must inevitably be regarded as an attack upon the present system of government in Germany.
>
> Whatever one may think of the Hitler regime, the prosecution [sic] of Jews etc. they are no direct concern of ours, so that the presentation of this picture of conditions on the British stage could not be regarded otherwise than unfriendly and lead to official complaint which would be difficult to answer. Besides which if we allow this in England, our authorities can hardly complain of retaliation by anti-British plays in Germany. At the present time it would be an unwise play to produce and will do no good, only possibly harm.

Cromer also hoped he could discourage the playwright from amending and resubmitting the script: 'I hardly think any alteration in the dialogue would remove the basic objection to the theme of the play', he wrote. But details of the case were evidently leaked to a newspaper editor, and in December 1933 Cromer felt obliged to respond to his probing and justify his own decision:

> The whole thing is a strong indictment of atrocities and excesses committed by the Nazis in Germany and, while possibly there is much truth in it all, I did not think that the British stage was a vehicle for this sort of propaganda, which would most certainly have led to protests from Diplomatic quarters which I always endeavour to avoid.
>
> For your personal information, let me explain that the political aspects of the play were such that instead of circulating it to the Advisory Committee, I referred it to the Foreign Office people, who were emphatic in deprecating the appearance of such a play in this country. Had such a play have [sic] been allowed here it would be futile for us to complain of the production in Germany of anti-British plays, and as naturally the Foreign Office are mainly concerned in maintaining good relations with Germany and other Foreign Countries, they were bound to take this line, and having advised me in this sense I could hardly do otherwise than abide by the advice given me.
>
> Personally I hate introducing any political element into censorship at all, but at times this is inevitable and *Who Made the Iron Grow* is a case in point.
>
> A verbal explanation has been given to the would-be producers, the Bradford Civic Playhouse.

Peters's play subsequently received a handful of private performances in Leeds, and in February 1934 the playwright himself wrote to Cromer to ask what he needed to do to obtain a licence for public performance: 'It has been suggested to me that if the play were re-written, and the scene placed in an imaginary country ruled by a political party not called Nazis or Fascists, that you might reconsider your decision'. Peters promised to remove specific references to actual statesmen, though he admitted that 'it would be impossible to hide the fact that the allusion is to Germany'. However, he intimated that the application need not be so narrowly defined: 'The production of the play in its altered form would be useful as propaganda against similar tragic conditions being forced upon England'.

At a meeting with the playwright's solicitor, Cromer confirmed that the Ruritanian route might be acceptable, and in March 1934 a revised script was duly submitted under the title *Whither Liberty*. Again Street reported, and again he did his best to persuade the Lord Chamberlain to grant a licence; he also questioned the logic of requiring so transparent a fictionalisation, though he recognised that this was an established strategy which had frequently been adopted. But above all, Street, who had been a Reader in the Office for some twenty years and was now approaching retirement, pleaded for the stage to be granted the freedom to criticise a regime which hardly deserved the protection and respect being granted to it:

> I gather . . . that the Lord Chamberlain hoped he would be able to license the play if an imaginary country replaced Germany, and other names were altered. This has been done. Germany becomes Nordia, Hitler Hacker, Nazi Nori, Brown Shirts Yellow Shirts, and so on. Otherwise the play is the same, with the outrages on Jews and the denunciation of the Nazi regime.
>
> That Nordia means Germany and the other imaginary names those for which they stand will of course be obvious to everybody. But that was certain when the author was more or less encouraged to make the changes. That being the case, however, I should be inclined to cut out the accusation against Hacker, i.e. Hitler, of himself having the 'Senate House' 'blown up' as being particularly offensive to the German government and as never having been proved, whereas for the outrages of the Jews there is a mass of evidence. But I think the play should be passed. The custom of allowing imaginary names when the real names would not be, even though everyone knows the identification, is open to objection in theory, but it has always existed and has saved many a situation. . . . My own opinion, for what it may be worth, and with the greatest respect to the Foreign Office, is that the stage should not be debarred from expressing an almost universal sentiment. I note that another anti-Nazi play refused here is being presented in France and America. Still more, do I think that this revised version with its imaginary names should be allowed.

Cromer insisted on some further amendments, but he then licensed the play—even while acknowledging that no-one who saw it would be in any doubt about the real subject matter. What he had effectively done, however, was to protect his own back (albeit with a somewhat thin covering) against the inevitable criticisms and accusations which would flow from the German Embassy. He said as much in an internal memorandum: 'Much as I regret resort to the subterfuge of a change from the real to an imaginary country, dictates of policy render this necessary. Although too transparent to hoodwink any audience, it is sufficient, or should be, to gainsay any official protests'.[11] Such a priority would be a central plank of his policy over the next few years.

But if a week is a long time in politics then four years was a very long time for St James's Palace. In 1938 it came to the attention of the Lord Chamberlain's Office that Peters's play was to be revived. Both Street and Cromer had gone by then and, under pressure from the government, which was now even more desperate to avoid upsetting Germany, the Office decided that 'in view of the national situation' the play should not be revived. In October 1938, the new Lord Chamberlain, the Earl of Clarendon, took the almost unprecedented step of seeking the surrender of a licence which had been issued four and a half years earlier:

> You may remember that even in 1934 there was some difficulty in granting a licence for the play 'Whither Liberty'.

International affairs have changed considerably since then, and if the play were submitted for licence at the present time, it would undoubtedly be refused.

In view of this the Lord Chamberlain requests you to return the licence which was issued to you in April, 1934.

I hope this withdrawal will only be temporary, but in view of the present situation the necessity for doing so is one which I'm sure you will understand.

Mrs Roberts, from the Bradford Civic Theatre, may have understood, but she was not willing to submit:

I hope you will pardon me for expressing my very strong feeling that it is just the present state of international affairs that makes it much more important that such plays as *Whither Liberty* should be produced, more important even than in 1934 when the licence was given. Glad as everyone is that peace has been preserved there is, I think, throughout the country a strong feeling of dismay that Nazism has, by the method thro' which peace has been maintained gained a considerable victory. Everyone to whom I have spoken, in the country or in the town . . . are united in their desire that we should somehow make it plain that England's passion for peace should not preclude us from expressing our detestation of tyranny. A play such as *Whither Liberty* . . . might enable many people to find an emotional and rational outlet for their scarcely formulated convictions and feelings.

Surely the Lord Chamberlain's office is not going to be the first to abandon the peculiar genius of the British people and their rulers, which has for so many centuries allowed the free expression of opinion, whether at Hyde Park Corner, in the press or in the Theatre, and has, by the use of this safety valve, escaped revolution for longer than any country in Europe—where such safety valves are not permitted.

It is not as if *Whither Liberty* was a gross exaggeration, it is very much an understatement of the case.

In a potentially awkward situation for the Lord Chamberlain's Office, Clarendon's silver-tongued Comptroller, Sir Terence Nugent, employed all his diplomatic expertise to try and persuade Mrs Roberts to accept a compromise:

In view of the international situation the Lord Chamberlain is naturally anxious to do nothing which may embarrass the leaders of this country.

For this reason, and because of complaints at other plays which have been received from foreign embassies, the Lord Chamberlain has decided that in plays which criticise or attack the acts or ideology of the leaders of Foreign States and their supporters, great care must be taken to avoid leaving anything in the script which may furnish a clue as to which State is aimed at by the author . . .

> In *Whither Liberty* there are many such passages, which the Lord
> Chamberlain will require altered before the play can be performed in
> public again.

Nugent invited Roberts for a personal interview, and sought to reassure her
that the Office's policy was rooted in an even higher sense of duty and
responsibility than her own.

> Finally, I am to say that the Lord Chamberlain would certainly not wish
> unduly to restrict a free expression of opinion, but I am sure that at such a
> time as this you will appreciate the necessity of not making more difficult
> the task of those who are working for a peaceful solution to the present
> International problems. The Lord Chamberlain feels that by the removal
> of clues that might connect fictitious characters and places with real ones
> no harm will be done to an author's work, nor will he, or she, be
> precluded from expressing those views which he has at heart.

Her reply seemed as obdurate as ever, implying that she would seek
support and publicity in high places and asking:

> on what authority your Office originally asked (in your letter of October
> 13th) 'for the return of the licence issued in April 1934' for *Whither Liberty*
> and what was the precedent for that action? The League of British
> dramatists, a part of the Author's Society, knows of no other case of a
> licence being recalled after it had been granted. It is a subject which
> interests them and which would also interest several friends of ours who
> are members of Parliament.
>   I heartily share the Lord Chamberlain's desire to assist in a peaceful solu-
> tion of the present International problems, and feel that to allow it to appear
> that England has no objection to persecution for race, religion or opinion, is
> not a good, nor in the long run, a safe method of seeking that end.[12]

In the event, a compromise was reached in which further cuts were
imposed on the text and the licence was not surrendered.

The other anti-Nazi drama alluded to in Griffith's 1934 article was *Take
Heed*, a warning play by a barrister, Leslie Reade, which had been privately
staged at the Piccadilly Theatre in January and then refused a licence for
public performance. The private performances by the Progressive Players
had attracted the sort of critical response which would inevitably provoke
the German Embassy, and though the censors remarked that the reviews
had been generally positive, this was far from an incentive to grant a
licence, 'since all state that the play is strong anti-Nazi propaganda'. The
Daily Telegraph described it as an 'anti-Hitler play' and 'an indictment of the
Hitler regime', and the *News Chronicle* predicted that while a ban would be
regrettable it was probably inevitable: 'I presume the censor will not allow
Take Heed to be played in public, although there is nothing in its picture of
Nazi intolerance and cruelty which has not been vouchsafed for by eye

witnesses'.[13] Street's report echoed this last point: 'The play is vehemently and fiercely anti-Nazi', he wrote, 'but in the light of what has been witnessed to of the early atrocities it is difficult to say it is unfair'. Yet even he reluctantly recommended that a public performance should not be allowed:

> I cannot advise the Lord Chamberlain to grant a licence. I should like to, because I dislike the brutality and ignorant 'Nordic' nonsense of the Nazi movement. But it would be 'asking for trouble'. I have read that when the play was produced at the Piccadilly they were apprehensive of disturbance. Nothing happened except enthusiastic applause, and I do not suppose there are many Nazi Germans in London. Protests from the German Embassy would of course be made, and I think would be unjustified on the facts if the abuse of Hitler were taken out. But it would be unwise to allow a theatre to become a centre of anti-Nazi feeling and I cannot advise the Lord Chamberlain to take that risk. I should be only too glad if he takes a different view, but I advise as duty dictates.

Street suggested that performances might incite confrontations and clashes in the audience, and reviews referred to similar apprehensions; the *Daily Telegraph* noted that 'It was feared in some quarters that a hostile demonstration might be made', while the *Morning Post* report clearly indicates that the threat was taken very seriously: 'The large number of police who surrounded the Piccadilly Theatre last night gave credence to the many rumours one heard within that the Fascists were due to make a demonstration against this play'.[14] In seeking a licence, the play's producer, Harold Mortlake, claimed that the audience had included 'many Germans who were not Jews' and that the theatre had 'specially invited members of the Fascist Party to come and see the play and there were many present, including Sir Oswald Mosley'; he insisted there had not been 'one murmur of dissent nor any suggestion of disorder'. Yet the play and its production were undoubtedly intended to disturb; one review described even the programme as 'provocative, for it contained a statement that the Nazi steel whip that was used on the stage was "kindly lent by Miss Ellen Wilkinson from her collection of such implements made on her recent visit to Germany"'.[15] Moreover, a powerful speech in the climactic scene evidently produced strong reactions, when a professor with impeccable Aryan credentials, whose Jewish wife has been driven to suicide in an effort to preserve her family from persecution, drags her dead body in front of a group of storm troopers:

> You ask me to salute your leader. I will do so over her poor body. (*He raises his hand slowly in a fascist salute*). Hail National Socialism! Hail Reaction! Hail Barbarism! Hail Torture and Murder! Hail Intolerance! Hail the destruction of Liberty and Culture. Hail the man who has shamed our country and defiled her in the sight of mankind! Hail those who have

caused the very name of our country to stink in the nostrils of the whole world! Hail Hitler![16]

Some reviews reported that this attack on the Nazis and their leader was drowned out by the cheers of the audience, and since part of the Lord Chamberlain's brief was to prevent performances which might lead to a breach of the piece, he had a ready-made justification for refusing a licence.

A further anxiety was that, as its title clearly signals, *Take Heed* was not intended simply as a dramatisation of events in Germany, but also as a warning about what could happen at home. In one scene, the professor is asked by his wife what Germany has done to deserve its present punishment and subjection. He replies that it was the 'indifference' of the ordinary population which allowed the Fascists to take power:

> We weren't accustomed to our liberties and didn't esteem them highly enough. Democracies must look after their rights, or they'll be gone before you've even counted them; for the enemies of democracy are always on the alert. We were too easy-going and tolerant. All that mattered to us was our own work, our own friends. Often enough we were so occupied with our little worries that we never even bothered to vote. We neglected the privilege which brave men had died to win for us; and then when the trouble came, we cursed the Republic light-heartedly, and sighed for a Dictator. We should have worked night and day for the democracy. We should have given our very souls for the preservation of the Republic just as the National Socialists gave theirs to destroy it. Instead, we did nothing; and in that way we were guilty of a fault . . . We have our Dictator now, and retribution has overtaken us. I pray God that the remaining democracies will escape our fate.

Like Street, Cromer did not dispute the authenticity of the picture the play painted of contemporary Germany, and he claimed that he had 'the strongest reluctance to allowing political motives to effect Stage Censorship'. Yet he was adamant that he had 'no alternative as the theme does not lend itself to alteration or modification'.[17] Although he sent the script to Sir Robert Vansittart at the Foreign Office, his 'confidential' letter accompanying it suggests that his mind was effectively made up:

> My dear Van,
> At a time when you have quite enough to occupy you at the Foreign Office without having to trouble about plays, I hesitate to inflict this one upon you. To save time I should be very glad if you could arrange for someone at the Foreign Office to look through the accompanying play by Leslie Reade entitled 'Take Heed', which is purely an Anti-Nazi Propaganda piece of a distinctly strong order.
> Even if it were cut about and modified, which would ruin it for the theatre, it would, I think, be most unwise to have it produced in England as you would be bound to have protests from the German Embassy.

Vansittart agreed, and his reply testifies to the government's priorities:

Confidential
My dear Cromer,
Many thanks for your confidential letter . . . I agree that protest would most certainly be made by the German Embassy. They have already protested about considerably less.
There is an answer when the press is concerned, but the answer is not so easy (and would certainly not be accepted) where the theatre is concerned and a licence has been granted. The Germans would of course look on this as an official encouragement, if not incitement.

The producer offered 'to make any cuts or changes desired', but had to be satisfied with two further private performances later that year.

Take Heed was resubmitted by Mortlake in December 1938, with the intention of presenting it immediately in the West End.

I have prepared a version of the play from which I have excised every reference to political personages, places, countries, and to Germany in particular . . .
I will of course, also alter all the uniforms worn on the stage so that, like the script, they no longer signify the Nazi regime

But with the government wholeheartedly pursuing its policy of appeasement, the Reader, Henry Game, commented:

The Lord Chamberlain has recently decided that these anti-Fascist plays must be satisfactorily ruritanianised, if they are to receive a licence. I do not think that this play will lend itself to such treatment—there is too obtrusive a background of the contemporary German politics of 1933. For this reason I think the Lord Chamberlain will be justified in refusing to lift the ban.[18]

Rather spuriously, Game attempted to draw a distinction between this play and the licensed *Who Made the Iron Grow*: 'there is much less political background woven into the narrative of that play, and the brutality is more personal to the characters concerned, than symbolic of the general brutality of a political party, as here'.

Mortlake continued the battle, showing himself ready to challenge a policy of intransigence which was effectively anti-Semitic. The Assistant Comptroller expressed his frustration, with a rather disquieting emphasis: 'This play has given a great deal of trouble—I have spent hours with this man Mortlake who is a Jew; he is not the author but only the present owner of the play'. He drew another distinction which teetered on the edge of political absurdity: 'I have tried to point out to him that we do not object to a play on the persecution of the Jews, but we will not have any direct reference to the persecuting country—even by inference'. In January 1939, somewhat surprisingly, Lord Clarendon agreed to license *Take Heed*—provided that the script was submitted to an extensive catalogue of alterations in line with this policy. Apart from replacing 'brown shirts' with 'coloured shirts' and insisting on no recognisable salutes or uniforms and no goose-stepping, the dozens of changes required included the removal of the term 'Herr', the substitution of 'King' for 'Emperor', 'Marshall' for 'Leader', 'Our' for 'Nordic', 'Hebraic' for 'anti-Nordic', 'Military Socialists' for 'National Socialists', 'All Hail' for 'Hail', 'crowns' for 'marks', 'Paris' for 'Basle', 'abroad' for 'England', 'terror' for 'monster' and, in order to avoid anything too specific or identifiable, of 'millions' for 'two million'. Whole passages of discussion were also marked for exclusion, and the censorship crucially excised the final visual image, in which 'a shaft of sunlight suddenly streams through the divided curtains' and catches the corpses of the dead professor and his wife: 'No sunlight to encircle the heads of Sophie and Opal', insisted the endorsement.

Mortlake expressed himself 'appalled at the ruthlessness with which your office is hacking the play to pieces', and railed against the particular limitations imposed on the stage:

> in deference to your wishes I have changed the locale, the names of my characters, the very characteristics of their speech, in order to make this play as harmless as a J.M. Barrie charade . . . Since you insist on cutting anything that is at all good in the play . . . Why this squeamishness, when the German Government openly brag about it. As this is now Ruritania, if they recognise it and protest against it, surely the more shame they? . . . I have reluctantly agreed to your chopping off of the head, arms, legs, and tongue from what was once a living play. That it has taken every literary virtue from the play does not matter very much to the Office. I pray you to have the understanding and generosity to at least let me keep the remnants of the plot in.
>
> Although—unlike the Office—I loathe mutilation in any shape or form, I enclose herewith a clipping from 'Picture Post' with a characteristic reference from a speech of Friend Goebbels. Picture Post may say it. The stage must not. Lowe can say it daily with the utmost impertinence, and temerity. The Stage? VERBOTEN! Queer situation in a country which boasts proudly, challengingly of its complete FREEDOM OF SPEECH!

The Lord Chamberlain sent the revised script to Dr Von Selzam at the German Embassy, and an internal Office memorandum recorded the German response: 'He said it was a pity such plays had to be as "they did not help" which of course is obvious but I explained our difficulties too, which I believe he understood'.

Although *Take Heed* had been subjected to very extensive and detailed cutting, one might ask why the Lord Chamberlain was prepared to consider allowing it at all in 1939, when it had been refused in 1934. Perhaps part of the answer lies in the review of the production published in *The Times*:

> The process of events ... may well have seemed the melodramatic exaggeration of propaganda when the play was first produced a few years ago. In 1938 the facts have so far outstripped Mr Reade's imagined horrors that one is more inclined to suppose that they have been deliberately toned down to suit the exigencies of the stage.[19]

In other words, the play no longer appeared extreme or excessive, and had been effectively censored. When it might have been shocking, it was silenced. Soon after war was declared, the original script was resubmitted: in November 1939, Game commented: 'As far as making the play an anti-Hitler and anti-Nazi play by restoring the original text, I see no objection'. The Acting Comptroller agreed:

> Mr Game now considers there is no reason why this play should not be licensed, since other plays of an anti-Nazi character, such as *Pastor Hall* and *The Crucible* have recently been passed ... it is simply a bitter denunciation of the Nazi Party and regime. There is no propaganda in it against any other country and it therefore seems logical to pass it for production.

Clarendon even managed a little joke: 'I agree', he wrote, 'for we need not now "take heed" of German feelings'.[20]

The Lord Chamberlain's Office had always been willing to consult the Foreign Office, and the interests of 'friendly' nations had traditionally been taken into account. But it had surely never found itself under the sort of sustained pressure that it experienced from the German Embassy during the thirties. What made it even harder for playwrights and producers who wished to engage with contemporary international politics were the changing strategies and positions of the British government. A further specific obstacle was the general principle, as stated in court in 1939, that 'the Lord Chamberlain will not permit rulers of foreign states to be mocked upon the stage'.[21] In September 1934, Henry Daniell's *Lucid Interval* was submitted for the Playhouse in London, but although Street admired the play he again doubted if it could be passed:

> This is a fantastic play about Hitler. It is clever and interesting and the only objection is that it is about him. There is no disguise at all, though of course the name is changed. ... I wish it could be licensed with an instruction against any personal make up. Given the admitted facts Hitler is not treated badly ... A man with a sense of a humour would not object to this portrait of himself. However I cannot advise a licence without further consideration. A sense of humour is not a strong point with Germans and there might be a fuss.

Cromer again sent the script to the Foreign Office, who were adamant:

Sir Robert Vansittart asked me to say that he has come to the reluctant conclusion that it would be undesirable to license this play. What ever the make-up of the principal character, there could be no doubt in anybody's mind that it was intended to represent Hitler, and there are many passages (apart from the general trend of the play) that would certainly provoke protest from the German Embassy: such for instance is the love-making scene which, so far as is known, would be quite untrue to life. Moreover and this is perhaps the most important aspect, Hitler is now not merely Chancellor but the Head of a friendly state and falls into a different category. It would be most unfortunate if there were any retaliation in Germany at the expense of the King.[22]

Over the next few years, any direct reference to Hitler was automatically refused; in 1939 a description of him as 'a tub-thumping little Austrian house-painter' was disallowed, and the phrase 'a rum little beggar' was cut as 'disrespectful'.[23] Lines referring to Hitler and Mussolini as 'those two dictator fellows' were removed from a revue in Peterborough, as a 'rude reflection',[24] while the briefest of references to Hitler as 'that awful man' was excised from a portrait of life in a Glasgow tenement, with the Office refusing even to allow a character to say of Hitler that he had 'never heard of him'.[25]

Nor was the Lord Chamberlain acting in isolation. In 1935, for example, the Chief Constable of Liverpool instituted a successful prosecution against a comedian for saying that Hitler was 'head of the Nancies',[26] and revues and pantomimes found the policy equally restricting—especially since it also covered visual representations. In January 1937, the London County Council noted in relation to the impersonation of Hitler in a Variety Show at the Paramount Theatre in Tottenham Court Road 'that steps were immediately taken to have the item complained of removed from the performance'.[27] Many pantomimes traditionally incorporated more or less harmless political gags, and in a 1935 report on a Christmas version of *Robinson Crusoe* Street pointedly observed that 'freedom of allusion to current events is an immemorial privilege of pantomime'.[28] Now, however, such freedom was under attack, and a week later the same Reader dutifully reported in relation to a *Jack and the Beanstalk* that he was 'very careful in all the pantomimes to note any jokes about Hitler or Mussolini'.[29] He clearly found such requirements rather absurd. Reporting on a *Dick Whittington* for Gateshead he recorded: 'As the German Embassy is so childishly touchy about Hitler I mark a harmless joke about him'; he added: 'it would be absurd to censor it and Gateshead is not London'.[30] The following month, Street made his feelings even clearer in relation to another slight piece:* 'Jill

---

* *Out of the Dark*, by Ingram d'Abbes

has a pony called Hitler . . . I mention this as there may be no limit to the stupidity of the German Embassy in this matter, but I think there should be a limit to its indulgence'. Considering that a few months earlier they had insisted on changing the name of a goose called Hitler (and a pig called Baldwin) in a particularly silly farce, it is actually surprising that Cromer ruled that Jill's pony 'Can be risked'.[31] In February 1936 a passing reference to 'that blighter Hitler' was removed from a one-act play,[*32] and cuts in that winter's pantomime season included a character in an Eastbourne *Cinderella* saying Hitler had deported him for refusing to salute a German sausage,[33] and from a *Babes in the Wood* at Hull[†] the verse:

> When Mary went out walking
> Along with Mr Hitler.
> One hand he kept to salute like this
> And the other hand to tickler.[34]

Occasionally, things got through. In the autumn of 1935, the German Embassy protested vehemently about the London production of a Hungarian play in which a page boy in a Budapest hotel has the name Hitler;[‡] 'the Permanent Under Secretary of State at the Foreign Office asked that the reference should be omitted in deference to German wishes', noted the Assistant Comptroller. (Bizarrely, the name of Ghandi was substituted, leading to complaints from both the India Office and the Indian National Congress, and to questions in Parliament.)[35] In 1937 references to Germany as 'the enemy' were removed from a revue sketch in Southampton.[36]

As some of the examples already cited show, make up and costume were as important as text, and any hint of a toothbrush moustache was removed. In November 1936, the Office inspected a dress rehearsal of a revue and complained that in a scene called 'Selling the Earth', one of the silent bidders was made up to resemble Hitler. When they were told to modify this, the management asked whether 'the male character may give the fascist salute and say "I should have a different face, but the Censor has cut it"'. Unfortunately, is not clear whether this was permitted.[37] However, one case which caught the national news occurred in January 1937, when the Office upheld the complaints of the German Embassy about another pantomime version of *Robinson Crusoe*. The Lord Chamberlain's secretary, George Titman, first heard about it through the Foreign Office:

★ *Their Majesties Pass By*, by Leonard Hines
† Written by Frank Dix, Fred and Jack Clements
‡ *Vicky*, by Ladislaus Bus-Fekete

> Mr Baxter telephoned to me yesterday that representations have been made to the Foreign Office by the German Embassy concerning the caricature of Herr Hitler in the above-named pantomime.
>
> After perusing the script and being assured that no such representation of Herr Hitler, or a dictator, had been passed, I attended last evening's performance at the theatre.
>
> I found that the German Embassy was fully justified in the protest made.
>
> I also found that there were many other unauthorised interpolations . . .
>
> After the performance, I interviewed the manager and told him that the representation of Herr Hitler must come out immediately and he assured me that this would be done. He said that it was not in the rehearsal and that the comedian must have slipped it in later—(which is the old excuse).[38]

Though often overlooked (or unknown), the interpolation of lines after a script had been licensed was technically an offence against the Theatres Act, and the *Daily Mirror* reported that summonses had been duly issued on these grounds:

> Because a gag about Hitler was introduced in the pantomime 'Robinson Crusoe' at the King's Theatre, Hammersmith, the Lord Chamberlain has summoned the principal comedian, the proprietress of the theatre and the author of the pantomime. He has also ordered the gag to be cut out of the show.
>
> The joke was introduced by Hal Bryan in a scene in which he is supposed to be making love to a dusky queen.
>
> One of the actors says: 'Don't let the queen get you or she will make you her dictator.'
>
> Bryan put on a little black moustache, pulled one lock of his hair over his forehead and came down the stairs shouting, 'Heil, heil, heil.'
>
> 'It seemed such a simple little joke,' said Bryan. 'You see I was not even dressed like Hitler. I had a pilot suit and a red wig.'[39]

Rather confusingly, the Lord Chamberlain's letter to the Director of Public Prosecutions seems to describe a different gag:

> Towards the end of the story of Robinson Crusoe, where the white people are defending themselves in the stockade against an assault by the 'blacks', a man is stated to be approaching bearing a white flag. The gate is opened and the comedian runs into the camp made-up to represent Herr Hitler, giving the Nazi salute and saying 'vot iss all sis about?' His appearance in this guise is quite short, but sufficiently long for there to be no doubt about his identity . . .
>
> His Lordship desires me to inform you that he has at no time permitted the representation of Herr Hitler in any stage play, for reasons which are obvious.[40]

The resulting court case was widely reported in national newspapers—
'Hitler Gag Alleged in Panto Summons' was the *Daily Express* headline—
and fines were imposed.[41]

If he was made aware of it, any 'guying' of Hitler in revues was invariably
disallowed by the Lord Chamberlain. From a Windmill *Revudeville* in April
1935, a feeble joke was cut in which someone asking for raspberries is told
to 'go to the corner house and make a noise like Hitler'.[42] On another
occasion the Chief Constable of Preston sent a report on a touring revue to
the Office, detailing a scene about which he had qualms:

> Two men walk on the stage from opposite wings, each wearing semi
> military uniforms . . . one of them wearing a black moustache in represent-
> ation of Herr Hitler the German Chancellor and the other, a thick set
> figure bearing a very strong resemblance of Signor Mussolini the Italian
> dictator. As these two men approach each other Mussolini's prototype
> raises his hand in a Fascist salute and Hitler's prototype gives the Nazi
> salute. They do this three or four times as they walk across the stage, halting
> at attention for each salute, and then when they are each disappearing at the
> sides of the stage, both turn round and each makes a disparaging sound
> with a rubber instrument, commonly known as a 'razzer'.[43]

The case was taken up by the Lord Chamberlain, and the revue was
inspected in several different venues. 'These "raspberries", which the
Director of Public Prosecutions describes as "a labial imitation of the passage
of wind through the rectum", are never allowed', reported Titman, and a
public prosecution was brought in January 1939. In February 1937, the
Office deleted 'a quite unnecessary reference to Hitler', noting: 'the fact that
all the characters in this sketch turn out to be inmates of a lunatic asylum
adds to the advisability of cutting'.[44] In October 1938, a brief mention of
Hitler was removed from a Boy Scout show in Lanarkshire, and a
Birmingham University Revue was instructed to cut a joke about a governess
being nicknamed 'Miss Hitler' and to her nephew having been born with a
small moustache.[45] On another occasion* they cut 'a most peculiar reference
to Hitler', in the line 'P'raps it'd 'elp if old 'Itler 'ad a baby'.[46]

Street described the Italians as 'less silly in such matters than the
Germans', but the Lord Chamberlain was still careful to censor anything
which seemed to tread on dangerous ground, and in December 1935 he
removed from another version of *Robinson Crusoe* 'Benito's Jazz-Band' and
references to Abyssinia.[47] In January 1936, Street described a scene within a
Windmill *Revudeville* as 'An absurd sort of imaginary parallel to the
Abyssynian troubles', and warned that '"Signor Captain Whale-Blubber"
for Mussolini might give offence'; Cromer was adamant: The whole thing

---

* *Heaven and Charing Cross*, by Aubrey Danvers-Walker

as it stands will not do. If they want any skit of this sort it must be entirely amended so as to be free of objectionable features to sensitive foreigners. The best course is to delete the scene entirely.[48] Later that month, Street found himself pleading to his superiors* that 'One cannot rule out <u>all</u> dictators', for it had become increasingly hard to include any such reference at all.[49] In June 1937, the Office cut lines from a revue sketch in Sheffield in which Mussolini was 'mentioned impolitely', and Game's report on a revue in Blackpool in 1938 noted that 'There are a bunch of Mussolini jokes which I have marked, and which in view of the recent Foreign Office letter should be cut'.[50] In 1938, 'an undesirable Hitler joke' was removed from a *Cinderella* but a reference to Mussolini allowed to stand specifically because 'it's complimentary'.[51]

In August 1938 the censorship effectively killed off a sketch for Manchester's Palace Theatre called 'Geneva in a Dream', in which leading international statesmen were made the subject of comedy: 'the Stalin is slightly offensive, and the Hitler more so—both being figures of fun', and steps were taken to ensure that it was rendered innocuous: 'By banning Hitler and Stalin we have actually practically destroyed this silly little sketch and this telegram . . . will give it its death blow'. Permission was given to perform the sketch 'subject to deletion of all dialogue reference and make up concerning Monsieur Blum, Anthony Eden, Stalin and Hitler'.[52] A revised version in which the international leaders had been replaced by unidentifiable delegates was deemed acceptable, provided no attempt was made to imitate or represent the original characters: 'it may seem silly in view of the plain speaking in the daily papers and elsewhere, but as we are a Censorship I doubt whether we should allow anything at the moment which could possibly exacerbate the German feelings'.[53]

As we have seen, references to swastikas, brownshirts, goose-stepping and marks were habitually excised from serious plays as well as revues, along with national anthems, military salutes, portraits of Hitler or Mussolini, Nazi or fascist emblems, the use of the word 'German', and any German or German-sounding names. In December 1937, the senior Reader, Henry Game, revealingly described Beatrix Thomson's *Sons of Adam* as too 'thinly disguised'.[54] While not recommending complete rejection—'I should be sorry to see any play which expresses hatred of persecution banned'—he insisted that the Nazis must not be implicated as the persecutors, and the censorship required the removal of 'all clues, which connect the action specifically with Germany and the Nazis'. A revised version was submitted in February 1938, but Game argued that although the script had been 'pretty satisfactorily denationalized', there

---

* On behalf of *Sweet Wine*, by Kenneth Bolton

were 'a few words still left in which point to Germany as the country aimed at'. With a rather disquieting detachment, Game pointed out that there was no need to disguise the victims, since 'Three European Powers seem to be busily engaged at the moment in persecuting the Jews', but he was adamant that the identity of the oppressor must not be indicated through costume. Indeed, he even contemplated whether a similar requirement should be extended into the style of acting: 'Felman, the villain of the piece, who is described as fair and bullet-headed, should not perhaps be made too aggressively Teutonic?' he mused. Again, the censorship insisted on removing all specific German references from Clifford Odets's short play, *Till the Day I Die*, licensing it 'On the understanding that the particular Totalitarian State aimed at is left indefinite'.[55]

It was not easy for the Lord Chamberlain to maintain consistency through the thirties. Probably the first significant stage criticism of the Nazis to be licensed for public performance was *The Crooked Cross*, a play written by Sally Carson and produced by Sir Barry Jackson for Birmingham Repertory Theatre in November 1934. This was essentially a realistic drama set in Germany, which again used a small group of characters and a domestic setting to examine the effects of recent events. It showed or alluded to relationships being destroyed by racial prejudice, to friends and families turning on each other, to Jewish professionals being sacked from their posts, to violence being perpetrated against Jews, and to the deaths of refugees attempting to flee across the border. In 1934, the presentation of such shocking and contemporary subject matter on the public stage was a breakthrough of considerable significance, and the judgement expressed by the reviewer in *Truth* was fairly typical, and not unfair:

> This is a great theme . . . It must be, for alone it has triumphed over bad writing and bad acting and made *Crooked Cross* move a quarter of its audience to tears . . . Miss Carson . . . is the first to have seen the dramatic possibilities of a subject which other Ivory-Tower-dwelling authors have scorned . . . The wish must be added that some more able dramatist will make a better play from the same story.[56]

Crucially, in terms of the censorship, the reviewer insisted on the play's willingness to be fair to all sides:

> she is accurate—the German consul in Birmingham, who saw the play, had no complaints—and she is fairer to the Nazis than more foolish opponents would have been. She has had the intelligence to see that the rank and file of the Storm Troopers were boisterous, bourgeois unemployed.

Of course, Carson and Jackson would both have known that such 'fairness' was essential to their hopes of securing a licence, and the play's tone and emphasis probably reflect conscious or unconscious self-censorship.

When *The Crooked Cross* was submitted in the autumn of 1934, Street's description of it as 'temperately written', and his reminder that it was based on accepted facts, amounted to a coded appeal to the Lord Chamberlain to approve it. 'If it is a rule that no play about contemporary Germany can be licensed I suppose this cannot be', he wrote.[57] Knowing that it was the portrayal of Hitler which might cause most concern, he stressed that the violence and prejudice were blamed entirely on the storm troopers, and that there were no grounds for resenting this 'now that Herr Hitler has given the Storm Troopers the cold shoulder and shot some of their leaders'. Cromer was prepared to support Street's position, and the Foreign Office evidently accepted his distinction:

> The opinion of the competent authorities in the Foreign Office whom I have consulted is that we cannot object on political grounds to all plays about Nazis. There is here no portrayal of Hitler himself, and we do not wish to interfere with your discretion if you regard it as suitable to license.

The Crooked Cross was duly licensed, though not without some significant cuts. One of these was a speech in a scene in which a young woman watches in horror as a group of Nazis beat someone up; she then asks her pro-Nazi brother what would have happened if the victim had been her own Jewish boyfriend:

> ERICH: Do you really want to know? Well, (*He is looking at her all the time*) if it was Moritz, your dear Moritz, your nice little Jew-boy (*He pauses, considering the effect he is making*) I'd have them beat him slower, much slower . . . beat him only on the raw flesh first, whip him in the eyes, flog his teeth in . . . beat him till the blood . . . till the blood . . .[58]

It was specifically the detail of the violence to which the censors objected, and the Lord Chamberlain recommended that 'the description of the atrocities might be toned down'. He did not, however, interfere with Erich's justification for the violence:

> He was a filthy little Communist skunk. Dirty lot all of them. If we teased a few more like that we wouldn't have so much trouble from them. Punishment, that's what they want and then all they got wouldn't pay them out for the dirty tricks they've done to us, all the tribe of them.

Also cut was a suggestion linking the Nazi love of regalia to a latent homosexuality, when the young woman says to her brother: 'You love the uniform and the noise and the flag-waving—and I don't imagine the Storm Troopers are immune to your charms'.

Under the headline, 'ANTI-SEMITISM DRAMATISED', *Truth* highlighted the absurdity of the Lord Chamberlain's policy of attempting to anonymise the subject:

He was right, though it seems to be against his previous principles, to permit the performance of this Anti-Nazi play; and rightly again he has left it almost uncut. But what he has cut! Every 'Heil Hitler' in the dialogue. Since any Nazis who did not thus begin and end their conversations would be considered traitors, the absence of these two words must be far more an insult to a foreign potentate than their presence.[59]

But it was January 1937 before *The Crooked Cross* reached London, and by then, it had lost its power to shock and its topicality. James Agate dismissed its predictability: 'Nothing is uttered by any character which is not taken for granted before he enters the theatre by any person above the age of ten who has ever thought for five minutes about religious persecution of any kind'.[60] Yet *The Times* praised the play for its 'restraint from propaganda' and its willingness 'to show us both sides of the question',[61] while W.A. Darlington in the *Daily Telegraph* also approved the writer's balance: 'Although she hates the things which Nazism did to the Jews, she tells truly and sympathetically how it put heart into the younger generation of Germans'.[62] Despite this, the Westminster production drew a storm of protest from right-wing elements in Britain. 'Several papers have "got us into trouble" over this play', wrote Cromer.[63] One extreme review described *The Crooked Cross* as 'an insult to Nazi Germany and part of a very dangerous anti-German propaganda'; it added that 'Anti-Semitism is inevitable in countries where Semitism makes itself conspicuous by its exaggerated ambitions, its obtrusiveness and its desire for domination'. This article was sent to the Office by a member of the public, accompanied by a long and disturbing rant penned in Gothic print on notepaper bearing an apocalyptic letterhead featuring a church window and a figure burning in flames:

Can you explain the criminal folly of your department in passing such a subject?

I have lived in Germany for five months in the last year, mixing with every class, in cities and villages and I am proud to number several members of the National Socialist Party among my friends. The people are happy, well-fed and putting up a magnificent fight to regain for their country the security and prestige she lost. There is no oppression of the Jews, merely certain regulations which they (as do any aliens in this country) have to abide by. The German people have two dominant desires, from the highest to the lowest; peace, and friendship with Britain. They are bitterly hurt by the persistent campaign of lying atrocity stories in our Jewish controlled Press. The mass of the British people is as anxious for German friendship as they for ours.

What would be the reaction of the British Government if a play, rabidly anti-British, were produced in Berlin, passed by a Government department? An official protest, at least, if not worse. Germany is hypersensitive, and there are limits to what she will stand in the way of insults from us. She has everything to gain (and we have everything to lose) from a declaration of war against us, a war which in our present lamentable state of weakness, we should lose. Are all our young generation (for whom I speak) and our splendid Empire to be sacrificed to pander to the revenge-instinct of a handful of Jew professors and profiteers, who have found it impossible to earn their livings in the country that puts patriotism and decency first?

I must most seriously ask you to have this play withdrawn. If there is any legal necessity for a private person to apply, as common informer, I am prepared to do so myself . . .

P.S. It seems to me so un-British and utterly against all our rules of fair play, to launch, or tolerate these attacks on a Government who have never shown us anything but friendship.

Another factor which sometimes influenced the Lord Chamberlain was the location in which a play was to be performed. After all, the German Embassy was unlikely to find out about productions which took place outside the main cities and theatres. In January 1935, Cromer approved a patriotic pageant for The Women's Unionist Association,* in which a group of factory workers moaning about life in Britain are transported by a fairy godmother to other countries, so they can discover how lucky they are to live where they do. 'It is all rather complacent, but mostly true', wrote the Lord Chamberlain's Reader.[64] But among the places they visit are Germany in 1930, and again in 1934; the former shows children happily playing, the latter children preparing for war in a world of anti-Jewish persecution. 'One can hardly interfere with the Woman Unionists representing known facts', commented Street, though he added: 'As a matter of expediency I think it a pity to rub in Germany's faults just now, and her alleged warlike intentions'. However, the saving grace was the venue: 'St Helens is not an important centre'. Cromer agreed: 'I hardly think in the circumstances of this production interference is necessary'. The following month the Office also licensed *Official Announcement*,† another play which sought to expose anti-Jewish persecution. The censorship decided the play was 'a trifle which could hardly cause any fuss'. Its performance was in Bexhill.[65]

Perhaps more surprisingly, in May 1935 the censorship licensed for Cambridge's Festival Theatre *Son of Judea*.‡ This was a short play set in Berlin, in which we see a worker being victimised because of his Jewish grandfather, and hear his grandmother being beaten up offstage by brutal storm troopers. There are also references to concentration camps, to 'thousands of quite innocent people massacred, butchered', and to 'steel rods beating out the rhythm of Nazi marching songs on the backs of some

---

    * *Tell England*, by Aileen M. Wood
    † Written by Eleanor Elder
    ‡ Written by Michael Walsh

poor swine'. Yet it seems that the only cut made was the removal of the epithet 'bitch'. Street commented: 'it is impossible to prevent an occasional protest against barbarous usage of Jews'.[66] By contrast, a few months later Street identified the satire of Auden and Isherwood's *Dog Beneath the Skin* as 'an obvious attack on Germany' and proposed a series of cuts; he added: 'I dare say if the Lord Chamberlain requires all these excisions the author will withdraw the play. It would not be a great loss'. A considerably altered script was staged in January 1936 by the Group Theatre, and Game, who inspected the performance, found a few elements to be still unacceptable: 'One of the characters carries a Swastika flag which won't do, another character wears a mask of Mussolini (unflattering) and another a mask which I took for Hitler with toothache'. The Office insisted on removing all of these.[67]

In November 1935, the censorship licensed without objection Friedrich Wolfe's *Professor Mamlock*. Already, Street was criticising the play for its use of cliché and for being out of date:

> Yet another play, and rather belated, exhibiting the irrational intolerance practised against Jews in Germany. Belated, because the events are two years old and contemporary intolerance is on different lines . . . The play is rather ineffective for an English audience. We do not need to be told as we are over and over again of the want of reason and logic in the persecution of Jews. . . . But there is no reason for refusing a licence. Much more violent plays on the subject have been passed.[68]

Cromer queried 'I suppose the Germans cannot object?', but he agreed to risk a licence. Tellingly, when the same script was (unnecessarily) resubmitted in January 1939, it received a much less generous judgement from Henry Game:

> This play is very definitely an anti-Nazi play, and as the development of the action is based on certain well-known events—such as the Reichstag fire—which marked the rise to power of Hitler and the Nazis, it will be extremely difficult, or impossible, to ruritanianise it without drastic re-writing . . .
>
> If we are to adhere to the rule, that if authors want to write anti-Nazi plays, they must cast them in a Ruritanian form, I cannot possibly recommend this play.[69]

It was then discovered that Wolfe's play had already been licensed some years previously, and there were insufficient grounds for revisiting it.

In 1936 a licence was granted for what Street described as 'the most uncompromising attack on the persecution of the Jews we have had'. *Do We Not Bleed** was a desperately old-fashioned melodrama set in the fictitious

---

* Written by George H. Grimaldi

province of Galania and featuring a completely unflappable English hero confronting and outwitting the villainous governor. Despite an absurd and fantastical narrative, there was no doubting the identity of the victims.[70] The Governor declares he is 'fighting to free Galania of the accursed Jew', and to keep 'the blood of the race as pure as my own'.[71] The play's twist is to reveal at the climax that during a previous visit to Britain this Governor received an emergency blood transfusion which came from the English—and Jewish—journalist now confronting him! Street described *Do We Not Bleed* as 'An extremely bitter attack, effective though crude, on anti-Semitism in Germany', but again declared that 'the subject is stale now and unattractive'. He even argued that 'Such plays, which stir up useless passion, are I think to be deplored, even though they may be based on facts'; but there were reasons why it was unnecessary to ban it: 'The play is to be produced by the Richings Players—patroness Princess Victoria and with a distinguished President—probably in the country and though it is an able play of its kind I doubt its coming to London'.[72]

One of the problems which the censors repeatedly struggled with was the issue of 'fact' and 'fiction'. While on the one hand they intervened to prevent the inclusion of false—or unproven—details and accusations, it was the documenting in dramatic form of what was widely accepted to be 'true' which frequently caused the most trouble. 'It is "la verité qui blesse"', as they informed the Foreign Office.[73] On one occasion they suspected that a playwright had included actual text taken from 'a recent Nazi edict' and, bizarrely, it was proposed that the author should be told 'that if he didn't make it up he must take it out'.[74] Which way could a playwright turn? The German Embassy was particularly sensitive to any suggestion that the Nazis themselves had burnt down the Reichstag in order to discredit the Communists, and the 1938 version of *Whither Liberty* was licensed specifically 'on the understanding that the accusation against Hacker of having the "Senate House" blown up is omitted'.[75] Yet as early as December 1934, the Office had licensed Elmer Rice's *Judgement Day*, even though Street's report described it as 'an unmistakable and bitter attack on the Hitler Regime and especially on General Goering and, equally unmistakably a parody of the trial for the burning of the Reichstag'. Though it was 'cleverly veiled', said the Reader, there was 'no doubt of the identification'.[76] But Street persuaded his superiors that 'the distinguished American author ought to "get away with it"' because the identification was not explicit: 'It seems to me difficult to insist with an author that he <u>must</u> mean such an application'. However, in 1937, plans were announced to stage *Judgement Day* in London for the first time. The Office realised that, despite its cloak of fiction, Rice's play was likely to attract protests:

> In the final scene the dictator . . . is, very rightly, murdered. This fact, in
> itself, will not commend the play to the German Embassy, and, when
> taken in conjunction with the flagrant injustice of the trial itself, the
> characterisation of both Hitler and Goering . . . will probably call forth a
> protest from the German Embassy. As Mr Street points out there is a
> possibility that they will not be so foolish as to suggest that the cap fits the
> German people, but I do not think that the Germans at the moment are
> over-burdened with a sense of humour, or a vision of proportion.[77]

Nevertheless, apart from ensuring that make up and costume were not
used to make the analogy explicit, Cromer refused to withdraw the licence
he had previously issued: 'It is usually an inopportune moment in our
foreign relations to stage any play likely to offend the Germans, so that
conditions in this respect differ little in April 1937 from those of December
1934'.

But Rice's play received such widespread publicity and acclaim that it
transferred from a small theatre into the heart of the West End. Meanwhile,
reviewers left their readers in no doubt about the real subject: 'Though its
scene is in an imaginary European State, it is by no means Ruritanian, but
locked to contemporary events', stated *The Times*.[78] Others were even more
explicit: 'The Storm Troopers' shirts . . . are Slavic green, as supposedly
worn in a totalitarian State in south-eastern Europe, but the green would
seem to be a dye from Teutonic brown, as worn at the Reichstag Fire
Trial'.[79] Some drew attention to the audience response: 'On the first night
the cheering was tremendous . . . Here, in the middle of the London
theatre, is the most effective piece of anti-Nazi propaganda yet devised';
according to this reviewer, the performance of Rice's play was 'worth a
million book clubs and demonstrations'.[80] The German authorities applied
pressure on the Foreign Office:

> Herr Fitz Randolph of the German Embassy told me this morning that
> they had instructions from Berlin to draw our attention to the play
> *Judgement Day* which had now been running in London for some months.
> The play was clearly based on the Reichstag Fire Trial, and in German eyes
> was objectionable in that it was meant to cast discredit upon German
> judicial institutions. He appreciated that there was no direct allusion to
> Germany, and that it had been quite cleverly disguised, but at the same
> time it was perfectly obvious that it was intended as an attack on Germany
> . . . He drew attention to the . . . article in today's *Daily Telegraph*, showing
> that the play had been banned by the Burgermaster of the Hague 'on the
> grounds of its likeness to the Reichstag Trial'.[81]

Opting for the gentlemanly approach which so frequently oiled the wheels
of the British establishment, the Embassy put its trust in a discreet, rather
than an overt intervention:

> He added that it was desired only to draw our attention to this matter and not to enter a protest, and he particularly asked that, if we did find it possible to take any action, we should be careful that the fact of a German Embassy's intervention should not appear in the Press, as this would only make matters worse.

By coincidence or not, the censorship was able to reassure the Foreign Office that the production would be 'coming off in about ten days time'.

The German Embassy's strategy of making frequent complaints was doubtless intended not only to affect the immediate case but to influence future decisions. And indeed, the complaints about *Judgement Day* probably bore fruit elsewhere. The following year, when the author of *Take Heed* cited the licensing of Rice's play as a relevant precedent, Game dismissed his claim: '*Judgement Day*', he wrote, 'would certainly not be licensed now, and was always an example of bad-censoring'.[82] In fact, as the British government pursued its overt policy of appeasement towards the Fascists, and as the political crisis in Europe deepened, so these were reflected in the decisions and the arguments of St James's Palace. In May 1938, the Lord Chamberlain sought advice from the Foreign Office in connection with *Lorelei** and its 'many references to German persecution and cruelty'. But it was the general principle that most concerned him: 'I can foresee that we shall receive an increasing number of plays bearing on Germany and the Nazi regime so it would be a help to us if you could give—not so much a ruling, but some hints as to subjects and situations which it will be well to avoid'. The Foreign Office replied:

> We have, of course, had to consider this point on several occasions in the past, often as the result of a protest from the German embassy. We have always taken the line with the embassy that it is impossible in this country to censor plays dealing with Nazi ideology in general, merely on the ground of their underlying theme and general tendency. On the other hand it is clearly important that we should do what we can to give Herr Hitler, as the head of the German state, the protection which is afforded to heads of states by international practice. The Germans are very touchy about criticism of Herr Hitler and they have often pointed out that in Germany the greatest care has always been taken to prevent the appearance of any objectionable references to the British Royal Family. We should therefore welcome it if, in dealing with plays about Germany you were able to remove all references to Herr Hitler and passages which might be considered derogatory to his dignity as Head of the German state.

---

* Written by Jack Duval

The application for a licence for *Lorelei* was voluntarily withdrawn by the management following subsequent private discussions with the Lord Chamberlain's Office.[83]

In June of the same year, the Office licensed *Spring Morning,*[*] a 'light satirical comedy' about a dictator and his home life; they accepted the argument that it was 'the species "Dictator", and not the Political system that is the chief target of the author's ridicule', and that 'the caricature of a Dictator is sufficiently indefinite'. Even so, references to Jewish persecution and to the country having been previously 'robbed of its colonies' were cut, and to ensure that there were 'no recognizable emblems' on costumes, the manager was actually required to submit for approval a specimen cream shirt with symbol.[84] In the same month, Shaw's *Geneva* was approved, despite the fact that the main characters included transparent representations of Hitler and Mussolini. The new Reader, Geoffrey Dearmer, who soon gained a reputation at St James's for being unreliable and prone to leniency, recommended only minimal alterations. He argued that the dictators were 'by no means unsympathetic characters' and that Shaw's treatment of them was far from negative: 'If anything it is too fair!', he remarked. Dearmer suggested that the 'Chaplin moustache' might be removed, but on this occasion Cromer chose not to insist even on this: 'So long as there is no attempt at impersonation, objection can hardly be taken to a "Chaplin moustache" on the stage', he wrote, and decided that 'GBS is such a self-extinguishing volcano', that the play would cause 'little commotion'.[85] But the decision to license Shaw's play soon came to haunt the Office when it was invoked as a precedent by other writers.

Cromer did not have to deal with the repercussions himself. He retired in July 1938, after a sixteen-year reign, to be replaced by the Earl of Clarendon, a former Conservative whip, chairman of the BBC and, most recently, Governor-General of South Africa. Almost immediately, Clarendon had to deal with one of the most remarkable plays about Hitler and the Nazis so far written, a satirical farce called *Follow My Leader*, by Terence Rattigan and Anthony Maurice. Though one might now question how far it was appropriate to use broad comedy to attack the Nazis, this was surely one of the most witty and successfully sustained political satires of the decade. The Marx Brothers and Chaplin's *Great Dictator* both come to mind, but there are also elements in *Follow My Leader* which prefigure the work of Dario Fo, and, though it lacks the essential toughness, of Brecht's *Arturo Ui*. It certainly got under the skin of the German Embassy, and censorship kept it off the stage until January 1940, by which time, once again, its moment had passed.

---

[*] Written by C. Carter

Set in the imaginary state of Moronia, the central conceit is that its dictator—Zedesi (as in the national greeting 'Up Zedesi')—is a harmless puppet controlled by hidden forces in the party. Zedesi is coached into performing speeches which are written for him and which he barely understands, and he never subscribes to the political positions he is required to espouse. He makes friends with the ruler of the designated national enemy, and eventually destroys the party by refusing to give a speech declaring war. In some respects, Zedesi is clearly not Hitler, and Moronia is not Germany; indeed, in a revised version of the script the playwrights introduced a gag to the final scene which may have been invented partly to persuade the censors that the whole narrative is a fiction: answering the telephone, Zedesi finds himself in conversation with another dictator

> ZEDESI: Oh, yes, I've heard about you, and how are things going? Not so good, eh? Well, I'm not surprised the way you're carrying on. You just take my advice, old chap, get out of it while you can, it's no job for a self-respecting working man. There's no need to shout! Who do you think you are? No, I'm not coming to Berchtesgaden. I don't care if your patience is exhausted, I am not signing any bloody trade agreements, so there! (*He holds out the telephone. A furious voice, shouting in German, is heard through the receiver*) Oh, put a sock in it! (*He leaves receiver on the desk, the voice continues till the end of the scene*) . . . he should have stopped at house-painting.[86]

Despite this, and as Game noted, 'The source of inspiration of a good deal of the authors' fun is unmistakeable'.

When *Follow My Leader* was submitted by Gilbert Miller in July 1938, Assistant Comptroller Norman Gwatkin characterised it as a 'bombshell' which had 'exploded with shattering force under the new Lord Chamberlain', and described it as 'unfortunate that the new Lord Chamberlain should be faced with such a play, on which even the readers seem to disagree'.[87] Game considered the play 'farcical nonsense' and 'immature', and he proposed a series of specific changes to head off the objections of the German Embassy. Unwilling to give a definite recommendation, he concluded that 'in view of the recent letter from the Foreign Office, in which their views on these questions were indicated, I think this play should be sent to them for an opinion'. Dearmer, however, drew attention to the fact that the writers had 'taken pains to make Zedesi as unlike Hitler as possible', though he criticised them for having 'lazily' included too many facts and recognisable details. 'His unlikeness to Hitler could be emphasised still more. This, I think, should be done'. He proposed that the script should be rewritten, and the writers required to show 'more ingenuity' in constructing a greater distance between fiction and reality, but he argued that, in the context of recent decisions, there were no reasonable grounds for refusing a licence:

If the play is sent to the FO I think reference should be made to plays on the same subject already licensed. *Judgement Day* was a much more formidable attack and bitter if not savage whereas this is not. Shaw's *Geneva* too deals directly with the subject without making any attempt to disguise the personalities whereas this play carefully alters them . . .

If this play were banned the authors might complain with reason that preferential treatment is given to the GBS's and Elmer Rice's of the dramatic world. The Censor has never been guilty of this.

I think the play is fair comment on national philosophies and politics, not an attack against particular nations exclusively and, as such, should be licensed.

The script and the Readers' reports were forwarded to the Foreign Office: 'It is perhaps better that I should worry you now', wrote Gwatkin, 'than that you should be worried later on by the German Embassy'. The Foreign Office took a hard line, and, at the end of July the Assistant Comptroller reported their recommendation to Miller.

The Lord Chamberlain has just received the views of the Foreign Office who are of the definite opinion production of this play at this time would not be in the best interest of the country . . . I have enquired if there is any time limit to this ban and am told 'This year anyhow'—and I rather gather that that time limit was a minimum.

It was suggested that the play might be revised, ruritanianised and the chief characters altered in such a way that they could not be identified.

Following the staging of Shaw's *Geneva*, Miller argued that there could surely no longer be any valid objection to this play. Gwatkin, however, maintained that 'the two plays are hardly comparable', and that the situation was unchanged. His justification was contrived and tenuous: '*Follow My Leader* is a farce in which certain of the German leaders are definitely burlesqued, whereas *Geneva* is a politico-philosophic discussion in which the characters are abstractions rather than personalities.'

Another source of problems during the summer of 1938 was a play by Vere Sullivan which the censorship had licensed as *Code of Honour* the previous autumn. Reporting in September 1937, Game thought the writer's aim was 'to contrast the conception of life and its duties of the British and German peoples'; he noted, with evident relief, that 'the Teutonic point of view, and its justification, is treated with as much sympathy, if not more, as the British'.[88] Game recommended the play as one which 'far from doing any harm, may do good', and Cromer described it as 'a good study in national characteristics'. But the writer was subsequently stung by the critical reception of her work as pro-German and anti-British, and in June 1938 a new version was submitted under the title, *Trumpeter, Play!*. Ironically, this attempted realignment of sympathies towards the British and against the Germans made the text more problematic from the point of view of the censorship; Game suggested that 'the admirable impartiality of the original version' had been replaced by a 'British smugness', and attributed this to a cynical recognition of the needs of the box office:

> The original play was written with considerable understanding of the conflicting national characteristics; and if any bias was shown it was towards the German outlook on life rather than the English. Since then I think that the authoress has been persuaded that too great sympathy with the Teutonic point of view is unlikely to prove popular in the Theatre at the present time; and so, besides bringing her play up to date as regards the state of tension in European politics, she has made concessions to national amour-propre.[89]

The producer, Leon Lion, pointed out that he had been 'strongly criticised on the grounds that the case for Germany is stated but that nothing whatever is said about the case for England', but the censorship preferred the slant of the original version. 'We allowed this play because it did not seem that it could be offensive to Germany', wrote the Assistant Comptroller; 'I don't think that it should now be altered to pass dubious speeches'.

Lion staged the play privately and invited the Lord Chamberlain to attend, assuring him that 'you would find there is nothing offensive to Germany, in fact the bias seems to fall too heavily on the side of Germany'. Gwatkin did indeed go and see it, and in a contradictory and revealing comment subsequently confirmed that he 'was much impressed by the fairness of this play which undoubtedly had a pro-German bias'. After consulting with the German Embassy, it was agreed that the revised version should be licensed, subject to further modifications. However, the effort to appease all sides had weakened the play in the eyes of critics: 'Never was work better intentioned', wrote *The Times*; 'the puzzle is to discover what precisely its intention is'. Everyone in the play is 'nice', complained the critic, and the script was 'palpably struggling to be fair to Germans, English, militarists, pacifists, and any one else who turns up'.[90] In the *Daily Telegraph*, W.A. Darlington suggested that the author had 'changed horses in the middle of the stream', and produced 'a propaganda play with the added disadvantage of seeming to be on both sides at once'.[91]

Meanwhile, Sullivan herself apparently felt that the balance remained inappropriate. The following week, Lion wrote again to the Lord Chamberlain to say the play was to be withdrawn and more substantially reworked:

> I must tell you that my author is very distressed—and justifiably I think— at these widespread aspersions that the play as it stands . . . smacks of propaganda for Nazism . . . Having now seen the play yourself, I am sure you will appreciate that if there is to be any bias in such a sympathetic presentment of two Peoples, it should fall definitely to our own country rather than seem against it. Though I had no idea such an effect was

possibly being produced, I have personally received too many protests and
reproaches to ignore the fact that this incredible impression <u>has</u> been
created in certain quarters.

In a remarkable reply, Gwatkin sought to intervene directly with the
process of rewriting. What others saw as an objectionable bias in favour of
the Nazis, he saw as its strength:

> I am really distressed to hear that *Trumpeter, Play!* is coming off . . . because
> I think, quite apart from anything else, it is a helpful play in the present
> continuous crisis. Do please persuade your author not to rewrite the play
> full of 'jingo' spirit.
>   I think I told you that the rather well-informed people who had spoken
> to me about the play were impressed with its fairness and helpfulness, but
> at the same time I understand too, that for many people, anything which is
> not 'contra' in red letters is considered 'pro' which isn't really very
> sensible.

In September 1938, Lion submitted a new script by Sullivan, with a very
different tone. Dearmer described *We, the Condemned* as 'a fantasy of pro-
Jewish, anti-totalitarian-state propaganda', and the Comptroller, Tim
Nugent, sought the advice of the Foreign Office. Nugent indicated that,
since the setting was fictional, a licence would normally be issued for such a
play; but he added that the Lord Chamberlain felt 'that during the present
situation it would be unwise to license any play dealing with this or a
similar anti-Nazi theme'. While waiting for the Foreign Office to reply, he
met with the manager and author:

> I explained to him [sic] that the Lord Chamberlain was not prepared to
> license this or any other definitely anti-Nazi play during the present crisis.
> . . . The Lord Chamberlain felt that as a responsible censor he would be
> not justified in allowing plays of this sort to be produced at a time that they
> may be embarrassing to the Government, and a source of danger in a
> delicate situation. I assured Mr Lion, however, that this did not mean that
> the play was permanently banned . . . The matter, therefore, was left that
> Mr Lion would communicate with the Office again when the present
> crisis was less acute.[92]

In an important and explicit document of 6 October, the Foreign Office
replied to Nugent's letter. It was, they said, hard to comment directly since
they had not received a copy of the script, but they were currently 'anxious
to discourage anti-Nazi plays whenever possible since they may do
considerable harm to our relations with Germany by needlessly and
uselessly annoying influential circles in that country'. The letter concluded:

> This is perhaps particularly true at the present moment when we hope
> that, as a result of the Munich Agreement, we may be entering upon an era

of more friendly relations with Germany and when we have in mind the possibility of getting the German government to co-operate in facilitating the exodus of Jews from Germany by allowing them to take a proportion of their possessions with them. We therefore hope that you may find it possible to withhold the licence from this play.

We, the Condemned was never licensed for performance.

Within a few days of receiving this policy statement from the Foreign Office, the Lord Chamberlain had to rule on the proposed Group Theatre production of Auden and Isherwood's new play, *On the Frontier*. Dearmer defended it in principle, though he accepted that the parallels between the imaginary Westland and the real Germany were unmissable, and that specific references which forced the connection would have to be removed. But Dearmer was a published poet from the First World War—he had also made a significant contribution to the discovery and 1928 Stage Society production of Sherriff's anti-war drama *Journey's End*—and had a genuine interest in the theatre and in contemporary writing. He argued that the play should not be judged in terms of immediate and political relevance, but from a quite different stance: 'I would like to put forward the significance of its claim as poetic drama', he wrote, and he declared that its authors were 'two of the leading young poets of their generation'. Dearmer went on to argue that the main thrust of the play was not political or anti-fascist: 'It has no reference to the recent crisis, nor is it directed solely against the Totalitarian states; the Democratic countries come off just as badly as advocates of the jargon of patriotic war fervour'. He then stated his view that even if the play did take sides, it would still be illogical and iniquitous to suppress it: 'A play that pleaded the case for the Democratic countries as opposed to the Totalitarian would certainly be permissible, indeed to ban such would be to remove the right of free speech altogether'. Dearmer offered a forceful and impassioned defence of the playwrights' approach, and his conclusion was unequivocal:

> Great care has been taken to create an impersonal Leader, but it is impossible to draw such a character without his resembling one of the two known living examples because they are to some extent mere advocates of a philosophy, a philosophy which it is the right, and duty, of modern English poets to attack.
>
> To forbid this would be to subscribe to fascist ideology.

Not all of Dearmer's colleagues were convinced. Gwatkin restated the Foreign Office opinion which the Office had recently absorbed, and was unapologetic about its implications for freedom of speech: 'At such a time as this the best interests of the country are served by avoiding any unnecessary exasperation to the leaders of the German people—even if this entails a certain muzzling of contemporary playwrights'. Game accepted that totalitarian states must still be subject to external criticism, but only if such criticism remained abstract and hypothetical. Responding to Dearmer's argument he concluded: 'I agree that the totalitarian principle is one which is abhorrent to the normal Englishman but I disagree that it is the duty of modern Poets to attack this principle'. *On the Frontier* was licensed for performance, but only after extensive cuts had been imposed.

The letter from the Foreign Office of 6 October had brought things to a head, and there were substantial disagreements and dissatisfactions in St James's Palace about its implications. On 21 October, Clarendon called a meeting 'To discuss the licensing of plays containing criticism, veiled or open, of forms of government or political policy of other countries'; in effect, the intention was to clarify and agree a policy in relation to plays about the Nazis, and the meeting was attended by Clarendon's Comptroller, Tim Nugent, and Assistant Comptroller, Norman Gwatkin, and by the three Readers of plays—Henry Game, Geoffrey Dearmer and Charles Heriot. At least two of the Readers expressed misgivings about the political restrictions they were now being asked to police, and despite the relative blandness of Gwatkin's condensed account of the meeting, it is evident that some deeply held convictions were expressed and that Clarendon found himself struggling to balance conflicting pressures:

The Lord Chamberlain opened the discussion by suggesting that any plays which contained criticism of Mussolini and Hitler should not be licensed, as their production would only complicate the present situation; and he pointed out that although there is no censorship of the Press, we unfortunately have one over Plays, and that this fact is well known.

Mr Game proclaimed his championship of free speech, both in the Press and on the Stage and said that the British Nation has always stood for that freedom, as against other nations' policy of hatred and tyranny, and submitted that if any definite Nation is attacked, the objections from outside could not hold water, if the play was Ruritanianised.

The Lord Chamberlain doubted if the Stage was the correct medium for any political anti-anything propaganda.

It was suggested that as long as a play was Ruritanianised and if no attack on the Leaders of other nations was permitted that it was wrong to prevent free expression of views on ideology and expression of disgust at persecutions: or criticisms of other forms of Government or political policy.

Mr Game suggested that if the censorship did not allow a certain amount of criticism on the stage, it would eventually endanger the position of the censorship.

Mr Game agreed that a compromise is found in Ruritanianisation.

The Lord Chamberlain suggested that the possibility of protests from the justice-loving Englishmen are sufficiently voiced in the press, in private correspondence, and by the ordinary man in the street.

A discussion then arose as to the Lord Chamberlain's actual position either as a servant of the Government or as servant of the King, but in fact the King has to back up his Government, therefore as the King's servant, in loyalty, the Lord Chamberlain has to go back to the King.

Colonel Nugent raised the point that in any very serious crisis it would be wrong to go definitely against the Government's policy.

Mr Game whilst agreeing partially, was very strongly of the opinion that the censorship should be of a judicial capacity and not biased by the political situation. The Comptroller added that the present position was of such seriousness that there would be very grave danger in not adhering to the Government's policy.

Mr Dearmer said that we are a democracy and stand for free speech, and to prevent this would cause unfavourable comment in the press and might eventually cause more harm to the Government's policy than to allow well-controlled public performance of a 'doubtful play'.

The Lord Chamberlain suggested that the type of play in question provided that it was skilfully Ruritanianised should still be allowed and that a good playwright should be able to give his message without having to resort to personalities, or actual politics.

The Lord Chamberlain has, therefore, decided that the type of play under discussion shall be allowed a licence provided it is 'Ruritanianised' and provided any pointers are removed which may indicate, even indirectly, foreign personalities or countries.

Much of this was effectively a restatement of the policies practised by the Lord Chamberlain's Office over the previous five years. But it was far from the end of the struggle, and in December 1938 the Lord Chamberlain's Office produced a statement for the Foreign Office which attempted to summarise its position. Some of the frustration about the political restraints they were being expected to impose on playwrights, and the implicit criticism of the policy of appeasement, are barely masked by the diplomatic politeness:

Political International Plays
Anti-semitism seems to be increasing in intensity on the Continent, both in violence and in the number of countries concerned.

The natural resentment felt by the free people of this country has found expression in public speeches, over the wireless, in the press and in Parliament, even by the Prime Minister himself.

The only individual who is not allowed to express his views is the playwright. This fact is constantly being referred to by playwrights themselves and in the Press—in fact, it has been suggested that the Censor is a special department of the German Embassy.

Shortly after Munich the policy of this country was, rightly, one of conciliation and every effort was made to avoid jarring German susceptibilities in the hopes of fostering a glimmer of a satisfactory understanding between Germany and this country.

At best, it must be admitted that this light is no better than it was, and that Jew baiting in Germany is a hundred fold more than it was at the time of the Munich Meeting.

Several plays have been received and more can be expected, with a plot woven round the difficulties of Jewish family life in anti-Jewish totalitarian States.

Some of these plays can, of course, be completely Ruritanianised, with regard to names, places and heads, etc., and be reduced to the status of an ordinary Drama; but to the general public, any play dealing with Jew-baiting suggests that the bait is probably Germans—possibly Italians. There are other more difficult plays bringing in reference to Nazi ideology.

Even if German names are excluded, like the rose there is no mistaking the smell.

Once again, St James's Palace sought advice:

The question really is this—is the Censorship always to ban references to other countries' policies, even if all the names, heads, etc., are eradicated which give a direct clue to the nation whose policy is the subject of the Play?

It will be obvious by inference which nation is referred to, but as I say, there will be no direct clues.

It is, of course, understood that no foreign Statesman is mentioned by name in any derogatory sense.

The indications are that when Germany has dealt with the Jewish question to her satisfaction she will then start the same form of persecution against the Catholics, this, too, in its turn will probably bring forth another spate of plays dealing with the hardships of Catholic families in the totalitarian States concerned.

Therefore a ruling on the method which the censorship should employ in dealing with these plays would be of the greatest assistance, and to my own mind sufficient satisfaction should be given to foreign Embassies if all direct clues were removed from plays, even if direct allusions make it clear by inferences the country concerned. In fact, that the Censorship should protect foreign personalities but not foreign policies.

It took the Foreign Office nearly a month to respond, but, when they did, on 9 January 1939, they urged caution. It was evident that the Foreign Office, too, was endeavouring to balance on a shifting tightrope of uncertainty and compromise:

Dear Gwatkin,

I am sorry that we have not been able to let you have an earlier reply to your enquiry about our attitude towards the licensing of plays of an anti-German or anti-Nazi character. The question is a difficult one, and we have given it very careful consideration.

We appreciate that circumstances have somewhat changed since Roberts's letter to Nugent of the 6th October last, and that you must be finding it difficult to maintain the attitude suggested in that letter, in view of the widespread criticism in this country of certain aspects of Nazi policy, particularly since the recent anti-Jewish measures. The German Government are, of course, aware that, although we cannot control anti-Nazi attacks in the press, we are in a position to control such attacks on the stage. We should, therefore, not recommend that the present ban on anti-Nazi plays should be completely raised, since the London stage would probably then be flooded with such plays, which would no doubt be very popular at the moment.

Although it is difficult to lay down any hard and fast rule, our general conclusion would be that in present circumstances a play should not be banned simply because it deals with an enormity of which the rulers of Germany are guilty. Plays would have to be 'Ruritanianised', and all direct offensive references to Germany, to Herr Hitler, or to other prominent German personages must be avoided. If this is done, whether the play deals with questions directly concerning German policy, such as Jewish persecution, or with ideological themes, the German Government would have no legitimate ground for complaint unless they wished to fit the cap. Provided, therefore, that this condition is complied with, we do not think that an absolute ban should be maintained.

We feel, however, that the above relaxation in the policy which we have recently been following should only apply to plays of real artistic merit and not to merely vulgar rubbish. I do not know how far you are empowered to distinguish between good and bad plays in exercising the censorship, but from our point of view we should certainly like you to endeavour to keep off the stage scribblings that merely aim at making money out of heated feelings.

In every case it is, of course, essential to prevent the appearance of any obnoxious personal reference to Herr Hitler himself and of any passages likely to be considered derogatory to his dignity as Head of the German State.

In view of the difficulty in drawing a definite line, doubtful cases will no doubt continue to arise from time to time, and we should be glad if you would give us an opportunity in all such cases to express an opinion before the play is passed.

Gwatkin forwarded the letter to the Lord Chamberlain, and informed him of his own recent discussion with a German representative:

My dear Lord Clarendon,
    I thought you might like to see our long-waited-for letter from the F.O. about German plays.
    I also had a long talk with Von Selzam, the councillor of the German Embassy. He admitted that there were excesses in Germany, unavoidable under the circumstances, but said it was a pity that these excesses should be brought out in high-relief and that anti-Nazi plays did not 'help'. I

think he was reasonable and our talk may help. His chief concern was that the names of the German leaders should not be used: this, of course, we do see to. . .[93]

Staff at St James's Palace were not united. In December 1938, Dearmer recommended *Exodus*★ as 'a high class and serious piece of well-written and legitimate exposition' and 'a sympathetic picture of Jewish persecution'. He noted that its setting in 'the Jewish quarter of a city in middle Europe' was deliberately non-specific, and that the whole play was 'carefully constructed to avoid the charge of it appearing to be anti-Nazi propaganda'. Despite his advocacy, no licence was granted.[94] In January 1939, Stephen Spender's *Trial of a Judge* was submitted for a licence for public performance in Leicester. Not only had the play already been privately produced in London by the Group Theatre, but the published script had, according to Game, been widely read. Game evidently thought it a more potent play than many anti-Nazi ones he had encountered, but he predicted that it might have a better chance than some of avoiding the attentions of the German Embassy: 'This play, dealing as it does with fundamentals is much more deadly in its aim than a more simple and objective anti-Nazi melodrama; but it is for that very reason, perhaps, less likely to wound the thick hides of its intended victims'.[95] Game had no doubt that, in spite of its non-specific setting, the events of the play were 'inspired by, and directed at, Nazi misrule'. But he was becoming more and more irritated by the specious strategy he was expected to practise:

> in this play, as in others with which I have dealt, the fiction that we try to maintain, that they are of general application, is in truth rather a farce, and I have increasingly a feeling of attempting a futility and of having of necessity to turn out nothing better than a botched piece of work.

Spender's play was licensed with relatively minor alterations.

A few days later, Game developed his argument further, when he reported on a private performance he had witnessed of *Juggernaut*, a chronicle play written by A. Heckstall-Smith and E.P. Hare. Game did not think it likely any management would attempt to stage this 'exhaustive— and exhausting—narrative of the tragic history of Austria from 1913 down to the Anchluss of last year', but he used his report as a starting point to explore the weaknesses of the current policy and to recommend possible revisions. He found *Juggernaut* a 'remarkably moderate' play in political terms, which 'handles the coming of the Nazis to power with fairness and discretion'; yet 'under our present policy it could not pass, because the action, being interwoven with historical fact, could not be ruritanianised.

★ Written by Robert Ellison and Emerys Jones

Thus we should have a mild play banned while others, much more provoc-ative, are passed.'[96] He described the recent attempt to ruritanianise *Take Heed* as a 'misplaced and futile effort', since it had resulted in 'acrimonious disputes between the office and the author and the making of a thoroughly unsatisfactory job at the end of it'. Game argued for a change in policy:

> I think the present position is an impossible one and that we should in future do one of two things.
>   a) Ban all anti-Nazi plays which are not pure works of fiction—that is with no historical background except the fact of the Nazis existence, or
>   b) Merely alter real names and remove violently provocative passages.

Despite Game's prediction, *Juggernaut* was in fact submitted for licence less than a week later. 'I suppose the Semite Backers consider that its topical interest outweighs its dramatic shortcomings', he disparagingly commented, and he restated his view that it would be 'futile' to insist on removing the real historical context. 'I do not believe' he wrote, deliberately echoing Gwatkin's description of Von Selzam, 'that any reasonable German would object', since this was not 'a real genuine anti-Nazi play'.

> It seems to me that it is a fair and detached statement of historical fact, with a little melodrama put in at the end to give it a dramatic climax and that no more bias is shown by the authors against the Nazis than is felt by any moderate minded Democrat.

Juggernaut was licensed in January 1939 with only minor changes, but some of the responses would not have endeared the censorship to the German Embassy. The *Daily Mail* reviewer described Herr Hitler as 'the dreaded bogey' of the drama; 'if the pro-Semite sympathy is laid on with a large trowel', it suggested, 'the season for making the chief representative of the anti-Semitic party a pantomime Demon King ... is pardonably appropriate'.[97] Yet when the play was revived in June, the authors included a note in the programme insisting they had documented events with objectivity and were not in the business of propaganda:

> We have always maintained that the playwright has no business to don the preacher's stole, using the stage for a pulpit. Rather it is his duty like that of the landscape painter, to present a picture of a scene as he sees it ... We have no message to give nor moral to point.[98]

Also in June 1939, the Office licensed a play staged by the Yiddish Arts Theatre from New York. *Professor Schelling** centred on a family of refugees who flee Nazi Germany and take up asylum in the United States. The focus of the drama was less on the persecutors than on the response of the

---

* Written by H. Leivick

victims, but Schelling is supposed to have spent five years in a Nazi concentration camp before the play starts, and Game guessed that the script was likely to contain offensive references to Germany. 'Normally we should Ruritanianise the play', he wrote, 'but as this is a play in Yiddish, it should be sufficient if we require all offensive references to Hitler to be removed'. The company were instructed that 'there should be no mention of Hitler and such remarks as "The fire of his poisonous and bestial doctrine in this country" should be omitted, or altered'.[99]

At about the same time, significant cuts were being imposed on two of Unity Theatre's productions. 'To remove possible points of offence to Foreign Powers', wrote Game in May 1939 in connection with Jack Lindsay's *We Need Russia*, 'I should suggest the alteration of the word 'fascist' on page 1, as this is too closely associated with the word "murderers"'. He was also worried about 'the imputations of aggressive intention made against Japan and Germany on page 3', despite their accuracy: 'It is all very true, no doubt, but can we give our official sanction to such provocative statements?' Clarendon decided that they couldn't.[100] Similarly, Game described Unity's 'Every Father His Own Führer'* as 'a well merited burlesque of Hitler's ideas'; but he questioned: 'whether it is expedient to allow it', and the direct references were removed.[101]

At the start of July, Unity submitted Stephen Spender's translation of Toller's *Pastor Hall*. The Office felt obliged to maintain its policy, though Game's report acknowledged that the time for change was fast approaching. For the moment, however, and in the face of all that was happening in the world outside, St James's Palace advocated the practice of a traditional, gentlemanly civility:

> It might make an effective propaganda play if war breaks out; but while peace is still pursued, I could not recommend the L.C. to pass it in its present form. To do so would be to jettison our present policy of ruritani-anising anti-Nazi plays . . . I see no sufficient reason to abandon diplomatic civilities just because others are beginning to lose their tempers.[102]

Although Dearmer found Toller's play 'powerful and moving', he admitted that it 'spares no pains to vilify the Nazis and exalt the Jews'. He described it as 'a violently prejudiced piece of special pleading however much truth it may contain'. As with Auden and Isherwood, Dearmer acknowledged the status of both playwright and translator, but discounted its relevance: 'One hates to tamper with the work of a dramatist of Toller's reputation or, for that matter, of Spender's, but such considerations are beside the point. One cannot jettison a policy for such reasons'. He confirmed that the text was

---

★ A scene from *Unity Revue*, written by Geoffrey Parsons and Robert Mitchell 'so riddled with references to Germany, Nazis, S.S. and Gestapo men, not to mention Hitler himself, that it would be tedious to catalogue', and he indicated that only if the 'promoters' of the production accepted the principle of excising the Germanic references and ruritanianising the script should the detail be considered. Unity responded by asserting that 'the transfer to Ruritania of the subject and of this play would spoil its effectiveness'. Meanwhile, Clarendon sent the script to the German Embassy to test their response. Their spokesperson replied to Gwatkin on 25 July:

> Dear Norman,
>   . . . If you ask for my opinion I can only say that the whole thing is the most abominable piece of anti-German propaganda I have come across since a long time. I have made a few additional corrections, but I do not think that it is possible at all to take away by occasional scratchings anti-German character. You can omit as much as you wish—a reader will always realise against whom the book is written. It is most objectionable from the German point of view.

A few weeks later the situation had, of course, changed irrevocably, and a licence for Toller's play was granted in October 1939.

Meanwhile, in the same month of July, the playwright H.M. Harwood was inevitably disallowed from including Mussolini and Hitler alongside some forty other characters in Hades in the epilogue to his anti-war play, *These Mortals*. An earlier version of the play had already been licensed, and Harwood was furious that he was not allowed to make this addition. He cited Shaw's *Geneva* as one of several theatrical and cinematic precedents, but the Office desperately tried to rebuff the connection:

> With regard to *Geneva*, it is true that an acute intelligence is not required to recognise Hitler and Mussolini in Mr Shaw's characters, but these are poetic and philosophical types rather than actual representations; whereas it is Mr Harwood's object to represent actual and historical people only.[103]

The censors also objected that one of his examples was irrelevant since it was a film rather than a play. Harwood launched a bitter attack on the Lord Chamberlain's policy:

> I gather that if I substitute the name of Basso Profundo for that of Mussolini, the character will then become a 'philosophic type'. This seems to me a thoroughly English solution . . .
>   I chose *Nazi Spy* as an illustration precisely because it comes under a different censorship. It seemed to me that if Lord Tyrell had come to the conclusion that there was no objection to 2–3000000 people seeing a representation of Hitler, the same thing could scarcely be harmful to the few hundred who might see a play. It seems however that the stage is still to be the only place where mention of things that happen to be [in] people's minds is taboo. The press, the seminar, the pulpit, the House of

Commons are allowed to comment, but not the stage, which is to remain in the condition of a myxoedematous child whose parents refuse to give it thyroid because it had not been discovered in <u>their</u> day! No wonder the English audience is cretinous!

On 24 July, with war drawing ever closer, Rattigan resubmitted *Follow My Leader*, arguing that 'circumstances, if not personalities, have considerably changed'. He claimed to have rewritten the text and removed everything to which the Lord Chamberlain or the Foreign Office might object, and his case was supported with passion and conviction by Geoffrey Dearmer. Dearmer's report focused on inconsistencies in the practice of censorship, and he argued that the play's arguments and positions were now close to official policy:

> I feel that the case against the play is now out of date. I don't think it can seriously be contended that the three chief characters ... resemble Goebbels Goering and Hitler. . . Shaw's famous Three are much more like their originals. Is it fair to Rattigan to take the view that GBS's characters are any more 'philosophic types' because his are comparatively favourable to their originals and Rattigan's are not. The fact that *Follow My Leader* is a satirical burlesque whereas Shaw's is a serious fantasy should weigh in favour of Rattigan's play.
>
> There were reasons for banning the play last year because of its central political situation and the policy of appeasement ... but this is now history. Surely a dramatist may echo by implication the Government's and the Country's political views? To take the opposite view and ban a play because it makes fun of fascist ideology would be to hand over as a gift to the Censor's enemies the most weighty of ammunition ... The play is a political farcical satire on European events and any foreign embassy which took exception to it would be suffering from a very far-fetched imagination and a guilty conscience.

Game was more doubtful:

> I have not seen the new version of this play; but if the authors have made no material alterations, the probability, or possibility, that the public will associate its chief characters with the personalities of the German leaders still remains the objection. The Czecho-Slovakian source of some of the incidents in the play are, I agree, of less importance now politically; but they remain of equal importance as an indication of the source of the authors' inspiration.
>
> If the politics of the play are obviously German, will this not lead the public mind to a belief that the chief characters are German too? If I were a fanatical Nazi I should feel much greater resentment at fun being made of my leaders than at criticism of my political ideals. If the characters could be made unrecognizable as the German leaders I dont [sic] think the political analogies would matter.

Gwatkin sent the script to the German Embassy, who duly complained that the play would 'raise unfriendly feeling in the audience' and be unhelpful in terms of Anglo-German relations. On 3 August, the Assistant Comptroller endorsed their position:

> I have just received the remarks of a reasonable German from the Embassy, and he has arrived at the conclusion I feared he would by just reading the play unbiased by any additional reports.
>
> I do not think that there can really be any argument that the whole play is, in fact, a burlesque of the German leaders and the German ideology. I had hoped, the play being an absolute farce, and all the characters being the antithesis of what they really are in life, that the Germans would take the point of view that the cap didn't fit.
>
> There is a divergence of views between the two Readers but I myself come down on the side of 'No Licence' in its present form.

Gwatkin struggled to think of how best to advise Rattigan:

> How it can be altered is for the author to puzzle out but he will ask for directions and I think the only ones we can give him are
> 1. 'Hitler' not a plumber but someone not in the 'housepainter' class.
> 2. No 'blowing up' perhaps—(but blowing up of an Embassy is quite another matter to burning the parliament buildings).
> 3. No field Marshal.
> 4. No 'minority' talk.
> 5. The personalities without the incidents or the incidents without the personalities.

But he acknowledged the absurdity of the situation: 'I dont think the play <u>can</u> be rewritten, but for the life of me I dont see how anyone could write a play in which the <u>characters</u> could be more opposite to those of the actual persons who the incidents in the play make one believe they are'.

Clarendon agreed that the play was 'indeed a teaser', and found himself equally torn:

> Personally I should like to ban all these anti-Nazi plays for they cannot help to promote a better atmosphere, on the other hand a policy of appeasement cannot be said to have done much good so far. But I do not think I can refuse to license this play having due regard to the fact that *Geneva* and other similar plays have been allowed, so that would give the authors of *Follow My Leader* a chance of complaining that Shaw and Elmer Rice are accorded preferential treatment. It is true of course that *Geneva* and *Judgement Day* are severe criticisms of the Nazi system, where this play is as you say a burlesque on the German Leader and German Ideology. Nevertheless they are also anti though from different angles. I think the best course is to insist on alterations on the lines you suggest in your memo of 3rd August.

Despite Clarendon's doubts that he had any reasonable grounds for refusing a licence, On 10 August, the playwright was informed that his play was unacceptable:

> I to-day interviewed Mr Terence Rattigan and explained to him that there could not be any question of licensing the play as it now stands. I pointed out that although the principal characters bear no resemblance to the three most prominent men in Germany, yet the fact that all the incidents in the play so closely pointed to Germany being the country portrayed would undoubtedly lead the public mind to believe that the chief characters were German too. I added that the Lord Chamberlain had naturally to be very careful in not allowing any guying of heads of Foreign States, and I reminded him that Germany were always very particular to prevent any objectionable references to the British Royal Family. I further told Mr Rattigan that as far as I could see, the only thing that he could do was to re-write the play, either with the personalities and without the incidents or with the incidents and without the personalities, but that I was afraid that this might prove a well nigh impossible task. I also said that he would have to change the 'Leader' from a plumber to someone not in the house painting class and that he would have to obliterate any question of the soldier rising from the ranks quickly to the rank of Field Marshal and that the Minority talk would have to be expunged.

Probably with his tongue firmly in his cheek, the playwright himself offered an alternative suggestion which was almost equally alarming:

> Mr Terence Rattigan was very charming about it all and professed that he saw all the points that I made. He admitted that it would be very difficult to re-write the play in the lines indicated, and he wondered whether it would be possible to make the scene England in the future and thus avoid all question of Foreign countries. I said that of course I could not give an opinion on that until I had seen the script, and warned him that he would have to be just as careful to avoid English personalities such as Winston Churchill or Mosley.

Six weeks later, on 23 September, some three weeks after war on Germany had been declared, Clarendon agreed to license *Follow My Leader*: 'This play can now be passed for there is no longer any reason why we should be anxious not to hurt Nazi feelings'.[104] Ironically, Rattigan was himself now working for the Foreign Office. But perhaps surprisingly, the censorship continued even now to equivocate over how much freedom it was prepared to grant to playwrights wishing to criticise the Nazis. In October, the manager of the Phoenix Theatre, Claude Luxemburg, planned to revive Elmer Rice's *Judgement Day*, but to make the subject explicit by setting it in Germany and using German names—including Hitler and Goering—for the characters. He had Rice's backing for this, and argued that the play 'should be of real interest and value at the present time'.[105] But his request was rejected by the Lord Chamberlain, on the grounds that mixing 'fact' with 'fiction' might hand the enemy a defence and a propaganda coup:

> If we agree to the play being Germanized, we lay ourselves open to the charge, which may be made by the Germans, that we are allowing lying propaganda. In my opinion there would be some justification for this charge, as it is reasonable to suppose that a proportion of the public that may go to see the play in its new form would accept the facts of the play as historically true. There is no lack of historical truth on which to base propaganda against the Nazi leaders without the necessity of having recourse to imaginary happenings, and it seems to me undesirable to weaken our position by any doubtful propaganda.

Whether Clarendon had other motives or was put under external pressure we shall probably never know. Luxemburg pointed out that 'the Author has expressed his desire that the play should be presented with the true characters upon which he based his story', and complained: 'we cannot understand that a subject of such paramount importance . . . should be barred from being performed'. He promised to specify in all publicity that the play contained fictional elements, and reminded them that since it ended with the killing of the dictator this was anyway self-evident. Yet Luxemburg simultaneously defended the play for its accuracy:

> *Judgement Day* is as true a portrayal as any play can be, in that it depicts the travesty of truth and justice which the present German Regime has imposed upon the people of that country. When it is considered that exposure of these methods are being made clear to the British public through the medium of the Press, screen and broadcasting, and that in many instances these exposures contain direct references to, and portrayals of, the Nazi leaders, it would seem that the living theatre might also be allowed to play its part.

The Office was unpersuaded, and the Acting Comptroller, Major Gordon, dismissively advised the Lord Chamberlain that 'Mr Luxemberg, being of Jewish nationality, is, I think, unduly optimistic in regard to the value of a play of this nature at the present time'.

Nor was this the only occasion when the censorship continued to protect the Nazis after the war had started. At the end of October, permission was refused for the actor playing the Hitler character in a tour of Shaw's *Geneva* to be made up to resemble him physically; bizarrely, the reason given for this was the fact that the Foreign Office did not want to risk upsetting the Italians:

> the making up of Battler to resemble Hitler must inevitably connect the character of Bombardoner more closely with Mussolini, which in the

present delicate state of affairs would seem undesirable . . . I think it is the case where we must simply lay down what is to be done without giving any reasons, since Mr Shaw might fasten on this as a pretext for a letter to the press, or some other form of publicity.

The removal of Hitler and the Nazis from the stage in the 1930s was by no means systematic; no-one can have believed that changing names or costumes or specific words would really have disguised the subject matter from audiences. It also seems unlikely that just because a handful of successful prosecutions was brought against comedians for brief impersonations of Hitler, this would have prevented performers up and down the country from slipping in quick imitations and impressions, trusting no-one would report them or be able to produce sufficient evidence to institute a prosecution. It would be wrong, then, to say that the Nazis, or even Hitler, were kept completely off the stage, and one might be inclined to think that the censorship had little effect or significance. This, I think, is refuted by two things: the detail and extent of the alterations which were imposed, and the seriousness with which censorship of the stage was taken not only by the censors themselves but by the Foreign Office and the German Embassy. And, perhaps, beyond. In September 1938, the Reader Henry Game wrote that he had 'gathered from a remark in Hitler's speech on Monday at Nuremberg that he has taken note of anti-Nazi plays produced over here'.[106] There is no doubt that the German Embassy would have liked the Lord Chamberlain to be more restrictive, and the battle to pressurise him, through the Foreign Office and through threats of theatrical retaliation, was a continuous one. As always, we must at least acknowledge self-censorship and the possible plays and scenes which remained unwritten because they could not have been licensed.

The German Embassy won some battles, lost some and drew others. The Lord Chamberlain never completely capitulated (though he effectively handed over authority in this field to the British Foreign Office), and the story of the censorship of plays about the Nazis is not one of treachery and betrayal. The censors were not fascists, and nor, obviously, did they know everything which we know now about Germany in the 1930s. Yet they were aware that they were denying permission to the theatre to depict 'the truth' and opinions which were widely voiced elsewhere. They were not all and always in agreement with the policies they were required to carry out, and were sometimes reduced almost to the level of naughty children, obliged to maintain the letter of the rules imposed on them but ready to transgress and annoy where they thought they could get away with it. As one member of the Office wrote in connection with the licensing of Odets's *Till the Day I Die*: 'What with *Seed of Adam*, *Judgement Day* and this the German Embassy will be quite upset with us'.[107]

But the censors had always to cover their own backs. In the spring of 1939, Game recommended cutting the line 'down with Mosley' from a left wing play about the East End clashes between Jews and Fascists,* even though it is only a line shouted from within a crowd and has no special status or endorsement. Game commented:

> It is not really necessary, and his followers are probably touchy about their chief; and taking the long view, as I should like to be a 'Reich-Examiner' one of these days, I feel it is safer to disassociate myself from any insults offered to one who may become my Fuerher [sic], Duce, or merely leader.

Beside his comment, in the margin, someone wrote: 'Vicar of Bray'.[108] Can one be confident that Game's comment was simply a joke in slightly bad taste? In any case, the cut he proposed was confirmed.

---

* *East End*, by Leonard Peck

CHAPTER TWO

'Prudes on the Prowl'

The Moral Gaze

The general assumption of that section of the public which has not carefully considered the facts about the censorship is that if its powers were abolished and all existing restrictions removed the stage and the cinema would at once debauch public morals.

There is only one reply to this, and that is to consider the moral tone of the entertainments which are consistently licensed by the Censor's office.

(Philip Godfrey, 1933)[1]

The Public Morality Council had been formed in 1907, and it remained an extremely active organisation through the thirties and beyond. With its offices just off the Strand, and under the long-term presidency of the Bishop of London, it had influential leaders. Many of its most active organisers were clergymen, and, though it had some paid officers, it relied heavily on volunteers to document and campaign against the immoralities it sought to police and defeat. In a typical annual report of 1938, the Council listed the following areas on which its 'moral welfare work' had recently been concentrated:

> control of Night Clubs and Bottle Parties . . . advertisements of contraceptives . . . Hyde Park Public Morality Meetings held daily for four months (17th yearly series) . . . Public Entertainments—Plays, Revues, Cinemas, Music Halls, and Cabarets . . . Prints and Publications . . . Complaints of abuses—Public Places, Open Spaces and Streets, Disorderly Houses, Night Clubs, Public Resorts, Souteneurs, Unnatural Offences, etc.[2]

Referring to the 119 meetings it had organised in Hyde Park the previous summer, the report declared that 'Our platform is the only one engaged in the task of lifting the moral tone of the nation, giving instruction and guidance on sex matters'; it also claimed that theirs had been 'probably the most popular platform in the Park', though it had faced 'a direct attack' from a neighbouring speaker 'endeavouring to break down Christian morality, advocating free love and even extolling homo-sexuality'. And the report insisted that 'Never was our platform more needed than in these days of loose morals'.[3] On the one hand the Council habitually saw itself as fighting to resist the rising tide of depravity and decadence which was swamping British society, and on the other it regularly claimed important victories in reversing that tide.

Theatrical performance had always been one of the Council's principal targets, because of its perceived influence on how people behaved in real life; the Council took very seriously its commitment to protect the less educated and the 'impressionable' from frivolous and unthinking exploitation. In 1933 it reported on 105 performances in London, and complained to the Lord Chamberlain about ten of them. In 1934 it positively commended twenty-three out of seventy-seven plays in London, as well as thirty-four 'touring in the Provinces', and complained about thirteen 'on the grounds of immodesty of extreme nudity, offensive language or gestures and suggestiveness in scenes or dialogue'. In 1935 it rated as 'commendable' seventy-one plays out of 115, and found twenty-nine 'open to criticism' because of

> exploitation of semi-nudity . . . scenes or dialogue suggestive of sex acts or homosexuality, caricaturing of religious observances, making light of marriage, or exhibiting degrading habits of humanity unrelieved by higher characteristics, and the production of offensive 'Restoration' themes and extreme vulgarity.

In 1939, the list of complaints included the representation of 'objectionable women', 'non-moral presentation of sexual type' and 'bedroom scenes'.[4] The relatively small (though not insignificant) number of performances on which the Council focused its complaints is partly an indication of limited resources, but it fails to reflect its determination to exert a real influence on what could and could not be licensed for performance. The Public Morality Council was evangelical in its attempts to shape the Lord Chamberlain's policy and practice. Specific productions were used as exemplars of contemporary problems, and it was forever trying to send deputations to St James's Palace to debate both specific issues and underlying principles. From one perspective, the Council's influence might be seen as inevitably limited in as much as it was always chasing the game. In other words, it generally had no access to plays until they were already in performance with the official approval of the King's representative, who was loathe to rescind decisions. Yet, while the Council might be thought to have been wasting its time in complaining about a play which had already been licensed, this was primarily a strategy designed to influence future policy and decisions. Moreover, sometimes the Council's campaigns did lead directly to the Lord Chamberlain intervening over a production that was already running, especially if evidence was produced showing that the conditions of the licence had been breached (for example, by adding lines not in the original script). Occasionally this also led to prosecutions and convictions against managers and performers. In 1933, the Council claimed that in ten of the twelve instances where they had objected, alterations were subsequently made or licensees cautioned, and that there had been five prosecutions. In 1934 they reported that thirteen convictions had resulted from their complaints, and in 1935 legal proceedings were instituted in five cases.

Explicit 'nudity and semi-nudity' was always the major focus of the Council's campaign, and to this we shall return later. But other 'harmful tendencies' regularly surfaced as well. In 1936, they reported that they had made official complaints about 'cabaret and kindred performances' taking place late at night in hotels; enquiries had been instituted, and the Council had made its own investigations and sent reports to the relevant authorities 'in spite of the special difficulties attaching to attending midnight performances'.[5] It had always strongly opposed the degree of independence from censorship permitted to private theatre clubs, where material which was so 'nauseous in character' that it had been banned from the public stage could be seen by anyone who bothered to become a member.[6] Having previously failed in their campaign against what they saw as an anomalous and illogical freedom, the Council now shifted its attack onto the incongruity of allowing such material to be publicly advertised:

> Both the Bishop of London and the Committee have received frequent complaints that the so-called private performances are described at such length in the Press as to indicate to the public the tenor and nature of the performance. The Council feel strongly that the process defeats the whole object of a private performance and have so expressed themselves to the Lord Chamberlain. The official reply is that his Lordship has no power to interfere, but it is felt by some that by a rearrangement of the conditions defining private performances, some satisfactory solution could be arrived at by placing the onus of presenting such reports on the proprietors.[7]

Another exemption to which the Council objected was that of older plays, written before the Theatres Act had been passed. Their report of 1937 noted that

> The Council has viewed with concern, from its inception, the practice of reviving Restoration plays. They protested on three occasions against the representation of the Wycherley play *The Country Wife*, and on the last occasion were definitely informed that at present the Lord Chamberlain did not intend to stop the play.[8]

Indeed, as part of its campaign after a previous revival of the same play in 1934, the Council had forwarded a letter of protest to the Lord Chamberlain, which itself showed some resemblance to a seventeenth-century satire on hypocritical Puritans:

It was such wicked dirty wit that I could hardly stay to the end, only I wanted to be able to judge for myself the sort of plays young people and even a clergyman seemed to be enjoying.

Oh can nothing be done by some influential person in the Name of Christ . . . it seems as if even nice people are beginning to get so used to things as they are, that they smile and say 'One must move with the times!'[9]

The Council failed to close down the production of Wycherley's comedy, reporting with regret that 'their appeal to the Governors of a highly esteemed theatre . . . had not been successful'.[10] Yet perhaps their campaign may have contributed to the rarity of Restoration revivals—and, one might even hypothesise, to the way in which those revivals were cut and presented. In 1938, the Council expressed concern about the dangers of another genre it saw emerging:

The Council recognised that in regard to plays, revues, films etc, the need exists for a careful examination of the teaching and moral tendency of a number of productions. Particularly does this apply to possible developments of the policy of what is termed 'Realism'.

It cited as an example a private performance of an unidentified play which a reviewer described as focusing on 'a lost and degenerate community of people . . . reduced by starvation and squalor to the lowest depths', who 'live like pigs and have the morals of pigs, but are more degraded than pigs because they can reason and speak'.[11] No Gorki and no Arden, then, for the Public Morality Council.

Beneath a rather cold and British politeness, there was little love lost between the Lord Chamberlain's Office and the Public Morality Council. In April 1939, the Council's Secretary, one H.M. Tyrer, visited St James's Palace to discuss policy with the Assistant Comptroller; Gwatkin's account of the meeting leaves one in no doubt about the Office's attitude to the Council:

I have had a long and tedious interview with Mr Tyrer. As usual he was unconstructive except in the sense of complete destruction, and rebuilding on a standard of nursery rhymes and red flannel bloomers.

He could quote no actual cases of either men or women who had slipped from the straight and narrow path by reason of attending or acting at the Windmill or other Theatres.

I pointed out to him that one could not arrange entertainments designed only for those who are weak minded and impressionable at the expense of the larger majority which is reasonable in its outlook, and that we tried to keep plays on a level with current speech and thought and at the same time to curb any undue licence. I showed him instances of this in certain plays.

> I really think he only comes here in order that his Committee may
> think him very active.

Clarendon even added to these disparaging and cynical views with a
comment in the margin: 'What a curse this fellow is'.[12] On another
occasion, in a perhaps unique reversal of usual practice, the Bishop of
London wrote as President of the Council to ask that a licence be granted
for a play which the Lord Chamberlain had turned down. Street had been
adamant that *Happy Event*, a farce, could not be allowed:

> The main theme, the plot to keep a young wife from having a child and
> heir, and then egging on the husband to make her break the contract, will
> surely not do. It is moreover treated broadly and salaciously and with sly
> innuendos ... It is not a question of altering or modifying: it is the
> essential idea which is impossible in my judgement.

In a case of special pleading which perhaps casts some doubt on his
integrity, the Bishop of London took it upon himself to speak in the cause
of the play's author, Major Browning: 'the poor Major (who has no
pension) has had an offer for this play which would make all the difference
to him. (His wife at present has to work at Harrods)'. Cromer allowed a
hint of acidic sarcasm to creep into his reply: 'Much as one's sympathies
may go out to a major who has no pension and whose wife is pluckily
working at Harrods, I am afraid this can hardly be taken into consideration
when it comes to judging a play on its merits'.[13]

The Public Morality Council was generally intransigent in outlook and
inclined to assume that moral values transcended historical and cultural
contexts. By direct contrast, an article appeared in *Theatre World* in 1937
which argued the relativity and insubstantiality of morality and taboos:

> we can no longer ask what the difference is between a moral and an
> immoral play, because it has been proved that there is sometimes no
> difference at all. Two plays that were immoral before the war were so
> moral during the war that performances of them were subsidised by the
> State for the good of the troops. So the question is: 'When does an
> immoral play become moral?'[14]

The Lord Chamberlain's Office heard passionate advice on all sides, and
however one defines their boundaries, moral questions continued to be a
major focus for censorship debates through the thirties. An earlier *Theatre
World* article asked 'Do We Need a Censor?'. Its conclusion was that we did:

> if the theatre in general is to flourish, we must not have certain theatres
> presenting plays that cannot hope to get the support of a family man who
> wants to take his wife and daughters to a play without being in a state of
> acute embarrassment throughout.

The writer, Horace Richards, identified a particular problem for the Lord Chamberlain:

> The great difficulty of the Censor is that when he has licensed a play for one particular theatre he automatically licenses it for production at *any* theatre. The standards of susceptibility between a smart audience assembled for a Cochran revue first night probably differ considerably from the standards associated with many of our provincial theatres, and because the Censor has to legislate for all parts of the country, he has to find a safe middle course.[15]

Richards argued that plays presented at private theatres should not necessarily be exempt and, should, where necessary, be 'stepped on by the Censor'; but he sought to reassure readers that no-one should feel too restricted by this: 'There still remain many serious subjects which the playwright can discuss to extraordinary lengths without getting his knuckles rapped'.

By contrast, the writer, Philip Godfrey maintained that the censorship was fundamentally ineffective in what it set out to do:

> It is well known in the theatre that almost any degree of pornography can be got past the Censor by keeping it *between the lines.* So long as there is nothing lewd or obscene in the actual text of the play it is unlikely to provoke any protest . . . The obscene gesture . . . is much more subtle, and therefore more potent than the word . . . The obscene gesture which does not appear in the text of a play can be, and often is, introduced into the stage performance. Unless it is so marked as to cause public protest the Censor is powerless.

Godfrey even revived the familiar Shavian claim that the effect of the censorship in practice had been precisely the opposite of its intent, in that it had encouraged rather than discouraged dubious material:

> The number of pornographic plays which the Censor has licensed during the post-War period is much greater than would have been the case had the censorship been abolished, as few of the managers would have dared to present such plays on their own responsibility.
>
> Anyone seriously concerned with public morals, after examining the lower levels of the stage and the cinema, which portray crime, adultery, sexual prostitution, and certain special kinds of depravity in such a manner that the moral issues are romanticized or sentimentalised out of recognition, must be forced to the conclusion that public morals, as reflected at present in the lower forms of popular entertainment, can sink no lower. If any attempt were made to present any further degree of pornography, obscenity, or depravity than that which the Censor at present licenses, the police authorities would intervene and prevent the performance . . . however much they may feel the need for intervention at present, they cannot act where the Censor has already licensed without

coming into conflict with an officer of the Royal household, whose judgements and sanctions are supposed to reflect those of his royal master.

Godfrey also offered a definition of the prevailing and official morality:

> Public morality consists of respect for the traditional worship of God, the sanctity of marriage, and the respect for social law. Anything which is calculated to ridicule religion, condone adultery, sexual promiscuity, or depravity, or to bring the law into disrespect is a breach of public morals, and must be suppressed.

He added 'That, at least, is how the matter stands in theory. How far the practice departs from theory can be judged by examining the lower levels of the stage and the cinema'.[16]

While we may now feel uncomfortable with some of Godfrey's easy delineation of levels, it is true that 'light' entertainments often did seem to enjoy a greater freedom—both in terms of innuendo and explicit display—than that permitted to 'serious' drama. Music halls were effectively exempt from the licensing system, and many of the attacks on stage immorality were targeted at these (Godfrey probably had them in mind as manifestation of the 'lower levels of the stage') and on the emerging genre of the road show, which the Lord Chamberlain was also keen to exclude from his responsibility. As an irritated member of his staff once disparagingly noted in response to yet more complaints from the Public Morality Council about what the censorship allowed: 'It is obvious that the Bishop of London does not go to Night Clubs, otherwise he would see . . . things said and actions given in the Cabarets which are far beyond what we should allow on the stage'.[17] Even in relation to the theatres for which Cromer was responsible, exerting his authority was not necessarily straightforward; St James's Palace must sometimes have been littered with photographs of nude or semi-nude women in the poses they were supposedly to embody on stage—the Lord Chamberlain insisted on these being submitted, and the Comptroller or his Assistant would sign their initials across the bodies of those they approved. Yet the care taken over approving these ignored the fact that the members of an audience would not all see the same pose since they would be observing from different angles! Again, while representatives of the Lord Chamberlain did inspect some revues to ensure that performers kept to what had been licensed, it was still easier to prove that a word had been altered than a visual image. We cannot measure the extent to which the Lord Chamberlain was able to impose his rulings effectively, because he did not have the resources to allow him to carry out more than a tiny number of inspections. But it seems likely that the surviving evidence of prosecutions and warnings to managers or performers for breaking the rules are only the tip of an iceberg.

In any case, the relationship between censors and certain theatre managers was sometimes decidedly akin to cosiness. Consider this exchange between Gwatkin and the manager of the Windmill after the Assistant Comptroller had been to check on a performance of the latest show:

> Thank you for putting my friend and me into such good seats last night.
> I thought there was a lot of unattractive Bottom showing just after I got in—perhaps this has always been so, but my usual line of sight is from up above and not down below!
> Also is that line something about 'Put manure on your rhubarb' in the script?

True, an unlicensed line had been noticed, and hints were being dropped, but the tone is relaxed rather than adversarial, amused rather than confrontational. The producer, Vivian Van Damm, duly replied:

> I purposely put you into what I call the 'full sight seats' . . . On hearing of your remarks next morning about the amount of bottom showing . . . I immediately had another frill put upon the three skirts . . . God knows why they should suddenly go crazy, but if you knew comedians as well as I do, I am sure you would agree that at times you are dealing more with lunatics than sane people.[18]

While the leaders of the Public Morality Council may have believed in unchanging codes of right and wrong, the Lord Chamberlain's Office was bound to follow—if slowly and with a degree of reluctance—changing public attitudes. Policies over what was immoral and what could be permitted on stage were constantly shifting; a letter sent by the Assistant Comptroller in May 1938, responding to complaints about the licensing of Ben Travers's farce *Banana Ridge*, signalled this quite openly:

> It has to be admitted that the play is rather 'modern' but it is produced in the lightest possible vein . . . and I do not think—and I believe that you will agree with me—it is either erotic or it is likely to put wrong ideas into the heads of the younger generation.
> It would be easy enough for the Lord Chamberlain to put a stop to all plays of this sort but the difficult part of Censorship depends for its effectiveness on the co-operation it generally receives from playwrights and producers, which co-operation is only forthcoming when the Censorship manages to keep pace with contemporary talk and thoughts.
> It is part of the Lord Chamberlain's responsibility to keep a balance between those who like and those who do not like 'modern' situations in the Theatre.
> I think one must admit that facts and situations which a few years ago were not mentioned in public, are now discussed openly . . . and if a play is to be 'contemporary' it must include discussions and references which are in common vogue. If this is not so then the stage will lose its value as a reflection of the manners etc., of its age.

For instance Wycherley's 'Country Wife' would not be licensed now but it gives a valuable insight into the thoughts and manners of the seventeenth century.[19]

The Lord Chamberlain's apparent liberalism over moral issues sometimes turned him into public enemy number one, so far as the Public Morality Council was concerned. In October 1933, for example, the Office had licensed *The Greeks Had a Word for It*.* They did so with some reluctance, and for pragmatic reasons: 'I find the quarrels and intrigues of vulgar and illiterate harlots and their men extremely nauseating', reported Street. But Cromer felt he had no realistic choice, and his decision partly reflected a shift in the location of cultural power: 'If this unpleasant story had not already appeared on the screen as a Licensed Film it is quite dubious enough to consider banning', he wrote; 'This course cannot now be taken'. The Public Morality Council had no such factor to take into account, and launched into a typical attack on the play on two fronts—first that it 'familiarises young minds with much that is regrettable in human nature', and second 'that there is no indication in the play of any condemnation of the conduct of the persons concerned'. Major Gordon, the Assistant Comptroller, pronounced that the play was 'no more shocking or subversive of morals than any other play which shows the wages of sin to be something much more like expensive clothes and a good time than Death'. It was precisely that moral which worried the Council, but Gordon was dismissive of its complaints:

> I expect that the general un-moral atmosphere of, and the types depicted in, this play are the cause of a Puritan reaction in the minds of some people which makes them take a prejudicial view. But the answer to these objections is that you cannot confine the drama to plays about children for children.[20]

The following year an attack on Terence Rattigan's *First Episode* received similarly short shrift. The Council had complained that it was 'A disgusting play . . . thoroughly unpleasant and immoral . . . full of irreverence, sex in its worst form, and filthy language'; the authors were 'sex obsessed', and the text deserved 'complete annihilation' since it had 'no redeeming feature'. Particularly aggravating was the social status of the characters: 'Young men and women, supposed to have had the advantage of good education are entirely engrossed in undesirable sex relationships and university life is depicted as evil and disgusting'. With complete confidence, the Council declared: 'The public do not want such plays. People of all classes, when questioned, say they seldom go to the theatre because they

---

* Written by Zoe Atkins

are afraid of getting the sex stuff'. Game viewed a performance on behalf of the Lord Chamberlain, and acknowledged that certain aspects of the play were indeed provocative: 'I hardly think University life as depicted here would appeal to the Authorities'. Yet he doubted that 'anyone can take this play seriously', and showed little respect for the objections made:

> Generally speaking the complaints of the P.M.C. seem to me entirely unjustified and probably arise from a confusion in the minds of its members between life at a university and that of a Public School and between the functions of the Theatre and a Sunday School.[21]

So far as the moral vigilante groups were concerned, then, the Lord Chamberlain's Office was lenient to the point of weakness and irresponsibility. In September 1934, Cromer licensed a comedy, entitled *Man is an Insect*:* 'It is the sort of American play about which it is difficult to prophesy the English reception', Street had noted; 'All the talk about mating habits of insects etc. and about amatory reactions may shock an English audience'. In fact, even the manager of the theatre took it upon himself to query whether it had really been approved:

> I've never before produced or had produced in this theatre a play of this nature. Perhaps I am somewhat old-fashioned but I did so want to be sure that the Lord Chamberlain had passed and approved of the play before allowing same to be presented here.

When the production opened, complaints duly flooded in, spearheaded by the Westminster Catholic Federation:

> We must all appear before the judgement seat of Christ begging him to not allow the play to be on. I do beg of you when censoring a play, to remember the Eternal welfare of our young people, and not to release any Play that will tend to drag them down.
>   This a mother's prayer.[22]

General promiscuity was an obvious area of concern for the censorship, and though the censors were not necessarily puritanical in outlook, they could not be oblivious to the pressure and the ire directed against them by moral campaigners. As so often, it is hard to find absolute consistency of policy—partly because an unusually tough line taken against one play is quite likely to reflect a reaction to complaints about a play towards which they had been lenient. Thus in December 1934, a licence was refused for a translation of Sacha Guitry's *A New Will* for the Haymarket, even though Street clearly wanted to recommend it: 'it is so light in touch', he wrote, 'and the philosophy so much predominates over the intrigues that I am

---

* Written by David Boehm

strongly tempted to advise a licence'. However, because of the extensive adultery and promiscuity, and because he doubted the ability of English actors to find the lightness of touch which would make it acceptable, he did not do so.[23] Yet earlier in the same year, licences had been issued not only for *Man is an Insect* but also for a translation of Valentine Kataev's *Squaring the Circle*, even though the themes of adultery and promiscuity were seen to run through the text:

> It might be taken as a satire on the facility of the present Russian marriages and changes of partners, but it is less serious than that, merely light-hearted fun . . .
>
> I do not think anyone could object to this gay farce. There is an entire absence of any unpleasant 'sex' business: the couples just fall in love like children. Nor could any sensible person take the change of partners seriously and call it immoral. Their sharing a room is simply for Box and Cox sort of fun with nothing nasty about it.[24]

Perhaps they were influenced here by the fact that the play was to be staged by the relatively obscure Ballet Club Theatre, for at the same time they turned down a transatlantic play because of its 'jocular attitude to fornication'. Cromer described *Sailor Beware*,[*] in which men make bets on whether or not a woman will yield, as 'American beastliness'.[25] Also rejected was an Austrian play, *There's Always Tomorrow*.[†] 'Personally I do not think this sort of frank and open immorality would do very grave harm', wrote Street, 'but it would be an affront to any ordinary audience and its production would cause a scandal'. Game went to see a private performance the following year, and confirmed that to license it would be to make the Lord Chamberlain vulnerable to attack. The distinction indicated through his bracketed aside is also telling: 'I agree with Mr Street that this sort of light cynicism probably does little, if any, harm; but our standards being what they are (or seem) I think any who objected to the play would have a good cause not easy to answer'.[26]

Anything judged seriously likely to undermine the institution of marriage was generally rejected. Examples of plays rejected on these grounds included *Fig Leaves*[‡] (1934), in which two women agree to share the same man; *Laughter Outside*[§] (1935), a 'very unpleasant play about very unpleasant young people' involving 'serious love-making', 'unbridled lust' and serial promiscuity; and *The Loving Wife*[¶] (1936), in which a married

---

[*] Written by Kenyon Nicholson and Charles Robinson
[†] Written by Archibald Norman Menzies
[‡] Written by Max Catto
[§] Written by Virginia Estes
[¶] Written by John Hoare

couple not only tolerate but actively encourage each other's adultery.[27] The more removed a play was from everyday reality, or the more it could be excused as harmless fun, the better its chance of being licensed. André Obey's retelling of the Don Juan story was saved because its subject matter was, according to Street, 'much less to be feared in a French stylised play than in an ordinary English one'; Cromer agreed that, because the play was 'so extremely stylised, expressionist and symbolical', it 'need not necessarily give offence'.[28] Perhaps more surprising was the decision to approve the translation of a French play* about the relationship between Elizabeth I and the Earl of Essex, which linked Elizabeth's inability to consummate her relationship with having been raped at the age of fifteen. One member of the Advisory Board, Lord David Cecil, argued that 'the softening remoteness of historic times' made it 'less likely to give people a violent shock'; though he also warned that the English were 'peculiarly sensitive to the unseemliness of a physical relationship between a man and a woman much older than himself'.

Another adviser, Professor Winifred Cullis, exposed an interesting assumption when she told the Lord Chamberlain that she thought the theme of the play was 'suitable for discussion in a psychological study where it would be recognised as a suggestion, but not for a play where it would be accepted by many as a fact'. However, after viewing a private performance in March 1938, Game recommended that it could be licensed: 'Theatre-goers are much tougher than they were a few years ago', he maintained—though he anticipated 'protests from members of the public, who think that because they have been shocked that they have been corrupted'.[29] On the other hand, a licence was refused for *Why Keep a Diary*,† in which a man finds a baby abandoned on his doorstep and then has to work out which woman he might have slept with nine months previously. Street thought it 'rather violently opposed to English taste', but Lady Violet Bonham Carter, a member of the Advisory Board, picked up Street's comment to query, not for the first time, the precise nature of the responsibility with which the censorship was charged. While she accepted that the plot might well be offensive 'to most people's taste', she was convinced that it 'could not possibly be a threat to anybody's morals'. This, she suggested, 'raises again the problem as to whether we have the right to act as arbiters of taste or only as protectors of public morality—a point on which I have never been certain, and which I feel only the Lord Chamberlain is competent to decide'.[30] This was just the sort of decision which Cromer resisted making, since all definite rulings reduced his

---

* *Elizabeth la Femme sans Homme*, by André Josset, adapted by Yvette Pienne
† Written by Leszle Fodor

flexibility to respond to the public mood and risked offering hostages to fortune.

Why Keep a Diary was rejected, but a couple of months later an American farce, *It's a Wild Child,** invited comparison, since it centred on the disputed paternity of two children, one real and the other imaginary. Street hesitantly recommended rejection:

> The theme of this farce, which has been popular in America, is of a sort which gives no offence there but is violently opposed to average English taste . . . It is not really a salacious play. Nevertheless, if it had not been produced here, I should have thought it unsuitable for licence for public performances, going by precedents. But I am shaken by the fact that *The Times* and *The Telegraph*, when it was done by the Repertory Players, praised it without suggesting that it would not do for ordinary audiences: that the special audience liked it means little. If one can get over the having or not having the baby being treated as a joke there is no harm . . . on the other hand it is to be produced by Mr Abrahams who has gone in for a *succès de scandale* before and might again. Acted broadly and advertised as 'hot stuff' or something of this sort it <u>would</u> become a scandal. On the whole I cannot advise the Lord Chamberlain to take the risk.

But this time, probably swayed by the reviews, the Advisory Board proved more lenient than Street: 'The venerable Seventh Commandment has been so often ridiculed and contemned upon the British stage that I do not suppose this further American effort to bring it into disrepute will do it much harm', wrote Sir Ian Malcolm, and Street switched sides to provide a justification of why this play could be allowed when the other had been refused:

> With regard to any inconsistency involved because another play *Why Keep a Diary* was banned I do not think that matters. That play is salacious and unpleasantly suggestive all through, whereas *It's A Wild Child*, apart from some coarseness and crudity in detail is farcical fun. Similarity of theme is not enough to necessitate identical treatment in licensing. Even the same theme, and a dubious one too, might reasonably be licensed in one case and banned in another. [31]

In other words, it was the tone and the lightness that saved it.

Yet if this had this been a clear and consistent policy then one might have expected that Street would have recognised it when he first read the play; in fact, his neat rationale was supplied only after the decision to license it had been made. Indeed, when *Flying Blind*† was staged privately with James Mason at the Arts Theatre in November 1937, with the anticipation of a West End transfer, the script was refused a licence: 'promiscuity is not

---

* Written by Larry Johnson
† Written by Pamela Kellino and James Mason

permissible even in farce', wrote Dearmer, and Game dismissed it as 'a non-moral play written by two young people who think that going to bed together has no greater significance than dining together'. There was, too, more than a hint of racism in the Readers' responses, with Dearmer denouncing the play as 'foreign to the English spirit in farce' and Game drawing attention to the play's 'Hebrew promoter'. When a revised version was sent in, Game insisted that the changes were insufficient: 'The authors are too pre-occupied with beds and their uses', he declared: 'I don't think these people should be encouraged over much until they have a clearer idea of what is permissible on the English stage'.[32] Dearmer found the theme of *Come Out to Play*[*] equally unacceptable:

> I do not think that this play can possibly be recommended for licence . . . It advocates the 'advancement' of sex education at all costs. Its burden is 'you may get illicit intercourse between young people—we don't shirk this possibility in our play—but isn't it worth it?' The answer, I submit is Certainly Not. The play is a gross reflection on schools as they are. It is preoccupied with sex from beginning to end . . . Is it consistent with truth, morals or the dignity of the theatre to let it pass?

But although extensive changes were imposed, including the complete removal of a seduction scene involving a senior prefect from a boys' school and a girl from a neighbouring school, the Office was persuaded that it might be provocative to ban the play entirely, given its serious intent:

> The question of sex education in the schools is a very difficult and important one, and to adopt an attitude that it is to be considered as tabooed in the theatre would be to lay ourselves open to the old accusation that we pass prurient filth and ban plays which deal with anything important . . . I fully expect that these authors are sincere and passionately interested in the question they write about.

Dearmer attended a dress rehearsal and agreed that 'No reasonable person could now take exception to the play's theme'—though his choice of words was slightly unfortunate: 'The scene in which the boy and girl wander in a wood . . . is greatly improved by the boy's control of himself. What would have been unpleasant if not repulsive is now rather moving if a little stiffly acted.'[33]

One subject which Lord Cromer never took lightly was impotence. In December 1934, the censorship rejected an American farce called *Stallion and Narcissus*[†] (the name alone was unacceptable) in which a woman leaves her impotent husband for a younger, virile man; 'I can't bear it', declared

---

[*] Written by John Sand and Fanny Jocelyn
[†] Written by Rose Albert Porter

Cromer.[34] He also insisted on banning the song 'Men are so Sexless' from another musical farce;* 'It may be true', he admitted, 'but it won't do'.[35] More significant, perhaps, was the banning of Toller's *Hinkemann*. Street, in one of his less reasoned assessments, described it as 'a mixture of obscenity and raving . . . written by an over-rated German'. But whatever else might have condemned it was immaterial: 'I cannot imagine that any version could be licensed', wrote Street; 'The theme, a man's impotence, rules it out'. Cromer agreed: 'It would be a waste of time to submit any other version', he decreed; 'Why women want to translate and force on the stage the works of this German author, whose only claims to merit are sadistic views and language, I fail to appreciate'.[36]

Another subject which aroused occasional flutters of excitement in the Office was spanking. In the summer of 1938, 'male spanking of female posteriors (both on and off)' featured in a farce called *Sexes and Sevens*.† 'Personally I have never seen spanking on the stage', reported Game, 'but Miss Webster tells me it has been known, and certainly recently the charming Claudette Colbert was spanked in a film'. Clarendon, recently installed as Lord Chamberlain ruled: 'Whatever is done in Films, let us keep spanking "off" the stage'.[37] A few weeks later, Game tried again in relation to *Behind the Blinds*:‡

> The late Lord Chamberlain frowned on spanking of the adult female by the adult male, and a similar scene was cut not so very long ago. Personally I doubt whether such a piece of business would do any harm in the Theatre or produce any other reaction than healthy laughter, except in an infinitesimal number of cases; but I seem to be in a minority.[38]

The censorship also took seriously a play about the moral and sexual degeneracy of a member of the upper classes. The original script of *No Way Back*§ depicted Lady Beresford as 'a loathsome woman of 50 who spends her life in dancing and drinking and keeps a gigolo', and who indulges to excess in alcohol and drugs. Street commented that 'a kept lover . . . begetting a child on his mistress's daughter is against all precedent of the admissible', but he pointed out in the play's favour that 'the mannerless, drunken so-called modern people . . . are presented with real contempt and not, as so often happens, half sympathetically'. An extensively revised version was eventually licensed: 'it does appear to be a genuine attack on

---

* *Let's Pretend*, by R. Jaye
† Written by Con West and H.C. Sargent
‡ Written by Vivian Tidmarsh
§ Written by Graham Hope

the degeneracy of a coterie which is able to corrupt a decent girl'. Titman inspected a rehearsal and reported positively:

> It is made perfectly clear that Toni is no more than a gigolo and general lackey to Caroline . . . [the] love making scene is entirely one-sided by the woman . . . there is no suggestion that the girl has been corrupted by her mother . . . The uselessness of the mother is rather overpowered by the strong moral sense of the Aunt—the latter being a fine character.[39]

For all the concern with narrative and language, in terms of sex and morality it was the issue of stage nudity and undress which surfaced most frequently. Cromer had decided in the autumn of 1932 to permit actual nudity on the stage, provided certain conditions were met, and the Public Morality Council campaigned constantly to have the decision rescinded. Reviewing Charlot's 'non-stop revue', *Red, Bright and Blue*, at the Vaudeville Theatre in 1937, *The Times* described its unclothed 'statuesque ladies' as 'motionless monuments to one of the odder rules of the theatre'.[40] And following a bout of complaints to the police concerning nudity at the Windmill Theatre, Gwatkin sought to explain the situation to Air Vice-Marshall Sir Philip Game, the Commissioner of the Metropolitan Police at Scotland Yard, who, coincidentally, was the brother of the Lord Chamberlain's Reader, Henry Game:

> The Lord Chamberlain decided some time ago that he would allow nudes on the stage provided that they remained absolutely still, and provided that the lighting was sympathetically done. He also insisted on the fact that, whenever nudes appeared, the sketch should be one which aimed at artistry. I think I can say that from the latter point of view the sketches at the Windmill definitely are aimed at the artistic, and frequently succeed in their object.
>
> The aim is rather to produce a thing of beauty than one which will cause excitement. I am sure that you will appreciate the difference, which is a nice one, between that which is daring and that which is indecent.[41]

The Windmill and the Prince of Wales's quickly became notorious for using nudity within tableaux as a primary attraction to their revues. Soon, too, flesh-coloured tights were being widely used in other theatres—not least in revues which toured the country—to deceive audiences into believing they were seeing actresses actually moving in the nude. Perhaps sometimes they were. In January 1937, one newspaper reported:

> An almost nude girl staring from a front-page advertisement for the London Casino in a respectable evening newspaper last week made readers gasp.
>
> Because to many it was news that the nightlife of the metropolis exhibited anything resembling what many Englishmen regard as Continental degeneracy. It seemed that the Lord Chamberlain must have erred.

Little-known was the simple explanation that the London Casino show, having no actual plot, does not come under the Lord Chamberlain's jurisdiction, but receives its licence from the London County Council. Nor are there any genuine nudes on the stage only an illusion which satisfies the authorities and brings in the public . . .

An elaborate hoax was this impression of nudity. Vega was wearing flesh-coloured tights from the tips of her rouges toes to her throat . . . But though there is counterfeit at the Casino, at the Windmill there is no welshing.[42]

It is certainly sometimes hard to detect whether it was the audiences or the authorities who were being taken in. In 1939 a touring revue, *King Revel*, ran into trouble at a number of venues. There were several investigations by local police authorities, and the report of a probably inexperienced Detective Inspector at Halifax reflects the difficulty of knowing who was tricking whom:

She definitely seemed to be nude as she approached the front of the stage and as regards the back of her body there appeared to be no doubt that that portion was nude. It is difficult to say whether she is nude at the front of her body. Although by all appearances she is I am of the opinion that some adhesive material covers the pubic region in such a manner as to give the impression of complete nudity.

After the dance she mounts a pedestal and poses with the veil open and the right knee flexed forwards and to the left as an effort to reduce the display of the pubic region.

When the authorities at Wolverhampton complained about the same revue, the Lord Chamberlain's Office tried to specify exactly what was and was not allowed:

in no circumstances whatever does the Lord Chamberlain allow an artiste when nude or in the semblance of nudity to move on the stage. Girls are allowed to be on the stage in the nude, provided there is no display of private details, when the action is in tableaux of an artistic nature.

It was pointed out that a representative of the Office, the aptly named George Titman, had already inspected this performance twice; on the first inspection the dancer had been

standing side view to the audience, with the lower part of her body shielded by a bunch of flowers. On the second occasion, however, he saw her standing full front to the audience, without the flowers, and though her parts were adequately covered with some adhesive material, the effects of the lighting caused a 'shadow' which was very suggestive. Both the producer and Lanueda were warned that she should stand side view to the audience and that the flowers should be reinstated.

The letter to the police surprisingly added that 'The question of lighting and position of the nudes is generally left to the good taste of the producers'.[43]

While it was hard to impose absolute and binding rules, there were certainly occasions when the Office intervened over performances. Following a series of complaints in 1938 about a particular dance in *Going Gay*, a touring revue which they had already had modified, Titman went to inspect it.

> In my opinion it is still indecent. There is an appreciable space of time while this girl remains on the stage, bare from the waist up, fully facing the audience . . . It is only a matter of seconds, but I do not think the Lord Chamberlain allows the exposure of a girl's breasts to the full view of the audience, except in tableau, at all . . . If this is allowed to pass, undesirable nudity will develop all over the place.

The management pleaded that the delay had been accidental and caused by the slowness of the lighting operator, but Titman insisted that in future they must not rely on the lights and that it was essential 'for Eileen to bring her arms down <u>immediately</u> after she had raised them above her head'.[44]

Inevitably, some managers were always looking to test the limits of how far they could go. In July 1933, Street reported on a Charles Cochran revue, *Nymph Errant*: 'In scene 1 desks conceal most of the nudity and in scene 2 bushes. But the concealed nudity is supposed to attract the audience as a joke and that seems to me much more offensive than nudity itself'. Cochran agreed to cut the scenes, in return for a licence.[45] In October, Titman inspected a revue entitled *Les Mille et Une Merveilles de Paris*, about which there had been a number of complaints. He had some reservations about what he saw:

> I dislike very much the display of navels, which is now getting so common. It is quite unnecessary, as the maximum amount of bare flesh is already permitted to be exhibited . . . With regard to Item 4 . . . 'Shew Them More' . . . I consider part of this scene suggestive, particularly as regards the half-figures of old men, upon the outstretched hands of each of whom stands a girl in a transparent black frock. The faces of the men are close to the girl's legs and apparently air is blown up through their mouths which lifts the frocks above their thighs. Although the girls are properly covered underneath, the action is certainly unpleasant.

It so happened that this production had also committed a technical offence by including lines which had not been licensed, and the Lord Chamberlain was able to use the threat of prosecution to persuade the producers to eliminate the blowing and alter the costumes.[46]

Another revue to excite attention on account of its display of human flesh was *West End Scandals*, in the summer of 1934:

The tableaux of practically naked women have no artistic merit and are merely produced to excite the lower passions of humanity, and the whole show ... is on a par with what one would expect to find in the lower quarters of Buenos Aires.

Surely the Censor must be asleep to allow such fulsome beastliness to be publicly shown in this great City of ours.

When Titman saw it he declared himself 'shocked', and the management was required to adjust the tableaux images. Later that year, a Dr Doris Odlum wrote from Harley Street to complain about another revue featuring

an objectionable spectacle which depicts a number of dancing girls ... in a tight-fitting skin-coloured garment with certain parts of the anatomy emphasised in dark colour. The suggestion conveyed is absolutely indecent and offensive ... This spectacle is calculated to have an undesirable effect on public morals.[47]

Again Titman inspected a performance and agreed that the complaint was justified: 'It is certainly beyond the limit of anything that to my knowledge has been allowed hitherto'.

So notorious did the issue become that an article entitled 'Stage Nudity' even appeared in *Sunbathing Review*, citing the supposed freedom of the theatre in support of the magazine's campaign to give people the right to take off their clothes in public:

what is permitted on the English stage as regards undress should also be allowed for sun and air bathing ... We hold no brief for stage nudity; its objects are entirely distinct from active sun and air bathing in the open air, but the fact that it is apparently being approved of by the authorities should surely influence the magistrates, the police and the public, to view sun and air bathing in proper places and at proper times with greatly increasing tolerance.[48]

And it was the war against undress on the stage which featured most heavily in the Public Morality Council's annual reports, and which dominated much of their contact with St James's Palace. Apart from his responsibility towards individual scripts, the Lord Chamberlain also had the duty of licensing certain venues, and the Council strove to pressurise him into refusing, or at least threatening to refuse, a licence to those which regularly presented 'immoral' performances. When this failed, they campaigned for that part of his authority to be transferred to the London County Council, which they believed might be more favourable to their demands. In 1934, the Public Morality Council had noted the 'growing practice' of 'semi-nudity' as a major cause for concern, and reported on the 'reasoned protest (accompanied by 41 reports of instances of extreme undress seen at 13 theatres)' which they had presented to the Lord Chamberlain in advance of his annual renewal of performance licences.[49] The Council maintained that such performances 'alienated many good citizens from attendance at theatres', and announced that they had therefore decided to 'beg your Lordship to exercise the great authority attached to your office in such a way as you deem best to check this practice which is a source of discomfort and annoyance to great numbers of those for whom they speak'.[50] Deputations were sent to the Home Secretary and the Prime Minister, expressing concern at 'harmful tendencies in publications, plays and cinema films', and the Council regularly fed examples to members of parliament who were likely to be sympathetic to their cause.[51]

In 1934, a revue at the Prince of Wales's Theatre entitled *Folies on Parade* provoked the Bishop of London to preach a sermon against stage undress, which achieved widespread publicity. The Public Morality Council had complained that the revue was 'harmful to impressionable minds' and 'of little benefit to the very elderly people who attend', and, following his inspection, Titman asked the Lord Chamberlain for 'a definite ruling' about navels. But he did not support the more general complaints: 'The reports from the Public Morality Council appear to me to be exaggerated— probably in justification of the Bishop of London's recent purity announcement'.[52] While the Council was good at attracting publicity which allowed it to campaign for support, it did not have things all its own way. In January 1935, the seventy-year-old actress and film star Marie Tempest— still sufficiently well-known to achieve front page publicity in national newspapers—launched an attack on the Bishop of London: 'I hate people who must go round seeing dirt in things that are quite natural', she was reported to have said; 'Much as I admire the Bishop of London as a man, I think his ideas on sex are silly. I do not think he is in a position to give opinions'. Tempest declared: 'I love the young people of today for their absolute freedom from stupid prudery', and she rejoiced in the absence within the younger generation 'of the obsession of sex which one sensed in Victorian days'. Tempest's counter-attack was not likely to give the moralists much pause for thought, but it probably helped the censorship to argue that it was occupying the middle ground.[53]

In 1936, the Bishop of London led a deputation to St James's Palace, again voicing concern about undress on the stage. Cromer, partly playing for time, explained the difficulty of defining limits, so the Public Morality Council subsequently drew up and proposed a specific regulation stating that 'female dress on the stage should, as a general rule, cover the front of the body from above the breast to below the hips'. It also published a list of twenty or so societies which apparently supported its position, many of them 'church armies', but also including vigilance societies, the Girls'

Friendly Society, the Headmistresses' Association and the terrifyingly named British Women's Total Abstinence Union. Publications including *Variety News*, the *Stage* and the *Spectator* were also said to have endorsed the proposal.[54]

Slightly bizarrely, one of the defences offered by the Lord Chamberlain's Office for allowing nudity was that it was actually less provocative than other displays. In the spring of 1937, Dearmer's report on 'three statuesque ladies' who appeared in the nude proposed that 'their appeal is not sexual, as it might be if they were suggestively and vulgarly draped'.[55] Game, meanwhile, attended what he called 'the first un-dress performance' of another revue, and discussed its use of nudity:

> as long as it is merely used decoratively, as here, I see no objection to it. To my mind it is less provocative than the female form seen through diaphanous draperies and movement ... for it is undeniable that aesthetically the female form looks less indecent completely nude than clothed in a garment more or less in the style of a fig leaf. But here the association of ideas in the mind of a Philistine in the audience comes into the question and complicates matters. In his eyes the nuder the girl the naughtier the thrill. A good guide in these matters is to recognise that sex is alright as long as it is amusing or beautiful.[56]

It was on the Windmill Theatre that most complaints centred. In early 1937, a police chief inspector reported on *Revudeville No. 87*: 'The whole performance reeks of Sex and many of the female artistes ... are very scantily attired. Nearly all the audience were males and I noticed the front rows of the stalls were almost entirely occupied by elderly men'. The stern caution which Cromer issued to Van Damm, the producer, almost suggested a betrayal of trust:

> You must realise that there are three alternatives open to you: that the actors should remain still, with proper lighting; that they should wear tights; or that the sketch will be definitely not allowed.
> I am quite certain that you already know these regulations, and it makes it extremely difficult for us to try and do our best for you, in view of the constant criticism we have, if you do not try and help us by adhering to the rules we have laid down.[57]

The Windmill's next programme was again inspected by a representative of the Lord Chamberlain. Although he objected to a couple of unlicensed lines which had been added ('Dick here is the finest Dick in the country' and 'She'll lead you up the garden path but you won't get a sprig of parsley') he had no objection to 'The Inferno', a scene in which 'the Tempter' exercises his wiles on 'the Maidens', but is repelled and vanquished by 'The Nun':

There was a flash of red fire. During this flash the Maidens removed their clothes, and were revealed naked, the one silhouetted on the steps at the left, and the other in a kneeling attitude facing the audience in the front centre of the stage, her hands were crossed over the lower part of the body ... This scene was artistically carried out, and once they had stripped (during the flash), there was no movement on the part of any of the performers. It was noticeable, however, that, after the tableau, the three front rows, consisting practically exclusively of men, were vacated.[58]

The Public Morality Council report of 1937 recorded 'a general improvement in tone and matter'. But a new threat to public morals had arrived from America: striptease acts. Volunteers from the Public Morality Council paid 'repeated visits' to such performances in order 'to ascertain exactly what transpired', and protests were made to the London County Council about 'disrobing for disrobing's sake' which, said the Council, resulted in 'lowering the prestige and dignity of the stage or screen'.[59] The Lord Chamberlain received a number of complaints, including this distraught and somewhat disturbing letter about, one might say, the body politic:

> In the name of every decent woman of the Empire I write with the greatest urgency to ask that immediate steps are taken for the suppression of the indecency known as the strip-tease dance and which, in direct defiance of the London County Council, is shortly to be shown at the Victoria Palace.
>
> It is not the question of the American woman standing nude, in beads, or in a flesh-coloured bathing-suit at the end of the revolting exhibition. The sin against morality is the UNDRESSING of this person in public, to slow music and with every suggestive movement.
>
> What is the good of us striving to do away with the slums? Striving to improve the young people's physical standard when we supinely allow the same young people's minds to be corrupted by this alien depravity. London is filling for the Coronation. Many Orientals will be over with their purdah women, Moslem women and others as strictly guarded from moral corruption. What kind of report on the British Empire will they, many of them British subjects, take back with them!
>
> If, my dear Sir, you do not suppress this outrage, you will be responsible for the very greatest harm possible being done to the morality of men and women who are, so far as entertainment goes, in your special care.
>
> ... I am writing to many others and if the revolting exhibition is NOT suppressed FOR GOOD, I am writing to lay the whole matter before their Majesties ... even with the Coronation close at hand.
>
> That indecencies such as this shocking dance should be not only suggested for England by aliens, but carried out by them in defiance of those in authority in this country simply leads one to believe that there is not a man strong enough in the Empire to see that orders are enforced.[60]

Gwatkin replied, pointing out that the performance was actually part of a variety act over which the Lord Chamberlain had no control.

Meanwhile, the Bishop of London endorsed a written protest about striptease acts, which was sent to West End managers, to the London Theatre Council and to British Equity; his letter addressed a series of specific questions:

> 1. Are these acts legal or illegal? Would they be deemed a nuisance under Common Law and thus become a misdemeanour . . .
> 2. Do they exploit sexual feelings?
> 3. Do they involve the exploitation of young womanhood for commercial purposes?
> 4. Do they enhance or diminish the prestige and dignity of Dramatic Art?[61]

Further complaints were voiced over a show at the Prince of Wales's consisting of 'repeated scenes which are simply a succession of the display of girls with little and, in some cases, nothing on'. Again, there was more than a hint of nationalistic racism behind the insistence that the revue was 'excessive . . . from the point of view of English morals', and also in some of the secretary's assumptions:

> I do venture to submit that financiers and producers concerned, especially if they are aliens or continentalised, should not be allowed this latitude . . .
> I do assure you that these shows are a matter of grave annoyance to people who want to be entertained in a manner that is in keeping with British traditions.

A comment written in the margin beside this last point by one of the Lord Chamberlain's staff reflects the lack of empathy with the Council's view: 'people who want to be entertained in this manner will hardly go to the P of W'.[62]

But on 7 May 1937, a photograph purporting to be taken from a Windmill show was published in the *Daily Mirror*, and caused embarrassment and outrage. Scotland Yard informed the Comptroller that they were receiving complaints about the Windmill as a result, and Cromer felt obliged to take steps. Gwatkin offered a firm proposal:

> STAGE NUDITY
> The only hard and fast rules at the moment are:
> 1) No movement;
> 2) Medium lighting.
> However, the original idea of a tableau pure and simple is being slightly departed from . . .
> Perhaps it would be better, and would show our sympathy towards those who have a real objection to this sort of entertainment if we tightened down the screw a little on the following lines, although I would

definitely deprecate abandoning our present views about the artistic worth of the uncovered human form.

I suggest therefore, in addition to no movement, and medium lighting, that:

1) No man should be allowed on the stage; and

2) The top half of the body, if bare, should not face full towards the audience, and should only do so if draped with a gauze.

The Office also told Scotland Yard that it was all a storm in a teacup, and implied that the police should concentrate their energies elsewhere. In effect, they came close to defending the Windmill:

> Since the receipt of your last letter of the 13th May, the Lord Chamberlain has insisted on certain modifications being made with regard to nudes on stage . . . frankly, however, I do think that there is a considerable difference between what apparently is a sort of Strip Tease act given in the intimate surroundings of a Bottle Party—when probably most of the people are half tight—and what takes place on the stage.
>
> As you will no doubt realise, all this trouble has arisen from that preposterous picture in the *Daily Mirror*, the inclusion of which no one deplores more than the Manager of the Windmill, and which was a direct breach of faith on the part of the photographer. I may say that that picture gave an entirely false impression of what the audience see.

Nevertheless, a tougher regulation was drafted which, had it ever become policy, would certainly have outlawed all nudity: 'In view of the considerable pressure of certain elements of public opinion, the Lord Chamberlain has decided that plain nudity on the stage shall in future be forbidden, and in addition, any "semblance of nudity" shall not be allowed'. This was what the moralists had been campaigning for. Cromer arranged to meet the managers of the Windmill and the Prince of Wales's theatres, as well as (separately) the secretary to the Public Morality Council; whether or not he ever intended to enforce such a drastic change is not clear, but some at St James's Palace evidently thought it was for real, and counselled against it. Writing on 25 May, Gwatkin urged caution:

> Nudity has now been allowed for some time, although I agree that abuses have crept in . . . I respectfully submit that the following points are considered:–
>
> 1) That to forbid nudity now admits that this Department has been wrong in allowing it before. There is no discredit in admitting a fault, but was this Department at fault?
>
> 2) There will always be commercialization of sex in some form or another on the stage—every other stage play introduces sex of some sort.
>
> 3) Admitted that sex is inevitable, is it not more reasonable to try to canalise it and allow the public what is an attempt at artistic sex, such as

tableaux, and definitely to rule out can-can, strip-tease, black stockings, etc., whose aim is eroticism impure and simple.

In conclusion I would suggest that we do not entirely cancel our policy with regard to nudes, but that we tighten up the conditions.

That we warn managers that justifiable complaints which prove that the conditions laid down by us have been contravened will result in the immediate withdrawal of the Licence.

That turns which have no artistic worth and which rely for their popularity entirely on the lowest form of sex appeal should be definitely forbidden.

Game also weighed in with his opinion:

The Nudity Controversy

1) This is the old fight between those who regard Sex as the Devil, and those who don't.

2) Nudity is thought to be, but is not in fact, more provocative than semi, or veiled nudity . . .

3) Nudity should either be forbidden or allowed—no half policy adopted, which only produces ridiculous results.

4) If nudity is allowed, an unobtrusive cache-sexe gives the most artistic result, otherwise let the female form be shown naked . . .

5) Explain what it is we intend to allow to the Managers and then let them go ahead, with a warning that if, on complaints received, we find them not conforming to the conditions laid down, to save further trouble nudity will be abolished entirely.

6) The managers want nudity in their Revues, as it is a new way of selling Sex, or a new-old way,—the old Gaiety of the nineties sold sex just as busily.

7) Our justification for allowing it is to be found in 2) above, as long as the nude is used solely to build up an artistic effect.

But Lord Cromer was about to go in for a bit of invisible theatre. On 26 May, the managers of the Windmill and the Prince of Wales's, Van Damm and Charlot, were summoned to see him at St James's Palace. His prop was the sheet of paper saying that henceforth all stage nudity was to be banned:

The Lord Chamberlain started by saying that he was extremely annoyed, in the first place with having to get these gentlemen down to see him, and secondly for the cause, and explained to them that they had brought what was coming to them onto their own heads. He then handed them each a copy of the attached piece of paper (which he subsequently withdrew from them) at which Mr Van Damm said that he would close his theatre forthwith, and Mr Charlot became almost hysterical.

Having got that over, the Lord Chamberlain was forced to listen to a long diatribe from Mr Charlot in which he protested his moral purity and the fact that he was only led into doing these things by 'force majeure'. Mr Van Damm said that he employed a hundred and twenty people, and Mr

Charlot said that he employed a hundred and fifty people. The Lord Chamberlain said that he did not care.

Mr Charlot then produced a long story about the impossibility of working on the lines suggested by the Lord Chamberlain when, outside theatres, music halls, cabarets and nightclubs, much more daring things were put on the stage . . .

After a certain amount of argument, the Lord Chamberlain decided, and told these gentlemen, that the paper which had been put in front of them would not necessarily be enforced, but it was given to them as a guide as to what might have to happen eventually.

Cromer then switched roles for his meeting with the secretary of the Public Morality Council:

Shortly afterwards, the Lord Chamberlain saw Mr Tyrer. Mr Tyrer talked rather indistinctly, but was quite non-plussed by the Lord Chamberlain's argument as to the beneficial effects of the sun on the human body, i.e. was Mr Tyrer going to attempt to stop sunbathing on the Serpentine or elsewhere, and what did Mr Tyrer think of mannequin shows and things of that sort? Mr Tyrer's contention that what went on in the theatre would not be allowed outside on the street, and was therefore a misdemeanour, was discussed and exploded by the Lord Chamberlain.

Once again, having destroyed his opponent by giving him the bad news, Cromer then extended a hand of comfort with the good news:

The Lord Chamberlain then explained to Mr Tyrer, and told him that he, in his turn, could explain to the members of his council the steps that were being taken with regard to a concerted effort at an all-round clean up, which apparently pleased Mr Tyrer, who went away quite content.[63]

Cromer had resolved matters to his own satisfaction, but he also needed to be seen to be doing something. On 3 June 1937 he called a meeting with representatives of the London County Council (LCC) and Scotland Yard, J.F. Henderson from the Home Office, and his own Readers, to discuss setting up a conference of interested parties. It was agreed that there was to be no wholesale alteration of policy, merely a tightening up and an increase in active collaboration between the Lord Chamberlain and the LCC.

The Lord Chamberlain started by explaining the reasons as to why he had called a meeting of this sort, and also explained that he had seen the two chief managers concerned, Mr Van Damm and Mr Charlot.

He then proceeded to ask Mr Henderson if he had any views. Mr Henderson's view on the nude was that, when artistically presented, it did no harm.

Major Conyers-Baker (Scotland Yard) said that there were certain repercussions from the point of view that, if the nude were allowed in all seriousness on the stage it might be made an excuse for the lewd in private, and less public places than theatres. (They have had a case, of which we have the correspondence, about a bottle party at a London nightclub).

Mr Stamp agreed, in that he saw no actual evil in the nude suitably presented.

The Lord Chamberlain then pointed out that a certain section of the public—admittedly probably those who have not seen the shows in question—were very perturbed by the question of nudity, and that possibly some sop should rightly be given to them, as representing a portion of the community, which the gentlemen present in the room were professionally bound to consider.

Points were raised with regard to the semblance of nudity, the partial draping of the nude, and various types of garment, and the conclusion was come to that it would be almost impossible to lay down what could be and what should be worn. The consensus of opinion was in favour of leaving matters as regards the nude as they were, and saying, in addition, that any moving nudity, as opposed to a tableau vivant, would require individual vetting.

Three weeks later, Cromer hosted a conference entitled 'Nudity on the Stage'; among the attending delegates were representatives of the Society of West End Managers, the Theatrical Managers' Association, The Association of Touring and Producing Managers, the Entertainments Protection Association, the County Councils' Association and the Association of Municipal Corporations. Nobody from the Public Morality Council was invited.[64] Again, while seeking to impress on managers the need for them to avoid extending their liberties too far, Cromer's tone and intentions were hardly draconian:

The Lord Chamberlain opened the Conference by informing those present that it had been called as the result of a volume of complaints which had been received from various sources both by his Office and by the London County Council, criticising various items of entertainment which had recently appeared . . . He felt that a meeting should be called to concert action and to bring to the notice of everyone the need for a uniform justice in regard to all places of entertainment . . .

His Lordship said that personally he would prefer to leave matters to the discretion of individual managers, but he feared that in some cases intensive competition might lead to their endeavouring to 'go one better than the other' . . .

The generally expressed opinion of the Managers present was that at no time do they attempt to attract custom by deliberately putting on unseemly acts or by encouraging indecency. They expressed their willingness to co-operate with the authorities at all times . . .

Summing up the Lord Chamberlain said that he preferred to leave the matter to the discretion of Managers, and assured the meeting that he, at any rate, did not intend to put rules into writing. In response to the request for guidance as to the type of act to which exception is taken he instanced 'Perversion' and 'Pansy' jokes.

The Conference, his Lordship said, had been deliberately confined to generalities, but he hoped that due heed would be given to what had passed.

The rather vague conclusion reached at this gentle and gentlemanly meeting was simply 'that every effort would be made to eradicate any undesirable elements' from future presentations.[65]

Some prosecutions did take place following the conference, and the Public Morality Council particularly celebrated a reduction in the juxta-position of verbal innuendo and comedians with 'deliberately unclad performers'.[66] But the Council could not claim to have made a break-through, and, to the disappointment of its campaigners, soon found that the new Lord Chamberlain was no more willing than his predecessor had been to embrace their policies. This is evident from the account of their first meeting with him in July 1938. It can hardly have boded well when Clarendon began by telling them that he had himself attended a performance at the Windmill the previous evening, accompanied by his youngest daughter and his married son. The Council then suggested that a new regulation was required, and questioned whether nudity was even within the law.

> The Lord Chamberlain replied to the effect that he was glad to meet the committee and to listen to all they had to say, but that he had not had great experience in his position as Censor yet, but he wished to make it quite clear, in these words, that with regard to nudity 'I do not see myself any objection to nudity so long as there is nothing obscene or suggestive about it' . . .
>
> To his way of thinking there are only two ways of dealing with nudity; the first was to allow the present state of affairs, but at the same time to stem off any obscenity, or to go back to Victorian times; there was no halfway house, and rules which were suggested by certain members of the Committee, apart from the difficulty of drawing them up, would not be advantageous.
>
> The Lord Chamberlain then said that his policy would be to carry on as in the past, and that he would welcome any complaints or suggestions, which the Committee cared to send in. He added that to the best of his knowledge no coercion was put upon girls to appear without any clothes on.[67]

Not surprisingly, the Council's account of the year voiced frustration and hinted impatiently that it had been 'necessary to protest repeatedly' before Lord Clarendon responded to their campaign against striptease.[68] In 1939 the Council reported that it had submitted to Clarendon 'an extensive summary of incidents of apparent nudity or extreme undress presented at two theatres in 1936, 1937, and 1938'. Indeed, it dared to question whether the theatres concerned were operating with the effective connivance of the Lord Chamberlain, and, given his failure to act against them, the Council now requested the co-operation of 'leading and representative citizens' to persuade the Lord Chamberlain to ban such performances.[69]

From a modern perspective, the Public Morality Council almost inevitably appears as a patronising, middle-class group of do-gooders and interfering busybodies, driven by a wish to suppress sexuality and whatever it deemed subversive of the strict moral and religious outlook to which it adhered. The 'Prudes on the Prowl', as Marie Tempest christened them. Yet, however narrow-minded its outlook may seem to us now, the Council's roots lay partly in the nineteenth-century liberal tradition which sought to protect the socially vulnerable against the rampant self-interest and market-driven logic of capitalist exploiters. The chair of the Council's Stage Plays Committee in the thirties was Miss Edith Neville, O.B.E., who was not only an Honorary Director of a People's Theatre, but also a social worker and for fourteen years the chair of the St Pancras Housing Society Ltd.[70]

Traces of the urge to side with the powerless against the powerful certainly remain in the persistent campaign against stage nudity. The Council's annual report published in 1933, for example, typically insisted that scenes involving the undress of (almost invariably) young women 'must affect the self-respect of young women, and certainly encourage undesirable men to treat them lightly, regardless of the fact that, doubtless, many young women have felt compelled to accede to this practice rather than lose employment'.[71] Similarly, the arguments in a four-page leaflet entitled *The Stage Plays Committee's Position in Regard to Stage Undress* merit serious consideration. In particular, the Council was surely right that cynical exploitation for financial and commercial profit was the major force behind the stage presentation of living statuaries, in which famous paintings of beautiful young women were reproduced 'live' for the benefit of male punters:

> Since 1931, the Council has continually expressed its concern and that of those it represents at the reports of the development in the presentation of females in a state of undress, commencing with brassieres and loin cloths. This practice has been carried to an extreme and, in some cases, to what is apparently the altogether nude. Repeated visits to certain theatres over a long period have established the fact that this is carried on habitually.
>
> The Council's submissions on this matter have been formally expressed to the Lord Chamberlain as follows:–
>
> 1 That such presentations of undress by their lack of modesty, their suggestiveness and the frequency with which they occur are calculated to sensuously excite impressionable minds and, in the opinion of a number of members, do tend to degrade audiences which include couples of opposite sexes and particularly those of an age susceptible to sex influences.

2 The Council strongly maintain that there is no legitimate comparison between nudity or semi nudity in art schools, bathing, sports or normal environments, and that which is displayed in the emotional atmosphere of a crowded theatre and often-times exploited in scenes of sexual interest or association.

3 . . . Doubtless, many young women have felt compelled to accede to this practice rather than lose employment.

4 Presentations such as those in question have undoubtedly alienated many good citizens from attendance at theatres.

5 Persons can get used to any practice but there is surely no necessity whatever for perpetuating subjects of this kind, which involve exploiting the female body and ignoring the elementary facts of human nature.

The Council cannot subscribe to the idea that the theatre is to become an instrument of introducing boys and girls brought up in the canons of ordinary decency, if not religion, to an atmosphere which must force the thoughts in a direction calculated to create emotional disturbance.

. . . It is most unsatisfactory that a person bathing in the Serpentine in the nude will be arrested and convicted of improper conduct, whilst women, practically naked, are permitted by the Lord Chamberlain to exhibit themselves publicly in theatres licensed by him.

It is a matter of regret to the Committee to learn that girls willing to appear in this condition in public can earn from £4 to £12 per week.[72]

On the other hand, following yet another concerted campaign by the Council against the Windmill Theatre in 1939, the Lord Chamberlain's Office adopted a commendably strong stance:

The trouble with the Public Morality Council is that its members seem to regard the Theatre as a pulpit. This is a fundamental misconception. The Theatre is the platform from which the dramatist may express his thoughts about life, its evil equally with its good. To deny him this freedom, as long as he expresses himself with a reasonable decorum, is to kill the living art of the Theatre.

In these days when there is so much freedom in speech and literature outside the Theatre, unduly to restrict freedom of speech and thought within would meet with strenuous opposition, and rightly so.

If you give the people nothing but fairy tales, they will become mentally emasculated. Those 'with impressionable minds' must take their chance within the Theatre as they have to take their chance without . . . the dramatist cannot be kept in chains while his brother artists are free.

It is probable that the present revival of dramatic art owes much of its vitality to the reasonable attitude shown by the Censorship.[73]

On issues of morality, the Lord Chamberlain's Office could probably be said to be occupying a position not too far removed from the middle ground.

In January 1936, Street predicted: 'I think that sooner or later greater freedom may be given the stage in regard to sexual facts'. He drew a distinction between, on the one hand, the mere discussion of ideas or relationships which challenged conventional morality and, on the other, their physical embodiment and visual depiction. All that would really remain excluded, he prophesied, was 'indecency in representation'. Although Cromer proposed a different criterion for judgement, his letter to the Advisory Board made it clear that he too believed that the times were a-changing, and that he endorsed his Reader's initiative:

> Mr Street's remark that 'sooner or later greater freedom may be given the stage in regard to sexual facts, apart from indecency in representation' entirely coincides with my own views and feelings.
>
> As I write this, we may be on the threshold of a new epoch, occasioned by the commencement of a new Reign in which public opinion will advance and alter.
>
> Censorship of the stage will necessarily have to move with the times, as indeed it has done during the last ten years or more.
>
> The essential question for censorship to decide in plays will become . . . 'what is harmful?' [74]

A couple of weeks later, Street recommended as a candidate for 'the extension of liberty' a melodrama set in Malaya and focusing on abortion. He described *Amok** as in itself 'a worthless play', but one which provided an opportunity to establish a principle and a precedent: 'if a better on the same subject were licensed and this not, it would be unfair'. Street was keen to initiate in practice the change towards which both he and Lord Cromer had recently pointed: 'Before he left England, the Lord Chamberlain, in a note on a play, agreed with me that the basis of the permissible would probably be broadened', wrote Street. However, with Cromer himself absent, the Advisory Board was less willing to embrace the spirit of change. 'One of the principle Yellow Perils issues from Malaya; even its plays are pestilential', wrote Sir Ian Malcolm. He then staked out his own alternative wish list for a new era: 'If "broadening" is to be the order of the day, I suggest broadening up, and admitting fine plays about Our Lord, the Apostles and the Royal Family', he wrote.[75] In a private letter to the Lord Chamberlain, he expressed his views at greater length, and sought clarification about the role of the Advisory Board:

> A question of first principles seems to be involved; and I for one feel that if you could lay down for us a policy which should inform our criticisms, not only should we all be very much obliged to you, but we might be of far greater assistance than at present.

---

* Written by Harold Simpson and Esmé Scott Harston

My personal experience may illustrate the comparative darkness in which I wander when I have to criticise a play that you have sent me. I am, by your invitation, a member of your Advisory Board. But I have not been officially informed upon what exactly my advice is sought. Am I, in a word, to try to assist your final judgement as to:

a) The matter

or

b) The manner (language and style)

or

c) The morals

of the play in question: And which of these three ingredients of every play is to take precedence before the other two?

Nor is it yet perfectly clear to me what is the precise function of the Censor himself. I conceive him to be the official protector of three distinct entities: the British Theatre, the English Language, the taste and morals of the British public. If this be a true, if not an exclusive, definition, then we advisors are (if so informed) in possession of valuable pointers towards the goal at which we can be of most assistance.

Mr Street . . . believes that 'the basis of the permissible will probably be broadened'. And from the context I gather that it is to be a case (*pace* Lord Tennyson) of

'"Freedom" slowly broadening <u>down</u>

From devilment to devilment'.

And that subjects (such as gestation, incest and abortion) which have not hitherto been considered proper to public entertainment, may in the future, if decently presented, stand a good chance of being accepted, 'facilis descensus Averno'. Here comes in the problem of the Censor's 'Protectorate'; if not over the Theatre, at any rate over the English Language and British taste and morals. In such a case, what attitude would he desire his Advisory Committee to adopt? Would it be within their functions—on the question of 'broadening'—to stand for the older tradition of the British stage, excluding some of the dramatists of the 'Restoration' period; or would they be expected to take the line that, in order that the Theatre may be as 'free' as Literature, it must be a true mirror of the laxity of living and the looseness of language of the present day, and submit to a 'broadening' in the downward direction? On this point I, personally, ask for guidance.

But, at the same time, I put in a respectful claim for 'broadening' in an <u>upward</u> direction also. As at present advised, I can see no good reason why, if the baser side of life is to be allowed a loose rein in the Theatre, the spiritual and better side should not be given an equal chance of making itself seen and heard. Passion Plays might then come by their own once more; dramas based on Old and New Testament stories might be written in prose or verse; poets and dramatists might then feel inspired to prepare Milton for the stage, or *The Dream of Gerontius*, or the old Miracle and Morality Plays. And, to hold the scales equally as between the Theatre and the Book-stalls, the ban might then be lifted on deceased members of the Royal Family . . . In this direction, such is the innate reverence for the House of God and the House of Windsor in the heart of the British public,

I feel that, whether the subject be religious or royal, no blasphemy or flippancy or disrespect would be tolerated by any British audience from any author or from any players. Let us therefore aspire to be up to date, if we are already preparing to be down to date.

Cromer remained vague and unwilling to offer specific guidelines:

As to the guidance that I seek from Members of the Advisory Board, it is more in the form of wishing to know whether they individually would be in favour of a play being licensed, or not . . .

With the march of time the views of what can, or cannot be presented upon the stage are bound to alter, although stage performances must of necessity lag somewhat behind the books of our most advanced novelists. Consequently what I really look to my Advisory Board to give me is a commonsense view of how to deal with any particular play that comes before them.[76]

A couple of months later, after inspecting a private performance of a banned play set in a 'mental hospital', Henry Game, made his own case for how the censorship might reposition itself. When *Moonflowers** had been submitted (and turned down) the previous December, Game had opposed a licence, but had admitted that he was not 'very happy about condemning a play merely because it is likely to offend public conventions as against being subversive of public morals'. Now he proposed that the new era should recognise and establish that difference:

Within a minute which he wrote towards the end of January, I think, the Lord Chamberlain threw out the suggestion that the beginning of a new reign, which places a representative of a generation more recent than ours upon the throne, might be a good moment in which to modify and broaden the policy of the Censorship in certain directions.

Personally I should welcome such a development, which I take to cover what I might call the 'Brieux' or 'astringent' group of plays: plays to which objection has been taken in the past owing to the fact that they might shock public susceptibilities. I have never thought this a valid reason for the refusal of a licence, for if the intention of the author has a worthy aim, it may well be an excellent thing that the public should have their susceptibilities shocked.

If then there is to be a broadening of policy, this play . . . might surely be included in the new order.

Game even proposed that 'less consideration for the prejudices of the average man (or woman) would be a tendency in the right direction'.[77] Yet there were clearly forces which would have vigorously opposed any increase in leniency, and, if 1936 and the start of a new reign was a

---

* Written by Jean Pinard

watershed in relation to morality, then from a distance of nearly seventy years it is very hard to detect it.

In 1938 a play called *The Hand of the Potter* became the subject of much debate for the censorship. Written by the American author Theodore Dreiser, the story was set in a Russian-Jewish family in New York, and centred on 'a sexual maniac in his relations with family and society'. It culminated in 'a plea for greater sympathy and understanding of these victims of fate', and Game was again in favour of licensing it—despite the problems it would create:

> This is the type of play which if suppressed by the Censorship, gives a basis and fact to the argument that it is WE who are responsible for the triviality and futility of the modern theatre. Personally, I should give the play a licence, oppose reason to any outcry that may follow, and leave it to the Management in its own interests, to exclude all but Adults from their Theatre.

The script was sent to the Advisory Board for consideration, accompanied by an angst-ridden letter which clearly shows a sense of the censors' own awkwardness and embarrassment about what they were doing:

> The question is, whether we are justified in refusing a licence to a dramatist because of the unpleasant nature of his theme, when . . . he has treated the subject with sincerity and compassion and constructively. The only serious criticism of the modern Censorship is the fundamental one— that it, by the very fact of its existence, tends to restrict the range of subjects which may be treated on the stage. It is not easy to refute this charge while we allow the endless succession of worthless plays about infidelity and adultery, and place our ban upon a writer of realistic force such as the one under discussion . . .
>
> 1 is this a permissible subject for dramatic treatment?
>
> 2 Does the realistic treatment make the play too strong meat for the ordinary theatregoer?
>
> 3 Is it likely to be harmful socially by pandering to sadistic or any such degenerate appetites?

The Lord Chamberlain received contradictory advice. Professor Winifred Cullis (and the medical students who accompanied her to watch a private performance) supported it as 'putting forward a social problem that needed recognition and suitable action'. Lord Cecil accepted it was a moral text, but was worried by the realism and by the fact that it showed rather than just talked about its subject:

> I also agree that the range of subjects allowed a licence should be extended. Serious discussions of sexual problems on the stage does good on the whole: . . . on the same grounds I should permit plays discussing homosexuality or incest.

But Mr Dreiser does not just discuss: he exhibits . . . the public has to
watch an unfortunate degenerate in the throes of an animal lust for a child:
which culminates, they learn later, in her murder.

The other reader, Dearmer, opposed a licence 'On all counts—policy,
public interest and the sheer unnecessity of its horrible subject'. He insisted
that if the production was commercially successful it would be so 'on
account of the morbid interest it would arouse', and certain elements
particularly distressed him: 'The presence of children on the stage in this
play, seems to me a public offence. The play might do incalculable harm to
expectant mothers and those subject to neurosis'.

Cromer canvassed more opinions on *The Hand of the Potter* than on
almost any other individual script—not only senior church representatives,
but judges, the Metropolitan Police and a range of public figures. He even
invited the views of the Public Morality Council, who actually approved of
the fact that 'No particular stress is placed on nauseous details', and that
'there is no condonation of the offence'. The Council also welcomed 'the
writer's evident sympathy with the position of the sexual maniac and his
desire for some remedy', but expressed disappointment at the absence of
'any concrete suggestion about what should be done, to which Act Four
might have been devoted'. In conclusion, the Council thought that 'a
detailed study of a sexual maniacal theme might reasonably be deemed to
be offensive to the moral sense of, at least, a majority of our countrymen',
and that it 'could not be justified unless there was overwhelming evidence
of a great evil and urgent need of reform'—which there was not. The Lord
Chamberlain refused a licence, on the grounds that it would be 'distasteful'
and because 'The need for such a play is no means vital'.[78]

In November 1938, under a new Lord Chamberlain, Game went further
than before in suggesting that the censorship needed to reform itself and to
resist more strongly the puritanical reactionaries who sought to influence
it. Eugene O'Neill's *Desire Under the Elms*, which had been rejected for a
licence in 1925, was now resubmitted, and Game's passionate and
polemical report—worthy of Street at his best—was surely designed to
persuade Lord Clarendon of the need to overhaul policy, especially in
relation to 'serious' dramas:

Perhaps a refusal was justified in 1925, but I hold very strongly to the
opinion that it is no longer justified now.
    The potential audience for serious plays has very much increased
during the intervening years, thanks to the work of the Sunday producing
Societies and such Theatres as the Westminster, and because of the great
increase in the number of published plays. The Censorship, recognising
this development in public taste, no longer treats the Theatre audience as
if it was entirely composed of children: and the Theatre is now in process
of attaining at long last a reasonable amount of freedom.

At the Westminster, where the play is to be staged, the Management has built up a numerous audience which wishes to see serious drama; and which by no conceivable flight of imagination can possibly derive any moral harm from the work of a man who is undeniably a poet and an artist.

It is to me a humiliating thought to think of all the comedies of adultery and fornication which we have passed—to say nothing of the salacious spewings of a Ronald Frankau—while a work of art such as this lies under our ban, just because it treats of the primal passions of a rude society.

To ban the work of an artist which . . . is invariably suffused with poetic feeling, and to pass salacious trash, is to lay the heavy hand of the Philistine upon the Drama with a vengeance!

In conclusion I might add that the play is now known to a wide circle of readers, which makes a continued ban additionally ridiculous.

And finally I would ask upon what grounds can the play be forbidden? It would be difficult to substantiate a claim that it is morally harmful, and to forbid a play because some people prefer drawingroom-drama or comedies is quite indefensible.

O'Neill's play was duly licensed, though a subsequent internal office memorandum in 1940 alluded to it rather disparagingly as one which 'got through soon after Lord Cromer retired'.[79]

Another play which 'got through' in the early days of Clarendon's appointment and then provoked controversy was Noel Coward's *Design for Living*, which was licensed with only minimal changes in the autumn of 1938. Game had commented that 'despite the immorality of its theme, the Public would not in my opinion be justified, after the successful revival of Wycherley's "Country Wife", in raising any serious objection to what is, after all, only an artificial comedy of manners'. In early 1939, however, the Office came under attack for having licensed such a 'pernicious play'. As one correspondent put it, the play was 'the more pernicious to my mind as it is very witty with amusing lines'. Complainants received a standard and carefully prepared letter of reply which framed Coward's play as one which, through its depiction of bad characters, would promote rather than undermine correct moral behaviour:

Mr Coward has taken the old theme of the 'Eternal Triangle' and has solved the problem in a new way which is, of course, entirely unsuitable for the majority of people in a reasonable world. It is made quite plain that those immediately concerned are Bohemians and not particularly good citizens—their lives are centred upon themselves, they are useless members of society . . .

The author has treated this theme with decorum—there is no erotic and suggestive indecency, the principals are objects for compassion rather than for disgust, and it may well be argued that the reaction to a play of this description is one of thankfulness that the majority of people lead normal lives: nor can it be believed that anyone seeing the play would be converted to that type of existence.

The Public Morality Council was unpersuaded: 'To decry vice is not necessarily to teach virtue', it declared, and insisted that 'The presentation of the three leading characters' would 'far outweigh by its harmful influence any good effected by exposing to contempt vicious living'. The play was 'not true to the real function of the Theatre or to life generally', and was 'a harmful study of decadence', particularly dangerous because 'the reputation of the author and the reception of the play by the audience ... with adoring and almost reverent attention' would have the effect of 'encouraging further productions of the same kind'.

In April 1939, the secretary of the Public Morality Council wrote again to explain that *Design for Living* had now been formally discussed by the Stage Plays Committee and that he wished to register

> a strong protest against the Play on the grounds that, as presented, it is not true to life in any real sense, and that its whole tenor is descriptive of people with no morals, which, the Committee felt, is likely to injuriously affect persons of 'impressionable minds'.
>
> The executive felt that the play has no real justification as representing life in this country, and noted the absence of any really healthy leading character in the play. They also feel that studies limited to sordid life (in this case a 'mild nymphomaniac') even if intended as a skit on morals must, by the cumulative effect, have an injurious influence.

Tyrer enclosed a series of reports on the play by some of the Council's adherents; one actually voiced qualified approval of the play, on the grounds that it 'would appear to be quite unprofitable to gloss over certain tendencies which are apparent in every class of society'; but most condemned it absolutely. Slightly ominously, at a time when books were being burned elsewhere in Europe, one report stated that 'A public which accepts it has forgotten how to defend its dignity, and should be saved from it'. There was certainly no underestimating of the potential of theatre to influence its audiences:

> If we care about morality, human dignity, decent home life, the play obviously offends in every particular. It is a curious view that the negation of all that is best in life is immaterial so long as it is treated in an amusing way. There can be no question that this view is responsible for much of the lower standard of morality in the present day. To the less educated, and these are far more numerous in theatre audiences than formerly, it is the statements that influence, not the humour ... If such plays are to have the support of the Censor, it would seem far better to abolish the censorship at once, for it is merely ridiculous.

Another reporter was relieved from dejection only by the 'decidedly refreshing' sound of the national anthem being played at the end of the performance (one wonders whether anyone might have perceived this as suggesting a more ironic relationship with what had gone before). However, this correspondent was worried about the lasting damage such a play might be inflicting on the nation: 'the government is anxious about national fitness, and modern acids that are breaking up home life are held to be dangerous. Such a play as this would accelerate these processes of degeneracy'.[80]

Design for Living was passed in spite of its apparent cynicism, and yet over a period of several years the censorship refused to license 'a tedious Hungarian play on the theme that marriage is war'. Cromer first rejected *Ehe*,* in 1938, as 'a revolting play and a wholly unnecessary importation from abroad'. The story focuses on two central characters, symbolically named only as Husband and Wife, who loathe each other but are persuaded to remain together by an elderly neighbour who tells them that 'He and his wife have been quarrelling all their lives and rather enjoyed it'. Dearmer called it 'confused, cynical, dreary balderdash' and 'an exercise in cynicism and contempt of the institution of marriage'; however, since it was a play of ideas and discussion, and contained 'no love making business or anything that could encourage eroticism or immorality', he reluctantly recommended it, subject to amendments. Dearmer was over-ruled, but in January 1940 the play was resubmitted in a revised form under the title *Marriage in Mayfair*. Although he professed no sympathy for the play's philosophy, Dearmer again advocated licensing it, in part because *Design for Living* had been permitted. He also contested the practice of favouring the light over the serious treatment of immorality:

> This play has now been given a Mayfair setting. The required cuts have been made. The plot remains the same. The play is a picture of pre-war garishness and cynicism in most of the characters' attitude to marriage. These are not shown in a favourable light. Their misbehaviour is implied not dramatised, and although there are opportunities for objectionable business (for which reason a dress rehearsal should be attended) I don't think the play should be banned . . . the characters in Coward's play are represented as sufficiently sympathetic in their amorality to be worthy of our attention, whereas these characters are not meant to be worthy of our sympathy. We dislike most of them.
>
> I dislike the play . . . but the author would have a strong case if a comparatively serious treatment of the subject were banned because it was about depraved and idle people of a kind which certainly exists, when

---

* Written by Johanne Vaszary, translated by Lawrence Wolfe and adapted by Count T. Zichy

light-hearted plays of the *Design for Living* sort are passed. These latter may be much more dangerous and subtly salacious.

Major Gordon, now acting as wartime Comptroller, disagreed:

> The removal of the locale from Hungary to this country makes it a materially different play . . . Had the Continental setting been maintained some of the unpleasant business in the play might have been regarded as symbolic of the country of origin . . . To my mind the play is chiefly a medium for portraying some very nasty depraved people in a series of unpleasant scenes.

Dearmer had found himself increasingly at odds with and frustrated by the dominant views in the Office, and his reasoned response to Gordon's arguments challenged both the specific details and the general principles he had advanced. Again, Dearmer insisted that there were no adequate grounds for refusing the licence:

> To ban this play or even to cut it as drastically as proposed, will, in my opinion, cause a good deal of justifiable protest. Very many plays, e.g. *Our Betters*, (Maugham) and *Dangerous Corner* (Priestley) may be described as 'a medium for portraying some very nasty depraved people in a series of unpleasant scenes . . .' Maugham's scene is sexually stimulating, the scene in this play is the reverse. It is questions of this sort with which the Censor is concerned, the effect of a scene, not the details of presentation unless the latter are indecent. The adaptor will point out that he is out to show a type of person which undoubtedly exists, not to excite sympathy for their indulgence but the reverse. It will be very difficult to counter this objection which in my opinion is valid.

Clarendon appeared at first to have accepted Dearmer's recommendation; now, however, he came down firmly on Gordon's side: 'It would, if it ever appeared on the stage, cause a storm of protest, and justifiably so, from all sorts of quarters. I have destroyed the licence I originally signed'.

In February 1940, *Marriage in Mayfair* was submitted once again with further alterations. Now even Gordon agreed the play should probably be licensed: 'I think it would be very difficult, and unwise, from a policy standpoint, to maintain the ban'. One might have thought that five months into the war against fascism the whole affair would have seemed trivial and not worth arguing about. But with the divisions in British society by no means bridged in unity against a common enemy, issues of class conflict were still perceived as significant. Clarendon consulted his predecessor in office, and although Cromer found it hard to justify a refusal he was still reluctant to recommend the play:

> Had it not been for the fact that he has now submitted a third version and would probably be prepared to submit even a fourth version, the play

could have been banned on the demerits of its theme alone. I hardly think
it would be justifiable now to refuse a licence.

It is a pity, too, that the setting of the play has now been transferred
from Hungary to this country, but it is too late now to alter this.

For political reasons, Cromer suggested reverting to the original title and
abandoning the new one, 'which gives it a definite and wholly unnecessary
label'. But he reluctantly concluded: 'it ought not really to do much harm
except that it is a subtle form of Socialist propaganda'. Other members of
the Advisory Board still opposed licensing, but Dearmer stuck to his guns
and continued to argue crucial points of principle:

> Professor Cullis says she 'Cannot see any possible reason for putting it on
> the stage'. I quite agree, but a licence does not carry with it a 'reason' or
> indeed anything more than a guarantee that reasonable playgoers of all
> classes will not be degraded or outraged by the play as a whole, or their
> moral philosophy seriously endangered by plausible arguments.

He also reiterated a crucial point which the censorship had always struggled
to accept: 'The play is not degrading because certain characters are
degraded'.[81] But the ban on *Ehe/Marriage in Mayfair* remained—perhaps
partly because Clarendon had dug himself into an entrenched position
against Dearmer and did not wish to seem to be retreating. In the event,
political events in Britain saved the Lord Chamberlain from having to deal
with further representations from Count Zichy, the play's adaptor: 'I think
he must have been interned', wrote Gordon in April 1940. The file could
be closed—though Dearmer's relationship with other members of the
Office had probably been further damaged.

For some people at the end of the thirties, the war over sexual morality
was still the one they wanted to fight. In April 1939, the Office had received
an angry protest about Emlyn Williams's *Night Must Fall*, a play which had
actually been approved four years earlier. Now, however, an angry member
of the public wrote to both the Lord Chamberlain and the playwright, 'in
the hope that something will be done to mitigate this evil'. It was, she said,
one of a number of 'indecent plays' which she believed to be the major
danger facing the nation at this time:

> While it is probably true that such plays do little or no harm to young
> people who have been brought up in good homes, and have been well
> educated, there are the large numbers of young people on the borderline
> of intelligence and mental deficiency to be considered. To the latter such
> plays might do incalculable harm.

Her letter to Williams, a copy of which she enclosed for the Lord
Chamberlain to read, was much more tortuous and disturbing:

Can't you see how paltry, how wrong it is to pander to that section of the play-going public that has little use for a play unless it is for the vile language or bald statements . . .

Have you any children I wonder. No, you can't have . . .

We all know that some countries or other revel in the kind of thing I am complaining of, but is there any good reason why England should copy the bad habits of other countries?

. . . I do wish you would reflect seriously on what you ARE doing and WHAT YOU ARE CAPABLE OF DOING at this critical time in the history of our country—a time when it behoves every citizen to give of their best. Hitler and Mussolini are not by any means the worst enemies of our country today, and it is the duty of all of us, and especially of people like yourself who have it in their power to influence others for good or evil, to give of our best in this time of need.[82]

Such a letter might have had no real immediate effect, but who was to say that it would have no influence on future decisions?

CHAPTER THREE

'The Author Will Probably Deny It . . . '

Naming the Homosexual

> I . . . do not personally think that reference to homosexuality can always be kept from the stage.
>
> (The Lord Chamberlain's Reader of Plays, 1934).[1]

Before his death following a heart attack in the autumn of 1936, George Street, an open admirer of Congreve, Ibsen and especially Wilde, had long been one of the more liberal voices in the Lord Chamberlain's Office in relation to issues of morality—at least with regard to serious drama. In 1934, he had dared to cast doubt on perhaps the greatest moral taboo of all, questioning in his report on Aimée and Philip Stuart's *Love of Women* whether it was even feasible to keep the stage free from all mention of homosexuality. The play which provoked his comment was refused a licence, and, despite much agonising at St James's Palace and consultation with 'experts', it would be almost into the 1960s before the Lord Chamberlain would quietly signal the removal of his ban. But even if was not officially acknowledged, Street was surely right in drawing attention to the practical difficulties of maintaining an absolute and rigid policy.

In making his comment, the Reader doubtless had in mind the recent controversy over Mordaunt Shairp's *The Green Bay Tree*. In fact, it had been largely due to Street's positive recommendation in November 1932 that Cromer had licensed this play—a decision which provoked outrage in some quarters, not least because it was identified as a precedent which could be cited in relation to other texts. Even in 1943, Game patronisingly accused Street of naïvety, insisting that Shairp's play, 'never would have been licensed if my predecessor had had a greater knowledge of perverted types'.[2] Elsewhere, he described its licensing as 'a very unfortunate lapse', which had damaged the Office because 'if you once make concessions it is very difficult to persist in a consistent policy'.[3] In retirement, Cromer would state that he regretted having been persuaded to license the play against his first impressions, while another member of the Office subsequently claimed that Shairp's play had 'always been held against the censorship as inconsistent with its ban on perversion'.[4]

The Green Bay Tree ran in the West End for over 200 performances, and many critics—whether they acclaimed its courage or denounced its decadence—interpreted it as a serious play about homosexuality. Street, however, always maintained that because there was no direct reference to the subject—let alone any physical representation of it—it could not be so defined, and that the play could not legitimately have been refused a licence. Yet Street was far too experienced and careful a reader to have missed the unstated but obvious implications of the text. Some thirteen years before the play begins, Dulcimer has bought for £500 the eight-year-old son of 'a man down on his luck and drinking'. Dulcimer has brought the boy up to a life of aesthetic pleasure and luxury, and is now horrified when Julian announces his intention to get married and to jettison Dulcimer's financial support and work for a living. The boy's 'real' father subsequently shoots Dulcimer, who has left all his money to Julian, but the young man's fiancée refuses to marry him unless he gives up this money. Julian cannot bring himself to abandon the luxury to which he has become accustomed, and ends the play alone with the apartment and the valet he has inherited, presumably to emulate the life of his benefactor and continue the cycle.

Street's report acknowledged in relation to Dulcimer and Julian that 'the former is and the other likely to be, a rather sinister and abnormal person', but he was adamant that there was 'no suggestion whatever of anything pederastic' in the relationship between them, and therefore 'nothing to censor'. His report gave no hint that anyone else in the Office should read the play to offer a second opinion, and Cromer signed the licence the following day. Street compared the theme to Wilde's *The Picture of Dorian Gray*; he acknowledged that the play worked through 'implication and suggestion', but claimed that its essence was 'a struggle for a young man's soul'.[5] Curiously, when the text was republished in a collection of 'gay plays' in the 1980s, the editor, while pointing out that 'Shairp's play treads as near to the dark edge of his subject as the times would permit', echoes Street's assessment: 'Looking back at the play 50 years later, possession seems a more central theme than homosexuality'.[6]

When the play opened in January 1933, however, most of the critics took a very different view, and some used it as a stick with which to beat the Lord Chamberlain. Under the headline 'PLAYS THAT OUGHT TO BE BURNT', C.B. Purdom could not bring himself to name the theme, but called it 'an unpleasant story' about a 'wicked man', which 'should never have seen the light of the stage'.[7] 'Which would you kick the harder?' asked the headline of another review, which went on to describe Dulcimer and Julian as 'two abominable people'. Others spoke of a 'repulsive topic' which was 'repugnant to the normal individual', and deplored the play's public presentation, though a more positive review saw it as a condemnation of Dulcimer and everything he represented: 'a subtle and delicate, but at the same time ruthless, attack on certain vicious elements in present-day society'.[8] More interestingly, Ivor Brown praised the production's refusal to exploit the 'effeminacy' of its characters by making them the butt of comedy; the play was written, he said 'without a single cheap or nasty line, such as this subject so often provokes', exposing the world of 'mimminy-pimminy aestheticism' to the gaze of 'cool detachment' in ways that encourage the audience to contemplate, and perhaps even to sympathise, with the characters' affliction: 'The effeminate is either a victim of physiological misfortune or a revolting poseur; Mr Shairp's Mr Dulcimer . . . is not put up to shock us vulgarly or to amuse us basely; he is there as the objectively studied specimen of a rare and unusually unhappy species'. There was, concluded Brown, a healthy and health enhancing purpose behind such a play: 'A dark place of society is uncovered; it is also disinfected'.[9]

For one critic, the play was nothing less than a theatrical herald to the dawn of an era ready to speak about such issues for the first time. Indeed, this particular review offered a revealing and in some ways surprising vision of the public and theatrical contexts within which the censorship was acting in relation to its theme:

> The English resolve to bury the problem of sexual abnormality beneath a deplorable mixture of schoolroom secrecy and smoke-room smut is at last weakening. Our ancestors and parents herded their adolescent young into monosexual barracks where abnormality became almost normal, then solemnly wrapped up the subject in the terminology of terrorism, injected into this melodramatic parcel a sulphurous reek of hell-fire, and, having deposited this dubious gift of knowledge on youth's doorstep, washed their pious hands and proclaimed a sacred silence. The collapse of the taboo was long delayed, but it is now fairly complete. The breach of the holy hush carries with it certain nuisances; more general knowledge about these facts of life has created a ludicrous eagerness to descry abnormal tendencies in normal friendships. In London nowadays it is almost impossible for two people of the same sex to share a flat or maintain a close friendship without some sniggering allusions to the flowers of the garden or the isles of Greece . . . However, these follies are but the growing pains of an enlightenment which is essential to social health and decency . . .
>
> Even the theatre, usually true to the Shavian taunt of being forty years behind the time, is losing its timelag in this matter. First the Pansy joke became the stock-in-trade of every touring revue; then it invaded the fashionable West End comedy; now it has been supplanted by the recognition that a male effeminate or unwomanly woman is not, of necessity, 'a scream'. One danger of the long silence was to create, in the small and persecuted minority, the tiresome quality of a sentimental self-pity. The Intermediate Sex had to choose, as it were, between prison and

the pedestal, between cells of penitence and wells of loneliness. Now at last we can escape from the two extremes of majority bullying and minority sob-stuff and such a play as *The Green Bay Tree*, admirable in its detachment and only a Moral Warning if you choose to make it so, is an excellent advertisement not only of Mr Shairp's skill in playwriting, but of a public opinion that is coming to its senses.[10]

Irrespective of the ideological positions they adopted, reviews which stated that a play about homosexuals was being staged in the West End were bound to cause a considerable stir not only in the offices of the Public Morality Council but also at St James's Palace. Nor would it have been unnoticed that the central part—'the elderly person-we-have-no-polite-name-for', as James Agate called him—was played by Frank Vosper, an actor who was himself widely believed to be homosexual. But with the censorship under fire, Street stuck resolutely to his guns:

I saw this play last night and was confirmed in the opinion I formed when reading it. There is no suggestion of physical homosexuality in it and indeed the play is inconsistent with it. The few critics who took the opposite view were I think influenced by a desire to appear knowing or by the unfortunate fact that homosexuality is in the air very much at present, or at least in the theatrical air. It is true that 'Mr Dulcimer' does not care for women and wants to have the agreeable young man about the place, but that is a very different matter. As John Pollock pointed out in 'The Saturday' if it had been a Miss Dulcimer and a young woman no one would have seen anything odd in it.

The Office had to choose between leaving its senior Reader out on a limb as a sacrifice or backing him. Ever wary of admitting that the King's representative could make mistakes, it chose to endorse his position. 'I saw this play with Mr Street and concur with the above report', wrote Major Gordon, the Assistant Comptroller.[11] But the decision to license *The Green Bay Tree* was a recurring area of contention.

Street resented some of the prejudiced responses to a text which he obviously admired. A week after recommending Shairp's play he reported on *The Warrior's Husband*,* a play based on the Hercules and Hippolyta myth which also had homosexual undertones. Street included some sardonic and bitter comments in his recommendation:

Sapiens with his girlish tricks is not pleasant to read and may be less so to see. But that is part of the sex-inversion scene, and not even the stupidest or most malignant critic ought to be able to confuse it with perversion in normal conditions . . . critics, however and other people too are so stupid that perhaps the point should be further considered.[12]

---

* Written by Julian Thompson

Perhaps Street was smarting from spoken or unspoken rebukes. In 1933 he drew attention to a passage in *Five Aces*[*] which 'might suggest that Mike was a homosexualist'; he added: 'we have to be so careful about that'.[13] Indeed, in this case Cromer pointedly over-ruled Street's recommendation that the allusion was 'too vague to notice and . . . probably not meant', and insisted on removing the reference.

In February 1934, Street referred in his report on *Distinguished Gathering*,[†] a crime thriller, to an accusation made against the villainous Sir Brian that his being unmarried proves him to be an 'invert'. 'I think the author must mean "pervert"', wrote Street, though he did not comment on the fairness or otherwise of the charge. 'I will not have "invert" or "pervert" characters on the stage', fumed Cromer, and the 'odious' character was removed.[14] In July of the same year, Street reported that 'Two "exquisite young men"' who were 'obviously homosexual' were among the characters of *That Certain Something*,[‡] a play submitted for the Aldwych. 'They might be cut out altogether with advantage', he suggested,[15] and for a while the Office became almost absurdly careful not to repeat 'the mistake' of *The Green Bay Tree*, excising anything they spotted as having even tenuous references to homosexuality. Cromer insisted on cutting the line 'Let's hope you satisfy the men better than you do their wives' from Emlyn Williams's adaptation of a play called *Josephine*,[§] even though the Reader—in this case Game—was confident that no 'perversion meaning' was intended.[16] In relation to *Spears Against Us*,[¶] Game highlighted references to a young man having been locked in a room at a club with a male companion: 'Some people will undoubtedly read the meaning of the scene as an accusation of perversion. I do myself, but am not quite sure that this is intended', he wrote. Again, the Lord Chamberlain removed the lines as suggesting 'an act of homosexuality'.[17]

The Green Bay Tree was almost unique for its time in that it placed a male-to-male relationship based on desire at its heart. It may not have been quite explicit, but as James Agate, himself a homosexual, pointed out under the headline ''Ware Censor', 'one cannot expect a playwright to go the whole hog when too obvious a hint of the *cochon* may suppress the animal altogether'.[18] One of the few texts submitted which was more overt was *Murder on the Ship*,[¦] a 1935 play in which John 'confesses to Diana that, in

---

[*] Written by Valerie Wynsgate (?)
[†] Written by James Parish
[‡] Written by Dayrell Webberley
[§] Written by Hermann Bahr
[¶] Written by Cecil Roberts
[¦] Written by Noel Langley

his despair at losing her, he has fallen a victim to Winter's perverted instincts and feels that he is now shut off from the world of normal people'. When John in turn deserts Winter, the latter throws himself overboard and is eaten by sharks. There was no question of licensing such a theme; it might have fitted Street's criteria for acceptance, since homosexuality was discussed rather than seen, but, whether by chance or design, the script was sent not to Street but to Game, who had no doubts: 'the play, as it is at present, will not do. The perverted relationship between Winter and John is made an integral part of the plot and the audience is not left in any doubt as to what it means'. He suggested that the play could only be reconsidered if the playwright rewrote it 'eliminating the perversion theme'.[19] Also adjudged too risky was an adaptation of a French play by Louis Verneuil,* in which a middle-aged man abandons his mistress to live in a dingy hotel in Huddersfield with a good-looking boy. 'At present his feelings for the boy are purely paternal', reported Game, 'but there are times when he is no longer sure that they are'. In fact, the boy turns out to be the man's son, but Verneuil's plot trod on dangerous ground; 'I think the Lord Chamberlain's way is quite clear, to ban this play', suggested the Reader; 'True there is no actual perversion, but the matter is ever present, and continually discussed'. Indeed, Game was convinced—on what evidence remains unclear—that the opportunity to exploit this theme for publicity was 'the sole reason why the Promoter wants to produce this nauseating nonsense'. Perhaps if it had been a comedy it might have been a different matter: 'Only a Frenchman, with his fondness for dressing up our animal passions in sentimental trimmings, and with little sense of the ridiculous, could bring himself to treat a situation seriously, which obviously cries aloud to burlesque'. Game also specifically advised that the licensing of Shairp's play had no relevance: 'The Green Bay Tree is no precedent for passing this play. In that play perversion was never made explicit and it was possible to witness a performance and leave the Theatre as innocent as one went'.[20]

In August 1934, the Office did license Hugh Ross Williamson's drama about Edward II and Gaveston, *Men Governing*; but only because, as Street pleaded in its defence, it carefully eschewed any mention of the forbidden subject:

> It is a matter of history that Edward and Gaveston were accused of homosexuality and some critics, knowing this, are likely to see it in the play. But they would be quite wrong. Not even Gaveston's enemies accuse him of it and in his talks with Edward there is nothing but a brother-like or David-and-Jonathan devotion. Moreover both he and Edward are explicitly stated to be 'without any suggestion of effeminacy'.

★ *A Man of Fifty*

Cromer accepted that 'This ought to absolve the play of any tolerance of the intolerable', and the drama's remote historical setting doubtless helped.[21] In the same year, Street also praised EmlynWilliams for having 'completely avoided any suggestion of homosexuality' in his historical meta-theatrical piece, *Spring 1600*. 'The central idea, that of a girl pretending to be a boy in order to take a girl's part in a play, is a good one', he wrote, and he added that the men who played female roles were shown as 'conceited but not effeminate'.[22]

In 1936, Street all but implored the Lord Chamberlain not to censor *Last Voyage*, a play about James I;* even though the real James's homosexuality was beyond dispute, it was barely hinted at in the text:

> I believe that the view of historians now is that he was a sentimental, not a practising homosexualist, and that is all that is shown in the play ... it really does not go beyond what every schoolboy who has 'done the period' knows—that James had 'favourites'. He only pats his cheek which would be innocent in a different man. It would be absurd for the censorship to whitewash him in this respect, since no indecency is involved.

Street admitted that how a character is presented to an audience on the stage is only partially defined by the script, and he volunteered the fact that 'an actor like Laughton might easily make him a horrible beast'; but he added: 'Laughton, however, is unlikely to play the part'.

Last Voyage was licensed without serious objection. 'Nothing and nobody', wrote Cromer, 'could successfully whitewash James'.[23] On the other hand, Leslie and Sewell Stokes's courtroom drama about the trial of Oscar Wilde appears not even to have been formally submitted for licence. Instead it was staged privately at the Gate Theatre Studio in the autumn of 1936. Two years later, while Robert Morley was reportedly 'taking New York by storm in it', *Oscar Wilde* was revived in another club production at the Arts Theatre. *The Times* noted that 'If the subject is to be treated at all in the theatre, it could scarcely be done less offensively'; however, the newspaper assumed and accepted that 'since the part of Oscar Wilde's life with which it deals is that which brought him into prison' it 'presumably must continue to appear only on private stages'.[24]

If there were few serious plays submitted which openly depicted or even referred directly to homosexuality, the Office was more often troubled with comic representations and men in drag. In 1934, *Never Again*, an American satire on theatre,† received a caution about its play within the play, in which one character was said by Street to be 'played very effeminately'. Cromer

---

* Written by Edward and Theo Thompson
† Written by Edmund Delby (?)

insisted: 'Caution as to no "Nancy boy" make-up etc'.[25] In January 1935, Game described a character in *Summer's Lease** as 'an effeminate young man'. Cromer would allow no such character to appear, though the word order he chose to use gives his ruling an interesting emphasis: 'There must be no definitely pervert character in the play'.[26] In the same month, concern was also voiced about *Oh Edward*,† a farce being staged at a Conservative club in East Molesey; though not favourably impressed, Street was prepared to recommend tolerance over most—though not all— aspects:

> A wearisome farce on old fashioned lines. . . . Edward and Cecil plot to score off Bob by Edward's making-up as a woman . . . We then have at great length the more or less unpleasant business of Edward's vamping first Nelson and then Bob and making both promise to marry him . . .
>
> For my part I loathe plays in which a young man pretends to be a woman and other young men fall in love with him even farcically. But this farce is obviously written in innocence of any suggestion of perversion, and is moreover clearly for amateur sort of production and will never be heard of again. I am inclined, however, to advise cutting out some business of Edward's kissing Bob and Nelson . . . as going too far.

Cromer agreed: 'I entirely share this aversion. This business should be cut'.[27]

Inevitably, language and innuendo were frequently at the heart of the debate. In 1937, Dearmer made a specific appeal‡ for the word 'cissy' to be permitted within a serious discussion: 'I am sure this means effeminate not homosexual'.[28] In February 1938, 'pansy' was still being automatically removed by the Lord Chamberlain's Office, despite Game's observation that the word had appeared in *The Times*.[29] In September, reporting on *Behind the Blinds*, Game again pointed out that not only 'pansy', but also 'cissy' had been used in a leading article of that most august of publications; in all probability he was referring to an editorial of July 1937, marking the death of the original childhood model for Little Lord Fauntleroy, which had indeed employed both words (albeit within quotation marks) in the final sentence of its discussion of the signification of dressing a boy in 'curls, collars, and velvet'.[30] The use of such taboo-shattering language in *The Times* was genuinely significant—not least because it would provide the Lord Chamberlain with an alibi in the event of future complaints—and Clarendon immediately ruled that the two words could in this instance remain uncut.[31] Yet less direct allusions remained susceptible to censorship.

---

* Written by Winifred Howe
† Written by J. Ernest Browne
‡ In relation to *Sing and Whistle*, by Milton Herbert Cropper

In considering a revue for Gateshead in February 1939, Game commented: 'I have queried one line which may be a perversion joke, but I don't see how we can be sure?' The gag appeared in the script as follows:

> – Do you know what we are?
> – No, but I shouldn't be surprised.

'I suggest cut and be on the safe side', proposed a senior member of the Office. The manager was forced to comply, even though he pleaded that the intention had been to play the relevant part 'as a Mother's darling type, or a "dude" and not as a "Pansy" type', and complained that he had 'seen similar presentations which might be termed the "pansy" type in West End productions'.[32]

'I detest men making up as women', wrote Lord Cromer in 1933; he was commenting on a revue set in occupied France during the First World War in which a female chorus was (appropriately) played by men. Street pointed out that there was no 'unpleasant suggestiveness' and that it was 'simply a question of clever make-up', and Cromer reluctantly approved it, with the familiar proviso that there must be 'no "Nancy" business'.[33] Cross-dressing was more common in sketches and revues than in plays, and always worried the Lord Chamberlain since it frequently led to complaints. Yet it would have been difficult to suppress all such caricatures, since they were sometimes dependent not on a script but on the performer. Cromer habitually outlawed 'effeminate' or 'pansy' behaviour: 'A caution must be given against any Nancy business being introduced'; 'No professional pansies should appear'; 'Suggestive of nancy business and should be cut'; 'I will not tolerate any "Nancy boy" stuff even in Byzantine setting'.[34] Yet in 1932, Ivor Brown praised the production and the author of *The Green Bay Tree* for avoiding clichés which were evidently all too familiar to theatre-going audiences: 'We are most of us, I suppose, wearied beyond words with the easy laughter raised by parading effeminate men with all the mincing movement of their kind. Neither Mr Shairp nor the players stoop to conquer by these methods'.[35] Just because the Lord Chamberlain's Office decreed that certain things were not allowed on the stage, it clearly does not follow that they were never to be seen there.

In 1935, the clerk to the Licensing Justices in Birmingham (always one of the more rigidly puritanical city authorities) complained to the Lord Chamberlain about some of the items being staged, apparently with his approval:

> I have been directed by the Public Entertainments Committee of the Justices to call the attention of the Lord Chamberlain to their concern at the inclusion in licensed scripts of humorous references to men described as 'nancies', 'pansies', 'cissies' and similar terms . . .

It is, of course, acknowledged that many people merely regard these remarks as referring to an effeminate type of man, but on the other hand others see in them objectionable allusions and humour of an unwholesome kind.

Seldom a week passes at these Courts without the Petty Sessions Justices being called upon to try men who are being charged with soliciting males for immoral purposes, and they are given to understand that the terms mentioned relate to this type of man. On these occasions such allusions have a very odious significance, and it is difficult to understand how they can be the subject of humour in places of entertainment.

The Assistant Comptroller replied: 'His Lordship is entirely in agreement . . . All such expressions and allusions thereto are always required to be taken out of the licensed Scripts'. It transpired that a 'pansy' had somehow been missed by the Reader, and that the other words had been added after the script was licensed. Managers who were found out for having allowed unlicensed lines to be included generally used comedians as scapegoats. It may well be true that whereas an actor playing Shaw or Strindberg would not expect to alter the script in an attempt to improve a line, the instinct of a comedian would have been to respond to current events, to the audience, to how a scene had played at the previous performance, or to the need for laughter, adapting, adding and subtracting in order to improve a gag. In any case, we must avoid assuming that the Lord Chamberlain's edicts were always religiously observed. Unless transgressions were brought to the attention of the Office, with evidence and a strong case, there was little that could be done; the Lord Chamberlain and the Home Office were understandably reluctant to start legal proceedings unless they were confident of winning their case.

One example of a successful prosecution occurred in November 1934 in relation to *West End Scandals* at the Garrick Theatre. The script for this revue included a dialogue which had been licensed because it was presumed to take place between a man and a woman; it was being played, however, by two men. The production was viewed by George Titman, the Lord Chamberlain's regular inspector of revues, and the Office's acknowledged expert on women's bodies and costumes. Commenting on the scene in question in *West End Scandals*, Titman reported that the acting relied on 'a lot of filthy "business" involving "Nancy" remarks and gestures', and Cromer moved to instigate legal proceedings: 'These people should be dealt with as severely as possible and if prosecution is advised by the Home Office it will be taken', he wrote; 'They have frequently been warned and deserve no mercy'. Titman's deposition to the court confirmed that 'From the affected manner of their speech and gestures it was clear that they were attempting to portray the mannerisms of persons of homosexual instincts'.[36] Fines were duly imposed, and the trial itself was widely publicised. Under the headline: 'Comedians' High-Pitched Voices', the *Evening News* reported as follows:

> Mr Lawson Walton stated that in a sketch, 'Try it Again', there were suggestions of indecency. Two comedians on the stage adopted the mannerisms and high-pitched voices of homo-sexual persons, and thus gave lines which would appear innocent in the script, and which would not be suggestive if uttered between male and female, an indecent meaning.
>
> In one case a comedian remarked to two other men: 'Why don't you two get married?' There were also actions which were suggestive.

As usual, the comedian got the blame:

> When the matter was brought to the notice of the management instructions were given to the comedian to delete it.
>
> In the stress of the first night performance the comedian forgot to do so, afterwards explaining that it was much harder to *unlearn* a part than it was to learn it.[37]

The successful prosecution of *West End Scandals* was a victory for the Lord Chamberlain, and doubtless the reverberations were widely felt. But such cases did not always go the Lord Chamberlain's way. In September 1939, an unsuccessful action was brought against Gerald de Vere, described by his defence lawyer as 'an eccentric dancer'. A police report described his act:

> The man De Vere came on from behind the curtain and stood between the two girls, wearing similar clothes. During the singing, off, of the song 'Lovely To Look At', the man slowly disrobed his feminine clothing. When the last top garment was removed he had let down hair from a wig which only partly covered dummy 'breasts'. He then put on a flimsy dressing jacket before removing the lower garment . . . He then turned to face the audience, displaying his body and with his legs close together. Although it was evident that his private parts were fastened with a jockstrap, the exhibition was none the less disgusting. A very respectable-looking woman sitting behind me exclaimed 'Good God!'

Yet to the embarrassment of the Lord Chamberlain and the Home Office, the magistrate ruled that because the Office had actually approved something described in the script as 'a female impersonation by Gerald de Vere assisted by two girls', this 'entitled the actor to give any sort of female impersonation he wished' without further intervention. 'You licensed a female impersonation act, believing it to be a proper one, without asking any questions, and what you are now complaining about is that it has turned out to be improper', the magistrate pronounced. To bring a prosecution now was 'locking the stable door after the horse had gone'.

The censorship was not prepared to let the matter drop so easily, and Titman wrote a memorandum to the Lord Chamberlain spelling out the serious implications and the drastic changes in procedure which he believed needed to be instituted:

> The action of the magistrate at Westminster Police Court, dismissing Summonses issued in connection with an indecent exhibition in the Revue *Cosmopolitan Merry Go Round* at the Chelsea Palace Theatre on August 2nd, aims an indirect blow at the Censorship and imposes upon the Lord Chamberlain the necessity for a closer scrutiny of the Manuscripts which are submitted for licence . . . that some direct action on the part of the Lord Chamberlain must arise from this case there is no doubt, and there is only one which will meet the necessity. All scripts in future must include full particulars of stage directions, actions, and complete descriptions of dumb acts. This has already been demanded in the case of the Windmill Theatre and it must now be made universal, and the Examiners should be instructed that no play should be recommended for licence until it is complete in every detail, including all action and business.

The Acting Comptroller and Clarendon agreed that Titman's proposal should be adopted, and informed the Readers accordingly: 'We must demand in every case a complete description of details of the entire performance . . . The Lord Chamberlain would be grateful if you will carefully scrutinise Manuscripts for references to Tableaux and Dumb Acts and mark them for further investigation'. Game had little choice other than to accept the instruction, but he cautioned that an over-reaction could lead to the Office being made to look even more ridiculous:

> I warned Titman that he might well lose his case. The fact that we allow female nudity on the stage brings the impersonation of a naked woman within the definition of 'female impersonations' . . . To cover ourselves legally I agree on the action you propose to take; but I think that in practice we need not be too exacting but continue to use what we fondly imagine is common sense. After all 999 silent acts out of a thousand are perfectly harmless . . . We don't want to encourage people to pull our leg by sending in, as the Windmill has done recently, pages of description of costume, when what we want to know about is the case where there is no costume to describe.[38]

The press, meanwhile, were not slow to point out the impracticality of stipulating that every aspect of a performance could be written down and submitted: 'under this order it is conceivable that George Robey would not be allowed to raise an eyebrow if the business were not mentioned in the script', reported the *Evening News*. The newspaper also sought and published the opinion of a well-known comedian, Vic Oliver:

'I just don't think it's possible to carry out this regulation,' he said, 'For one thing, it's not possible to describe a facial expression in words. And for another, every comedian varies not only his expression, but his actual gestures, in every performance, according to the response of the audience'.[39]

While issues of male 'perversion' often centred on cross-dressing and comic caricatures, a number of serious plays were refused licences in the thirties because they referred to 'unnatural' relationships between women. The best known example is Lillian Hellman's *The Children's Hour*, which was first turned down in January 1935 and approved only in 1964. Even Street found it 'horribly unpleasant ' and 'obviously impossible to licence', pointing out that 'Plays with not a tenth of the Lesbian element of this one have been banned'.[40] Two representatives of the Lord Chamberlain attended Norman Marshall's private production the following year, but advised that it would be a waste of time and money to resubmit it. But Hellman's play (and the treatment of it) were not unique. In 1933, the censorship had insisted on cutting 'the Lesbian passages' from a French language production of André Obey's *Loire*, and had excised the briefest reference in another play,* even though the lines they cut explicitly asserted that the character is not a lesbian:

> – You never seem to care for men Gypsy. Why? You are not the other sort?
> – I am not, though I can understand some of the other—with so many rotten men about.[41]

In October 1934, a licence was withheld from *Emergency Exit*,† which Game thought had been written 'by an obviously inexperienced author, who seems unaware of the attitude of the Censorship to the question of perversion'. The play made reference to both female and male homosexuality, though the Reader acknowledged that nothing tangible was supposed to occur:

> There is nothing the least immoral in the action of the play, but there is a good deal of talk hinting at perversion . . . We gather that Marian who has a masculine appearance is supposed to be a Lesbian and that her name is coupled with that of Lois and that John and Tony have a similar reputation . . . There is no real perversion in the play and no pervert except Tony in the past. The perversion merely exists in the imagination of some of the characters.

But Cromer was taking no chances, and insisted he was 'not prepared to license this play until the author removes all traces, or references to perversion'.[42]

---

* *Hemlock*, by Marius Underwood
† Written by W.S. Plymouth

Soon afterwards, Street agonised over *Love of Women*;* though there was evidently much in the play which commended itself to him, the writers had strayed just too far beyond the boundary for him to support it. Like many censors, Street wanted a slightly different play from the one its authors had chosen to write:

> Unfortunately the whole play is dubious, to say the least, and one of the most difficult to report on I have ever had. Homosexuality between two women is much of the theme: it does not exist but it is talked about. . . . Lesbianism is never mentioned, but it is obvious that this is what the gossip implies and Brigit's parents fear. Mrs Wingate says 'it is worse than I feared', having seen the girls kiss. . . . The girl Jacqueline's advance is Lesbian, but that could easily be cut out. In fact there is no reason why the author should not have written a play about the devotion of two women—like *The Ladies of Llangollen*—and the sorrow of one when the other marries without any suggestion of lesbianism at all. But they do suggest it, not as a fact, but as an unfounded rumour . . . They will perhaps plead the precedents of *Children in Uniform* or *The Green Bay Tree* as being occupied with homosexuality— wrongly in the latter case . . . in view of the rules and precedents I cannot possibly advise the Lord Chamberlain to license the play.

When Cromer consulted his Advisory Board, Violet Bonham Carter spotted the weakness in the Reader's suggestion that the unacceptable elements could be surgically struck out: 'You cannot—as is suggested— eliminate the parents' anxiety as to the situation, the references to "gossip" etc., without robbing the play of its only point and completely puncturing its plot'. Most of the Board were instinctively opposed to licensing such a play—Lord Ullswater, Lord David Cecil and Professor Winifred Cullis all dismissed it without much hesitation— but Bonham Carter wanted a more precise boundary to be defined:

> There is a technical question of principle, i.e. are all plays in which the theme of homosexuality is discussed, or hinted at, to be automatically barred from performance on the English stage? If the answer is 'Yes' (just as the appearance of The Almighty on the stage is automatically banned) then this play most certainly comes within the scope of the ban.

In June 1935, one of the Lord Chamberlain's staff watched a private performance and recommended that, even though the script had been amended, it should not receive a licence. Cromer communicated his final decision to the authors:

> It might possibly, as you say, be argued that the play is even a moral one, but the fact remains that it introduces a perversion as a factor in the plot,

---

* Written by Aimée and Philip Stuart

thus giving advertisement in the emotional atmosphere of a theatre to a fact in life, which appears undesirable for public discussion on the stage.[43]

Only two days after reading *Love of Women*, Street found himself faced by another play with an implied lesbian relationship at its centre. He was unable to recommend Gilbert Wakefield's *Lady of the Sky*, primarily because he knew from experience how it would be received:

> Another play with a suggestion of lesbianism. It is less on the surface of the dialogue than in *Love of Women*. The author will probably deny it altogether, but the critics will certainly find it. I do not see how the lesbian proclivities of Karin can fail to be obvious. She takes a young woman from her husband and tries desperately to keep her away . . . On the other hand Jane's innocence of lesbianism may be accepted,—though it is unfortunate that she should share a bed with Karin. She is merely out for her freedom and a good time and is dominated by the stronger woman.

The Reader concluded: 'These plays are horribly difficult to deal with. Perhaps the author might remove the lesbian suggestion somehow . . . Apart from the lesbian idea the only thing to notice is a passage about pinching a behind.' Cromer was adamant: 'The whole motive of this play appears to be a study in lesbianism and as such unsuitable for public performance'. He insisted that nothing less than a fundamental rewriting of the entire plot would be enough to earn a re-evaluation. He also took the opportunity to spell out his intention to try and preserve an absolute ban on the exploration of homosexual relationships in serious drama. Yet his remarks contained a hint of uncertainty as to whether he was likely to succeed:

> This play may not be technically either indecent or demoralising, still its fundamental theme is that of passionate and unbalanced love on one side and passive acquiescence to the point of attraction on the other side as between two women. A lesbian relationship between the two women is the obvious conclusion . . . I fail to see how this play can be licensed without appearance on the part of censorship of condoning illicit love between two women . . . Albeit the manner of presenting the theme is not offensive or blatant.
>
> Still the germ is there and either in its female or male form, I have no intention of seeing it fostered on the British stage if I can prevent it.[44]

In July 1935 yet another play was turned down because of its 'tinge of Lesbianism'. Reporting on Henry Broadwater's *Riviera*, Street again agonised, before deciding that to issue a licence would lay the Office open to attack:

> Madeleine and Elizabeth are both likeable and decent woman [sic] and their friendship certainly does not involve any physical perversion. But Madeleine's repulsion from male embraces of course suggests an

abnormal woman and if the play is licensed the Lord Chamberlain might
be accused of licensing a Lesbian play . . . Therefore I cannot advise a
licence, though to my mind the question of Lesbianism is so faint that I
think it a pity to refuse it.

He tentatively suggested that it was only in the last few pages that the issue
of lesbianism became visible, but that was sufficient for Cromer: 'The
obvious lesbian implication at the end of this play precludes me from
granting its licence', he declared.[45]

With four plays rejected outright between the autumn of 1934 and the
following summer because they made reference to possible lesbian
relationships, playwrights and managers would have been left in no doubt
that the subject would not be licensed. Occasional and passing references
continued to be removed; in January 1936, for example, Street spotted
some 'veiled references to Lesbianism' in *Children to Bless You*,* and the term
'ambisextrous' was duly removed.[46] Doubtless, too, some playwrights who
might have thought of exploring the subject had been effectively silenced
before opening their mouths, or themselves imposed restrictions on their
own scripts. Small wonder, then, that, as Helen Freshwater rightly
identifies in her discussion of such dramas, contemporary projects to
reclaim and celebrate lesbian theatrical writings face such difficulties; as she
says, 'dramatic images of lesbian desire created during the first half of the
twentieth century are often homophobic, prurient, and deeply
conventional in their reinstatement of the heterosexual norm'.[47] We must
ask, how could they have been other?

One further case is worth citing. In December 1936, Game reported on a
play set partly in the staff room of a girls' school. The characters in *Dawn*†
included two junior teachers, between whom existed what the Reader
labelled as 'one of those sickly friendships which can hardly be defined as
Lesbian'. But despite specifically indicating that the relationship, and
therefore the play, fell outside what could reasonably be constrained,
Game's comments did not end there; he hypothesised that the author had
deliberately underwritten the theme in order to try and secure a licence,
expecting that a production would find non-verbal ways of communicating
her real intentions :

> The only objection to this play is in the relationship between Hill and
> Tyler. Personally I think that, taking the text at its face value, it would be
> unfair to read more into this than a somewhat unbalanced friendship, but
> that does not mean that the author did not wish to imply more but was
> restrained by the fact of the Censorship and that in production the most

---

* Written by G. Sheila Donisthorpe
† Written by Henry Stare

might not be made of the material. I think a warning against this being done might well be given, and the play seen in rehearsal to ensure that our intentions are carried out

The script was rewritten to Game's approval, so as 'to make it more difficult to give a lesbian interpretation in the relationship between the junior mistresses'. Although he still recommended that it should be checked in rehearsal, the Reader was now prepared to stand up to those who might criticise the Office for its leniency: 'the critics and others may find in this play a chance to belabour us', he wrote, 'but I do not think we can entirely bar all question of these mawkish friendships between women from the stage'. However, though not officially turned down in its revised form, *Dawn* remained unlicensed in the Office's Waiting Box.[48]

After homosexuality, incest remained the other great perversion from which audiences needed protection, though plays with historical settings and accredited with a classical status (such as *Oedipus* and *The Cenci*) were, by now, often exempt. But the merest whiff of it was usually sufficient to disqualify a modern text, In 1933, Street recommended rejecting 'a disgusting play' called *The Gay Generation:*[*] 'It makes a joke of the idea of incest—the prospective marriage of a half-brother and sister—and although at the very end we are told that they are not really so related . . . it remains a very ugly affair'. A revised version was submitted which dropped the word 'incest' and made it apparent to the audience from earlier in the play that the two characters were not related. Even this was not enough to gain a licence.[49] The following year, a play translated from German as *Lord Byron Goes Out of Fashion*[†] was also rejected—the historical setting here being outweighed by the explicitness of the allusions; Street was adamant that one scene 'treats the subject of the incest in too sensuous and unmistakable a manner to make the play a possible one for an ordinary commercial production'.[50] However, in the same year he recommended licensing another play on the grounds that its performance would be too obscure to be noticed; *A Marriage Took Place*[‡] was not only set but also due to be staged in the Orkneys: 'Incest is a tabooed subject and by the rules the play should be banned. But as it does not happen <u>in</u> the play and the play is so utterly silly and unimportant I suggest to the Comptroller that it is hardly worthwhile to ban it'. His superiors were not prepared to take the risk, and the licence was refused.[51]

In 1936, a historical setting was the passport for Arthur Hood's *The Lord of Ferrara*. Street argued that, since its subject mirrored the Hippolytus

---

[*] Written by Anthony Gibbs

[†] Written by Elisabeth H.C. Corathiel

[‡] Written by David Tower

myth, 'the particular form of incest is not so terrible as some'; equally importantly, 'The remoteness of the period and Byron's poem dispose me to think there will be no great shock to anybody'. Most of the Advisory Board agreed that performances would neither damage nor shock audiences: 'I am being driven to the conclusion', noticed Sir Ian Malcolm, 'that if murder, incest and other pleasantries are made to occur several centuries ago and are dressed up in Italian costumes and are spoken about in pseudo-classical language, the public will look on them not as bestialities but as picturesque incidents which never occurred'. Historical distancing excused almost anything, since it was apparently accepted by audiences:

> My conscience tells me that murder, poison, rape, incest, et hoc genus omne do not matter to morals if the plays dealing with them are dated 'classical' or even 'Cinque cento'; and if they are richly furnished with marble columns, Italian brocades, tapestries and with what is supposed to be the language of the period. To the general public such performances represent merely melodramatic episodes ... which have no more deleterious effect upon the minds of a twentieth century public than have 'Macbeth' or 'Die Walkurie' or innumerable pictures and books concerned with similar unattractive practices ... I hasten to add, quite definitely, that I should advise against a licence to any play of the same kind laid in the present day or any date near it.[52]

Another play about Byron in the same year, Catherine Tracey's *Bitter Harvest*, focused on the poet's 'too cool attitude to his wife, and too warm attitude to his half-sister'. More than one reviewer of the private production speculated that the author had actually been deliberately vague in order to try and secure a licence; James Agate reckoned she had been 'ogling the censor', and Sydney Carroll that she had deliberately eschewed 'accuracy' and 'truth', watering her play down through 'the glossing over of biographical facts'. Who could blame her? Even the script she did produce ran into difficulties with the censorship—not simply because of what was in the text itself, but because of an audience's pre-knowledge about the subject, which might encourage them to read into it more than what was stated. Street was hesitant, for it was possible that 'An ignorant or unsophisticated spectator might conceivably think there was "nothing in" the scandal'; yet he suspected the play had itself been inspired by the recent publication of Byron's correspondence, and that the truth was 'so well known that the play could not be taken as other than one with incest as its theme'. Cromer consulted his Advisory Board: 'Incest as a theme naturally is harmful, but extenuating circumstances may at times be admitted in historical cases'. Though not without equivocation, Malcolm thought the playwright had sufficiently masked the facts, and was therefore prepared to support it:

> I have no patience with people who shout 'Bravo *Oedipus* and Incest'
> (especially for public school-boys) and in the same breath mumble 'À bas
> *Bitter Harvest*' on the same account. As a moralist, I must say 'a little Incest
> is a dangerous thing'; though I feel that, like cocaine in homeopathic doses
> given by an expert, it need not be fatal ... I must realise that theatrical
> best-sellers have long been the worst enemies of the Decalogue; and that
> the most we can hope for from a Comédie de moeurs is for a robe of
> sufficient length and texture to cover what used to be considered a
> multitude of sins. Such a garment is certainly provided by the author of
> *Bitter Harvest*.

On Cromer's instruction, Game attended a private performance at the
Arts Theatre, but was still undecided: 'a decision one way or the other is
really dependent on the view taken of the functions of Censorship', he
unhelpfully advised. However, he attempted to sum up his 'impressions' of
the performance:

> Firstly the Incest theme dominates the play to the exclusion of any other
> interest. Secondly, the author does not seem to have made up her mind as
> to whether it is to be understood that actual incest has taken place or not.
> There are lines that can only be taken as inferring that it has, and others
> that can only mean exactly the opposite. In the end she seems to plump for
> no incest . . .
> Thirdly, it seemed to me that the theme did excite an unhealthy
> reaction in the audience, especially in scenes where there was any
> demonstration of physical attraction between Augusta and Byron.
> So far plays about incest (with the exception of *Oedipus* and *The Cenci*)
> have not been passed and although my personal inclination is more
> towards using the censorship for the suppression of harmful plays, rather
> than for the suppression of plays that can at the most only offend people's
> prejudices, after actually seeing a performance of this play I am less sure
> than before as to whether I am in favour of interfering with this particular
> taboo.

The application for a licence was turned down—a decision condemned
by a number of leading theatre critics who enthused about the private
production of *Bitter Harvest*. To the *Observer* it was a 'monstrous decision'
which 'takes us back to the time when the Censorship, instead of saving us
from unpleasant and unnecessary twaddle, was really getting in the way of
decent work'.[53] Even Sydney Carroll in the *Daily Telegraph*, a sometime ally
of the Bishop of London, spoke of the Censor's 'inexplicable refusal',
blaming 'old-fashioned prejudices and outworn regulations'. He insisted
that such a 'deplorable' action raised fundamental issues:

> It is difficult to understand the decision. We are never in such cases
> furnished with any of the Censor's reasons. My personal view is that all
> objections should be stated publicly. There is no more reason or

justification for withholding the arguments from the affected parties than there is for depriving a litigant of the terms of a judge's decision.

He went on to dispute the whole basis of stage censorship, as currently practised:

> How arbitrary and autocratic is the system that allows the personal opinion of a State official, or a combination of officials, however fair-minded or tolerant, silently but unalterably to override all other views and destroy with a single verdict, unexplained and unargued, the work of months.[54]

Cromer lacked the courage to change his mind immediately, and royal duties took him to the West Indies for several weeks. But on his return he swiftly reversed his decision, apparently in the light of the press campaign. This probably also influenced his decision to approve 'Yet another half-brother-and-sister affair' a few days later; 'We seem to be in for an epidemic of them', commented Street in his report on *Deep Waters*,[*] and Cromer warned: 'These "near-incest" themes will require watching, especially when the setting is modern and not historical'.[55] But that discreet and almost imperceptible signal, combined with recent decisions, marked a shift away from the previous policy.

However, it took another decade, another Reader and another Lord Chamberlain to license Jean Cocteau's version of the Oedipus myth, *The Infernal Machine*, for which the Group Theatre sought a licence in October 1935. Street had found himself torn but ultimately unable to recommend it:

> The Group Theatre seems destined to give the censorship more trouble than all the other theatres put together. I do not blame them. In the present instance, for example, they are offering an ingenious play of considerable artistic merit and naturally they wish to try if it can be passed. That is very doubtful.

Street found it 'difficult to advise'; he noted that *Oedipus Rex* had been licensed, and that while 'a translation of a great ancient classic is a different thing from a modern play', this did mean that 'the incest of Oedipus and Jocasta has been admitted as a theme for our stage'. But some of Cocteau's treatment of his material made him doubtful: 'in Sophocles we are simply told of the marriage; here we see the couple in their bedroom and witness playful love making between them'. The occasional post-Freudian references also made him uneasy, since they were 'wholly unSophoclean', and meant that 'the irony of Sophocles is vulgarly emphasised'. And though he acknowledged that 'In a way it is a brilliant play', he remained undecided: 'What will, I think, horrify an ordinary audience is the love-making of Mother and son . . . but the play is only meant for "high-brows"

---

[*] Written by G.K. Mowbray

who do not mind'. He recommended that the Lord Chamberlain should seek further opinions, and Cromer consulted members of his Advisory Board. David Cecil was a strong advocate. It was, in his view, 'a most distinguished and venerable work of the imagination . . . a most remarkable piece of work—an ornament to the stage'; though he expressed some minor reservations about the potential realism of the bedroom scene between Oedipus and Jocasta, overall the play deserved a licence because it 'removes its subject to an unrealistic and symbolic state where it could give no real offence'. Sir Ian Malcolm, however, took a contrasting view of the Lord Chamberlain's responsibilities: 'if, as I hope, he is privileged by his functions to forbid the exhibition of so flashy and unscholarly an adaptation of a great and ancient drama upon the British stage, then I trust that he will exercise his aesthetic powers and influence in that direction'. Looking for a compromise, Street proposed some discreet textual modifications to avoid reminding the audience too often of the relationship between Oedipus and Jocasta, and also an endorsement specifically insisting 'that the acts should be played in a formal and stylised manner and reality eliminated as much as possible'. But though Cromer was willing to accept Street's solution, the play was not rewritten and was licensed only in 1943.

Almost more disturbing than incest was the narrative in which a man has a relationship with the daughter of his mistress—a fantasy which cropped up with surprising regularity. In 1935, Street thought *Margorie Crocker's Lover** not worth banning: 'A man's intending knowingly to marry the daughter of his ex-mistress is horrid enough, but it comes to nothing'; Cromer took a stronger line and rejected it: 'A nasty plot. Not to be encouraged'.[56] Two days later, Street found Elsa Malik's *The Chequered Board* to be far worse:

> 1) In the other play the affair with the mother is twenty years old, here only three years, which I think makes the daughter-marriage idea much more repellent. 2) In the other nothing happened; here the two are married. If Robert's marriage with Julia is not technically incestuous it is more repulsive than many cases of incest might be.

Joseph McLeod, who had taken over Cambridge's Festival Theatre where Malik's play was to have been staged, was outraged when the play was turned down, insisting that it was a highly moral play written by 'a young woman barrister . . . of great responsibility'. He was even more furious to discover at an interview he attended at St James's Palace 'that you have confused me with my flippant and irresponsible predecessor in this theatre'. Unless it was tongue in cheek, McLeod's moral conformity would

---

* Written by Elizabeth Carfax

have shocked Terence Gray, a natural subverter if ever there was one, but what is most striking is the power which McLeod claimed to wield:

> I would like to point out that this theatre—since I took it over in 1933—has always considered itself a training ground of an extremely powerful, because oblique, character, for the youth of England in the middle classes. My programme each term is selected with the utmost care, in order to influence these young men so that they shall become virtuous and good citizens; both of which qualities the present generation stands in great need of.

Highlighting the perennial difficulty of judging whether the depiction of vice is condoning or condemning it, he declared that 'The theme to which you take exception is the theme of the morality of the play', and he attacked the Office for licensing other plays which were, in his view, genuinely immoral. He concluded rather pompously: 'I do not understand, Sir, the principles on which your Office works, but I am doing my best to ensure that morality shall triumph'. Game went to see a revised and private performance of Malik's play under its new title of *Cul-de-Sac*, but recommended that it was still not acceptable. (There was, incidentally, a certain irony in the censors relying on an inspection of a private performance to help them make decisions, since the very advantage of such performances was that producers were not required to conform to the wishes of the censors!) In this case, Game tried to have it both ways, advising that there was no reason to reconsider the ruling, but that he himself would have favoured granting a licence in the first place:

> It is to all intents and purposes the same play . . . I cannot therefore recommend the Lord Chamberlain to reconsider his decision . . . Personally I should be in favour of licensing the play; my view being, as regards the sexual relationships here dealt with, that they are unfortunate and unpleasant but not fundamentally revolting, as in the case of incest where near blood relationship is concerned.[57]

But Malik's play remained unlicensed.

In discussing *Love of Women*, Helen Freshwater draws attention to the 'glaring inconsistencies' in Street's original report of October 1934:

> First he declaims, 'homosexuality between two women is much of the theme', only to add the proviso: 'It does not exist but it is talked about.' He then contradicts himself completely: 'Lesbianism is never mentioned . . . The girl['s] advance is Lesbian but that could easily be cut out.'

To be sure, Street's uncertainty is apparent in his anguished musings. But, as was evident in the arguments over *The Green Bay Tree* two years earlier, what is effectively under discussion is the right of the censorship to censor the invisible, and it may be helpful here to try and categorise four different levels at which homosexuality (for example) might have been seen to be signified in performance. The first, and absolutely taboo level, would have been the actual physical manifestation of it on stage—Jacqueline's lesbian 'advance' in *Love of Women*, which Street knew could and must be removed, was perhaps a relatively mild example of this; a reciprocated advance would have been much worse. The second level would have been onstage discussion of, or direct references to the subject, and the suggestion that a character whom we actually see is homosexually active would doubtless have been the most provocative example within this category; also significant at this level was whether the language actually named its subject, and this, I think, explains the distinction Street draws (and which Freshwater sees as a contradiction) when he says 'homosexuality between two women is much of the theme . . . It does not exist but it is talked about . . . Lesbianism is never mentioned'. The third level (which might well have provoked more ire than the second level) would have been onstage dialogue indicating that definite physical actions are supposed to be occurring or to have occurred off stage. And the fourth level would be where there is no direct mention of homosexuality at all, but audiences and critics might take it to be implied. Cutting across all but the first of the four levels is the question of whether or not we are to take the references in the script as being 'true' within the fiction; it is surely no coincidence that playwrights of this period so often chose to address the subject in terms of 'false accusations', consciously or unconsciously believing that this gave them more chance of staying within the Lord Chamberlain's parameters. Cutting across all four levels was the problem of the gap between script and performance, whereby action, gesture and expression could be used either to convey definitely or to imply what was not stated in words.

Street's stubborn and very deliberate insistence that he had been right to recommend *The Green Bay Tree* for licence was based on the belief that the playwright could not be held responsible for, and the censors could not act upon, the fourth level—for how audiences interpret and read into a performance something which is never mentioned. But he also went further on other occasions, as when he offered the 'personal' view quoted at the start of this chapter. Of course he was right. While plays about Edward II and James I, for example, might not have contained censorable lines, the knowledge and expectations that members of the audience would have brought with them would almost certainly have rendered the invisible visible. After all, if you could not keep the Nazis from the stage (or, at least, from the minds of the audience) by banning recognisable costumes, terminology and moustaches, then it would surely have been much harder to keep the door locked on homosexuality.

CHAPTER FOUR

'These Communist Effusions'

Testing Tolerance in Politics and Religion

Politics

> All Communist propaganda as such should certainly be checked in plays
> (The Lord Chamberlain, 1936)[1]

In the so-called 'pink decade', many on the left viewed theatre and performance as potentially crucial to the processes of informing, educating, propagandising and even organising. Those who threw themselves—unpaid—into the work of umbrella movements such as the Workers' Theatre Movement and the hundreds of branches of Unity Theatre all committed themselves, to a consciously greater or lesser degree, to the philosophy that theatre could be used as a tool to serve political ends. Although the balance of aesthetic and political priorities varied, there were other companies, too—Left Theatre and Group Theatre among them—which were driven at least in part by ideological imperatives. While it was not the only factor, the control of public theatres by censorship was certainly one of the factors which influenced such groups in their decisions to perform in the street or in venues which were not subject to the same restraints or policed with quite the same rigour. Having a performance disrupted by the uniformed forces of law and order may be more immediately confrontational and frightening, but, by contrast with the system of pre-censorship practised in official theatre, at least there was a chance that some or all of the piece could be presented before it was disrupted, and that the physical presence of a supportive audience might further hold back interventions.

Given that elements within the British establishment clearly identified a significant threat to the social, economic and political order coming from the left, it may seem slightly surprising to discover how little the Lord Chamberlain's Office chose to interfere with many plays which overtly addressed contemporary political matters. The degree of relaxation is perhaps typified in a comment by the Reader in 1936: 'The play contains a few sound arguments for a communist state of society, badly expressed. Communists will like it, others won't; and that's all there is to it.'*2 But, as always, we must take note of the plays which were not submitted for licence; whether or not the average Workers' Theatre Movement script would have been passed is extremely doubtful. Moreover, positive decisions were frequently informed by the conviction that it was safer quietly to license a play which was unlikely to catch a wide public eye, than to draw attention to it—perhaps thrusting it onto the front pages of national newspapers—by banning it or entering into prolonged arguments over amendments. Finally, there was no equivalent of the Public Morality Council constantly campaigning about the staging of politics. There were, of course, individuals who wrote to the Lord Chamberlain's office to voice their concerns, but no organisation to amplify and co-ordinate such views. True, there were ministers and a government to avoid upsetting (not to mention the King), and it was common practice for the Lord Chamberlain to send scripts to the Home Office for a view on whether a particular play might be dangerous. But with the exception of the anxiety over aggravating Germany, politicians usually seem to have doubted the capacity of the theatre to create or amplify dangers. Yet one should certainly not misread the apparent leniency of the Lord Chamberlain's Office for real freedom, since it rested on the secure knowledge that there were clear boundaries which few playwrights or managers would consider crossing. Put simply, if more plays had dared to challenge political assumptions then more plays would have been subject to political censorship.

On the whole, however, the Lord Chamberlain's Office was relatively relaxed about the likely impact of passionate revolutionaries. The commercial conditions of the industry, and the convictions of the performers, both helped to ensure that such work tended to be ghettoised and was often presented by and to its disciples. The censorship could afford to be patronising, as it was in 1937 over *Who Are The English?*, Jack Lindsay's powerful choric recitation for Unity Theatre. This mass declamation sought to ally the revolutionaries of the present with a suppressed historical tradition of rebellion against autocratic rulers, but as Game commented:

> The people who take part, as performers or audience, in this sort of thing are ninety-nine per cent already potential, but happily ineffective, revolutionaries. They may sing until they are as red in the face as their flag, without bringing the day of revolution a day nearer. It does no harm to allow people to let off steam.[3]

He confidently dismissed it as 'an improvement on that dingy hymn "The Red Flag"', which was 'unlikely to prove a Marseillaise'. Similarly, Unity's

---

* He was referring to a play called *The Pacifist*, by James W. Hugill

Where's That Bomb?*—a comic satire on anti-communist propaganda—caused few political hesitations. Game thought it 'a somewhat unusual play ... more suited to a private performance, at Oxford say, or in the seclusion of a Bloomsbury menage'; he acknowledged that although it was unlikely to 'do any harm in Bethnal Green', where it was to be performed, 'it might not end there'. But he judged it 'no worse than the usual Communist, or extreme Socialist, propaganda'. To add insult to injury, the text was subjected to censorship on rather different grounds; the plot is founded on the Orwellian Big Brotherish notion that the government plans to use toilet paper as a vehicle for propaganda, in order to penetrate the last refuge where people can still think for themselves. This proved unacceptable, on grounds of moral decency: 'we can hardly swallow the toilet roll theme', wrote Game, and the Office insisted on modifying it to 'shaving paper'. Even then, a risk remained: 'except to the expert, a roll of w.c. paper is indistinguishable from a roll of shaving paper', worried the Reader; 'I suggest that this is rather a dubious property to use'. So the theatre was specifically informed that 'The shaving paper should not be in rolls, to avoid confusion with toilet paper'. So despite the popularity of *Where's That Bomb?* with Unity theatres up and down the country, and the play's celebration as 'a magnificent proletarian guffaw at the propaganda of the capitalist class', it was not the political content which the censors cleaned up.[4] Another Unity satire, *The Fall of the House of Slusher*, also failed to disturb St James's Palace: 'It may amuse the "Comrades"', wrote Dearmer, 'but I doubt whether the production will change the course of history'. And *The Case of the Baffled Boss* was similarly perceived to be harmless: 'the squib may be recommended for licence'. Cromer was explicit: 'too much interference only gives a handle to propaganda'.†[5]

The fundamental question for the Lord Chamberlain was whether or not a play was potentially dangerous in its likely effect. In January 1933, *When the Crash Comes*‡ showed the Communists coming to power in Britain after winning a general election. The Reader's report described it as 'a very tame play' which could be safely licensed because it was 'not nearly strong enough to arouse any political feelings', and Cromer agreed it was unlikely 'to have any serious influence and so need not be taken too seriously'.[6] In the same month, Street summed up *Power and Poverty*§ as 'a crude, one-sided play, calculated to embitter class feeling', containing a strong speech about the need for workers to develop 'a greater will to resist

---

* Written by Herbert Hodge and Buckland Roberts
† Both collectively written
‡ Written by Beverley Nicholls
§ Written by W.J. Throup

oppression'. Yet he recommended that the play, which was to be staged at the Weavers' Institute in Earby, should be licensed because it was 'unimportant' and 'it would be unwise to interfere with it'.[7] An even more revealing example is *Mutiny*,* in which a military detachment is sent by the government to control striking miners in Durham, which was submitted in 1934 by Barry Jackson on behalf of Birmingham Repertory Theatre. The play centres on an army captain who is in the process of training a machine gun to fire on the strikers when he is shot dead by a superior officer, but many of the miners and their wives are massacred. The major is court martialled for shooting the captain, and is offered the choice between being certified as a lunatic or given an honourable discharge with pension if he agrees to live abroad and to take the official blame for the slaughter of civilians. Street thought the plot 'improbable', but rather bravely suggested that 'as a satire on the way that politicians might deal with an awkward situation' it was 'certainly not censorable'. He acknowledged that the depiction of the military might be thought a reason for rejecting the play, and that the decision on licensing needed to be made at a higher level, but his own position was informed by both liberal and strategic factors:

> I do not think that the presentment of what is a possible sequence of events in this relation should be banned from the stage, and I think its banning would give much more trouble than a licence. If the play became widely known, opposite schools of thought could fight it out.

Cromer sent the script to the War Office rather than the Home Office, explaining that a ban 'might be difficult to justify, and lead to more publicity being given to it than if it was produced by a Repertory Company, beyond whose auspices it is hardly likely to go'. While it was reluctant to become involved, perhaps the War Office reply contained a hint that a less direct way to suppress might be sought:

> Though we do not like it very much and it is full of inaccuracies, we do not see that we could advise the Lord Chamberlain to refuse a licence.
>   We share your view that to appear to ban it would give unnecessary advertisement and your hope that it may not be very widely played.

Cromer did insist on some cuts, but ruled that, subject to those, the 'unnecessary play' could 'reluctantly pass'.[8]

In the same year, there was no significant objection to the stage version of *Love on the Dole*† being licensed for Manchester Repertory Theatre. Indeed, the Office could almost be said to have anticipated Brecht in

---

* Written by David Stewart
† Written by Ronald Gow and Walter Greenwood

indicating that although the depiction of 'reality' within the hidden frame of naturalism might create empathy, it would not encourage an audience to see those conditions as capable of change:

> This play could not fairly be described as propaganda except in so far as any play on this subject must cause a feeling of distress and discontent with present conditions in the beholder. Some things are said in the course of the action which would not appeal to other than Socialist ears, but they come naturally within the framework of the play, and so are justified, aesthetically at any rate.[9]

Similarly, Game reported a few months later, on 'a dreary play about unemployment in Lancashire' in which one of the characters expressed 'subversive sentiments';* he recommended licensing with some minor changes: 'The play shows a painful picture of unemployment but it is not a revolutionary play', he wrote; 'Its general effect seems to me to be more that of domestic drama than that of a play meant to be politically disruptive'.[10]

A pageant† presented at Crystal Palace in the mid thirties included in its list of characters Luddites, Chartists, the Rochdale Pioneers, the Co-Operative Movement, and striking Matchgirls and Dockers. According to Street, its theme was 'the evils of the unreformed industrial system', and the script quoted from speeches by politicians including Lloyd George, Ramsay Macdonald and Churchill. The Reader acknowledged that the evils and the suffering were 'not exaggerated', but commented that 'what is unfair is that the rich—politicians, bishops and whatnot—are all shown as smugly indifferent to them'. Yet the script was licensed without interference: 'A very one-sided propaganda picture with which I agree it would be impolitic to interfere', wrote Cromer.[11] Again, Left Theatre's touring version of Gorki's *The Mother*‡ (which, according to the Reader, 'conforms to the most exacting standards of Slavonic gloom'), was disapproved of, but allowed. 'This play, addressed to the sort of audience which will go to see it in East Ham is intended, no doubt, to have a revolutionary appeal', noted Game; but he doubted it would have any significant impact: 'as the opinions expressed in it seems [sic] hardly more violent than those of the Red Flag (as far as I can remember them) or than those of the more extreme type of street corner orator, I do not suppose it will being [sic] the day of revolution any nearer'. The play was safe because 'the conditions depicted here are so remote from those we know in this

---

* He was referring to *Harvest in the North*, by James Lansdale Hodson
† *The Pageant of Labour*, by Matthew Anderson
‡ Adapted by F. Polionovska and Barbara Nixon

country that the propaganda effect of the play is lessened thereby'; (though Cromer insisted on emphasising this distance by stipulating that the national anthem played within the action should be the Russian rather than the British one).[12] Similarly, while Odets's *Waiting for Lefty* was identified as 'crude American Communist propaganda', Street could see no legitimate reason for refusing a licence: 'It is most unlikely to cause any disturbance in an English audience being intensely American'.[13]

Even in November 1939, a vaguely expressionist musical, inspired by *Love on the Dole*, was granted a licence for a community hall in Sheffield because it was deemed safer to allow it than to refuse it. *Symphony in Awakening**—its alternative title was *1936 and All That*—showed two young lovers on the dole getting married, and the man forced to accept employment in the rearmament industry, as the only work available, even though he has previously denounced it in a powerful piece of polemic:

> Life on the dole. There's just nothing decent ahead. Nobody wants you. You're just in the way. Human surplus production. You know what they do with wheat Jim, when they've got more than they can sell at the price they want? They burn it!—Well maybe, that's what they're going to do with us one day. Burn us—with machine guns and bombs . . . What else can they do with us without cutting their profit?—Go on, Jim, go to your shop. Turn out your guns and shells. They're all for us one way or another. We'll fire with them and we'll get them back. <u>We</u> make them and they kill <u>us</u>. It's just a little vicious circle that the chosen few keep spinning.—Hurry, Jim, the shells are waiting. You mustn't be too late. There's two million unemployed. Something has to be done for them.

This speech was marked in blue as being perhaps too dangerous and explicit to be spoken on a public stage, and Game understood clearly what the writer was getting at and where his main interest lay:

> the narrative is of course not the point, it is merely a vehicle for propaganda—the general argument being that the Capitalist Social system condemns the surplus labourer to unemployment, denies him the normal rights of citizenship, frustrates his desires to build a better world, and can find no other work for him to do but in creating the engines of death with which to destroy his fellows, victims of like circumstances to himself.

But he concluded by reaffirming a familiar position: 'my opinion of these Communist effusions is, that you do more harm by suppressing them than you do by allowing them their limited appeal'. Gordon, the Acting Comptroller, surprisingly added: 'There is really no harm in this, and a great deal of truth'.[14]

---

* Written by Norman Brown

However, there were some occasions when tolerance of left-wing ideology was tested more severely. In March 1937, the London Labour Choral Union submitted a script for its *Peace and Prosperity Revue.** 'This so-called Revue is really a communist tract in dramatic form: anti-capitalistic and anti-fascist, and identifying the one with the other', warned Game. He found it full of 'political mis-statements which strain my natural tolerance to explosive point', and predicted that it might cause actual confrontations, but he reluctantly accepted that 'In a normally functioning Democracy it is probably wiser to tolerate than to suppress this sort of thing' and recommended non-intervention.

> As regards the general questions raised by this work; lies and mis-statements about the Government are nothing new and have to be put up with in a free country; the references to Fascism may arouse opposition possibly, but if so the Police may well be left to deal with the matter.

Cromer was less blasé, and sent the script to the Home Office. Significantly, he warned them that he was expecting more plays of a similar persuasion, and that it was therefore vital to establish a precedent.

> Under the guise of fun and nonsense . . . the whole tendency of this Revue is frankly communistic, and other plays of the same sort will probably reach us in increasing numbers as well as in intensity of feeling as time goes on.
>
> I agree with the Reader . . . in thinking that it is probably wiser to tolerate this sort of thing, but it is not an easy matter for the Censorship to know where the line should be drawn . . .
>
> There is also an obvious intention of trying to impersonate Mr Ramsay MacDonald, and possibly other British statesmen, but we can prevent any make-up to resemble them.
>
> However, the object of my sending you this play is that the Home Office authorities should know the kind of thing that is brewing, and I hope you will agree with me that the whole play should not be refused a licence, although it should be considerably pruned.

The Home Office agreed that a licence need not be refused, but forwarded the script to the Foreign Office', who recommended removing one scene completely. Cromer duly complied: 'The dialogue is offensive to various Foreign Nations and if complaints are made by the Embassies to the F.O.—as would be probable—they would only have to come out later, as this sort of thing is indefensible'. And apparently oblivious of the protection his Office unquestioningly and habitually provided to British politicians, monarchs, public figures and institutions, he repeated as a justification for

---

* Alan Bush was credited as the author

his censorship the familiar and groundless cliché: 'Besides no Foreign Nations . . . appreciate the particular form of humour known as British'.[15]

Inevitably, the thirties produced a number of plays about war. 'I wonder if these plays reminding people of the horrors of war do good or harm', mused Street in response to *Peace In Our Time*,* in which 'England is supposed to be at war with an unnamed Foreign Power'.[16] For the censorship, it was usually more problematic when the foreign power was identified, as in *Skyscraper* in March 1936:† 'The enemy is made out to be Japan', wrote Game; 'Perhaps it might be as well to have some fictitious nation'. Changes were duly insisted upon. 'In the present state of international tension, the references to Japan and Japanese had better be altered'.[17] By contrast, in the same year, and on Street's recommendation, they licensed *Everlasting Hills*:‡

> It is an old-fashioned play of Anglo-Indian intrigue and the Khyber Pass, and I seem to have read or seen a hundred just like it, full of sentiment and heroism and thoroughly artifical . . .
> Nearly all such plays . . . talk of Russia as the enemy and I think it would be quite absurd to object to that now. The play, though written with sincere emotion, is too utterly unconvincing to have any vogue and I cannot imagine any emissary of the Soviet Government hearing about it or being ass enough to complain.

Cromer's additional comment is personally and politically revealing: 'I entirely agree', he wrote; 'Russia always has been (secretly) and always will be (secretly) jealous and so an enemy of England'.[18]

In the first half of the decade a strong peace movement developed, evidenced in a series of well-known occurrences: the Oxford Union resolution passed in 1933 that 'this House will in no circumstances fight for its King and Country'; the Fulham by-election of the same year in which a Conservative Party advocating rearmament had a substantial majority overturned by a Labour Party arguing that this was a preparation for war; the campaign begun in 1934 by a clergyman inviting people to send him postcards renouncing war; and the resulting Peace Pledge Union, which by 1936 had 100,000 members.[19] Though Street's reports often showed some sympathy for the peace movement, the political propaganda and the targets of anti-war plays often caused irritation in the Office. *Dragon's Teeth*, for example, was an American play§ given its first European performance at Manchester Repertory Theatre in 1934; Street called it 'a trenchant peace propaganda play', and the *Manchester Guardian* described it as the work of 'a

---

* Written by Bernard Upton
† Written by F. Sladen Smith
‡ Written by Evelyn Millard
§ Written by Shirland Quin

Pacifist who believes passionately in the theory of war as a conspiracy of vested interest, with Capital as the arch villain and armament manufacturers as his willing dupes'.[20] Theatrically, noted the reviewer, it was 'an essay in the advanced form of dramatic technique, which has evolved out of "expressionism", the cinema, and the rediscovery of the medieval mystery plays'. But it was the political slant that concerned the censorship, and even Street was goaded by its 'hysteria', and 'the author's zeal', especially when one of the characters declares: 'I have realized that to invent methods of warfare is a profession of the damned'; Street took a different view of the theory of deterrence:

> I am disinclined to discourage any propaganda for peace, but this is rather a strong order. To attribute war to greedy financiers is common form. But to make it a sin for a soldier to invent lethal contrivances is a different thing. While other countries have them the country which has the best is least likely to be attacked.

Yet he concluded: 'I do not think any inventive officer is likely to be put off. And on the whole I think it would be a mistake to the ban the play'. The Lord Chamberlain agreed.[21]

Sydney Box's *Bring Me My Bow* provoked much greater outrage in the autumn of 1937. A satire, set in a girls' public school and written for an all female cast, it had already been performed by women's institutes in private productions when Welwyn Garden City Theatre sought a licence for public performance. The story centres on a visit to a school speech-day by the wife of the Minister for War, and her announcement there that the government has been forced to drastically cut the money available for scholarships to Oxbridge in order to fund the massive rearmament programme needed to defend the country. Only a single scholarship is available, to be awarded to the girl who produces the best essay under the title: 'A Britain armed means a world at peace'. The second half of the play shows Mary, the most able and deserving of the sixth formers—and whose father was killed in the previous war—refusing to write an essay to fit this closed title; she falls asleep, and the audience witnesses her dreams, which derive from a series of nursery rhymes, adapted into quite potent and effective anti-war verses:

> Humpty Dumpty was hit by a shell.
> Humpty Dumpty was blown to hell.
> All the king's doctors and medical men
> Couldn't put Humpty together again . . .

At the climax of the sequence Mary asks 'Who killed my father', and the chorus replies:

'I', said the shell,
'I sent him to hell;
'I killed your father.'[22]

Bring Me My Bow was a strongly emotional piece of anti-war polemic, but it is still surprising to see the fury and resentment it caused at St James's Palace. 'The whole thing preaches a superficial and flabby pacifist doctrine which to a realist mind is pernicious', declared Game, 'and I have little doubt that this sort of thing in its small way does actual harm'. Cromer was even more hostile, and equally alarmed by the script's potential:

> I consider this play a most pernicious form of pacifist propaganda, capable of doing much harm in ignorant minds. Once licensed, the play is liable to be performed elsewhere than in the Welwyn Garden City, which may already be a hotbed of Pacifist doctrines.
>
> For this reason I should prefer to see the play banned as being 'subversive of National interests' . . .
>
> It may lead to trouble in the Press but 'Sidney Box' and his followers deserve no mercy in these days of international crisis.

He sent the script to the Home Office, and must have been disappointed by the refusal there to accord it a similar degree of seriousness. 'I cannot understand Women's Institutes performing this sort of rubbish', declared one civil servant, but it was agreed overall that 'To give this play the cachet and the advertisement of the Lord Chamberlain's ban would be most unwise'. The Lord Chamberlain was sent a copy of the minute detailing the comments of the Home Secretary, in which he tried to establish a general code. His rather dismissive comments may have caused some embarrassment at St James's Palace:

> I do not know the principles on which the Lord Chamberlain bases his decision on the question whether or not to license a play.
>
> As regards a play of a pacifist propaganda character, the criterion to be applied in my view is
>
> a) whether or not the play is seditious or subversive within the meaning of the criminal law. i.e. would a speaker expressing these views expose himself to the risk of a prosecution—and
>
> b) whether the treatment of the subject matter is so grossly offensive to public opinion, or any large section of it, that the presentation of the play on the stage is likely to give rise to disorder or to incite to breaches of the peace.
>
> Judged by these standards the play does not seem to me to qualify for the refusal of the Lord Chamberlain's Licence. The play is a fourth form effort, and it would indeed be a bad outlook for this country if ever it became necessary to treat jejune propaganda of this kind too seriously.

The script was licensed with only a couple of specific changes.[23]

This was not the only occasion on which the Home Office was less worried than the Lord Chamberlain expected. In the summer of 1938, shortly before he retired, Cromer forwarded a copy of *A.R.P.*, a Unity Theatre script* which satirised the advice being offered by air-wardens to the inhabitants of slum tenements: 'It is anti-Fascist and anti-National Government, which does not matter', wrote Cromer, 'but it also pours ridicule on anti-gas precautions, which seems to me under present conditions to be mischievous and subversive'. The Home Office saw it as 'a stupid production, and very dull', but declined to see it as a cause for concern: 'The fact that a Play ridicules the Government A.R.P. policy is not a reason for banning it, and we think that not to pass it would exaggerate its importance, more especially as it is being produced at an obscure Communist Club'.[24]

As we have already seen, by far the most contentious area of political censorship in the 1930s centred on the depiction of Nazi Germany, and the attempts by the German Embassy to influence the Lord Chamberlain. It was much rarer for the Italian Embassy to notice plays, but in September 1938 it complained about Robert Sherwood's anti-war play, *Idiot's Delight*, in which Italy is said to be dropping bombs on Paris. The play had been licensed two years earlier, having supposedly been ruritanianised both in its script and its costumes, but after a run of some 200 performances at the Apollo Theatre, complaints were received that the Italian identity was still evident. The Foreign Office informed the Lord Chamberlain about a meeting held with a senior member of staff from the Italian Embassy: 'The impression created on those of his countrymen who had seen the play was that not only was Italy being pilloried as wilfully setting alight a European conflagration for mean ends but that fun was made of the Italian army'. The representative had specified that

> He was not making an official protest but would be very grateful if something could be done to persuade the Producers of the play, which he understood was now being withdrawn from London and going to tour the Provinces, to alter the uniforms and the foreword so that no question of insult to the Italian army could arise.

Having inspected the production, the Foreign Office accepted the basis of the protest:

> I must say that the uniforms to which Signor Crolla referred do look to an inexpert eye, very like Italian uniforms. In these circumstances we should be grateful for anything you might be able to do in the way of inducing the

---

* Written by Vance Marshall

management of the play to arrange that all traces of Italian uniforms, decorations, etc., might be eliminated from the dress of the cast.

The Lord Chamberlain was then reminded that the matter must be handled with discretion:

it is hoped that you will not regard this letter as an official one . . . It goes without saying of course that if it leaks out that there has been anything in the nature of an Italian protest or Foreign Office intervention, the play's publicity manager might make very undesirable use of it and more harm than good would be done.

So the Comptroller duly contacted the producer:

I did not mention that I had received any complaint from the Foreign Office, or from the Italian Embassy, but I told him that owing to the present crisis the Lord Chamberlain felt it right to look round the various political plays now running to see that nothing was being done that might cause embarrassment.

Fortunately, the producer proved 'most helpful', and ready 'to eliminate any cause for embarrassment to foreign visitors', since 'at the present moment one cannot be too careful not to offend in these ways'.[25]

In the last year of peace, a number of other political dramas also ran into trouble. In the autumn of 1938, *Crisis*, Unity Theatre's* 'living newspaper' which reflected the changing national and international political situation, was submitted. The new Reader—Charles Heriot—described it as 'an exciting piece of work', which, while 'not, of course, free from bias', need not offend either the Prime Minister or the German Embassy. Game observed that it was 'as much an attack upon Mr Chamberlain as upon Hitler', and that 'This from the International point of view is something in its favour'. However, documentary drama depended on incorporating the actual words of real people, and even representing them on stage, and Game reported that 'the Prime Minister, Lord Runciman and Mr Duff Cooper appear in person'. *Crisis* remained stuck in the Waiting Box and, though it was staged at Unity's own private club, it never received a licence for public performance.[26]

In March 1939, the censors excised socialist versions of nursery rhymes from a provincial Unity revue on the grounds that they made insulting reference to the Prime Minister, and in August they cut as 'subversive of national morale' part of a new sketch in the same revue which echoed the Communist Party line that the British government only wanted to fight Hitler in order to avoid the economic problems which would result from closing down factories producing arms:

---

* Collectively written

> Though British boys are butchered, tis for a glorious end
> So war shall be our watchword, and every foe our friend.
> Our policy on land and sea, shall be the one that clears,
> A few more hundred thousand pounds
> For the British Profiteers.[27]

In the same month they rejected *Leave it to Me*,[*] an American musical comedy which proposed a novel solution for avoiding the impending European conflict:

> the German army is to march into France and the French into Germany, and to remain for one year. Then they march home again, and in twenty years time France and Germany are full of Franco-Germans. The Franco-Germans then march into Russia and in the course of time Russia is peopled by Franco-German-Russians and the United States of Europe is an established fact.

The script, said Game, was 'in the most deplorable taste . . . humourless and utterly puerile', and its authors had 'the mentality of worms'. He was firmly against licensing:

> I don't see how we can pass a play in which the German Ambassador is kicked in the belly by his American confrere who is thereupon congratulated by the English and French Ambassadors, to say nothing of the Latvian.
>
> I suppose it would be possible thoroughly to ruritanianise the wretched thing, but the play is undesirable and worthless trash.

He also produced a substantial list of the specific incidents and features which could not be allowed; these included

> Reference to the Duke of Windsor, the joke about German methods of aggression, references to Mussolini, reflection on Russian habits, a slighting reference to the Romanov family, agitators, as applied to the Bolshevicks [sic], this seems tactless at the moment. References to Stalin, or Stalin in person. German Ambassador's speech. The incident of the belly kick. A reference to Lenin's corpse, jokes against the Japanese Ambassador.[28]

In April 1939, an updated version of Guy du Maurier's 1908 melodrama *An Englishman's Home* was staged. The original play had been written, as Game now reminded the Lord Chamberlain, 'in an endeavour to wake up the youth of England to the danger of German invasion, and their duty to be prepared to defend their country'.[29] Before the First World War, the play had caused an outcry and accusations of war-mongering; though it did not

---

[*] Written by Bella and Samuel Spewack

quite attract comparable attention in 1939, the lines were drawn on familiar ground. Indeed, the stipulation that 'no German uniform should be worn by the Invaders' was an almost exact echo of the requirement from some thirty years earlier, and the Reader noted that 'It is a melancholy reflection on the English character that in 1939 the play still has its topical application!'. Neville Chamberlain's attention was drawn to the revival by a letter from a member of the public, suggesting that it was not the time to revive anti-German propaganda: 'it was used tremendously in 1914—and as we were at war with Germany, it was excusable—but surely we do not want to work up hate and suspicion and all the devilish atmosphere of war now'. The letter asked the Prime Minister to 'stop this outrage', and was duly forwarded to the Lord Chamberlain. But the censors maintained that

> The author's object is not to work up hate and suspicion against Germany, but to persuade his countrymen and countrywomen that one of their duties as citizens is to be ready to defend this country. The only thing to be deplored is that there should be any necessity for such a play in 1939.

Plays dealing with political conflicts in Ireland continued to be a focus for debate, though to some extent the censorship could afford to be more lenient as events receded. In January 1934, Street recommended allowing *Mountjoy*,[*] 'A moving little play of the troubles that followed the Irish treaty in 1922'; as he pointed out: 'Ten years ago there might have been a reason for refusing a licence on the chance of the play's arousing passion, but that hardly applies now, certainly not on this side of the Irish Channel'.[30] A couple of months later, the Office also approved a play about the 1921 conflict,[†] even though it contained what the Reader called 'a bitter animus against the Black and Tans and a rather (I think) idealised picture of the IRA'. Again Street was certain it would have been banned ten years earlier, but now he was confident that there was 'no danger of disturbance in an English audience'. It was also convenient that the play could be classed as moderate rather than extreme, since it extended sympathy and understanding towards the oppressor as well as to the victims:

> The author is so far fair to the Black and Tans that he admits that misconduct is due to nerves and one of them is a good fellow. I imagine few English people approve of what they did and I never heard an Irishman of any party do so. Their conduct was provoked and that is all that can be said.[31]

---

[*] Written by Andrew Anderson
[†] *Nothing in his Life*, by Louis J. Walsh

More provocative was *Easter*, a dramatisation of the 1916 uprising, written by Montagu Slater and staged by the Left Theatre at the end of 1935. Slater was a regular contributor to *Left Review* and a member of the Communist Party, and his play was worrying partly because it broke the fourth wall of naturalism to involve the audience directly in the action. Although the censors were concerned about references to police brutality against strikers, which were seen to carry contemporary as well as historical echoes, they thought it would be 'difficult to object' because similar arguments could be heard 'at any Socialist meeting'. They also thought that the specific subject matter was unlikely to generate much response since

> except among the more extreme Socialists and Communists, who always love our enemies best, the Southern Irish get very little sympathy over here anymore: so that the play should not rouse any very violent passions on this side of the Irish Sea (except perhaps in the Irish quarters of such places as Liverpool.) The story, has of course, a moral for English revolutionaries, but in the circumstances of English politics I think I need hardly discuss that.

Interestingly, the accusations against the police seem not to have merited intervention because they were *not* derived from acknowledged facts but 'only hearsay'. However, what did alarm the Office was the final scene in which James Connolly, the Irish leader, is murdered in cold blood by the British army as he lies injured on a stretcher. The accuracy of the event was not disputed, but public audiences were not to be reminded of it:

> The shooting of a helpless man is abhorrent to one's instincts and, although justifiable legally, is a tragedy best forgotten by both sides. The scene is unnecessary to the play and is only dragged in here to sow hatred of the upper classes. I should cut this out completely.

Cromer was undecided about the advisability of granting a licence at all, but after checking with the Home and Dominions Office he ruled that it could be allowed, subject to the changes proposed by his Reader.[32] These included cutting the murder of Connolly.

One play about Ireland that did cause problems for the Lord Chamberlain was *Parnell*, by the American playwright Elsie Schauffler. Schauffler's play focused on the leader of the Irish parliamentary party, who had been the architect and head of the campaign for Home Rule until shortly before his death in 1891. But when it was submitted in February 1935, the Office had recently turned down another script with the same name and subject matter by Dr W.M. Crofton, a former professor from Dublin University. Writing about this first *Parnell* in October 1934, Street had reported that 'A large part of the play is extracted from newspaper reports and they can hardly be censored'; however, the way in which the real-life figure of Captain O'Shea was shown was another matter. O'Shea had been a follower of Parnell, but it was an affair between his wife and the Irish leader, and his own subsequent divorce from her, which had led to the discrediting of Parnell in the eyes of many of his followers, causing considerable damage to the campaign for Irish freedom. The playwright was by no means the first person to pin much of the blame on O'Shea – Cromer described him in a private letter as 'an unmitigated blackguard'— but the public stage had special rules:

> 1. Whatever Captain O'Shea's demerits, it is a strong order to represent him as a complete scoundrel while probably children of his and other relatives survive.
> 2. Apart from him the thoroughly ex-parte [sic] presentment of events only forty years or so old—such as the accusation against 'The Times' of inciting O'Shea . . . seems to me extremely undesirable.

Cromer ruled that 'Whether a travesty of history or not, it is too recent in date and would certainly arouse objection from living descendants'. Indeed, even Street's assumption that documentary material already in the public domain was beyond censorship proved false. Crofton protested that his play kept 'meticulously to history', and he found it 'astonishing . . . that speeches delivered in Parliament . . . must not be said on the stage because they are unpalatable to some one or other descendent [sic]'. His sense of injustice was exacerbated when Schauffler's play was eventually approved, but a licence eluded Crofton because of his failure to secure permission from the family.[33]

When Schauffler's *Parnell* was submitted in February 1935, it faced the same objections which had originally met Crofton's, and Street thought that rejection was inevitable: 'Since a play on the same subject was refused a licence last October on the ground that the events were too recent, it seems idle to trouble the Lord Chamberlain with a minute account of this one'. He explained that this one, too, heaped venom on O'Shea, and amounted to a 'preposterous falsification of history', which would be 'quite as offensive, if not more, to descendants'. The licence was refused, but in November 1935 Schauffler's play premiered in New York, and in April 1936 Norman Marshall staged it privately at the Gate Theatre in London. Marshall's production was generally well received by the critics, and the press was full of demands that the ban should be lifted. Game went to see the production, but he still confirmed that 'descendants of Captain O'Shea . . . would have cause for complaint' about the characterisation: 'for the sake of heightening the drama and to whiten Parnell and Mrs O'Shea, the dramatist has made O'Shea very very black', he reported. Nevertheless, *The Times* published a leading article calling for the Lord Chamberlain to license the play, on the grounds that its aesthetic merits outweighed other factors: 'good plays are rare', said the editorial, 'and ought not to be sacrificed to quibbles'.[34] Marshall issued a statement claiming he had been told that the Lord Chamberlain would reconsider the ban if descendants promised not to object, but O'Shea's son, Captain William Henry O'Shea, had made his opposition clear in correspondence with both the Lord Chamberlain and the press:

> my father . . . is made out to have been a blackguard and a blackmailer, which was certainly not the case . . . you may imagine it was very painful for me to see this play at the Gate Theatre last night as it unburied the scandal of 50 years ago, and drew renewed attention to the Divorce case which brought misery into the lives of my sisters and, in a lesser degree, into my own.

Cromer was challenged on all sides about the principle of providing protection in such a case. *The Times* even suggested that he was less concerned with safeguarding O'Shea, and more with the reputation of Gladstone. Cromer was driven to send a private letter to the newspaper, not intended for publication, but written 'in order that the dramatic section of *The Times* may be enabled to visualise the problem in aspects which are far wider than those merely involved in this particular play'. He insisted the issue was whether or not it was

> the duty of the Lord Chamberlain to protect individuals from their forebears being traduced upon the stage. Personally I hold that it is his duty to do this so far as is reasonably possible . . . I have always held that a certain measure of protection should be afforded to the living over episodes of an unsavoury nature in family histories . . . no hard and fast rules can naturally be maintained about historical periods, but as a guiding principle I have hitherto taken an interval of 50 years as the period beyond which playwrights would tread at their peril.

He explained that he had had 'a strong appeal made to me by Captain G.H.W. O'Shea to protect his father', and he believed that

> within reasonable limits the Lord Chamberlain is in duty bound to protect families from being caused pain, and from being outraged by the presentation on the stage of their deceased relatives whose characters, according to them, are being objectionably represented, or whose actions and motives are presented in a distorted light, merely for the purpose of obtaining dramatic effect.

The Times replied, citing R.C.K. Ensor's *History of England 1870 to 1914*, to argue that the dramatist's version of events was historically accurate: 'I suggest, therefore, that O'Shea's reputation is one that ought not, in the public interest, to be protected at the expense of a play the banning of which will do harm to the theatre and inflict grave hardship on those who have put it on the stage'. Cromer insisted this failed to take sufficient account of the sensitivities of living descendants; his principle, he maintained, was to protect the present generation, whatever the truth about the relatives of previous generations. He drew on an extreme analogy:

> Your Dramatic Critic's arguments only hold good in this play, and any other play of a historical nature, if no consideration whatever is to be given to the feelings of relatives whose forebears are in their opinion traduced upon the stage . . . and if no protection whatever is to be afforded them against what they consider to be a slanderous exploitation of their family's misfortunes, merely for the entertainment of public and for the benefit of the Box Offices and Actors.
>
> Surely this country has not yet reached the stage of adopting the 'Nazi' doctrine that minorities not only suffer but must be made to suffer acutely in the so-called 'public interest'!

In July, Marshall submitted a revised version of the play, and Cromer persuaded O'Shea to visit him and discuss his objections. At the meeting, a crucial revelation emerged which gave the Lord Chamberlain the way out he had been seeking:

> In the course of conversation Captain O'Shea admitted that he had a contract in his pocket, the terms of which were that he was to proceed to Hollywood at an early date to assist in the preparation of a scenario dealing with the life of Parnell, in return for a fee and his expenses.
>
> The Lord Chamberlain pointed out to O'Shea that it was hardly a consistent attitude to oppose the presentation of a play in this country dealing with the life of Parnell and his father and mother, while agreeing to go to America to assist in the preparation of a film in return for financial payment.

In August, with O'Shea now in Hollywood, Cromer signalled from his holiday retreat at Gleneagles that Schauffler's play could now be licensed; he insisted that the change in policy was not the result of pressure, but because O'Shea's decision to sell himself to the film industry had changed the situation.

> My original reasons for refusing a licence were twofold. 1) Because it was too recent history 2) Because the subject matter and characters portrayed were offensive to living descendants of the originals.
>
> The first objection has been removed by Captain O'Shea himself co-operating in the production of a film . . . as to the second objection, this too has been weakened by the modifications introduced in the revised version as well as by Captain O'Shea forfeiting any further obligation on my part to protect him or his family by his own action in not sticking to his guns . . .
>
> Had he maintained this attitude out of high principles of family honour I should have felt, as I did at the outset, in duty bound to protect him.

In any case, Cromer was not convinced that the controversy and public debate of the last few months reflected the artistic worth of the play. He speculated that 'public interest in this play has largely evaporated' and that 'All the fuss that has been made in the Press and elsewhere about this play is entirely out of proportion to its merits'.[35]

Through procrastination, Cromer had found a way around the specific obstacle. But as usual, the principle remained unresolved. In 1935 he refused to license a play about Rossetti until it was proved that his living relatives had no objection to it. In a letter to Cromer, the writer and critic St John Ervine launched a furious attack on the implications of such protectiveness:

> I realise that the objections made to biographical plays are usually sincere and apparently reasonable. It cannot be pleasant to have your grandfather shown up as a sadist, or a treacherous lover, or a man of perverted affections, or as one who bungled his business as a soldier and sent thousands of men to dreadful deaths. But the unpleasantness is no less when it is exposed in a biography or a novel than it is when it is exposed on the stage . . .
>
> Why is it always the dramatist who is hampered and hindered by bans and prohibitions? Are they right who say that the English hate the theatre, and will tolerate it only as long as it is trivial and insincere and unrelated to life? Imagine what our novels would be like, what sort of history we would have, how empty of value our biographies would be, were there operating against novelists, historians, and biographers such a rule as now operates against dramatists. The Censorship, in its inception, was a device of politicians to prevent themselves from being adversely criticised. We have seen the establishment in Russia, Germany, and Italy of censorships more rigorous and widespread than any hitherto established, so that any criticism, any expression of opinion, any utterance that is not sickeningly fulsome in its praise of the governing body, is prohibited, and those who try to make it are heavily punished. In such places the mind is languishing, art is in danger of death, and the people are dwindling to the stature of slaves. A great people can endure and profit by the most searching enquiry and criticism and the frankest statement of opinion. It is only a mean and servile people who cannot.[36]

Ervine claimed that he was considering writing a play about an American general, William Booth, but had been informed that Cromer was now insisting that relatives down to the fourth generation would have the power of veto:

> In my *Observer* article I said that if your new rule were as I had stated it to be, I should have to obtain the consent of a hundred persons for the performance of the play before I could obtain yours, but I realise now that that number is a grave under-estimate. The number would be about a thousand; for in addition to Booth's immediate surviving relatives who are

numerous, there are the immediate surviving relatives of all his associates, of whom many would have to be brought into the play . . . I mention these facts to show you how oppressive your new rule . . . must be.

The Lord Chamberlain replied that no such absolute rule had been invented, and that it was not the practice to seek trouble by immediately sending scripts to relatives: 'what I do is to invite would-be producers to use their best endeavours to obtain the concurrences of the nearest relatives and, in certain cases, when subsequent information has been asked for, the script has been shown to them'. Cromer again insisted on the difference between a written biography and the impersonation of someone in the flesh, and, in relation to Ervine's own proposed play, reminded him of the extent of his duty:

> I should not, of course, pay any heed to objections based upon the stage in toto, but in this particular case I venture to think that extreme care would have to be exercised to avoid protests by salvationists and others, which might lead to an uproar in the theatre which it is part of the Lord Chamberlain's duty to prevent.

Religion

The Public Morality Council was uncompromising in its demand that plays should actively take sides. In 1934, it complained about the lack of clarity in Sean O'Casey's *Within the Gates*: 'whilst it is true the "whore" is shown as dying and therefore presumably punished for her life, the representations of the ecclesiastic and the Salvation Army officer tend to hold these persons, and consequently religion, up to contempt'. The Council's correspondence with the Lord Chamberlain continued even after the play had closed in London:

> as the play is withdrawn, this protest would appear belated, but I am writing in the hope that very drastic censorship of this play may be exercised in the event of its being sent on tour in the provinces, when I am sure very great exception would be taken thereto.[37]

Given that the constitution of the Public Morality Council was so dependent on the Church, it is hardly surprising that it took a strong interest in religious subjects. However, what does seem ironic is that the Council was so often opposed to allowing the most pious religious dramas to be performed. Depictions of, or words spoken by, God, Jesus and the Virgin Mary had been more or less banned for some time, largely at the behest of the Church, though by the mid thirties the policy was changing slightly. In F.J. Bowen's *The Three Kings* at the Rudolf Steiner Hall in early

1934, Mary was allowed to sing a lullaby on stage, and the following year the Lord Chamberlain, 'after obtaining ecclesiastical and legal opinion' agreed to license *Public Saviour Number One,** even though it was described by the Reader as 'an analogue of the life of Jesus Christ … set in the present', in which the three wise men were represented as a New York financier, a London scientist and a Berlin collector.[38]

Alterations in the Church's stance were inevitably confusing for the censorship. In 1934, Street reported on the 'considerable difficulties' caused by *In Darkness—Light*, a 'mystical play'[†] evidently written out of belief and religious devotion, and intended to be preceded by a service. It was, as Street made clear, the Church itself which created the problems

> The difficulty of such plays is the changing attitude of the clergy. Some time ago the appearance of Christ on the stage—and in this case there can be no doubt at all as to who is meant—was disallowed as a matter of course. The rule has been relaxed but I am not sure if it has been relaxed as far as this. But it seems difficult to refuse a licence.

He suggested that 'Perhaps a condition might be made that the play must be part of some service, or an ecclesiastical authority might be consulted', and even though the ruling had no basis or justification in law, Cromer followed a precedent established for religious plays some time earlier whereby his licence was tied to a specific occasion, and any subsequent performance would have to reapply.[39]

If reverential attitudes towards God were no guarantee of securing a licence, any other attitude surely led to rejection. In September 1934, a licence was refused for Alfred Savoir's witty *Congress in Switzerland*, in which a group of freethinkers staying in a hotel in Switzerland all vote for the non-existence of God, with the exception of one who insists he is God. 'There is no real harm in the play', acknowledged Street, 'but the joking about God and his attributes would cause a scandal. It is a play for a private performance'.[40] They also refused *A Strange Case of Miss Sippy*[‡] for its 'light-hearted treatment of what is sacred to Christians', and, for its 'unfortunate jocularity', *The Needle's Eye*,[§] in which St Paul complains that the Corinthians are not answering his letters. According to the Reverend L.J. Percival, to whom the Lord Chamberlain referred it, this last play was 'a gratuitous slap at Archbishops, Bishops, Clergy, and the like'.[41]

---

* Written by John Frushard
† Written by Ronald C. Grant
‡ Written by Maurice Browne
§ Written by T.M.W. Watson

Generally, the censorship (and the Public Morality Council) liked its religion orthodox. In January 1934, Street recommended *The Brides of the Lamb** as 'a strong indictment of the evils produced by hysterical revivalist preaching among ignorant women, with a special note of the ease with which so-called religious emotion passes into the erotic'. Since the play was 'attacking an undoubted evil', he argued that there was no reason to turn it down. Game supported him:

> I see no justifiable reason for banning the play or the theme and I consider that if it did anything to discourage the revivalist movement in England it would be all to the good: and I have seen something at close hand of the effects of emotionalized religion upon the semi educated

However, Cromer objected to 'the nauseating use of biblical phraseology' and described it as 'the sort of play I detest seeing on the stage'. After consulting Church representatives some amendments were made, including a change to the 'abominable' and 'blasphemous' title, which was 'likely to give real offence to numbers of religious people'.[42]

Not upsetting religious believers remained a fundamental plank of Cromer's policy, and in August of the same year he rejected a play which revealed the founder of the Christian Scientists as 'a scheming impostor . . . illiterate and partially unbalanced'. There was no doubt that the public performance of *The Faith Seller*† would have upset the movement's followers. 'I should personally be inclined to defy them', wrote Street, but he conceded that 'given the precedents there would be a case for humouring them'.[43] In 1936, they also turned down *The Sickness of Salome*,‡ described by Street as a 'guying' and a 'burlesque' of a Bible story, in which John the Baptist is actually the name of a peacock. 'This play will not do', wrote Street. But the script had actually been submitted on behalf of Bristol Y.M.C.A., and its indignant author was adamant that the play was not intended to be comic. Perhaps Street's exasperation at its triteness and absurdity had encouraged him to treat as a spoof something which he knew was intended to be serious.[44]

Whether and how Christ could be represented on stage was the subject of some agonising, particularly where the representation was oblique. In June 1937, there was confusion and partial dissent within the Office over 'An embarrassingly ingenuous anti-war propaganda play' called *The Great Atonement*,§ in which Christ appears in a vision. Given the context of the

---

* Written by William Hurlbut
† Written by Francis J. Mott
‡ Written by Wilfred H. Westlake
§ Written by Dorothy Elliott

performance, the new Reader, Geoffrey Dearmer (himself a committed Christian and the son of a high churchman who had been Canon at Westminster) considered it safe to recommend a licence, subject to amendments:

> The piece is written on behalf of the Cancer Research Fund, for one performance at the Savoy Cinema, Lincoln. It is too shockingly crude to see the light elsewhere, and is recommended subject to the elimination of an actor visually representing Our Lord.

Cromer, however, proposed the elimination of 'all impersonation and words spoken by Christ', which, he declared, had 'never been allowed on the stage'. Rather pedantically, Dearmer challenged this: 'I submit that it is untrue to say that no words spoken by Christ are ever allowed on the stage . . . There is no doubt that authors and managers could quote hundreds of examples where the sayings of Christ have been reverently quoted'. Dearmer argued that it was rather Christ as a character which was unacceptable, and that a firm principle needed to be established:

> But it is ludicrous and therefore irreverent to represent Christ on the stage. It is equally objectionable to represent him as a speaking character off—as in this case. Whether a character is seen and heard or not seen and heard is, I think, immaterial and whether He says things He did say or invented stuff is equally immaterial. I think we shall find ourselves in difficulties unless we make this quite clear.

He offered a solution:

> Why not say that no actor representing the character of Christ is permitted to be seen or heard in the theatre—this solves the difficulty without prohibiting the 'influence' of the direct use of much of the Gospels which people may say will be done if you prohibit 'quotations' from words spoken by Him? . . .
>
> P.S. Game agrees with what I have said.

Cromer conceded that he had expressed himself poorly, and accepted his Reader's recommendation; however, since this represented a change in policy, he was effectively obliged to include a caveat of exemption in his ruling:

> 1) No actor representing the character of Christ is permitted to be seen or heard on the British Stage.
> 2) Quotations from words spoken by Christ are permitted in appropriate cases when spoken on (or off) the Stage by other characters in a play.
> 3) In certain cases a Voice 'off' the stage is also permitted as in some cases already licensed.[45]

But attempts to establish absolute rules of censorship were almost always doomed to failure. Within a few months, the Lord Chamberlain found himself consulting the Archbishop of Canterbury over *The Birth of Christmas*,* which, unsurprisingly, included a representation of Christ as a child. It was, said Game, 'A nativity play for children . . . naïvely reverent in its treatment and highly moral in its effect; but the character of the Christ-Child presents a difficulty'. He pointed out that 'We have, so far, not allowed Christ as a child to appear on the stage, even as a silent character', and then tentatively suggested a possible, if rather tortuous, way out of the quandary: 'I don't know whether the Lord Chamberlain can pass this play, taking the view that here the Christ-Child is more an abstraction of an idea than a historical character?'. The Archbishop conceded that performances of Christmas nativity plays were widespread, and that often 'the Christ-Child figures in such amateur productions and sometimes takes a small vocal part'; he expressed a willingness to exempt this play from the general rule, provided it was not seen to establish a new precedent.[46]

Where Street had sometimes tended to be gently mocking of the Church and religion, his successor as Reader, Geoffrey Dearmer, had a very different attitude. His own faith had triumphantly survived his experiences at Gallipoli and on the Western Front, and the death of his brother in action. He was also a published poet, and even his verses about the First World War have been characterised as suffused with a Christian perspective in which nothing is in vain or futile and 'hope and faith shine through the murk of mud and blood'.[47] Dearmer was the author of a hymn, 'The Healing Christ', included in *100 Favourite Hymns for Today*, as well as of texts for some religious choral works and a play about St Paul. So it is not surprising that his anxieties over religious plays extended to protecting the clergy from criticism, as his 1937 report on the 'tedious and wordy' *Spug*† demonstrates. What worried him here was the characterisation of a clergyman named Fluke, and he asked Cromer to adopt an unequivocal stance:

> an undertaking should be required that this character is not made offensive to the church-going public . . . Characters like Fluke are intolerable in the theatre. Jejune authors like Mr Latimer are blandly unaware that a great number of Theatregoers regard religion with more than academic reverence. I feel sure that the Lord Chamberlain will strongly caution the Management.

Cromer duly endorsed the cuts proposed by his Reader, and, since there was concern not only over what Fluke said but also how the character

---

* Written by Anne Cundall
† Written by Rupert Latimer

might be played, Dearmer attended a dress rehearsal, with the authority to require further changes in the acting style. In the event, this proved unnecessary:

> Yesterday I suffered a four hour dress rehearsal . . . I am pleased to report that the interpretation and playing of Fluke, the parson, were both as good as the script—duly cut as required—allows. The actor made him a kindly, wooly old gentleman.[48]

For Dearmer, the author's intention was the key, and superseded the letter of the law. Moreover, as Street had argued in relation to sexuality, there was a crucial distinction to be made between the philosophical discussion of religious ideas and their stage embodiment; between spirit and flesh. As he wrote in relation to Alfred Savoir's *He Himself** in 1938: 'A play, . . . that deals with God as a concept is very different to one in which He is actually represented. I think to ban the representation of the concept of God on the stage would give our critics a very strong case . . .'.[49]

Although power lay ultimately in the hands of the Lord Chamberlain, and his Readers enjoyed no authority to make decisions, they could certainly influence through the framing and emphasis of their reports. In October 1938, Dearmer described *The Unknown Artist,*[†] in which a picture of the Virgin Mary comes to life, as 'a devout piece and wholly to be recommended'; it was licensed without hesitation.[50] In February 1939, *The Voice of Love*[‡] was also licensed on his recommendation and without reference to any religious authority, even though it included a resurrection scene in which Christ's final words on the cross are spoken aloud: The script, said Dearmer, was 'written by a woman who is evidently a very devout Christian'.[51] Nor was his religious outlook necessarily parochial. In September 1938, Game was ready to recommend a revised version of *He Himself*, in which one of the characters believes himself Divine. A previous version had been turned down because it had invoked the name of Christ, but Game thought that the rewritten text was close to being acceptable:

> My reason for thinking that the play would not prove too offensive to Christian susceptibilities is that Harry now announces himself as Buddha —this is no doubt a pseudonym for God, or even Christ, but would nevertheless make a considerable difference in a London Theatre.

Dearmer disagreed strongly: 'I doubt whether the use of the idea of Buddha should be allowed. My friend Clifford Bax, for instance, professes

---

* Written by Roma June, 'adapted from the French of Alfred Savoir'
† Written by Reginald Garden
‡ Written by Margaret Duncan

to be a Buddhist, and won't write a play about Buddha for this reason. For Harry to say he is the Buddha is cheap and in bad taste'. The Lord Chamberlain accepted Dearmer's view and turned down the play. 'I suggest you might achieve what you want by putting the play into the realms of mythology and letting Harry think that he is Jupiter', he helpfully advised the playwright.[52]

The presence of Dearmer made it less necessary for the Lord Chamberlain to seek the advice of the Church, but there were still occasions when he consulted the Archbishop of Canterbury. In February 1938, Dearmer had recommended—after some agonising—*The Love of Judas*,* in which 'Judas is represented as desiring Mary, and Matthias as having already "bought her love"'. It was, said Dearmer, 'written with a genuine religious motive and purpose', and he found the character of Mary 'entirely without offence' because she does not respond to Judas's desires. But some questions of principle remained: 'how far are authors to be allowed to pervert the facts of the New Testament to their advantage?'. Cromer was prepared to support his Reader's conclusion that in this instance 'the "pros" will outweigh the "cons"':

> The decision may, I think, be based upon two guiding principles. a) That censorship is not responsible for and therefore concerned with historical accuracy and b) That so long as distortion of historical tradition is not made offensive interference is not imperative.

However, he also consulted the Archbishop of Canterbury, who, while not questioning the 'general motive and purpose of the play', was nonetheless disturbed by the fact that 'The background of the Gospel story has been definitely falsified'. He expressed particularly grave reservations about the characterisation of Matthias, and the dangerous messages this might impart:

> What is the justification for implying that the man specially selected to take the place of Judas had before his conversion been a man of immoral life . . . It seems to me highly undesirable to put into people's heads the idea that one of the Twelve Apostles who were instrumental in founding the Christian Church had, in his earlier days, had immoral relations with Mary Magdalene.

The name of Matthias was amended.[53]

Inevitably, religion sometimes spilled directly into politics, and the Lord Chamberlain had to prevent the stage from becoming caught up in interdenominational conflicts. In January 1935, he refused to allow the

---

* Written by Teresa Hooley and Cedric Wallis

City Hall in Glasgow to stage a play submitted by the Scottish Protestant League and described by Street as 'the crudest anti-Catholic propaganda'. Written by 'a fanatical propagandist', *The Trial Of Father Diamond** showed a Catholic priest inciting a bank clerk to rob his employers. 'I should advise the Lord Chamberlain to ban this play as likely to cause a breach of the peace', warned Game—though he himself seemed not unwilling to swallow the propaganda: 'There is, I believe, a logical basis for the point of view here presented but we have not to deal with logic but with the probability of riot'.[54] Another play which was approved and duly upset Catholics was *Family Portrait*, written by two American playwrights, Lenore and William Joyce Cowen. The licence was issued in the summer of 1939, with Dearmer's recommendation—and enthusiasm:

> Free from the pious propaganda which is the ruin of 99% of religious plays, it presents a strong and convincing picture of Mary's difficulties, and, indirectly, some valuable sidelights on the teachings of Jesus.
>
> Plays, properly treated, in which Mary appears are now always allowed. This is a full length portrait. But no sensible person could object to it . . . in a play handled with religious impulse of the right kind, and calculated to do nothing but good.

But to Catholics, the effect of focusing on the family life of Jesus and his mother was to humanise their relationship and deny the essential divinity which was fundamental to their faith. The play became the eye of a furious storm of protest and doctrinal argument which persisted for over a year. The Office was bombarded with angry correspondence from, amongst others, the Catholic Women's League and several cardinals, and disagreements raged about the exact meaning of specific passages in the Bible. For some, the representation of holy figures by actors was itself still taboo: 'the people to whom Our Lord is a now living Divine Person will regret the portrayal of His home in the secular surroundings of a modern theatre', wrote the Bishop of London. He also had specific concerns over the issue of casting:

> I think it is also germane to the matter to say that if the play is performed, it becomes a possibility that Christian opinion would be shocked by the part of the Virgin Mary being taken by unsuitable people . . . It cannot be left out of sight that if the play is released, it might be that an actress who, for instance, had been divorced might be found taking this part.

Clarendon tried to remain above the religious intricacies of the dispute, defending his decision on the grounds of reasonableness and tolerance:

---

* The playwright was Alexander Ratcliffe

> As Censor of Plays I do not consider that I am justified in refusing to
> license a play for the sole reason that its narrative is based upon doctrinal
> facts about which there is a difference of belief, as between one section of
> the Christian church and another.
>
> If I were to adopt such an attitude I should find myself in the
> impossible position of having to ban certain religious plays which reach
> me from sources closely allied with one or another section of the Christian
> church. This would lead to severe restrictions being imposed on the scope
> of Religious Drama, which surely deserves encouragement rather than
> suppression. Some Christians believe in the perpetual virginity of the
> Virgin Mary, others do not. The authors of *Family Portrait* are clearly
> amongst those who do not; but they have written their play with sincerity
> and reverence, and most certainly had no wish to give pain to anyone.
>
> This being the case there does not seem reasonable cause for anyone to
> feel offended.[55]

But a massive file of correspondence built up in 1939 and 1940, indicating
that very many people did indeed find cause to be offended. Again, while
Lords Chamberlain never liked withdrawing licences he had issued, such
an affair was likely to influence future decisions.

Monarchy

According to the historian Charles Loch Mowat, at the time of King
George's silver jubilee in 1935 'The institution of monarchy had never
been stronger in Great Britain; the wearer of the crown never more
beloved'; George had raised the monarchy 'to a place of strong affection in
the hearts of the people', and he himself was 'the father of his people', a
reassuringly solid and unchanging centre in times of uncertainty.[56] Given
the Lord Chamberlain's position as head of the royal household, it is
unthinkable that any direct criticism of either the King himself or the
institution of monarchy could have been approved for public performance.
Perhaps the closest to it was Hugh Ross Williamson's *Mr Gladstone*, which
the censorship angrily turned down in 1937. Williamson's play was already
being staged privately when it was submitted, but Dearmer, strongly
opposed a licence:

> The author in his preface to this play now running at the Gate Theatre,
> boldly states . . . that Queen Victoria to him 'Appears to be one of the more
> unattractive characters' and 'certainly one of the most unconstitutional
> monarchs who have occupied the English throne.'

Dearmer, no doubt accurately, suggested that 'Unlike most of the
Houseman plays, I think this play would give offence to the Royal Family
and a large section of the public'. He noted with disapproval that 'Many of

the sentiments attributed to the Queen are venomous', though she was not the only one to be unfairly treated: 'Dizzy is here a dreadful creature, Gordon a religious fanatic. Only Mrs Gladstone is drawn with sympathy'. The Reader also pointed out that 'to license it would make it more difficult to ban worse and more biassed plays of the sort'. Cromer agreed that it was 'an offensive portrayal', and the play was rejected. Even when it was resubmitted nearly a decade later, Lord Clarendon was adamant that the ban should remain in place.[57]

There were three broad areas within which the Lord Chamberlain was engaged in protecting the King. The first was putting Queen Victoria and her family on the stage, where the official attitude changed in 1936 with the change in monarch, from an automatic refusal to a cautious and very selective freedom. The second issue, which emerged after 1937, was the theme of abdication; the third was the portrayal of other (real or imaginary) monarchs in ways which might be taken to reflect on the British throne. Nor should it be forgotten that the throne retained an effective and total power of veto on any play. Although we have some specific evidence of cases where the opinion of the King was sought or where he intervened, the extent to which informal nudges were applied remains unclear. What we can be sure of is that any such nudges would surely have been treated as commands. In 1937, *Theatre World* published 'a timely and controversial article on the working of censorship' under the title *The Throne is the Censor*; its author, Willson Disher, acknowledged the greater degree of lassitude afforded in recent times, but raised the question of 'whether the theatre is still under "Star Chamber" rule'. In fact, questioning the assumption that things had completely changed, he compared the arguments over Granville Barker's *Waste* in 1906 with the recent ones over *Parnell*, claiming that the latter 'were so similar in manner and matter that reading them gave you the feeling of having picked up, by mistake, a thirty-year old newspaper'.[58]

Comparisons between censorship of cinema and of theatre reveal that whereas the film censors published lists of themes and images which were prohibited, often citing examples of what they had rejected, there was never any equivalent statement from the Lord Chamberlain about theatre. The effect of this was that there existed a degree of transparency in the censorship of film which did not exist in theatre. The point was well argued in another article in *Theatre World* in 1932:

> I think everybody interested in the theatre would be relieved if the department responsible for the censorship of plays would come out into the open and take the public into its confidence. The Film Censors are not nearly so reticent. Periodically we read lists of the 'Thou shalt not's' which film companies have to follow. We read that wild parties, prolonged embraces, lengthy bedroom scenes, feminine nudity, certain oaths,

depiction of the Deity, and flogging and torture scenes are not looked upon with favour. But no such lists are issued in connection with the stage, and consequently we are a little hazy about what is and what is *not* permitted in the theatre.

But film censorship was not the responsibility of the monarch, and the absolute discretion enjoyed by the Lord Chamberlain certainly allowed him the possibility of responding to the hints or whims of his master, without needing to justify them. Disher's 1937 article drew attention to the lack of accountability in theatre censorship, and suggested that the power still residing with the monarch was not nominal and dormant but was being widely exercised in practice. He advanced little or no hard evidence to support his argument, though it is tempting to speculate about possible sources within the Lord Chamberlain's Office which might have inspired his conclusions:

> What exactly are the principles of censorship. No one knows because, so I have been assured at St James's Palace, they are incorporated in no written laws . . . I have never studied a subject so elusive in 'documentation'.
>
> Further enquiries have led me to the conclusion that the throne is the censor. Even though his powers are derived from successive Acts of Parliament, the Lord Chamberlain is a court official, solely concerned with divining and interpreting the wishes of the King as a private person, as head of the established church, as guardian of his subject's [sic] morals and as head of the State.
>
> There you will discern difficulties enough. Yet in the past year we have seen even those bounds set 'wider still and wider'. The Lord Chamberlain appears to have been concerned with the wishes of the King as safeguard of his subject's hurt feelings for neither in *Parnell* nor *Rossetti* were any living persons represented.
>
> Of course, if Parliament has been so careless of its own duties and the people's rights as to set down no rules and regulations for the guidance of the Lord Chamberlain (or of the perplexed playwright who never knows what obstacles have been set up or are likely to be set up against him) what can we expect?[59]

There is certainly evidence that George V insisted on enforcing key principles in respect of plays which he thought impinged directly on the monarchy. In 1933, Lord Cromer consulted the Foreign Office over a French play, *Tsar Lénine*,[*] which criticised the founder of the Communist state and featured a brief appearance by Stalin. Though Cromer had noted elsewhere that he had 'no wish to protect . . . the Soviet Government' since 'they do not deserve protection',[60] there was a particular factor which it was necessary to take into account here:

---

[*] Written by François Porché

I have to bear in mind that one or two plays of late years, in which it was intended to impersonate the late Emperor and Empress of Russia, have been banned, mainly because The King objects to the tragedy of His relatives' murder being exploited on the stage.

The Russians might logically argue that we forbid plays about the Russian Royal Family while allowing plays of still more recent date about the Bolshevist Regime. This really is the point upon which I would welcome the opinion of the Foreign Office.

The Foreign Office doubted whether 'the Soviet Government would have reasonable grounds to complain', but the brief appearance of Stalin was cut by Cromer—either on the instruction of the King or because Cromer himself believed he was shielding the King from potential criticism.[61]

It was, too, George V who was responsible for maintaining the absolute ban on presenting Queen Victoria and her family on stage—a ban which was lifted almost immediately after his death. In November 1923, Louis Parker's *Queen Victoria* had been refused a licence when tentatively sent in by Basil Dean. Cromer, who had only recently become Lord Chamberlain, had told Dean:

that in deference to the feelings of the King and other members of the Royal Family, some of whom are actually the children of Queen Victoria, the attitude hitherto adopted by my department has been to discourage the impersonation on the Stage of Queen Victoria and of historical incidents during her late Majesty's reign in which Queen Victoria figures.

Yet recognising that the script was not in any way intended to criticise or embarrass the monarchy, Cromer had also sent it to the King—carefully signalling both his discretion and his complete subservience to the monarch's wishes:

the Lord Chamberlain could not submit that any such idea be considered by the King during the lifetime of the generation of the Duke of Connaught, quite apart from the very natural feeling the King and Queen and Queen Alexandra would entertain in regard to any such play. . . .

The Lord Chamberlain's endeavour will be to keep the whole of this question within the bounds of private negotiation with Mr Basil Dean and to avoid his raising the matter officially and thus possibly risking comment in the press.

In so doing the Lord Chamberlain ventures to hope that he will be faithfully interpreting the King's wishes.

If His Majesty would graciously spare the time to read this play which . . . is written in all seriousness and good faith . . . The Lord Chamberlain ventures to think the King would be interested to see the manner in which published works have been assembled and utilised so as to construct this drama.[62]

It was the unambiguous reply of the King's private secretary, Lord Stamfordham, which confirmed and set in stone the policy which would last for the next thirteen years: 'The King has read Mr Louis Parker's play *Queen Victoria* and considers it is vulgar and in many instances historically incorrect: and permission for its performance in this country ought never to be granted during His Majesty's lifetime'.

There were no exceptions. In April 1934, Street reported on a proposed pageant to be staged in Ramsgate; he suspected that the Lord Chamberlain would feel obliged to refuse it, but went as far as he dared in suggesting that such an inflexible policy was not only unnecessary but perhaps counter-productive in encouraging support for the monarchy:

> Ramsgate attaches great importance to it, being proud of the Queen's sojourn there as a girl. I cannot imagine how it could possibly give offence, and with great respect submit that to ban it would be a mistake as tending to a snub to loyalty and a needless unpopularity, in Ramsgate at least, for the Lord Chamberlain's Office.

Cromer did not query his Reader's assessment, but indicated that the decision was out of his hands and, for the present at least, beyond discussion: 'In itself the question appears trivial and harmless', he wrote, 'but the King has a strong objection to the impersonation of his Grandparents on the stage and this must be respected during the present Reign'.[63] In practice, Cromer knew it was doubtful whether such performances were even subject to his control. The following year, Wigan staged a pageant without seeking consent, but newspaper reports of the event came to Cromer's attention. He wrote to Buckingham Palace:

> I have taken up with the Chairman of the Centre Pageant Committee of the Wigan Carnival the question of the impersonation recently made of the King and Queen.
> From Mr Arthur Hawkes' letter enclosed you will see that he takes full responsibility for what took place, and is extremely contrite offering to Their Majesties his most humble apologies.

He went on:

> I should explain that these provincial Pageants present certain difficulties because, strictly speaking, they are not Stage Plays according to the Theatres Act unless any dialogue is introduced.
> In this case, as in many Pageants, there was no dialogue so that they did not require a Licence, and did not therefore come within the Lord Chamberlain's jurisdiction.

Cromer received a reply:

His Majesty quite realises that the Lord Chamberlain has no jurisdiction where there is no dialogue, and the only thing that can be done when people make these applications is to tell them that Their Majesties would view anything of the kind with disfavour.[64]

In April 1935, Street tried once again to shift the policy in relation to *Vickie*,* 'a chronicle play illustrating the life and character of Queen Victoria from the age of seven to her accession'. He insisted the play 'does nothing but honour to its subject', and that its effect might even be beneficial to the throne: 'For my part I cannot imagine any possible harm in it—quite the contrary':

> if the play concerned recent events some of it would be indiscreet. But it is all one hundred years old . . .. It keeps to the facts and . . . so far as the Queen is concerned it presents her as a charming child and girl and with a real and pathetic dignity on her accession.

Moreover, Street pointed out that the play had already been staged privately, and that it was to be broadcast by the BBC, and went so far as to declare: 'I think the rule a pity'. Cromer's response hinted that he shared his Reader's view but was powerless to intervene: 'I am bound to prohibit the impersonation of Queen Victoria (even as a child) during the present reign', he stressed.[65] When Sydney Carroll in the *Daily Telegraph* criticised the Lord Chamberlain's policy as 'oblivious to common-sense', Cromer dutifully replied that it was motivated 'out of respect for the feelings of a Sovereign'. Carroll was not persuaded. He wrote to Cromer at length, suggesting that George and the monarchy actually needed the sort of boost which the right kind of play about Victoria might supply, and detailing the political ramifications:

> I cannot but think it is unfortunate that He should persist in viewing the problem as a personal one . . . [it] implies a desire for secrecy and the possibility that some scandal attaches to her glorious career which it may not be desirable to disclose.
>
> I quite agree as to the undesirability of exposing anyone who cherishes an affection for a mother or a grandmother to the possibility of being hurt by the portrayal of those dear to them, but as unfortunately and most unhappily for the theatre the practical interest taken by the members of the Royal Family in the cause of the theatre is negligible, and as no visit to the theatre has been undertaken or is likely to be undertaken by either the Duke of Connaught, Princess Louise or Princess Beatrice, they cannot possibly be exposed to something that they are never likely to see.
>
> Moreover, a character drawing that is little short of a panegyric of some person real and distinguished cannot be anything but helpful to the

---

* Written by Consuelo de Reyes

memory of that person, to say nothing of its benefit to the cause of the monarchy in general.

Such plays act, in my opinion, as invaluable reactions against the innumerable anti-social propaganda plays of a Communist or Bolshevist character which are allowed to be performed without let or hindrance and which cannot under our legislature be forbidden. It seems to me both illogical and indefensible to permit the lives of such recent destroyers of social serenity as Lenin to be given on our public stages and their characters held up to admiration and idolisation, whilst a tender, affectionate and living picture of such a monarch as Queen Victoria remains taboo . . . I think the attitude adopted by His Majesty completely opposed to the best interests of all who love the Royal Family and all they mean and stand for in the State, and my criticism has been couched in a spirit of intense loyalty and a regard for what I consider the best interests of the reigning family.[66]

But there was little Cromer could do.

The censorship was almost equally rigid over distant and oblique references to the monarchy. In December 1934, the Office had refused to license *Four Ducks on a Pond*,* a play based on a Hungarian short story. Street described it as 'an effective Ruritanian play with dubious elements from the point of view of the Censorship', and he voiced concerns about the play's immorality:

The chief objection is the plot, with its . . . talk of the Crown Princess's unpopular sterility, her rather unnecessary talk about her virginity and the means she took to correct it. Immorality is certainly condoned, but it is the 'broadness' of the sterility and virginity theme which will shock a good many people.

Members of the Advisory Board confirmed the Reader's suspicion that the plot, in which the Crown Prince refuses to cohabit with his wife and maintains relationships with several mistresses, was intended to refer primarily to the Habsburgs. Lord David Cecil was adamant that the play should be turned down as 'a vulgar attempt to exploit . . . the public's prurient curiosity'. Crucially,

It shows up royalty in a bad and wholly false light—and it is full of passages that would be taken—and I believe are meant to be taken—as referring to current events and living personages . . . It is a play that might definitely have a harmful effect.

Professor Winifred Cullis also sensed a danger to the institution of monarchy embodied not only in the sexual immorality depicted, but also in other aspects of royal behaviour:

---

* Written by Cosmo Hamilton

An unpleasant feature is the presentation of Royalty turning so naturally and easily to trickery to deceive its subjects. Foreign uniforms and setting would probably give rise to a smug feeling of satisfaction of how different things are in this country but would not really lessen the doubtful taste of this aspect of the play.

The licence was refused.[67]

On 20 January 1936, George V died. On the same day, Lord Cromer found time to send a letter to his Advisory Board: 'As I write this, we may be on the threshold of a new epoch, occasioned by the commencement of a new Reign in which public opinion will advance and alter'. His confidence that the death of George signified the start of a new era in stage freedom is striking not least because his letter was written to accompany *Bitter Harvest*,* a play which itself had nothing to do with monarchy; this would seem to imply that perhaps the hand and mind of the monarch had indeed been influential in a variety of ways. Cromer was convinced that a new (and younger) King would breathe freshness into the spirit of the age and the institutions of the establishment, and that the Lord Chamberlain's Office would inevitably be caught up in the movement. 'Censorship of the stage will necessarily have to move with the times', he told the Board.[68]

By the time the lifting of the ban on plays about Queen Victoria was officially announced in December 1936, the British monarchy had been through the much greater crisis and public agonies which culminated in the abdication of Edward VIII. Parliament was told on 10 December that the King intended to resign, and the Declaration of Abdication bill was passed on the following day. At the very height of the crisis, and little more than a week before Edward's decision was confirmed, the Lord Chamberlain published his proposal 'to allow production after 20th June 1937 of plays dealing with the life of Queen Victoria'.[69] It is hard to know whether the timing was coincidental or whether the seriousness of the crisis now facing the monarchy made the shielding of Victoria from all possible contamination seem too absurd to sustain. Perhaps the royal household even judged that performances of plays which celebrated and praised the monarch of a previous (but not too distant) age might divert public interest down a more positive route. The decision also followed extensive negotiations between Cromer and the Duke of Connaught, the third and only surviving son of Queen Victoria, who was now in his mid eighties, and without whose consent the policy could hardly have been altered. Laurence Housman was undoubtedly the playwright who had most invested in a change of policy; he claimed to have had some thirty-two plays (most of them about Queen Victoria) banned during the previous

---

* Written by Catherine Turney

thirty years or so, even though his attitude towards her seems closer to reverence and worship than to interrogation or criticism. He had endured many confrontations with the Lord Chamberlain, and reviews of his autobiography, published in January 1937, hailed him as 'Britain's most censored dramatist'.[70] Now some of his plays could find a place on the public stage, and as the Lord Chamberlain explained to him in a letter of August 1937, it was Connaught who was

> the person primarily concerned in all these plays about Queen Victoria, as being the only surviving son of the Queen and it is largely due to His Royal Highness's broad-mindedness and courtesy that permission has been granted to me to issue licences for Victorian plays.[71]

The shift in policy came just too late for Street to witness—he died in November 1936—but the year 1937 did indeed witness a small explosion of plays about Victoria. The St James's Theatre and Laurence Housman were first off the mark, submitting *Victoria Regina*—a collection of short plays which had previously been staged privately at the Gate Theatre and in New York—in early December 1936.[72] But it was not intended that the lifting of the absolute ban should give playwrights freedom to say whatever they wanted about Victoria and her family: 'all references to doubts as to Prince Albert's legitimacy must of course come out', noted Cromer in relation to Housman's play, and he insisted, somewhat nervously, that 'When this play is eventually in rehearsal it should be seen and a report made to me in case any further adjustments prove necessary'. The lines cut were a reference to the absence of haemophilia in Albert, which might have suggested that he was of a different stock to the royal household. Over the coming months, detailed discussions took place with the new King, George VI, about the principles of precisely what was and was not to be allowed. In April 1937, the Comptroller recorded:

> I would like to make a note that I asked the Lord Chamberlain for a ruling on certain points in connection with the Queen Victoria Plays. He layed down that there should never be any death-bed scene of Prince Albert or of the Queen, and that mention can be made of Queen Victoria's children and grandchildren, but that they are not to be represented on the stage. Also that any other distinguished contemporaries in the plays may be left in, provided they are shown in a pleasant light, but if they are represented in an uncomplimentary manner their relations and descendants should be consulted.[73]

In July 1937, Gwatkin went in royal company to watch a public performance of *Victoria Regina*, and subsequently passed on to the producer suggestions which seem to reflect the pedantic accuracy and superficial adherence to 'truth' and 'authenticity' which the Office assumed would be the goal of plays about the Queen:

> I took Princess Helena Victoria who, from a long personal experience of Queen Victoria, is a very great expert on matters appertaining to her. I thought it would interest you to know her criticisms . . . Her Highness was delighted with all the scenes except the last two . . . in the last scene but one the Queen is worried by wasps, and the handkerchief-waving is a little over-exaggerated . . . The two jokes with Brown about fruit and the garden of Eden and clothes, and the cat and dog joke . . . Her Highness said the Queen would never have made . . . The Queen never called Brown 'Dear Brown'; the most she ever said was 'My good Brown'. He had grey hair at that time and not such a jutting out beard.[74]

Similarly, in the case of Housman's *Queen's Ministers* in July 1937, a descendant of Gladstone wrote to point out that his grandmother would not have knitted, as depicted, (though he generously made no objection to this invention). Arthur Ponsonby, the son of Queen Victoria's private secretary, and himself a former Labour MP and Socialist who had led the party in the House of Lords, also enjoyed pointing out one or two of the playwright's gaffes:

> With regard to the statement attributed to Lord Roseberry that Pepper's Ghost came to Windsor on one occasion for stud purposes, and sired Peppercorn out of Cornucopia, I think it only right to let you know that no mares were ever at Windsor. Queen Victoria kept her mares at Hampton Court: and in any case the mare goes to the stallion, not the stallion to the mare.

In practice, the censorship did not insist on altering such details. When the leading theatre manager (and former Conservative MP) Sir Alfred Butt resubmitted Louis Parker's *Queen Victoria* in January 1937, Cromer defined an important principle: 'Censorship cannot take the responsibility for historical accuracy of detail and in such plays must be confined to the elimination of all objectionable matter', he wrote. However, he confirmed the need for certain minor amendments, and Sir Malcolm Murray, who had been Comptroller of the Duke of Connaught's household for the last thirty years, passed on his master's reservations to the Office:

> I think the treatment of Prince Consort's death, i.e. 'a dreadful scream being heard from the other room' should be altered . . . The Queen's treatment and dismissal of Lord Granville and Lord Clarendon seems overdone and is scarcely dignified . . . . Is it necessary for Her Majesty to say to the Prince of Wales 'You reek of tobacco—what do you want?'

He had one other requirement: 'If the play is produced, I do think it is absolutely essential that an Englishwoman and not an American represents Queen Victoria'.[75]

Restrictions remained tight, and Cromer was far from relaxed about Housman's wish to stage more from his back catalogue of banned plays. In August 1937, he wrote to Gwatkin:

> On the whole, it seems as if Housman is much tamer now, but it remains to be seen what other surprises he may have up his sleeve in wanting to produce some of his other playlets . . . I specially have in mind one where King Edward the Seventh, as a boy, gets a dressing-down from his parents.[76]

Nor was Houseman alone. In March, Game had also reported cautiously on *Vickie*, the cycle of four plays about Victoria's life, written by Consuelo de Reyes.

> There are various matters of state which I have queried throughout, notably the deathbed of the Prince Consort, which obviously wont [sic] do . . . I think it would be advisable for someone in the Duke of Connaught's Household to read through the plays.

It is hard not to feel some sympathy with Cromer's response: 'This cycle of four plays is intensely tedious, long-winded and in parts cheap and in bad taste. I can hardly imagine them being relished by British audiences who will be sick to death of plays about Queen Victoria'. More specifically, he advised that 'there can of course be no deathbed or illness scene, which would not only be very painful but in the worst of taste', and that it was 'obviously impossible too to introduce Princess Beatrice in the character of a child'. A couple of weeks later he passed on a further stipulation: 'I am sorry to say that we must insist that Queen Alexandra, the grandmother of the present Queen, is not impersonated on the stage'.[77]

In the same year, *Victoria, Queen and Empress** raised a new issue for the censorship in that it contained 'invented' scenes, openly mixing 'fact' with 'fiction':

> If the Duke of Connaught raises no objection to his mother appearing in fictitious drama, there seems no serious objection to the scene being licensed, although . . . I think it should be realised that the granting of a licence will slightly extend the limits within which the character of Queen Victoria may be exhibited on the stage.

Connaught seems not to have objected to the principle, and following extensive correspondence on minute points of detail and permission, the script was duly licensed. A rather droll letter sent to the playwright in July 1937 reflected the Office's growing sense of impatience and exhaustion:

* Written by Gerald Wynne Rushton and Thomas South Mack

The Office is on tenterhooks to receive your Act Three, Scene One; all leave has been stopped, and the entire Staff is feeding on Vitamin B.

I return to you Lord Aberdare's letter, as you probably want to file it amongst your treasures.[78]

In July 1937, the censors also removed references to a German waiter, and to 'abdicating Kings' from *Vickie and Albert*.* The endorsement included the following proscriptions: 'The business of the Prince of Orange being drunk not to be played in any offensive manner . . . The Queen not to kneel down as described in the stage directions'.[79]

In December 1936, the Office had insisted on removing several individuals, including Queen Victoria, from a collection of some forty characters (others included Hitler, Mussolini and Greta Garbo) in the Epilogue to *These Mortals*, H.M. Harwood's anti-war play, designed, as the Reader put it, for 'the very educated public'. In July 1937, 'In view of what has happened both on the stage and in films with regard to the representation of Queen Victoria', Harwood cheekily sought permission to reinstate the monarch. The Lord Chamberlain was not amused:

> Mr Harwood should understand that the licensing of plays dealing with the life of Queen Victoria based more or less on historical records is quite a different proposition to introducing Queen Victoria as a character in a play like *These Mortals*, especially as the setting purports to be in Hades.

The playwright was accused of lack of taste:

> I am sure you will agree that it cannot be entirely pleasant to see someone taking the part of one's own mother on the stage . . . and it would be even more wounding to see her after death in Limbo with such company as appear in your Epilogue. Had the Duke of Connaught envisaged such a possibility, I know there would have been no question of the action which he would have taken when the question of plays about Queen Victoria was put to him[80]

A year later, the censorship was equally adamant about not allowing Victoria to appear at Streatham in a comic satire alongside Michelangelo, Helen of Troy and Queen Elizabeth, expressing her 'opinions on art, politics, manners and the state of the world generally'. According to Game, there was 'no dramatic justification for the Queen's presence' in such an 'unseemly' and 'frivolous' context. Cromer took the opportunity to establish a further general position:

> While serious plays about Queen Victoria are now permissible in certain circumstances, it would certainly be offensive to the Royal Family if Queen Victoria were to be introduced into 'comic satire'. Consequently

---

* Written by Consuelo de Reyes

this cannot be allowed in this or any other comic play or revue in which the intention is to make fun of Queen Victoria.

The manager was informed of the decision in a letter which was pained and reproachful:

> When permission to portray Queen Victoria on the stage was sought from Her Majesty's children, it was given on the understanding that these portrayals would be in serious plays.
>
> It cannot be denied, I think, that it would not be very pleasant for anyone to know that their mother was being represented in any circumstances on the stage, whilst to think of her in a 'comic satire' would be most painful . . . I am sure you will understand.

The playwright, Mary Basil Hall, replied with a letter of fulsome apology: 'I quite appreciate the fact that the frivolous atmosphere of the play would be likely to have an effect on Her Majesty's portrayal which might pain Their Royal Highnesses, and that is the last thing I would wish to do'.[81] Queen Victoria and her champions could hardly have guessed what would one day come her way from the pen of Edward Bond.

Abdication was too hot and touchy a topic for most managers or playwrights to entertain, though at the end of January 1937, the Office reluctantly licensed a Ruritanian play* in which an imaginary King abdicates his throne. The script contained 'Some rather unfortunate remarks in view of the happenings of a few weeks ago', but Game argued that 'Although this theme inevitably brings to mind recent historical events, I think the treatment is far too trivial and superficial for the play to be taken seriously'. As usual, the fear was that to clamp down unnecessarily would draw attention to something which would otherwise remain obscure, and the Comptroller agreed it would be safer to issue a licence:

> I have seen the producer and author . . . the play is due to be put on in Birmingham and some time will elapse before it is played in London—if it ever is.
>
> In view of this it seemed to me of doubtful value to stress all the objections, which appear to us to be so obvious . . . I fear that if other rather minor points are insisted upon it will get into the Press and that would be unfortunate.

Cromer accepted the recommendation: 'It is to be hoped this will stay in Birmingham!', he observed.[82]

A year later, Game again reluctantly recommended a musical† which featured Mrs Fitzherbert and the Regent and incorporated 'some rather

---

* *Lèse Majesté!*, by John Beanes
† *Hearts Beloved*, authors unknown

unfortunate dialogue ... which has a topical application'. He suggested, however, that it was 'best to accept these oblique reminders of the recent Abdication as unintended and inevitable'. Cromer agreed that it would be counter-productive to try and excise every reference to abdication, though he did demand modifications to sections of the dialogue he considered 'unnecessarily unhappy'.[83]

More problematic was Noel Coward's *This Happy Breed*, submitted on the eve of war, in July 1939. Although the text appeared patriotic and celebratory of the national way of life, it included a scene in which the last words of the abdication speech are heard onstage by a family listening to the radio. Dearmer was full of praise for the play and its timing: 'It proves Coward capable of genuine uplift in terms of character in a deeper sense than in his comparatively theatrical *Cavalcade*'. However, while generally supportive, Gwatkin wrote to the Lord Chamberlain expressing reservations:

> The play itself is a serious picture of contemporary life and the incident of the abdication, treated as it is at the moment, is not used for Box Office effects; nor do I think that if this was allowed that it would open the door to the use of the Abdication by other playwrights, which in some ways is a consideration of more weight to us than any other.
>
> I do not know if you feel that the King should be asked about this. If so, I could take the thing over to Alec, or perhaps get a chance of explaining it myself direct, which would be in fact so much better.

Writing in late August 1939, the Assistant Comptroller added: 'It seems rather fantastic to write a lot about this sort of thing at the present moment, but there it is!'. Clarendon confirmed that 'H.M. should be asked', and Gwatkin sent the script for his attention, with an explanation and justification of the play:

> Noel Coward's new play is on the same lines as *Cavalcade*, his object being to show that the strength of this country lies on the sound common sense and inherent virtue, which is the heritage of the ordinary middle class family.
>
> The play shows the reaction of this family to various important incidents during the last few years, amongst which must be the abdication.
>
> The last thing that Noel Coward wants to do is to hurt anyone's feelings but to ignore that occasion in a play of [this] sort ... would give rise to comment—perhaps adverse ... I can but ask you if you would choose a time to ask The King what His Majesty's wishes are in this particular play which is a serious picture of the England of recent years.

In the event, not only was the scene excised, but requests in 1942 and 1950 to restore it were also rejected. A spokesperson for the King wrote to the Lord Chamberlain from Buckingham Palace in 1942, definitively confirming that the scene should be disallowed; typically, he suggested that this coincided with the wishes of the nation, with which he was apparently and conveniently in tune:

> I always feel that the British people look upon the abdication as a discreditable episode which they would like to forget altogether. I believe that it would be distasteful to them to rake it up again—and definitely repugnant to the royal family.[84]

Ultimately, then, the throne was indeed still the censor, and the removal of the automatic ban on the representation of Queen Victoria did not signal a willingness to open up the monarchy to scrutiny or debate—much less to allow criticism. Nor was there any wish to hasten the end of the age of deference. In December 1937, a female character in a light musical staged at Boscombe Hippodrome speaks of having dreamed she has dined with the King; 'it is impudence and quite out of place to bring in the King's name here', wrote Cromer, and the line was banned.[85] At the end of October 1939, when one might have expected priorities to be elsewhere, Game found time to note in his report on a revue, 'I have queried a line which seems to suggest that it is possible to get tight at Buckingham Palace after a Levee'. Gordon responded: 'Omit "Buckingham Palace". Levees are not held there anyway'.[86]

One of the few occasions when Unity Theatre managed to needle the establishment was at the end of May 1939, with their version of *Babes in the Wood*.* This 'political pantomime', in which Hitler and Stalin were represented as the robbers, and with Chamberlain as the wicked uncle, had already been performed privately with considerable success; when Unity sought a licence for public performance it was the portrayal of 'King Eustace the Useless' which caused most upset in the Office. As Game reported, the performers in the private production had actually been made up as the current King and Queen, and it remained 'clear who the originals are intended to be'. The Office could not afford to license royal mockery:

> it is widely known that these people have guyed our King and Queen in their legally private, but all too public, performances. If we now license the show, many who do not see the pantomime again will be under the impression that we have granted official approval to this insult.

Game also knew they were bound to refuse to license a play which attacked and satirised contemporary political leaders:

> Even if we insisted on the characters of the King and Queen being eliminated, and on the Wicked Uncle and the Two Robbers not being

---

* Written by Geoffrey Parsons, Robert Mitchell and Berkeley Fase

made up as Mr. Chamberlain, Hitler and Mussolini, it would still be perfectly obvious to all but the more idiotic of village idiots who these characters were meant to represent.

Rather than risk drawing attention to the criticisms of royalty, Game therefore advised the Lord Chamberlain to base his official objection on the portrayal of the political leaders and dictators. Clarendon did indeed refuse the licence, but it was the mockery of the monarchy which really upset him:

> I am sorry that it has been played privately. The references to the King and Queen are rude and insulting intended no doubt to ridicule the Throne and undermine its status, and this alone would I think justify . . . refusing a licence.[87]

Perhaps things had not changed so much after all. Writing in June 1940 out of frustration and exasperation at the continuing conflicts over *Family Portrait*, and his decision to license it the previous year, Clarendon asked rhetorically 'why should beliefs, which we tolerate outside the Theatre become suddenly intolerable when they are made the theme of a dramatic work?'.[88] It was, of course, a question which might well have been directed at the Office itself on numerous occasions. In expressing his regret that it was not possible to reject outright the anti-war play *Bring Me My Bow*, Game had observed in 1937 that 'ours, for better or worse, is a Country of free speech, and I suppose it must be allowed'.[89] But in terms of politics, religion and the monarchy, it continued to be free only so long as you were willing not to transgress boundaries, and to remain deferential towards certain taboos. Would the war alter that?

SECTION TWO
1939–1945

CHAPTER FIVE

'Everybody Bombs Babies Now'

Politics in Wartime

> Better make a small cut on p. 13 as we are at peace with fascist Spain, and anyhow everybody bombs babies now!
>
> (Reader's Report, February 1945)[1]

In the autumn of 1939, the Lord Chamberlain's office was evacuated from the vulnerability of St James's Palace to the safety of Windsor Castle. The Comptroller, Tim Nugent, was called to military duties, and Major Colin Gordon, who had retired from his post as Assistant Comptroller in 1936, returned as Acting Comptroller, until his death the following August. When war was declared, and in anticipation of imminent air raids, the government immediately prohibited 'all gatherings for purposes of entertainment and amusement' involving 'large numbers', and with theatres closed, it looked like being a quiet time for the Readers of new plays.[2] On 10 September, Game wrote to Windsor, hoping that a position could be found which would enable him to compensate for his anticipated loss of income and activity:

> There have already been, as you will have noticed, some slight signs of life from the ... Theatre; and I hope to God they come to something, as besides being financially disastrous it is very depressing to be idle these days. Personally I don't foresee more than a limited revival of entertainment in the evacuation areas. The black-out at night will make it impossible to open theatres and music halls except for matinees.

Game was not enjoying life in London: 'The black-out is extremely black', he reported, 'and it is easier than ever to get squashed by a bus; as some people have already found to their cost'. Nor was there much evidence yet of the famous national unity in adversity: 'Edgware Road is beset by footpads', complained the Reader. Gordon's reply on behalf of the Lord Chamberlain was not optimistic:

> I am afraid I cannot suggest anything for you here; in fact, you might be more bored than you appear to be in London, except that you would be further away from the footpads and the danger of being squashed by a bus.
>
> So far as Theatres are concerned I cannot visualise them re-opening in London unless there is some relaxing of the black-out arrangements, even for matinees.
>
> Meanwhile I will send you any plays that come in and let you know if it is advisable for you to return here at any time.[3]

It was not that theatre was seen as an unimportant activity in wartime. The decision to close the theatres on 4 September 1939 had been described by *The Times* as 'the heaviest blow that had struck the theatrical profession since September 2, 1642'.[4] The newspaper accepted the immediate necessity of closing theatres for a trial period: 'Until the dangers of modern aerial warfare to urban life have been more fully assessed, and our defences against them tested, it would be manifestly rash to permit any unnecessary assemblies of people in a confined space'.[5] But while accepting the decision, it argued that it was 'no less essential to review it at the earliest possible moment'. Indeed, a couple of days earlier a leader column had unreservedly endorsed the words of a former Dean of Rochester: 'When all hearts need uplifting and inspiring the door of the theatre should be set open as widely as the door of the church, that the hour of recreation as well as the hour of devotion may be rightly used to meet the human needs of the nation'.[6]

More provocatively, Bernard Shaw described the decision to close the theatres as 'a masterstroke of unimaginative stupidity', and even raised the question of whose interests the closure was designed to serve: 'What agent of Chancellor Hitler is it who has suggested that we should all cower in darkness and terror "for the duration"?'. *The Times* pointed out that by the middle of the First World War there had been more theatres operating than in peacetime, and Shaw argued that rather than closing them down it was the duty of the 'now all-powerful authorities' to do the exact opposite and to expand the number of theatres and cinemas.[7] Basil Dean, the director of ENSA, (the Entertainments National Service Association), agreed that

> the importance of entertainment's task in upholding the moral [sic] of the nation in wartime can scarcely be over-estimated, for in the modern holocaust the strain upon the occupants of what might be termed the civil trenches will be almost as great as that imposed upon those who man the firing posts.[8]

Dean called for the organisation and distribution of entertainment throughout the country to be taken over by a Central Entertainment Authority, which would be part of (and responsible to) the Civil Defence Administration. In the first week of the war, plans were announced to establish touring companies to take plays to areas where schoolchildren were being evacuated to, in order to contribute to their education. Others argued passionately for the cohesive and social value of 'home-made entertainment' in the extraordinary circumstances now prevailing:

> I am convinced that people (both young and old) in the new reception areas would not find the substitution of a rural for an urban background quite so strange if they could take part in some elementary musical or dramatic activity alongside their new neighbours.[9]

The Times was adamant that 'the maintenance of the theatre under war conditions is a national service', and that re-opening theatres must be seen as a priority:

> The theatre provides three necessities of civilized life—an art, a relaxation, and a livelihood. On its highest plane it is the shrine of one of the supreme arts, both the product and the aliment of the free civilization we are fighting to defend; to allow the enemy to deprive us of the enjoyment of great drama, even temporarily, is a measure of defeat. On the lower but still important level, the theatre in its lightest moods was found during the last War to supply one of the most valuable forms of solace and refreshment for nerves strained to their limit.[10]

As it gradually became clearer through the autumn of 1939 that the anticipated aerial bombardment was not for the moment to be unleashed, theatres across the country began to re-open. Within two weeks, the government had largely rescinded its banning orders and recommended that most places of public entertainment throughout Britain could open until 10.00 p.m. Part of central London was an exception, and venues within a mile and a half of Leicester Square were still required to close by 6.00 p.m., but before long that restriction too had been lifted. Some venues, such as London's Little Theatre, were ambitiously reported to be fully prepared to cope with an attack: 'This theatre has the good fortune to have beneath the stage an A.R.P. shelter capable of holding the audience several times over', reported *The Times*, 'and should the worst come to the worst, a piano has been installed'.[11]

The role of theatre and the stage during the Second World War has never been documented or subjected to a general analysis comparable to L.J. Collins's appraisal of their place in the First World War.[12] It is striking, and symptomatic, that an excellent collection of essays about the period produced in 1995 under the title *War Culture* addresses not only the role of cinema, cartoons, radio, art galleries and fiction, but also fashion and professional football, without having anything at all to say about theatre, other than in relation to Olivier's cinematic version of Shakespeare's *Henry V*. Yet from the very beginning of the war, live theatrical performance was identified as having a vital function, and the need to keep theatres open was seen as vital in helping to preserve national morale. By comparison with the 1914–18 war, its importance as an instrument for conducting overt political propaganda may have decreased, and cinema and radio had become as (or more) influential. But there was a rich and varied range of dramatic activity which was identified as contributing, not peripherally but centrally, to the war effort. ENSA, which had initially been formed in 1938 as a voluntary society but was now supported from a government grant established to provide amenities to the armed forces, was soon installed in new headquarters in the theatre at Drury Lane. From here, under the control of Basil Dean and Seymour Hicks, it could effectively co-ordinate the entertainment of troops. ENSA aimed mostly to entertain but also to educate the armed forces, through programmes which included not only variety acts and comedians, but also Shakespeare and ballet. Companies performed at army, navy and airforce bases within Britain and overseas and, by the end of 1943, ENSA was giving over 3,000 dramatic performances per week to the armed forces. According to the subsequent claim of its director, although film had initially been the most popular entertainment with the troops, this gradually changed, and live shows proved more efficacious:

> . . . as the war progressed, the demand for living personalities to relieve the tedium . . . grew in something like geometrical progression. Men and women divorced for long months from their normal lives sought unconsciously for the renewal of their humanity by contact across the footlights . . . Purpose was renewed, enthusiasm rekindled and the lift to morale noticeably greater by these means than in the case of mechanized entertainment.[13]

Possibly the human contact which troops sought may more often have been with comedians or singers rather than with actors in serious plays, but the historian Angus Calder cites a Mass Observation report suggesting that on occasions more 'straight stuff' was actually requested by some audiences.[14] Furthermore, in 1943, a Play Unit was set up by the Army Bureau of Current Affairs (ABCA), which reputedly gave fifty-eight performances to 20,000 troops in the first six months of its existence. Drawing heavily on Unity Theatre for both its writers and its theatrical forms, ABCA's propagandist slant was sufficiently radical to lead Churchill to investigate it for political bias.[15]

By January 1940, the Council for the Encouragement of Music and the Arts (CEMA) had also been established with government money. A roughly equivalent body to ENSA, CEMA's primary commitment was to organise touring performances for civilians in Britain. Its self-declared principle was 'to maintain the highest possible standard of the arts in war-time and to distribute them as widely as possible', and its achievements included sending Sybil Thorndike, Lewis Casson and the Old Vic Company on tour to Welsh mining villages, and to Lancashire and Durham; the Pilgrim Players and Mercury Players into village halls; Ballet Rambert into factories and hostels; and the Sadler's Wells Company into industrial towns.[16] Aside from the performances given under the auspices of ENSA and CEMA, traditional and temporary theatre spaces continued to function through the war; a glance at the scripts of melodramas inhabited by heroic Russians and fiendish Germans, or at the often naïve slogans in pageants celebrating Anglo-Soviet unity, provides plenty of evidence that in this field, too, theatre had an active role to play.[17] In a celebration of current mainstream theatrical activity in 1943, *The Times* described the range of work on offer in London as something of which 'no theatre, even one at the height of a dramatic Renaissance, would need to feel ashamed'. It claimed that audiences were flourishing, and theatres were 'hard pressed to entertain all who wish to be entertained'.[18] At the end of 1944, the newspaper reported that Shakespeare was 'enjoying more popularity on the stage than at any time since the days of Napoleon', and declared that 'this interest in our greatest genius argues a serious-mindedness which everyone who has anything to do with the educational side of service activities insists is more general and widespread than is commonly supposed'.[19] Nor was there any shortage of revue and lighter material. Overall, the point had certainly been well taken by the government that, as the Home Secretary told Parliament in 1942, 'entertainment and relaxation were needed to bolster efficiency in wartime', and that he therefore had 'no intention of imposing needless hindrances'.[20]

Many of the performances given by such organisations as ENSA, CEMA and ABCA were effectively excluded from the scope of the Lord Chamberlain, and fell under the auspices of the Ministry of Information and the government; apart from anything else, the Lord Chamberlain's authority did not extend beyond venues located within the British Isles. Moreover, since the first head of CEMA was in fact the Minister of Information (Lord Macmillan) it could be argued that beneath the government's unprecedented (and, since it led directly to the formation of the Arts Council, far-reaching) decision to fund the provision of art and entertainment, lay a strategic wish to ensure that these were subject to government control. Almost inevitably, state subsidy, however desirable, itself becomes a covert form of censorship. Equally, while it is true that even in peacetime it was not unusual for the Lord Chamberlain to seek 'advice' from government ministries, the practice greatly increased in wartime. In effect, the Ministry of Information and the armed forces were given powers of veto.

Other kinds of performance also escaped the Lord Chamberlain. Unity Theatre, through its variety arm, adopted the role of entertaining people forced to camp out at night in London's underground railway stations, and though their work relied to a great extent on cheering them up with music hall songs and revue sketches, these sometimes contained an immediate political dimension.[21] On another scale were some of the pageants and public performances presented after May 1942 in order to express and demonstrate Britain's support for its newest ally. The most spectacular of these was *Salute to the Soviet Union*, scripted by Louis MacNeice and staged in the Royal Albert Hall with not only the official support but even the participation of government ministers. The performance was certainly subjected to censorship, but this came directly from the cabinet, and it seems that the script was not at any point sent to the Lord Chamberlain's Office.[22]

In September 1939, supporting calls for theatres to be re-opened as soon as possible, *The Times* had proposed that 'they must, of course, be ready to submit cheerfully to many restrictions that in peacetime would be irksome'.[23] While the newspaper was thinking partly of issues such as starting times, provision of shelters and guarantees of quick evacuations, the notion of an instantly united Britain, speaking to itself in one voice and offering unanimous support to the war against Hitler, is a naïve one. In fact, changing political allegiances and situations were the subject of sometimes didactic theatrical performances, and the censors were always ready to intervene where they thought the effect of a performance might be subversive. Moreover, if theatre's key function was being identified as the maintenance of morale, then any play considered liable to have the opposite effect was likely to find itself in difficulty. There was a danger, too, that plays focused on contemporary events might, however patriotically intended, be at risk of giving military or other information to the enemy. Finally, the representation of leaders, politicians and national figures from other countries was always a focus of anxiety in the Lord Chamberlain's Office, and the potential for conflict and debate here was also considerable.

The decisions made were not necessarily always predictable. It is perhaps not too unexpected that in November 1939 the Office should have insisted in relation to a revue sketch: 'The acrobat in this scene must not be made up to resemble Stalin'. Perhaps it is more surprising to find that they also cut the line: 'Hitler, one, Goering, very small, Himmler, similar, Goebbels, none at all'.[24] But although newspaper cartoons were free to make fun of the Nazis in more or less any way they liked, the outbreak of war did not immediately lead the censors to abandon their presumed duty to preserve Hitler from mockery and insult. After all, there was a possibility that peace terms could be agreed quite quickly. In the summer of 1940, a successful prosecution was actually brought against a revue at Aldershot for adding to a song an unlicensed verse 'regarding the sticking of a pitchfork up a certain part of Hitler's anatomy'. Although ostensibly the prosecution was based on the fact that unlicensed lines had been added rather than on the nature of the lines, we can be certain that the content was significant to the decision to prosecute. Police evidence was given against the comedian

> who is dressed to represent the devil and carries a pitchfork in his hand. I noted the words of the verse sung by this person, which are as follows:
>
> > 'If I were not on the stage something else I'd like to be.
> > If I were not on the stage the devil I would be.
> > Stoke the fire up
> > Stoke the fire up.
> > Hitler's here at last.
> > If he does not get a move on I will poke this up his ——'
>
> It is not possible to hear the last word of this verse as at the time that it is sung a drum is struck by the Orchestra drummer and Pleon makes an upward motion with the pitchfork which is very suggestive.[25]

We might note in passing that the performer was not saved by the fact that he left the crucial part of his 'offending' line unsaid.

By September 1940, the Office was prepared to license for the Windmill a sketch which it had previously banned featuring both Hitler and Mussolini. However, the King of Italy had now been added to the scene, and this they were not happy with:

> I think this character should be altered. It would seem to me most unchivalrous to make fun of the poor little man, just because fortune has placed him in a humiliating position, and forced him for the time being technically to become our enemy.[26]

Moreover, while it might now be acceptable to represent Hitler, there were still limits regarding what could be said about him. Given the political context, some of these seem so trivial as to be barely credible. In September 1941, Game objected to 'a joke which reflects on the virtue of Hitler's mother', and asked for its removal: 'Personally I think it is a case of hitting below the belt and should not allow it'.[27] In December he objected to a similar joke in another show: 'I think it beneath our dignity to call our opponents bastards'.[28] Even in 1943, derogatory references to the private lives of German leaders were being cut on the grounds that it was 'beneath our dignity to be vulgar about the wives of the Nazi officials'.*[29] The depiction of the other European dictators was equally problematic. In March 1941, the Office refused to license a duet sung by Hitler and Stalin in one of Van Damm's revues.[30] The following month they refused to allow

---

* The play in question was *Downfall*, by Douglas Reed

a revue sketch entitled 'The Dictators'. 'This will have to be entirely re-written with Mussolini and Chamberlain eliminated', wrote Dearmer; he also queried: 'Possibly this should apply to Stalin too?'. The Office opted for the easy solution: 'Better ban the sketch. Hitler can't play alone!'.[31]

In May 1941 a licence was refused for *Cats and Dogs**—'A satirical fantasy in the form of a light opera; probably from the pen of some undergraduate'. The allegory drew on a struggle for power between Fiddler, the Dictator of The Dogs, and Ratin, the Castigator of the Cats:

> Fiddler and his lieutenants, Boring and Dropabrick, are Hitler, Goering and (I think) Ribbentrop. We can hardly object to that under the circumstances of war. Ratin, and his men Snoopin and Breadbasket, are to be identified as Stalin and one or other of the Russian leaders. This is a different matter, as we still maintain the semblance of diplomatic relations.

Some of the other equations also worried the censorship: 'Diablo seems to be Bernard Shaw, and the badgers the Americans and both are treated with very dubious respect', wrote Game. The censorship concluded:

> The author should be requested to prepare another version, in which any identification of Ratin and his lieutenants with Stalin and the Russian Statesmen, or of the Cats with the Russians, is made impossible. The same thing should also be done with Diablo and the Badgers.[32]

A similar ruling was made in the summer of 1941 in relation to *Exeunt the Dictators*,[†] which again included obvious embodiments of the leaders of Germany, Italy and the Soviet Union: 'There must be no character in the play resembling Stalin in view of the fact that the Russians are now our allies', ruled Clarendon.[33] In fact, the need to avoid causing offence in that direction escalated, and in July 1942 the Lord Chamberlain felt obliged to remove some references from a melodramatic thriller:[‡] 'To be on the safe side "Bolshevists" and "Bolshy" should be altered where they occur . . . as the term "Bolshy" is not used over here in a very flattering sense'.[34]

Predictably, there was great sensitivity about references to the royal family. Indeed, in March 1940 the censorship even threatened to clamp down on theatre clubs and withdraw the freedom which they had traditionally been granted. The Gate Theatre was planning a private production of *The Jersey Lily*, a historical play which focused on the 'not very elevating story of Edward, Prince of Wales'. The Office considered 'That it is not in the public interest, especially in these critical times, to stage a play which may in any way undermine the dignity of the crown'.

---

* Written by Winston Dean
† Written by J.B. Fell
‡ *Murder Without Crime*, by J. Lee Thompson

Although private performances had long been assumed to be outside the scope of the Lord Chamberlain, there was no actual basis in law to support this position, and Game now proposed warning the Gate 'That the production of the play will necessitate the reconsideration of the legal position of the Private Theatre'. When Gordon invited him to amplify the point, he explained:

> The position of the Private Theatre under the Theatres Act 1843 has never, as far as I know been legally determined. The official policy so far has been to let matters drift, the idea being that the Private Theatre affords a useful safety valve for disgruntled authors. This was, I believe, Lord Cromer's view, a typically English solution of the problem, and probably a wise one. But if, in these days of extreme licence in thought, speech, and authorship, plays, which are against the public interest, are to be produced . . . in these semi-private theatres, then sooner or later the legal standing of such theatres will have to be reconsidered. If not the position of the Censorship will become farcical!

He admitted, privately, that in the event of a court case, the Office's lenient attitude hitherto might 'be found to have weakened our position', but even to hint at the possibility provided a useful card for bluffing managers.[35]

In the same month, the Office received a letter of complaint about a performer appearing as 'Afrique' in a Moss Empires revue in Manchester. The letter accused the comedian of having 'quite clearly imitated the mannerisms of the Duke of Windsor which brought up immediately all the unfortunate talk of he should have been King and Mrs Simpson banished [sic]'. The complainant protested that he, like many others, disliked 'artists on the stage imitating any members of the Royal Family especially during the present crisis'. In fact, Afrique's act was not a new one, and successful attempts had been made some years earlier at the behest of the Lord Chamberlain's Office to have it excluded from a variety performance, even though this was not officially subject to his control. But in licensing the script for the revue, the Office had failed to notice that the figure to be impersonated was not specified, and the fact that it turned out to be the Duke posed an embarrasing problem. Gordon contacted the Chief Constable of Manchester, asking him to check Afrique's act for unlicensed interpolations:

> I have to inform you that no such item has been licensed, nor would the Lord Chamberlain have allowed it had it been submitted. Further, representations were made to this comedian regarding the elimination of this impersonation from his Act when it was being performed in a variety bill.

The actual holder of the licence was also asked about the act, and Alfred Black sent a deliberately vague and obfuscating reply on behalf of the General Theatre Corporation Ltd & Moss Empires: 'All that happens is that

Alfrique puts on a trilby hat, walks up and down the stage a couple of times—without a single word being uttered, and walks off the stage'. Gordon called this response 'an evasion', and contacted Black again: 'The description now given by you of what Afrique does is quite meaningless, unless it is explained who he is supposed to be impersonating'. Black continued to stonewall, refusing to give anything away:

> I regret to say that no further description can be given . . . No mention is made of whom the impersonation is to be, and it is left entirely to the imagination of the audience, and who they think it is, is entirely a matter of conjecture.

But writing, perhaps appropriately, on 1 April, the Chief Constable of Manchester reported on the scene in performance and the resulting confrontation:

> With regard to the impersonation given by the artiste at the conclusion of his performance, this he announced in the following words:– 'And my next impression, ladies and gentlemen, I leave entirely to your own imagination'. The impersonation which he then gave to an accompaniment by the orchestra of 'Rule Britannia' left no doubt whatever that his subject was the Duke of Windsor . . . I then told Afrique that to my knowledge his impersonation of the Duke of Windsor had not been licensed and he had therefore committed an offence under the Theatres Act, 1843, and he would be reported with a view to proceedings being taken against him. He replied:– 'In fairness to me, you must admit that there is nothing offensive in my impersonation, and besides who says it is the Duke of Windsor I impersonate? The audience might think it is Winston Churchill'. I told him that the question of the subject of the impersonation did not enter into the matter. He was reported for acting a scene before the same had been allowed by the Lord Chamberlain.

Gordon wrote again to Black, demanding that the impersonation should be excluded from the performance. He also encouraged the Chief Constable to institute legal proceedings:

> Such an impersonation has never been, nor would not be [sic] , allowed in any play licensed by his Lordship. As a matter of fact this is the type of offence which was responsible for the passing of the Theatres Act nearly a hundred years ago.

Meanwhile, he warned Buckingham Palace of the background to the case, and of the intention to issue a summons:

> In 1937 this same artiste, while on a tour of provincial Music Halls, started to give a similar impersonation. Although these performances did not come under the jurisdiction of the Lord Chamberlain, representations were made by my predecessor to the Association of Municipal

Corporations, and allied Bodies, with the result that the impersonation was discontinued.

A few days later, he received a reply:

> I have shown your Memorandum of yesterday, about the stage impersonation of the Duke of Windsor, to The King, who will be prepared for the publicity which will inevitably attach to the prosecution of Moss Empires Limited.
>
> His Majesty thinks it quite right for the prosecution to take place.

But although the prosecution was duly upheld in court at the end of May 1940, the Lord Chamberlain's Secretary, George Titman, was frustrated at the outcome:

> There were three defendants: Moss Empires, Ltd and George Black for presenting, and Alexander Witkin ('Afrique') for acting . . . The magistrate took a ridiculously lenient view of the matter and awarded penalties as follows:-
>
> George Black was fined 20/– + £5 5/ costs.
>
> Alexander Witkin ('Afrique')—fined 10/– total £6 15/ . . .
>
> Mr R.H. Gillespie, managing director of Moss Empires, was present at the hearing, and as he left the Court I discerned a 'smile on the face of the tiger'.
>
> A very disappointing result.

Clarendon agreed: 'Though it is satisfactory that convictions were procured I am sorry the penalties were not more severe'.[36] Perhaps some people thought there were more pressing matters to worry about.

As often seems to be the case during war, increased censorship was widely (if not universally) accepted as a necessary strategy. The newly formed Ministry of Information used its powers to control stories about the war in the press, and in the summer of 1940 an Emergency Regulation was passed which made it an offence for anyone to distribute any statement about the war 'likely to cause alarm or despondency'; examples of this regulation in action reportedly included the imprisoning of a Cardiff bricklayer for talk 'likely to create breaches of their duty among certain persons' and of a schoolteacher for teaching 'defeatist' theories to his pupils.[37] Such censorship was founded partly on the highly plausible belief that there were people on both the left and the right who, for different reasons, opposed the war. Mosley's Fascist Party, of course, allied themselves to the Nazis. But on the other side of the political spectrum were the activists and supporters of the peace movement which had developed in the thirties. Furthermore, although the left and the Communists had actively supported the International Brigade's defence of Spanish democracy against Franco, Hitler's pact of non-aggression with

Stalin caused confusion and reversals. Some were prepared to see the war as a distraction from the real fight which should be taking place against the class enemy, and were even ready to embrace the possibility 'that the defeat of Britain would create chaos in which a Communist coup would be possible'.[38] The government's nervousness in the early years of the war that the left was winning too much support in its demands for a 'People's Government' is evident in such decisions as the closing down of the *Daily Worker* in January 1941, and the covert instruction reportedly issued by the Ministry of Information to the BBC, requiring them to cease broadcasting J.B. Priestley's talks, on the grounds that they were too political.[39] The Ministry of Information established its own Film Censorship Division, and although both the press and the BBC more or less willingly self-censored in order to demonstrate that they were fully behind the war effort, the knowledge that the government could choose to impose more overt control may also have influenced their policies.

The Lord Chamberlain's Office was on its guard against anything it identified as dangerous and likely to influence audiences in unhelpful directions. In January 1940, the Women's Committee for Peace and Democracy submitted a script by C. Haldane and R. Swingler under the title *Children Calling*. Through a Commentator, a Chorus, and English and German working class families, the script offered a perspective on events in Europe between 1918 and 1938 which was described by the Reader as 'of a distinctly communist and pacifist complexion'. Game noted that the performance culminated 'with an appeal by a Chorus of the Unborn for the abolition of riches, poverty, and War, and the building of a better world'; however, he was supremely patronising about both the content and the form, and dismissive of the play's significance:

> This is one of those amorphous dramatic tracts—generally the work of some over-earnest female—which are intended to arouse us to instant action against the Forces of Evil and in this case the Wicked Capitalist in particular; but which, and it is perhaps as well, prove in the performance far less socially disruptive than a good marching song, such as the Marseillaise.
>
> The message to suffering humanity which this play ... seems to contain is 'Women of the World, Unite to Abolish War and Poverty!' An objective far more admirable than the means here used to attain the consummation of so desirable a millennium.
>
> It would be a mistake to take this flabby propaganda too seriously. This sort of production has a very limited appeal, as most people wisely prefer the cinema or the wireless; and less harm is done if such simple minds, as are these authors, are allowed to have their say without opposition.

Nevertheless, despite his confidence, he was not prepared to approve some sections, and changes were required to lines which impinged on and implicated British policy: 'there are certain statements . . . which as far as I know are mis-statements, or distortions, of fact, and which seem to me mischievous at the present time. I do not think we should set the official seal of our approval on them'.[40]

A few months later the censorship chose not to intervene in Merseyside Left Theatre's staging of Toller's *Requiem*, a poetic tribute in which the ghosts of Rosa Luxemburg and Karl Liebknecht return. Although the script was 'communistic', the Office decided it was 'too idealistic to be dangerous and too subjective to be subversive'.[41] Similarly, in the autumn of 1940 they decided it was unnecessary to censor an allegorical drama called *Freedom On Trial,*[*] which was to be staged at an event organised by the British Youth Peace Assembly. The script depicted several historical heroes of the left being arraigned in court as personifications of freedom, and ended 'with Youth's triumphant challenge to the Enemies of Freedom'. Game again saw no reason to reject it:

> I do not know who 'The British Youth Peace Assembly' are, probably Communists; but whatever or whoever they may be, this effusion is a harmless ebullition of idealist minds, too wide in its scope to be either topical or precise in its intention.

Clarendon accepted his recommendation, though he was not quite so blasé about the implications: 'Try and find out something about "The British Youth Peace Assembly" and their ideals', he ordered; 'If you cannot I will try'.[42]

Yet the Office's arrogance was combined with a surprising degree of nervousness. In the same month that Toller's *Requiem* was designated as safe, the censorship refused to license the third act of Sean O'Casey's explicitly pro-communist play *The Star Turns Red* for public performance by London's Unity Theatre; 'this play is subversive', wrote the Lord Chamberlain, 'and in view of the necessity of preventing anything of this nature in these dangerous times I cannot grant a Licence'.[43] In July 1940, he rejected another Unity application for a play called *The Second Helping.*[†] Heavily under the influence of the Communist Party, Unity was defining the current conflict as a capitalist enterprise and peddling the anti-war line which was necessitated by Hitler's pact of non-aggression with Stalin. This had been a difficult and a bitter line for many on the left to swallow, and *The Second Helping* reproduced some of the debate:

> After supper in a lower-middle class home. Father, Mother, a Son and an Aunt, argue about the war and its problems, Father with the unquestioning

---

* Author unknown
† Written by Robert Mitchell

resignation of the 'little man', Mother with the outraged sanity of a wife and mother, the son from the point of view of an egoist and Conscientious Objector, and the aunt as a selfish capitalist. Ultimately the discussion is put to an end by the return of the Daughter with the news that her young man has been killed.

Almost inevitably, the play ultimately endorsed the party's position:

> This being a Communist production the author tips the scales in favour of the pacifist and subversive characters . . . and the general effect of the play is to encourage such views in the mind of the beholder, rather than to strengthen any will to victory which he may have.

The question for the censorship was whether it was likely to have any real effect on audiences, and whether it was necessary to intervene. 'It is only fair to say that the whole thing is very mild propaganda', reported Game; 'In normal times we should pass the play without question'. Not now, however: 'but in these abnormal times the matter is not so simply dealt with . . . Its effect, if it has any, will be to weaken rather than to strengthen the country's resolution, and therefore it is not recommended for licence'. The Lord Chamberlain agreed that he was bound to take seriously any risk of promoting negative feelings about the war:

> Such propaganda, mild as it is, is calculated to impede our war effort. I suggest the best course would be to tell the Unity Theatre Society (a 'Left' Organisation) that the Lord Chamberlain is not prepared to issue a licence for it 'in existing circumstances'.[44]

Once Britain became an ally of the Soviet Union, Unity quickly reversed its position, producing several plays which attacked those sections of society and the establishment which they accused of sympathising with Hitler and of being reluctant to accept the Communist ally. Such attacks were hardly welcome on the stage. In the autumn of 1941, the Lord Chamberlain refused to license *The Spectre that Haunts Europe*, a Merseyside Unity Living Newspaper* in which scene after scene showed the British establishment—both in the past and in the present—as favouring the Fascists over the Communists. Understandably cynical about Unity's volte-face, Game was concerned about the intentions behind the script, and its likely effect:

> Two or three previous 'Newspapers' have been staged by the communists at their theatre in St Pancras, and I believe that we have licensed at least one of them. This particular Newspaper, which is full of the usual misleading historical half-truths, is supposed to be a warning against the fifth-column; but is in fact mostly an attack on certain public men, whom

---

* Written by George G. Banks

the Communists regard as their special enemies, coupled with vague warnings against certain unspecified persons in high places . . .

One of the unwritten rules of the censorship has been that no offensive personalities will be allowed. This rules out a good part of this play. But apart from that, does the pillorying of a number of probably quite harmless old gentlemen, and the mis-representation of the characters and aims of a deceased statesman, really strengthen our determination to win the war?

I think not, but rather that it is more likely to cause despondency and alarm—and class-hatred, which is no doubt the author's chief aim. I might add that an attack on the Fifth-Column comes ill from the Communists, until recently in effect their allies, and still giddy from their summersault from the anti- to the pro-war position![45]

In February 1942, the censorship excised lines in Unity's *Comrade Enemy** which referred to the need to 'fight the English Nazis', and which claimed that some people in Britain 'wouldn't be too sorry to see the Red Army in difficulties'.[46] In August, Game was agitated that another Unity Living Newspaper, *Lift the Ban,*† was designed to stir up trouble and internal conflict at a time when the country should have been united:

> This so-called play is nothing but propaganda . . . for getting the ban on the *Daily Worker* lifted . . . The play ends with an argumentative appeal to the Home Secretary to lift the ban and an emotional appeal to the audience to put pressure on him to do so. If we were still in the days of peace, I should recommend a licence being granted for the public production of this play, with some few excisions of course, following our usual policy based on the belief that hot air is better exhaled than bottled up. But in war time it is a different matter. This play attacks the Home Secretary, and encourages the class war, and its effect must be to disrupt, rather than to strengthen and cement, the common determination to see the war through to a victorious conclusion.

The script was sent to the Home Secretary, who, as so often, was more relaxed:

> After examination of the play he does not feel that it can be regarded as calculated to foment opposition to the prosecution to a successful issue of the war, and so far as the Home Office is concerned we can find no grounds for suggesting that a licence ought to be withheld.[47]

Perhaps his confidence was helped by knowing that the ban on the *Daily Worker* was about to be lifted, thus rendering the whole basis of Unity's attack rather pointless.

---

* Written by K. Penty and Alec Baron
† Written by Miles Tomalin

In February 1943, Unity came into conflict with the Lord Chamberlain again over *We Fight On*,* described by Game as 'A Communistic glorification of the International Brigade'. The focus was less on the Spanish civil war itself, and more on the spirit of the Brigade and its subsequent diffusion through political conflicts in Europe and beyond. In the opening scene, as the war in Spain ends, members of the Brigade pledge their support to a perhaps rather portentous declaration: 'We are returning to our respective countries for celebrations in our honour, not to rest, but to continue the fight we helped to wage in Spain; we are merely changing the fronts and our weapons'. This commitment is subsequently reinforced for the audience through the rhetoric of the play's narrator:

> And so the International Brigade fights on. The war against the evil forces of bestial capitalism, which started in Spain, has become a global one, and wherever the battle is raging, there you will find one of the Volunteers for Liberty to the fore.
> The living fight on; they take with them the spirit of those who died that Democracy might live; the unconquerable spirit of their comrades who gave their lives in the shell holes of Jarama, Teruel and the Aragon, to defend their native countries from the coming storm.

Game reported that 'most of the scenes are unexceptionable', but suggested that the Foreign Office should be consulted, since one scene in Spain and another in a North African concentration camp 'impinge on two rather ticklish international relationships'. The Foreign Office duly required both scenes to be excised:

> the first on the ground that it ridicules the Head of the Spanish State and might, with some justice, give rise to a protest from the Spanish Government, and the second on the ground that it would be likely to involve us in difficulties, not only with the Spanish Government, but with the United States authorities and the French administration in North Africa, with both of whom we have already had a good deal of trouble on this and connected issues.

In fact, the Foreign Office disliked the whole script, but recognised that it might be counter-productive to have it entirely suppressed:

> The whole theme of the play, and in particular the opening references to the Battle of Jarama are distinctly unfortunate from our point of view, as they revive the issues of the Spanish Civil War, external and internal, which are much better left to rest in peace. But clearly any attempt to ban the whole play at this stage would cause even greater difficulties than may arise from its production. So we do not wish to press for more than the

---

* Written by S.T. Frieze

removal of the two scenes mentioned in the preceding paragraph, to which
we attach considerable importance.

Unity submitted revised versions of the censored scenes—amongst other
things, they deleted all references to Franco—and claimed that the motive
of the play was to support the struggle against fascism: 'There is no attempt
to offend any country or nationality and the message of this show . . . is to
whip up the enthusiasm against the Nazis, which is expressed in all the free
countries of the world'. But Clarendon refused to negotiate or to
reconsider.[48]

Although many saw the primary role of theatre in wartime as being to
distract audiences from the reality around them, there were some attempts
to reflect and pay tribute to how people were living in contemporary
Britain. In January 1942, the Office licensed a patriotic drama entitled *We
Are the People:** 'A realistic and moving picture of the reactions of a working
class family in a North West industrial town to the horrors of the total war
. . . [which] pays a richly deserved tribute to the cheerful heroism of so
many of our people'. Game even proposed incorporating an additional little
dig at those who refused to fight by altering the always dubious word
'pansies', as a term of abuse, to 'conshies'. However, another version of the
text, submitted a few months later, contained an extra line which was not
permitted; Stan, a conscientious objector, protests that 'they pack us off to
some outpost of Empire without guns, or tanks or planes'. Even though the
sympathies of the play were not with the speaker, the censors required this
accusation to be deleted: 'Stan . . . might well make a bitter statement such
as this, but to my mind it has just enough truth in it to make it an unhelpful
criticism'.[49]

German aerial attacks on British cities also produced a spate of plays. In
October 1941, the Office licensed *The Morning Star*, Emlyn Williams's play
about London under the Blitz. It was, said Game, 'distinctly grim at times
and I should have thought an unsuitable entertainment; but there is no
accounting for tastes'.[50] By the following summer, the genre was well
established and popular, though not without its critics. In August 1942,
Game described *London West One*† as relying for its interest on 'a realistic and
violent air-raid, and the usual but less dramatic local colour, which are
becoming inseparable in a play about Londoners in wartime'. Picking up on
recent views, Game expressed his dislike of such plays: 'I must say I rather
agree with Mr Agate when he questions the good taste of these commercial
dramatists who are busy exploiting the tragedies of war'. But he

---

* Written by A. Burton Cooper
† Written by Aimée Stuart

acknowledged that it was not up to the censorship to intervene on those grounds: 'the public have the remedy in their own hands. If they disapprove, they can stop away from the theatres'; and he admitted that 'As they flock to such plays as *The Morning Star*, they evidently do not disapprove'.[51]

Agate's argument actually provoked *The Times* into responding with a leader column entitled 'War on the Stage'. More willing to condone the propagandist, celebratory and jingoistic nature of the genre condemned by Agate, the article challenged the right of the critics to object to such work on ethical grounds:

> It would seem that dramatic critics have lately had a moral problem thrust upon their consciences. A flush of plays reflecting the work of the Royal Navy, the Air Force, and the Merchant Service has set them wondering how far the theatre may be justified in making dramatic grist out of the lives of our fighting men . . . In war-time, the conscience-stricken argue, it is not a minority but a majority of every audience which has a personal interest in the fighting men and would deem intolerable any unworthy image of their lives.
>
> It is popularly believed that dramatic critics have no conscience, but the qualms they now appear to be suffering suggest that, on the contrary, they have too much.

The Times insisted that critics should confine themselves to analysing imaginative and artistic weaknesses, and avoid suggesting that the lives of fighting men were an inappropriate subject for the stage. Productions in which narrative and characterisation failed to match 'the plausibly constructed background of crashing aircraft and blazing ships' were 'occasions of failure in art, not of sins against decency'; indeed, 'Only by an excessive activity of the conscience, or by a confusion of thought, can the problem that troubles them be considered a moral problem'.[52] Since the press was far closer to the state than it would have been in peacetime, it is probably safe to assume that the government would have endorsed the article's tone and was happy to view such plays as patriotic and useful rather than exploitative.

Alternative perspectives were less welcome. The historian Angus Calder long ago demonstrated that the narrative of the Blitz, which shows the British people as stoical, united and almost unmoved, is a fabricated and partial construction. Probably the best-known of the Crown Film Unit's accounts of the bombardment, commissioned by the Ministry of Information for presentation in America, was *London Can Take It*—shown in a shorter version at home as *Britain Can Take It*. Citing its narrator's calm assurance that 'there is no panic, no fear, no despair in London Town', Calder comments that it is 'hard to believe now that such blatantly propagandist assertions were ever accepted as the factual observations of a neutral'.[53] Theatre clearly had its ordained part to play in confirming (or at least not challenging) the agreed view, and the need to control anything which failed to conform is evident in relation to a Glasgow Unity play, *The Night of the Big Blitz*.* In March 1941, Clydeside had been subjected to heavy aerial bombardments; two nights of raids had killed 500 people and injured 800, and almost every house had been damaged. A later historian suggests that Clydeside was known as a place where 'continued bitterness between employers and employed had remained strongest, and where there was still a great sense of remoteness from the war'.[54] The heavily positive reports issued by the Home Intelligence after the bombings suggested that the attack had encouraged the people of Glasgow to experience 'much greater interest in and enthusiasm about the news than is usual' and 'A new feeling of partnership with the English blitzed cities'.[55] Unity's play stood in partial conflict with this comforting analysis, and Game drew attention to 'a misleading speech on economics', and to some 'unhelpful statements' about attitudes to the war. The 'misleading speech' occurs when someone casts doubt on the truth of government statements about the economy:

> You remember in the pre-war days the struggle they used to have balancing the Budget. It was a tremendous feat balancing the Budget. Couldn't give sixpence to the unemployed or it wouldn't have balanced. Now they don't bother to go through with that farce. The Budget doesn't balance by hundreds of millions. But nobody's any the poorer. In fact there never was so much money going around. And is there any sign of us going bankrupt? . . . Of course they've got to keep up the face by making periodic collections for Tank weeks and Warship weeks to deceive you into thinking that money's still important.

The 'unhelpful statements' were claims that 'There's plenty folk here in this country who'd rather lose the war than win the peace', and that 'They can talk till doomsday; but I don't see Winnie Churchill and Jo Stalin agreeing about the peace'. Game commented:

> The first is certainly not true. There may be some who prefer defeat to the political uncertainties of the future, but after the experience of the French there cannot be many; and the second, although naturally one cannot expect the PM and Stalin to see eye to eye, is a falsification of fact by simplification of statement.

But on balance, the reader's tactical recommendation was to avoid too heavy an intervention:

> I expect worse things are said at by-elections, and these Unity Plays are performed mostly to audiences whose minds are already set. Even in war

---

* Written by James Barke

time, except in cases where we can pin down an obvious mis-statement of fact, it is wisest, I think, for the Censorship, associated as it is with the Crown, to support the rule of freedom of political utterance.

However, the censorship did insist on cutting one scene in *The Night of the Big Blitz* in its entirety. This was 'the Mortuary scene', which reads now as the best and by far the most disturbing scene of the play. Bleak, brief and savagely comic, it is set in a temporary mortuary in a bombed out church hall. A woman in search of her husband's remains roots urgently through a pile of unidentified bodies as though sorting through clothes at a jumble sale in search of the best deals: 'Steady there, mistress', says the attendant; 'This isn't the bargain counter'. Having supposedly found the body and taken it away in a coffin, she returns with it at the end of the scene: 'I took the wrong man. His mother recognised it wasn't him'. Others cannot bring themselves even to come into the hall to look for the bodies of loved ones: 'It's worse than death should be', declares one woman. Meanwhile, a working man, Dunlop, who has already searched in vain through a dozen mortuaries, arrives to look for the body of his wife and children:

> I told her to go to the shelter if the sirens went. I'm on night shift. We copped it pretty bad. When I got home in the morning she wasn't there. Not a trace. And I knew she'd taken the weans to her mother's. Not a bomb fell anywhere near Moor Street; not even an incendiary. I went round to her mother's—nothing but a heap of rubble.

Eventually he finds the bodies, and his emotion comes out in the form of an appalling anger directed against his wife:

> (*He speaks with a strange harshness*) So you went to your mother's after all I said, eh? What was the last thing I said to you? But you paid no attention. You never did, damn you! Well, you're with your mother now. And the bairns. You're all with your mother. I hope you're satisfied. You'll be happy now. If it wasn't—

It seems as if only the attendant prevents him from venting his anger physically on the dead body, and this provokes another confrontation in which he abandons the bodies of his loved ones:

> ATTENDANT: Steady, mate, steady.
> DUNLOP: Who asked you to interfere? I suppose a man can get talking to his wife even if she is—
> ATTENDANT: Take it easy.
> DUNLOP: Take it easy? Shut your trap or I'll paste it in for you.
> ATTENDANT: I know how you feel, mate.
> DUNLOP: Don't mate me. <u>You</u> know how I feel? (*He walks towards the door*)
> ATTENDANT: Are you making any arrangements?

DUNLOP: (*Turning as he indicates the mortuary*) That's what you're paid for.

The scene ends with the undertaker and the attendant, unable to cope with the pain and horror, going off to drink whisky together, while the sound of a siren signalling another imminent air-raid is heard from off-stage. Game described the scene as 'unseasonable realism' and its humour as being 'in execrable taste'. It certainly did not fit with the image of steadfastness in adversity that the Ministry of Information was keen to promote. Indeed, the mortuary scene questioned whether Britain could, in fact, 'take it'—or at what cost.[56] Such a question was too dangerous to be allowed.

Even more serious was the risk of giving significant information or encouragement to the enemy. Reporting in 1941 on *The Morning Star*, Game noted 'a reference to the bombing of Buckingham Palace, which I mention because I cannot remember whether there has been any announcement in the Press of the Queen being bombed'. On the stipulation of the Home Office, they also removed a reference to landmines, a word which was evidently banned from the press.[57] A similar reference was removed the following year from *To Dream Again*,* a fantasy in which Shakespeare, 'uneasy at the sounds of battle rising to Heaven from this "Sceptred Isle" descends to earth'; Game noted: 'if "landmine" is still taboo it must be erased from the script here', adding, 'It seems absurd, but ours not to reason why'.[58] Again, the Reader queried in connection with *London West One*: 'I suppose the Germans know about all these details of buildings destroyed in London? If there is any doubt a phone call to the MOI seems indicated'. A subsequent memorandum recorded that cuts would be made in line with the policy of the Ministry of Information and the Air Ministry: 'For "landmine" substitute "bomb", and the sound in Act Two p. 69 must be that of a bomb . . . omit Victoria Station, St Pancras and King's Cross'.[59] Even in 1944, Game queried a reference to a landmine in *The Road That Beckons*:† 'does the Air Ministry still fuss about such things?', he asked. Evidently they did, and the reference was amended to 'flying bomb'.[60] Detailed modifications required by the Air Ministry in connection with Flight Lieutenant Terence Rattigan's *Flight Path* included (for no obvious reason) the substitution of Littlehampton for Margate.[61] The same ministry also intervened over *Tomorrow's Eden*,‡ though they appear only to have found out about this play after it had been licensed and was in performance:

> Strong exception is taken to two sentences . . . by the leading character, a Squadron Leader, to the effect that the only way in which Bomber crews

---

* Written by Veronica Haigh
† Written by Guy Vaesen
‡ Written by M. Charles and D. Sutherland

could keep going—owing to the intense strain—was to go up to London, and get drunk, and return by the 'drunk special' (actual words). The next sentence talks about living on drink and drugs . . . it is considered that the sentences complained of represent Bomber crews in a completely false manner, cause resentment in the RAF and damage its reputation in the eyes of the public.

The censors were reluctant to act against a play which had been running for several months without any other complaints, so the authors were quietly persuaded to make voluntary amendments—even though they insisted that the lines were being misinterpreted.[62]

In the case of *The Admiralty Regrets*, it was the naval authorities who became involved in censorship. The play was written by Sir Patrick Hastings, a respected barrister and politician as well as a playwright, who had served as Attorney General in Ramsay Macdonald's first Labour government of 1924. Game described it as 'An exciting naval thriller', but recommended that the script should be sent to the Director of Naval Intelligence. Here, there was serious unease at the military details which Hastings had included:

> I regret to say that, for technical reasons, it is considered undesirable that this play should be licensed for public performance . . . censorship, from the technical aspect would have to be so drastic that it seems that the play would be ineffective after such censorship.

Hastings submitted a revised version, but the Admiralty still had reservations: 'Greater emphasis requires to be laid upon the fact that the scene of the play is laid during the last war and not the present war', it insisted. The letter listed further details and references which it wished to see altered or removed:

> the tactical employment of the 'cue' ships . . . Civilian passengers in hospital ships, and the statement about carriage of guns and arms in hospital ships . . . the methods of interrogation of prisoners, particularly suggestions of an ill-treatment and making prisoners drunk . . . all remarks referring to anti-submarine range and classification of the optic . . . the use of the word 'echo'; all details of attack on the submarine . . .[63]

Eventually the Admiralty's Director of Anti-Submarine Warfare went through the text with Hastings and produced a script which could be approved.

Also rejected in 1942 because of the secret and potentially dangerous military information it contained was *To Stall the Grey Rat*,[*] which had been scheduled for the Globe Theatre by Tennent and Beaumont productions.

---

[*] Written by Mary Bell

Set in Occupied France, it showed British airmen carrying out clandestine operations from their base in a disused mill on the French coast, including organising escape routes for soldiers trapped in the country. Game assumed it was probably 'A work of pure imagination, . . . not inspired by any exact knowledge' and that it 'probably gives nothing away'; but he added 'obviously we are not in a position to judge', and recommended sending it to the Director of Military Intelligence in the War Office, who would 'probably know if there is any organisation for getting men out of France, and who deals with such matters'. Understandably, the War Office took the matter extremely seriously, apparently irrespective of whether there was much truth in the specific details contained in the plot:

> It is very undesirable that any publicity whatsoever should be given to incidents connected with escapes. The constant re-iteration of this theme undoubtedly serves to draw the enemy's attention to the subject, with the inevitable tightening up of measures designed by him to prevent them, thereby prejudicing the chances of future escapers.
>
> There is already a complete stop on all escape stories of British personnel in the Press, and everything possible is being done to include in this ban fiction or films and broadcasts which are in any way near the truth.
>
> For these reasons I hope that you will be able to prevent the production of this play.

Beaumont was informed that the licence was being refused at the express wishes of the Director of Military Intelligence, and a revised script was submitted for the Edinburgh Lyceum a couple of months later under the new title of *Men in Shadow*. Game reported on it:

> This is a new version of a play which was recently banned because the DMI objected to its theme—the adventures of some men engaged in helping airmen and others to escape from Occupied France
>
> In explaining why he wished the play suppressed, the DMI expressed a wish that, if it were found impracticable to ban the play in its entirety, certain amendments should be made in the dialogue. To meet all these objections the authoress has now made alterations in her play.
>
> The incidents which take place on the stage remain the same, but the leading characters are no longer supposed to be members of an organisation concerned with helping men out of the country. Their activities are now confined to sabotage, the assassination of German officials like Heydrich, the organisation of the 'V' Army . . . and the lending an occasional hand in Commando raids. Whether the DMI will consider such activities innocuous from the Intelligence point of view I cannot say.

Perhaps surprisingly, this script was licensed after only minor amendments; evidently it had been the focus on escape, and especially the co-ordinated planning of escapes, which was seen as risky.[64]

Predictably, the censorship had little time for the sympathetic depiction of those who refused to fight, but such characters were not automatically banned—provided they were not too persuasive. In February 1942, the Office patronisingly approved Fay Myddleton's *This Dreamy Waste*:

> Why do earnest but sloppy minded females write sickly sentimental twaddle about conscientious objectors ... I suppose because they are earnest and sloppy minded, but as we allow conscientious objectors we must allow plays to be acted about them, and in fact I do not think our morale is so weak as to be in the slightest degree affected.[65]

But in October of the same year, they refused to license Joe Corrie's *Dawn*, which was set in and around German and English working-class homes just before and during the war. Game reported:

> There is nothing in the narrative as such to which we can take exception, but the author's treatment of his theme is quite another matter. He is presumably a pacifist, anyhow he is at pains to excite sympathy for his pacifist characters to the disadvantage of those who are ready to help their country in a healthy mood of bellicosity. Pacifists are sometimes deeply sincere people and are no doubt worthy of respect, but this seems hardly the moment to exalt them as the real heroes of the War.
>
> The play in so far as it has any effect, is likely either to irritate or depress the audience and certainly will do nothing to fortify their morale.
>
> The promoters have evidently felt that some passages went too far and have blue-pencilled them themselves.
>
> I suggest that the Lord Chamberlain will do well to go one better and ban the whole thing.[66]

The banning was widely reported in the Scottish press, and the play's producer insisted that the company had been 'completely surprised by the announcement'. She explained:

> Personally there seemed to me nothing in the play that could raise objection to it. It is the story of two families, one English, the other German ...
>
> Neither of the sons want to fight. The young German's fiancée is an English girl. The story comes back to the mother in each case, and I think the theme might be summed up as suggesting that all mothers think the same way about war.
>
> Mr Corrie does not spare the Nazis ... Hitler, the Gestapo, and all their works are ruthlessly dealt with. But *Dawn* suggests that there are good Germans still living.[67]

Titman wrote to the theatre on behalf of the Lord Chamberlain, explaining the rationale and the context of the decision:

> It seems clear that the author's purpose was to excite the sympathy of the audience in favour of his pacifist characters and their views in contrast with the bellicose patriotism of more normal youth.

His Lordship has during the past few years licensed plays in which the
point of view of the pacifist or conscientious objector has been
sympathetically expressed; but he does not consider that it would be
helpful to a vigorous prosecution of the war to license a play in which the
purpose of the argument appears to be to exalt the pacifist or conscientious
objector into a hero, and to exhibit the ordinary patriotic young man or
woman in as unfavourable a light as possible.

When Corrie asked what he could do in order to secure a licence, he was
informed that the Lord Chamberlain 'regrets that he would have no
suggestions to make whereby the play could be altered or re-written in
such a way as to make it suitable for public performance at the present
time'. A Labour MP took up the issue in January 1943: 'I hardly think that
appeals from the stage or the platform have the effect of influencing youths
in the way suggested', wrote Rhys J. Davis. But Clarendon's reply to 'this
inquisitive MP' was unyielding:

> *Dawn* . . . is obviously propaganda, the author being at pains to show his
> pacifist characters in a very sympathetic light in contradistinction to
> normal bellicose youth, which is made to look almost ridiculous. The
> Censorship has to proceed on the assumption that the Theatre does to
> some extent exert a cultural influence upon the public mind, and in my
> view the effect of such special pleading, as in this play '*Dawn*', cannot but
> be detrimental to a vigorous morale. I am not therefore prepared to license
> the play at a moment when we are fighting for our lives, and when
> depressing and emasculating views are certainly not helpful to the victory
> we all desire

A separate area of political sensitivity was the portrayal of Britain's
allies—and in particular the French. In November 1942, Game reported on
Roly-Poly, 'a very free adaptation' of Guy de Maupassant's *Boule de Suif*,
transposed to 1940 and incorporating a German officer.* He worried that,
given recent history, it would be taken by the French as an insult. 'The
author . . . has gone out of his way to make it topical', he noted, suggesting
that in this version 'de Maupassant's tale becomes something in the nature
of anti-French propaganda'. Game suggested it was 'not the moment to
produce such a play', and offered a somewhat condescending explanation
of his position:

> The play satirises certain types that are not as uncommon in the France of
> to-day as one might wish, though one gathers that material loss at the
> hands of the enemy is converting many amongst them to the advantages of
> patriotism; but is this the moment for such a satire? The free French
> amongst us are quite as aware as we are of the egotism and materialism

---

* Written by Lennox Robinson

amongst their people, which has helped to bring about their downfall; but will they care to be reminded of the fact? I doubt it.

The licence was refused, and when a revised version was submitted early in 1943, Game reminded the Lord Chamberlain that the original script been turned down because 'it seemed a somewhat tactless moment in which to give the supine French a kick'. The later version returned the action to 1870, and Game could no longer find reasonable grounds on which the ban could legitimately be maintained. But he still preferred to pass the buck:

> I do not think from the Censorship point of view we can object to the play . . .
> Beyond wider implications which concern human nature in general, de Maupassant in particular satirises certain types of French society, who one would imagine would still be held in contempt by all patriotic Frenchmen. But French psychology is quite beyond my understanding, and I cannot usefully advise the Lord Chamberlain as to how any free French in our midst, who may chance to see this play or to hear of its production, are likely to react. Perhaps someone in the Foreign Office could help us?

Clarendon sent the script to the Foreign Office, which in turn consulted Charles Peake, the British representative on the French National Committee. Peake was forthright in his opposition:

> I have no doubt at all that its presentation upon the stage during the times we are living in would cause the gravest offence to the Fighting French in this country, and not to them alone. I do not think the fact that the scene is laid in the France of 1870 and that the original idea was contained in a story written by a Frenchman, nor the fact that the story is itself a masterpiece would alter the situation from the French point of view. I have no doubt at all that they will think their country and their people are being gratuitously insulted. The fact is that the France of 1870 has passed away, and to bring back so crude and cruel a representation of one aspect of it, while there are Frenchmen here who, whatever their faults—and I admit they are many—have given up everything to fight at our side, and who, in many cases, have had to leave their wives and children in a German-occupied France, is both unwise and uncalled for.

Clarendon had little option other than to refuse the licence again. Even in June 1945, a further attempt to secure a licence for *Roly-Poly* failed, despite the fact that it had been broadcast on radio. The Foreign Office argued as strongly as ever that it would be politically inexpedient to allow a public performance, and the potential attributed to a stage adaptation of a nineteenth-century French classic in the context of post-war negotiations and settlements is remarkable indeed. If the political significance of theatre was declining, then its demise had hardly been recognised in diplomatic circles:

I still think that it would be inadvisable to let this play be performed on the English stage in present circumstances. Anglo-French relations have been a good deal strained lately by our inability to do more to help the French in the economic field and by events in Syria. De Gaulle is in a particularly intransigent mood and there seems to be a widespread feeling among the French that we are bent on relegating them to a secondary role in world affairs. We in the Foreign Office are doing all we can to overcome these difficulties, for we regard close and friendly relations with a strong France as an essential factor in our own future security. It is, however, an uphill task at the moment and the French are more than ever on the lookout for imagined slights and insults. The production of *Roly-Poly* in the near future might be regarded by many Frenchmen as a calculated attempt to discredit their country and thus cause us some political embarrassment.

I therefore hope that you can see your way to a further postponement of *Roly-Poly*, at least until next year. By then our present difficulties with France may have been resolved and the question of the treatment of collaborators should be a less burning one.[68]

The text remained unlicensed.

There was uncertainty as to whether such sensitivities needed to be extended to all things French. In October 1943, Game's report on *That Freedom** referred to 'some rather rude things' being said about Henri Philippe Pétain, the French Marshal and Nazi collaborator, by a 'Communistic' young woman. 'I don't know exactly what the Foreign Office line is about the Marshall, but the speeches are in character and the production obscure, so I doubt whether it matters'. In the margin someone added: 'Pétain's behaviour not only as regards his former ally, but his own countrymen has been scandalous. Why should he be protected? The production is in a Village Hall!'.[69] Yet in January 1944, Game queried in relation to *The Bowl of Night*,† a play focusing on French patriots: 'I don't know whether Pétain is still under our protection. If he is, his name and picture had better be altered to that of the hated Laval'. This time—possibly as a result of representations following the previous case—the Lord Chamberlain decreed that Pétain's name and photographs should be omitted.[70]

One play which evidently irritated the French when it was licensed at the end of 1944 was Irwin Shaw's *The Assassin*, a 'romantic drama written round the assassination of Admiral Darlan', and described by Game as an 'apocryphal treatment of recent history'. The young American playwright had been in Algiers with the army in 1942 at the time of the assassination of François Darlan, the former right-wing collaborator with the Nazis and Vice-Premier in the Vichy government. The circumstances of the real-life

---

* Written by Phoebe Rees
† Written by Roger Williams

murder were still unclear, but although the play inserted imaginary names and fictionalised elements within its melodramatic narrative, the central event—the assassination of an Admiral Vespery by a French royalist—was too recognisable for Shaw's interpretation to be dismissed as fiction. As Beverley Baxter's review put it when the play eventually opened in London in March 1945: 'this play is not only for the theatre, but is intended as a contribution to contemporary history'.[71] Moreover, while the foreground of the narrative concentrates on the royalist who commits the murder in the hope that it will save the life of the woman with whom he is in love, the background focuses on the intrigues of corrupt and sinister Vichy officials, and their struggles with the underground de Gaullist movement. Indeed, it is one of the corrupt generals who instigates and tricks the young royalist into committing the assassination, hoping to seize power and establish his hero as King of North Africa and subsequently of France. *The Assassin* therefore dabbled in some murky waters. When it was first submitted towards the end of May 1944, the Reader suggested: 'as far as I can see there is nothing to which either the Americans or the French can reasonably object'. The Foreign Office saw it differently. There were two issues which concerned them—the likely impact on French–American relationships, and the risk of exposing something which Sir Alexander Cadogan, the Chief Adviser to the Foreign Office and one of Churchill's most trusted diplomats, believed would be better left interred:

> I must say straight away that on general political grounds I see considerable objection to the play being produced in public at the present juncture. The assassination of Darlan . . . is a matter which still rouses bitter controversy here and amongst Americans as well as amongst Frenchmen. The subsequent execution of his assassin is an even more controversial matter. We do not know to this day the inner history of his fate nor to what extent, if any, the American authorities were involved: indeed we have always felt that it might be embarrassing for all concerned if we were to probe too deeply into the question. If . . . Mr Irwin Shaw's play were to be given a public performance now, the whole sordid Darlan story would be dragged into the limelight again and old passions revived at a moment when it is more important than ever before for Frenchmen to pull together and to forget their past differences with the Americans and ourselves . . .
>
> We are having a good deal of trouble trying to explain away the bad reputation of American troops among the French in North Africa and it would not help matters to have their misunderstandings with the local inhabitants represented on the London stage.

In July, a revised version was submitted, and Game recommended that the Foreign Office should be consulted again: 'I think we should write to them and ask whether the recent accord between the American government and General de Gaulle modifies their objections'. Yet even though the play was about to be staged in America, Cadogan and the Foreign Office remained reluctant to allow it in Britain:

> I still feel that it would be inopportune for this play to be produced in London at the present juncture . . . . It is one thing for the Americans to blacken their own people on their own stage, but they may not feel the same way about it if we allow the process to be undertaken first over here.

But at the start of December, apparently following a direct appeal from the play's putative producer, Frith Shepherd, to the Secretary of State, Sir Alexander Cadogan informed the Lord Chamberlain that the Foreign Office no longer wished to oppose a licence:

> In view of all that has passed in France since we first asked you to withhold permission for the play, the Secretary of State feels that the political objections which we raised at the time have lost some of their strength. We are therefore prepared to reconsider our objections.[72]

However, Cadogan still maintained that it was 'important that the New York production should precede the London production', and he also insisted on examining the script once more in order to make amendments 'In the interests of Anglo-United States relations', and 'so as not to draw attention to the ideological differences between the Americans and the De Gaullists'. When Shaw's play finally opened at the Savoy Theatre in March 1945, it seems still to have provoked the French. At the conclusion of a letter to the Lord Chamberlain the following June, (in which they recommended that *Roly-Poly* should not receive a licence), the British Foreign Office told him:

> I might add that the French Ambassador was rather upset by the production of *The Assassin* (to which, as you will remember, we reluctantly agreed last year) and made an unofficial protest at the Foreign Office about it. I expect that he would react more strongly to *Roly-Poly*.[73]

At a more farcical level, concerns over insulting the Americans had also surfaced in 1944, when the Lord Chamberlain rather bizarrely attempted to intervene after receiving a complaint from a clergyman about a scene in a revue. He requested that the police in Bristol viewed the performance of 'A Lonely Yank' in *Showtime*, and it was their detailed report on the acting style to which the Office responded:

> In my opinion, Lester's representation was such as might conceivably cause offence to United States' subjects. He slouched on the stage in a most undignified manner, his shoulders were slumped together, his back was badly bent and his stomach 'caved in'. In short, he presented the picture of a very poor specimen of American manhood, and the fact that he continually chewed something in a very exaggerated manner did

nothing to relieve it. I feel that, in certain circumstances, unfortunate circumstances might result from such a representation. One can easily imagine, for example, that a party of American soldiers present in a theatre where the revue is shown, might give some very tangible expression to their disapproval of Lester's conception of one of their kind.

When the censors informed the theatre that 'The Lord Chamberlain cannot permit this', the manager asked with understandable irritation: 'How can I be expected to define the correct limits of slouching, slumping or chewing?'. Having no wish to stir up a hornet's nest of satire against himself, Clarendon effectively backed down, and the manager was informed that he was 'prepared to leave a moderation of the "business" to your discretion'.[74]

More seriously, in February 1945, sensitivities towards Polish nationals necessitated significant interventions by the censorship in relation to two plays, *Beyond the Mountain*[*] and *Jacobowsky and the Colonel*.[†] In the former, an Englishman dreams of capturing Hitler and handing him over for punishment, but it was the identity and behaviour of those doing the punishing which worried the censors, and Game recommended the text should be rewritten so as to

> make the character Count Czerny, of indefinite nationality rather than a Pole as at present, as he is one of Hitler's tormentors—not that most Poles wouldn't like to have the chance to get a bit of their own back; but they might object to being singled out as the Villains of the piece . . . though we share the honour with them.[75]

Jacobowsky and the Colonel was an even more provocative political comedy, which had already been staged in America, and which poked fairly mild fun at the actions and attitudes of an aristocratic Polish colonel in exile in France who, as the Germans approach once again, is now trying to escape to England. His outrageously selfish behaviour is contrasted with that of another Pole from a much poorer background, who is used to being persecuted and who manages to combine good-humoured and earthy innocence with an ability to stay calm and do the right thing. The two find themselves as unlikely allies in their efforts to escape the German invasion and reach England. To most people, the play might have seemed a gentle if unlikely piece of escapism, but Game's embarrassingly patriotic report highlighted the problem with it:

> A play which is both extremely entertaining and at times exciting, but unfortunately there is more to it than that, there is the Polish problem!

---

[*] Written by A.C. Stevenson Cottam
[†] Written by S.N. Behrman

The author, no doubt, intended, amongst other things, to hold up the Polish Military Aristocrat to kindly ridicule . . . But not everyone possesses the sane and healthy faculty of being able to enjoy a joke against themselves (at which the English are past masters, thank God!). And I understand that the Polish Ambassador has already made frantic representation about the play.

Game believed that the effect of the play would be positive rather than harmful, but doubted whether Polish officialdom could be persuaded of this:

> Personally I am convinced that *The Colonel and Jacobowsky* would do more for Anglo-Polish relations, if allowed to appear on the stage than reams of propaganda about Polish rights and wrongs. We English understand humour at one's own expense, and laughter is the shortest road to our hearts. But whether the Poles can be made to see the point . . . I very much doubt . . .

He also recognised that there were rather darker elements involved, and recommended that the Foreign Office should be consulted: 'One doesn't need much more knowledge than can be obtained from the daily press to realise that there may be both political, class, and anti-Semitic elements in the official Polish reaction'. The Foreign Office agreed that the play would indeed cause problems: 'the Poles and the French (both of them touchy people in a particularly touchy frame of mind) would be likely to be critical and resentful'. A licence was issued only after extensive cuts had been imposed.[76]

In the same month of February 1945, a licence was refused for a satire set around the table at a post-war peace conference in the Balkans. *Sweet Liberty*[*] created a fictional conflict between the Savonians and the Banjaks, to mock the political posturing which might take place at a conference tasked with reconciling the rights of independence-seeking minorities and the interests of the dominant power. 'The British, Russian and USA and Chinese Delegates are all drawn into the discussion which involves a good deal of international criticism and mutual mudslinging very much in the Shavian manner'. Dearmer saw no serious objection, but 'the international political implications in both the theme and the dialogue' worried Game:

> I am afraid I must disagree with Mr Dearmer's conclusions . . . Personally, far from finding the play tedious, it strikes me as amusing and likely to act well on the stage; but I think it highly probable that the Foreign Office would object to many of the speeches as likely to give offence to both the Americans and the Russians. . . . That we are equally held up for ridicule

---

[*] Written by Bernard and Muriel Jaeger

would, I fear, not carry the weight it should with foreign critics, who would probably only consider it a true statement of fact. And apart from the rather barbed humours of the dialogue, is not the theme untimely? To an elderly sceptic like myself the play, of course, appears to be too absurd to be taken in any other than the spirit intended by the authors; but it undoubtedly treats present, and impending problems in an unquestionably flippant manner; and to others it might well appear to be an ill chosen subject for farcical comedy just at this moment in the world's history.

The Foreign Office identified 'certain passages in this play which are particularly calculated to offend American and Russian susceptibilities', and pointed out that 'a comparatively large number of American soldiers might be expected to visit Birmingham Repertory Theatre', where Sir Barry Jackson was intending to stage the play. There was also much 'to which the Russians would take very strong objection indeed', such as

> treating the Soviet Embassy flippantly and accusing it of throwing a spanner in the works . . . a jeer at Stalingrad, which would be regarded as in the worst possible taste, as we should regard a similar jibe about Dunkirk or the Battle of Britain, and as a slur on the Red Army's honour. Nor would the Russians like to be represented as sneering at the US Army . . . since they are always very correct in these matters in public. In general they would regard it as insulting to have a Soviet Ambassador represented on the stage as a participant in a game of verbal mud-slinging.

The Foreign Office concluded that 'the performance of the play is undesirable at the present time owing to the invidious and flippant way in which it treats the problems of international co-operation'; it feared serious international repercussions might result from licensing it:

> The Russians in particular, who have very different ideas from ours on the subject of political censorship, would be likely to misunderstand His Majesty's Government's action in licensing the play as it stands, and, in the department's opinion, there is a real risk of an adverse effect on Anglo-Soviet relations.

Sweet Liberty was approved only when resubmitted in 1948; Game wrote then: 'In 1945 we were still in the Age of Innocence, as far as past war conferences were concerned, and what then was an ill-timed joke has now become but a pale reflection of the real thing'.[77]

Angus Calder's discussion of wartime censorship of the media has little to say about theatre, but he identifies three main dimensions to the government's imposition of ideas:

> One was to suppress news and views which should not be known. A second was to release, or to invent, news which should be known. A third was to give writers special facilities to report what was happening . . . with

concomitant restrictions on the liberty both of the chosen few, and of those who were not given special privileges.

He also distinguishes between 'security censorship'—that which was designed to prevent the broadcasting of information which might be useful to the enemy—and 'policy censorship'—which 'had no set rules' and was broadly defined by the need to avoid publishing anything likely to 'give comfort to the enemy, cause despondency among the troops, or alienate neutrals and allies'. Examples of the former included not only details about military positions and manoeuvres—'so determined was the navy that the Germans should not know where its ships were that ignorant and nervous censors at various times deleted mentions of *H.M.S. Pinafore* and the *Marie Celeste* from press items'—but also the weather, which 'was always top secret'. Examples of the latter included not referring to the Americans as 'Yankees' or mentioning anti-war movements, while even newspaper astrologers were required to discover signs in the alignment of stars and planets which would enable them to make predictions compatible with military outcomes and objectives. Scripts of radio programmes were scrutinised and, where necessary, amended; but the censors in this case had a facility which gave them a significant advantage over the Lord Chamberlain and his Examiners:

> When live talks were delivered, the announcer would sit in the studio, carefully comparing what the speaker said with the censored script in front of him, with a special switch to hand by which he could cut the speaker off instantly if he strayed.[78]

Calder also draws attention to the extent to which many artists not only signed up as active contributors to the war effort, but were prepared to participate in considerable self-censorship. It was not that the British people were being fed a diet of lies. Calder is adamant that 'considerable cultural and political freedom still existed', and that it remained possible to 'express quite openly heterodox views on any subject'; and a more recent analysis of the creation of myths about the war similarly insists that 'Deliberate lies were rarely spread during the war'. The historian Malcolm Smith argues convincingly that 'the myth was actually formed on a base of unassailable facts', and proposes that the effective slogan of the establishment was 'the truth, nothing but the truth and, as far as possible, the whole truth'.[79] Nevertheless, Calder argues that 'history, some history, was rewritten'. And after the Soviet Union joined the war against Hitler, it was not only the left which was willing to commit ideological contortions:

> Mention of the crimes of Stalinism was as unfashionable and contemptible, as, ten years later, would be any suggestion that Marxism was not identical with Nazism or that not all Russians were robots. 'Block

thinking' was the rule of the day, and long memories were discouraged. Like the Germans, the British devised 'black propaganda'—the creation of fake 'underground radios', the forgery of documents, the fabrication of rumours—justifying this on the grounds that such lies were necessary if a Nazi regime based on lies was to be defeated . . .

Because Britain was fighting a regime which burnt books and suppressed the truth, journalists and other intellectuals in Britain consented to the suppression of the truth, and gladly took part in the fabrication of mendacious propaganda, arguing with themselves that the ends must justify such means.[80]

Theatre was not excluded from the process.

Probably the enduring image of cultural propaganda from the Second World War is Olivier's film of Shakespeare's *Henry V*, famously dedicated to the troops currently at war. As has been well argued, partly by the judicious exclusion (one might say 'censoring') of some 1,700 lines of the original text, this adaptation constructed 'a picture of Henry as man of the people with a Churchillian resonance', and ensured that the play's tone and message unequivocally supported the convenient, and perhaps necessary, myth of national unity: 'Olivier's deft excision of images of conflict, usurpation and historical discontinuity creates a patriotic celebration of Henry's heroism and victory'.[81] In the press, too, Calder concludes that 'The attitude of newspaper editors made the efforts of the Censorship Division remarkably easy'; they were 'generally amenable to suggestions' that nothing should be published which went against the 'national interest'. But such concepts can only exist, of course, when a single 'national interest' can be identified (or constructed) as applying equally to everyone. Calder argues that, although 'the authorities had no great hankering to resort to it', if the chips had ever been down then 'behind all velvet gloves, lurked the mailed fist of coercion'.[82]

Many of the principles and details which Calder itemises in relation to wartime control of the press, the radio and the cinema are—as one might expect—recognisable from the practice of theatre censorship which had existed even during peacetime; self-censorship, the art of persuasion, and the (usually) hidden fist were all central to the process, and 'national interest' equates quite closely with what the Lord Chamberlain's Office believed it was always serving. Although censorship on grounds of tightly defined security needs was more or less a new phenomenon—and resulted in the Lord Chamberlain's passing more responsibility than usual to government ministries—in some respects, and specifically in terms of overtly political drama, the theatre was probably less altered than other media by the new wartime censorship instituted by the government and the Ministry of Information. Indeed, because even during wartime theatre was, on the whole, a much less centralised institution than other media, it potentially offered more gaps and cracks within which a range of voices and opinions could find expression.

Inevitably, just as with the cinema, most domestic theatre-going audiences probably sought escape from, rather than engagement with, issues to do with the war or the body politic. The next chapter focuses on the issues surrounding stage entertainment during wartime.

CHAPTER SIX

'Lubricating the War Machine'

The Nude in Wartime

Let us remember the soldier who is away from his woman and his family. That chap has his emotional problems and if he goes into the theatre and sees nudity nobody imagines that he will come out with less emotional problems than he had when he went in. He had far better have a cold bath! It is not cheering him up, it is only making his emotional worry greater at the end than it was at the beginning.

(Herbert Morrison, 1940)[1]

Uncertainty about the future and a sense of impending doom caused a shift in how people behaved. The inevitable rupturing of the patterns of normal family life by the evacuation programme and the creation of military garrisons hastened what some saw as a breakdown in codes of behaviour, and a decline into decadence and immorality. During the First World War, live performance had become associated with an almost desperate frenzy of light-hearted and distracted pleasure-seeking. This time, it was not only the troops who lived with the fear of destruction; the expectation of aerial bombardment and invasion by a superior and ruthless army was a reality for every citizen, and there was an almost self-fulfilling prophecy that things which might in more genteel times have been censored would now dominate the world of live entertainment. The centre could hardly hold. As we have already seen, there were people for whom the disintegration of moral principles was as, or even more urgent than the threat from Hitler. In January 1940, the Public Morality Council cited Lord Halifax's injunction: 'We ourselves must see that our own standards of conduct do not deteriorate because the day that we lose our respect for our fellow men, our democracy will have lost something on which its vitality depends'.[2] In an earlier letter to the Lord Chamberlain, the Council had registered its horror at 'such gatherings as the ball described recently in the papers, where members of the Forces, A.R.P. wardens and many others danced in complete nudity'. The Lord Chamberlain disputed the extent to which theatre affected behaviour:

Experience tends to show that it is possible to exaggerate the influence of the Theatre on public morals, as it is only in very rare cases that a play has any profound or permanent effect upon members of an audience, and it would be nearer the truth to say that manners and morals of the world outside affects the manners and morals which we see pictured in the theatre, rather than that the contrary is the case.

The Council did not accept this:

My Committee venture to suggest that the opposite view has been taken in most countries and by many leading thinkers in all ages . . . and would endorse a recent statement that 'there is no pulpit from which it is so easy to fire imagination, stir emotion or sow seeds of revolution or patriotism'.

To his credit, Clarendon also defended the right of the stage to reflect the world beyond: 'if the Theatre is to remain a living art it must be allowed to draw its inspiration from contemporary life outside. Standards change from decade to decade, and this fact must inevitably be reflected on the stage'. In principle, it was not what you said but the way you said it that mattered:

The duty of the censorship is to ensure, as far as is possible, that, while the dramatist is allowed every possible licence in the expression of his views, these are expressed with a reasonable decorum in the theatre. The treatment of the theme in a play is in reality the key to the problem, and in considering a play for licence my department is guided by what, in the light of their experience, will be the emotional reaction of the audience.

But the Council utterly rejected the justification that the stage had an inalienable right to reflect real life:

while the theatre draws inspiration from contemporary life, it is surely essentially its function to give inspiration and, even though standards partly change, to endeavour to present those which uphold right living and good citizenship. The contention of my Committee is that some plays now running do the exact opposite and tend to encourage and develop tendencies that are deplored by the best thought in the country. They would suggest that opinions that are universally recognised as evil, such as the upholding of unrestrained sexual intercourse, cannot be expressed, however decorously, without much harmful effect on many individuals and on the good life of the country.

In the winter of 1939 the Council insisted that 'some of the plays now in London are doing serious injury to the country in that they are making self-control more difficult for an audience exceptionally impressionable in this time of unrest'. The main focus of complaint centred not on plays, but on entertainments of other kinds, which were not necessarily subject to the control of the Lord Chamberlain. The censorship was adamant that no drop in moral standards had occurred in the field of straight drama, and, in any case, there were far more revivals than new plays on the stage. Revues, however, were a different matter, and it was this form of entertainment that Lord Clarendon had in mind in October 1939 when he issued a strong reminder through the press that he required much more than the spoken word to be included in manuscripts submitted for licence:

> We are asked by the Lord Chamberlain to draw the attention of Theatre Managers and Producers to the necessity of including a complete description of the whole performance when submitting for licence Stage Plays which include Acts in which there is no spoken dialogue, such as Variety Acts, Ballets or a Tableau etc. A sufficient description of the action, business, or dress, should be included in the script to give a clear indication of the significant features of such Acts.[3]

Comedians were also the subject of moral outrage, for their supposedly increasing vulgarity, but it is the continuing war over nudity on which the current chapter will primarily concentrate. It was not a war to be taken lightly. As the Lord Chamberlain's own Reader put it in July 1940:

> How the censorship survives such going-on defeats me! Nobody but a hypocrite could maintain that it is anything but a bare-faced—and bare-bodied attempt to fill the theatre by the indecent exposure of a lot of young women. From Lord Cromer's original restricted ration of one or two nudes (with no exposure of the breast) this monstrous growth has now developed. I am very strongly of the opinion that the Lord Chamberlain should put his foot down and put an end to this sort of thing, which brings discredit upon our office, and gives Hitler some justification for saying that we are a decadent Democracy.[4]

Although the Theatres Act of 1843 had long been taken to apply only to certain kinds of performance, many people assumed that the Lord Chamberlain's powers extended much more widely than they did; as a result, he was regularly blamed and criticised for permitting things which were beyond his control. The issue became particularly acute in the early months of the war. In November 1939, the Home Secretary was questioned in parliament about 'semi-nudist Cabaret shows at nightclubs'; he sought advice from St James's Palace regarding the attitude there towards nudity. 'This is a subject which has given the Lord Chamberlain's Office a good deal of trouble in recent years', replied Titman. But he was quick to distance the censorship from the more earnest and extreme moralists, informing the government that the Lord Chamberlain's aim was 'to maintain the balance between the enterprising theatrical producer and the narrow-minded citizen, who complains of what he or she sees, and probably enjoys it as much as those who don't'. On the other hand, he insisted that, despite the war, revues in London were still being regularly inspected, and that the Office had not abnegated its responsibilities: 'The fact that we have evacuated to Windsor does not mean that we have in any way relaxed our efforts to keep the more venturesome producer within reasonable limits'.[5] Indeed, although the limits of what was permissible were being tested more and more frequently, the censors were adamant that they were not allowing standards to slip.

Perhaps partly because there were fewer new plays to report on, and partly because of campaigns and pressure against the spread of on-stage nudity, the Lord Chamberlain's Office seems to have increased its vigilance by checking up on more performances. In January 1940, Titman reported in typical detail on a worrying dance in the revue *Black Velvet*:

> The girl possesses a normal figure and performs slow evolutions on the stage, . . . she is covered by a loose transparent veil, through which can be seen the movement of every part of her body. The lighting is limed magenta and reduced to about half strength. At the end of the scene, the girl opens her arms and stands facing the audience. Her private part is covered by a glistening star. I sat in the centre of the third row of stalls and the impression I received was that this star was placed over the pubic hair. I have no doubt that this was not so, but I do know that others have been given the same impression . . . I was fortunate on this occasion of having my wife with me. She corroborates the impression I received about the star.

The Acting Comptroller, Major Gordon, warned the manager that such evolutions were 'a departure from precedent', and noted that the positioning of the star 'draws attention and emphasises that particular part of her anatomy over which it is placed'. He also expressed concern that 'The dropping of the Veil at the end with outstretched arms, as if in invitation, might be so construed by some'. But Gordon adopted a gentlemanly rather than a confrontational approach:

> Having allowed this particular artiste to perform this dance for so many weeks the Lord Chamberlain does not wish to formulate any definite modifications . . . but he desires me to suggest that you might consider some alterations . . . the fact that you deemed it advisable to omit it on the occasion of Their Majesties' visit naturally provokes the suggestion that what is not fit for a King to see, may not be fit for his subjects.[6]

In the same month, the Office expressed concern about a proposed nude dance in the latest Windmill *Revudeville*. Movement in the nude was, of course, forbidden; the issue was what counted as 'nude', and whether fans and snakes were the equivalent of clothing. The producer sought to reassure the censors that nothing new was being attempted: 'the lights are lowered to between ½ and ¼, the Javanese movements calling for nothing that is likely to put the snake, which is her covering, out of position, as this would entirely spoil the effect of the dance as it is intended'.[7] In February, following a number of specific complaints, Titman inspected another revue, and described it as 'one of the type that I wish we could evade licensing'. However, he felt it hardly 'exceeded the limits which, unfortunately, are now allowed'. One change was demanded, in relation to a nude Britannia, who was guilty (at least on the occasion Titman saw the performance) of smiling. The management was officially informed that the performer must 'remain rigid in every feature until the fall of the curtain'.[8]

Not everyone agreed how far such things really mattered. Following complaints by a clergyman in Leigh in March 1940, the local Chief Constable was asked to investigate a revue featuring a naked young woman clinging to a cross. The subsequent police report hinted broadly that the complaint had been an over-reaction:

> The particular item to which Canon Eastwood appears to take exception was La Moya's act which consisted of artistic studies representing famous pictures. A tableaux in which she clings to a cross is named 'Renunciation' and whilst it may be considered hardly a subject for a stage show, one of my Inspectors who witnessed the performance assures me it was effectively staged and was in no way irreverent. The Inspector also states the girl was not nude, but wore flesh coloured briefs and a brassiere, together with a quantity of flimsy drapery.

It was also reported that 'the Reverend gentleman admitted he had never been near enough to the stage to see whether or not the girl was nude'.[9]

What seems to have been changing was less the content or nature of individual acts involving nudity, but rather the quantity of shows incorporating such acts. What had previously been confined, at least so far as the Lord Chamberlain was concerned, to the Windmill and one or two other London venues, was now becoming a staple ingredient of touring revues, and thus of provincial entertainment. In effect, the special freedom granted to the Windmill had been comparable to that allowed to private theatre clubs; now it was as if the special status was being removed. Moreover, performances away from London were difficult for the Lord Chamberlain to control. It might be hard to credit when one reads descriptions of some of the acts licensed for it, but there was an assumption (or prejudice) at St James's Palace that touring shows lacked the taste and discretion of the Windmill:

> When it comes to semi-nudity there is a right and a wrong way of presenting it. The skill of the producer, the technique of the lighting engineer, the art of a dressmaker, all can contribute towards either an artistic unobjectionable act, or to a crude exhibition of the worst type.[10]

Even some managers came out against the touring nude. Mr George Black, who was employed by the prestigious Moss Empires, and was a member of the Executive Committee of the Entertainments Protection Association, wrote to the Lord Chamberlain in March 1940:

> As a responsible theatre manager, I am very perturbed indeed over the recent invasion of Strip Tease artistes, and other nude displays now being presented in the many Touring Companies.
>
> Probably due to War conditions, this form of entertainment is found to be highly successful from a financial point of view, and accordingly a large number of Revue proprietors are adopting it. Naturally, there are reasonable exceptions, in which scenes of this description are done in a highly artistic manner, but generally this is not the case, and it is just a frank exposure of the female form.
>
> In a number of instances, we have caused such items to be deleted, or else more covering to be worn, but this type of entertainment is increasing at such a rate that if we refuse to book all Touring Shows including these exhibitions, we shall have no Shows to put in our Provincial theatres, for which it is very difficult to find attractions at the present time.
>
> Furthermore, I am of the opinion that the general public do not want to have this form of entertainment thrust upon them, and I should very much welcome any suggestion you can make for the total elimination of this class of performance.

Gordon expressed support in principle, but explained that although 'everything that is possible is being done by the Lord Chamberlain to curb, or eliminate, this form of entertainment', to ban something which had previously been allowed was a hard step to take:

> Once a principle has been admitted, and it has been admitted in the past in cases where the Act has been done artistically and in a tasteful manner, it is very difficult to curtain it when it spreads to provincial productions, and is exploited by less reputable Managements, who seem to have an idea that the more nudity and suggestiveness that can be introduced, results in increased patronage and higher takings.

Moss Empires announced they were taking unilateral action:

> We have issued instructions to all the Managers on our Tour to the effect that no nude bodies are to be allowed on the stage, unless they are lightly covered by gauze or netting, and we have given our Managers full authority to prevent nudity of any description at our theatres . . .
>
> We have also written to a number of producers who are prone to this class of entertainment, and have advised them that we will have no nudity on our stages, and every girl must be covered.[11]

Black had referred specifically to the spread of striptease performances, something which had particularly exercised the Public Morality Council and the Lord Chamberlain during the late thirties. In February 1940, the police brought a successful prosecution in relation to one such dance in a revue in Carlisle, and following complaints from a local watch committee at Sunderland about Phyllis Dixey, who had recently attracted much publicity for incorporating a 'burlesque' striptease into her variety act, Clarendon took the potentially decisive step of removing his licence from her 'Confessions of a Fan Dancer'. This left the manager and the licensee (as well as Dixey herself) without the security of official approval, and much more easily liable to police action. The implications were far-reaching, and an official announcement was made:

> His Lordship . . . has decided, under the powers which he possesses under the Theatres Act, 1843, to disallow all strip-tease scenes and acts of a similar nature, in view of difficulties which have arisen resulting in prosecutions in various parts of the country.[12]

In March, Vivian Van Damm, whose work at the Windmill had brought him into very regular contact with the Lord Chamberlain, branched out by launching a revue at the Garrick through his no doubt carefully named company, V.D. Productions Limited. The revue provoked further outrage, not least for a scene in which a group of mermaids relied on nothing other than long hair to hide their nudity. Van Damm sought to reassure the censorship:

> We find that the wigs are sufficiently voluminous, coming below the knees, to cover the girls if and when they move behind the gauze, which has a further sea effect in front of it making the whole scene opaque.
>
> Their movement is very slight as their action is coming from behind the shell to take up positions on a rock each side of the stage, where they remain throughout the scene.

Gordon ruled that this was acceptable in theory, 'provided no portion of the girls' private parts are visible to the audience'. But Titman's report on the actual performance was less generous:

> In view of the numerous warnings given to Mr Van Damm in the past no one should know better than he what is allowed in the way of nudity, and what is not. He knows very well that any movement of a nude woman, or of a woman in the semblance of nudity, is forbidden . . .
>
> The breasts of the Mermaids were <u>not</u> covered by tresses from the wigs . . . their breasts were visible most of the time.

Titman also offered a list of specific objections about the exposure of flesh in other scenes:

> Item 1 The last of the three show girls . . . was big-figured. Her left breast was insufficiently secured and was visible and moving as she turned on the stage . . .

Item 7 A girl sitting in the driver's seat of a coach containing a can-can chorus—both breasts bare. It was not an artistic pose, and the girl was not still. It was simply an opportunity to display nakedness . . .

Item 9 The artist (Elsie Hunter) who, as Ghost of the Borgias, wore a long transparent veil, through which her moving breasts were visible . . .

Item 16 Two Show Girls . . . wore transparent coverings over their bodies, through which the breasts and the 'division' of the private part could be seen . . .

Elsie Hunter did a shawl dance in such a way that at different times every inch of her body could be seen. She appeared to be absolutely nude and the shawl was raised and lowered during her dance to show her breasts, the other place and her bottom.

It seemed at first as if the Director of Public Prosecutions (DPP) was willing to institute proceedings, which because of the high profile enjoyed by the show's producer might have had significant repercussions.

In his opinion a prosecution of this show for the offence of an indecent exhibition would be a test case of the very first class and would affect almost every show in London. You will understand that if you (and better still some other people also) express the view that you and they were shocked by what they saw upon the stage, then we have a very good case not only against the show at the Garrick but almost against any show in London which has a doubtful act in it.

However, other witnesses were needed to support Titman's claim:

the fact that you yourself were shocked would bear little weight but if three or four other persons from various walks of life would come forward and say that they also were shocked, it would strengthen the case very much indeed.

A successful prosecution would have strengthened Clarendon's hand in relation to similar performances, but, remembering recent experiences, he signalled his concern to the DPP about the risk of losing the case, and the adverse publicity which would result:

You will remember that in a recent prosecution undertaken by your Department at the request of the Lord Chamberlain, the summons under the Theatres Act failed because the female impersonation by a man—although described by the Magistrate as indecent—was referred to in the licensed script. A bare reference to the shawl dance also appears in the script licensed for Van Damm's revue, and his Lordship feels that a summons in this case might similarly fail, which would be most unfortunate in the present circumstances.

Given the enthusiasm of the Public Morality Council, it is hard to credit that witnesses to support Titman could not have been found if Clarendon had looked for them; instead, he chose to inform the DPP that there was 'no corroboration of Mr Titman's evidence'. For whatever reason—perhaps out of fear of becoming embroiled in a difficult court case, perhaps because he did not wish to side with the moralists, or perhaps because he did not want to sour a generally amicable relationship with Van Damm—it seems as if the Lord Chamberlain did not wish a prosecution to be undertaken. Gordon had already told the DPP that steps were being taken to deal with the wider issue:

> As you are aware, probably due primarily to war-time conditions, the question of nudity on the stage has been extended to a point where some action has been found to be necessary, and the Lord Chamberlain has called a conference of Licensing and Theatrical Associations for next week.

The DPP had himself questioned 'whether it would be advisable . . . to proceed against these people now or to leave it till after the conference', and no doubt it was partly because Clarendon hoped this event would clarify matters and establish a firmer and less ambiguous policy that he was inclined to hold back on the possible Windmill prosecution.[13]

In the early months of 1940, the issue of stage undress was very much in the public eye, as sections of the press highlighted the supposed decline of theatrical standards, and the fight to reverse this. Under the headline 'THE CHORUS FIGHT "NUDE" SHOWS', the *Daily Mail* reported in February that 'London's chorus girls are fighting for the right to wear more clothes on the stage', and that they had appealed to Equity for support 'in their resistance to managements who ask chorus girls to appear in scanty costumes or no costumes at all'. According to the paper, these performers felt 'degraded' by the demands put upon them, but lacked the power to resist:

> One of the girls' leaders, well known on the London stage, told me their views. But she would not give her name 'because managers stick together, and to be black-balled among them means no more work'.
> She said: 'The war seems to have gone to the head of some managements'.[14]

In March and April, the letters page of the *Daily Telegraph* ran a prolonged and passionate debate on the subject of 'indecorous stage acts'. According to the newspaper's leader column, 'the rank growth with which the evil has increased in recent months has roused general indignation'.[15] Some correspondents identified themselves only as 'VIGILANTE', or 'A MOTHER OF SONS', and the majority voiced antipathy and strong disapproval towards 'Vendors of indecency' who had stooped to 'take advantage of exceptional times to sell their contemptible wares'. They called for a clamp-down on the 'degrading exhibitions' and the 'national disgrace' pervading the country:

> The poison has now spread far beyond the West End of London, and to an extraordinary extent the suburban and provincial theatres are suffering . . . Could anything be more blatant than '*Strip-Strip-Hooray*', which is the name of a show advertised this week in Warrington.

Politics and nationalism were woven quite explicitly into the debate:

> The great mass of the people in this country do not want the bad imitations of Montmartre entertainments that are being thrust on them, or the even more futile emulation of American 'strip-tease'.
>
> We protect ourselves against infectious diseases. Why are we so lax over the pernicious form of sensuality that is being allowed to go unchecked on the stage?

Concerns were expressed about 'whether the gibes of foreigners about our race becoming decadent are not true?', along with fears that 'we are becoming, if we have not already become, a second-class people'. One correspondent was anxious about the potential impact on the empire, as students and businessmen from places such as Hong Kong, Malaya, Burma, India, Iraq and Africa visiting the 'home country' would be taken aback by what they found:

> They come with a high opinion of English morality and with a deferential respect for English women. But what a shock awaits them. They find that those whom they had put on a pedestal have feet of clay, and women may be seen parading the stage in nudity for the price of a theatre ticket.

Others suggested that the 'nasty business which is creeping into our entertainments' must undermine the war effort, and that 'the nation's strength is impaired by letting such things be'.

Most sinister, perhaps, were those who identified the decadence with the pre-Nazi culture of Germany:

> To anybody who remembers the appalling conditions in Berlin between 1918 and 1930 the present trend of affairs in London is terrifying . . . Is this the 'freedom' we are fighting for? . . . A young girl, even a young man, coming inexperienced to Berlin in those days had hardly a chance of escaping corruption. A whole generation was corrupted in this way. The first duty of patriotism, of which we hear so much, should be to protect the youth of Britain against this exploitation.

It was only a short step from here—and some took it—to argue that 'the "clean-up" of this sort of thing in Germany I will always put to the credit of the Nazi party', and that a similar process was required in Britain: 'The one thing that National Socialism did, which even its most inveterate enemies, including myself, were unanimous in praising, was to stamp out the revolting conditions which the Weimar Republic allowed to develop in Germany'. It was left to E.M. Forster to turn such claims on their head:

Mr Douglas Reed's correspondents are correct in emphasising the connection between Nazism and 'purity drives'. The connection is all too close, and that is why it is disquieting that anyone should want a purity drive here.

The moral 'clean up' is one of the most familiar weapons of Totalitarian tyranny. It can be employed against anyone and anything, and it is the more insidious because no one can criticise it without incurring the charge of being himself unclean.

There was no doubt that female performers and (predominantly) male audiences were being cynically exploited by managers whose only concern was to make money for themselves. But Forster knew that the alternative was surely worse:

Let the people who dislike nudity shows (like Mr Douglas Reed and myself) keep away from them and not get into a fuss about them. And let the people who like them, or think they like them, go to them; they will probably soon get bored and stop going, and the whole thing will fizzle out quietly by itself.

This is not a high-minded solution, I know. But it has the advantage of common-sense. And it is infinitely preferable to that dangerous clamour for a moral Gestapo—an organisation, which, once established, would be rapidly diverted to other uses. A warning from Germany should suffice: the Nazis there adroitly utilised the 'purity-drive' to vilify and discredit the Roman Catholic church, and to plunder and maltreat various religious communities . . .

Let us realise that there is something sinister in a 'purity-drive', however much it gratifies our desire to meddle in other people's affairs. And let us get on with the war.[16]

By coincidence, Forster's letter was published in the *Daily Telegraph* on 16 April 1940—the very day on which the Lord Chamberlain held his widely anticipated and publicised conference on stage nudity and the supposed decline in moral standards. The stated aim of this event was to establish new standards and principles, and to secure widespread agreement and co-operation in their maintenance; but although it was officially convened and presided over by the Clarendon, as Lord Chamberlain, it had not been his idea. In fact, the impetus had come directly from the Home Office, in response to the volume of complaints they had apparently received 'from various sources, including a number of Members of Parliament, regarding the bawdiness of the jokes and the tendency for increased nudity, particularly in the Music Halls'. In February, they had sought an urgent meeting with representatives of both the London County Council and the Lord Chamberlain's Office:

Various representations have been made to the Home Office to the effect that the standard of decency and propriety in the London theatres has been lowered since the outbreak of war. The complaints I think generally relate to the revues rather than to the straight plays and I understand the grounds of the complaints are partly the bawdiness of the gags and jokes and partly the indecency of the clothes, or lack of clothes.

I know how difficult it is to prescribe a standard in these matters, but from comments by people who are by no means prudish, I get the impression that there may be some substance in these complaints.

On 6 March, Gordon, along with representatives of the LCC, attended a meeting at the Home Office to discuss 'the alleged deterioration in plays, and in Music Hall entertainments presented in London, and elsewhere since the outbreak of War'. It was chaired by Sir Alexander Maxwell, the Under-Secretary of State at the Home Office, who, reported Gordon, 'began by explaining that he personally knew very little about the matter, and confessed that he had not been to a place of entertainment for over a year'. Maxwell identified dress and comic gags as the main causes for concern, but the Acting Comptroller pointed out that the problem was not primarily centred on plays:

Mr Gordon said that he did not think that standards in the straight play had deteriorated, but it was certainly true that there were many more shows of the revue type since the outbreak of war. This meant more opportunities for slackness of standards and also a greater chance that attention would be drawn to that kind of show, because the public went to these and not the more serious plays.

The meeting also discussed 'the cause of the deterioration' in moral standards, reaching the rather vague conclusion that 'it was mainly due to war conditions'. Privately, Gordon described the debate as 'rather desultory and disjointed', and he remained unconvinced of its value: 'I have attended several such conferences in past years', he wrote, 'but I think this one was the least satisfactory and most inconclusive one of them all'. He had tried to convince Maxwell that the roots of the problem lay outside the scope of the 1843 Theatres Act, and that there were other fields where it would be more appropriate for the government to initiate action:

I told Sir Alexander Maxwell that if the Government would start from the bottom and stop the Bottle Parties, and exercise a more stringent control over Cabaret Entertainments at the less reputable Restaurants, the undesirable jokes, gags and nudity would not permeate upwards and come before the Lord Chamberlain, or the London County Council, to deal with.

I pointed out to him that a good deal of these things originated in America, and, although they were not permitted on the stage, they could be put across in Cabarets and Music Halls.

But Gordon doubted that there was any real commitment to tackle the issue: 'I left with the impression that the Home Office are no more anxious to cope with the "Bottle Party" and Cabaret questions than they are with the aliens', he reported.

The Comptroller had not responded enthusiastically to the suggestion that the Lord Chamberlain should organise a meeting of interested parties and organisations, pointing out 'that several such Conferences had been held in the past', and that 'he was not persuaded this really did much good as any improvement was often only short-lived'.[17] But Clarendon was more or less obliged to submit to the Home Office's suggestion, and the April event took place in a highly charged context. The *Daily Mail* sought to maintain the pressure on the morning of the conference; under the headline 'GIRLS BARRED AT NUDITY ENQUIRY', the paper complained that 'London chorus girls who began the outcry against "strip-tease" and nude shows are not to be allowed to voice their protests'; indeed, the newspaper claimed that the views of those most involved in the theatre industry were liable to be ignored:

> The chorus girls' spokeswomen have spent weeks preparing and presenting evidence to British Equity, the L.C.C., and other authorities. But they are not the only theatre workers who hoped to give evidence.
> Mr Tom O'Brien, Secretary of the National Association of Theatrical employees, said to me yesterday: 'I understood when the inquiry was first planned that theatrical employees would be able to present their case.
> The views of such of our members as stage hands and other theatre technicians who are against the present nudity cult should, I feel, be represented'.[18]

Clarendon and the conference needed to come up with a firm policy and commitment.

In addition to Gordon, Titman, Game and Clarendon himself, those present at St James's Palace on 16 April 1940 included, the Right Honourable Herbert Morrison (An MP and leader of the London County Council), the Assistant Under-Secretary of State at the Home Office, the Assistant Commissioner of the Metropolitan Police, and senior representatives from the LCC, the County Councils' Association, the Association of Municipal Corporations, the Society of West End Managers, the Theatrical Managers' Association, the Association of Touring and Producing Managers, the Entertainments Protection Association, the Variety Artistes Federation, the Hotels and Restaurants Association of Great Britain, the Cinematograph Exhibiters' Association, and the British Drama League. Clarendon's opening address drew an almost obligatory, if vague, connection between the need to control the stage and the need to defeat Germany:

I am quite satisfied that we shall all be agreed that in these times, when the efforts of everyone should be devoted to securing the complete Victory in War of our Allies and ourselves, it is very desirable that the whole standard and tone of public entertainments, whether in Theatres, Music Halls or any other places, should be maintained on a decent level of propriety. (Hear, hear)

The aim of the conference, he said, was to produce an agreement to control public entertainments, for although the event held by his predecessor in 1937 had initially had a positive effect, it had become necessary to deal with the 'marked increase in nude exhibitions, objectionable dialogue and business since the outbreak of War'. He therefore sought a stronger and less ambiguous resolution than the one produced three years earlier. From his own perspective, explained Clarendon, the difficulty lay in the discrepancy between what was permissible in performances controlled by his licence, and the liberty granted to those which were outside his authority. Often, the same artists and the same acts were involved:

The chief difficulty experienced in dealing with objectionable features in Revues, both as regards dialogue and indecency of dress or gesture, is due to the fact that Variety Artistes are permitted to do their Acts without previous examination when performing in Cabaret, or under a Variety Bill at a Music Hall. Any such Acts, or parts of them, when submitted for inclusion in a Revue, are disallowed.

Clarendon identified the other source of the current crisis as the infiltration of the British stage by foreign influences. With the United States not yet an ally, there was no need to worry about giving offence:

The 'Strip-Tease' Acts, and many of the objectionable jokes and gags are importations from America, and were first introduced here through the medium of so-called 'Bottle Parties', and the less reputable type of Cabaret entertainment. Thence they spread upwards to the Music Hall, and the Revue.

Nudity itself, he explained, had been introduced to revues 'some six or eight years ago', but he insisted that 'steps have always been taken at all times to control indecent exhibitions of the female form, and suggestiveness in action'. Rather disingenuously, Clarendon claimed that 'no objection as far as I know has ever been raised to "still" artistic poses', and he summed up the current official line:

My policy, and that of my predecessor, has been never to allow any movement when in the nude, or in the semblance of nudity. This prohibits naked Strip-Tease Acts, and dancing where any portion of a female artiste's private parts are visible, even through transparent veiling, or similar devices.

The real problem was the 'marked increase in nude exhibitions', and their growing popularity: 'Since the outbreak of War, the public taste for amusement has tended towards the lighter entertainment, and there has, in consequence, been a marked increase in the number of Revues, not only in London, but in the provinces'.

Reginald Stamp, the Chairman of the London County Council's Entertainments Licensing Committee, also voiced his objections to the current 'craze' for 'questionable entertainments which include provocative nudities, strip-tease acts, exceedingly vulgar jokes and gestures'. It was, he declared, part of a wider problem, and a society which permitted pictures of naked women to be posted through the letter boxes of ordinary houses was storing up 'acute problems' for the future:

> during the progress of the War the general social life of the community has undergone a tremendous upheaval, soldiers are separated from civilians ... the War itself has produced acute problems for civilians and soldiers alike. It is because of that that we feel that undue provocation should not occur in the realm of entertainment, which is likely to bring about difficulties both for the soldier and for civilian relatives whom he leaves behind him.

If the traditional British way of life was to survive, then it was necessary to guard against enemies within as well as without:

> We are at war. Human values are in the balance. Things are being done which are a crime to civilisation. Ordinary decent men and women are being torn from their homes, relatives and friends to carry out the national will of England. Are not the resulting problems serious enough for all concerned? Are we to add to the pitfalls and complications of the soldiers and their relatives by provoking them in a dangerous setting and playing up to the worst elements in human nature?

Herbert Morrison, who would shortly become Home Secretary and Minister of Home Security in Churchill's wartime cabinet, agreed that the effect of such performances could be dangerous for the future of family life. It was the influence on the young and on the future that most concerned him:

> I am not too much worried about the grown man or the grown woman. But I am worried about the youth and the girl of fourteen, when the emotions of adolescence are beginning to work. We have all gone through that period. It is really a wicked thing to stimulate these urges that are growing in these young human bodies.

Some delegates, notably George Black, seized the opportunity to call not just for a halt in the proliferation of nudity, but for a resolution which would actually reverse the tide. Black said he was unable 'to see the necessity whatsoever of nudity on the stage in any guise at all, whether as art or otherwise'. The spokesperson for the Variety Artistes Federation agreed: 'It should be stamped out . . . the girls cannot take a firm stand themselves and it is up to us to protect them if we are decent people'. Forced onto the defensive, a speaker from the Touring and Producing Managers conceded that 'the strip-tease is being carried a little too far', and cautiously expressed himself 'willing to take it out in its entirety, as long as it is made a general rule and all producers do the same'. But to lose even the right to stage nude tableaux would have been a concession too far, and some speakers suggested that the problem had been overstated:

> One is apt to gain the impression, reading the remarks of certain non-theatregoers, the whole of the Stage is covered with nudity. Nothing of the kind. Many of the letters appearing in the Press are written by people who have never seen a show.

The President of the Association of Touring and Producing Managers endorsed the view that 'the whole matter . . . has been exaggerated'; however, he was forced to acknowledge that there were 'very many objectionable things done on the stage', and to promise that 'my Association are prepared to do everything possible to assist Mr Stamp in cleaning it up'.

Perhaps following the principle that attack is the best form of defence, representatives from the theatrical side tried to locate the blame elsewhere: 'you are overlooking the most dangerous part of the whole subject, and that is, bottle-parties', declared one; 'Stop the bottle-party and you will stop the whole thing' agreed another speaker, and the Assistant Managing Director of the Savoy Hotel confirmed that 'nudity is a very frequent occurrence in those parties'. Such events were effectively unregulated; 'The bottle-party is an uncontrolled institution at the moment', he declared; 'there are no powers, Parliamentary or otherwise, by which it can be dealt with'. Herbert Morrison eagerly joined in, pledging that Parliament had a duty to bring bottle parties 'under proper control'. A scapegoat had been found onto which most of the objections could be projected. Some delegates did wonder whether they had been sidetracked by a strategically placed 'red herring', and questioned whether if there had been any representatives of bottle parties present, they too would have declared themselves as anxious as everyone else to maintain standards of decency and propriety.

As the morning drew to a close, Clarendon attempted to steamroller through a complete ban on nudity, presuming to have identified a more or less unified agreement for such a policy:

> I think I have sized up—if I may use that expression—the general feeling . . . that it would really be more desirable than anything to eradicate nudity entirely from all our shows. (Hear, hear). I think I have not gone too far in making that statement . . . so far as my Department is concerned . . . if

nudity were entirely cut out . . . it would make our task much easier and simpler.

But even the LCC—the other major licensing authority alongside the Lord Chamberlain's Office—had no particular wish to outlaw nude tableaux. Such an extreme solution was also resisted by Sir Joseph Lamb, from the County Councils' Association, who argued that it would be both unjustified and ineffective to issue a blanket ban on stage nudity. Not all nudity, he argued, could reasonably be considered offensive: 'I have never heard it said that a baby when born was an indecent thing'. Lamb maintained that it was in 'the spirit in which it is presented that indecency really lies', and that to simply 'do away with nudity' per se would only 'lead to a worse aspect—that is, the "nudity" which is not really nudity, but leaves behind it that spirit of suggestion'. Clarendon agreed, and conceded that it was also 'extraordinarily difficult to define what nudity actually is'. Lamb made this the substance of his argument: 'I do believe that it is impossible for us to say that we are going to do away with nudity unless we say what we mean by "nudity"'.[19] It is not hard to imagine the silence and the pre-lunch slump of helpless despair likely to have rippled through the delegates at the thought of having to define the concept of nudity. But Clarendon gained approval to reconvene the meeting in the afternoon with just himself, the President of the Society of West End Theatre Managers, and the Chairman of the LCC Entertainments Licensing Committee, to formulate a statement which could be passed to the expectant press. Probably most of the other delegates couldn't get out of the room fast enough.

The statement issued later that day declared, as such statements generally do, that 'a gratifying measure of unanimity was evident' among the delegates. It summarised the conclusions and impending actions:

> That immediate steps should be taken to check the greater tendency which has become evident since the war at some places of entertainment, both in London and in the provinces, towards the giving of performances including nudity and impropriety of gesture and speech . . .
>
> That the powers of control over places where music, dancing and other entertainments are given which are not subject to any form of licence should be greatly increased, and that the Government should promote legislation for this purpose at an early date.[20]

Significantly, however, the emphasis was put on the pledging of co-operation rather than on enforcement. As Stamp explained in a press interview:

> Because we do not want to take legal steps we have asked theatre managers to co-operate voluntarily. I feel sure they will do so.
>
> If some do not co-operate, and the L.C.C. feel their present powers are inadequate, we would not hesitate to move.[21]

With the conference over, some steps were taken in the Lord Chamberlain's Office to institute a tougher code of practice. Within days, Game reported on 'an extremely dirty revue' to be staged in Birmingham. It included a dancer dressed in brassiere, pants and a white diaphanous robe; 'This is, I suppose, still allowed', said the Reader, doubtfully. But Gordon ruled forcefully: 'This seems to imply semi-nudity in dancing. Not now allowed. The dancer must be fully clothed or the item omitted'.[22] A few days later Game recommended in connection with a dance set in an Eastern Harem that 'A tassel is certainly inadequate clothing, and a veil is little better. They will have to give the girl more clothing to conform to the recent decisions'.[23] And the following week in relation to a 'dirty' provincial revue he noted: 'We should ask for an assurance that there are no nudes, or partially clothed dancers, or anything of that sort about which we now require more particulars'. Gordon asked Game to: 'explain that the fact they have been allowed previously makes no difference. The L.C. has withdrawn previous permission and now requires them to be omitted'.[24] In its next annual report, the Public Morality Council claimed with delight that its anti-nudity campaign had at long last been brought to a successful conclusion.[25] But the Council was surely overstating its success. There was still a lack of clarity regarding exactly what was and was not allowed, and it seemed unlikely that everyone would fall willingly into line. In July 1940, the Lord Chamberlain sent a letter to managers informing them that he was 'not now prepared to grant any further permission for the inclusion of any scene where there is movement in the nude, or in the semblance of nudity; neither will his Lordship permit anything in the nature of a Strip Tease Act'. Yet this seems little more than a restatement of previous policy. Indeed, George Black, representing Moss Empires, wrote to complain that 'the question of nudity on the stage has not been definitely cleared up' and that 'further guidance' was required. 'I am afraid I cannot define very much more closely the position in regard to nudity than that given in the last paragraph of my letter', replied Gordon, unhelpfully.[26]

Crucially, nude tableaux had not been disallowed, and even though the censorship might have wished to do so, these could not easily be confined to one or two theatres in London. Indeed, they continued to proliferate, even though licensing was strictly subject to photographs of actual individuals and their poses being submitted and approved. In theory, the censorship also maintained a rule that tableaux were never to be accompanied by the spoken word; as Clarendon insisted in relation to one revue in July 1940:

> Jack Taylor must be told that permission for <u>artistic</u> (if these are) representations of nude females, can only be given when they are unaccompanied by accentuating dialogue. He must either have his

tableaux without the dialogue, or the dialogue, with cuts required, without the naked ladies.

Gordon issued the manager with a strong reminder of the rules: 'I am surprised at your expression of ignorance of the Conference held last April to discuss the question of nudity on the stage. The matter was fully reported in the press at the time'. The manager's 'excuse' was an improbable one:

> on looking at the photographs that were taken I find that the Photographer has carefully touched out the bust bodices and trunks that the girls are wearing which does in fact make it appear on the pictures that the girls are nude, when such is not the case.

Far from apologising, Taylor presumed to challenge the aesthetic judgement of the censors:

> I notice that his Lordship does not consider these Tableaux to be artistic and in reply to this I can only point out that they are faithful copies of works hailed as masterpieces, one of which was painted by Bourne Jones [sic] and has for years been exhibited at the Manchester Art Gallery and the other is by G.F. Watts and is at the Walker Art Gallery in Liverpool. The girls in the tableaux were posed by Professor Ernst Stern who made the models which were copied by Alick Johnstone, both of whom are acknowledged to be England's greatest and most artistic designers and painters of scenery.

Clarendon initially stuck to his position, insisting the poses were pornographic and inadmissible, but a compromise was achieved and a licence granted when new photographs were submitted, accompanied by letters from local dignitaries—including a justice of the peace—supporting their claim to be works of art.[27]

In August 1940, nudes were again banned from *Ladies Be Good*. Game reported:

> This Revue is chiefly remarkable as containing the most grossly pornographic scene which in my experience has ever been submitted. I had the promoters of the show down from London this morning and informed them that it was sheer insolence to have submitted such filth.

The censorship ruled that the tableaux were 'nothing but nude girls posed within a frame, and have no artistic justification whatever'.[28] In an effort to resolve uncertainties and pre-empt further conflicts, the Office finally issued a statement articulating what Titman called 'the policy which we are inflicting upon producers' in relation to nudity:

NUDES
All stage scenes in which nude figures are introduced must be submitted in photograph form to the Lord Chamberlain.

a) They must be accurate representations of actual works of art, paintings or sculptures, and/or

b) They must satisfy the Lord Chamberlain as having sufficient artistic merit, as against being merely an excuse to exhibit nude figures upon the stage.

The use of 'and/or' had been a subject of internal debate; Game had wanted 'or' on the grounds that 'We cannot rule out all original work' since the Windmill 'uses the nude in original settings with taste and discretion'. Titman, however, insisted that 'and' was essential to qualify the right to stage established works of art:

I deliberately altered the word 'or' to 'and' because there are many works of art, paintings and sculptures which could never be represented by flesh and blood upon a stage. I have in mind, amongst others, a noted picture at Hampton Court Palace.

By combining b) with a) it gives the LC the right to reject a) if it does not comply with b).[29]

Additional clauses were added subsequently, stipulating

c) There must be no movement whatsoever.

d) Photographs of nude poses must be submitted and approved before they can be performed.

e) The lighting on the stage must be subdued or otherwise made appropriate to the scene.[30]

Other factors which were never written down nevertheless informed some of the decisions made. Commenting on a Windmill revue in 1942, Titman observed that 'Fortunately all the girls are young and slight in figure, otherwise the present condition of scantiness would not suffice';[31] after watching another show at the same theatre in 1944 he reported:

One of the new girls is on the big side and hardly suitable for nude poses and scanty costumes.

Before I left the Theatre I asked the Assistant House Manager to make minor alterations regarding this particular girl.[32]

The censorship had no hesitation about considering not merely a pose, but the shape of the performer doing the posing. A pose licensed for one individual could not automatically be transferred to another. As Titman explained to a senior police officer: 'You will appreciate that each naked lady must be dealt with on her own merits. What could be allowed to one would be objectionable in another with a different figure'.[33] It seems doubtful whether this discrimination would have stood up in a court of law, but no such case was ever tested.

At the April conference, Sir Joseph Lamb of the County Councils' Association had defended nude tableaux: 'if I am allowed to go to a picture gallery or sculpture gallery and see the same thing, I do not see why I should not be allowed to see it on the stage'.[34] But one of the things the censorship found hard to swallow was that the audiences at revues doing the looking were probably not of the same class as those visiting art galleries. Unschooled in art appreciation and ignorant of aesthetics, as he presumed them to be, Game thought their motivation and gaze were fundamentally different and less refined:

> From an artistic point of view these nude poses are very good. But the great majority of the public have no aesthetic sense, and to them the girl will appeal as a nude young woman of very pleasing appearance, and nothing more.
>
> The real object of such turns, which have become a feature of so many of these provincial Touring Revues, is not really to present something which is beautiful, and which will appeal to the latent aesthetic perceptions of the beholder, but to help fill the theatre by exciting a quite different interest.[35]

He accused managers of cynicism, describing one tableau in a Windmill revue as 'just framed up naked women, with a prop or two to make them respectable ART, but not to obstruct the view!'.[36] Patronising he may have been, and no libertarian, but Game was far from coy. It surely was the exploitation of sex rather than the sex itself to which he most objected:

> Sex is one of the great natural facts of life and not one which we could, or should, try to suppress in the Theatre. Sex always has, and probably always will, play a great part in both the matter and manner of theatrical entertainments: but as trustees for the standard of public morals in the Theatre, we have very doubtful justification for allowing sex to be used in this blatant manner, merely for the commercial purpose of filling the producer's pocket.[37]

On another occasion he was even more explicit in acknowledging that, by its actions, the censorship itself was implicated: 'I don't think nudity is immoral, but I am quite sure its exploitation for financial profit is; and I consider our position in being accessories to the fact is one that is to be deplored'.[38]

Meanwhile, the Lord Chamberlain attempted to pressurise the Home Office into taking some action in relation to activities which fell outside his authority but for which he was mistakenly blamed. In July 1940, Gordon submitted a letter to Clarendon for his approval and signature: 'I have taken the opportunity of referring ... to the Bottle Party question. I rather suspect that the Home Office have taken advantage of the exciting Military and Political events of the last twelve months to shelve the latter question'.

Gordon had always doubted the Home Secretary's commitment to taking action, and his letter to Sir John Anderson was written with some force:

> I continue to receive written complaints from various sources regarding incidents at Bottle Parties, which in each case I have passed to your department . . .
>
> I should be glad if you could tell me what action you have been able to take in regard to these places. I would venture to remind you that at the Conference over which I presided, at your suggestion, at St James's Palace on April 16th, great stress was laid by the Theatrical and Licensing interests represented upon the urgent need of some action being taken to curb the activities of these unlicensed places of Entertainment.
>
> In view of the general measure of agreement reached at that Conference with the Theatrical interests to eliminate nudity, suggestiveness, and objectionable dialogue from Theatres and Music Halls, there is some tendency in these quarters to think that while they have done, or are doing, their best to carry out their side of the bargain, it is not apparent, or at any rate no announcement has been made public as to, what steps are being taken by the government to deal with the less reputable type of Cabaret Entertainment and Bottle Parties.[39]

A few weeks later, Anderson did indeed introduce a defence regulation under the Emergency Powers Act, which gave the police greater powers to deal with bottle parties.

The prosecution of offenders who broke regulations may have seemed vital to the Lord Chamberlain's Office, but not everyone was willing to prioritise such matters in the middle of a war. In the autumn of 1940, the Director of Public Prosecutions sent a rather disparaging letter to the Office: 'Without belittling the importance of these theatre cases, I feel obliged in present circumstances to put them in a category of rather minor importance'. Clarendon had to concede that the German aerial bombardment, which had finally begun, did create certain difficulties:

> <u>Decision for abandonment of certain prosecutions for contravention of the Theatres Act</u>
>
> In addition to the foregoing (fifteen) prosecutions for contravention of the Theatres Act, there were four others, in the London area, which the Director of Public Prosecutions had undertaken to conduct. In the month of September, however, a communication was received from him to the effect that in view of the situation in London, which rendered proceedings in all Courts unusually difficult, particularly in connection with the attendance of witnesses and defendants, and in view also of the almost entire cessation of theatrical activities, he did not propose to proceed with the prosecution of the delinquents in these cases.
>
> The Lord Chamberlain expressed his agreement with this decision.[40]

Still, perhaps fearing that the intensification of the war would heighten the temptation for theatres and audiences to seek solace in ever more extreme rudery, Clarendon was determined that the Blitz should not excuse or eclipse all issues of censorship. In October 1940, Van Damm sent in a series of photographs for the next Windmill revue, asking that allowance be made for the fact that they appeared so bright, and claiming that it was currently impossible to photograph under the lighting states which would actually be used in the performance. Titman, writing from the relative safety of Windsor, ignored this appeal and sent a stern warning: 'The Lord Chamberlain desires me to warn you that unless more reasonableness is shown in the inclusion of nudity in your programme he will have no alternative to prohibiting it altogether'. As Titman commented to Clarendon, 'I am sure you will agree that Van D is slipping again. He is one of those people who need to be brought up with a jerk periodically'. However, Van Damm responded with hurt innocence: 'I regret very much that you should have to again warn me about my "unreasonableness" in the inclusion of Nudity in my programmes'. Accused of holding back photographs as a deliberate tactic to prevent the Lord Chamberlain from intervening, he insisted:

> I do not withhold these one minute longer than I can help, but with things happening in this City at the present moment, I am sure you will appreciate that we cannot work in that Department as in most others at the same speed as we have always done. Two of our Photographers have been bombed out in the last three weeks, and pictures which I took of 'Gavotte' were destroyed in the studio before they could be printed.

Perhaps more tenuously, he also claimed to be serving the national interest by keeping performers in work, and he thanked the generosity of an altruistic benefactor for enabling him to do so: 'With the tragic unemployment of Theatrical Artistes and Musicians . . . she feels that she is being more than patriotic in devoting so much of her private fortune to helping those who would be in very dire straits'.[41]

In January 1941, Van Damm helpfully sent the Office a set of coloured 'mediums' through which to view the poses so as to get a more accurate sense of how they would appear in performance. The Office rejected one particular photograph: 'the position of the hands of the girls will not do and some other means must be found for obscuring those parts which must be covered'; even if one allows for exaggeration and an element of spuriousness, Van Damm's reply surely highlights the absurdity of the activity in which the head of the royal household was engaged in the middle of the Blitz: 'This was taken on the night of Monday, April 7th', when there were two alerts from 10.30 pm till 5 in the morning', pleaded the producer; 'everybody in this part of the world was feeling a bit jittery at the time as the gunfire was very heavy'.[42]

It was not only the poses themselves but their number within individual shows which became the focus of the censors' increasingly arbitrary attempts to exert some sort of control. Of the Windmill's *Revudeville No. 143*, in March 1941, Game observed: 'the Nude ration is rather generous'; he warned that 'six nudes is too much, and the old men in the front row of the stalls will think that they have wandered into paradise instead of the Windmill Theatre'.[43] Generally he advocated a policy of 'limiting the Nude in the Theatre to the minimum', and permitting 'merely the sparing use of an occasional nude as part of the decoration'.[44] Of the nudes in a revue at Wolverhampton, Titman remarked: 'Individually, I could find no objection . . . my only doubt is whether there are too many of them, although we have never before fixed any limit'. After consultation, the management was informed: 'The Lord Chamberlain has decided that the number is excessive and must be reduced. Sixteen nude poses exceeds by three or four times anything that has hitherto been allowed'.[45] On another occasion, he again complained about the number of nudes at the Windmill: 'His Lordship feels that the extension of nudity to scenes covering one-third of the production . . . is more than he can be reasonably expected to allow'. Van Damm answered that 'Although these may look in number very considerable, they are used only in such a way as to enhance the artistic presentation of the scene'. He added: 'I do hope Lord Clarendon is not under the impression that I am forcing unnecessary nudes into my scenes. I am merely improving the artistic presentation of these scenes by the occasional introduction of statues'. And he insisted that they were 'in no way put there for the purpose of the Box Office effect'.[46] As always, the difference between the artistic and the exploitative depended on what angle you looked from.

It would be naïve to imagine that all managers strictly observed the regulations, and ways could often be found of evading them. Following a complaint about a Windmill show by the Bishop of Chichester, for example, Titman inspected it and commented:

> It was lucky that the Bishop 'could not stay to see the whole programme' because in the final scene there was some 'can-can' and one of two 'hula-hula' girls, wearing a string skirt and a brief garland of flowers had a slight mishap—the garland slipped down, but she quickly restored it!

Correspondence suggests that a surprising number of such 'mishaps' occurred, and it seems highly probable that some were deliberately built into the performance. Certainly, at the start of the 1950s, when the Office was vainly trying once again to turn back the tide and clamp down on the

Windmill's growing use of nudity, Clarendon issued a strict warning to Van Damm:

> [you have] now had sufficient experience in this method of production to know where the danger lies and to take proper precaution as to avoid accidental exposure in view of the audience . . . I have overlooked these incidents in the past, but they must now cease, and after this warning a failure in dress which involves exposure of any of your artistes will be treated as negligence.[47]

One kind of performance which the 1940 conference had railed and ruled against was the striptease. Even here, however, there were practical problems in maintaining an absolute ban. For example, how many clothes could be removed on stage before the compulsory blackout came? In the early fifties a proposal was even made to disallow 'the removal of garments (other than an outer coat or wrap) by or from a performer while that performer is within the view of the public'.[48] But it would probably not have taken managers long to realise that this begged the question of how much a performer was required to wear under the coat! If it was hard to define 'nudity', then the same was surely true of 'striptease'. In January 1943, the Association of Touring and Producing Managers wrote to query whether a 'burlesque striptease' could be included in a revue:

> It does seem to me that there are certain forms of what are probably wrongly described as strip-tease which are of a comedy and burlesque nature, which from my observation have appeared to be perfectly harmless and without any quality of suggestiveness about them.

The managers suggested to the Lord Chamberlain that 'your Department must naturally be placed in some difficulty in judging the nature of an act of this kind merely from a written description on paper'. Was there a hint of corruption and bribery in the proposal that 'a much better decision could be arrived at if the actual act could be seen by yourself or one of your representatives'. It would hardly have helped the Office's reputation if the press heard that striptease artists were demonstrating and refining their act in private audiences at St James's Palace or Windsor Castle. In this case, the 'burlesque' involved a girl being supposedly hypnotised by an illusionist, and then taking off her clothes down to brassiere and trunks. According to Titman it occurred within 'one of the worst revues we have had for a very long time', and over which a prosecution was already pending. He argued 'that having rigorously wiped out this objectionable feature, it would be most unwise to allow the thin end of the wedge'. Game was equally suspicious:

> I may be dense, but personally I don't see how a strip-tease can be burlesque. I don't suppose they select a plain girl for the job, and either she

takes off her clothes or she doesn't! How do you burlesque a pretty girl undressing?

He added: 'We cannot begin viewing acts before production, which would be necessary if strip-tease in any form was to be allowed'. Clarendon agreed, and Titman informed the Association accordingly:

> His Lordship wishes me to explain to you that, while he does not find it altogether easy to understand how a strip-tease act can be 'burlesque' (a disrobing act is always a disrobing act, is it not?—and even absence of 'suggestiveness' would not alter that fact), that is not the main reason for his being unable to agree to the request you have made. Even if he were convinced of a real and definite distinction between genuine and burlesque strip-tease, to permit the latter would inevitably be 'the thin end of the wedge', and lead to frequent trouble with second-rate and perhaps unscrupulous producers, who would not hesitate to overstep a line which would in any case necessarily be a vague and indefinite one. Inspections . . . could not be arranged by this Office.[49]

In May 1943 the Public Morality Council accused a sketch in the current Windmill show of having 'a flavour of the strip tease of other days'. Game commented:

> It must be nearly two years since we have received a complaint about the Windmill Theatre. I like to think that it is due to my vigilance and the fact that I make a point of visiting every edition of REVUDEVILLE. It is certainly a coincidence that I had been unable—through more pressing affairs—to see the current edition before it had run for five weeks—and then comes a complaint.

But after watching a performance, Game dismissed the complaint:

> I do not consider it objectionable in the circumstances. If it were in the nature of 'strip-tease', I should certainly not allow it, but the girl is sufficiently covered with brassiere and 'panties' to enable her to perform an energetic dance at the end of the number.[50]

Some latitude was certainly permitted to the Windmill even in this area. In February 1945, Titman approved a 'Dance of the Seven Veils':

> Strictly speaking, such a dance cuts across our ban on striptease, but as this particular dance is now rather traditional and has been included in early editions of *Revudeville*, it would be extremely difficult to interfere with it now. Moreover, it was extremely well done.[51]

But the following month Van Damm went a step too far and the Public Morality Council complained about an item which was 'manifestly a revival of the Strip-tease, since the performer completely disrobes in the course of the song she sings, pausing a moment completely nude before putting on her nightdress and going to bed'. The censorship felt obliged to support the objection, though their letter to Van Damm was openly apologetic: 'Since this act was included in your programmes before the war there has been a definite regulation forbidding any form of "strip-tease"— to use a vulgar term . . . I am sorry to have to ask you to alter this item'. Titman politely commented: 'I have no doubt that even the disrobing was done in a delicate and artistic manner'.[52]

One of the performers whose disrobing on stage provoked the controversy which led to the 1940 conference was Phyllis Dixey. Dixey's career and fame were built entirely on her willingness not only to appear in nude tableaux, but to perform a striptease act, and even to dance while apparently in the nude. The ambivalence with which the establishment— including the Lord Chamberlain's Office—treated Dixey is an indicator of its conflicting attitudes. What moralists saw as a decline into decadence and evil, others saw as morale-boosting. In March 1942, questions were asked in Parliament about the government's policy on public entertainment: 'Mr Stokes asked the Home Secretary when the Government proposed to introduce regulations restricting . . . activities not considered in accord with the true spirit of determination of the people in this crisis'. The implication was that diversions and frivolous leisure pursuits were peacetime activities which had no place in a society focused on the serious business of war. But in reply, the Home Secretary—now none other than Herbert Morrison— offered a very different perspective:

> The Government's war-time policy with regard to entertainments has been to permit them to continue on a restricted basis in the belief that, within reason, *popular entertainments act as a lubricant rather than a brake on the war machine.* [my emphasis][53]

Probably few performers acted as more of a lubricant than Phyllis Dixey. She had first achieved public notoriety in 1940 as 'The Girl the Lord Chamberlain Banned', after a Cardiff Watch Committee had complained about her 'satire' on striptease—which, of course, included a striptease act. She subsequently took to ending her fan dance by singing 'That bit was simply grand,/But that's the bit the Lord Chamberlain banned', before going into a sequence of nude tableaux.[54]

There was no shortage of outrage from moralists about the standards embodied in Phyllis Dixey's act. Yet although Dixey herself complained that she had never been formally invited to contribute to raising the morale of the armed forces—a song in one revue declared, 'Though I'm frowned on by the Censor/And I'm not attached to ENSA'—her act seems to have been particularly popular with serving troops, to whom she regularly performed on her tours around Britain. Indeed, it was claimed that the government had expressed official appreciation of her efforts:

The more troops in the area, the more enthusiastic was the reception. The army started to make a fuss of Phyllis. She and the company were invited to officers' messes and to give Sunday night performances in camp theatres and local cinemas. After Canadian troops had gone on the rampage in protest at poor billets and nothing to do, Phyllis was flattered to receive a grateful letter from the War Office for her efforts in restoring morale with a series of appearances.[55]

In the autumn and winter of 1940/41, Dixey spent four months performing—reportedly to packed houses—in 'the garrison town to end all garrison towns', where she became known as 'The Queen of Aldershot'. Even allowing for some exaggeration by reviewers (and ignorance of the tricks habitually employed by performers to fake complete nudity) descriptions of her act suggest how ineffective the resolutions of the April conference had been:

> Miss Dixey gives an exhibition which you can't see in the West End: she appears with no clothes at all, dances, walks that board round the orchestra as well. There's no boldness about her performance and no simpering modesty. She appears nude as unconcernedly as she might play a game of tennis in her native Surbiton. Miss Dixey is an artist.[56]

These performances took place in a venue outside the Lord Chamberlain's licensing authority, and it would have been impossible for him to countenance granting a licence for such an act, but as he repeatedly said, it was equally difficult for him to impose standards which were being flouted elsewhere. In February 1942, the London County Council wrote to theatre managers reminding them of the obligation to which they had signed up in April 1940:

> The Council has recently observed with regret a tendency in some quarters to overlook or disregard the conclusions reached at the Lord Chamberlain's conference. The council would prefer to deal with this matter by co-operation with those concerned, and confidently looks to the management and profession for that co-operation.

Titman commented, 'This is probably the outcome of that recent furore in the *Daily Telegraph* about Miss Phyllis Dixey'. Titman himself was sympathetic towards Dixey.

> You will remember that I personally investigated this young lady's Act, although it was purely a variety turn, and I only wish I never saw any worse on the stage. I have constantly to be after the Windmill Theatre to keep their nudity within the bounds of Miss Dixey.[57]

Presumably the performance to which he refers was not the one reviewed above.

Yet by all accounts there was an offstage gentility and respectability about Dixey. Even her act was described as being 'as if teacher were taking off her clothes',[58] and, according to her biographers, she impressed the censors as 'a decent, respectable girl who neither drank nor smoked'. Titman, at least, was appreciative: 'We thought the photographs of her were quite good', he was later quoted as saying, and she had always shown a proper respect: 'At no time did she try to enforce any of her own will on things, she was always ready to accept whatever the Lord Chamberlain or the office thought fit to impose on her'.[59]

Within the Lord Chamberlain's Office, Titman was known as the 'expert' on 'the question of the brassières and trunks'. In February 1943 a script and photographs were submitted for *Step Out with Phyllis*, a revue: 'As there is a good deal of nudity whenever Miss Dixey is about', reported Game, 'Mr Titman is having a pre-view before production'. So much, then, for the impracticality of seeing acts before licensing them. One particular photograph was rejected, but Titman actually reversed the decision after seeing the pose in rehearsal—with the proviso that the lights were less bright. He also attended a performance, and was quite charmed by what he saw:

> The chief attraction is, of course, Miss Phyllis Dixey. Her performances are difficult to judge, but my own opinion is—after careful consideration—that she goes as far as possible but just keeps within the bounds of the regulations. In her favour I can say that she has a small figure, and although she is a strange mixture of demureness and provocation, she knows just how far she can go without giving any justification for interference on our part.

Titman insisted that he had 'looked at the question from both sides', and while continuing to assert 'I personally am against <u>any</u> display of nudity', he concluded:

> I do not think the Lord Chamberlain would be justified, so long as the regulations permit this form of entertainment, in interfering with any part of her current performance. I listened carefully to comments from other members of the audience, and I heard nothing but complimentary [sic] to her acts.

Unless he had coincided with a visit by followers of the Public Morality Council, the lack of criticism from audience members is less than surprising. However, Titman sent a courteous letter to Miss Dixey, making some minor suggestions:

> With regard to your four poses in scene 7, these will comply with the regulations provided you remain perfectly still and that the lighting is still further cut down. More care must be taken in your 'dance' at the end of

this act so that no intimate portion of your body is disclosed during movement.

The following year, the Public Morality Council did complain about Dixey's act in the non-stop revue at the Whitehall Theatre, *Good Night Ladies*. They did not see her stage demeanour in quite the same light as Titman. 'Serious objection is taken by my Committee to Miss Dixey's sly manner at the front of the stage and to her asides', wrote their secretary; 'in addition a booklet of nude studies featuring Miss Dixey is offered for sale'. Clarendon agreed that the material in her act was 'of border-line character', but Titman's report registered no significant concern: 'I found two small adjustments necessary in Miss Dixey's act. These, I think, were more of accident than intention'. Indeed, he self-consciously blamed his own presence for having affected her: 'I believe she saw me in the front of the auditorium, and that might have made her nervous!'. Titman rose to Miss Dixey's defence, acknowledging her 'sly manner' but suggesting this could not easily be amended since 'it would be difficult to detach this from the performance'. He described her as 'a woman of refinement, small of build and fair of skin', possessing 'a mixture of charming simplicity and subtle audacity', and he insisted that 'Possession of these qualities enables her to transform vulgarity into artistry'. Titman even persuaded Clarendon to attend a performance and reported (could the double entendre have been unintended?) that 'It would be difficult to ban her out of hand'. For once, he was prepared to endorse the liberal argument that since people knew what to expect, it was ridiculous to go to a performance and then complain. However, following widespread publicity in what Titman called 'a cheap periodical', the Home Office passed on objections they had received from a Scottish parson, specifically querying the fact that Dixey was being allowed to 'patter' during the poses: 'once the actress begins to talk she ceases to be statuesque and becomes a human figure'. Titman retorted with conviction that the article was 'exaggerated', the picture 'misleading', and the poses 'quite separate from the patter'. Clarendon, however, required 'that her gestures and remarks to the audience should be curtailed' and that the lighting should be made lower; he also intervened to prevent the theatre from selling the book of pictures entitled *Phyllis in Censorland*.

In January 1945 Titman noted disparagingly: 'The Public Morality Council seems suddenly to have come to life again'. It had complained that the current Windmill show was 'more bold' and 'brazen' than usual, and was guilty of 'increasing the weight of its broadside attack on the male weakness and susceptibility'. Clarendon's response was slightly unguarded and offered an unfortunate hostage: 'While I am prepared to agree that the performance is "bold", I do not feel that any offence is caused to those who desire this particular type of entertainment'. The Council picked up on the implications of this remark:

> The Committee . . . must dissent from the implied suggestion made, that if any section of the community desires a type of entertainment which might be described as salacious or indecent, they may be permitted to have it because it does not offend them.
>   The Sub-Committee venture to suggest that the effect on the standards of public behaviour, as well as on the private conduct, of official sanction being given to such a practice, could be nothing other than highly dangerous . . . I trust that some reassurance may be received.

The censorship had to dig its way out from an awkward position. It did so by avoiding the line on which the Council had made its attack:

> With all due respect to the Public Morality Council, there is a world of difference between 'bold' and 'salacious' or 'indecent'.
>   To ask . . . for an assurance that the Lord Chamberlain would not be prepared to admit a 'salacious' entertainment . . . seems barely polite.

Clarendon told the Council that he stuck to what he had said, 'with the proviso that the word "bold" . . . is strictly confined to its generally accepted meaning and not taken to imply anything worse'. He promised that there was 'no relaxation whatever in the standards of propriety on the stage which I and my Department require, nor of vigilance in upholding these'. Trying to turn defence into attack, he rounded on the Council's criticism and mistrust:

> I am very sorry to observe that this statement of mine . . . appears to have been stretched—or misunderstood—to such an extent that your Council has felt impelled to ask me for an assurance that as a matter of general principle, no 'salacious' or 'indecent' entertainment would ever receive my official sanction . . . I am sure you will agree that this query hardly requires an answer.

Reporting on photographs for a Windmill revue in 1941, Game had commented, 'I should like to see them disallowed as such, for once you begin permitting these exhibitions of nudity, it is extremely difficult to control them on any logical basis'.[60] In fact, the censorship frequently expressed the intention of revisiting the issue once the war was over. 'I hope the time is not far distant when the whole subject of nudity can be again fully considered', wrote Titman, and in 1944 Clarendon informed the Home Office:

> It is the Lord Chamberlain's intention after the war to call another Conference at St James's Palace when a further and stronger attempt will be made to obtain full agreement amongst the various sections of the

theatrical profession to rid the stage of nudity, and the semblance of nudity.[61]

Repeatedly, the Lord Chamberlain expressed regret that the 1940 Conference had not been willing to go further; 'all stage nudity should be stopped and I want to fully discuss this at the earliest moment', he declared in August 1941.[62] Titman, too, regularly professed that he had no sympathy for it: 'I dislike this type of act intensely and I would find no interest in going to see these exhibitions voluntarily', he noted after watching Phyllis Dixey in *Good Night Ladies*.[63] But the Office felt itself trapped and unable to do more than tinker at the edges: 'Whilst I have always been against nudity on the stage', wrote Titman, 'it would, I feel, be very difficult to suddenly stop these Windmill poses after so long, and without any warning'.[64] In 1941, the Bishop of Chichester enquired of Clarendon: 'is it really the case that public performances are allowed now where all but completely naked women are so clearly displayed on the stage?'. The bishop bemoaned 'the present state of public taste and ethical attitude', and expressed a hope 'that the day will come when it will be possible for the regulations to be made stricter'. Clarendon explained that his wish to ban nudity had been 'overruled by other licensing authorities much more so than by the theatrical people themselves', and that he was obliged to act 'in unison' with those authorities'.[65] This seems a slightly spurious argument, since logically it could have been applied equally to other aspects of theatre censorship. In 1942, Clarendon spelled out his position in response to another enquiry:

> I am glad you have written to me on the subject of nudity on the stage as it will enable me to explain my position.
>
> Soon after I was appointed Lord Chamberlain I called a conference at St James's Palace of representatives of all the licensing authorities and theatrical interests in the country in the hope that this matter, as well as vulgarity by comedians, might be eliminated by arrangement. Unfortunately, while everyone was in accord as regards vulgarity, I was unable to get nudity banned, the chief objector—to my intense surprise— being the London County Council.
>
> I thereupon had to set about formulating conditions governing exhibitions of nudity ... These have worked well in the circumstances, and although I shall endeavour after the war to carry my original intention, I am persuaded that the present is not an appropriate time to take any further action.[66]

Did the Office really believe it would ever be possible to push the genie back into the bottle?

CHAPTER SEVEN

'Beastly Practices'

Sexual Taboos in Wartime

> This chap complains
> Because I keep the Drama bound in chains—
> Of decency, of course . . . Morality
> (As I conceive it) . . . for the merest fee
> For every play: He pays me my two guineas,
> And then, no matter what his moral sin is,
> The Law can't touch him—he's <u>above</u> the Law!
> A sound insurance. Thus I censored Shaw,
> Ibsen and Barker,—Housman—Maeterlinck:
> Fellows whose names, like their opinions, stink!
> (*Genius Limited*, 1945)[1]

During the campaign against stage nudity, the censorship maintained that any slip in moral standards was confined to revues and similar entertainments. In February 1940, the Comptroller responded with caution to the Lord Chamberlain's suggestion that they were perhaps guilty of being too lenient in other fields:

> I agree that we must keep a tight hold on productions . . . but I am sure you will agree we must not go too far in the one direction, or there will be an outcry from the Theatre Managers and Producers. This would be much more difficult to combat.
>
> I am satisfied that during the last five months there has been no play licensed that can give rise to any complaint.

In March, Gordon also emphatically informed the Home Office that there had been no deterioration in the standards of 'the straight play'.[2]

Nevertheless, Game was clearly taken aback at the start of 1940 when he read *Queer People*:*

---

* Written by Colin Dale

In my ten years experience as an Examiner of Plays I have never read anything which was so impossible for public or private production . . .

Not only will it have to be banned, but every effort should be made to prevent it being produced by one of the bogus Theatre Clubs. I should suggest a consultation with the Home Office, with a view to warning the promoters that any attempt to produce it anywhere will at once provoke interference by the police, if this is legally possible.

It was the explicit references to homosexuality which so shocked him: 'The play opens and ends with a farewell homily on the penalties of sodomy spoken by a headmaster to a boy whom he is in the act of expelling'. This theme, said Game, was woven right though the text:

A neurotic young man, Clifford Terry, who has just become engaged to be married to Janet Rutherford, meets after a ten years interval Jim Marlowe, his lover when at school—the boy being the elder of the two was the one to be expelled. Jim . . . realises that he is incurably in love with him and proceeds to try and get Clifford away from his girl. By persuading the young man that . . . he is still abnormal sexually, and will only court disaster by marrying a woman, Jim ultimately persuades Cliff to marry him, as they euphemistically define their future relationship. Janet's distress . . . is so extreme that he agrees to give up Jim Marlowe and to marry her. . . . There is an hysterically dramatic and emotional scene, only ended by the arrival of a woman friend of Marlowe's, Mavis Burtle. . . . She uses her own experience as a Lesbian to induce Jim to send Clifford back to Janet. Clifford . . . shoots himself!

Game insisted that 'The play is even more unpleasant than my précis might suggest', and Clarendon supported his assessment: 'this revolting play cannot be allowed'. He also expressed the hope 'that if any bogus Theatre Club produces it a prosecution will follow', and the management was informed that 'His Lordship considers it a piece of impertinence that such a play should have been submitted'. The Duchess theatre immediately caved in, trying to deflect the criticism away from themselves and onto the playwright, and claiming they had submitted the script in error after two manuscripts were mixed up: 'Queer People . . . should, of course, have been sent straight back whence it came'. The censors doubted the truth of this story: 'I cannot see that your explanation as to how this particular play came to be submitted is very convincing', replied Gordon, and he took the unusual step of sending the script (and Game's comments on it) to Osbert Peake at the Home Office:

I do not know whether it is legally possible to take action as suggested by the Reader . . . I certainly think that the Home Office and, possibly, the authorities at Scotland Yard should see it.

I can confirm that in some twelve years experience of this office I have never before had such a disgusting play submitted . . .

> *Queer People* is so disgusting that possibly no publishers would accept it,
> but I would not put it past one of the Theatre Clubs producing it.

Gordon reminded the Home Office that the Lord Chamberlain had no
effective control over theatre clubs, and that there had been previous
occasions when a 'banned' play had not only been published but had used
the ban to promote itself. Peake replied:

> Dear Snapper,
>   I am sending it on to the division of the Home Office which deals with
> such matters . . . I have looked through it, and fully share your views about
> its character.

Ultimately, the Home Office and the Director of Public Prosecutions
decided it would be impracticable to prosecute either a published text or a
private production. This was regrettable since

> Even according to the lax and liberal standards now prevailing with regard
> to the drama and literature it appears to me to be impossible to defend the
> presentation on the stage of the sexual perversions so plainly indicated in
> the dialogue.

However,

> While it is clear enough that members of an unsuspecting audience would
> (or might) be horrified . . . I doubt whether, if it were printed as a book,
> any Court would find the book obscene. There is not a word of any
> description or account of the practice—there are a phrase or two on the
> question whether the practice is a vice or an illness, and broadly speaking
> there is just an acceptance of the existence of the practice.

Apart from the fact that the writer had been 'clever enough to imit [sic]
from the dialogue . . . a description or account of the beastly practices
which the several perversions involve', another obstacle to prosecution was
the fact that, by contrast with a play about lesbianism submitted ten years
previously, people already knew of the existence of male homosexuals:

> Sir Charles Biron told me after his retirement that in dealing with the
> 'Well of Loneliness' his decision was due 1) to the fact that he thought the
> practice repulsive and 2) to the fact that he believed that very few women
> or girls in the country knew of its existence, and he wanted to protect them
> from such knowledge.

Recent precedents made the prosecution of a published version almost
impossible: 'this sort of subject is commonplace now in the medical or
pseudo-medical books on sex which are not prosecuted', wrote one civil
servant, and he cited a previous decision 'not to prosecute the
Encyclopaedia of Sex which mentions every imaginable form of
perversion'. Gordon passed the Home Office minutes on to the Lord

Chamberlain: 'It seems to me a reflection on successive Governments, and Home Secretaries', he wrote, 'that "present standards" should have been allowed to become so lax'.[3]

Perhaps surprisingly, there is no definite record of *Queer People* having been either published or privately performed (and it seems as if the script has not survived either). But it was probably no coincidence that, in early 1940, the Lord Chamberlain's Office, with the assistance of plain-clothes officers from the Metropolitan Police, instituted a series of under-cover investigations of private venues. These were officially undertaken 'In pursuance of the Lord Chamberlain's policy of making periodical tests of the bona-fides of soi-disant private Theatre Clubs operating in London', and where it proved possible to buy tickets or to acquire membership too easily, as in the case of the Torch Theatre, prosecutions were promptly instituted.[4] But these were probably also intended to put the frighteners on club theatres generally, and to discourage them from thinking that, with the country at war and the Lord Chamberlain removed to Windsor, rules could be easily flouted.

The Lord Chamberlain's Office had no intention of encouraging any further laxness. In February 1940, 'insinuations' of 'an abnormal relationship' were removed from *Take Back Your Freedom*, Winifred Holtby's political drama about a repressive dictatorship coming to power in Britain; and in March they excised as 'hardly necessary' a 'reference to the female climacteric' from 'an abnormal thriller' about devil worship.'[5] *A Woman of Forty*† was also rejected on the grounds of its extensive promiscuity:

> It might be made into an amusing and not too outrageous Comedy of Manners; but at present much too much of the dialogue is embarrassingly sophisticated . . . If the author is willing to tone the whole thing down . . . less talk about the facts of sex for instance, and less insistence on Hubert's adultery with Joanna . . . I think it might be considered.[6]

In April, they received a request to lift the ban on Edouard Bourdet's play, *La Prisonnière*; 'It has never I think been disputed', wrote the prospective manager, 'that the dramatist castigates most severely by implication a certain unnamed vice with which the play is in part concerned'. He pointed out there was 'no slightest impropriety or innuendo anywhere in the play', and that 'so serious a play by so distinguished a dramatist' should now be licensed. Game remained uncompromising:

> The theme of this play is lesbianism and it is therefore taboo. However discreetly the subject may be handled, as admittedly it is in this play,

---

  ★ *Temporary Residence*, by C. Campion
  † Written by Henry C. James

performance in the theatre gives most undesirable advertisement, under emotional conditions, to something which is evil and anti-social.[7]

The following year the Office turned down another play touching on homosexuality, not because of anything explicit in the text, but, at least in part, because they thought that the actors might play up a latent theme. Set on a ship sailing from New York to England, *Flower of Grass** was widely supposed to be based on the mysterious death of the actor and playwright Frank Vosper in the mid thirties. It centred on a triangular relationship involving Larry, a cynical and disillusioned actor-author, Mike, his manager and friend, and Deirdre, who knows her love for Larry is hopeless and who, in turn, is loved by Mike. Larry eventually kills himself by jumping overboard, and, as Game reported, 'There is a lot which is left purposely vague'. But despite the non-specific nature of the text, the Reader recommended refusing a licence:

> The play is based on the suicide of Frank Vosper under similar circumstances a few years ago . . . Nothing very clear was allowed to come out, but Vosper being a notorious pervert, it was said of course that he drowned himself because the boy deserted him for the girl. . . . It will be said, and with truth, that this play is intended to furnish an explanation of the tragedy. Further it will be said that it is intended to imply an un-natural relationship between the men, Larry and Mike, although there is little evidence in the script to suggest such a thing. There is also the possibility that in the acting greater point could be made of this, and it might well be so. This of course would give the play an ugly twist, and one which we could not countenance.

Because there was no evidence to authenticate such suspicions, the Office fell back on the convenient justification that it was 'undesirable that plays should be based on recent tragedies'.[8]

In August 1942, the censors were dubious about *No Pansies for Mr Standish*:[†] 'The authors of this play will have to put their heads together and think up a new title', they insisted; 'Besides being suggestive the present one is misleading. There are no pansies in this play'. But the level of implicit sexual violence at the climax of the second act was also too provocative:

> Stephen has threatened to spank Betty in return for two slaps on the face, which she has given him. He has attempted to carry out his threat earlier in the act; but has been interrupted . . . Betty's skirt having come off in Stephen's hands during the struggle, she being left in panties, and he with the skirt in his hands . . . I see no harm in this curtain scene, but in case it may shock the old fashioned (Betty is in pyjamas) and excite the 'tired

---

* Written by Frank Charlesworth
† Written by John Sayles and Ireland Cutter

business man' too effectually, perhaps it would be better to bring down the curtain on Stephen advancing upon Betty.

The endorsement accompanying the licence duly stipulated that the act 'should end with Steve advancing towards Betty, with the stage direction "as he places her across his knee and starts the spanking", to be omitted'.[9]

In December, they rejected *Husbands Can't Help It*,* because of its sexual immorality. As Game explained, it was 'always a rather uncomfortable business on the stage when a young girl is the seducer'. In his view, the treatment of the material was exploitative:

> Sex is of course one of the legitimate subjects of drama in its comedic equally as in its tragic aspects, but the problem for Censorship lies in how the matter is handled by the author . . . I feel the author is out to shock and at times succeeds, or would if allowed to try. I am all for healthy frankness, as long as it is healthy and not licentious, frank and not pornographic; but it is undeniable that a good deal of what is claimed to be modern freedom of expression is just dirt for dirt's sake.

Game was prepared to consider simply making a series of cuts, but Nugent, who said his 'first and really only reaction is one of nausea', was not willing to make concessions:

> I do think that if a play is as near the knuckle as this one, it deserves little consideration if in addition it has no merit. As Mr Game put so clearly, sex is a legitimate subject of drama if it is handled properly by the author, but when it is used as the sole theme of a play, not to point an argument, or bring out a point of view, it merely becomes dirt for dirt's sake . . . I do not believe that any number of cuts in the play as it now stands will make it presentable . . . It is all such dirty post-card stuff.[10]

In January 1943, they also toned down *Striplings*,† a drama about 'the complications of adolescent passion' involving 'a hearty youth and a child of nature', of sixteen and seventeen years old. 'This is really rather young for an affair', wrote Game, 'despite the example set by Romeo and Juliet'.[11]

In March, the censorship intervened in relation to Michael Robinson's *Baltic Passage*, a 'queer play' set among the passengers on board a Swedish cargo boat, which evoked memories of *The Green Bay Tree*:

> The trouble from our point of view with this play is of course the character of Bunny and his relationship with Zadek. The author in his endeavour to make his villain particularly loathsome has given him both a mistress and a boy-friend, and in doing so has presented us with the problem of Mr Dulcimer and his choir boy over again . . . before this play

---

* Written by Eliot Crawshay-Williams
† Written by Nina W. Hooke

is given a licence I think the author should be required to remove, as far as he can, any suggestion that there are immoral relations between the man and the boy.

The Office required that this element should be, if not suppressed, then at least made less visible.

> The nastiness of the character Zadek and the presence in his following of an effeminate young man must always give rise to speculation, by the sophisticated, but at least, I think, we should demand that the unsophisticated (if any) don't have the facts shoved right under their noses. If the relationship between Zadek and Bunny is left sufficiently vague—the boy is a pianist and might conceivably be taken round by Zadek as a tame musician (the author could perhaps work on this idea) the play can then, I think, be allowed.[12]

The following year, the censors again insisted on removing 'the perversion theme' from an amateur play at Godalming;* the author was 'amazed and puzzled', insisting that his work was intended as 'a warning and a lesson to a thoughtless generation', and that 'far more horrible and loathsome things' were regularly passed. He cited Priestley's *Dangerous Corner* as a case where perversion was 'a loathsome fact', whereas in his own play it was merely a false accusation made against one of the characters. 'Is all you require a different and more veiled wording, or elimination entirely?', he queried. Titman uncharitably requested Game to 'lend a hand with a reply to this old fool?', and they spelled out the situation more directly:

> The Lord Chamberlain is very definitely of opinion that sexual perversion is a subject best excluded from the theatre. His Lordship is quite prepared to agree that a brief and oblique use of such a theme, as in your play, is probably neither offensive nor harmful; but experience has shown that once the subject of perversion is admitted as permissible, inevitably it becomes increasingly difficult to limit its use.

The playwright maintained that he would 'never have dreamt of using the accusation of perversion had I not heard it brought into *Dangerous Corner* by Priestley'. However, he rewrote the play: 'I think you will have to agree that perversion will much more require to be guessed at now'. Game did agree: 'I think the author has wrapped his meaning up so successfully now that to all intents and purposes there isn't any!'.[13]

One play about heterosexual promiscuity which provoked a response almost matching that caused by *Queer People* was *The Marry-Go-Round*, first submitted in 1940, and one of a series which brought the playwright, Charlotte Frances, into direct conflict with the Lord Chamberlain. The

---

* *Judgement and the Sifers*, by George Tanner

focus in this case was on husbands and wives who agree to swap partners for a night, though one of the men is swiftly rejected by his new partner and retreats to the bath. 'I felt like a bath myself after reading the first act', wrote Dearmer. He had no doubt that 'the play should be banned as thoroughly sordid and depraved', and he insisted it was

> no defence to point out that . . . the four characters are all too drunk to do anything but speak. The mere exhibition of an intended exchange of wives would be bad enough, but here we see the deal being put into effect . . . blatant is the only word for a play leading up in the first act to a climax of intended double adultery . . . It is not as though there is a glimmer of theme in the author's mind. Whatever she may say this play must be demoralising since it introduces an artificial glamour to refined debauchery. It is not as though the audience (particularly at the present time with so many visitors in the country) consisted entirely of hard-boiled theatregoers whom such stuff would not affect.

Clarendon agreed, and was adamant that 'No encouragement must be given to the writer to submit an amended version'. But Frances, while admitting that her play was 'modern and sophisticated', again claimed it was a highly moral piece, intended as a corrective, and that the judgement was unfair:

> I passionately wish to plead that this is not a prurient play, neither is it a play for the lewd-minded. . . . Not once, during the entire three acts, is one piece of infidelity perpetrated, nor does any act of adultery occur . . . unlike many of our present day dramas.
>
> Moreover, it is my earnest hope that when my play is finished it teaches and advises a closer adherence to marital laws . . . I seriously wish to state that both I, personally, and my play, are against promiscuity . . . as extolled and magnified by such plays as *Design for Living*, etc, etc. I wished the moral of my play to teach the danger of desire frustrated by denial (as happens in most cases of middle class domestic life) which can grow to terrific proportion if not recognised for the transient thing it really is when opposed to the solidarity and reality of the blessings of the marital state. . . . In writing this play I had hoped that, in revealing the weaknesses of the male partner in modern marriages, I might help his female in some small way to understand the 'strange beast' a little more, and, in understanding him, to give him the compassion and tolerance that every struggling man needs from his woman.

Reading her play in the light of these claims, Game was disposed to accept the writer's good faith. Perhaps he was caught up in the sense that a new age might be about to sweep away the past:

> we should not forget that most of us, who have to deal with dramatic censorship, are Victorians, and that the young of today enjoy, and I think on balance it is no bad thing, a much greater freedom of thought and

expression. To blindly oppose them when they try in all sincerity to express and discuss their ideas, would be as unwise as it would prove fatal.

The characters, he said, were 'not really bad, only unhappy', and in any case, 'to ban plays because the characters were unpleasant would lead to some very strange decisions'. Game suggested there should be a note in the programme spelling out the good faith of the drama, and he went beyond the call of duty in annotating the script and proposing a detailed series of amendments in relation to the drunkenness and the adultery: 'I have performed a major operation on it, and have done my best to make it possible', he wrote.

The Marry-Go-Round was sent to members of the Advisory Board, including Clarendon's predecessor as Lord Chamberlain. Cromer acknowledged Game's arguments, but doubted the wisdom of issuing a licence:

> It is unwise and fatal to oppose attempts at sincerity on the part of the young in ventilating a sociological problem on the stage and thereby endeavouring to point a solution and remedy.
>   But the question is, does the Authoress succeed in her object?
>   The answer to my mind is that she does not.

He concluded that it was 'a play that the majority of playgoers would consider to be radically sordid and depraved', and Game accepted the decision to reject it:

> Miss Francis [sic] has now had a very good run for her money . . . she is the author of her own disappointments. Her intentions were, I believe, excellent, but her methods unfortunate! I have privately urged her to give up these violent sex themes, and to turn her undoubted ability to the writing of plays less likely to bring her into conflict with the Censorship.[14]

A few months later, Frances did submit another play, *Strange Sport,** which focused on the wife of a psychology professor whose 'chief amusement is in arousing passion in her admirers, which she has no intention of satisfying'. Game was again prepared to believe that the play was written from a moral standpoint, but he doubted whether this was sufficiently transparent: 'As with *Marry-Go-Round*, the author hides a serious intention behind her comedy but she hides it all too effectually to be easily visible to an audience in the theatre'. Even more than usual, war was a time for striking unambiguous positions, and the 'extremely sensuous love scenes' were adjudged likely to 'shock an appreciable portion of the public' and to prove 'a somewhat misleading method of pointing a

---

* Frances submitted it under the pseudonym of Jean Longdon

moral'.[15] *Strange Sport* was again refused, and two years later the same author's contemporary adaptation of *Lysistrata* was also rejected, even though Game acknowledged that translations which were 'rather more bawdy than this' had previously been licensed.

> it might appear illogical to ban this play and to allow Aristophanes to have his say. The answer to that objection is, I think, that costume does make some difference in the Theatre, that the Greek play has only a very limited appeal to the more or less intellectual, while this play would be seen by the ordinary audiences of the commercial theatre, and finally that it is very doubtful whether the Greek author would have got his play licensed, if he had lived in England in 1942 instead of in Athens in the 5th Century BC.

Nugent was more prepared to grant a licence, but this time Game was unpersuaded:

> Colonel Nugent is apt . . . to judge these matters too exclusively from the point of view of the sophisticated London audience . . . to the many, who know nothing of Aristophanes and this play, I fear that the theme of this farce may appear somewhat startling.[16]

However, it was Game who, in 1943, persuaded Clarendon to issue a licence for Jean Cocteau's version of the Oedipus myth, *The Infernal Machine*, which had previously been turned down because of its references to incest. 'My predecessor had a somewhat uncertain sense of the Theatre, which at times led him astray', wrote Game, 'and I consider this play a case in point'; he argued that the Office 'would make itself supremely ridiculous by refusing a licence'. It helped that Cocteau's play enjoyed respectable advocates and that its performance would be safely away from the public gaze:

> The production is now sponsored by The Cambridge Arts Theatre Trust, of which the trustees, as the Lord Chamberlain will see from the list printed at the head of the covering letter, are a galaxy of Economic, Municipal, Musical and Scholastic eminence. The play will be performed before a cultured audience, and there is no fear of it later being performed before an un-cultured one: they would be bored to death and would never sit it out; the ordinary theatregoer shuns the high-brow Theatre like the plague-house. [17]

Clarendon accepted his Reader's recommendation, even though the previous year Lenormand's *The Simoun* had been turned down because 'the king-beam of the play's architecture' was incest:

> There have of course been other plays about incest before now, mostly *Oedipus Rex* and *The Cenci*, but there is a world of difference between poetic drama about remote Greeks or Italians and a Lenormand play about modern French. I may be getting squeamish in my old age, but I really

think the play rather strong meat for an ordinary audience in a Commercial Theatre.[18]

Plays from classical Greece were, of course, subject to the Theatres Act because they were being presented in modern translations; while this was not true of seventeenth-century English dramas, this does not necessarily mean they were free of unofficial censorship. In 1939, Her Majesty's Office of Public Works, which was responsible for activities in the Royal Parks, had been so apprehensive about Robert Atkin's planned open-air production of Shakespeare's *Pericles* in Regent's Park that they sent a copy of the already cut script to the Lord Chamberlain, asking for advice: 'If you think that it would be desirable to make further cuts would you very kindly suggest them?'. The Comptroller pointed out that they could take no official responsibility, but he was willing to help:

All I can do is to tell you unofficially how it appears to us.

Mr Gwatkin has read the play very carefully and his opinion is that it would be unnecessary and, indeed, impossible to make any further cuts.

Mr Atkin has obviously been very careful to take out the most blatant cuts . . .

At the same time one cannot get away from the fact that it is a strong play on two unpleasant subjects, to say the least of it. The theme of the first part being incest, and the second the procuration of a young girl, both of which are presumably hardly suitable for an audience of children.

I must make it quite clear that I am only giving you an unofficial account of the play, and obviously the Lord Chamberlain in his official capacity would have no objection to it; but whether it is politic to present a play of this sort to an audience such as you describe must be a matter between the Office of Works and the producer.[19]

In 1941 an MP sent the Lord Chamberlain a letter from a constituent 'drawing attention to the title of a play at the Strand Theatre'. *'Tis Pity She's a Whore* had been briefly revived the previous April by Donald Wolfit, when the Theatrical Managers' Association had taken it upon themselves to ask the Lord Chamberlain 'whether you consider it advisable to submit this play to your department'. Gordon had replied that if it were produced 'strictly in accordance with the original version' it was unlikely to be of direct interest to the censorship; 'If, however, any alteration has been made to the original version', he warned them, 'it would become a new Stage Play, within the meaning of the Theatres Act, and as such would require to be submitted for the Lord Chamberlain's approval'.[20] In 1941, Titman reminded the MP that the drama was too old to require a licence, and informed him that 'the Lord Chamberlain did not feel justified in interfering with this Jacobean tragedy'. Titman had evidently done his homework, and instructed the MP that 'The principle characteristic of

John Ford's works' was 'the powerful depiction of melancholy, sorrow and despair'. It is tempting to wonder whether his choice of words might have evoked echoes of the national mood in early 1941—a mood which the government's wartime powers of censorship had an obligation to discourage. Was Titman perhaps hinting that there were other avenues which the MP could pursue if he wanted to keep Ford's work off the stage? Even though he knew that the production had been mounted only for two private performances, which had already occurred, Titman wrote to the Lord Chamberlain: 'I happened to come across a critique of this play from the *Stage*, from which I discovered that the theme is as bad as the title, and the dialogue possibly worse!'. Clarendon certainly took it seriously: 'This play had better be put on the blacklist or a note made about it so that we can be on the watch . . . it may appear again'.[21]

While the hostilities of war tend to encourage an instinctive rejection of the enemy's culture, an increased identification with the characteristics and traditions of allies is perhaps likely to occur at both a conscious and an unconscious level. Thus a series of melodramas and pageants extolling and idealising the Soviet Union penetrated British culture to a remarkable extent at this period.[22] Similarly, the arrival of America in the war—and of its G.I.s in Britain—seduced individuals and aspects of the home culture into aping aspects of the American way of life. Certainly, the influence of American cinema led to conflicts, particularly over the issue of violence, and in July 1942, the Public Morality Council complained about the stage version of *No Orchids for Miss Blandish*.* In comparing the stage version with the recent film, *The Times* focused on the way in which the violence functioned:

> A good gangster film and a good gangster play are not quite the same thing. The film has a way of registering the brutalities as part of a smooth-running and exciting game; on the stage the same brutalities appear raw and are either more shocking or more boring.

Yet the review recognised that the production was in tune with the mood of theatregoers:

> This is a good gangster play, and it moves with certainty from shooting to knifing and on to the torture of a lovely young debutante through the agency of homicidal mania and imbecile viciousness. Playgoers who do not happen to be squeamish will probably enjoy the impact of its brutality . . . Each new revolution brings a brutal murder bespattered by brutal jokes; and the applause last night seemed to promise popularity.[23]

---

* Written by J.H. Chase and R. Nesbit

The Bishop of London wrote to the Office, uncertain whether 'there was any specific thing to which exception can be taken', but worried by the reputation of the playwright: 'The author of this play was recently convicted at the Old Bailey for causing an obscene book to be published. This play is based on a different book, but the same mind has produced both'. He was concerned about the general tone and the likely impact of the performance on the nation:

> The play is of a gangster type. Some gangster plays and films are alright, but there is a stage in which they become really demoralising and degrading in their influence . . . We feel that the influence of this play cannot but be really undesirable. The whole setting and suggestion is degenerate. . . .
>
> The Council was very disturbed at the thought that this play should be coming to London. The morale of the people in this present struggle is on trial. People judge England very largely by London, and representatives of all the Allied Nations are to be found in London. No-one would object to plays which are a temporary distraction and a relief to the spirit, but serious exception can be taken to a play whose general atmosphere is one of violence, bloodshed, blackmail and lust in a violent setting.

Clarendon conceded some of the Bishop's points, but defended with some eloquence the genre to which the work belonged. In an important declaration of principle—which he must have known could easily be leaked to the press—he refused the logic that demanded that everyone should be prevented from seeing a work of art simply because a few people might be adversely influenced by it. And not for the first time, he doubted how far the theatre had the power to influence behaviour:

> The play is admittedly violent and sordid, but there is this to be said in its favour, that in it evil is shown as evil, and not as in so many films, and even in some plays, dressed up in romantic glamour.
>
> 'Horror' plays have ever since Elizabethan days been an intermittent feature of the English theatre . . . It does no more than satisfy in the adult audience the same emotional need that attracts a child into the Chamber of Horrors at Madame Tussauds, or anyone of us into an easy chair with the latest thriller. Except, perhaps, in the case of a very few abnormal persons, for whose interests alone the Censorship cannot legislate, the effect of such plays as this ceases at the theatre exit.

Clarendon also pointed out that the book on which the drama was based had already been widely read, and that his own Examiner had judged the play to be milder than the novel. However, he did reassure the Bishop that the management had promised 'to tone down as far as possible the more violent incidents'. After watching the play in performance, Titman and Game agreed there was no need to intervene; 'Personally, I dislike this type of play', wrote Titman; 'shooting, knifing and other brutalities. Mr Game is bored with them'. But they echoed Clarendon's insistence that horror and violence were nothing new to the theatre: 'it is not so bad as the old-time melodramas, or the grand guignol plays which crop up from time to time'.[24]

On the other hand, there were some traditions of taste to be defended, and the Lord Chamberlain's Office was ready to emphasise the different standards of Britain and her transatlantic cousins. In October 1942, they rejected *Early American Murder,*[*] a play set around a New York brothel in the 1830s which focused on 'a young blaggard who lives largely on the earnings of the most famous tart in the town'. Game commented: 'it may be alright in America, but over here I think that people would find brothel scenes and fun amongst the whores rather strong and unusual meat'.[25] In December, they also refused a stage version[†] of 'that lugubrious American ballad', *Bonny and Clyde*:

> The play is a theatrically effective picture of the crude and violent world it depicts, and is quite possibly written sincerely and with no intention of shocking anyone's sensibilities; but American taste is much more robust than ours and the play which is one of brutal realism, seems to me quite impossible for production.[26]

And in January 1943, they required some cloaking of the explicit approach of Hemingway's *The Fifth Column*:

> A good many of the scenes are played in or around the beds of the adjoining rooms, there is nothing suggestive in this, not even really when Philip . . . gets into bed with Dorothy; but as a concession to English prejudices it will of course have to be altered. . . . The character, Anita, is quite inoffensive, but 'tart' might as well be omitted from the list of characters . . . We being less outspoken than the Americans, some cuts seem desirable.[27]

In 1944, the censorship rejected *Wallflowers,*[‡] an American comedy about two sisters at college; one of the sisters attracts more male attention than the other, but these roles are reversed when people are led to believe that the less attractive one has actually slept with someone. It made no difference that the belief turns out to have been wrong:

> Recently we licensed another comedy written around a somewhat similar idea; but in that play the audience was always aware that there was smoke but no fire. Here the audience are left for a time with the conviction that there is a regular blaze.

---

* Written by Bayard Veiller and Martin Vale
† *Frankie and Johnnie*—American authors unknown
‡ Written by Reginald Denham and Mary Orr

Some scenes were 'indecent and embarrassing, or should be so considered in a civilised society', and, despite its resolution of innocence, the play was potentially disturbing. 'Sexual precocity is a topical, and to all serious minds, a distressing problem and therefore as a dramatic theme requires careful handling. In this play I do not think it gets it'. A substantially revised version was submitted which removed 'practically all the embarrassing dialogue', and Game thought it sufficiently innocuous to recommend: 'the buzzing of the boys around Jackie in the third act is reduced to one young man who comes to try and make a date'. But Nugent still had reservations:

> It is so American in its so-called humour that the ordinary English theatre-goer will not think it in the least amusing and a number will undoubtedly be shocked. It is a dubious story, and even though it may be satisfactorily cleared up in the end from the moral point of view, the fact remains that the whole point of the play is that a well-brought-up girl of 18 years goes off to bed in a low night-club with a young man who is so drunk as to be impotent. Not a very nice idea whichever way you may look at it and not made very much better by the fact that the boy and girl had, in fact, been married that day, but with the bridegroom already too drunk to be aware of the fact.

He recommended further alterations: 'great care must be taken to avoid underlining the essentially dirty bits'. In the event, the script remained unlicensed and apparently unperformed.[28]

The censorship even required changes in an American service revue, to ensure it conformed to British traditions:

> American taste in humour is distinctly cruder than ours is, and with every desire to be indulgent to our Allies, I think that there are things in this Revue which we should cut out. It is inadvisable to set up one standard for our own people and another for foreigners.

It is striking that one of the things they most objected to was the attempt to insert a moment of seriousness and tragedy into a light and bawdy show:

> a short scene in which an Air Force mechanic learns of his brother's death . . . leads in to Rupert Brooke's lines . . . 'They shall not grow old' and 'there is no death' sung by the mechanic. Of course this scene is not censurable, but is it suitable in the middle of a revue? In my opinion it is not.[29]

The company were persuaded that the scene should be played only within private and not public performances.

Under the threat of military invasion, the censorship saw it as more than ever their duty to resist attempts to subvert the national taste, as they defined it. In 1941, they had refused to license *Seven Houses*, a play by the Hungarian-born playwright Lajos Biro, which argued for recognition of 'our country's responsibility to all enslaved and exploited nations, at whatever cost to ourselves'. Though championed as a work 'of deep ethical and political import', the central metaphor hinged on the inheritance by a young English woman of a chain of South America brothels:

> I do not think we can pass a play which is all mixed up with prostitutes and prostitution, although there is little in the situations which is offensive. It may be hypocrisy or it may be decent reticence, but it is our English way to ignore such things, and my own feeling is that if an author chooses to place the action of a melodrama in a brothel, he has only himself to blame if his play is banned.[30]

Maurice Browne, the manager, did his best to persuade the Lord Chamberlain to change his mind:

> Mr Biro is not only one of the most famous among living European dramatists—a naturalized British citizen (I believe) who is passionately pro-British and has made his home in this country for a number of years—but was also, as recently as Wednesday last, appointed by the P.E.N. Club the official representative of expatriated Hungarian writers, with a view to his forming a federation of pro-British writers throughout all the Danubian countries. This might perhaps be thought an additional reason for reconsidering the decision.

But it was another five years before an amended script was finally approved.

Another boundary which seemed to be in danger of collapse during wartime was the natural and essential division between classes. In May 1943, Game became rather agitated over Reginald Beckwith's *A Soldier for Christmas*, a comedy set in the country home of 'a charming conventional woman who does her best to live up to the standards of the Brave New World in which she finds herself involved by war'. As an expression of her willingness to embrace the spirit of unity, she invites an ordinary soldier into her home for Christmas; in an echo of *Miss Julie*, a play which had caused great problems for the Office in the preceding decades, the aristocratic daughter then finds herself sexually attracted to the working-class male. The relationship comes to nothing, and Game approved of the satire targeted at those who believed the war would lead to the disintegration of class barriers, and the play's reassertion of their naturalness and inviolability.

> The central idea of this comedy is to make a little good tempered fun at the expense of this New Democracy which the war has thrust upon us all. There is nothing wrong with that of course, a little mockery is timely with the idealists queuing up to make post-war life unbearable.

Near the end of the play, the soldier conveniently goes off with a Cockney girl and the daughter falls into the arms of a young scientist who is also in love with her. 'So much', mocked Game, 'for the "Brave New World"!'. But there were still aspects which worried him, for 'in developing his theme the author creates a situation which . . . raises a rather difficult question of censorship'. At one point, the daughter actually takes the soldier to her bedroom, and it appears to an audience that the relationship may indeed be consummated: 'Subsequently, of course, we learn that nothing did happen in Phoebe's room', explained Game; 'Bill very sensibly kept talking: class barriers are not broken down in a night'. But the Reader was anxious about what audiences might anticipate was *going* to happen. Or at least, some audiences:

> This is a play for a sophisticated audience . . . it is to be produced at the Cambridge Arts Theatre, where it will be quite at home. . . . If the matter ended there I should recommend it right away, but I cannot guarantee that it will not be produced elsewhere, and I confess I feel a little dubious about it being suitable for the ordinary audience.

He agonised at length about the extent to which audience expectations had become modified:

> would a comedy scene in which a father and mother dispute the question of interference, while their daughter is possibly losing her virginity upstairs, shock a modern audience . . . when one reflects how both old and young lap up the appalling indecencies of the Restoration, one feels that they have no right to boggle at anything. I don't suppose the younger generation would see anything in the play to worry about, but no doubt some of the older would.
>
> There is no question to my mind of the play doing anybody any harm. It will have no other effect except to amuse, and to argue otherwise would be to show an ignorance of the psychology of theatre audiences. This being the case should we bother about the possible objections of a few old women (whether in skirts, trousers or aprons)? Not unless, as the Lord Chamberlain once said to me, the few become many. That to me is the problem, will they? I should like Colonel Nugent's views.

This time, Nugent was less worried than Game; he decided that the play was 'written with such discretion that it never becomes even unpleasant':

> Personally I can see no harm in it. . . . I cannot believe that anyone except the most puritanical (and they would be shocked at anything) could take the least exception to it.
>
> To make the author take out the idea of sexual intercourse altogether would, I think, ruin the play.

Nevertheless, Game and Nugent went carefully through the text together, toning down and removing the innuendo.[31]

However, there is little sign of a general shift in what audiences were ready to tolerate, or of any relaxation on the part of the censors. Indeed, in the autumn of 1944, the Lord Chamberlain took the very rare step of withdrawing a licence he had already issued. *Felicity Jasmine** focused on relationships between a woman and her two daughters (one of whom is married) and American soldiers, and it had been approved on the recommendation of Geoffrey Dearmer. But after reading the reviews, Titman went to see it and was appalled:

> The play is wrongly described as a farce. It is a sociological drama which endeavours to prove that the English woman (of all ages) belongs not to the home but to the barnyard, that she is disloyal to her husband and to the recognised standards of living, and that if she cannot entice a man to her bedroom she will force him there.

Titman also undertook a little audience research:

> During the first interval I walked round the corridors to listen for criticisms. I hung on to two American officers: one said it was 'raw', and the other said it was 'a bit too dirty' for him. I heard plenty of adverse comments, but not one remark in favour of the play.

He was convinced that the Office had made a mistake in licensing it:

> I have no doubt in my mind that the play should never have received a licence. Mr Dearmer read the script and I can only suggest that either he did not see the point of the theme clearly or that the acting came over in a much worse light than the script implied.

Titman said that even the theatre staff agreed with him, and he was prepared to take a drastic step: 'I told them I should advise the Lord Chamberlain to withdraw the licence, unless, of course, they would be willing to surrender it voluntarily'.

Game agreed that for such a play to be presented with the Lord Chamberlain's imprimatur could inflict real harm on the censorship:

> Yes, it is a pity that this play was licensed; it does our reputation no good in quarters in which one would wish it to stand high: I refer to the Critics Circle and to all who take the Theatre seriously, not the old women of the Public Morality Council.

Rather than allow the situation to continue, Clarendon decided to intervene, even though it risked making the censorship look foolish. Not surprisingly, the precedent created some unease, and the League of British Dramatists wrote to the Lord Chamberlain to express concern about 'The question of principle and practice' of withdrawing a licence. Internal Office memoranda reveal that the censorship was unsure how to respond: 'Will you be so kind and help with a cocked-hat reply to this? It is not easy, and

---

* Written by H.B. Sheridan, under the pseudonym of Gordon Sherry

we must be careful what we say. Is it advisable—although it is true—to admit that the Lord Chamberlain made a bloomer?'. The Office sought to play down the significance, replying it had been 'an exceptional situation', which 'should not be taken as intended to inaugurate a new policy or to establish a precedent'. It insisted that the Lord Chamberlain was acting to support the views of the public:

> Although a Lord Chamberlain's power is autocratic, in a democratic community he is bound to take notice of responsible opinion. Since the play was not supported by the public in London, an amicable arrangement for its withdrawal was easily arrived at with the management concerned.[32]

The situation was almost repeated soon afterwards. In October 1944, a licence was issued for *Gather No Moss*,* originally, and more dangerously, entitled *Ladies Like Them Bad*. This 'silly, vulgar, farcical comedy' centred on Roderick who, in his relationships with women, 'comes almost to believe that he is a cave-man, and proceeds to act like one'. It concluded

> in a struggle between the two women as to who is to have Roderick, a problem ultimately solved by Roderick, himself, who decides that he will have both women. This unconventional solution brings the girls to their senses. They return to their respective husbands considerably shaken.

Following extensive amendments, a licence was issued, but the production provoked some strong protests:

> The whole object seems to be to arouse an unhealthy interest in sex . . . The moral standard of most people in this country today is high, and we should be proud of the fact, but the production of *Gather No Moss* and of similar plays cannot . . . have other than a detrimental effect . . . A few doses of this type of play . . . cannot fail to have a bad moral effect on a proportion of the average audience, which is certain to contain some young and not too well balanced members.
>
> No thinking man or woman with the welfare of the nation at heart can look on with equanimity.

Titman warned his colleagues: 'The reactions of *Felicity Jasmine*, which started in the same way at Bournemouth, have not yet died down. I am anxious that there should be no repetition of this difficult and unpleasant business'. But Game, who blamed the previous debacle on Dearmer's liberalism, insisted that he had censored this script with care, and that he had no wish or need to re-read it. He feared establishing a pattern in which the Office was seen to respond too easily to public protests, and argued that, although 'long term changes in taste must of course be taken into

---

* Written by Max Catto

account', it was necessary to avoid making knee-jerk reactions to individual objections and cases. This time the Office did not withdraw the licence, but Game's comments suggest a tightening, not a loosening, of moral taboos:

> This sort of play always produces complaints; and we must expect more of them than usual in the sixth year of a war, when there is a, probably quite temporary, reaction of prudery from those whom fear has chastened. But we can't alter our standards to follow every word of the public; censoring would become impossibly difficult if we did.[33]

During the First World War, the Lord Chamberlain of the time had been persuaded to license the previously banned *Damaged Goods* on the grounds that its warning about venereal disease had become a potentially useful— even vital—piece of health propaganda.[34] In 1942, a new translation of Brieux's play was submitted, and Game's report again recognised it as a 'cautionary tale against the insidious evil of venereal disease', of direct contemporary relevance. 'Let's hope it does good', he commented of the production, which claimed to enjoy the support of the Ministry of Health and the Central Council of Health Education.[35] Clarendon discovered that the programme for the original production had stated that the performance was being staged as useful propaganda, and he stipulated that this justification should be replicated: 'In this way we might be able to stave off criticism from such bodies as the London Morality Council'.[36] But soon after re-licensing Brieux's text they refused a play* about a man who murders the prostitute from whom he has contracted syphilis, after he unwittingly passes the disease on to his wife:

> Syphilis has been dealt with upon the stage before now . . . but in a very much more austere manner than in this play, where the subject is treated in the realistic and uncompromising style of the present day. My personal reaction to this drama is, that it is an attempt to cash in on the War-time interest in Venereal disease, and to get a play through the Censorship, which would have little chance of being passed in more normal times.

The Office rejected the management's plea that this author, too, had intended to be helpful:

> It is not the fact that the subject of the play concerns syphilis to which the Lord Chamberlain objects, but to the way in which the theme is treated. Whatever the author's intention may have been, the crude realism and the sordidness of the story make the play, in His Lordship's opinion, quite unsuitable as helpful propaganda in the fight against Veneral [sic] disease.[37]

---

* *Fear*, by Victor Dillon

However, attempts to draw a meaningful division between helpful propaganda and exploitative commercialism were inevitably problematic. In the autumn of 1943, the Office found itself in a dilemma over *Out of the Blitz:** 'Molly is a very young and pretty girl, who represents herself to be a refugee from the blitz. In fact she is a syphilitic prostitute who wanders about the country spreading disease in her path!' Game was inclined to accept the claim that it was 'more than merely an attempt to get a dirty play through the censorship, using the present interest in venereal disease as a passport'. Yet he feared what might follow from its theatrical ineptitude:

> As far as I can tell the author of this play is sincere, and is writing about a subject which he rightly regards as extremely serious. Unfortunately his style is that of Victorian melodrama with the result that his dialogue is full of unintended humour. The play simply cries out to be burlesqued by the actors or guyed by the audience. I do not think the producer would dare burlesque, but a sophisticated audience would have to keep a tight hold on themselves not to laugh in the wrong places.

Game suggested that the producer should take responsibility for ensuring that the audience took it seriously:

> I doubt very much whether such crude nonsense does any good, but on the other hand the dirty minded can hardly get much kick out of it. For these reasons I do not feel justified, as I did with another play about venereal disease, in recommending the Lord Chamberlain to refuse a licence ... but I should warn the promoter, Mr Fortescue, that if audiences take it in the wrong spirit and guy it, the Lord Chamberlain will withdraw his licence.

The production was specifically approved 'on the distinct understanding that the play is produced as a serious propaganda play', with the Lord Chamberlain reserving the right to withdraw his licence 'if it should be guyed by the audience'. Again he required 'that a notice is inserted in the programme stating that the play is a propaganda one'.[38]

The danger of audiences refusing to take propaganda in the spirit in which it was intended was not a new one. In August 1943, a licence had been withheld from a play† attacking artificial insemination: 'It is not very easy to advise the Lord Chamberlain about this play', wrote Game. 'The subject is certainly a little embarrassing, but as it has been discussed in the Lords it is difficult to say that it should not be referred to in the theatre'. He acknowledged that the author treated his subject with 'perfect sincerity',

---

* Written by William Melvyn
† *The Great Void*, by Walter Knight

but 'as is invariably the case with didactic propaganda plays, it is trash'. Yet
this did not necessarily justify refusing a licence:

> that his arguments are superficial and based on unsubstantial premises,
> and his play laughable trash, makes no difference to the intention . . . I
> don't see why authors should not write plays about important questions
> such as this one . . . as long they write sincerely and with suitable restraint.

Nugent agreed:

> The play is so badly written and some of the lines so stilted and absurd that
> it is quite possible . . . it will be ridiculed . . . I can picture the gay young
> sparks going night after night, laughing uproariously at the wrong places,
> and joining in . . . the thing might become a riot of fun! . . . I don't suppose
> this is a justification for banning the play but it would obviously be very
> unfortunate.

Titman confirmed that a ban could hardly be enforced 'in respect of a
problematical guying of a play by the audience', and that 'The censorship
must be applied only so far as the play itself is concerned'. But he reminded
his colleagues that the Lord Chamberlain had another arrow to his bow:
'He has power to close a theatre if there is likelihood of a breach of the
peace, and this should be sufficient safeguard in this present case'. In the
event, although the play was not actually forbidden, it remained unlicensed
and in the Waiting Box.[39]

As we saw in the previous chapter, the censorship was under sustained
attack in the early months of 1940 for its supposed leniency; while many
objections centred on the display of the female body, the liberty being taken
by stage comedians was denounced with equal vehemence. Moralists
protested that the war was being used as 'a beautiful excuse for smut' and
accused popular entertainment of having succumbed to an invasion by a
'blue epidemic'.[40] Language, too was a problem. In January 1940, Gordon
wrote to Game:

> I have had a certain amount of trouble with some of the producers of
> Revues over the elimination of the word 'bloody'.
>   My impression is that it has always been the policy both in Lord
> Cromer's time and also in the present Lord Chamberlain's to delete this
> expression where it is used flippantly and unnecessarily, but to allow it
> where the sense of the dramatic seems to render it essential from the
> producer's point of view.
>   In one or two cases lately it has slipped through in the former
> connection.

Game was offended at the implication that he had allowed anything to 'slip
through': 'Your letter seems to suggest that I have been inconsistent. I very

much doubt it'. Importantly, his reply, 'written more in sorrow than in anger', also disputed the Comptroller's distinction:

> There is a comedic use of the word 'bloody', which is sometimes as justified as when the word is used in moments of dramatic tension. In fact the first time the word was heard in a London theatre was when it was used by Shaw for a comedic effect in his play *Pygmalion*. If I have left it in recent revues, I have little doubt that it is for this reason, and because I consider that, taking the show as a whole, it would do no harm. I do not miss these things and as a rule give them more consideration than they sometimes deserve . . . You are asking me to alter a policy which has up to now, as far as I know, been quite satisfactory to the Theatre people and to the public. I do not think this fair! . . . I am not at all prepared to admit that a cuss word is never to be used to get a laugh . . . Has there been an outburst of popular indignation or what?[41]

However, the media campaign against comedians continued. In January 1940, the entertainments page of the *Sunday Dispatch* complained:

> 'Broader and bluer' seems to be the slogan of entertainment these days and nights.
> A rash of rudery-crudery has broken out since the war started, and jokes called the 'doubtful' kind are being heard in unusual places from unexpected lips.

The stage was by no means seen to be the only or the chief culprit: 'Radio, stage, cabaret have all been affected (and infected) and only films have kept their pre-war purity'. Indeed, according to Moore Raymond on the Entertainment Page of the *Sunday Dispatch*, 'The most surprising relaxation in censorship has been that of the BBC'; in his perception 'There seems to be very little supervision now, and the comedians are slipping in a surprising number of hot ones'. Raymond had no doubt that

> Stage censorship, both official and unofficial, is obviously slacker . . .
> . . . comedians are at their broadest when performing at troop concerts in this country . . . a singer I know is always entertaining the forces, and he tells me that the comics are putting over the most sizzling gags to mixed audiences at troop concerts.
> HE SAYS THEY DON'T LAUGH MUCH, BUT THEY LOOK EMBARRASSED.
> As for West-end cabaret, it is always expected to be rather warm. Now it is running the highest temperature in its history.[42]

Although the Lord Chamberlain had no responsibility for many of the performances referred to, such public attacks did create pressure on the Office. In February 1940, Gordon, no doubt mindful of Game's recent riposte to his own letter, responded with some indignation to Clarendon's suggestion that, with regard to revues, they were erring on the side of leniency:

> I have gone rather further than may perhaps have been customary recently, in excising jokes or allusions of a doubtful character, particularly perversion, and what are termed 'w.c.' jokes, also 'bloodies' used frivolously or unnecessarily. I have also taken particular trouble to treat all producers of this type of entertainment equally.

Gordon declared that the problem was not laxness on the part of himself or the Reader, but rather that comedians had become more daring in adding gags which had not been in the approved script. Managers and producers claimed there was little they could do to curtail such practices:

> It had been represented by certain managements that comedians would put in some gags which were not in the licensed script and when reprimanded for doing so, would threaten to walk out knowing that they could not be replaced. [43]

In a revealing admission to the St James's conference of April 1940, Lord Clarendon conceded that 'the interpolation of unauthorised and objectionable "gags" has grown to such an extent that, in spite of periodical legal action, no certainty now exists that a script, once licensed, will be adhered to'.[44] The result of subsequent attempts to clamp down was that the censorship found itself in direct confrontation with comedians, who argued that the freedom to include topical gags and improvised repartee was fundamental to their skills and traditions. While the censors could legitimately maintain that the letter of the law had always forbidden such interpolations, and that no new principle was being introduced, it is evident that the law had not been strictly observed, and that a typically British blind eye had often been turned. George Black was far more reluctant to accept the imposition of a new standard on comedians than he was to restrict nudity :

> I have written to all the comedians in our employment in London productions, giving them the Lord Chamberlain's ruling, i.e. that no gags or business of any sort must be put into the Show until they have been submitted and approved, and the comedians themselves are all very perturbed about this ruling, as they allege this is jeopardising their business, and they point out that gags are often put in on the spur of the moment, and tried out in two or three ways, until they get the laugh from it, and the Lord Chamberlain's ruling precludes them from doing this in the future, and they claim it is not possible for them to carry on their business of comedians under this ruling.
> Might I suggest I agree with their contention, and I would ask that before any definite decision is arrived at, the comedians have an opportunity of laying their views before the Lord Chamberlain.

The idea of a delegation of comedians arriving at St James's Palace or Windsor Castle may not have appealed to Lord Clarendon (though it would surely have tempted playwrights), and there was no hint of negotiation or accommodation in Gordon's reply:

> The Lord Chamberlain desires me to tell you in reply that he cannot possibly agree to the course suggested as, apart from the fact that it would appear to him to be an entirely new contention, it is quite definitely against the provisions of the Theatres Act . . .
>
> If the contention of the comedians to whom you refer was upheld, and they were allowed to try out gags and jokes in various ways and then, when it was found that they came over sufficiently well to satisfy themselves, and the Management, they were to be submitted for the Lord Chamberlain's approval, it would nullify the whole basis of censorship.

In reality, Gordon must have been well aware that what the Lord Chamberlain was now forbidding was a well established and widespread practice. The comedian Vic Oliver suggested a compromise:

> I have been informed by the producer of our show *Black Velvet* currently running at the London Hippodrome, that in future no new jokes or bits of business or any spontaneous remarks must be made, without first obtaining permission from the Lord Chamberlain's Offices.
>
> I do hope, in the interests of the top-line comedians, as well as the young, aspiring comedians, that you will be gracious enough to modify this ruling as otherwise our profession will receive a serious setback, and the inventing of any jokes and witty remarks will have to become a thing of the past. As you know, spontaneity is the basis of every joke, and the biggest laughs of all are produced from topical patter. If the comedian was supposed to submit beforehand every topical joke he wishes to tell his audience, it would, by the time it could be dealt with, cease to be topical, and the comedian's reputation of being original and different would severely suffer.
>
> Would it not be possible to grant us the privilege of telling a joke once, and then immediately submitting it to your offices? I do not believe that any comedian in the top-line class would willingly say or do anything which might offend his audience, which after all is his bread and butter, and if a flagrant violation of this rule were to happen, I am quite sure that all comedians would be very pleased if the culprit were to be severely punished.

Perhaps never more like the Malvolio to whom Shaw had famously compared the Lord Chamberlain, Gordon remained firm:

> no new principle is involved in regard to the interpolation of jokes, or business which has not been submitted for approval.
>
> Such has always been the rule, and is in accordance with the provision of section twelve of the Theatres Act, 1840 [sic] . . .
>
> Certain comedians have recently taken upon themselves to introduce unauthorised gags and business into current entertainments, not only

topical or spontaneous—but old and objectionable, often disallowed on previous occasions.

It was in consequence of this that the Lord Chamberlain was constrained to remind managements of the law in this matter.[45]

Next to appeal, on behalf of his members, was the secretary of the Association of Touring and Producing Managers. Lewis Casson tried to separate the theatrical understanding and natural sympathy, which he graciously attributed to the censorship, from the pedantically unimaginative approach of the police. The zeal of the latter, he complained, was

> having a detrimental effect upon many of the comedians who state that they cannot carry out their work satisfactorily under this watch-dog form of supervision.
>
> I feel sure that you will appreciate this point when I tell you that it is no uncommon practice for two representatives of the police to sit in a box with the script before them and make notes of any variation from the script. Action has been taken and threatened because of trivial departures from the script. If such departures involved indecency their action might be justified, but such is not the case. A comedian by the very nature of his work cannot help at times introducing a topical or other gag. These gags are spontaneous and are the hall-mark of a really good comedian and are by their nature not capable of being licensed beforehand. Most of these comedians are Variety Artists and in that capacity have full scope for gagging without any restrictions save that of decency, with the result that when they appear in Revue their work suffers in consequence and the manager does not get the value from their work for which he pays . . .
>
> I feel sure the Lord Chamberlain would not wish to insist upon a too literal reading of the Act to the detriment of the Manager.

Casson took up the cudgels again in another letter, in which he insisted that he had no complaint about police action in relation to genuinely objectionable material, but that 'The feeling amongst our members is that they [the police] are rather trying to catch them by finding a few words which are not in the script'. He claimed that

> A small amount of license [sic] has always been allowed to comedians in the past and my experience has been that this license has not been abused to any serious extent. After the battle at the River Plate there was hardly a comedian who did not introduce a joke about scuttling and perfectly harmless topical jokes of this kind frequently occur both in West End and Provincial productions.

Gordon still maintained—he could hardly have done otherwise—that the Lord Chamberlain was 'bound to concur in the action taken by local authorities', and that to allow any special freedom to comedians 'would nullify the whole basis of censorship'. He pointed out that 'The Lord

Chamberlain has to administer the law as it stands, and it is for this reason that his form of licence for Stage Plays contains the words "Without any further variations whatsoever".' However, following a private meeting, the Lord Chamberlain did yield an important concession. At the start of July, the Comptroller wrote to Casson:

> On the general question of the institution of prosecutions for infringement of the Theatres Act, I may perhaps take this opportunity of confirming what I told you verbally—that the Lord Chamberlain only advises, or recommends, legal action to be taken in cases where either unauthorised gags, dialogue, or business of an offensive nature, which would not be passed if submitted, had been interpolated, or when material, which had already been disallowed, was re-included.
>
> In cases where there has only been slight deviation from the licensed script, and the additional material would in any case have been passed, legal action is not recommended.[46]

The door, which had seemed to be closing, was to be left ajar.

Casson expressed his 'deep appreciation' of the shift. He added: 'We have only one point remaining of concern to our members and that is the question of so called Road Shows'. Twenty years or so earlier, the Home Office had advised the Lord Chamberlain that this new branch of entertainment should be taken as falling outside the scope of the Theatres Act, but there had often been doubts about how road shows were defined and how they differed from revues. Clearly, Casson was professionally jealous of managers who were, as he saw it, evading the censors and profiting from a freedom to which they had no right:

> We contend that these in no way differ from the majority of Revues. They all contain dialogue of some kind even if only between the compere and some other artist, and in many cases contain questionable jokes for which revue managers have been punished and which have been dis-allowed by the Lord Chamberlain.
>
> I would submit to the Lord Chamberlain that he has full power under the definition contained in section 13 of the Theatres Act to require these Road Shows to be licensed by him . . . Our chief reason for urging that they should be licensed is that they constitute unfair competition to the Revue Manager who is bound by the terms of his licence. The Road Show presents precisely the same type of entertainment, differing little in make up yet they are free to introduce any jokes, questionable and otherwise, which they think fit . . . I understand that they are still presenting 'strip tease' acts, as are places in the West End of London.

Titman reminded Gordon and Clarendon of the rather unclear definition adopted by the Office in excluding the road show from the process of censorship:

The definition of a stage play in section 23 of the Act is very wide, but I have always understood that a stage play is 'an entertainment <u>of</u> the stage' and that a Road Show or a Variety performance is 'an entertainment <u>on</u> the stage', the latter definition not coming within the scope of the Act.

A road show, he explained,

consists of a programme of variety turns given under a general title, each turn being individually introduced by an interlocutor who may say two or three words relevant to the performance to be given: at the close of the entire series of turns the whole of the artistes coming together on the stage is an 'ensemble'.

The Home Office ruling had assumed that none of the individual turns should normally be classified as a stage play.

If, however, one of the turns <u>is</u> a stage play, the continuity of artistes and compering, and the fact that the show is given under a general title, would, in my opinion bring it within the same category as the present day Revue, and should therefore be subject to the Lord Chamberlain's licence.

The Lord Chamberlain had no wish to be drawn into another debate on the issue, but Casson warned them that he was 'going to press the point', since many revue managers felt that a 'great injustice' was being done under the present system:

I think you will agree that they are justified in this view when they find doubtful jokes, for which revue managers have been heavily fined, being introduced in 'Road Shows' with impunity. The vast majority of revue managers do not want dirty jokes on the stage because they believe it is a bad policy and tends to drive away many of the better class of people in the audience and that is one of their main reasons for resenting the introduction of dirty jokes in Road Shows which are entirely uncontrolled.

Privately, Titman conceded that there was 'something in Casson's contention', and advised that the best procedure would be 'to submit the matter to the legal experts at the Home Office'. He accepted that 'Revues have altered considerably and the gap between them and Road Shows has definitely narrowed'. However, on going to see two road shows which Casson had specifically accused of misrepresenting themselves in order to bypass the licensing requirements, he changed his mind. Both, he said, had been genuine variety shows, comprising individual turns such as accordion and harmonica solos, a dance band, a thought-reading scene, and song and dance numbers. He admitted there had been 'Comedians' double patter', but 'no sketch of any kind, no Cameo, Black Out or Gag which could, with the greatest stretch of imagination, be considered a stage play, or part thereof'. It is doubtful whether a distinction between 'dialogue' and

'Comedians' double patter' would have stood up in court, and there was probably an element of bluff in Titman's urging that the Office should stick to its guns:

> I have not the slightest hesitation in saying that there is no case for the Lord Chamberlain to put before the Home Office. Variety has never been brought within the scope of the Theatres Act since it was passed a hundred years ago and I see no reason why it should be now. If the Lord Chamberlain had to licence [sic] such entertainments as are under review it would mean that every entertainment on the stage had to be censored. This would create an impossible position and a staff running into hundreds for examination and inspection purposes would have to be employed.

While acknowledging that 'the contention of the Association is fully justified', Titman cleverly turned Casson's accusation on its head: 'The crux of the matter is this', he wrote; 'Variety entertainments have not altered in the least. It is the Revues which have back-slid towards Variety'. And he dropped the broadest of hints that the solution for revue managers would be to follow road shows and exclude themselves from the censorship process—even if this meant altering the nature of their programme by excluding acts which could be classed as stage plays. Such a move could, of course, have made life much easier for the Lord Chamberlain's Office. But Titman alleged that there were ulterior reasons motivating producers to stay within the system:

> Why do Producers of present-day Revues go to the trouble and expense of getting a stage play licence for their material? Because most of the provincial theatres are unable to open their bars unless they have a licence for the production. But for this, the majority of producers would not subject themselves to censorship, and would either eliminate sketches, etc., altogether, or would obtain individual licences for them. We should be rid of an immense amount of worry if they did this—but they won't.

Casson was sufficiently provoked to dispute the final point of Titman's argument:

> the Revue manager has no interest whatever in the bars of a theatre, financially or otherwise and you may accept it as a definite fact that no Revue manager ever has any thought upon this subject in projecting a production. It is quite immaterial to him whether a theatre or music hall has a drink license [sic] or not.

But Titman did not back down:

> we have often been informed by such Managers that they have been requested by the theatres to obtain the Lord Chamberlain's licence solely for this purpose. This has necessitated what was really a variety bill being

reconstructed in order to make the material suitable for a stage plays licence.

Casson had made no impression, but he continued his campaign, declaring that shows were being put on 'with the <u>sole</u> object of evading censorship' and that 'Road Show managers openly boast of this fact'. Perhaps the distraction of the Blitz in the autumn of 1940 helped to end the argument and the correspondence for the time being. By the following spring, Titman had effectively taken over Gordon's duties after the latter's sudden death, and he wrote again to Casson, citing a recent successful prosecution against the comedian Frank Randle:

> I do not know whether you saw a report in *The Performer* of February 27th of proceedings at Oldham police court the previous week concerning an entertainment entitled 'Randle's Scandals'. This entertainment was one which the proprietors chose to call a 'Road Show', but which I had no hesitation in deciding was a stage play within the meaning of section 23 of the Theatres Act.
>
> I mention this to show that the passage of time has not caused any relaxation in my efforts to ensure just and consistent treatment for all concerned.[47]

This was by no means the last occasion on which Randle would come into conflict with the censorship, and other comedians also continued to create controversy. In February 1941, the Office licensed *Nineteen Naughty One* for the Prince of Wales's Theatre, after making a number of amendments: 'The comedians, headed by that cess-pool minded Ronald Frankau, are a dirty lot', moaned Game; 'the humour is rarely inspired by anything but sexual intercourse and WCs'. He noted: 'I have cleaned up the worst of the mess'. But there were others who thought a far more thorough deinfestation was required, and in May, the Office received an extraordinary letter of complaint. One almost wonders if this was a pre-echo of the Ortonesque strategy of drawing attention to your own work by writing outraged and spurious letters of complaint about it, but it would appear the letter in this case was genuine. Headed 'Not to be read by Women', it began with an assertion of credentials:

> I do not think I am a crank, as I have lived at sea, in Rhodesia and many parts of the world, been Managing Director of Rolls Royce Ltd and am not a parson. I believe I am just a typical Englishman with ordinary ideas of decency.

The object of his ire was the inclusion of the word 'Nancy' in humorous contexts:

> Every ordinary man knows that Nancy equals bugger. Is it your opinion that buggery is a good basis for public humour? . . . do you think that the

peoples of other countries and British dominions will form a good opinion
of the British people when they hear jokes about buggery being broadcast?
Do you think that the people of Britain will feel satisfied to go through the
present war when they realise they were fighting for a government and a
country whose soul is so low that they encourage comedians to raise a
laugh by using the lowest type of filth? . . .

Is your staff either so inexperienced, or so low minded and lacking in
ordinary decency that it allows jokes about buggery to be put across to the
public?

Are you aware that the underlying great majority of the Forces are
decent minded, mainly Britishers, and not the sweepings of Paris and
Berlin, and therefore they resent being entertained by low filth? I served
through the last war and am serving in this war and know what I say is
right.

Titman warned that 'The complainant is certainly of some substance', but
he believed that, provided the cuts were being dutifully observed, there
should be no problem: 'we ruined all his "best" jokes'. However, he
decided to pay an unannounced visit to the theatre: 'It may be that the LCO
being at Windsor is considered too far away to keep up its accustomed
vigilance'. Whether the management had been tipped off, or whether the
complainant had had some personal or financial reason for 'exaggerating his
information', as the Office suspected, Titman's inspection discovered
nothing untoward: 'I found the complaint unjustified', he reported.
Indeed, he could detect 'nothing in Frankau's dialogue or actions . . .
bearing on the subject of perversion'.[48]

Sometimes the interventions were rather more heavy-handed, as when a
successful prosecution was brought against a comedian who cross-dressed
as a Girl Guide and made reference to women's periods. Clarendon
portentously declared: 'I do my very best within my powers . . . to protect
the Girl Guide movement and similar national organisations'; in this case,
he certainly earned the gratitude of its staff:

As so-called head of the organisation, [I] feel so very strongly that it is very
hard on the thousands of Guides up and down the Country who are doing
such a magnificent bit of work to know that they are held up to ridicule by
men such as this comedian.[49]

The Public Morality Council was less generally exercised over
comedians than over the female body, but worst of all was when the
comedians and the nudes joined forces, as in Tommy Trinder's famous gag
as compere in a 1942 London Palladium revue: 'Never', he promised the
audience, 'was so much shown to so many by so few for so little'.[50] The
Council described this as 'a most appalling travesty of the Prime Minister's
noble utterance', but the Lord Chamberlain's Office was less than
delighted to receive the protest.

> Alas, the Public Morality Council has come to life again, after a silence of
> nearly two years. I hope the new secretary is not going to be so tiresome as
> his predecessor, who looked a depraved old man and was very efficiently
> dealt with by Major Gwatkin and Major Gordon.

But the lines about the chorus had not, in fact, been licensed, and the
manager, when challenged, offered the usual defence that Trinder was 'apt
to slip in gags while he is on the stage'. Somewhat disingenuously, he
claimed that no innuendo had been intended by Trinder's lines:

> He used them during the scene where he undresses the girl wearing the
> Victorian bustle dress, and when the remark was made the girl was quite
> respectably clad from above the knee to her shoulders. She is very tall and
> towers above Trinder and the point of the remark 'so much' refers to her
> extraordinary height.

Titman inspected the show and found not only that further
interpolations had been added, but that lines which had been specifically
banned were included. The management received an extremely strict and
threatening letter:

> The Lord Chamberlain does not accept your remarks regarding
> spontaneous comedians. No special concession can be granted to Mr
> Trinder, nor does His Lordship feel inclined to transfer to him the rights of
> censorship. This matter has already been thrashed out before. If
> manuscripts are altered and added to by 'spontaneous comedians' and
> others, after they have been passed by the Lord Chamberlain, the whole
> act of submission for censoring becomes a farce.

Legal action was threatened, but, after receiving a letter of apology, Titman
concluded: 'I think perhaps it would not be wise to prosecute. Some good
must result from the severe shaking up they have received'.

Trinder's act also featured a mock anatomy lecture on the physiology of
the human female figure, to which the Public Morality Council had
strongly objected. The comedian manipulated lights positioned on the
body, supposedly to illustrate the lecture, and the Council complained that
'the switches are worked in such a way as to be extremely offensive and
disgusting'. Titman described the act as 'extremely amusing, but harmless',
and Clarendon informed the Council that nothing offensive had been
detected. The Council then went into more detail: 'The offence was that as
Miss Daniels used the words "but of course the most important part is
here" she paused and the light was switched on to the location of the genital
organs'. Titman refuted the allegation: 'This was not so', he informed the
Lord Chamberlain, 'the light was higher'; Clarendon duly informed the
Council that 'My representative paid very special attention to the lighting
of the dummy'. Unsatisfied, the Public Morality Council then took the

almost unprecedented step of challenging the authority and even the word of the Lord Chamberlain by asking the Public Control Department of London County Council to investigate. An inspector duly attended the show, and a copy of his report was sent to the Lord Chamberlain. From his description of the same moment, it sounds as though Trinder perhaps adopted the attitude which later became a trademark of Frankie Howerd, whereby the comedian feigns surprise that the audience have discovered a vulgar meaning in something which was innocently intended:

> . . . 'which', she asks discursively, 'is the most important part?'
> Here Trinder touches a switch which illuminates an irregular patch about the size of a hand and with serrated edges, situated in the region of the genital organ.
> The audience reaction is instantaneous, and on this occasion stopped the show. . . . Mr Trinder stands by with coy, shocked look.

Of course, this pose has the effect of heightening the comedy, especially since the audience is simultaneously aware that the pose adopted by the comedian is itself an act. However, it does provide an alibi for the performer—and one which is hard for the censor to challenge—against accusations of vulgarity. Rather than engaging with the report itself, the Lord Chamberlain's Office wrote to the Public Morality Council, challenging its strategy and playing the role of being affronted: 'His Lordship does not understand why you found it necessary to communicate with the London County Council, which has no jurisdiction over Revues and Stage Plays'. On the same day, Titman advised the LCC:

> After a long period of inactivity following the retirement of Mr Tyrer, the Public Morality Council seems to have come to life again and I should imagine that both the Council and the Lord Chamberlain are going to have a busy time keeping them quiet.

Another revue to provoke controversy was *The Air Force*,[*] in 1944. This time, the chief complainant was Alfred Denville, a Conservative MP and Justice of the Peace, who was also a former actor, comedian and producer, now known as 'the actors' MP'. Denville told the Lord Chamberlain he was 'never more astounded in all my life' than by the 'filthy language and disgusting sexual actions' he had witnessed; the show was 'the worst example of sexual vulgarity that I have ever seen', made worse by the fact that it 'purports to show what takes place in the air force', and that the actors were in appropriate costumes. So upset was Denville by what he saw as an insult to the services that he threatened to raise the matter in the

---

[*] Written by Con West and Herbert Sargent

House of Commons. But once again, the censors were not as impressed or conciliatory as Denville would have hoped: 'As you probably know Mr. Denvill has rather warped ideas', wrote Game; 'We have had similar complaints from him before, which have turned out to be unjustified'. Clarendon invited the MP to be more specific, and Denvill wrote again:

> The sexual actions are difficult to describe, but his hands wander everywhere. They speak of putting things up people's bottoms; and in the last scene he comes on and says 'Ah, there's the old bugga' . . . It is disgusting from an airforce point of view.

Game inspected a performance and found some of these accusations to be justified, and meriting intervention:

> The business of sticking the electric poker up the nurse's bottom, to be omitted.
> The business of looking inside the bedclothes after the reference to 'my Waterloo' to be omitted.
> The business of looking into the bed after the line 'cut off your verbosity', to be omitted . . .
> There must be no fingering of 'breast', and in one instance, the private part . . . the line 'keep your mind above your waistbelt' to be omitted . . .
> The business of putting the hand in trousers pocket when kissing the girl to be omitted.
> The line 'if she asks you to cough, say you haven't got one', to be omitted . . .

However, the Lord Chamberlain informed Denvill that the show contained 'nothing derogatory to the Royal Airforce', and instructed the Home Office that it was 'little worse than many others going round the country' and 'far from the damning description given by Mr Denvill'.[51]

Some protesters were accorded more respect. The following year, the Lord Chamberlain recieved a complaint by a Lady Howitt about *Panama Hattie*, a revue which had been touring for some time:

> It seems to me very regrettable that, particularly in war-time when many young people are visiting the theatre, a revue which is completely lewd from beginning to end should be permitted . . . .
> I should like to know, sir, whether young people are likely to feel that going to a brothel is wrong when they see this treated as a frivolous incident.

She expressed particular disapproval of the use of a red light, of a scene showing people queueing for a toilet, and of a dance in which the woman 'permits herself to be held out by a man as if she were a child in a lavatory and a receptacle brought to her'; she added 'I, unfortunately, took three daughters, aged 26, 22, and 16'. Once he appreciated the identity of the complainant—'I apologise to Lady Howitt for not having realised the letter was from her'—Clarendon took the unusual step of making amendments to material which had previously been licensed.

The comedian who enjoyed the reputation of being riskier and more provocative than any other was probably Max Miller, but he seems to have had supporters in high places. In December 1944, Miller's business manager, Julius Darewski, contacted the Lord Chamberlain with a letter which positively crowed:

> My reason for writing to you is because I know that at times you have had complaints about this artiste's material, and, with all due respect, I thought it might be interesting to record that on Sunday last Max Miller appeared before Their Majesties The King and Queen at Windsor Castle.
>
> He was specially asked to appear there and he made a very big success, being on the stage for nearly half an hour.
>
> After the show he was presented to Their Majesties. He had a long and interesting chat with the King and Queen and was highly complimented on his performance.

This had the potential to create an embarrassing and even damaging situation for Clarendon, especially if it should be publicised in the press. Since the Lord Chamberlain acted with the express authority, and in the name of the monarch, any future attempt to censor an act which the King himself had not only approved but even enjoyed would be seen as an act of hypocrisy which could be used by his enemies to discredit the whole system of stage censorship. The Office obtained a detailed report of the event from Sir Owen Morshead, the King's Librarian, who had organised the entertainment for the occasion. Without completely denying Darewski's claim, he sought to play it down:

> It is true that Their Majesties knew Mr Max Miller's form, wanted to hear him, and would have been disappointed if he had not come. It is true that he was on the stage for (say) twenty minutes, and that T.M., like the rest of the audience, enjoyed his accomplished performance. After the concert I assembled the whole cast in an adjoining room and Their Majesties had a word with them all . . . Their Majesties were very nice to him, as they were to them all.

He was adamant that the act had not been excessively vulgar or, by implication, censorable:

> I do not personally know Mr Miller's form. On this occasion he was pretty outspoken, but his material was delivered with such extreme rapidity and aplomb as to pass muster quite happily. For my part I thought his opening song, 'I have a packet of <u>BLUE jokes</u>' in questionable taste—and I remember with relief feeling at the time that it was not borne out by the majority of jokes which he proceeded to retale.

Indeed, Morshead then quoted the testimony of the chauffeur who had driven Miller straight from his Windsor engagement for his appearance in the second house at New Cross, and who had been allowed to watch his routine there from the wings: 'you should have heard the stuff he put across . . . Well, I never knew such things could be put across—what he gave you here was nothing at all—child's play'. Morshead concluded by asserting that nothing had occurred which merited concern:

> It will be seen then a) That it was not a command performance . . . b) That he gave them asses-milk-cum-water in comparison with the full cream of his normal outpourings. And hence c) The argument that what is not too strong for The King and Queen should be admissible for the general public, besides being in all the circumstances improperly advanced, falls to the ground on its own demerits.

Still, it was not an occasion which the authorities would have wished the general public to hear about. Morshead cautioned that his report was 'only for the confidential information of Mr Titman and his confrere of the LCC', and that 'The incident should never be brought into the limelight, nor committed to paper in correspondence with Mr Darewski'.[52]

When Charlotte Frances resubmitted her script for *The Marry-Go-Round* in 1945, she claimed that Game had privately admitted to her that the original rejection five years earlier had been 'unfair and biased'. Understandably embarrassed, the Reader was quick to distance himself from the claim: 'Miss Frances is a little inaccurate (if not wild) in her statements'. In resubmitting it now, the playwright had claimed that: 'Our theatre has broadened considerably during the subsequent five years of war'. Game refused this analysis: 'Miss Frances is wrong in thinking that the theatre has broadened considerably during the War years. It has not'. And he insisted that 'except for Revues perhaps, it has marked time'. Nugent also denied that that there had been any shift in standards: 'If a play was not fit to be licensed in 1940, it certainly is not in 1945'.[53] But the world outside the theatre was changing. Cracks had already appeared in some of the pillars holding up British society, and the balance of power was beginning to shift.

In March 1945, the censorship became involved in a bruising confrontation with a tenacious and uncompromising young playwright, Wallace Wilfred Blair-Fish. A rebel and an angry young man well before James Dean or Jimmy Porter, Blair-Fish announced that his aim was to secure the abolition of theatre censorship, which he compared to a 'Star Chamber authority' and 'an absolute tyranny in an absolutist State'. He was more than willing to take his fight to the heart of the establishment, and neither his rhetoric or his tactics were naïve. In a Shavian attack on the nation's enthusiasm for authority, he argued passionately that it was not only armies and military power which allowed totalitarian regimes to govern and flourish: 'Anomalies, anachronisms, or other abuses are customarily tolerated in a democracy through sheer ignorance, inertia and indifference or on grounds of mere convenience or expedience long after their indefensibility is recognised'. And Blair-Fish came surprisingly close—perhaps closer than any individual before him—to succeeding in his attempt to destroy the censorship.

The impeccably trivial starting point for the confrontation was his play, *Genius Limited*, which focused, probably rather narcissistically, on a left-wing and unconventional playwright living in an attic study in north-west London. The text caused no real difficulties for the censors, but the author was incensed by the stipulation that he remove the 'gratuitous indecency' of a reference to a 'Nice, comfortable Chesterfield', on the grounds that the line was deliberately implying that the sofa in question was an appropriate location for sexual intercourse. The manager of Amersham Theatre was willing to accept the censors' ruling that these three words should be cut, but Blair-Fish was so outraged that he preferred to withdraw the text in its entirety; he then launched a passionate attack on behalf of freedom and against a system 'by means of which one man seeks to dictate his own personal view on author and public alike'. He conceded that the line in question was 'in bad taste', but argued that 'if it were not, I should be a bad playwright, because it is a character of very bad taste who utters it'; moreover, in comparison with other licensed texts which he cited, 'it would be at once agreed by anyone outside the walls of a mental hospital that the censored line in my play is delicacy itself'. The playwright accused the Lord Chamberlain of 'gratuitously abusing his already inherently abusive function', and questioned his right to cut this line: 'I was not aware that the Act empowered him to be the arbiter of taste but only of blasphemy, sedition or indecency'. He also threw down the gauntlet by signalling his intention to embarrass the Office by publishing full details of their correspondence.

Always loathe to rescind a decision, the censorship could not afford apparently to concede to threats and direct challenges: 'the Lord Chamberlain can yield to reason but not to compulsion', wrote Game, and, misjudging their opponent, they condescendingly charged Blair-Fish with having 'foolishly adopted an attitude of defiance to the Lord Chamberlain's authority'. The playwright not only refused to back down, but sought to ally the dictatorial control of the censor with the fascistic instincts of the Nazis:

> treatment such as this is not merely discourteous but exhibits the Censorship as a wholly arrogant, irrational, and arbitrary authority. For, unless his Lordship holds himself bound to observe reasonable and consistent standards of judgement and to reply rationally to arguments

against his judgement ... he is functioning merely tyrannically in mutilating or suppressing ... in a manner which must be held to be intolerable in a supposedly free community which for more than five years believes that it has been waging a war for ... freedom of expression.

Following a further exchange of politely vicious letters, Blair-Fish's next step was to submit for licence a short dramatic allegory set in 'a limbo in Britain', and featuring as its principal characters Drama, Public Opinion and Dramatic Censorship; the latter was to be costumed so as to resemble 'the Minotaur or Mammon: half beast, half man, ponderous, gross, hairy, with a rough, roaring voice'. As Game dryly commented, 'The Lord Chamberlain and I have only to look in the nearest looking glass to feel reassured'. The sketch was witty, if somewhat laboured and over-stated, and it was supposedly to be performed as a prologue to *Genius Limited*. It was targeted quite directly at the Lord Chamberlain, and reads like an early forerunner of the sort of anti-establishment satire which would flourish in the sixties:

> CENSORSHIP: I, Censorship, who keep in servile chains
>   The British Drama—and you never heed 'em—
>   I am the smelly drains of British freedom!
>   Oh, what a joke! Before a play is played
>   I, and I only, say if it has strayed
>   Beyond decorum: I decide what is
>   Or is not decorum. That's my biz.
>   Democracy! Freedom before the Law!
>   I'm the dictator!—I have censored Shaw!
>   Fee, fi, fo fum!
> (*Enter DRAMA*)
> DRAMA: And now you've censored Blair:
>   An insignificant creature—but beware!
> CENSORSHIP: Blair? Who the devil's he?
> DRAMA: A chap whose play,
>   Censored by you, they're playing here today.
> CENSORSHIP (*furiously*) Not with the words I cut!—With unconcealed
>   Depraved intent he mentioned 'Chesterfield'.
>   A most suggestive word, a nasty line!
> DRAMA: He's put [it] in the programme.
> CENSORSHIP: Oh, the swine.

While recognising its intention 'to hold the Censorship up to ridicule and contempt', Game professed, as victims of satire must inevitably do, to be unworried by the attack: 'It is of course unfair, but our reputation will survive'. Nugent agreed that there were 'no grounds for refusing', and that it would be 'much more dignified to pass it without comment'.

Whether or not the Office was as relaxed as it claimed, their assailant certainly succeeded in stinging them with a tactic, alluded to in the lines above, of threatening to print the banned line in the programme. Game called this 'an ingenious and malicious way of circumventing the Lord Chamberlain's ruling'. However, it proved the most effective strategy yet, for it lured the censorship into overstepping the bounds of its authority. Blair-Fish was informed that a licence for performance could be issued only 'on receipt of your written undertaking that no reference whatever will be made to the excised line in the programme, nor any other attempt made to circumvent the Lord Chamberlain's authority under the Theatres Act'. Sensing he had drawn blood, the playwright immediately asked the Office to cite the section of the Theatres Act which gave the Lord Chamberlain the right to impose such a demand:

> I was not aware that the Act gave His Lordship authority over anything other than words spoken on the stage as part of a play. It would appear from your letter that he is now claiming authority indirectly to censor a theatre programme, which is a publication.

His prologue had mistakenly referred to the fact that playwrights were not allowed to represent Queen Victoria on the stage; on being informed that because this was no longer the case the accusation could not be licensed, Blair-Fish acknowledged his error, but, in a brilliant riposte, managed to turn the situation to his own advantage by challenging the right of the Lord Chamberlain to cut something simply because it was untrue:

> I must also ask whether it is his Lordship's practice to exercise his veto over falsehood in accordance with any regular rules: I mean, does he ignore some factual untruths and censor others (such, for example, as affect his own function of Censor); does he scrutinize plays for certain classes of untruth only, such as historical, political, medical, etc., or for untruths of any and every kind?

The censorship was on the run, and resorted to bluffing. After considerable internal debate as to what it would be safe to say, the Office informed its tormentor that the Lord Chamberlain's 'power to attach any rules or conditions to his Stage Play's Licence was confirmed many years ago by the Law Officers of the Crown'. Hoping that the matter could be allowed to rest (and, as it were, offering him a draw), the Comptroller added:

> The Lord Chamberlain feels that no good purpose will be served by continuance of this correspondence, which has provided so little benefit to His Lordship or to yourself, and he suggests that the time has now come for it to cease.

But Blair-Fish knew he had them going. In a letter worthy of Shaw at his best he told them he was 'distressed to hear . . . that His Lordship himself has derived so little benefit from the correspondence', and insisted that, for his own part, he was finding the correspondence highly informative in exposing the previously hidden practices and assumptions of the censorship:

> First, His Lordship's admission that his exercise of his deplorable office of Dramatic Censor in a supposedly democratic community should be based, not upon personal or individual views but upon his estimate of what public opinion will and does tolerate: and secondly, in your latest letter, the startling information that the Law Officers of the Crown have actually empowered his Lordship 'to attach any rules or conditions' to the granting of a licence to perform a play.

He magnanimously offered them another opportunity to back down and reverse the decision which had begun the argument, but in the meantime he requested legal rulings in relation to various alternatives he claimed to be considering as ways of presenting the banned line. Could it be included in a speech 'made by any person from the stage before the curtain (not speaking as one of the characters in the play)'? or in a lecture given 'in the theatre or in another building in the same town about the time when the play is to be played'? Would he be within his rights

> if I communicate it in a letter to the local Press?
> If I print it in the programme and sell the programme <u>outside</u> the theatre?
> If I print it in a separate leaflet and sell or distribute the leaflet outside the theatre?
> If I publish it in the printed text of the play?

Attacking on all fronts and with all guns blazing, the playwright also complained that he had received no reply to his query concerning his 'right to state in a play, if I choose, something which is untrue'; and finally, since it was, he said, his intention to bring the whole case before Parliament and the public, he asked the Office to 'quote me the date, circumstances and precise wording of what amounts to an extra-legislative authority, alleged to be granted to the Lord Chamberlain by the Executives, to censor a play . . . on any grounds whatever'.

It was almost game, set and match. The Comptroller sent the entire file to the Home Office and, as Blair-Fish pressed for answers, sought to fob him off. 'It has not been found possible as yet to reply to the legal points raised in your letter', wrote Nugent. 'Surely an interval of now very nearly a month should be more than long enough to obtain legal advice on the points raised in my letter', replied their nemesis; 'I really must press for the matter to be accelerated'. Worse was to follow, when the Home Office eventually informed the Lord Chamberlain that, although they knew of no legal way in which his decisions could be challenged through the courts, the position he had taken and the claims he had made were not ones which they were willing to condone or support. In effect, the censorship had dug itself into a hole, and the Home Office saw that the only real reason for maintaining the ban on publishing the line was to avoid conceding that an error had been made:

> If the facts of this case were made public in Parliament or elsewhere, could a reasonable defence be put up for the action of the Lord Chamberlain in refusing to license the play unless the author undertakes not to print in the programme the words 'nice comfortable Chesterfield this, anyway.' . . . It is important to maintain the authority of the Lord Chamberlain, but in view of the general public and of the authors of dramatic works it is equally important to ensure that the extremely wide powers of the Lord Chamberlain should be used reasonably. Accordingly it would be out of the question to use publicly the argument that the Lord Chamberlain felt it necessary to require this undertaking from the author for the purpose of maintaining the Lord Chamberlain's authority.

Probably acting on the advice of Law Officers, the Home Office suggested that the legitimate grounds for censoring a programme were actually extremely limited. They applied

> only if, in the view of the Lord Chamberlain, the presentation of a play, which in itself is sufficiently innocuous to be licensed, would nevertheless, if accompanied by something objectionable in the Theatre programme offend, in the words of Section 16 of the Theatres Act, against 'good manners, decorum or the public peace'.

And they queried whether it could

> reasonably be maintained that the printing in the programme of the words 'nice comfortable Chesterfield this, anyway' would turn the presentation of a play which is otherwise innocuous into a presentation which offends against good manners, decorum or the public peace? Would such an argument carry conviction in the minds even of persons who are generally prepared to support the Censorship?

The Home Office warned that to try and dig in further could have far-reaching and damaging implications: 'to insist on this stipulation would be very dangerous and might well revive the agitation, which has been for many years quiescent, in favour of some method of limiting the Lord Chamberlain's powers'. If this were not embarrassing enough, the Lord Chamberlain had also claimed an authority which the Home Office was not prepared to substantiate:

> This danger is increased by the statement in your letter of 19th of June that the Lord Chamberlain's 'power to attach any rules or conditions to a Stage Play's Licence was confirmed many years ago by the Law Officers of the

Crown'. We have been unable to ascertain what opinion of the Law Officers you have in mind; but, in any case, the statement seems dangerously wide and likely to provide ammunition for those who want to attack the Lord Chamberlain's powers.

Embarrassing though it was, the only way for the Lord Chamberlain's Office to save its skin was to back down. It is tempting to think that the doors of the citadel were ajar, and that a concerted putsch in the brave new world of 1945 could have brought the whole system of theatre censorship crashing down in ruins. But perhaps Blair-Fish did not quite realise just how close he was to securing the ultimate prize, or quite how exposed the censorship had become. He was invited to attend St James's Palace to discuss the case. At first, he remained splendidly unwilling to be duped or to negotiate:

> With reference to our telephone conversation yesterday, although I agreed to come and see you next Wednesday on your pressing your request that I should do so, I must confess myself to be still very much at a loss to imagine what useful purpose can be served by such a meeting, in view of the fact that, as I told you, I am not prepared to compromise in any way with the censorship: my quarrel with that institution is à outrance, like the national quarrel with Nazidom (of which censorship is a part)—and it would be hardly necessary for me to attend in person to receive His Lordship's unconditional surrender!
>
> I do beg you, therefore, not to cause me a wasted day in town but to cancel the interview, unless, in the light of the above, you should still have good reason to believe that you are warranted in desiring it.

But, not for the first time, the diplomatic skills of the men patrolling the watchtowers of the British establishment prevailed, and opposition was nullified and absorbed. Blair-Fish came, and Nugent reported on the meeting that he and Gwatkin had held with him in August 1945:

> I told him that it had seemed to me that it was all rather a fuss about nothing. I said that I felt that if he, Mr. Blair-Fish, had adopted a less defiant attitude in the outset, and had come and talked the matter over amicably, the Lord Chamberlain would, in all probability, have allowed him the line. I then told him that I had again approached the Lord Chamberlain, and had pointed out that it seemed a pity that the play could not be produced simply because there had been a quarrel over a . . . detail. The Lord Chamberlain had agreed to this, on further consideration, and had decided not to demand the cutting of the line . . .
>
> We then spent twenty minutes in rather aimless and abortive discussion of the censorship in general. Mr Blair had certain strange, and to me, impracticable ideas about it, but Colonel Gwatkin and I were able to point out to him that it was not quite such an easy matter as some people seemed to think.

The matter, I hope, is now at an end.[54]

In a humiliating and perhaps unparalleled climb down, on 8 August 1945, the Comptroller wrote to the secretary of the Amersham Repertory Players 'to inform you that the Lord Chamberlain has now agreed to the reinstatement of the line which was originally objected to. A fresh licence, without any endorsement, is enclosed herewith'.

Blair-Fish's tenacity had paid off and he had won his battle. But it was only a minor victory, and nothing had really changed. The giant may have been scratched, but it had bought the time to retreat and allow its wound to heal. The established order had survived, and the censorship lived to fight another day. Or several days. As for Blair-Fish, not unlike one or two who followed after, he seems to have trodden the path from left-wing rebel to establishment Conservative, leaving the Labour Party in the fifties over its failure to endorse the theory of nuclear deterrence. This from the man who nearly brought down the Lord Chamberlain and theatre censorship.

> PUBLIC OPINION: Oh, keep us moral!
> CENSORSHIP: I'm glad, ma'am, you support me in this quarrel.
> PUBLIC OPINION: (*severely*) Of course I do! You're there for my protection
>   From plays to which I might find some objection.
> DRAMA: . . . 'What! Have we fought for freedom from our prime
>   To dodge and palter with this public crime'—
>   This Censorship?
> CENSORSHIP: (*roughly*)   Freedom? Go, hug your chain!
>   D'ye think they care? Listen to them again!
> (*Back-stage voices are heard again. Public Opinion listens in wrapt delight, Censorship grins broadly, Drama bites his lips in angry despair*)
> 1st MAN'S VOICE: Government by the people!
> OMNES: 'ip-'oorah!
> 2nd MAN'S VOICE: A free press!
> 3rd MAN'S VOICE: Magna Carta!
> CENSORSHIP: (*roaring with laughter*) Ha, ha, ha!
> OMNES: (*more feebly*) Democracy!
> DRAMA: (*angrily*)   Humbug!
> CENSORSHIP (*cynically contemptuous*)   Yes—humbug! Yah!
> (*The lights fade. Curtain*)[55]

SECTION THREE
1945–1952

CHAPTER EIGHT

'Two Ways To Get Rid Of The Censor'

> The Lord Chamberlain is not a horrid ogre. The gentlemen in his department do not simply say, 'Out with this line.' They sit there and think 'How can I help these people?' They are the most kind, considerate, helpful people in the world.
>
> (MP and playwright Sir Alan Herbert, opposing the bill to repeal the Theatres Act, March 1949)[1]

At the end of the war, Nugent and Gwatkin returned full-time as Comptroller and Assistant Comptroller, but Clarendon still had some sorting out to do. Game was already in his sixties, and though he let it be known that he wished to postpone his retirement indefinitely on account of the loss in reading fees he had suffered during the war, the Lord Chamberlain was keen to manipulate the succession. Geoffrey Dearmer had never quite fitted; on a number of occasions he had challenged the assumptions of his superiors—sometimes forcefully—and some of his colleagues thought his judgement was unsound and that he had too often created problems by missing or misinterpreting elements in the material on which he reported. Clarendon therefore wished to ensure that Game's permanent successor as senior Reader was Charles Heriot, even though he had only recently joined the staff:

> Dearmer is the senior but he is already employed at the BBC. He is, also, not an absolutely reliable examiner of all types of plays. Heriot is the junior and is first-class—well able to take on the post of senior examiner when Game retires.
>
> Dearmer has been approached and agrees to Heriot jumping him whilst he (Dearmer) is employed by the BBC. This is unsatisfactory and, I think it must be made quite clear that Dearmer remains second reader until he retires.

It was agreed that Game should be allowed to stay in post for a further two years beyond his sixty-fifth birthday, and that he would continue to oversee the distribution of plays to the various Readers until he retired. Heriot would deal with over half the plays, and receive the due income.

Furthermore, in order to avoid the risk of losing Heriot (and finding himself landed with Dearmer), Clarendon approached the King's Treasurer with a somewhat patronising but well-intended appeal for an extra £200:

> we have had a 'boy', Heriot, training up since before the war to take Game's place when he returns [sic] . Heriot is a free-lance writer and has kept going since the war (during which he married) on his occasional writings, his gratuity and his savings.
>
> He is faced with financial difficulties now, which will be removed when Game becomes 65 in March next year.
>
> It is really important that this office should not lose Heriot, he is a most suitable successor to Game and has had quite a lot of experience.

The application was successful, and 'a special grant' was provided to deal with the 'exceptional position'.[2] Dearmer, while continuing to act as a Reader, went on to become a household voice as one of the presenters of *Children's Hour* (the radio programme rather than Lillian Hellman's banned play).

Clarendon was also keen to resurrect the Advisory Board, which had largely slipped into abeyance during the war, and in 1946 several new candidates were canvassed and recruited. Lady Violet Bonham Carter remained a member, as did the former Lord Chamberlain, Lord Cromer, and Professor Allardyce Nicoll; other members of the Board were Professor David Cecil, of Oxford University; Dr Winifred Cullis, a professor of physiology and expert on health and social hygiene, who had worked on behalf of both the Colonial Office and the Ministry of Information; Colonel Peter Fleming, brother of the creator of James Bond, himself an explorer, author and regular contributor to *The Times* and the *Spectator*; Mrs Miles, the daughter of the theatre manager and former member of the Board, Sir Johnston Forbes Robertson; the Reverend F.H. Gillingham, probably best-known to Nugent as a first-class cricketer and through the MCC; and a light comedy actor and theatre manager, Cyril Maude. In joining, they were assured that their names would not be made public and that 'the work entailed is negligible, as it is only very rarely that plays are sent'.[3] As well as consulting government departments when he judged it appropriate, Clarendon also continued to make regular use of the Archbishop of Canterbury, the Dean of Westminster and the Chief Rabbi.

The political upheavals and changing social attitudes of post-war Britain were bound to lead to a sustained campaign against the censorship, and the previous chapter ended with an example of that. In many ways, the only surprise is that the system survived to stagger on for a further twenty-three years. If it is impossible to pin down the moment when its death throes began, the roots of its gradual demise are visible well before the arrival of Osborne, Beckett, Brecht, Genet and the theatrical revolution of the mid fifties. The final section of this book will therefore begin by discussing some of the direct and indirect attacks on what was increasingly exposed as an anachronistic system born in a country in which things had been done differently. Although the walls of the old structure may still have been standing when a new monarch and a new Lord Chamberlain took office in 1952, beneath the surface the foundations had been rattled. Indeed, it was possibly more apparent to the staff at St James's Palace than to most outsiders that their days were numbered. Like the colonised nations of the Empire, the theatre wanted its independence, and the question could not be 'whether' but only 'when'. The task for the Lords Chamberlain was to find a way to beat a dignified retreat.

In February 1948, a four-day British Theatre Conference, which was probably justified in its claim to be 'easily the most representative' event of its kind, was addressed by the Chancellor of the Exchequer. Stafford Cripps spoke of his plans to supply more funds to the Arts Council, but he noted that the funding of the arts through the Treasury 'brought the Government directly into contact with the problems of cultural development'. He therefore cautioned delegates 'to think many times before advocating that all theatres should be owned by the State, unless they wanted a State censorship of all plays', and *The Times* identified Cripps as being 'on the side of the angels' when he warned that 'a planned drama may so easily become "an art made tongue-tied by authority"'.[4] The conference approved a series of resolutions and recommendations which it passed to the government, including an all but unanimous call for the abolition of theatre censorship through the Lord Chamberlain's department. However, one group which had refused to participate in the conference, and which certainly did not sign up to the recommendations, was the rather provocatively named Theatre National Committee. This was a composite body representing theatre managers from a number of organisations, such as The Society of West End Managers, the Theatrical Managers' Association, the Independent Theatres Association, the Entertainments Protection Association, and the Association of Touring and Producing Managers. All were suspicious of anything connected with the Arts Council, and anyone who challenged the assumption that theatre was primarily about entertainment and profits. For the same reasons as in the past, managers continued to support the licensing of scripts through the Lord Chamberlain, and the Society of West End Managers responded immediately to the conference's declaration by passing its own resolution calling for the retention of the current system. Yet perhaps there was already a hint of desperation in the leader column of the *Stage* when it took issue with the Conference's insistence that censorship and the Lord Chamberlain were obsolete hangovers from another era:

Surely the fact of the office having lasted so long, in spite of abuse of all kinds . . . is in its favour rather than otherwise. It suggests some reason for survival. A statement has been made that there is no censorship in other forms of art; but this is hardly so. We have a British Board of Film Censors. Books and pictures are both liable to police action—an obviously undesirable thing in the theatre. With a local censorship there would be perpetual rows from anti-theatrical cliques and publicity-hunters. As things stand, much of this is avoided under a broad-minded and approachable Lord Chamberlain, not averse to changing his mind . . . and above political prejudice.[5]

This was just a foretaste of the clash which would occur twelve months later when Edward Percy Smith, the playwright-turned-Conservative MP won a ballot which gave him the opportunity to present a private member's bill to the House. Smith, who claimed to be descended from Nell Gwynne, had been campaigning for alterations to the practice of theatre censorship for forty years, and had already clashed with the Lord Chamberlain over the banning of *Mr Lincoln Meets a Lady* and the withdrawal of the previously issued licence from *Felicity Jasmine*.[6] In 1944, he had raised an objection to the fact that the Lord Chamberlain was effectively situated above and beyond both parliament and the law, and that MPs therefore had no right or opportunity to ask questions about his activities or decisions. In anticipation of a difficult debate, Sir Alexander Maxwell, the Under-Secretary of State at the Home Office, had produced a lengthy briefing paper tracing the principle of how censorship should operate back to the recommendations of the 1909 Joint Select Committee:

No doubt in the last resort if the Lord Chamberlain proved to be totally out of touch with public opinion in the matter of the licensing of plays, it would be necessary for the Government to make representations with a view to his removal and replacement by someone better qualified, and so long as this power exists in the background there are advantages in leaving the responsibility for the particular decisions to someone who is not answerable to the House of Commons. As the select committee of 1909 recognised, it would be quite intolerable if questions or debates could be raised in the House of Commons on particular decisions which must frequently be merely matters of opinion and can be hotly argued both ways by partisans. If, for example, the censorship allowed a play with a Fascist tendency or quite properly interfered with a play with a Communist tendency on the ground that it contained offensive personalities or did violence to the sentiment of religious reverence, or was calculated to cause a breach of the peace, suggestions would certainly be made that the interference was based on political prejudice, and it would be most undesirable [that?] a Minister belonging to a particular political party should be the final arbiter on the question whether the play should be licensed or not.

The broad defence for the present system is that though from time to time the Censor may give decisions which some people think are mistaken, this would happen whatever were the system of censorship. If the archangel Gabriel were Censor, he could not hope to avoid giving offence on some occasions. All that can be asked for is that broadly speaking the censorship shall be exercised in accordance with principles that are acceptable to public opinion in general. So far as the experience of the Home Office for the last twenty years goes, there has been no serious complaint against the general method by which the censorship has been exercised. Complaints have been rare, and as already stated, complaints in particular cases are inevitable.[7]

On that occasion, the parliamentary discussion which followed Smith's question turned out to be brief—'abortive but amusing' as the MP himself put it in a letter to the Home Secretary. But though Smith evidently accepted the specific and private information he was subsequently given by Herbert Morrison—which probably amounted to the fact that the King objected to one of the plays he was asking about—it did not change his mind about the principle. Indeed, he had described the Home Secretary's letter as

the finest evidence there could be of the soundness of my contention that the Censorship should be under a Minister of the Crown. Here, in a few lines, you give me information about a matter of public interest . . . which not weeks of work, questions to Ministers and general Parliamentary artfulness were able to elicit.[8]

The argument over how MPs could ask questions about stage censorship was one which regularly surfaced. In the summer of 1948, following a complaint by an MP about a performance by Phyllis Dixey, the Lord Chamberlain's Office received a letter from the Law Officers asking who had responsibility for dealing with questions. Nugent hedged his reply cautiously:

I believe I am correct in saying that although the Lord Chamberlain derives his powers from the Theatres Act, 1843 that Act merely confirms his exercise of the Royal Prerogative in this respect. No Minister can, therefore, answer for the Lord Chamberlain in the House of Commons. At the same time I think it is true to say that the Home Secretary would be the appropriate Minister to make observations upon the conduct of the Stage were these called for.[9]

In March, Percy Smith had tabled another question in the House, querying whether or not the Chief Constable of Birmingham could demand changes in a script, as he was trying to do, when that script had already been approved by the head of the King's household.[10] This was a trap, as the Lord Chamberlain's Office realised. The argument most frequently used by theatre managers and others to support the current system of censorship was that to remove the security of the blanket licence would result in different local authorities imposing different standards of censorship, making it all but impossible to plan a tour with any guarantee that it would not be disrupted. It followed that if those seeking to abolish the system could prove that the licence did not in fact provide such a guarantee, then a large hole would have been blown in their opponents' case. In preparing an answer to Smith, the Home Office rang the Lord Chamberlain's Office to discuss their draft response; as provisionally formulated, this stated 'that the Local authority had power to make rules for ensuring order and decency in a theatre, that such rules might include a prohibition of profanity, and that on the strength of such a prohibition the local authority might require deletions from a play already licensed'. Ronald Hill, the secretary to the Lord Chamberlain, spotted the danger:

> I did not think that this was on the right lines from the practical point of view, and I told her that whatever constructions could be put upon the Theatres Act, I should like to make it plain that any diminution of the Lord Chamberlain's absolute powers of censorship and aggrandisement of the claims of a local authority could have only one end, which was the material weakening of the Censorship.

He proposed an alternative spin:

> I said that we had an unbroken record of co-operation on these matters with Local authorities, but that *we should not like it publicly owned* [my italics] that there was a possibility of their vetoing the Lord Chamberlain's decision. I therefore said I thought she ought to stress that interference by Local authorities in support of their rules had never yet stood the test of the Courts, and to emphasise that the Lord Chamberlain was the sole authority for allowing or disallowing a play.

To ensure that they would be singing from the same songsheet, Hill also suggested that the Home Office should send them a revised draft for further corrections. Regrettably, avoiding Smith's snare also meant that instead of supporting the Chief Constable of Birmingham, the Office would in effect be joining a strategic alliance with the MP who was himself seeking the dissolution of the censorship!

> There would seem here to be a possibility of hard words in Parliament as to the Ch. Constable at Birmingham exceeding his authority, and our line I take it is to minimise whatever trouble there is as much as possible, without admitting (which is still very doubtful whatever the Home Office may say) that the Lord Chamberlain's decisions can be questioned or altered by anyone. It is a difficult position, but if we do not to some extent support the MP we are bound to suffer for it later, as we shall be putting a powerful weapon against the Censor into the hands of our adversaries with the Theatre Conference. At present almost the only supporters of the Lord Chamberlain in the Theatre world are the Managers who side with

us purely on this point that the Lord Chamberlain's authority is universal and unquestionable.[11]

Smith's ambush had been avoided for the time being, but as Hill warned them: 'We shall obviously hear more of this!'. A year later, in March 1949, Smith's Censorship of Plays (Repeal) bill was duly published. Previously, Smith had seemed content to settle for a rearrangement which involved shifting the power and responsibility held by the Lord Chamberlain to a minister who could be officially asked questions. But his bill raised the stakes by calling explicitly for abolition of the system. Its stated aim was to

> Amend the Law relating to the Censorship of Plays and Licensing of Theatres so as to exempt the Theatre from Restrictions upon Freedom of Expression in excess of those applicable to other forms of literature; and for purposes connected therewith.[12]

Although the bill was never close to becoming law, the arguments and counter arguments which raged in the debate and in the public campaign surrounding it are important and instructive. Inevitably, there was much retreading of old ground, as echoes or even reruns from earlier parliamentary discussions were heard. Again, one of the most basic arguments centred on whether theatre should be governed by the same laws which operated in relation to the other arts, or whether it was such a distinct form and medium, with so much more potential for influencing audiences, that it required different standards and policing.

In February 1949, the Home Office wrote to Titman to warn him of what was coming, and to let him know that it would soon be all hands to the pump to help stave off the attack: 'As soon as we receive a draft of the Bill we shall, of course, want to consult you and have the Lord Chamberlain's views'.[13] St James's Palace did not even wait for the publication of the bill, to begin preparing for the conflict ahead by producing detailed briefing papers which justified the present system and denigrated the alternatives. These they fed to the Home Office and to friendly MPs who could be trusted to speak against the bill. On 3 March, the Comptroller wrote to one such, Captain Malcolm Bullock. Nugent assured the MP that the censorship argued its position not from selfishness or to defend its own territory, but out of altruism and duty: 'we in the Lord Chamberlain's Office gain nothing by censorship and would, therefore, lose nothing if it was taken away from us'; he then rehearsed a series of arguments as to why censorship of the stage was so important:

> 1) Although the Lord Chamberlain seldom has to ban a play in toto (out of 1200 plays submitted in 1948 less than half a dozen were refused a Licence) a great many require cuts and alterations to make them fit to be played before a mixed audience. This particularly applies to Revues and

Pantomimes. The former may not matter vitally as they are usually played before a sophisticated audience but Pantomimes should be primarily for children and I can assure you that a great deal of the stuff submitted nowadays is totally unfitted for such an audience.

2) The Lord Chamberlain has few defined rules and tries to judge every individual play on its merits but there are certain themes, e.g. homosexuality and lesbianism, which are taboo now but which would undoubtedly be used if there were no censorship. Such plays as *The Children's Hour* (lesbianism), *Queer People* (homosexuality and lesbianism) and *Oscar Wilde* have all been played in theatre clubs where the censorship does not obtain and these subjects would, I think, if given unlicensed scope on the commercial stage be an influence for ill.

3) A censor can exercise a restraint on religious themes which, even if not actually blasphemous, would give pain and distress and cause embarrassment to religious-minded people. The Lord Chamberlain never allows the personification of the Deity on stage. To do so would undoubtedly offend many people.

4) The censor can use his tact with regard to plays in which offence might be given to friendly foreign powers, or even unfriendly ones with whom we are technically at peace. For instance, out of courtesy we do not allow Heads of foreign states to be guyed on the stage.

5) The Lord Chamberlain is able to protect individuals from offensive representation on the stage. It is a misconception to think that he protects political parties or the Government of the day from justifiable banter but he does see to it that an individual, whether he be politician, public servant or private individual, is spared the distress of ill-mannered gibes . . .

It may be argued that the common law should be sufficient to defend the rights of the community from the above dangers but if there is no pre-production censorship this will have to be done by recourse to the law and it would be cumbersome and certainly irksome to the players and producers if the police were constantly walking in and stopping the performance. In effect, they probably would not do so except in very serious cases, with the result that the standard of decency on the stage would tend to go down.

Nugent also restated the old argument that, without the insurance the system offered, managers would take fewer risks and that therefore even the authors who most opposed the system would actually suffer if it were abolished.

The second part of Nugent's case was to provide ammunition which would allow the Office's supporters to demonstrate why it was the Lord Chamberlain, rather than any alternative, who remained 'the most suitable authority' to carry out the task:

Perhaps I am not the right person to give an opinion on this but in my view the qualifications for the office of Lord Chamberlain are very suitable for that of a censor. He is non-political, non-sectarian, has no axe to grind and, owing to his position, is in ready touch with the best opinions of the day. He has only to ask the opinion of the highest authority, be it the Archbishop of Canterbury, the Lord Chief Justice, the Foreign Secretary or other prominent authorities, to be vouchsafed an immediate and courteous reply.

The Comptroller argued that although it was easy for the enemies of censorship 'to sneer and to say that it is ridiculous that an elderly peer should be the sole arbiter of the dramatic taste of the nation', in practice the Lord Chamberlain drew on the knowledge of expert examiners and 'an Advisory Council drawn from a good cross-section of modern thought'. Nor was it accurate, insisted Nugent, to claim that the Office refused to explain decisions or to negotiate:

> The Lord Chamberlain insists that any author or producer who wants to discuss any part of his play that has been cut, should be interviewed by Norman Gwatkin or myself. No-one, therefore, can say that they do not get personal service. Indeed, I think you would have to go a long way to find a more impartial and benevolent censor than the Lord Chamberlain.[14]

On the same date, Clarendon wrote to the Home Office, affirming the principle that theatre required its own unique and stricter form of control because 'the emotional and psychological effect of a stage play is recognised as being much greater than any other form of art'. He also sought to elucidate the benefits of censorship:

> 1) It protects the public from excessive vulgarity, especially in pantomimes which are largely intended for children.
> 2) It prevents the production of plays on perversion and other unsavoury subjects.
> 3) It controls religious intolerance and blasphemy.
> 4) It checks plays and passages which might give offence to foreign governments.
> 5) It protects the individual or the family from hurtful publicity, which might arise from the personification of real people.
> 6) It protects the managers, producers and employees from loss of contract and financial hardship.

Post-production censorship would be unsatisfactory, he explained, because it would put extra strain on the police and the judicial system; moreover, it would be 'undesirable because the play or passages in it have already caused offence and the subsequent action—if the case is upheld—will be the withdrawal of the play, with consequent considerable financial loss and unemployment'. While acknowledging that there were other authorities which could replace the Lord Chamberlain's Office and carry out his duties, 'the present system appears to have worked satisfactorily for hundreds of years and at no cost to public funds'; it satisfied managers and producers, and was, he claimed, 'agreeable to the majority of playwrights and actors (as far as any form of censorship can be)'. Once again, he averred that 'the author of an ordinary decent play has nothing to fear from the censorship, whilst the author who wishes (probably under some guise) to exploit an unsavoury theme, incident or fact, will always be against any form of censorship or control as tending to cripple his genius'.[15]

Nugent's and Clarendon's letters were both adapted from a much more extended paper written by Hill. 'It may be thought long', the secretary had admitted when he first shared it with them, 'but if anyone is to speak on our behalf and cannot spare an hour or so in reading up the case, then I feel we are better without his services'.[16] There was probably nothing in Hill's version with which his superiors would have disagreed, but there were elements which it might have been injudicious to express in public; for example, Hill called into question the disinterest and impartiality of the MPs who were sponsoring the bill, on the grounds that they themselves were also playwrights: 'The bill is therefore being promoted by partisan interests, who although they may represent that they are actuated solely by the interest of the community, cannot deny that they have personal motives'. This line of attack was withheld by the Comptroller and the Lord Chamberlain. Hill also complacently dismissed the argument that censorship was having a stultifying effect on thought and experiment in the theatre: 'The best proof that these fears are unfounded lies in an examination of the present state of the British theatre', declared Hill, arrogantly; 'It compares most favourably with that of any other country'. He admitted that the system was open to abuse and depended on having 'the right administrators' to control it, and tried to define the requirements of the post of censor:

> He must be a man of such standing that
> i) His rulings carry conviction and acceptance everywhere amongst those who realise the need for some control in the interests of moral welfare, international necessity, or the maintenance of religion and the less material aspects of life.
> ii) Unfortunately this means he may sometimes be at variance with playwrights and actors who are apt to consider dramatic quality the only criterion.

He argued that 'The censor chosen must be both aware of topical thought and opinion, yet detached from the makers of it', and that 'He must be manifestly impartial and have sufficient inherent authority for his writ to run unquestioned throughout the Kingdom'. But had they not been discreetly toned down and, one must say, censored by his superiors, Hill's attempts to demonstrate that the Lord Chamberlain alone fitted the bill and was uniquely qualified might have exposed hidden assumptions and given some openings to the opposition:

The Lord Chamberlain as Censor

a) As the senior Member of His Majesty's Household he is demonstrably removed from any exclusive natural political or sectional partiality.

b) As the holder of one of the great ceremonial and social offices of the Crown he has considerable intrinsic importance, quite apart from his function as Censor. This fact gives additional weight to his decisions, already known to be completely impartial, and leads generally to their willing acceptance.

c) i) The Lord Chamberlain's appointment as Censor of Stage Plays is not an arbitrary one.

ii) He has censored plays for over four hundred years, practically speaking since secular plays commenced to be performed in this country.

iii) His function originally derived from the Royal Prerogative, but has been confirmed by two Acts of Parliament, in 1737 and 1843.

iv) In the past his detached position has enabled him to protect the Stage from oppressors, as well as to protect the public from the occasional irresponsible or worse dramatist.

v) He has appointed Examiners of Plays since 1737—there is always a Deputy currently learning the work. This provides for continuity of treatment and logical decision.

vi) But, Examiners are only ADVISERS, and the final decision is always taken by the Lord Chamberlain. His general responsibilities require that he shall be a man of wide experience and liberal outlook. These qualities super-imposed on the work of the Examiners, ensure that tradition shall be tempered by current thought and the Censorship shall be a balanced instrument.

c) The Censorship is NOT a VESTED INTEREST.

Fees have been unchanged for one hundred years, and all are devoted to the actual Examiners of Plays. The Lord Chamberlain his Official and Clerical Staff give their services without reward from the Stage.

Indeed, Hill could hardly understand why people were not falling over themselves to express their gratitude: 'The duty of Censoring Plays is one which by ancient custom devolves upon the Lord Chamberlain and which he is glad to perform for the Common Weal'.[17]

It was true, of course, that theatre managers still favoured the current system. On 9 March, the Theatres National Committee wrote to the Home Office. They sent a similar letter to all MPs, in advance of the parliamentary debate:

The Theatres National Committee does not favour any alteration or amendment of the Theatres Act 1843 . . . for the following reasons:-

1) In our opinion the Lord Chamberlain, through his office, has always carried out his duties with broadmindedness and erudition, and the system has worked most satisfactorily and expeditiously, resulting in benefit both to playwrights and to the providers of public entertainment.

2) In the event of abolition of the present censorship, my Members feel that they would be at the mercy of unilateral action by different bodies in

various parts of the country ... the booking of a consecutive tour throughout the country would be impossible.

3) A play licensed by the Lord Chamberlain acquires a certain 'hall-mark' which indicates that it has received official approval ...

5) ... If the present censorship ceases to exist, the Theatres National Committee will have no alternative but to set up its own Board to grant licences for the presentation of stage plays on lines similar to those prevailing in the Cinema Industry.

6) We maintain that the present system of censorship is not in any way derogatory to the work of the dramatist ... On the contrary, we believe the enlightenment of the Lord Chamberlain, his tolerance and willingness to consider favourably any arguments against objections he may raise to a play submitted to him are of great assistance to authors ...

The present system has worked satisfactorily for over a century and has proved an adequate safeguard against the presentation of what might be considered improper plays by some, and we trust that if the proposed Bill is presented to Parliament the House will reject it as being unnecessary and not in the public interest.[18]

The letter was signed by Horace Collins, the secretary of the committee. Although there were some playwrights who supported the Lord Chamberlain—including William Douglas Home, Warren Chetham-Strode and the MP Alan Herbert—the battlelines were formed on familiar and predictable grounds.

The sponsors of the bill were well aware of the legitimate argument that removing the licensing system might have the unfortunate effect of silencing the more challenging work, as managers elected to play safe. There was a real and serious risk that power could be placed in the hands of local authorities and moral activists, and theatre would suddenly find itself, as Chetham-Strode put it, 'at the mercy of any crack-pot who wants for this or that personal reason to stop the show'.[19] Indeed, the *Stage* predicted, not without some justification, that the removal of the system 'which the Lord Chamberlain so well and tactfully exercises' might not only hand power to what it called 'a hugger-mugger' of 'bawlers and scrawlers', but that rival managements would adopt a deliberate strategy of sabotaging competitors by promoting objections. A touch obsequiously, the newspaper also reminded its readers of 'the treasured privilege our theatre enjoys of being in direct touch with the Throne', and it questioned whether there was really anything to complain about: 'Looking round at current plays which have received the Lord Chamberlain's benison it is difficult to gain any other impression than that of remarkable freedom'.[20]

In drafting the bill, the MPs had tried to anticipate and nullify the potential for disruption by individuals or small groups of fanatics, by incorporating a clause based on the Newspaper Act of 1888. This was overtly designed to disarm frivolous or serial objectors, by ensuring that no criminal prosecution could be instituted until a judge at chambers had been persuaded of the validity of the case. However, Smith was rightly convinced that the immunity which managers presumed they currently enjoyed through the licence was 'chimerical' and of no value in law, though he conceded that 'it may be of some value to them in practice'.[21] Introducing his bill to parliament on 25 March 1949, Smith made 'freedom' the moral and political heart of his appeal; he declared that freedom of the word was the most important freedom for a society, to which 'all other freedoms shall in the fullness of time be added', and described the Lord Chamberlain as 'the last official chain upon the word'. Walpole's licensing act of 1737 was 'the evil parent of the Act of 1843', which had 'destroyed the theatre as a vehicle of ideas and graciously allowed it to become the Mannequin of Contemporary Manners':

> It is inimical to the drama as a cultural force and . . . contrives to protect the public not from impropriety, because that seems easy enough to slip past the censor, but from the impact of ideas which, however startling or irrelevant or however absurd and far-fetched, may not happen to appeal to the Lord Chamberlain's clerks . . . it compels the theatre to lag behind public opinion instead of being, as it should be, in the van.

For the playwright, said Smith, it was 'an intolerable humiliation, to be compelled to submit every word he writes to the close scrutiny of a public official'.

Seconding the bill, Michael Foot sought to answer the objections raised by the Theatre National Committee, while also undermining their authority; 'the theatre managers are not speaking for the theatre', he declared, 'they are only speaking for themselves', and any 'hall mark' which they claimed was acquired through the licence and of which they were so proud was merely 'the whim of the Lord Chamberlain'. Foot said he could see no reason why anyone other than the Communist Party would oppose the bill, and told the House that even if the current system of censorship were removed, there would still remain 'full protection under the common law of England against blasphemy, profanity, libel, treason, sedition, obscenity and the rest'. Importantly, he also tried to reach beyond the visible examples of censorship, insisting it was not simply 'a matter of considering those plays whose heads have been cut off by the actions of the Lord Chamberlain's guillotine', but that 'we must also consider the plays killed in the womb'. For Foot, censorship was 'an issue which touches the roots of freedom'; perhaps his rhetoric, powerfully though it reads even today, could be accused of exaggerating the importance of theatre:

> These are cruel times in which we live. Freedom is being suppressed in one land and another, and perhaps the most obvious symbol and example

of that suppression are not [sic] the prisons of Buchenwald and Saxen-hausen, and the slave camps of Siberia. It is not the bodies of the men in such camps which the dictators fear; it is the words they seek to speak and the thoughts they strive to utter. The most evil thing in the world today is censorship which divides nation from nation and people from people . . .

. . . It would be a splendid thing if at this time, when new and more barbarous forces are being unleashed upon the world, we took steps to enlarge the Empire of the human mind and to widen the territory where heresy and inspiration can bring new life to the people.

Although Foot had tried to demonstrate that the bill contained clauses specifically designed to protect productions against individuals or organisations trying to close them down, his parliamentary opponents continued to raise fears that the effect would be to hand power to 'old women and goose-necked cranks', and devolve too much responsibility onto local authorities: 'The last state will be worse than the first. We shall bring chaos into the country on this matter and into the industry'. They stressed the indulgent and non-interventionist approach of the current Lord Chamberlain ('We have more freedom on the stage than any other country, with the possible exception of the French stage'), citing the fact that *The Respectable Prostitute* and *No Orchids for Miss Blandish*, as well as works about artificial insemination and venereal disease, had all recently been approved: 'Can it be said that the Lord Chamberlain's office is motivated by intolerance or narrowmindedness? Certainly not'; they insisted that the bill's supporters had been largely unable to cite actual examples of injustices or complaints against the current system: 'we have not heard, with the exception of three cases, of any real grievance against the Lord Chamberlain's office of today or within the last 20 or 25 years'; and they made much of how few of the 20,000 plays submitted during that period had been banned: 'a little over 1 per cent. Does that sound like the denial of freedom? Does that sound as if authors were committed to the Tower, as if they were living in concentration camps?'. Strangely, although Foot had already alluded to unwritten plays, no-one raised the issue of how many scripts received licences only after they had been cut and altered; the Home Office had been prepared for this question by Clarendon, who informed them that some 40 per cent of scripts submitted in 1948 had required alteration. But such information was probably not in the public domain or known to supporters of the bill; perhaps the drive to end censorship might have been more powerful if it had been.[22]

Those speaking against the bill claimed that there were no serious restraints on the theatre— 'If there is any country in the world today that can claim the greatest freedom for words, whether oral or written, it is Great Britain'—while nevertheless insisting on the need for controls to be exercised:

There are such things in life as good taste and delicacy. An audience is a cross-section of the community and does not represent one class . . . there are sensitive people with susceptibilities as well as the more raucous elements. There are people sitting in the stalls or in the galleries who have very tough skins and stomachs. The managers of the industry have to cater for all these people, and they want in self-defence to have some kind of censorship.[23]

Captain Bullock made full use of the dossier supplied to him by Nugent; he explained why the Lord Chamberlain was the right person to exercise the power of the censor ('He is above party politics; he has no axe to grind') and why it was important to avoid the excessive liberty allowed across the channel:

If we compare our stage with the theatre in France, it will be found that the quality and wit of our plays are infinitely superior . . . If there is no censorship, except that of the police as in France, one is wearied by the same kind of wit and gesture on the same kind of subject. We have the impropriety of the head of the State being guyed daily, as happens in France.

He then gave a round-up of the grounds on which censorship was still essential, in order to protect others:

It is most desirable that there should be a censorship on religious themes so as not to give offence. There are also certain sex questions which should not be enacted in public on the stage. Those of us here do not suffer spiritual or moral setback by seeing that sort of subject because we have reached an age when we can take it, but for the young it is certainly a moral setback. There are also political matters which should not be produced on the stage. I do not think there should be any violent praise of Communism at the present time; I think the Censor would be right in stopping it.

Bullock argued that the prime duty of the Lord Chamberlain was to judge and follow the public mind, and to license plays only when audiences were ready for them:

I am sure that in the Victorian days of hypocrisy and smug morality they were right not to allow *Ghosts* and *Mrs Warren's Profession* to be performed. It would have offended many people; it would have upset the thought of the time. People were not ready for those plays.

This point, if granted, effectively shifted the responsibility away from an individual, constructing those writers and managers who complained about the censorship as outsiders from society, or mavericks. It also anticipated and hoped to deflect criticism of the fact that licences were almost bound to be granted eventually for plays which had once been beyond the pale. As one of the bill's advocates pointed out, Bullock's argument seemed to be that 'we need not worry terribly if anything worth hearing today is being suppressed, because in 1990 it will be the accepted thing', since 'if one waits long enough, any of the Lord Chamberlain's sins will be remedied'.

The House was not split on party lines. Indeed, Bullock's fellow Conservative, the well-known theatre critic Beverley Baxter, was one of the bill's strongest supporters. He took a diametrically opposed view to his parliamentary colleague, passionately attacking his complacent and patronising attitudes, and accusing Bullock of having 'moved back the calendar' with his argument:

> I thought I was listening to my grandfather. The sentiments he expressed were those which made the Victorian stage so inept and unworthy of this great people. Ibsen and Shaw were striving to be heard, yet there was an idea that people must be protected from thought and controversy—a most astonishing idea . . . What matter if some feelings would be hurt? Such a play would be one for thought, and the stage is a great debating chamber.

Baxter urged that 'the public should be trusted', and challenged the assumption that they needed sheltering: 'He said he would not like to see a play in praise of Communism. As a dramatic critic, if such a play was well written I would urge everybody to see it'. He accused Bullock of wanting 'to reduce the theatre to a maiden aunt's charade, where nobody is allowed to see anything except what is pleasant', and described opponents of the bill as a 'mass of cotton wool'. Baxter even embraced and relished the possibility that without a centralised authority to issue licences, different parts of the country would disagree and impose different policies: 'I should like to think that the public would take the theatre so seriously that they would even have a civil war between one town supporting something and one town rejecting it'. In any case, he insisted, theatre was not a mass activity in the way that cinema was, but 'a selective medium' where audiences knew what sort of play to expect when they went to see it. In refuting the argument that the small number of plays banned could be taken as proof that all was well, Baxter followed Foot in emphasising the international context in which a debate on the exercising of power through a centralised dictatorship was taking place:

> Surely tyranny is always exerted on a minority. That is the meaning of the word 'tyranny'. That is the very thing we hear from Moscow. We heard in the House yesterday of a lady who is visiting us at the present time and who says: 'We have freedom in Russia and those who oppose the Government are sent to gaol where they are taught the error of their ways'. The hon. Gentleman's is the same process of thought.

Indeed, Baxter was prepared to embrace the paradoxical and seemingly perverse argument that liberty should, if necessary, be forced on those who preferred to remain prisoners:

There comes a moment in the affairs of people, and of nations very often, when, if people will not accept freedom, it must be imposed upon them. When a nation is ready for freedom it must be imposed upon it, even if its people still ask for the manacles to hide the fact that their hands are trembling.

In the final speech before the House divided to vote on the bill, Ben Levy summed up the case for the abolition, and sought to counter some of the arguments which had been used to defend the censorship; he insisted that the dispute was not with the present incumbents of St James's Palace but with a principle:

> The office as at present operated works in a civilised and tolerant manner. The argument is not against the personnel but against the ridiculous position in which the personnel inevitably finds itself, because it is invited to make objective judgments in a field where only subjective judgments are possible.

He even maintained that 'If the Lord Chamberlain from time to time covers himself in ridicule, it is not really he who covers himself with ridicule but we who have put him into that ridiculous position'. Yet he also mocked as absurd the notion that the other functions required of a Lord Chamberlain somehow conferred upon him a facility to act as censor of the stage: 'It seems to me that the qualifications which may fit a man admirably to conduct a Sovereign to and from his carriage are not necessarily immediately connected with the qualifications which might entitle him to be an arbiter of the arts'. He insisted it was a mismatch, and that the task was an impossible one:

> I would say that the Censor is there to ensure that a sensitive public is not allowed to see things which will do it more harm than good and is only allowed so see things which will do it more good than harm. The man who has to decide that has to decide something . . . If he has to make decisions of that kind it requires not only that he should be able to look into the hearts of men, but also that he should be privy to the unforeseeable concatenation of cause and effect, which is one of the aspects of eternity. In other words it requires that he should have the omniscience of the Almighty. Now whenever we decide to install somebody into the position of the Almighty, we must not be surprised if we encounter a certain difficulty in finding a candidate with the necessary qualifications.
>
> I have looked up the qualifications of the present incumbent of the office and I note that his qualifications, among others, are that he is a director of Barclays Bank, an ex-Chancellor of the Primrose League and a member of the Turf Club; all of them estimable things in their way, but none of them, perhaps, quite achieving the level which I have previously predicated.

Levy also launched a tactical attack on the credentials and the assumptions of the Theatres National Committee and the managers, who had written to all MPs urging them not to pass the bill. He drew a telling distinction:

> But perhaps those not connected with the stage were not fully aware that the circular was from the managers alone, who were not, of course, entitled, as their circular implies, to speak on behalf of the entire theatrical industry. The phrase 'theatrical industry' is, in fact, a new thing . . . It used to be an art. The thought may conceivably very well have passed the managers' minds that to control in this arbitrary way an industry might be less offensive to our susceptibilities than to control an art, and, of course, in that they are perfectly right.

And he again insisted there was 'concrete evidence' that 'important and considerable writers' had been 'deterred from writing for the stage'; it was, said Levy, 'hard to calculate the destructive effect of censorship . . . because we do not know the unborn children'.

To the chagrin and disappointment of supporters of the bill, the Labour government had declared itself neutral. The Home Secretary, Chuter Ede, spoke in the debate, but he urged caution because of the risk that if such a bill became law the resulting difficulty would be 'at least as great as the difficulties which the present system creates'. He also warned of the need to ensure 'that in giving liberty we do not assure a licentiousness that may very well have repercussions and lead to something far more drastic than anything that the present censorship has done'. Although Ede indicated that he would not be voting either way, every word he said reeked with the claim voiced so repeatedly over the previous forty years that the current system, even if wrong in principle, somehow 'worked', almost in spite of itself: 'I do not intend to defend the existing position on the ground of logic', said Ede; 'But there are many things that work in the British Constitution which cannot be defended on the ground of logic'. It was precisely this complacent and very British model for apathy which defenders of the censorship always fell back on, and which Levy knew it was necessary to refute:

> The real basis of most of the opposition this afternoon has been the argument that, although the present system may be unreasonable and even ridiculous, in some way it works . . .
>   Let us examine the claim that 'it works' . . . Let me say, first of all, that that is the defence of the censorship in Russia. It was also the defence of censorship by Mussolini and by Hitler. It has always been the defence of censorship that it works . . . And it is perfectly true that there is one sense in which it always works. It is always true that there is less friction and life goes more smoothly when only one man's opinion is allowed to prevail and in that sense it does work. But does it work well?

If we really think that censorship works better than free speech, why are
we not clamouring to extend the boon to other fields of creative activity...

... Novelists, for example, might be put under the supervision and
control of the Crown Equerry, historians could be under the Keeper of the
Privy Purse, philosophers under the Master of the Horse, poets under the
Hereditary Grand Almoner ... preachers could come under the Mistress
of the Robes and politicians under the chief Lady of the Bedchamber ...

This argument that it works is supposed to present a dialectical
dilemma, because to rebut it involves one in the necessity of proving a
negative ... It works and it works well only if we believe that the plays of
great creative writers should be destroyed or mutilated at the whim of a
bank manager and that other great writers should be deterred from writing
for the stage at all ...

... It works, does it? Yes, indeed: it works steadily and inexorably
towards the impoverishment of our theatre.

Smith's bill to repeal the Theatres Act was comfortably passed by
seventy-six votes to thirty-seven, and the outcome generated considerable
publicity and excitement. Some sections of the press hailed it as heralding
the imminent demise of the Lord Chamberlain's control over theatre.
'THE CENSORSHIP FARCE MAY BE ENDED AT LAST', declared
Hannen Swaffer in the *People*; 'The Man Who Cuts Out Purple Passages
may lose his job', danced the *Daily Mirror*, telling its readers that the Lord
Chamberlain had been 'under fire for five hours in parliament yesterday'.
Under the headline 'Away with that Censor', the *Tribune* asked, 'Can we
now rejoice that this monstrosity is to be brought to an end?', and
concluded that 'If we could, it would be another feather in the cap of the
Labour government'.[24] On the other side of the propaganda battle, *John Bull*
published a homely and sympathetic portrait of Clarendon, which
bordered on the sycophantic, and which was clearly written with his co-
operation, or perhaps connivance; 'Who is he?', asked the author of the
article, before offering some romanticised fragments from Clarendon's
daily routine to demonstrate the essential decency of both the man and the
system he operated:

Well, during a long, full life devoted to public service he has been
Parliamentary Under-Secretary of State for Dominion Affairs, Chairman
of the Overseas Settlement Committee, Chairman of the BBC, and
Governor-General and Commander-in-Chief of the Union of South
Africa. He belongs to various clubs, is a director of a bank, a keen
theatregoer and a real man of the world ...

... Lord Clarendon has a red carpeted, quiet and by no means
pretentious office in a corner of St James's Palace. The censorship of plays is
only one of many duties carried out in this discreet, secluded corner of the
Palace. Royal Warrants, the supervision of all ceremonials, the care of all the
furniture and pictures in the various palaces take up most of the time ...

> . . . Occasionally a leading actor will come round in his greasepaint
> from rehearsals to the Lord Chamberlain's Office asking permission to
> alter a sentence simply because it does not sound well when spoken on the
> stage . . .
>   . . . Some playwrights have complained that they have no redress in the
> event of a rejection by the Lord Chamberlain. This is completely untrue.
> Any author can query anything and can always make a point of seeing the
> Lord Chamberlain personally and discussing the matter with him.
>   The truth is that if a playwright writes a good play he need have no fear
> of the censorship, but if he writes something obscene for the sake of
> exploiting obscenity he will be up against it.[25]

Sometimes, the bitter arguments sometimes descended to the level of
insult and abuse. In a letter to *The Times*, the writer James Bridie declared,
'If the "theatrical industry" is perturbed by the Bill, those who regard the
theatre as an art and a branch of literature are delighted'. He disputed the
claim that the licence of the Lord Chamberlain offered any sort of
guarantee that a script was safe from interference, citing a recent occasion
when he had been required to alter a script which had previously been
approved. He also denied that the Theatres National Committee was 'of
great theatrical and national importance', insisting he had 'only once heard
this body mentioned'. The secretary of that organisation replied in another
letter, listing the managerial organisations which together made up the
federation, and allowed it to represent 'the interests of the entire theatrical
industry'; this, in turn, goaded Levy to assert that 'managers are not the
theatrical profession, even though Mr Horace Collins strives to magnify
them, like a stage army, by splitting them up into a long list of little
component organizations'. The playwright William Douglas Home joined
in, claiming that there was very little support for the bill in 'the theatrical
profession' or 'the theatrical world'; co-writing with the manager S.E.
Linnit, Home inveighed against its dangers:

> It seems to us that the attempt to abolish the duties of an official whose
> activities are conducted with such admirable tact and discretion is an
> unnecessary and wanton assault on an institution which has stood the test
> of time. And, in any case, who will replace him? We see dark visions of a
> demand by the public for some form of censorship, and of that demand
> being met by watch committees, police supervision, and Home Office
> officials. It is for these reasons that we dread a Cromwellian era in the
> theatre brought about by the desire of a Parliamentary minority to execute
> tradition in the name of progress.[26]

Elsewhere, it was reported that at a debate held by the Gallery First
Nighters' Club in May 1949, during which Smith's motion for abolition
was 'very vigorously' opposed by Sydney Carroll, the argument became so

intense that the chair was moved to suggest that 'a section of the room would have to be roped off for combatants'.[27]

Despite the heat generated, as a private member's bill which had gained the right to parliamentary time only through the luck of a ballot, Smith's repeal bill never had much chance of passing into law. It had supporters and opponents on both sides of the House, but we have to note (as the Home Secretary did within the debate) that, for all the passion and argument in the chamber, it was a fairly small numbers of MPs who had bothered to attend. It seems likely, too, that a disproportionate number of those who had made the effort to be there had a commitment to seeing theatre censorship abolished, and there is no guarantee that, even if the government had sought to introduce legislation, it would necessarily have received the support of a majority of MPs. Any hopes that the Labour government might have been persuaded to adopt or adapt the bill were finally scuppered by the announcement of the general election for February 1950. Yet perhaps notice had been served.

In opposing Smith's bill, the Theatres National Committee had argued that the existing system did not have the effect of silencing playwrights, as was sometimes claimed:

> We would point out that if a playwright has such advanced ideas that they might offend against the rules and regulations of the Censor, he can still present his work to a section of the community through the medium of the many Societies and experimental theatres, to which only members are admitted to performances.[28]

Private theatre clubs had indeed long been seen by the Lord Chamberlain's Office as a deliberate 'safety-valve', permitting the performance of certain texts which could not be licensed for public performance. Sometimes the authorities had become worried about what they saw as an 'abuse' of this system, and there had been legal prosecutions against clubs for being lax in maintaining rules or following procedures, and for making it too easy for people to see banned plays. In the twenties, the Home Secretary of the time, Joynson Hicks, had been keen to see the loophole closed entirely, and during the Second World War, the Lord Chamberlain's Office had carried out secret checks to see how clubs were operating. But although the system had never operated on the basis of complete freedom of expression, it had often been used to allow 'highbrow' audiences to see work considered too challenging or provocative for a general audience. Ironically, this relative freedom had generally been recognised—at least by the Lord Chamberlain's Office—as a help rather than a hindrance in maintaining censorship, by 'buying off' some of those who might have campaigned most vigorously for reform.

However, doubts were increasing about the actual legal status of clubs and whether or not the Theatres Act technically allowed the Lord Chamberlain to exclude them from normal regulations; they had been largely ignored because they were seen as helpful, but it had become apparent that, if tested in a court, there were almost certainly no legal grounds for allowing such exemptions. By the late forties, this was known and accepted by the Lord Chamberlain's Office. In 1949, Manchester Experimental Theatre Club enquired about the definition of a club, and whether admitting press representatives might automatically redesignate a private performance as a public one. The Assistant Comptroller warned in his reply that

> The present situation of the so-called 'Private' Theatre Club is an artificial one based upon the individual constructions which Theatre Managers have taken the risk of putting upon the term 'acting for hire' as defined in s.16 of the Theatres Act, 1843. These constructions are very vulnerable, being unsupported by any legal authority, and they may possibly be proved false by the High Court decision upon the matter when it comes.[29]

As for their query about the press, Gwatkin advised them 'that in certain conditions their presence does convert an otherwise private performance into a public one'; but it was the broader point which has more significance. In effect, the Lord Chamberlain's Office was protecting itself from future liability or complaint, by stating that it was the managers and owners of clubs who were taking a risk in choosing to interpret the law in the way they did, and assuming it was not applicable to private clubs. As well as covering their backs, there was doubtless some value for the Office in being able to hold the vague threat over a club that it might be taken to court and prosecuted if it took too much advantage of the degree of freedom being allowed.

In 1951, following a successful prosecution against the manager and producers of Unity Theatre Club for presenting an unlicensed script in an unlicensed venue, the *New Statesman* raised through its columns the general issue of the legality of theatre clubs. The article began by expressing relief at 'the unwritten legal convention' in Britain that laws were not always enforced, but applied with discretion, and pointed out that theatre clubs were only allowed to function thanks to 'a tendency to overlook section 11 of the act'; at best, said the paper, they enjoyed a 'tenuous legality'. But in the light of the recent prosecution, the article went on to argue that the Lord Chamberlain and the Director of Public Prosecutions now appeared to be threatening to remove the effective immunity of clubs in such a way as to endanger their continuance per se: 'the result of the case might reasonably have been regarded by all theatre clubs as the writing on the wall', it declared, and it reported that the National Council for Civic

Liberties had now written to all theatre clubs warning them of 'the danger in which they stood'. The author also hypothesised that the reason why the authorities were changing their policy was that the increasing size of such clubs, and the numbers of people involved, was threatening to undermine the whole basis and purpose of theatre censorship:

> A theatre club with, say, twenty-five members or less would not, perhaps, interest the Lord Chamberlain's men. A membership running into thousands, which is not now unusual, approaches the point where a 'private' activity might be thought to merit a new description. When does it become 'public'? . . . There must come a point at which, on a numerical basis alone, the meanings of 'private' and 'public' begin to merge.

But a question was also raised regarding the extent to which the content of the performance might crucially influence the attitude of the censorship:

> In looking for reasons behind the recent prosecution by the Lord Chamberlain's Department (who could prosecute a theatre club every day if they wanted to), you must take your choice between size of 'membership' and Unity Theatre's declaration that it is 'a people's theatre, built to serve as a means of dramatising their life and struggles, and as an aid in making them conscious of their strength and of the need for united action'.

Rather than bemoaning the implications, the *New Statesman* approached the issue from the opposite direction, suggesting that 'the theatre club could before long reduce the censorship to complete impotence', undermining and eventually destroying the control of the Lord Chamberlain:

> There are two ways to get rid of the censor if we don't want him. One, gallantly tried by Mr. E.P. Smith in the last Parliament, is to abolish him by Statute . . . The other is to develop the theatre club to a position of such dominance as to enforce its recognition in a new Theatres Act.[30]

In the Lord Chamberlain's Office, Ronald Hill accepted that the basic premise of the article was correct:

> Not only has the legality of the Private Theatre never been endorsed by any Act, By-law or rule, but it is virtually certain that by reason of s.11 of the Theatres Act, it is an offence to exhibit any play for hire whether privately or publicly.
>
> Basically therefore there can be no doubt that the great majority of theatre clubs existing to-day are illegal.

He also acknowledged the article's assessment of the implications for the future of censorship.

Hill warned his colleagues and superiors that clubs should no longer be seen as a useful device which helped to reinforce and maintain the censorship system, but as a potential threat which could eventually destroy it. He agreed, too, that the practice was now becoming so pervasive that the distinction between private and public had effectively ceased to exist:

> We have now reached the present day situation where allegedly 'private' theatre clubs have so established themselves that:-
>
> a) Their performances are openly advertised in the same way as public theatres.
>
> b) Admission is generally by the formality of paying an extra 2 shillings 6d the first time one goes—i.e. membership is a sham.
>
> c) In certain cases such as the Unity a system of affiliated membership is springing up . . . How does this differ from a public theatre?
>
> If the private theatres have gained so much ground in the past ten or fifteen years, what is the rate of progress to be in the next fifteen years . . .
>
> At present the law is on our side, but cases are getting more difficult to prove and eventually custom will supervene over ill-defined law, and we shall lose.
>
> If this censorship ever goes I agree with the writer of this article in thinking that it is just as likely to be by being 'outflanked' by the Private Theatre as it is by Act of Parliament.[31]

A decade or so later, some of the longest nails hammered into the Office of the Lord Chamberlain would be the decisions of the Royal Court and the RSC to challenge him and bypass his authority by temporarily, and somewhat spuriously, turning their theatres into private clubs. Nor were they the first theatres to seriously threaten the very basis of his authority through such calculated tactics. If in 1951 the end was not yet nigh, then the endgame had surely begun.

CHAPTER NINE

'This Infernal Business of Sex'

We live in a period, consequent upon the war years, when considerable freedom of speech and action has been accepted in public, in literature, the Press and the B.B.C. and the theatre—if it is to live—must keep abreast of contemporary thought and fashion.
(Norman Gwatkin, November 1950)[1]

Although it was specifically homosexuality which dominated much of the debate in the post-war years, this was not the only item on the moral agenda. In the autumn of 1945, a short play called *The Celibate* was submitted to be staged at London's Granville Theatre as part of a season of Grand Guignol dramas. Dealing, as it did, with a corrupt and abusive clergyman, Frederick Witney's play was bound to excite controversy; 'The Curate, poor fellow, is over sexed', reported Game; 'his wife is an invalid and can therefore afford him no relief, with the result that he is in a terribly erotic state'.[2] In the opening scene, the sweating curate invites his vicar to his study, its walls covered in erotic art, and announces that he intends to resign:

CURATE: It's—it's this awful business, Vicar, this appalling business (*he breaks off, stammering and sweating*)
VICAR: (*patiently impatient*) What awful business?
CURATE: This infernal business of sex.
VICAR: I beg your pardon.
CURATE: I am a man in Hell . . . A Hell of the imagination.
VICAR: What on earth are you talking about?
CURATE: That Hell where the starved senses, cheated of their rights, revolt. That Hell where desire, thwarted and frustrated, revenges itself in dreams of unattainable delights—the Hell of convicts, of celibate priests.
VICAR: Celibate priests! But you are married!
CURATE: Vicar, my poor wife is an invalid . . . A wife who is no wife, who might as well be lying in her grave . . . And when a priest of the Church of England finds himself regarding every girl he sees as a—
VICAR: (*outraged; jumping up*) Stop! Stop! I will not have this! I will not listen!

> CURATE: When he cannot walk along the streets—without
> VICAR: (*shouting*) Silence! I order you—silence!
> CURATE: When every little blonde sets him speculating as to the cost of a
> weekend at Brighton—
> VICAR: (*sinking back into his chair*) My boy, my boy, I beg you! One knows
> what you mean, of course, but still . . . We are all tempted occasionally—it
> is for our good—discipline. We must struggle against it. But you—you
> appear to be giving way to it.
> CURATE: . . . I bow to the inevitable.

The curate shows the vicar a series of prints of pornographic etchings he
has purchased, then a series of obscene photographs; appalled (and
fascinated) though he is, the vicar is desperate to retain the curate's services:

> VICAR: What of the Scouts? And the Young Man's Bible Class? And the
> Institute? And the Athletic Club? And the Folk Dancing? And the
> Shakespearean Evenings? . . . I have never had a curate who has worked so
> hard, who has flung himself so wholeheartedly into the social work of the
> parish, who has had so much influence with our adolescents—that
> difficult problem. They bring all their troubles to you, I understand.
> CURATE: They do. I see them in here . . .

When the vicar has gone, we watch the curate attempting to seduce the
daughter of his housekeeper as he sits her on his knee to show her the
photographs, until finally his sick wife—'a thin, pale ghost of a woman'—
limps in and shoots him: 'you shall expiate your wickedness in eternal
torment'.[3]

Game, having read other works by Frederick Witney, recommended that
the play should not be licensed: 'I have come to the conclusion it will be no
bad thing to discourage him. He has a too fertile mind for what is really
nasty'. The Office invited Canon Gillingham, who had recently been
invited to join the Advisory Board, to see a private performance; he was one
of a group of eight clergymen, whose attendance at the theatre was reported
in the national press, and who were unanimous that the play should not be
shown. Remarkably enough, Gillingham found it 'a very powerful play,
very dramatic, very well acted with no pounding of the seamy side of life';
he had no doubt, either, that it would 'hold the audience spellbound'. But
not surprisingly, he was unable to recommend it: 'after all those enconiums
[sic] you will say it is only logical that it should receive the Lord
Chamberlain's permission for public performance; but we are an illogical
race and much of our national strength depends upon our illogicality'. One
objection was that it had 'not a very helpful ending', since no real solution
was proposed to the curate's problems:

> Had he fought and overcome the tremendous struggle finally coming out
> on top owing to his wife's and his vicar's and his own spiritual powers I

should not have queried it but the poor devil is cut off in his sins by his wife's action.

Gillingham also had other reservations:

> 1) Is it true that there are such sexberidden beggars among the ranks of the Clergy? That there are moral lapses amongst them I am prepared to admit but in my 46 years experience I have never come across a man so obsessed as that man seemed to be yesterday. I think it would give to many people the idea that such a type was common rather than exceedingly rare amongst the Clergy.
>
> 2) There is no moral lesson to be learnt from the play—not that you are an adjudicator of morals but only an adjudicator of 'immoral', but there is no moral in the play which can in any way be helpful because the poor devil is shot at the end . . .
>
> 3) The old Mother Church in this land is not going too well at present and is losing influence (despite the efforts of a few) over the lives of the people. Is this the time to give her another dig in the ribs . . .
>
> 4) Despite of what I have said under (3) there are still a good many people who have faith in the Church and look to her as the means of pulling this country around and those people, many of them the mainstay of our national life, will I think be genuinely hurt and wounded by such a powerful presentation of what after all is a very very exceptional case.

What seems most remarkable at this distance is that the Lord Chamberlain's Office should have ignored this view and decided to license a play which derided and disparaged not just an individual clergyman— who, we are encouraged to think, is almost certainly involved in dubious and possibly illegal activities with local adolescents—but the Church itself, which seeks to retain his services. Changing times indeed—especially when one thinks of the exaggerated protection guaranteed to clergymen before the war. Gwatkin wrote to Gillingham, expressing appreciation of his argument, but warning him that a licence would probably be issued:

> Goodness knows that the last thing one wants . . . is anything that is unhelpful to the Church and her works but unhappily (perhaps luckily) for this 'seldom-right' Department, our legal responsibility is to guard against a breach of the peace etc. and, as you say, we are concerned more with the immoral than with the moral.
>
> The Theatre is a mirror in which times, and the manners of those times, are reflected . . . I certainly would not pay money to see that play, but does it do enough harm to justify the Lord Chamberlain . . . in forbidding its production?[4]

In fact, the Office took it as an opportunity to try out a system of issuing discretionary licences, which would remain valid only for a specific production at a specific venue rather than for general application. This, Clarendon hoped, would permit him to give a little more slack to those managers where he deemed it appropriate, without letting dubious scripts off the leash completely. However, it was a scheme which was quickly scotched by the ruling of the Law Lords that this would not be legal within the 1843 Theatres Act.

Another sign of new times was the decision over *Patricia's Seven Houses*, Lajos Biro's play which focused on 'a young and unsophisticated English girl inheriting from an old and unknown elderly relative a chain of houses of ill-fame'. A licence had been refused more than once during the war. When it was resubmitted in January 1946, Game saw the decision of whether to overturn those judgements as one which carried some very significant ramifications:

> what is in question is not this particular play . . . but the standards of dramatic censorship, which I take it to be the duty of the Lord Chamberlain to preserve. Those standards are based on what the Americans would call 'the English way of life', or what I should describe as 'decent reticence', which in its turn is based on Puritanism. That there is a great deal to be said for 'the English way of life' surely the past six years are proof enough. Puritanism is still a great force in the country, and it is as well to remember this fact and not to allow the sophistications of the Capital to override one's judgement entirely. English prudery may be absurd when carried too far, but in its essence it is healthy, and I should be sorry to see it further undermined by Continental standards.
>
> To take the case in point—could one sit unembarrassed beside many women of one's acquaintance, both old, or elderly, as well as the very young, during some of the scenes of this play? We do not tolerate brothels in England, and as far as my experience goes decent people do not talk about them in mixed society . . . should one be embarrassed in the theatre?
>
> A play in which the scene is quite openly laid in a modern brothel, will . . . establish a precedent . . . and however much one may claim, and attempt, to judge all plays on their merits, a precedent inevitably has an effect on subsequent events.
>
> It is for this reason, that taking the long view, I think it will make it more difficult for the Lord Chamberlain to uphold our English standards in the future and will tend to undermine those standards by Continental influences, that I oppose the licensing of this play.

But England was a changing country, and the Lord Chamberlain was beginning to do things differently. Clarendon ruled that 'it is no part of our duty to be biased by the fact that the play . . . cannot be regarded as a useful contribution to "the theatre"', and a licence was issued for Biro's play, albeit with the provisos that the brothel should be changed to 'a low night club' and that 'the production must absolutely ensure that illusion'.[5] In the event, most newspaper reviews still referred to 'a chain of foreign brothels'.[6]

In the autumn of the same year, a new translation of Gantillon's *Maya* was submitted. A previous version had been submitted by Terence Gray for the Festival Theatre in Cambridge in 1929, but had been turned down as 'too grossly offending English feeling in the picture of a prostitute's promiscuity'.[7] Now, however, Game was positively enthusiastic about it, and perhaps gently mocking of the first Lord Chamberlain under whom he had served:

> The subject is factually sordid, but poetical in treatment—that is the magic of the artist, to take mud and transmute it into gold.
>
> The play would no doubt shock the squeamish, as Lord Cromer would say, but no reasonable person could argue that it could possibly do anybody any moral harm—in fact everybody who is capable of aesthetic stimulation will receive both pleasure and benefit from seeing it acted.
>
> No doubt the adverse verdict was the right one in 1929, but times are very changed now; the public is more catholic in its tastes, and the Censorship consequently can afford to be more reasonable in its judgements. You cannot allow the Commercial Theatre to stage plays like 'Patricia's Seven Houses' . . . and then refuse to allow a high-brow Theatre like the Arts Theatre of Cambridge to play 'Maya' to its intellectual audience—there is little fear that the Commercial Theatre will try and exploit the play, and if they did they would not find it too easy to vulgarise it unless they cut out everything except the dirt.[8]

However, the production never took place, and the play remained unlicensed.

A few months later, some changes were demanded before an English version of Sartre's *La Putain Respectueuse* was approved for production at the Lyric, Hammersmith, in association with the Arts Council. Originally submitted as *The Yankee Tart*, its title was quickly amended to *The Respectable Prostitute*, but it is a sign of a shift in standards that even this was deemed acceptable. 'This is a violent play and if it is to be licensed at all, a lot of the violent language and implications will have to remain', warned the Reader; but after a series of alterations to tame the vocabulary, the Office passed the play. However, the production led to a number of complaints, not least over the advertising used to attract audiences. When it was staged at the New Cross Empire in 1950, it was promoted as 'THE DARING VIVID TRUTH ABOUT A FORBIDDEN SUBJECT WHICH DEALS FRANKLY AND INTIMATELY WITH A TREMENDOUS HUMAN PROBLEM', and 'The Most Talked of Play of the Century'. Camberwell Youth Committee informed the Public Morality Council that 'strong exception was taken to the presentation of the play . . . and to the sensational nature of the posters', and provided details of the advertising:

> There are three types of poster exhibited—a large one (Type A) an extra large one (Type B) and a small one fixed to a small board which is propped up outside the place . . . the only difference is the size and layout . . . The

words in capitals and those underlined can be read across the street from the smallest size of posters.

At the entrance to the theatre is a verandah or alcove, with four pillars. At the foot of each pillar is a board displaying the small poster. At eye level there is a board on each pillar displaying 'stills'. 'Stills' are also displayed in the alcove, together with normal poses of the stars. There are 24 stills of scenes from the play. Of these, thirteen show a woman in a negligee, either alone, with a man, or as part of a group; the majority depict a bedroom scene.

The Westminster Public Control Department joined with the Public Morality Council to complain

that the effect of such plays and advertisement must render largely nugatory the work which Youth Organisations are endeavouring to carry out among young people to fit them to make the best possible use of their leisure time.

A national tour of Sartre's play brought further objections. As one police report informed the Lord Chamberlain:

I would point out that much of the dialogue when read, is not so offensive as when played on the stage accompanied by actions and inflections of voice. It is certainly not a play suitable for young persons, and is billed as for 'Adults only', neither do I think that decent men would care to let their womenfolk see it.

A further aspect, and one which requires careful consideration, is the possible effect on the coloured population. The theme of the play is the American 'colour bar'; and the action is fairly strong.

In Liverpool, a successful prosecution was brought against the actor manager for ending a scene by carrying the woman to the bed and lying down on top of her as the curtain fell; because there was no stage direction in the licensed script which specified such an action, it was deemed to be an interpolation and in breach of the Theatres Act. As the Lord Chamberlain subsequently stated: 'The dialogue is but an ingredient of a play ... the necessity to describe business is well known in the Theatrical Profession'.[9]

In the spring of 1947, the Office was somewhat startled by a version of the Heloise and Abelard story* which featured 'an act of castration (done off of course) and its consequences (and no bones made about the matter)'. However, Game argued that the factual basis of the narrative was in its favour, and that, after some toning down of the details, it could be passed:

Taken as a whole, the treatment of the story does not suggest that the author had any salacious intention in writing his play, but merely that he

---

* *Heloise*, by David Monger

does not suffer from squeamishness' (I see he is a doctor). In these days when most of us have heard a good deal about the nasty little tricks the Abysinnians [sic] play on one another and a native festival of circumcision has been portrayed in a film, I do not think it would be reasonable to be shocked by this play. . . . Still I don't see the necessity to harp too much on what is after all a somewhat embarrassing incident, one needs to establish the fact of the mutilation . . . without any underlining being needed.

Having checked the authenticity of the details in *Chambers Biographical Dictionary*, Clarendon agreed that 'although it is a new departure for us' a licence could be granted with, as Game might have said, appropriate cuts. In 1951, the producer of an uncut version of the play, which had won an amateur competition, sought a licence to perform it in public; he professed himself 'amazed to find no less than twelve lengthy omissions, which completely destroy the value of the play'. The Office was not impressed:

It is nonsense to say . . . the play is 'mangled' . . . Mr. Game's suggested cuts seem to me to leave all that is necessary about the operation. The play is still a play . . . Mr. Gaston should be told that if he doesn't like the play as licensed, he can lump it, and that we shall send someone to see that he doesn't monkey about with the text during the performance![10]

Another French play which caused some hesitation at St James's Palace was Roussin's *La Petite Hutte*. Binkie Beaumont, the producer, submitted the original text, in the hope, he said, of receiving a licence 'before we approach an author to have an adaptation done for the English and American stage'. No doubt his choice of the word 'adaptation' rather than 'translation' was intended to signal that he recognised that some details might need changing. Dearmer wearily described the action of 'this rather silly play' as being based 'on the eternal triangle of which the French never tire'; but he thought there was 'no harm' in it, since there was 'No violence and no love-making' in the script; 'Suzanne leaving the men tied up while she goes off with the beau garcon sauvage . . . does not matter'. However, although he thought that 'if well and discreetly adapted it could be made passable', he was unwilling to promise that 'carte blanche' would be given to an English version: 'I recommend that the Lord Chamberlain refuses to license the French version as requested, and I do not think that any more will be heard about a play which we can well do without'. Heriot was even more doubtful:

I feel that the question on which a licence depends is whether we can countenance a scene where a man leads a woman into a hut on the stage with the intention (shared by her) of having what the newspapers call 'relations'.

It was, he said, 'essentially gallic' in the 'association of Sex and "Snobbisme"'—'Suzanne is quite willing to be ravaged by the cook so long as she believes him to be a native Prince'—and he thought this would be 'surely incomprehensible to most Englishmen'. Heriot recommended that it was 'only the trimmings that we need to worry about', but he proposed two fundamental changes: first 'to have the Hut itself less obviously on the stage, so that the audience does not spend its time . . . wondering what is happening behind the curtain of the door'; and second:

> to restrain the detailed conjugation of the verb 'to violate'
> (I am violated,
> Thou art being violated,
> He, She (It) is violating (you),
> We watch you being violated,
> You seem to like being violated,
> They discuss at length your being violated.[11]

Beaumont was informed that an English version could not be licensed without 'considerable modification', and although he seemed ready to enter negotiations it appears that no English version was submitted.

In the late forties and early fifties, the Lord Chamberlain's Office clamped down on a series of home-grown melodramatic pieces on moral grounds. In December 1949, they rejected *Modernity*,[*] the tale of a young woman called Hermione who 'shrinks from physical contact but wishes to have a child'. She is impregnated by a doctor who is carrying out research into artificial insemination, but after fears that the semen may have come from a criminal, a pervert or an animal, it turns out to have been supplied by her own brother and that she has committed involuntary incest. 'A play written from a depraved imagination', said Heriot, and the licence was refused.[12] In September 1950, they turned down *House of the Red Lamp*, in which an innocent young woman who has been seduced and sold to a brothel keeper escapes by finding a virgin to act as her substitute; twenty years later she is wealthy and married to a baronet, when the father of the woman she once betrayed tracks her down and demands her daughter as his mistress. 'I should have no compunction hacking this play about; it is cheap sensationalism', wrote Game. A revised version was submitted under the title *House of Shame*:[†]

> the dialogue has been considerably modified . . . the moral of the play is unexceptionable: repentance and expiation. It is only that whores and brothels are a bit of a shock as a background, anyhow to those of us who

---

[*] Written by Wilby Morris
[†] Uncertainty over author(s)—Bruce Walker, Mary Preston and F. Mabelle are all identified at different times

can remember good Queen Victoria's glorious days, when if such things existed they were never mentioned—and in my opinion quite rightly so—but times change.[13]

Game was prepared to recommend it for licence, but was over-ruled, and, in the same month, the Office also rejected *Sex for Sale.** Game described this as 'a basically moral anecdote made dubious by its characters and setting'. But he also thought it was 'an attempt to cash-in on whores', and reported that 'if *The House of the Red Lamp* was in bad taste, then this is much worse'. He concluded: 'despite the fact that I very much doubt whether a generation that not only accepted but defended the publication of *The Naked and the Dead* would raise an eyebrow at either of these plays, I am not going to recommend it for Licence'. The manager strove to defend his play as one designed to inform and assist:

> Regarding the organised traffic in women, which is now being exposed elsewhere, my play should prove a powerful weapon in the campaign against the thugs who wax fat on this vile traffic, causing untold misery to the women they hold in virtual bondage. But the message cannot be given popular appeal unless it is put over in a popular way

Clarendon agreed with his Reader that it was 'a loathsome play which I cannot on any account pass'.[14]

A week later, the Office refused another 'white slave trade' play, *Woman of the Streets,*† in which the central character is an innocent girl who is forced into prostitution. 'This is a piece of deliberate pornography', wrote Heriot, 'written by an illiterate who cannot conjugate the verb "to lie" in his stage-directions'. Gwatkin agreed it was 'very dirty and frightfully bad into the bargain' and 'far worse than either *The House with A Red Lamp* or *Sex for Sale*'. He informed Clarendon: 'I read it through last night and could hardly believe my eyes!'. The Lord Chamberlain confirmed: 'It is muck all the way through and I have no hesitation in banning it'. When the manager again claimed that it was written in good faith and to warn young women of the dangers facing them, he was told that it seemed

> unlikely . . . that the audience who went to see such a play would contain many who were in need of saving from the White Slave Traffic, or a fate worse than death! It would consist of hard nuts who were anxious to have their appetites whetted !

In April 1951, a rewritten and toned down version was licensed under the title *City of Sin*, with the action transferred to America. 'The play still remains the product of an ignorant, grimey little mind', grumbled Heriot.[15]

---

* Written by Eddie Kaplan
† Written by Richard C. Ford

In the autumn of 1950, the Office also rejected *Street Girl*,* a play about 'A Maltese gangster and ponce who operates in the neighbourhood of Tottenham Court Road'. Heriot said it was 'more subtly titillating than *Woman Of The Streets* because it is more life-like', and found 'the whole thing . . . salacious and disgusting'.[16] Two days later, he slated *The Naked Lady*† as 'A cheap and nasty American "pulp-magazine" thriller', set in a Soho night-club. 'Sex and sadism are the keynotes of this nauseating rubbish', choked Heriot, though he thought that with thirty or so cuts it might just be possible to pass it. Nugent spoke to the playwright: 'I pointed out that if he took out all that the Lord Chamberlain would insist upon only a skeleton would remain and that the Lord Chamberlain did not even like the skeleton'.[17]

The censorship considered such work as cheap and exploitative, and a reflection of declining moral standards in wider contemporary culture. In June 1951, the secretary in the Lord Chamberlain's Office, Ronald Hill, summed it up:

> The standard of what is acceptable in literature, the drama and everyday conversation has been considerably lowered since the War. The criterion of what constitutes legal indecency has altered . . . and has enabled such books as 'The Naked and the Dead' to be published without prosecution.

He characterised it, somewhat euphemistically, as a 'relaxation of previous good manners', but he had no doubt that it had been 'exploited by the cheap theatrical touring companies, and by some of the better class producers too'. Hill identified 'two unpleasant trends on the contemporary stage'; the first of these he named as 'A Cult Of Viciousness', citing as examples not only *Sex for Sale* and *Women of the Boulevards*, but also *A Streetcar Named Desire*. To Hill, at least, the difference was not apparent or material.

The second target of Hill's contempt was 'The Commercialisation Of Nude Women'.[18] There had probably never been any real likelihood that the Office would be able to impose a more draconian rule after the war—even if they had been committed to doing so—and clashes with the Public Morality Council continued to occur. In April 1946, the Council complained about 'An attempt . . . to introduce something very much like a strip-tease', claiming that a performer could be seen changing behind a screen. 'I confess the idea of "strip-tease" never occurred to me', commented Titman, who had also seen it as part of his continuing commitment to inspect every new Windmill show in person; 'I sat in the box, which is the nearest point to the stage, and although the screen is

---

* Written by Clem Harris
† Written by Irving St John

transparent, and it can be seen that a girl is changing her clothes, the lighting is so dimmed that no detail is visible'. In a jibe at the complainant, Titman teased, 'perhaps his imagination is greater, or was it wishful thinking?'. Nevertheless, the Lord Chamberlain required that the screen be made opaque. Following another complaint about 'scanty and transparent dress' at the same theatre, Gwatkin injudiciously informed the Council that such costumes 'could only be permissible in the case of young girls such as are employed at the Windmill theatre', adding that 'the Lord Chamberlain gives particular attention to this'. When the Council queried why such a degree of special licence should be permitted to the Windmill, Clarendon had to dig himself out of a difficult hole:

> I should like to explain that my object, when licensing shows of the type to which you refer, is to eliminate all cause for unhealthy excitement, without the use of excessive severity, which could only bring the censorship into disrepute, and would ultimately result in a weakening of its control . . . the sentence upon which you seek further enlightenment, therefore, which should not be read out of its context, is to explain that after individual inspection of the performances, I have found it possible to permit greater latitude in dress by young and athletic women, such as those employed at the Windmill theatre, without inducing the morbidity which I want to avoid, and which would result from the same permission being extended to those of a fuller and more mature figure.[19]

The Public Morality Council's annual report for 1949 condemned what it called the 'disastrous toleration of nudity on the stage', which, it claimed, had had 'the inevitable effect during the year of multiplying the number of productions which make a special feature of this element in stage entertainment'. Indeed, they alleged that 'Many salacious and most harmful productions are now touring the country excusing themselves on grounds of "art"'. The same report implicitly attacked the Arts Council, criticising the 'continuance of the policy of providing financial support from government sources for the revival of Restoration comedy', a genre which it railed against as 'bawdy, decadent and unfit for public presentation'; the report denounced it as 'lamentable that public funds should be forthcoming for plays which present religion as contemptible and sexual morality as absurd', and expressed the wish that 'the BBC will not, in future programmes, find room for the Restoration comedies'.[20]

In May 1949, the Council wrote to Clarendon once again, to 'draw your Lordship's attention to the development, which has now taken place (as we foresaw) of the introduction of the moving nude' to the Windmill's latest show.

> The Jungle Woman and the Snake perform their dances with uncovered breasts . . . the Water Lily who performs a dance behind a flimsy

transparent curtain is completely nude, carrying only a wisp of tulle . . . the dancers permit the exposure of the breasts in spite of the scarf which is worn . . . the chorus appears repeatedly in dresses which are so transparent as to exhibit the whole body clearly . . .

Clarendon was adamant that no permission for such a development had been, or would be, granted, and the theatre was told to amend the dance: 'I do not question the artistry of the scene, but . . . It should not be possible for any member of the audience to see any detail of the artiste's bosoms whilst moving about the stage'.[21] Every now and again the censors continued to fire warning shots at the Windmill management, but they knew that they were in retreat. As Hill lamented in 1951:

> The increase in the 'daring' aspect of nudity will be apparent if what was permissible in 1939 is contrasted with what is allowed to-day. Then we only permitted profile views and very severe lighting for individual models. Nowadays full body views are permitted and in some cases half the chorus is allowed to strip. Another disturbing feature is that two photographs have recently been submitted for approval in which naked girls are shown obviously without even a cache-sexe . . . We never say anything in our permits as to a cache-sexe being worn and in the present state of public opinion it is doubtful whether the Police would prosecute for indecency.[22]

The Public Control Department of the London County Council had also become concerned about the spread of nudity in variety and music hall, and produced a paper called 'Nudity on the Stage' which traced what had occurred during the ten years or so since the St James's meeting of April 1940 had tried to define a common policy: 'The Council has endeavoured—probably with little success—to ensure that performances involving nudity shall be kept within the limits agreed upon at the Lord Chamberlain's Conference'. In 1951, The LCC suggested three alternative positions which could be taken up in order to turn back the tide:

> a) To exclude entirely the presentation of nude acts of any kind . . .
> b) To permit still poses . . . without any dialogue, song, recitation, monologue or other accompaniment . . .
> c) To send a circular to licensees, on the general lines of the circular sent in 1942, reminding them of the agreement reached at the 1940 Conference . . .[23]

Hill wrote a paper, commenting on and corroborating most of what the LCC had stated, and adding his own detailed account of the shift in the standards of what was being approved by the Lord Chamberlain's Office:

> Originally the only nudes we permitted were tableaux specially staged with subdued lighting and appropriate scenery. There was no talking and

no movement in the entire scene. There was also no need for rules to govern this simple procedure.

Once having attained their point of getting nudes on the stage however . . . the following innovations have gradually been introduced:–

a) Lights have been brightened until ordinary stage lighting and frequently spot-lights are used.

b) Nudes have been moved from their special set to ordinary stage backgrounds, sometimes a questionable association such as 'apache cafes' . . .

c) Introduction of a compère to present each pose—often with salacious or even indecent remarks. The police have prosecuted here at Blackpool and at Cambridge to my knowledge.

d) Instead of special artistes engaged only for posing, the artistes who act in the show, often in seductive roles now have to strip at some point in the show and pose—whether they like it or not. This gives the boys a chance to confirm their opinion as to the full beauty of some girl who was attracting their attention earlier in the show, and completely destroys the impersonality of the former (formal?) tableaux which did approximate somewhat to works of art.

e) The poses have crept round from side views to full-front. The cache-sexes have grown demonstrably slighter and slighter and recently their have been two cases where the vagina was completely uncovered.

f) Moving figures have been introduced into shows clad only in a tinsel star—one on each nipple and one on the vagina. This passes for clothing and is held to defeat the Lord Chamberlain. I have also seen others clad only in gold paint.

g) Normally only one tableau was allowed in a show. Nudes are now interspersed throughout it.

While officially the censors had 'never really departed from our original standpoint of allowing only artistic nude tableaux', in practice they had been 'defeated in our intention by Managers'. And Hill had no doubt that acts were now being permitted which were damaging to audiences and performers, and were leading to improper and offensive behaviour in society at large:

From what I have seen in the cheap theatres such as the Granville Walham Green, and Collins Music Hall, Islington, and in my talks with Police Officers at the Police College, I am convinced that the type of nude show at present going the rounds in the Suburbs and the Provinces is harmful both to the ill-educated adolescents who frequent them, and to the very young girls (often only sixteen we are told) who are procured to pose in them.

I have seen the intent rush from the back of the theatre to get in the front rows at half-time; at least one case has been reported of a man exposing himself in the front row at one of the shows. I had a man in today who alleged that at the Windmill men in the audience spent the time of the show fingering themselves, and I have heard remarks shouted from the auditorium at the nude girls, who in some small theatres are very close to the audience.

I think that some of the younger men leave these shows in a highly excited and sexually stimulated condition.

He thought there were only two possible ways for the Office to proceed:

a) To wipe the nude entirely off the stage and lay down in every licence a rule that two thirds of the breast including the nipple will be covered and a loin cloth worn as the minimum dress . . .

b) The alternative is to reassert the standpoint from which we have never officially departed.[24]

Titman agreed that the Office should clamp down: 'I have always advised more care in the approval of photographs', he hinted, and he complained about the lack of rigour being exercised: 'Only recently one of the examiners passed a strip-tease with a remark something like "I don't think this matters", but I either got it stopped or withdrawn after it had been passed'. But he pointed out that even if they managed to institute a tougher policy now, there would still be a problem in respect of poses which had been previously approved: 'It would be almost impossible to go through the many Revues in the last few years and withdraw permission previously given'. Titman also reasserted the view that complete nudity was not necessarily the only or the most important issue, and that in his experience 'the flimsy covering of some artistes' was 'the worst type of sex stimulant'. He cited some of the acts at the Windmill: 'almost in every report I have made on my visits to this Theatre I have called attention to the continuance of flimsy covering, resulting in transparency or lack of control of certain parts'. He recommended that the focus of tightening up should be on 'titles, salacious dialogue, and dress' rather than on nudity, and that they should begin with one venue: 'If the Windmill Theatre is brought to book—and this will not be easy—we shall at least be able to hold up our heads when we are dealing with producers generally'.[25]

In August 1951, Clarendon wrote to Van Damm, introducing a threat which he knew was really a bluff:

I am deeply concerned with present-day trends in the exploitation of nudity and semi-nudity in performance on the stage, a matter which has decidedly worsened during the last few years. The time cannot be far distant when the whole question will have to be reviewed, which might quite easily result in the banning of nudity of any kind.

He asked for an assurance that those performers who were not in nude poses would be 'adequately covered', and made it clear that Van Damm's habitual practice of blaming the excessive display of flesh on accidents and unfortunate slips, (many of them supposedly caused by dancers of different sizes trying to share the same costume), was something to which the Office would no longer turn a blind eye.

In August 1951, and again in September, members of the Lord Chamberlain's staff met with LCC representatives 'In pursuance of the long-established policy of complete co-operation between the Council and the Lord Chamberlain'. It was agreed that 'the voluntary obligation hitherto laid on the theatrical industry to confine scenes depicting nudes to unexceptional representations had proved a failure, and that future action should be by regulation'. They also agreed that since it would be 'impracticable to ban nude poses entirely from the stage at this time', they should more clearly define common limits of what was permissible. Striptease was to be banned from variety stages, as it was by the Lord Chamberlain, but they decided 'it was not possible to forbid patter and dialogue accompaniments to nude presentations'. Two conferences were proposed; the first would be restricted to those responsible for administering and controlling public entertainments, such the Home Office, local government representatives and the Magistrates Association, and would be charged with formulating a common policy; once that policy had been agreed, there would then be a second event, which would include representatives of the entertainment industry, who would in effect be presented with a *fait accompli*. Additionally, a draft for a proposed new section to be added to the Lord Chamberlain's licence was drawn up, which would spell out some very precise codes of practice:

> The undernoted are disallowed, and may not be performed by the authority of this licence:
>
> i) Any performance requiring the removal of garments (other than an outer coat or wrap) by or from a performer while that performer is within the view of the public—including a performer whose movements or a reflection of whose movements can be seen by the public through or on a translucent screen, mirror or similar device (—that is to say a performance of a kind commonly known as a 'strip-tease' act) . . .
>
> ii) . . . the appearance of any performer while that performer is within the view of the public (including a performer whose movements or a reflection of whose movements can be seen by the public through or on a translucent screen, mirror or similar device) with any private part of the body (which expression so far as a female is concerned shall also include the breasts) exposed or seeming to be exposed or visible through flimsy veiling or other semi-transparent material or by any other means whatsoever.
>
> iii) Any nude or semi-nude pose unless . . . specifically allowed by this Licence, and then only provided that:–
>
> a) The artist wears an efficient cache-sexe or 'g' string.
> b) No footlights are used.
> c) All other stage lighting is suitably dimmed.

d) The artiste assumes the pose out of sight of the audience and remains motionless for the entire time that it can be seen by the audience . . .[26]

In the spring of 1952, a further meeting took place to produce a final version and agree the detail of a common policy; but suddenly the whole plan collapsed when the LCC—presumably under pressures from elsewhere—suddenly backed down and told Nugent that they were giving 'fresh consideration to the whole question of controlling the display of nudity on the London Variety stage'. They were now against the proposed conferences 'on the grounds that Provincial Committees might consider it an attempt on the part of the Council to impose "London" views on the rest of the country'. Moreover, 'In view of the considerable controversy which the issue would arouse', they had decided to go no further than placing a ban on strip-tease.[27]

Whether the attempt to clamp down could ever have succeeded is doubtful, and it seems extremely unlikely that the Lord Chamberlain had the right to amend the format or content of his official licence other than through the route of government legislation. But certainly, what the Lord Chamberlain's Office viewed as a last-minute betrayal by the LCC, made it much harder to revise his own practice. And for all their warnings, the Office—and specifically Titman—continued to exercise a surprising degree of leniency towards the Windmill: In 1952, Titman reported on *Revudeville No. 248*:

> It was a fortunate evening for 'the boys'. There were at least three occasions where the covering 'came away' from the girl . . . I saw both Mr Van Damm and Miss Mitelle afterwards. They were obviously concerned and assured me that it could not occur at the next performance because they employed a man who did nothing else but watch each performance and take any necessary action afterwards. Miss Mitelle nearly had a heart attack when she saw what I did—she was sitting with me in the box.
>
> I think one can put these lapses down as accidents. The Windmill has been much better recently since we sent a strong letter from the Lord Chamberlain. I have no reason to believe that the incidents were intentional.[28]

There were still some limits to defend. In April 1952, a firm of Westminster solicitors acting in a case involving obscenity wrote to enquire about the Lord Chamberlain's policy on female nudity: 'We are specifically interested in the Lord Chamberlain's views on the exhibition of pubic hair on the stage', they wrote; 'Does his Lordship think that any scene in which named women display their pubic hair could not ipso facto have artistic merits, or are there circumstances in which such a scene might be permitted'. Gwatkin replied that that he was 'authorised to say that the

Lord Chamberlain would never knowingly permit any person to expose the pubic hair during the course of a stage play'.[29]

When the Lord Chamberlain sent out his 1951 letter seeking opinions on his policy for plays featuring 'perversion', one reply, from Rose Henriques, suggested that his attention should perhaps be focused elsewhere:

> What I consider to be far more harmful to the general public, and what is bound to have a reaction, not only on young manhood going to see the performance, but on young people in general who see the posters, are the Folies Bergeres type of performers in advertisement.[30]

She was referring to a recent controversy which had provoked complaints against the censorship for its failure to intervene. In December 1948, newspapers had reported that a Parisian revue was coming to London, and the Office received letters of protest:

> no less than sixty-to-eighty artistes are to flaunt themselves throughout the country, commencing in the season of Lent, and probably showing even in Holy Week itself . . . The obvious thing to do is to forbid their entry into this country, as it will otherwise become an annual event, to appeal to the baser instincts of many of the populace.

The Comptroller pointed out that the Lord Chamberlain's Office had 'no power whatsoever to interfere with the entry of foreigners into England nor to give pre-dated decisions on plays of which he has no official knowledge'. When the script for *Folies Bergères* was submitted, along with photographs of the nudes, the Office required only minimal changes to bring it into line with the standard they had already accepted at the Windmill. Following complaints about the performance, Heriot went to see it but found little out of the ordinary:

> The nudes are certainly static—except 'purity' in the Hell scene who throws off her white veil when the devil has played Liszt's Liebestraum at her on a white and gold violin, appearing in an adequate cache-sexe and a few gold sequins gummed over her nipples. I feel that this is not a very efficient substitute for a brassiere, especially when the body is in violent motion.

They required that the dancer 'should wear an efficient brassiere', and other minor changes were made, but in fact it was the advertising for the show which provoked most complaints—and specifically 'the large female figure'. The Office carried out an inspection:

> I had a look at this female figure. It's about 30 inches high and adorns the theatre façade. You can therefore see sex, even if you can't sense it, as far away as Trafalgar Square. The figure is nude except for a brassiere, a large advert covering the unmentionable and an odd feather. It is sex-clamant

but it is not obscene. The build-up of advertising of this show has concentrated on sex. The theatre front is full of representations of nude females—three dimensional photographs, photographs and drawings. The cut out is in keeping but I suppose the Morality Council objection is that it acts rather like a sexual lighthouse, drawing people from afar. Personally I thought the whole display was 'cheap' but I don't think there are adequate grounds for prohibiting any of it.

To the dissatisfaction of its campaigners, the Public Morality Council was informed that 'The Lord Chamberlain does not question the lack of taste in this advertisement but he does not feel that it is indecent'.[31]

However, the way in which shows were advertised became a subject of increasing complaints to the Lord Chamberlain, though his legal writ barely extended to this aspect of production. In an internal memorandum of June 1951, Ronald Hill listed the venues about which protests had recently been received; these included (within London) the Casino, the Hippodrome, the New Cross Empire, and Chelsea Palace, and Hill added: 'Every complaint sent to us represents many unuttered, and we have received a greater volume on this subject than on most others in recent years'. But he pointed out that the Office's powers were strictly limited: 'The Lord Chamberlain has authority to control the display of posters and photographs on the actual theatre building only, and then only in the areas proscribed by s.III of the Theatre Act, 1843, roughly the centre of London'.[32]

The censorship tried one of its bluffing strategies; it selected what seemed to be the two worst offenders—the Casino and the Hippodrome— and sent them letters which combined advice, an appeal for assistance, and a hint of a threat:

> For the last three years the Lord Chamberlain has received intermittent complaint of the form of display used ... to advertise the various productions ...
>
> This rather obvious appeal to the lower instincts is found offensive by those who write to his Lordship, and is creating an antagonism which I should think you could well do without ... The Lord Chamberlain is receiving an increasing volume of complaint against you, which he feels you would do well to placate by moderating the too frank appeal to sex which at present constitutes the theme of your advertising. This could be done by making your posters proportionately representative of the various types of entertainment included in the show, instead of exaggerating one small aspect of it. As regards the last poster, it is being represented to his Lordship that this is provocative and of such a size as to attract to it persons, possibly adolescents, whose thoughts have no bent towards 'sex' until they are diverted by this poster. The inference drawn is that if they enter the theatre such persons will be subjected to depraved influences.

This is not, of course, true, and if the poster has this effect, there is certainly a case for its replacement by some less provocative picture.

I will also be quite frank and say that a modification of your policy would relieve the Lord Chamberlain from considerable embarrassment.

The Hippodrome evidently made some attempt to respond positively to this letter, but the Casino ignored it.[33]

Replying in 1950 to a complaint about the use of oaths on stage (in phrases such as 'For God's sake), the Assistant Comptroller pointed out:

> Were the Lord Chamberlain to employ his powers as harshly as you suggest he would make the stage so remote from real life as to endanger it; and there is no doubt that it would be the Censor who would not survive the ensuing conflict.

He concluded with an important statement of principle: 'I think it must be accepted that the Censorship cannot be used for the purpose of raising the moral standards of the Nation: that is a matter for the Church and the Educational authorities'.[34] But in abnegating and abandoning that responsibility, not just in practice but in principle, was the censorship helping to seal its own fate?

CHAPTER TEN

'But Perverts Must Go *Somewhere* in the Evening'

> I do not know what form of sexual perversion the Lord Chamberlain has in mind. If he is mainly preoccupied with the question of homo-sexuality, a case can, I think, be made out that this practice is stimulated by wars. Large numbers of men are thrown together in abnormal circumstances in all the three services, and opportunities for associating with people of the opposite sex are restricted. An increase of homo-sexual practices is to be expected. But the phenomenon is a transient one and does not long outlive the aftermath of the war.
>
> (Letter from the Eugenics Society to the Lord Chamberlain, 1946)[1]

The Lord Chamberlain's Office regularly clashed with managers over revues in which men impersonated women and wore women's costumes. Such revues derived partly from the necessarily all-male wartime entertainments which Peter Nicholls would later draw on for his play *Privates on Parade*. In 1945, prosecutions were brought against participants in *Meet the Boys*, a show which had originally been entitled *Boys will be Girls* and later became *Soldiers in Skirts*. The military overtones were particularly offensive to some. 'What an insult to our soldiers who died for this country', fulminated one letter to the Lord Chamberlain; 'We expect to see genuine discharged <u>men</u> not a Bunch of Filthy Puffs'.[2] On another occasion, the Theatre Royal at Stockport was informed 'that the Lord Chamberlain is unable to sanction the appearance of a man, whether in tights or not, in a Dance of the Seven Veils', and, in the same month, Game reported on *Get in for Laughter*,* another all-male revue: 'they seem to be busy demobilising the pansy age groups now!'.[3] Even in 1953, a military captain objecting to 'the filthy and disgusting type of shows that are touring the provincial music halls', cited *Soldiers in Skirts*, in which 'obvious moral perverts' posed as ex-servicemen, as the sort of all-male revue he was

---

★ Written by Ralph Marshall

objecting to: 'It makes one feel quite sick to see these creatures going around the town'. He insisted that such people could not possibly have served in the military 'as this would be a menace to any self respecting body of men', and was particularly outraged by the 'nerve' of the promotional tag line: 'They were proud to serve their country, now they are proud to serve you'. But the Office did not automatically capitulate to such prejudice:

> The MSS of these shows as submitted to the Lord Chamberlain are not of a type that he would have any reason for banning. His Lordship must exercise his functions as Censor in a judicial and impartial manner, and he has no evidence that the shows to which you refer are performed in other than a proper manner: neither can he accept unsupported aspersions against the character of the performers.

It may be the Office had half an eye on the possibility of hoax protests designed to fuel publicity, but the response also had a faintly sinister undertone:

> The Lord Chamberlain is most strongly opposed to the portrayal of perversion in drama or burlesque and has incurred much criticism for his attitude.
>
> If you are able to provide me with legally supportable evidence of any of the allegations which you make against the Company concerned, I shall be glad to arrange for it to be investigated, and proper action taken upon the findings.[4]

And if the censorship disliked all male revues, they were no happier with the female equivalents: 'I particularly dislike blue-pencil dirt from women at any time, in or out of the RAF', commented Game in relation to the teasingly named *Girls out of Uniform.** Clarendon added: 'I don't think this deserves much mercy'.[5]

It would be 1958 before the Lord Chamberlain's Office would officially relax its policy and rule that, in certain circumstances, plays dealing with the subject of homosexuality, or including identifiably homosexual characters, could be considered for public performance. There would be much anger, prejudice, disappointment and confrontation before that would occur. Yet it would be wrong to assume that the decision to maintain the ban till then was taken easily. At the start of 1946, George Titman wrote a lengthy memorandum to the Comptroller and the Lord Chamberlain:

> I have recently met a good many people connected with, or interested in the Stage, who express great concern with the state of dramatic art both now and in the future.

---

* Written by Cecil G. Buckingham

> They have little to complain of the censorship as a Department so long
> as it exists in order to put a stopper on sheer dirt, the hurting of feelings or
> plays of political danger.
>
> They agree that the standard of plays, playwrites [sic] and actors is
> generally low.
>
> This is largely attributable to six years of war and they hope that a new
> brood of playwrites and actors, who have been otherwise employed, will
> appear and automatically raise the standard of the types of plays produced.
>
> They point out that these new playwrites, many of whom have been
> very close to reality during the last years, may produce unusual works and
> hope that the censorship will not be too rigid; or that it will fail to
> recognise the effects of war on the younger generation; and will not forget
> that the contemporary theatre is a valuable contribution to present day
> thought and to future history.

It was particularly in relations to issues of sexuality and morality where
Titman felt there was a push for change:

> Many question our attitude to homosexuality, lesbianism and prostitution
> and, although they do us the kindness not to brand us as ignorant of the
> very existence of these things, they are doubtful, at least, that our attitude
> towards these subjects has marched with the times.
>
> They point out, with absolute truth, that talk on these subjects, their
> consequences etc. is much more open than it was and, what might shock
> the older generation, is as nothing to the contemporary.

One of the perennial problems faced by each generation of censors was to
decide whether plays which inhabited or entered 'dangerous' areas must
necessarily be seen as promoting and encouraging anti-social practices, or
whether it could be plausibly argued that they might achieve the opposite
effect. Titman cited the decision to allow certain plays about venereal
disease to be performed:

> The contraversial [sic] question was raised as to whether harm or good
> was done by ventilating certain social evils which all people should know
> exist and it was maintained that if a play was a serious work, intended as a
> deterrent, it would be of social benefit.[6]

Titman was writing at a time when a number of plays touching on
homosexuality had recently been turned down. In July 1945, a licence was
refused for *Outrageous Fortune*:[*]

> It is extremely difficult to follow what is happening in this play, as the
> authoress gets her effects by implications and half-statements and is rarely
> explicit . . . Unfortunately the authoress has given Bert a brother, Julian,

---

[*] Written by Rose Franken

who is a pervert . . . As plays including perverts are taboo, and wisely so, this one is not recommended for licence.[7]

Then in August, the censors had turned down *Surface*,* which centred on a writer and a musician: 'both are pansies', reported Game, and the fact that they were not even condemned within the play made it potentially more dangerous:

> David and Peter share a flat, the same bedroom and there is every indication that they share the same bed! . . . The play . . . as far as possible, considering the theme, is emotional rather than sordid; the sentiment- alising about perverts is a most insidious method of encouragement, and I have not the slightest hesitation in advising that the play is not recommended for licence.[8]

A few months later, they only agreed to license *A Man about the House*† after removing all references to homosexuality:

> the only objections to the play from our point of view are the more obvious clues to the relationship between Salvatore and the Uncle, Salvatore and the American, and so forth, which are definite references to perversion . . .
>
> Of course it is all in the past, before the play begins, and except in retrospect is not part of the actual action; but it establishes the fact that Salvatore has been a kept-boy in his youth and it introduces the subject of perversion.

The Office required this aspect of the narrative to be 'much less insisted upon', and demanded changes. If failing to condemn homosexuality in the characters rendered a play irresponsible, then using it as a signifier of evil was no more acceptable : 'There is no need to stress all this perversion to make Salvatore a more unpleasant character. I think it is an effort to get cheap sensation by bringing in homosexuality'. After discussions with the manager and the writer the script was made safe:

> The American man has been turned into an American woman, and some additional lines have been put in to make it clear that the orgies attended by the old Uncle, about which Salvatore attempted to blackmail both the Uncle and the two spinsters, were not in any way homo-sexual. Where necessary lines have been altered so that there is no implication of perversion in them.[9]

Titman's memorandum invited the Lord Chamberlain to consider whether it might be possible 'to further the cause of the production of plays hitherto banned for general exhibition' by taking steps

---

* Written by Dail Ambler
† An adaptation by John Perry from the novel by F. Brett Young

(1) To encourage a 'season' of plays on hitherto forbidden subjects at a place such as the Lyric, Hammersmith (to which the general pleasure-seeking public do not penetrate).

(2) To limit his Licence to that theatre and then only for a certain length of time.[10]

One of the people to whom Titman had been speaking was the well-known manager Binkie Beaumont, who was seeking permission to perform both Sartre's *Huis Clos* and Lillian Hellman's *The Children's Hour*. In March 1946, Beaumont proposed 'that a special licence should be granted for plays of this nature for performance only at the Lyric, Hammersmith, under the auspices of The Company of Four in association with the Arts Council of Great Britain'.[11] In both plays, it was the references to homosexuality which caused the censors to hesitate. Had the time come to officially relax the policy? In February 1946, Gwatkin sent a 'strictly confidential' and explicit letter to members of the newly reconstituted Advisory Board, and to selected religious leaders, canvassing advice.

> Up to now the Lord Chamberlain has not, wittingly, licensed any plays dealing with perversion.
>
> It will be agreed that the present generation is outspoken on subjects which, previously, were not matters for open conversation. The subject of perversion occurs frequently in contemporary literature, both in fiction and autobiography.
>
> It may be these facts or, indeed, it may be part of the aftermath of two major wars but there is an impression that perversion is on the increase.
>
> The contemporary theatre is a valuable contribution to future history: it is also a powerful weapon for propaganda.
>
> It has been suggested that the production of serious plays dealing with the subject of perversion, its evils and its consequences, would act as a deterrent and would be of social benefit.
>
> Against this can be placed the opinion which prefers to draw a curtain over the existence of very unpleasant aspects of life . . .
>
> Lord Clarendon would be most grateful if you could give him the benefit of your opinion on this matter.[12]

Of course, this was no democratic survey, and the choice of whom to consult carried assumptions which slanted the whole exercise in particular directions. Nor can we know what the Lord Chamberlain would have decided if the balance of advice he received had strongly favoured licensing. But there is no reason to suppose that his mind was made up or that he was going through the motions. On the other hand, the way in which his request for advice was framed, hardly presented the possible revision of policy as a positive liberalisation or a call for tolerance. Rather, the debate centred on whether the exposure would help society to control and suppress something evil, and comparisons were made with government decisions to use the press and advertisements to warn people about venereal disease.

Most respondents realised that, although he had not named the actual subject, the Lord Chamberlain was enquiring in respect of homosexuality. 'If by "perversion" is meant yet more abnormal sexual practices (of which most people are mercifully ignorant)', wrote the Dean of Westminster, 'the less said the better'. The Chief Rabbi, however, evidently assumed he was talking about sex and promiscuity more generally, and replied that it was 'the regular triangle plot in romantic novels that causes most of the mischief'; possibly the real focus of the enquiry never occurred to him as one which could be under serious consideration. A majority of those whom the Lord Chamberlain consulted came out against licensing plays dealing with homosexuality, and most were unconvinced that the use of the theatre as propaganda against 'perversion' was likely to prove effective. The Eugenics Society, for example, thought it would be 'a catastrophic mistake' to allow the theme at all:

> To license plays dealing with this subject would, in my opinion, have the sole effect of drawing attention to them and of widening the practices which it is sought to restrain . . . Plays designed to deter from such practices would excite the opposition of sexual reformers, who consider themselves 'broadminded' and are ready with their pens. A campaign against homosexuality cannot, in my opinion, be compared with a campaign against venereal diseases. If you contract a venereal disease, dire consequences ensue for you in the shape of illness and personal discomfort. No such consequences ensue from the practice of homo-sexuality.

The Dean of Westminster also refused the comparison with venereal disease, which was merely 'the direct result of a normal though undisciplined instinct'. It was much more dangerous, he suggested,

> To draw attention to vices to which the ordinary healthy minded people are not normally inclined and indeed of whose nature most people are probably ignorant. Why poison their minds by acquainting them with perversions to which they are not naturally disposed? What good will that do to anyone? It will not turn the pervert from his ways—and it may suggest ideas to normal people which otherwise would never have entered their heads.

The Free Church Federal Council also feared 'that the production of such plays would be likely to spread the infection'. The Council accepted that the existence of homosexuality should not be hidden and that 'it would be well for many people to realise that it is far commoner than is generally supposed'; but theatre, it argued, was not an appropriate vehicle to use for publicising it. Lord Cromer, the former Lord Chamberlain, agreed there was a danger people might be 'encouraged in these pernicious practices', and reaffirmed his belief that just because the subject was now common in literature and conversation 'there is no reason why latitude should be given for it to be proclaimed from the stage'. One letter warned that 'after the Oscar Wilde case a whole speight [sic] of trouble started because people who hadn't thought of it before felt it would be worth trying if Oscar Wilde did it'. And the Archbishop of York worried that it might stir up hatred of the aristocracy, where he clearly supposed homosexual practices to be located: 'The great mass of middle class and working class opinion strongly condemns perversion, and is only very slightly affected by it'. He also suspected that productions would attract only 'those who are either morbidly minded or addicts', and that the granting of licences might 'still further undermine the condemnation which perversion has received in the past'—in effect, promoting homosexuality by normalising it:

> It would encourage the tendency to regard it as something that is normal rather than abnormal and, while the actual play might stress the evil and unhappy consequences of perversion, the mere fact that it was dealt with on the stage might encourage some to remove the restraints which hitherto they have shown.

The Reverend Gillingham, who was about to become a member of the Advisory Board, was reluctant to state a definite view but, for all his earnest agonising, most of his arguments were against licensing: 'By my age I am of the Victorian era but I am trying to forget these things in coming to a decision on Buggery and Lesbianism', he wrote; 'Pardon my frankness but that is what you really mean—Victorian or no Victorian'. Again, he worried that to draw attention to such things on the stage would 'open the eyes of a lot of people who don't know anything about it'. He also thought that 'Whereas many men know about buggery—from public school onwards— the great majority of women don't know about Lesbianism and are not drawn to it as men are to their perversion'. Gillingham concluded by facing the argument that it would be healthier to bring vice into the open than to suppress it:

> But if the vice be of the 'underground' why not let it remain there? I . . . know there is an 'underworld'—but I have always tried to direct the eyes and ears of people away from the black things of life. I know ignorance is not innocence but I also know that Lot <u>looked</u> toward Sodom and eventually finished up in it.

Writing from a Catholic perspective, Father Cavanagh, of Downside School, saw it as one of the Almighty's oversights that there were no 'physical sanctions of perversion'. He was convinced that 'foreseeable evils would far outweigh the good' if the Lord Chamberlain removed his ban:

1. Such plays will nearly always be written by perverts themselves, to justify their wrongful actions and to secure sympathy . . .

2. There would be at least a tendency to exalt an abnormal condition and to minimize its essentially anti-social basis.

3. There would be a great danger that many, especially young people, not acquainted with these matters . . . would . . . be led by curiosity and desire for new sensations into indulging in such practices.

4. Part of such plays would be the portrayal of perverted conduct, which has no beauty, dramatic or otherwise, in it.

5. The theatre would be used to attack the existing law.

6. Almost all women, particularly of the respectable middle class, would strongly resent the public exhibition of plays dealing with this problem.

7. Once the principle of admitting any plays about perversion were admitted, even though at first their scope might be severely restricted and narrowed, it would be impossible to resist the tendency to widen that scope until it included plays of an evil nature and gravely harmful to public morals.

Cavanagh declared that perversion was 'repugnant and no fit subject for anyone save a doctor or a priest', though he had some sympathy for 'inverts'—people with 'more elements in their nature pertaining to the sex opposite to that of their physical bodies'. A pervert, by contrast, was someone who 'being normally sexed . . . commits sexual acts with another man' out of a wish for experimentation or 'because there is no other opportunity of allaying his merely physical appetite'; such acts were 'aberrations on the part of normal people'. He concluded:

> While plays about perversion should be entirely banned, one can make out
> a case for allowing those about inversion, provided that they keep the
> subject in its proper perspective, emphasize its rarity, do not excuse evil
> acts on the part of the invert, and do help to dissipate the unfair prejudice
> against the true invert.

But he recognised that, in practice, 'censorship on these lines would be unmanageable' since most people would 'draw no distinction between inversion and perversion . . . and the press would read into them what they did not contain'.

Some replies favoured lifting the automatic ban, but these were no more reflective of any liberal enlightenment than those which wished to maintain it. The National Council of the YMCA, for instance, recommended that if the subject was 'skilfully dealt with and tackled in such a way as to reveal the nature and good potentialities of man', there should be no objection to anything which helped 'to break into the secrecy which lends false and attractive colour to the topic'. Violet Campbell agreed that 'serious plays dealing with immorality and perversion could do nothing but good', provided that

(a) the subject is <u>not</u> treated as something specially interesting, salacious or romantic: (b) it is made quite clear that these actions are wrong actions which could easily be avoided by the use of sufficient self-control: (c) eventual retribution is shown to be certain.

Rejecting the 'ostrich-like attitude' which ignored it, and the 'equally foolish' extension of understanding and sympathy towards those who practised it, as 'unfortunates, more sinned against than sinning', she demanded an unambiguous condemnation of those who transgressed the social laws. Pressure was needed to encourage homosexuals to resist temptation, and it was here that 'the dramatist is of service in drawing that picture of mental and domestic suffering, consequent on ill-doing, which is within the special scope of art'.

A newer member of the Advisory Board, Peter Fleming, also thought it would be 'wrong to withhold a licence from any sincere <u>and</u> skillful [sic] play dealing with perversion' or 'to suppress or run away from the truth'; however, he itemised a series of dangers and potential consequences:

Whether the effect of having one or more 'much discussed' plays about perversion running in the West End would in practice be deterrent [sic] is very difficult to say. Whatever the dramatist's approach to his subject, it is probable that the caste [sic] and certain that the audience would include a 'hard core' of perverts; thus the theatre concerned might tend to become a stamping (or mincing) ground for perverts and for the morbid or silly people who like to watch these creatures going through their paces in public. But perverts must go <u>somewhere</u> in the evening and there seems no great harm in providing them with a rendez-vous since they will provide themselves with plenty anyhow. On the whole there is at least a fair chance that a good play about perversion would lessen the numbers and impair the influence of these poor creatures . . .

The Lord Chamberlain has obviously considered the possibility that the production of one distinguished or reasonably successful play about perversion may, as often happens in the theatre, start something of a vogue. The influence of even one play on the subject will be wide within the London theatre, for it will automatically become a favourite topic for music-hall jokes, skits in revues etc; and it would presumably not be in the interests of national prestige for an undue proportion of the capital's dramatic output in any one season to be inspired by unnatural vice.

Violet Bonham Carter, an experienced member of the Advisory Board and now a governor of the BBC, took a rather more liberal view, doubting that plays would affect actual behaviour. 'I am not an authority on the psychology of perversion, but in my view those who suffer from it would be most unlikely to be influenced by any public dramatisation of the subject'. It was therefore more a matter of taste, and questioning 'how far the public should be "paternally" treated and "protected" in the field of art', she declared herself 'loth [sic] to exclude any subject from artistic treatment'. She therefore supported a change in policy:

> If the arbitrament of the Lord Chamberlain is to be exercised in matters of taste as well as morals (and in practice it is hard to draw a distinction between them) my opinion is that this subject should not be excluded, but that each individual case should be most carefully considered on its merits, (its <u>artistic</u> merits being given their due weight in the scale).

There was also an element of broad-mindedness in the recommendation of Maxime Miles that the ban should be lifted because the theatre should be allowed to reflect its age and because social attitudes had changed. However, she was concerned about 'the difficulty of neither frightening nor comforting the people concerned', and warned that the campaign against venereal disease had been in some respects counter-productive: 'Much harm was undoubtedly done by the weapon of terror, so that the sufferer was encouraged to hide his state. It is probably equally unfortunate to encourage the idea that "it may happen to anyone and is nothing to be worried about"'. She thought that 'while a play may be good propaganda for or against any subject it is unlikely to be effective if written <u>as propaganda</u>', and advised that in order to be effective, 'homo-sexuality must be a necessary part of the story and not just a necessary text for homily'.

Finally, David Cecil from Oxford University confirmed from his own experience that 'young people of the most intelligent and respectworthy type' were now discussing homosexuality openly. 'The old taboo is gone', he insisted, and the subject 'should surely be ventilated as cleanly and fully as possible'. He argued passionately that homosexuality was 'the source of crucial and painful problems in the normal and emotional life, not just of criminal and degenerate types but of persons otherwise often valuable to society and even remarkable'. Yet even he stopped well short of advocating freedom or a change in the law, and was obliged to subscribe to the view that sexual preferences could somehow be detached from the personality. He argued that because of recent advances in scientific understanding, it was now 'possible to approach the subject in a cooler and soberer spirit and to discuss how to prevent it and cure it with profit', and that theatre could play a part in this. But even though he called for 'rational discussion' to help 'get the subject viewed more sanely', his cautious conclusion was all too familiar in its assumptions: 'the wrong sort of play about perversion could stimulate a desire for it in some members of the audience', he warned, 'So . . . I should act with great circumspection'.[13]

In a sense, then, there is little to choose between those who favoured retaining an absolute ban on references to homosexuality, and those who were prepared to relax the principle. Almost all the correspondents seem to have accepted that the only plausible reason for changing the policy was to allow the waging of a more effective propaganda campaign against it. Nor was there any real attempt to distinguish, as the Lord Chamberlain's Readers had often done in practice, between the explicit and the implicit; was any play centring on a same-sex friendship a play 'about perversion', or was it so only if the subject was specifically identified and 'dwelled on' within the text?

Titman's memorandum urging the Office to consider moving with the times had acknowledged the 'obvious and recognised danger' of the fact that productions were essentially commercial enterprises, and that if restrictions were removed then business imperatives would surely dictate. This was crucial to his proposal that some theatres and venues could be given greater freedom than others, and his belief that such plays 'definitely require handling only by first class actors and actresses'. Titman believed that the Lord Chamberlain enjoyed 'wide and almost indefinable powers', and he had even considered whether it might be possible for the Office 'To take a more active and decisive role in the selection of actual actors and actresses asked to play certain parts'. In the end, he had reluctantly discounted that particular idea:

> I question the desirability of this—we already have enough stones thrown at us from the playwrites [sic]: to adjudicate on the suitability of actors or actresses would be far more dangerous than refereeing a football match between the Germans and the Poles, although it was said that this could only be possible in England where public servants are still more or less incorruptible.[14]

However, the censorship did explore the possibility of issuing 'a restricted licence'.[15] The advantage of such a licence would be that it 'enables us to gauge the public reaction to any play' before setting it free. But was it within the rights given to the Lord Chamberlain by the Theatres Act? 'I think we have the power to do this—or rather I don't know if we have not the power', wrote Titman, optimistically.[16] In March 1946, Nugent, as Comptroller, wrote to the Home Office 'to obtain the opinion of the Law Officers of the Crown as to whether the provisions of the Theatres Act, 1843, would entitle his Lordship to issue his licence for a stage play to a particular theatre for a specified time only'. Unfortunately for Titman's plan, the reply was negative:

> I am directed by the Secretary of State to say that he is advised that this power is not available . . . He is also of opinion that there are no provisions in the Act which could be construed as authorising the Lord Chamberlain to issue a licence embodying the requirement that the play should not be performed after the expiration of a certain period . . . It does not, therefore, appear to the Secretary of State that there is any room for doubt about the answer to the question put in your letter.

The Home Office even included a copy of a letter sent to Sir Douglas Dawson in 1913, informing him that 'there is no doubt that when a stage-play is once allowed, anyone can produce it without infringing the provisions of section 12 of the Theatres Act'.[17]

Clarendon had little choice other than to confirm that the ban on plays about homosexuality should remain in force. Earlier in the same month, Beaumont had written to the Office: 'I am very anxious to know whether you have been able to arrive at any conclusion with regard to *Huis Clos* and *The Children's Hour*'. Gwatkin's reply suggests that he, at least, had recognised the need to reform policy: 'Since we last met I, like Cranmer, have lit a torch (or was it a candle) but I think gales and gusts from various angles have blown it out'. He added: 'I shall have all the material to hand very shortly, and then I suggest we meet again and I can give you some pointers'. However, after receiving the negative assessment of the Law Lords, Gwatkin wrote a more formal letter, which not only made clear that there was no likelihood of a change in policy, but also implied that there never had been:

> There are, as I think you know, very few hard and fast rules in the Censorship. . . . But the main rules which do exist cover the exclusion of the actual Presentation of The Deity; the protection of living personages, and the close relations of the celebrated or notorious dead; and themes which are about or which include unnatural vice.
>
> The Lord Chamberlain has never wavered, wittingly, from the above rules and with regard to the final rule he is fortified by the very great majority of feeling in this country as to the undesirability of allowing such plays for public performance.

Turning to Hellman's play, Gwatkin stated that he had witnessed a private production:

> There are, of course, degrees of the presentation of unnatural vice, and in this play *Children's Hour*, it could not be more delicately handled . . . The play does not centre round this attitude, which is anyhow shown as deplorable, nor indeed do the principals practice this vice—the reverse— but it is introduced into the play and therefore the Lord Chamberlain cannot give the play a licence.

And he was adamant that the censorship did not consider it a play liable to simple modifications in order to secure a licence:

> To suggest that this forbidden subject should be exorcised from the play is, in my opinion, fruitless, because no other accepted social evil could be substituted and to attempt to do so would mean the ruin of a fine piece of work.

Beaumont forwarded the letter to Hellman, who in turn wrote pointedly to the Office:

> The Lord Chamberlain's reasons for censorship of *The Children's Hour* are to me shocking, and, to use what is evidently a favourite word, immoral.
>
> There is a paragraph in your letter that worries me . . . I don't know who could have suggested to you that I would be willing to alter the play. I do not make alterations for other people's rules, and I would not like you to think that I do.[18]

The Office had little respect for such principles; 'Frankly I don't care a damn what she does!', wrote someone in pencil on her letter.

Sartre's *Huis Clos* stood even less chance of being allowed. It had been submitted, 'somewhat tentatively', by the British Council in the autumn of 1945, and they had been unofficially advised that it was unlikely to be passed. In December, the producer H.M. Tennent Ltd. sent it in again, but Game was clear that it could not be licensed:

> The play illustrates very well the difference between the French and English tastes. I don't suppose that anyone would bat an eyelid over in Paris, but here we bar Lesbians on the stage. Some years ago we had quite a run of plays about Lesbianism, and of course we turned them all down. Our taboo is understood by informed opinion, and is accepted as reasonable; and I think that it would be extremely unwise to take any step which weakened our position. This play has, of course, merits, and the Lesbian theme, for what it is worth, is treated on a fairly high plane and not unduly exploited; but there it is! I am all for treating the claims of the high-brows (Sartre is all the rage amongst the Intelligensia [sic] at the moment) with as much consideration as those of the low, who, to say the least of it, are well catered for: but it would need a clever advocate to persuade me that British culture needs the introduction of such queer themes from the Continent for its healthy life. It is not a play which you can cut.[19]

Translated as *Vicious Circle*, Peter Brook directed a private production at the Arts Theatre with Alec Guinness, Donald Pleasance and Beatrix Lehmann. In August 1946, Charles Heriot attended a performance on behalf of the Lord Chamberlain, and, although he recognised it to be 'a serious work of art' with 'an ingenious and interesting exposition', he had no difficulty in identifying its philosophical weakness: 'it fails', he said, 'because it presents (however convincingly) only one side of a system of moral economy and totally ignores the possibility of redemption either by faith <u>or</u> works'. This was convenient:

> This failure to develop completely a theme which must stand or fall by its metaphysical verity makes it easier to withold permission for public performance on the obvious grounds, already indicated by Mr Games [sic]

of eroticism and Lesbianism, without feeling that an important work of art is being stifled.[20]

When the BBC broadcast a radio version of Sartre's play the following year, the Conference of Repertory Theatres pointed out the inconsistency to the Lord Chamberlain. Gwatkin replied:

> At first sight it would appear anomalous that a play banned by the Lord Chamberlain should be broadcast by the BBC. But I am sure that you will understand that there is a difference between words coming over the air and the same words spoken in the more personal atmosphere of a theatre, by visible characters. It is interesting to note that many people who listened to the broadcast of the play did not notice the perversion of one of the characters, whereas this particular thing was quite apparent when produced in the theatre.[21]

One long-standing policy was over-turned in June 1946, when the Lord Chamberlain allowed the term 'pansy' to be used in *But for the Grace of God*, a Frederick Londsale play; 'as *The Times* uses the word it would seem rather over nice to cut it', wrote Game. However, the Office required that 'The character of Gerard must not be played in an effeminate manner'.[22] On another occasion,* it demanded 'an undertaking that the aesthetic young men will not be played as homosexuals', and issued a licence only 'on the understanding that the part of the Princess is not to be played as a Lesbian'.[23] In July 1946, the play by Leslie and Sewell Stokes about Oscar Wilde's trial, which had been privately produced at the Gate a decade earlier, was again submitted. Game's general views had not been officially sought in Clarendon's consultation exercise, so he took the opportunity to voice them now:

> This play is about perverts and perversion, and that its central character has been erected into a sort of literary martyr does not alter the fact. We do not license plays about pederasts, and in my opinion, rightly so. During the period between the two World Wars a mistaken toleration gave a deplorable stimulus to the practice of abnormalities, and the Censorship is undoubtedly right in making perversion taboo as dramatic theme.

Two years later *Oscar Wilde* was produced privately once again, earning positive reviews and demands in the press that the ban should be lifted. The co-author, Leslie Stokes, who was working for the Third Programme on BBC radio, invited the Lord Chamberlain to see it: 'I do not believe that anybody who sees a performance will find that perversion is the main theme', he insisted; its subject, he said, was 'the downfall of a man unable to overcome a defect in his character', and the authors 'did not seek in this

---

* In relation to *Atalanta*, by Jay Davenport and Bridget Chetwynd

play to condone or to explain the defect which resulted in Oscar Wilde's conviction'. Again, Heriot, was sent to watch a performance; his report was not sympathetic to Stokes's argument:

> The authors claim that they present a study of a man ruined by his own pride. I do not agree with them. To me, this play seemed a study of a convicted homosexual ennobled to the point of sainthood ... There was little or no indication of the psychological disintegration which is symptomatic of the last stages of most homosexuals. Now this implicit condonation of the vice is precisely what I presume the Lord Chamberlain tries to prevent in stage presentations.
>   Further, the ignorance of the general public about what may be called the technical aspects of the crime has bred fear and its counterpart levity about the crime, so that there is on the one hand an unwholesome curiosity that would undoubtedly be stimulated by public performances of this play, and on the other, a brutal kind of humour.

Heriot specifically drew attention to the fact that, once licensed, the Lord Chamberlain had no powers to prevent other productions:

> The text, when well acted as it was last night, seemed to skate perilously on the thinnest of ice, so that what was <u>not</u> mentioned loomed with a reality larger than if it had been dragged into the open. What would happen to this play in the hands of bad actors or those themselves perverse, makes one shudder.

Even ten years later, when the automatic ban on plays about homosexuality had been lifted, a licence was refused after Wilde's son, Vyvan Holland, notified the Lord Chamberlain that a public performance 'would certainly cause distress to my wife and my son'.[24]

At the end of September 1948, Nugent had told Stokes, 'The Lord Chamberlain does not license plays in which perversion is the main theme'. The slight shift in emphasis hinted at in the penultimate word here is significant, for in fact the Office had quietly eased its position. The licensing in February 1947 of 'Now Barabbas . . . ', William Douglas Home's prison drama, based on his own experience during the war when he was locked up for refusing to obey orders, became something of a landmark. The script had been admired by Dearmer, and a private production had received good reviews. But the Reader's report also drew attention to the 'questionable side of the play', which centred on one of the characters, Richards, whom Dearmer described as 'a not unpleasant 100% pansy'. He was reluctant to see the play condemned on that account:

> The only suggestion of perversion, and the subject is treated with complete reserve and delicacy—indeed barely hinted at, exists in Metcalfe's mind. Metcalfe is a gentle, educated prisoner with a possible tendency towards abnormality himself. He complains to the Governor ... that Richards's influence in the prison is unhealthy and he is sent to

another prison. One gathers that Metcalfe is 'inside' for some similar offence himself . . . There is no suggestion that any improper behaviour has been practised at any time and the subject is so remote and briefly treated that I do not think any offence can reasonably be sustained. It could not be removed from the play without doing it irreparable damage, and no doubt this is a problem in prison life . . .

The tone of the play is not the least morbid and no attempt is made to excite any morbid instinct.

Gwatkin worried about creating a precedent:

if we allow it in this play, however 'remote and briefly treated', I cannot see that we have any justification for disallowing this subject in other serious plays—and more particularly in those which deal primarily with this complex—and which point a moral.

But in the end, because there was 'no suggestion that any actual improper behaviour takes place', they agreed to license it after some other relatively minor amendments ('You behave yourself' instead of 'We'll stand no funny business here') had been made.[25]

Several critics had no hesitation in announcing Home's theme: 'The present play swims in homosexuality', wrote James Agate. Despite his own sexual orientation, he expressed no overt support for the play: 'I hold that this highly specialised subject is not one to which the stage should be much beholden, but that if there is to be treatment at all that treatment should be adult'. In the *Evening Standard*, the MP Beverley Baxter was much nastier:

Frankly and openly the play has the background of homosexuality running through it. One lad in prison is represented as being so soft and mincing that the normal section of the audience giggled with embarrassment while sleek young men in the audience with their black bow ties and effeminate manners smiled with professional approval.

While professing to 'loathe censorship of any kind', Baxter made some unpleasant and disturbing observations:

I do not denounce the author . . . But everybody knows that the actual or posing or imitative homosexualist has far too great an influence in the West End theatre, either as actual theatrical people or as their hangers-on, and that this play may extend that influence.

I take no pleasure in writing these words nor do I want to be regarded as a crank, but there comes a time when tolerance is mere spiritual flabbiness. The power of these mincing elegants with their sexless vocal affectations is too widespread in the West End theatre. We shall never have the long overdue Renaissance of great dramatic writing until they are destroyed or at any rate diluted . . .

But if, as everyone knows, there is camaraderie among these gentlemen in the West End theatre and its antechambers, and their influence extends even to the casting of plays, may we who believe them to be a degrading and pernicious force not also combine to limit the extent of their kingdom?[26]

In some respects, more than a decade before *A Taste of Honey* arrived, and well before the Office announced it was changing its policy, *'Now Barabbas . . .'* was a mini-watershed for the censorship of homosexuality. A few months later, the Office had little hesitation in licensing *Baffled Spring*,* in which the central character was 'an aesthetic youth, very unhappy because his father has compelled him to learn farming instead of dabbling in art'. Even if that had been sufficiently coded to be taken at face value, the plot centres on how the aesthetic youth, Penn, is so charmed by an agricultural student called David that he too begins to take an interest in farming. When David falls in love with Penn's (female) cousin, Penn becomes jealous, and eventually shoots himself 'after David discovers the emotional disturbance he has caused and expresses his distaste'. Heriot not only dared to name the theme, but did so without expressing automatic disapproval: 'This could have been an interesting and unusual study of adolescent homosexuality: actually, it is dismally long and deadly dull'.[27] In October 1947, the Office also licensed *The Shadow of our Night*,† in which a man and two women compete for the affections of a young pianist whose mental health has been disturbed by his imprisonment in a Japanese POW Camp. Bernard 'has a genuine affection for the young man' but, as Game put it, 'has the making of a pervert'. In trying to persuade Peter to come with him, Bernard 'makes the fatal mistake of telling Peter that he has planted ideas about their relationship in the minds of the women'. As a result of this 'Peter is revolted and quarrels with Bernard'. Turning a remarkably blind eye, the censors were prepared to accept that this was 'only talk and has no basis in fact', and to leave the scene intact, provided an alternative reason could be substituted for the argument between Bernard and one of the women:

> I don't see why some other cause for the quarrel between Celia and Bernard . . . could not be substituted, which would merely leave the scene in Act Two where Bernard tells Peter what he has been hinting at to the women in the hopes of warning them off. It really would have greater dramatic effect thus, unprepared for by anything in earlier scenes, and would not put ideas into the mind of the audience at such an early date . . . the cause of the break between Bernard and Peter is necessary and will be too brief to make the play offensive as the earlier introduction of the idea of perversion will tend to do. Not that post-war audiences mind anything.[28]

---

* Written by Falkland L. Cary
† Written by Michael Sherwood

Alterations were required to ensure that the performance 'will not stress the theme of perversion so much', but there was no attempt to excise the theme entirely.

In the same month they also licensed *The Hidden Years*,* described in the *Sunday Times* as 'a fine play about the dawning consciousness of sex in a boys' public school'. Or, as the *Evening Standard* put it: 'This play deals with the frustrated emotions of boys who form attachments for each other. It pleads the innocence of them and decries the brutality of condemnation and expulsion'.[29] In the Reader's words, 'Digby conceives one of those schoolboy "pashes" (a form of sublimated love), for a younger boy, Martineau'; when a teacher, Mr Johnstone, discovers the boys together and reports it to the headmaster, 'Martineau, who is in fact a peculiarly virginal boy, is made to doubt the purity of Digby's friendship, and is so distressed that he runs away'. Game insisted that 'the boys' virtue is never in doubt' and that 'There is nothing dirty in the play except Mr Johnstone's mind'. Clarendon sought advice from Lord Cromer, who suggested that 'refusal would cause more trouble than the play is worth' by lending the play the publicity its author and manager probably craved.[30] They cut a line in which Johnstone actually refers to having 'caught them flagrante delicto' and claims 'The boys confessed', but the script was licensed with only these minor amendments.

In December 1947 the Office was split over whether or not to license *The Gingerbread House*,† which was already running in a private production. Gwatkin thought it was a step too far:

> Very briefly this is a fight between a doting mother and a middleaged homosexual to prevent a young man marrying . . . That the young man has had active homosexual experience with the older man, and others, is made quite clear.
>
> This play is far worse than THE GREEN BAY TREE the passing of which has always been held against the censorship as inconsistent with its ban on perversion.
>
> If we pass this type of play, for the second time (with our eyes open) we allow perversion as part of a plot and we shall have radically to revise our ideas about plays dealing with sexual perversion of either sexes, or be accused, and rightly, of gross inconsistency.

The Reader, Charles Heriot, saw it differently:

> This seems to me to be a serious, well-written, adult play, in which the subject of homosexuality is treated with care and discretion. I do not believe that it would offend any audience and it is certainly not an apology

---

* Written by Travers Otway
† Written by Shirley Cox

for, or a defence of, homosexuality. I therefore suggest that it be recommended for licence.

Heriot stressed that 'there is no indication that Terry is actively homosexual', and that although he 'has formerly been too friendly with more than one homosexual', he is in the process of trying to make 'a clean break with his past'. This is being made difficult for him by his former associate, a solicitor who is 'is petulantly jealous and masochistically humble by turns'. Game had severe doubts and regrets, but his comments, which ultimately supported a licence, are also revealing:

> Heriot is of course wrong in saying Terry, the hero, is normal, as he obviously has had Pansy adventures in the past, but now wants to lead a normal life. This is, of course, a quite common situation in real life; lots of young men are a bit Pansyish at Public School and University, and become respectable married men in the early twenties. I do wish these women authors would leave the perverts out of their plays; but there it is, too many people no longer consider the subject taboo, and we have to move with the times. As this play very cleverly shows perversion as an evil and as good triumphs in the end, I do not see how we can object to it.

Clarendon again consulted his predecessor, who compared it with *The Green Bay Tree*, which he now regretted having licensed. While admitting he was out of touch with contemporary thinking, Cromer sought to turn back—or at least to halt—the tide:

> To my mind, which has no pretensions to being in tune with 1948 audiences, the very fact that this play treats homosexuality 'with care and discretion' and is neither 'an apology for or a defence of homosexuality' renders it all the more of a danger to youth.
>
> Here is an opportunity to cry 'Halt' to these sort of plays, and so to discourage other young women or men from writing them.

Game was not impressed by these comments. In his view, the censorship was not in a position where it could any longer afford to make such a stand:

> I cannot follow Cromer's reasoning about the play being a danger to youth, although I would agree that there is much to be said for taboos of the unmentionable. Though we live in 1948 and not in the age of Victorian prudery; and the world outside seems to me to think otherwise, and the Censorship ignores such a fact at its peril. The first consideration in censoring a play is, what is the author's intention? And one can hardly maintain that in The Gingerbread play, where evil is shown as evil and good is triumphant, that the authoress's intention is bad. So the only justification, as far as I can see, for banning it would be that any mention of perversion on the stage would be offensive to public decorum; and it obviously isn't after the very favourable reception of NOW BARABBAS by the critics and the more responsible public. In a democracy the

Censorship cannot set itself up as the autocratic arbiter of taste, and survive; it is because I do not think we are supported in a rigid ban on perversion as a dramatic theme, that I have supported Heriot's recommendation.

He added, pointedly: 'I should like to see some young minds on the Advisory Board'.

Rather surprisingly (and it is hard to say exactly why) *The Gingerbread House* was turned down. A revised version was submitted the following month, and Heriot reported that 'The author has very tactfully suppressed all the homosexual implications in the plot'. He insisted 'there is now no word in the text that could be construed as having a homosexual significance', that the crime had been amended to dope-peddling, and that whole scenes had been cut or fundamentally rewritten; 'In a word, THE GREEN BAY TREE has been cut down and the silver cord considerably strengthened. I confess that the play suffers in consequence, but I do not think that even Lord Cromer could now regard it as being in any way "a danger to youth"'.[31] Perhaps the play had been too much ruined, for it remained in the waiting box and no licence was ever issued.

A year later, extensive changes were demanded in *The Miraculous Miss Mann*,* a farce about a woman who has changed sex as the result of an operation following a skiing accident. S/he has now married as a man and is expecting to become a father, but finds himself obliged to dress as a woman once more in order to secure an inheritance. Again, Game thought the time had come to stop worrying about such plots:

> In earlier days this would have been considered a dubious farce; but I should not think many present day theatre-goers would be embarrassed by the hermaphrodite theme—after all such cases are written about in the press. But I think the references to the operation . . . should come out.

Titman, however, took exception to it:

> I have read this play and did not like it one little bit. . . . I do not think that hermaphrodites are subjects for farces in the theatre; indeed they are very great tragedies and by no means as rare as some people imagine . . . very likely the cases amongst the theatre-going public are so small as to be negligible but the fact remains that, like blindness, or any other affliction of the body, it is not a subject for levity.

Presumably he had never read *Volpone*. Titman worried about one particular character 'who will clearly be portrayed as a roaring pansy and in this setting this will be particularly nauseating'. Gwatkin shared many of Titman's doubts:

---

* Written by Percy Robinson

Personally I feel that a misfortune like an indeterminate sex is not a subject for a joke and I can hear some difficult anatomic questions being put to parents who are misguided enough to take young children to such a show.

But I would not object to it if it was mentioned once as essential to the plot and left at that. In this play it runs through the whole play and is treated 'dirtily'—in fact I think the whole play might have been written on the wall of a public lavatory by a nasty-minded adolescent.

With the Office split, and on Titman's suggestion, the decision was made to consult a member of the Advisory Board, Peter Fleming, 'who is of the modern generation and who will also have the advantage of the opinion of his very knowledgeable and intelligent wife, Miss Celia Johnson, who is not only a very distinguished actress but a mother and a woman of the world'. Fleming agreed that the play must have been 'Written by a man with an exceptionally vulgar mind. The trouble', he added, 'is that he is unaware that he has a vulgar mind'. However, Fleming did not believe the play was dangerous, and thought it simply a matter of taste, on which he understood the Lord Chamberlain was not 'empowered or intended to be an arbiter'. He concluded that the play 'may offend, will almost certainly bore but is unlikely to corrupt', and a licence was issued.[32]

There can no doubt, then, that the drawbridge had been discreetly lowered, and that by 1948 the censorship was knowingly allowing some references to the supposedly banned subject of homosexuality to appear on the stage. But, as usual, one looks in vain for absolute consistency or for clear definitions. Perhaps, too, there was a backlash, and a feeling that St James's Palace had been in danger of going too far too quickly. Certainly there is a sense at the end of the forties and the start of the fifties that the pendulum was beginning to swing back the other way, and the liberal advance of the previous few years was halted or reversed. Perhaps it reflected a wider political retreat from the post-war radicalism which had apparently so decisively swept away the old order in the general election of 1945.

In 1949, Binkie Beaumont submitted *Seagulls over Sorrento*,* a drama set on a naval experimental base on a remote Scottish island. The focus was primarily on the tensions and relationships among the all-male group working there, and Dearmer identified 'a discreet but definite suggestion of homosexuality'. However, since it 'could not be better handled', he suggested leaving it. Others at St James's Palace were less sure: 'Surely it is still a matter of the "subject" regardless of its handling—I feel if we allow "this subject" in yet another play . . . we are going to make it more difficult to prevent it creeping in future plays'. One crucial passage concerned Herbert, a thirty-year-old officer 'with a twisted cruel mouth and a

---

* Written by Hugh Hastings

jaundiced complexion', who invites a young and naïve sailor named Sims into his cabin to play cards. This is followed by a confrontation when Lofty, who has befriended Sims, challenges Herbert:

> HERBERT: Nothing to do, Mr. Turner?
> LOFTY: Yeah. Quite a lot in fact.
> HERBERT: For instance?
> LOFTY: Well, for instance, I'd like to have a little chat with you.
> HERBERT: Me?
> LOFTY: Yes. That's if you're not too busy.
> HERBERT: I am busy. You'd better come to my cabin. (*Herbert turns to go*)
> LOFTY: To your cabin, did you say?
> HERBERT: Yes.
> LOFTY: To play cards, I suppose!
> (*Herbert's face is twisted with anger*)
> HERBERT: Now look here, Turner. I've heard about you. I know you're a skate, so I don't want no nonsense, see?
> LOFTY: (*smouldering*) And, Petty Officer bloody Herbert, it so happens I've heard about you! Quite a lot of rather dirty stories—unpleasant little tit-bits that get whispered around the Fleet. And I'm not referring to the well-known fact that apart from everything else you're a confirmed yellow-belly! . . . Listen, Herbert, I'm warning you now. We don't know exactly wot's in store for us but we do know that wotever the game is it ain't kiss-in-the-ring![33]

Beaumont insisted there was 'no double-meaning or suggestion of homosexuality intended' in this passage, and attempted to convince Gwatkin that the identity of the actors made any such angle unimaginable: 'there could be no possible question in the audience's mind of there being anything unpleasant between the two characters as they are played by Nigel Stock and William Hartnell'. The Office was not convinced: 'Mr Beaumont is in no position to argue about homosexual implications when these have been perceived even by Mr Dearmer'.[34] The scene was rewritten to remove overt sexual implications, though it would not have been hard for actors to layer suggestions within their performance which an alert audience would have picked up.

The censors' first encounter with Tennessee Williams in the late forties was also challenging. *A Streetcar Named Desire* was again submitted by Beaumont in June 1948, while it was still running in New York. Game described it as 'a mixture of the lurid and the high-brow', and thought that judicious handling might be required:

> Although the central character is, if I understand the author's intentions rightly, a tragic nymphomaniac, or something of the sort anyway, there is nothing in the story which would justify a ban . . . One cannot tell everything as the stage directions are limited to entrances and exits, and

THE CENSORSHIP OF BRITISH DRAMA

> one is left to infer from the dialogue what the characters are up to and they seem up to a good deal at times! . . .
>
> . . . one is left in the dark by the script about much of the business on the stage, which is perhaps why the impression the play makes upon one is blurred. It certainly is with me . . .
>
> I have an idea that a general warning to Tennents that they must see that reasonable restraint is exercised in production to suit the (still) milder taste of an English audience compared to the American, might be salutary.

Nugent agreed: 'It is strong stuff but I quite agree with Game that there would be no justification in banning it, or even altering it much . . . I think in order to obtain the atmosphere of toughness it would be a pity to err too much on the side of squeamishness'.

However, one line in particular worried them and led to prolonged argument and negotiations—Blanche's statement that she had walked in on her husband with another man. 'I think we ought to keep the homosexual part out of it', commented Gwatkin, who, as Assistant Comptroller, was noticeably less willing than some of his colleagues to embrace change in this area; 'This rule used to be rigid'. He recognised that *'Now Barabbas . . .'* was being cited (not least by Beaumont) as evidence that the Office had already relaxed its attitude: 'if we allow a gradual slide, like nudity, I think we forge a stick to beat ourselves with', he warned. It was decided to ask for Blanche's speech to be amended, 'leaving it vague beyond the fact that she "found out in the worst of all possible ways"'; this, Gwatkin told Beaumont, would be 'enough for the sophisticated without going into details'. However, Beaumont's response was to say that he had discussed the matter with Tennessee Williams, who 'feels that the speech under discussion is the entire basis of Blanche's character'. Moreover, Williams was supported by Sir Laurence and Lady Olivier, who were due to direct and star in the London production. An acceptable compromise was reached shortly before the play opened in the autumn of 1949.

Ironically, in 1951 Gwatkin leapt to the defence of *Streetcar* (or, at least, of the Office's decision to license it) when reports of a production in Edinburgh provoked an outraged letter of protest to the Lord Chamberlain:

> In an Edinburgh newspaper it was described as 'portraying moral and physical disintegration, violence, and final insanity'. Do you seriously maintain that plays like that come under the category of 'pleasant and satisfying entertainment?'.

Gwatkin's reply focused less on the detail of the play, and more on the changing principles and policies which the censorship was having to adopt in order to reflect a changing society:

> Thank you for your letter of 1st of November, in which you ask for a reasonable explanation as to why plays are released to which a section of

the British public object. The Censor of plays has the unenviable task of
holding a balance for the general public as a whole, between those who are
surprised that such-and-such a play has been licensed and those who are
astonished that there should be any doubt about it being passed.

It is undoubtedly true that plays nowadays are much more outspoken
and on subjects which would not have been permitted at the turn of the
century. I think you will find the same tendency in much modern
literature, in art and in the Press, in particular in such matters as sexual
abnormalities and artificial insemination.

If the Play Censorship exercised its powers to such an extent that the
Theatre ceased to be a mirror of contemporary life, apart from causing
great hardship to the entertainment world, it would do irrevocable harm to
the future study of this epoch. One has but to consider the restoration of
Victorian playwrights, and the insight which they give into their times.

The Play in question, *A Streetcar Named Desire* is not at all a pleasant play
. . . but it could not be said that anyone visiting the play would have their
morals impaired. They might be shocked but they could not be debauched
and, in any case, they are under no compulsion to go at all.

I must repeat that it is not the task of the Censor of Plays to ensure that
the public gets 'pleasant and satisfactory entertainment'. Among the
Censor's duties is that of trying to ensure that modern playwrights and
producers do not exceed the contemporary standard of language or
situation.[35]

Williams's play benefited from having some high-profile supporters with
the capacity to embarrass the Lord Chamberlain's Office. Others fared less
well. In 1950, the Office refused to license *Hiatus*,[*] which focused on 'an
invert' who struggles against his desires; he eventually 'conceives a passion
for his son-in-law and when he finds it is anything but reciprocated, jumps
under a car and is killed'.[36] The following year they turned down *The
Ostrich Eggs*,[†] in which a father 'suddenly wakes up to the knowledge that
his 19-year old son Charles . . . is a pansy', and 'explodes, with just the kind
of outraged bourgeois reaction that one might expect'; Charles is jilted by
his male lover, but after making a lot of money is reconciled with his father.
'For obvious reasons', wrote Heriot, 'the play is not recommended for
licence'.[37] They also rejected *Third Person*, 'an attempt to examine the male
friendships that exist and which are intensified by the atmosphere of war'.
Andrew Rosenthal's play was performed privately at the Arts Theatre, and
eventually licensed after being 'severely pruned of the homosexuality
inherent in the original script'. Reporting on the revised version, Heriot
noted that 'The homosexual element has been soft-pedalled and the end of

---

[*] Written by Thomas R. McKay
[†] Written by André Roussin and translated by David Lewis

the play made less ambiguous'; specifically, 'Hank does not show any tendency to leave his wife for Kip':

> What is left now is one of the rather over-emphasised friendships which were formed abroad under the stresses of battle and propinquity. In this case it is a friendship or comradeship between an elder and a younger man—properly reasonable and normal. . . . Of course one can suppose a physical association between the elder and the younger man . . . but that is quite an unnecessary angle on this play . . . *The Third Person* even as now produced, will in some minds reek of perversion, but I don't think that it need do.[38]

In May 1951, the Office refused to license *The Lonely Heart,** in which 'a Lesbian living with the fluffy but normal Suzanne' is so upset when the latter falls in love with a man that she assaults her and then tries to commit suicide. 'The whole thing is on the intellectual level of an article on popular psychology in the *Daily Mirror*', wrote Heriot, disparagingly.[39] In September 1952, two further plays were refused licences on similar grounds; 'There seems to be a spate of these Lesbian plays', noted the censors. *White Terror,†* which focused on relationships in a guesthouse in Switzerland, was 'quite impossible by our present standards', as was *Two Loves I Have,‡* which Dearmer described as 'a study of a violently possessive woman' who contemplates suicide when the woman she is in love with leaves her for a man.[40] As with *The Green Bay Tree*, what was invisible was a matter of interpretation, and Alec Clunes of the Arts Theatre wrote to Nugent, questioning the decision:

> I believe that your objection lies in the fact that you assume the relationship between the two women, Pauline and Janet, to be one of sexual perversion . . . there is in the script submitted to you, no such suggestion.
> Nowhere, even by implication, is there anything to indicate that their relationship is anything other than the complete <u>intellectual</u> domination of the younger woman by the elder. . . . The women's relationship is admittedly unhealthy, it is neurotic and evil perhaps, but in it is no suggestion of homosexuality.

The Lord Chamberlain refused to change the decision.

Geoffrey Dearmer had noted in relation to this play that if a licence were granted then it would be difficult to maintain the ban on *The Children's Hour*. In November 1950, Peter Cotes, the author of what the *Daily Telegraph* had called 'a provocative book on the theatre', took over the

---

* Written by Judith Warden
† Written by Marjorie Squires
‡ Written by Dorothy and Howard Baker

Bolton's Theatre in South Kensington. Cotes had previously run the New Lindsey Theatre Club, where he had staged the controversial *Pick-Up Girl*, and the Library Theatre in Manchester, and the Bolton's already had a reputation as an interesting and experimental theatre. When Cotes announced his first season here it contained several plays described by the *News Chronicle* as being 'on the Lord Chamberlain's "stop" list'. The opening production scheduled was *The Children's Hour*; 'Mr Cotes says that our attitude towards this subject has altered', reported the *Telegraph*, 'and he hopes to persuade the Lord Chamberlain to change his mind'.[41] Cotes was perhaps rather closer to the zeitgeist than Clarendon and his staff, and his private production was acclaimed by the critics. Under the headline 'CENSOR HOLDS BACK THIS ADULT PLAY', the *Daily Mail* reviewer found himself 'wishing there could be grades of censorship in the theatre, as in the cinema', while the *Evening Standard* asked loudly: 'Why Ban this Problem Play?'. Beverley Baxter was scathing:

> The Lord Chamberlain apparently takes the view that providing sex is presented frivolously, enticingly and suggestively it is in keeping with the nation's conscience. But let sexual abnormality be treated sincerely and depicted as the tragedy that it is then he is moved to righteous wrath.[42]

An agent in Shaftesbury Avenue who hoped to transfer the production to the West End sent extracts from the reviews to the Lord Chamberlain:

> You will have noted that those touching on the subject of the ban were of the unanimous opinion that it should be lifted and on this point I enclose herewith extracts. I also note that you have not seen the play since before the war and I think; i), that public education has advanced quite considerably in matters of this kind ... and ii), that the play, I am confidently advised, is handled with much more delicacy and restraint than when you saw it previously.

Gwatkin attended a private performance the following week; but although his confidential letter to Cotes signalled regret, his response was negative:

> Thank you for letting me visit 'The Children's Hour' last night, which I have not seen since before the War.
> It is a most moving and sincere play, but whilst the present ban remains on such sexual irregularities the Lord Chamberlain will not license the play.
> I am sorry to give you such a disappointing answer.

Cotes said he was 'prepared to make any deletions in the script of the above play, which you may consider necessary for public performance', but in a memorandum to Nugent, Gwatkin noted: 'If one admits this "subject" it could not be treated more delicately: but it will lead to a spate of similar plays and make it difficult to say "no" to the male counterpart which I consider a far greater and more dangerous evil'. His reply to Cotes offered little hope: 'I am afraid the only alteration you could make in this play would be to substitute for the lesbianism some more normal vice—such as dope or men'. He acknowledged: 'I do not pretend that the play would not lose a great deal of its value, or that the re-writing of it on these lines would not present a formidable task'.[43]

Ironically, from today's perspective *The Children's Hour* is more likely to be lamented as a 'deeply homophobic' drama.[44] But in the 1950s, Hellman's play had attracted a lot of attention and champions, some of whom, like Gwatkin, realised that it was a test case which carried significant undertones. In January 1951, Sydney Carroll, an experienced critic and man of the theatre, asked the Lord Chamberlain to receive a deputation 'on behalf of a number of people prominent in the arts and in public affairs' who had concluded 'that there were many and strong reasons for asking you to reconsider your decision'. Carroll assured Clarendon that

> Anything said at such a meeting would, of course, be regarded as strictly confidential and no publicity whatever given to it. It is hoped that in the course of discussion new aspects of the question would be opened up which might enable you to find a way round the difficulties—not at present known to us in detail—standing between the play and the normal course of public performance.

The Lord Chamberlain received the deputation on 2 February. Carroll stressed that it was expressing 'a very large body of representative opinions', which believed *The Children's Hour* should be licensed, and that their aim was 'to discover, if they could, just what particular objections the play presented to the Lord Chamberlain and whether it was possible for them to suggest any way of meeting them'. The deputation again promised that 'If any particular passage of the play was objected to, they would be willing to meet the objections'. It was a multi-pronged attack. Beverley Baxter said the play embodied 'the cleansing power of tragedy' and repeated the familiar accusation 'that if sin was presented in an attractive and enticing form, it has the blessing of the Lord Chamberlain's department'. Another speaker pointed out that since the law identified homosexuality but not lesbianism as a legal offence, 'the Lord Chamberlain had reversed Society's view of these two particular offences against Society's code' by licensing *The Green Bay Tree* and *'Now Barabbas . . .'* while rejecting Hellman's play. Lady Buckmaster, expressing 'the woman's point of view', declared that there was no actual lesbianism in the play and that its theme was 'the appalling unjust prejudice' vented against two women who find themselves living together, a situation currently all too familiar 'owing to the housing shortage and the predominance of women'. Examples were given of other plays, such as *Children in Uniform*, which were 'more pronounced and provocative' and which had been licensed even in the thirties, and it was noted that Hellman's play had been performed in many other countries 'including New York and the dominions'. Someone else questioned whether, if 'this was not the time to air the theme of Lesbianism, could not the same apply to murder, which was the theme of many plays'. The deputation even sought to encourage Clarendon by guaranteeing that if the granting of a licence provoked an outcry against him, he could rely on the active and public support of important individuals and organisations.

Gwatkin told them that the crucial question, on which the Office had previously taken advice, was whether 'the shaking of the red flag of perversion would do good, do nothing or do harm'; and he reported that most of those consulted had been opposed to any reform of policy: 'The few who had thought it could be put on had so hedged it about with suggestions that they were not practicable'. Yet the censorship was uncomfortable and forced onto the defensive. On being told that 'the main objection was the mentioning in public of an unmentionable vice', the deputation pointed out that the vice never actually took place and asked 'what distinction could be drawn between imaginary misdemeanour and actual homosexuality and incest'; Gwatkin was reduced to informing them that 'notice would be needed of that question'. In conclusion, Baxter asserted 'that the theatre had to grow up', and that more credit should be allowed to the public to make their own choices and to discriminate appropriately.

At the end of the meeting, Clarendon announced 'that he could not, of course, give a decision straight away but that the Deputation's opinions would be given very careful consideration'.[45] He then immediately embarked on another major consultation exercise, similar to the one carried out five years earlier. Four days after the meeting, a letter was sent to, among others, the Home Office, the Lord Chancellor, two Harley Street doctors, the Bishop of London and, more surprisingly, Laurence Olivier:

> I am under heavy pressure from some shades of public opinion to lift the ban upon plays in which references to homosexuality and Lesbianism occur.
>
> As you may be aware, reference to these two perversions has hitherto been taboo. I have as few hard-and-fast rules as possible and try to judge every play on its merits but neither I nor my predecessor have allowed these subjects. The main reason given for lifting the ban is that the general public is much more outspoken and broad minded than it was and that to ventilate vice and its tragedies would be to the general social advantage. Further, that the theatre is the mirror of the age and that any fettering of modern playwrights is a bad thing.

> I am, however, advised from other quarters that the ban on this type of play should be retained, the argument being that the subject would be very distasteful and embarrassing in mixed company of all ages and also that the introduction in plays of these new vices might start an unfortunate train of thought in the previously innocent.[46]

He promised that if a change were made he would ensure 'that the subject is not treated with levity in stage plays', but reminded them that he had no such control over music-hall artistes, 'who might tend to give the subject distasteful notoriety'. He added:

> Moreover, if these subjects were allowed, they would open up a new field for playwrights and a considerable number of plays of this type might be expected. This will make my already difficult task harder because I shall have to differentiate between those plays that treat the matter with sincerity and those that are written for sensationalism. But this is my problem and should not affect the principle of the matter.

He concluded by admitting that there was 'a certain urgency about the matter, as a play on the subject of Lesbianism is under immediate decision'.

The response of the Bishop of London, as president of the Public Morality Council, was entirely predictable: 'I certainly hope that you will not yield to the pressure that is being brought to bear upon you. I cannot see that the subjects you mention are suitable for public discussion before mixed audiences containing members of many different ages'. Another clergyman, the Reverend Michael Hollins, took a similar line:

> Living as I do in the middle of the London Theatre land, one might say of London's vice as well, I come into contact with many of the things which are going on. Frankly, the moral standard could not be very much lower! Both men and women 'pick-ups' are 'two-a-penny' (only figuratively, as I understand their charges are more exorbitant), and organized brothels pretty frequent in some streets.
>
> My answer must be that I would deplore this step, as in my opinion inevitably leading to further loss of moral standards. And I would back that argument by saying that as far as I can see, the 'ventilation' of the sex question in general in recent years does not appear to have had a very cleansing effect upon our lives or upon our morals. As you know discipline is a most essential thing in our lives, military or civilian. I would be inclined to think that if these two subjects became common sources of jokes, stories and wireless programmes, as they will do once they come into the theatre, the effect will be definitely lowering.

William Moody, a Harley Street psychiatrist, argued that

> repression is normal and healthy, (it is the power by which our minds keep our unruly animal drives out of consciousness) and that in our publications, as in our private lives, we have a certain control over our

cruder impulses. As a social individual I feel that we should strive towards
beauty and health rather than towards the ugly and pathological.

He also undertook some unofficial research among friends and colleagues:

> I discussed the matter with a psychologist of the modern school, who said
> that he thought that all aspects of human thought were better brought to
> the surface, because thus they became more healthy and lost their
> unpleasant flavour. This is, of course, the attitude of the analysts who are
> often, I fear, not very normal people.
>
> I got the opinion of an extremely cultured and intelligent young
> woman of twenty-two, who works as a secretary and who has some
> experience of dramatic work. Her feeling was that, if these matters were
> portrayed, they would attract audiences of perhaps rather an abnormal type
> for a while, but this interest would fade.
>
> I have tried to get the opinion of some of the people working at the
> hospital, but my impression was that they had not thought very much
> about it, because they take it for granted that matters of this kind are best
> left alone because they have such an abnormal flavour.

And Moody considered the question in relation to his own medical
experience:

> From my own experience of patients, and I have seen a number of people
> who are abnormal sexually; I have gained the impression that quite a
> number are seeking for justification of their abnormality and they could
> quite well get this from a play, they already get it from books; a large
> number detest the whole thing and would hate to have it paraded. The
> average person would far rather discuss such matters in private if
> necessary, otherwise leave them alone.

Game said he was opposed in principle to 'rigid taboos', since 'in the end
as tastes change they generally have to be broken'; he cited 'VD in *Ghosts*,
perverts in *'Now Barabbas . . .'* and now God in the Festival of Britain'. But
he came down strongly against any relaxation of the policy in relation to
women:

> I do not consider that the moment, or the necessity, has yet come for
> advertising Lesbianism to the general public. For that is what the licensing
> of *Children's Hour* entails, and the Theatre with its emotional atmosphere is
> hardly the best forum from which to draw attention to unsavoury sexual
> practices.

He was dismissive of the praise which some had heaped on Hellman's play:

> It is absurd to pretend, as some of the play's supporters do, that it is an
> important play and a serious work of art . . . There is no real necessity for a
> Lesbianism theme except for its commercial value as a bait to attract
> audiences into the theatre . . . The play is a sensational rather than an

exceptionally good one, and it would never have received particular notice if it were not for the perversion theme—of that I am absolutely certain.

But it was the threat of establishing a precedent on which he particularly dwelled:

> If *Children's Hour* receives a licence, it will not be easy to refuse to licence [sic] other plays about Lesbianism, and there are a number lying in authors' cupboards that may well see the light of day again—we had quite a shower of such plays in the early thirties.
>   . . . there is a tendency, I think, for our Office to pay too much attention to the views of the Metropolitan intelligentsia, which are not in fact very widely representative. The Lord Chamberlain has to take a more comprehensive view.

Some of the 'experts' contacted thought that perhaps the time had come for the Lord Chamberlain to abandon his rigid position. Peter Fleming argued that 'the more unpleasant the truth, the greater are the evils that may arise from its suppression', and doubted whether the theatre would really have an adverse effect on audiences—though he was far from advocating complete freedom for playwrights. Strategically, though, he thought it would strengthen the censorship to loosen its position:

> Films about gangsters may help to increase the numbers (and to improve the technique) of juvenile delinquents, but licences would presumably continue to be withheld from plays which glorified the pervert and I doubt whether sincere plays on the subject would make perverts out of people who were not already abnormal. It would, I am afraid, shock and embarrass some people; but plays on more ordinary subjects, like war and marital infidelity, are already liable to do this . . . I also think (though this does not come into the question and has not affected my answer) that any decision to perpetuate or prolong what is after all an arbitrary embargo gives critics of the present system of censorship a stick to beat it with

The Labour Home Secretary, James Chuter-Ede, also gave half-hearted backing to a change in policy:

> I am inclined to think that at the present state of public opinion it is no longer necessary to have a hard-and-fast rule that in no circumstances should a play dealing with or mentioning these perversions be licensed. Much depends on the way in which the subject is treated and I think a distinction might well be drawn between a play containing casual and inoffensive references to perversion and a play devoted wholly or mainly to this subject. The ideal is no doubt to consider each play on its merits, but I realise how difficult this would be and, if you do not consider it practicable, I think you would be right to take a stricter view of plays dealing with perversions than of those dealing with normal sexual activity.

You could justify this course on the ground that there are still happily few people for whom the former represent a serious personal problem.

The Conservative MP, Basil Assheton, expressed dislike for 'hard-and-fast rules in such a matter' and thought that plays which treated the subject 'unsensationally' might be allowed. Basil Henriques, a well-known juvenile magistrate and leading activist in the Boys' Club movement, favoured simpler criteria:

> I think I would like to make a distinction between homo-sexuality among men, and Lesbianism. There are, in my opinion, comparatively few men or young people, who know about Lesbianism at all, or even of its existence, and to show plays of any kind which depict this form of sexual expression among women would be putting fresh and undesirable ideas into the heads of men and boys which might have disastrous effect.
>
> With regard to homo-sexuality among males I consider that this form of sexual perversion is well known and talked about by both men and women, boys and girls, and therefore any play depicting it would not be putting fresh ideas into people's heads.

It is not at all clear what 'disastrous effect' he had in mind as likely to arise from informing, not women, but boys and men about the existence of lesbianism. In some respects, Henriques adopted a liberal position, pointing out that 'Homo-sexuality among <u>adult</u> males is not a criminal offence in a large number of countries', and even that 'many people today are advocating that it should not be considered a crime among willing parties'. He suggested that 'Plays presenting that kind of problem cannot, I think, do great harm, but probably good on account of the blackmail which goes so often with it'. Yet he was unable to avoid the assumptions of his time:

> I think however, that it would be undesirable to show any plays which were not purposeful; by which I mean that it would be bad to show homo-sexuality as a form of relationship which is not frowned upon, or which is accepted as more or less normal . . .
>
> Anything that shows the fearful effects of turning a more or less normal boy in his bi-sexual stage of development into a homo-sexual, can only be helpful and good . . .
>
> On the other hand, plays which accept homo-sexuality as a normal relationship, would be offensive to most people.

Henriques's wife, Rose, who worked with her husband and was committed to similar causes, also argued that 'the deciding factor should be the sincerity of purpose with which the author has set to work and not the actual fact as to whether homosexuality and Lesbianism are mentioned'; but there were certain taboos on which she insisted: 'I think that under no circumstances should acts of perversion take place on the stage and that even if a scene might lead the audience to surmise that such practices would take place, the preceding scene should not contain actual physical contact'. She also drew the same distinction as her husband had made, though it was the effect on girls and women rather than on men that concerned her:

> I think that plays about Lesbianism are more likely to instruct girls and young women who knew nothing of it than are homosexual plays in the case of young men. I have dealt with adolescent girls and young women for thirty five years and the proportion who were very knowledgeable on the subject of Lesbianism was extremely small . . . I remember that when *The Well of Loneliness* was published, it created a certain amount of excitement amongst a few of the girls between eighteen and twenty one in the factories and workshops, but the great majority did not bother about it. I therefore think that greater care should be taken in assessing the general value of a play in which Lesbianism figures.

Another recipient of Clarendon's letter was Kenneth Walker. Walker was one of the more broad-minded and progressive British authorities on male sexuality—a subject on which he had already published widely—and he saw himself as a disciple of Havelock Ellis and Ouspensky. The opening page of his *Sex and a Changing Civilisation* defined 'immorality' simply as 'that which is "contrary to custom"', and elsewhere he followed Ellis in substituting the term 'deviation' for 'perversion', because the latter was an 'antiquated and mischievous method of looking at sexual anomalies' which embodied a moral judgement and constructed it as a sin. Walker cited both Egypt and Greece as cultures which had treated homosexuality with reverence, and asserted that it was most frequently found today amongst 'people whose culture and intelligence raise them above the ordinary level'. He discussed whether it should be considered 'a natural phenomenon', daring to admit that it would be much more visible 'were the private desires and lives of many distinguished people today fully known'. Such people 'hide it from the world' and, being 'possessed of high ideals', were able to 'find an outlet for the urge which has been forbidden sexual expression in art, music, literature or social welfare'. Again following Ellis, he claimed that 'the frontiers of sex are often uncertain', and that there were intermediate stages between a complete male and a complete female. In considering recent medical attempts to 'cure' homosexuality by injections, by psychological hypnosis, or by the surgical grafting of testicular tissue, he declared that he had witnessed no evidence of success. But even Walker could only go so far in challenging the climate, and since he defined as abnormal any sexual activity which had no procreative potential, it followed that 'Homosexuality, therefore, cannot be deemed normal since by its very nature it has no connection with the normal function of sex'. Even while questioning whether it was right to intervene and try to alter the 'condition' of homosexuality, he described it as 'an aberration' and 'an evil', and warned that 'tolerance must not be made synonymous with licence'.[47]

Walker's reply to Clarendon's request for advice reflected some of his thinking:

> I find it impossible to answer your letter without first stating my attitude to the whole problem of homosexuality. By doing so you will understand my justification for my answer. First, I cannot accept the idea that homosexuality is a vice, if by vice is meant a deliberate choice of evil rather than good. The real homosexual is not responsible for the fact that his sexuality has developed along wrong lines. He is the victim of circumstances . . . I am bitterly opposed to the law's so-called remedy for homosexual practices . . . It is as out of keeping with modern knowledge as would be a revival of trials for witchcraft.

Yet he was wary of advocating a change in theatrical policy: 'what should be allowed or not allowed on the modern stage is an entirely different question'; while theatre might be a mirror of contemporary life, Walker said he could 'see no reason why this mirror should have to reflect the more pathological side of humanity'. He doubted—and not without reason— whether the world of entertainment would be capable of avoiding the temptation to trivialise and mock:

> If a serious play were to be written around the subject of the unfortunate homosexual and around the difficulties he encounters in adjusting himself to life, such a play might well be sanctioned. But . . . the difficulties of the unfortunate homosexual or Lesbian are far more likely to be treated pornographically, or as a naughty joke. I do not suggest for one moment that a play about homosexuality will have the power to corrupt a normally constituted youth, but I regard it as a subject more suited to a book than a play.[48]

Once again, Clarendon decided to leave the official policy unaltered. He explained his decision to Carroll:

> I am sorry for the lapse of time since you came to see me but not only have I been considering the problem very carefully myself but I have taken an opportunity of getting the opinion of a number of people who represent a wide cross-section of the theatre-going public. It may be of interest here to tell you that shortly after the end of the war, in view of the upheavals and readjustments which it had caused, I wished to find out then, as far as I could, the public reaction to plays about perversion: I was advised, in general terms, by my advisory committee and others to continue the ban which had been in force. Those whom I have consulted just recently were not the same as those I wrote to before, although they too were wise people in varied positions and of various ages . . . Therefore, together with the important point of view which your deputation represented, I now have many additional opinions. Now, I know that the public decision is

mine and mine alone, but I would ask you to believe that I am very conscious of the difficulties of my office and I would agree with my critics, or rather with the critics of the censorship of plays, that if the power was exercised by myself in isolation, it could well be intolerable, or should I say to you, even more intolerable than it is at the moment. Therefore, as you will perhaps see, I try my best to keep in touch with contemporary thought of all shades to ensure that the decisions which I make are those which are acceptable to the majority . . .

. . . I put the points in favour and against as judicially and impartially as I could. Of the answers I received most were unequivocally 'no', the remainder were in favour, in varying modified forms, none of which I am legally permitted to implement. I cannot, as does the Film censorship, give a licence for adults only: I cannot, mercifully, license a play to one producer, to certain artistes or to special theatres: I cannot limit my licence to specified areas. I cannot control lewd allusions on the Music Hall stage, nightclubs, etc.

You will readily understand that whilst a play well produced and acted to a broadminded London audience can be one thing, it can be quite another in the hands of a second-rate touring company in the less sophisticated north.

In view, therefore, of these reasons, I am afraid that the ban on *The Children's Hour* and similar plays must still remain.[49]

In 1952, Nugent's 'confidential' reply to a senior lecturer in law at Manchester University, who was researching various forms of licensing activity in Great Britain, summed up the Office's current position on 'Unnatural Vice', which it would carry into the start of the new Elizabethan era.

After taking the most experienced general, medical, and psychological advice open to him on two separate occasions within recent years, the Lord Chamberlain is satisfied that at present more harm than good would result from the presentation of plays dealing with Pederasty and Lesbianism, and he refuses to pass such themes.[50]

It was surely not chance that he avoided the term 'homosexuality', for a distinction had certainly been established in the Office between censorship of male and female examples of same-sex attraction. Although the Lord Chamberlain's policy may have recently hardened again, it was certainly not set in stone. And to suggest that homosexuality had been entirely absent from the post-war stage would be a long way from the truth. If the taboo was losing its power elsewhere, then the stage was bound to follow.

In the same year, Gwatkin contacted the British Board of Film Censors after watching 'a film involving a theme of lesbianism' which had been approved, querying what their attitude would be to a possible film based on Hellman's play. 'I envy you your "x"', he wrote.[51] No such demarcations were available for St James's Palace.

CHAPTER ELEVEN

'The Crazy but Satisfactory Ethics of the English'

> The Lord Chamberlain's office would not dream of imposing any
> restriction on a play because it was political. That factor would not
> come into the purview of that Office.
>
> (K. Lindsay, MP, March 1949)[1]

During the 1949 parliamentary debate on Smith's repeal bill, some MPs
expressed concern that since it was the duty of the Lord Chamberlain to
prevent public performances of any play he deemed likely to upset a
friendly foreign state, it followed that 'it would be possible under the rules
of the present censorship to have pro-Communist plays in this country but
not anti-Communist plays'. Several speakers, including Major Legge-
Bourke, were adamant that political propaganda must be kept out of the
theatre in order to protect the public:

> I believe that if we take away censorship altogether there is a great danger
> that we shall inject into the theatre a political antagonism which does not
> exist at the moment, and I hope never will.
>
> I think there is a great danger that we may have people with violent
> opinions making sure that certain plays get produced. They may be able to
> arrange it with the manager who may be of the same political feeling. As
> soon as that happens we shall have exactly the same thing happening from
> the opposite point of view. Then the theatre will be a chamber where the
> most violent political dramas are put on.

More specifically, he insisted that 'It is undesirable that we should have a
wave of Communist productions', followed by 'a wave of productions
deliberately directed against Communism'; and he maintained that the
country had been saved from such a state of affairs because the Lord
Chamberlain exercised his powers so wisely.[2]

For the most part, the censorship could afford to remain fairly relaxed
about post-war propaganda plays. In the middle of the argument with
Blair-Fish over the Chesterfield line in *Genius Limited* in 1945, a much
more explicitly political play by the same author was submitted. *Blimpton*

Won't Budge centred on a character who gives up his job and 'goes off to London to educate himself for the Class War'. Game thought that 'on the whole the political views are stated with fairness', and that even though the playwright 'seems to show a leaning towards revolutionary views, I don't think one could say the play is definitely subversive'. While remaining 'a bit uneasy', the Reader felt that banning the play would have the effect of advertising the 'extremist views' of the author; moreover, he speculated that it was likely to push him into proceeding with his threat to publish the correspondence over *Genius Limited*, with perhaps embarrassing consequences for the Office. Fortunately, Nugent agreed that the new play was not dangerous: 'You can hear all the Communist's arguments any Sunday afternoon in Hyde Park', he commented; 'Indeed it seems to me quite good Tory propaganda!'.[3]

Similarly, in the early days of the war, the Office had refused to license the final act of Sean O'Casey's pro-Communist play *The Star Turns Red*. By 1946, when Unity Theatre resubmitted the play, its politics were still anathema, but no longer considered as dangerous:

> Communist propagandists should grow up. This jejune mixture of realism and bad blank verse can appeal to none but adolescent intellectuals. Now, however, that the war is over, I do not feel that the pronounced Communism of this inferior piece of work will have a greater effect on the public than any other Unity theatre production already licensed.[4]

Nor did they object to *The Gorbals Story*,* an everyday picture of life in a city slum, staged by Glasgow Unity in the summer of 1946, and greeted with acclaim. When the company brought the play to London's Garrick Theatre in 1948, it was reasonably well reviewed by critics, but the Lord Chamberlain also received protests: 'It is none of your affair that it is crude, vulgar, sordid, badly acted and produced', wrote someone from Sussex, 'But it is your affair that it is Communist propaganda'. What really grated for the writer of this letter was that 'The Arts Council are allowing this degrading and badly written play to run—TAX FREE, because of its cultural value', when it was really 'a charming piece of Communist claptrap, which in view of the present Russian inroads on civilisation, made my blood boil'. The 'claptrap' was in fact a criticism of Franco; 'How do these things get past the Censor?', he asked. Hill inspected a performance on behalf of the Lord Chamberlain and described it as 'a social document set in the sordid surroundings of a Glasgow tenement slum, where all the characters seem to have hearts of gold'; and he was confident that there was no chance of its functioning as effective propaganda: 'apart from a few political cracks, the cast confine themselves to moral platitudes'.[5]

---

* Written by Robert McLeish

In 1949, the Office also had little hesitation in licensing—again for Unity Theatre—Ted Willis's *The Jolly George*. 'A Communist propaganda play inspired by the refusal of the London dockers to load arms, destined for use against Russia, in 1920', reported Game. Yet the terms in which he expressed his recommendation for licence may also be revealing:

> Like most communist propaganda it is muddle-headed and emotional, and as far as the author's pacifism is concerned one suspects he is only a pacifist when the Bolsheviks are concerned as the enemy; but I don't see what we can do about it. This is a country of free speech, and to try and suppress it, only makes matters worse.[6]

Despite the relatively *laissez faire* attitude adopted by the censorship to such plays, anything which criticised or mocked the royal family would still have been completely unthinkable. Even in relation to the past and Queen Victoria, while some of Housman's plays—which in their obsession with that monarch seem to be closer to sycophancy than to attack—had been allowed since 1937, this did not indicate that playwrights enjoyed anything like carte blanche. In 1944, the Office was informed that the MP E.P. Smith had signalled his intention to ask a question in the House about two recent plays over which he considered the Lord Chamberlain had been unreasonable. Titman described Smith as 'a busybody MP', who had 'evidently been "got at" by a disgruntled author' whose play about a imaginary meeting between Queen Victoria and Abraham Lincoln had recently been turned down:

> There can be no doubt that one of these cases is that of the play *Mr Lincoln Meets a Lady* by Mr Monckton Hoffe, about which he recently wrote to the Home Secretary. He complained that Lord Clarendon had refused to license the play because it involved an impersonation of Queen Victoria and pointed out that Lord Cromer, the previous Lord Chamberlain, had licensed *Victoria Regina*. He seems to have been under the impression that Lord Clarendon had gone back on Lord Cromer's policy and would not allow any stage representation of members of the Royal Family. This, however, is not the case. Strictly biographical representations of Queen Victoria have been permitted since 1937, but *Mr Lincoln Meets a Lady* is a fantasy and members of the public might well have thought that the imaginary scenes (many of which approach the realm of absurdity) were authentic episodes . . .[7]

The play was indeed a fantasy, in which Lincoln and Victoria travel through time and meet in the present. At one point, however, Lincoln declares: 'Our reputations are largely bogus. We are dummy figures used for purposes of moral propaganda'. In spite of this, Dearmer saw no reason to intervene: 'The figure of Queen Victoria is, throughout, a blend of duty and dignity', he reported, noting that 'The author ventures no criticism of her character'. Game was more cautious because of the genre in which the Queen had been placed: 'Queen Victoria so far has only been seen on the stage as a central character in biographical drama. It would be something quite novel if she were now to be allowed to star in fantasy!'. Clarendon decided 'to take The King's Pleasure', and the script was sent to Buckingham Palace; a few days later, he was duly informed that the King and Queen were 'strongly of the opinion that the play should not be granted a licence'. This fact, of course, was not made public knowledge and probably not known to Smith: 'The King and Queen who saw the script, did not like it and expressed the hope that it would not be licensed, but this of course should not be made public', emphasised an internal memorandum.[8]

In 1951, Clarendon again wrote to Buckingham Palace about *Birthday Bouquet*,* another play with the same monarch at its centre: 'I have kept a fairly tight hand on plays in which Queen Victoria plays a secondary or incidental part', wrote the Lord Chamberlain, 'and of course, any remarks of a derogatory character have been exorcised from scripts'. The problem with this one, he explained, was that it 'breaks new ground as it is a musical comedy with Queen Victoria and Prince Albert in the lead'. Clarendon described it in quite positive terms as 'a Housman with music, and in places rather charming'. But for Heriot, 'the thought of the young Victoria played as a conventional musical-comedy hoyden, or the Wicked Uncles eating muffins' was 'very distressing', and Clarendon agreed that to allow it would certainly be 'to extend the licence a little more'. The response from Sir Alan Lascelles, the King's private secretary, was unyielding:

> I think this work attempts the impossible. . . . Whatever Victoria and Albert may or may not have been, they were certainly not 'musical-commedy' [sic]—even in 1838. W S Gilbert himself could not have fitted them into that particular frame; to try and do so is as un-natural (and as inartistic) as to try and present the Battle of Waterloo as a ballet, Mr Gladstone as the hero of a Wagnerian Musik-Drama, or the Day of Judgement as a pantomime . . .
>
> Some of the dialogue is nice enough, though almost always out of character—and Housman has already done it much better; the buffooneries of the royal Uncles and the dancing-mistress are rarely funny; and the lyrics recall the Gaiety theatre at its lowest ebb . . .
>
> My view is that it is all rank bad theatre, and consequently dangerously near the ridiculous. Queen Victoria, who many of us can remember, and whose name, in many parts of the Commonwealth, is still the centre of an almost religious legend—Queen Victoria should not be associated with the ridiculous.

---

* Written by Norman Ginsberg and Eric Maschwitz

Helpfully, he added: 'On a matter of canine detail . . . I don't believe that either Cairn terriers or Chow dogs were known in England in 1838'. The theatre was informed 'that Queen Victoria is still too much modern history to be portrayed in a Musical Comedy role', and even when the script was resubmitted in 1954, the Office ruled that it could not be considered for as long as any of Queen Victoria's grandchildren were alive.[9]

In February 1951, the censorship also rejected *My Good Brown*:* 'If we do not allow musical comedies about Victoria and Albert I do not think we should allow comedies that present the Queen as a silly conventionalised "Victorian" and her son, later King Edward VII as a frivolous ass'.[10] A few months later, Clarendon went so far as to establish a general and supposedly absolute principle that 'the presentation of Queen Victoria is not permitted in a fictional role'.[11] Yet in 1952, the Office allowed *The Glorious Days*,† described by Heriot as 'A sentimental musical vehicle for Miss Anna Neagle', in which the actress reprised her well-known film portrayal of Queen Victoria.

> The Victorian scenes are concerned merely with the Queen and the Prince Consort waltzing together . . . the Queen also sings 'Drink to me Only' and later appears as the old Queen presenting the Victoria Cross to a veteran of the Boer war. All of this is, of course, familiar ground to Miss Neagle, who has done exactly the same things in her films about Queen Victoria. Since the Royal items are treated very carefully and since, with the accession of the present Queen, Victoria has slipped back a further generation, I suppose there can be no objection to her first appearance in musical comedy. But I suppose it should be made clear that this does not constitute a precedent and that, for instance, we should be doubtful about licensing the other musical comedy script in which Victoria and Albert sing popular libretti and behave in the coyly insane manner usual in such circumstances.

The Comptroller was a little more cautious about precedent: 'we must dismiss from our minds the fact that Anna Neagle is playing the part and will therefore do it with impeccable taste. We must be prepared for other and less accomplished artistes to take the role'. On balance, however, he agreed that it was safe to license this play, since the device of removing the events from reality by situating them within a dream meant that they were not to be taken as 'real':

> It seems to me that you are not breaking your principle of not allowing Queen Victoria as a fictitious character in a musical comedy. In this play

---

* Written by Robert Kemp
† Written by Harold Purcell and Robert Nesbitt

the 'character' throughout is Carol, and Queen Victoria and the Prince Consort are mere figments of her brain when she is dreaming.[12]

The following year, however, a revue sketch containing 'a devastating parody' of Anna Neagle's impersonation of Victoria was banned. Heriot had recommended it: 'I don't see why we shouldn't permit a caricature of a caricature—the impersonation . . . is of Miss Neagle rather than the Queen'. But he was over-ruled: 'Anything which brings Queen Victoria into ridicule does not come within the permission which can be granted. Although this sketch purports to take off Miss Neagle, in fact it ridicules Queen Victoria & must come out'.[13]

The representation of royalty in amateur spectacle was also restricted. In 1948, a Somerset village sought permission to represent the silver jubilee of the King and Queen in a tableau within a pageant; Nugent informed them that this could not be allowed:

> We well understand that in proposing this scene your villagers have nothing in mind but loyalty and respect for the Royal Family and we are very sorry to have to disappoint them. There are, however, so many . . . factors attendant upon Royal representations that they have had to be generally banned, and I am afraid that your Gymkhana must conform to the rule.

In fact, Ronald Hill, who made it his job to understand the Theatres Act more fully than anyone else, knew that the event almost certainly lay outside the Lord Chamberlain's jurisdiction: 'I have little doubt that we have no right to say this', was his comment on Nugent's letter. But he was more than ready to maintain the bluff by providing disinformation:

> Such representations are obviously unsuitable however, and we ought to stop this one if we can. The villagers aren't very likely to question our authority but if they do we can always approximate between a pageant and a stage play.[14]

Four years later, the Office took a similar line with a gentleman from Sheffield who sought permission for his five- and nine-year-old daughters to attend an event, dressed in costumes similar to those worn by the Queen in the Trooping of the Colour ceremony:

> It is most courteous of you to write to me on the subject of the dress you would like your daughters to wear at gymkhanas in Coronation Year.
> I hope you will not pursue your idea of copying the uniform worn by The Queen at Her Majesty's Birthday Parade, because in fact this is a regular military uniform of sealed pattern, and cannot be worn with propriety except on suitable military occasions, and then only by those of a requisite rank and Corps.[15]

Trivial though examples like these may seem, it is only by recognising how careful and sensitive the censorship was in such cases that we can imagine how impossible it would have been to stage anything remotely critical of British monarchs. At least in its attitude to the monarchy, the censorship had not moved. It was as though the country was unchanged.

In certain other respects, that was clearly not the case. In April 1946, the Home Secretary made a speech warning about the expanding pattern of juvenile delinquency in the country, and suggesting, among other things, that the typical age of girl delinquents had changed from eighteen to fifteen years.[16] One of the most controversial and shocking plays on the London stage that year was *The Pick-Up Girl*, Elsa Shelley's American courtroom drama about a girl who by the age of fifteen has already had an abortion, and has contracted syphilis from a forty-seven-year-old man.[17] Elizabeth has become trapped in a world of crime and prostitution, and despite its American context, the play struck a disturbing chord for British audiences, who feared that changing social values were destroying the moral order. The programme included an extract from a recent statement by the Home Secretary in which he blamed inadequate parenting for teenage crime and immorality, and it was where the play located the blame for the girl's harrowing experiences that was most calculated to jolt audiences. At one point the judge describes Elizabeth as 'typical of hundreds of other juvenile delinquents', and Peter, the faithful young man who still loves her, makes a heartfelt interruption:

> I'm studying languages. I know what delinquent means! A delinquent is one who—who fails to perform a duty . . . Well, then your Honour, why don't you call the mothers and fathers delinquents? Or the teachers and the ministers?.. and even the law-makers! It's <u>adult</u> delinquency . . . Why does everyone call it 'juvenile delinquency' now? And why does everyone say it's all because of the war?

Later, the judge pins the blame specifically on Elizabeth's mother:

> You've neglected your daughter. You're largely responsible for her present plight . . . No child is born bad. No child is <u>born</u> a thief or a liar or a sex delinquent . . . but children learn quickly good <u>or</u> evil. Therefore they must be taught the right things . . . they must be <u>taught</u> the virtues!

But when the mother breaks down, the judge broadens his accusations in a way reminiscent of Priestley's *An Inspector Calls*:

> No, it's not your fault alone, it's the fault of all of us . . . it's our indifference, our greediness that's at fault. We didn't realise that the <u>real</u> natural wealth of the world is in children . . . there is the seed of divine goodness in every child. But we adults must cherish that seed, and we

must nourish it! . . . If we neglect it, a young life is ruined, and we've no-one to blame but ourselves.[18]

The programme also quoted a justice of the peace who advised that the production 'should be seen by everyone interested in social problems'. He warned that there were many similar cases now coming before British juvenile courts, and lauded the play's 'deep seeing and relentless analysis'.[19] One of many positive newspaper reviews even identified *The Pick-Up Girl* as the modern equivalent of Ibsen's *Ghosts* and Brieux's *Damaged Goods*, crediting it with 'the quality of Zola in the relentless inevitability with which the play moves to its tragic climax'.

The same review also praised the 'courage and wisdom' of the Lord Chamberlain in licensing the play.[20] But thereby hung a tale. Game's original report had indeed responded positively to it:

> The play is certainly not one, as Lord Cromer would say, for the squeamish. But as it was decided in the case of *Patricia's Seven Houses* recently that the squeamish were not to be over-considered, I think it would be highly illogical to pass that play, which was after all only a sensational melodrama, and to ban this one, which is aesthetically of much greater worth and sociologically much more profound.
>
> Censoring becomes impossible unless one at least tries to act on rational lines, no easy matter in itself, but if you allow sociologically superficial drama about the adult white-slave traffic and cheap shockers about concupiscent curates corrupting little girls, then it would seem utterly illogical to ban a play of greater merit, which deals more profoundly with much the same sort of unsavoury subject.

The Reader concluded:

> the play cannot do anybody harm, and if it brings home to some people the supreme importance of parental responsibility, it may do some good; and judging by what happened during the war years the lesson is badly needed.

Gwatkin concurred: 'this may be rather strong meat but it is sincere and if we pass propaganda plays on V.D. we should be thought inconsistent if we put a stopper onto this play which deals with another social evil, which is a "natural" one'. So did Lord Clarendon:

> The theme of this play is certainly unsavoury and will probably make the squeamish squirm! But as it is sincere and brings home the great importance of parental responsibility it can receive a licence subject to all the cuts recommended.[21]

However, they all agreed it was necessary to make a series of cuts, including the references to abortion. These changes were resisted by the management, and the play was performed unlicensed at the New Lindsey Theatre Club in Notting Hill Gate. Then it was reported in the press that, on the personal recommendation of one of the royal ladies-in-waiting, Queen Mary had been to watch the private and uncut production on the eve of her seventy-ninth birthday, accompanied by the Princess Royal and Princess Alice.[22] When the Home Secretary also gave the play his tacit support by attending a performance, the Lord Chamberlain had little choice other than to back down as quickly and quietly as possible, and issue a licence.

The Pick-Up Girl caught the zeitgeist. The *Daily Mail* said it was 'forthright and forcible', the *Sunday Express* that it 'succeeded magnificently' and was 'THE BEST REALISTIC PLAY NOW TO BE SEEN', and the *Daily Telegraph* recorded that it was 'received with rapturous applause at the Prince of Wales Theatre', to which it transferred after its initial club run. One reviewer described it as a 'documentary' and reported that in watching it 'we really feel that we have strayed into a New York juvenile court'. *The Times* also referred to the play's 'unrelentingly matter-of-fact realism', and the *Picture Post* called it 'a raw and bleeding slice of life slapped bodily onto the stage'. Indeed, this last review questioned whether the performance qualified as fiction or theatre, and insisted on its absolute power and significance: 'How Elizabeth got this way is partly Elizabeth's story and partly the world's, or America's, or the twentieth century's, or womankind's . . . it is really the world which is on trial in this tortured microcosm'.[23] No wonder, then, that in his parliamentary speech in support of the repeal of the Theatres Act, Michael Foot should cite what had happened over *The Pick-Up Girl* as a demonstration of the absurdity and abusive power of the censorship:

> It was only an accident that a Lady-in-Waiting was present at a private showing of the play and informed Queen Mary that she ought to see it. Queen Mary did see it and said it was a wonderful play. Then the Lord Chamberlain also commended the play. Is this the protection and the bulwark of liberty for the theatre and the author?[24]

Elsa Shelley's play was one of a whole number of post-war dramas to worry the censors, with their exposure of a young and often violent generation which seemed to mock the morality and the values of their elders. 'Standards of decorum [have] become almost non-existant [sic] in our degenerate age', lamented Game,[*][25] and in March 1948 he described Richard Pollock's *Symphony in Violence* as a 'Study of the modern gangster, the youthful immoral savage, the product of two world wars, loss of faith,

---

* He was commenting in relation to *Away From it All*, by Val Gielgud

and of our many social disorders'. But however much they disapproved of the modern world, the censors could not prevent the theatre from reflecting it—even if they had wanted to:

> one might moralise about the degeneracy of taste, which makes an author write about such people and the public take a sadistic pleasure in witnessing their acts, but every age has its horror plays and Mr Pollock is right . . . to go to contemporary life for his facts. With such characters . . . it is no use expecting them to talk pretty all the time and they don't.[26]

The following month, the censorship licensed Ted Willis's *No Trees in the Street*, 'a drama of the "Brighton Rock" type' about an eighteen-year-old rebel against society who becomes involved in violent crime and is finally shot dead. When the production reached the midlands, the Chief Inspector and five justices of the peace complained that it was 'one of the worst types of entertainment played upon any stage in Birmingham', but there was no realistic likelihood of persuading the Lord Chamberlain to reconsider his decision.[27] Similarly, Oldham police complained about *Cosh Boy*,* which again dramatised how a young hooligan becomes involved in crime. Such plays were often fiercely moralistic, and—ostensibly at least—were far from championing their anti-heroes. *Cosh Boy*, for example, indicated that Roy's problem (and, by implication, that of his generation) was the post-war absence of fathers to control them in childhood, and Heriot considered it 'A sound tract for the times'. Roy backs down only when he is confronted by a stepfather who is tough enough to call his bluff and demonstrate that he is prepared to administer physical chastisement to control him: 'The moral seems to me that if boys are beaten by their parents they won't become menaces to society', said the Reader; 'The language is pretty strong in places, but I believe this to be a serious attempt to present a solution to the problems of the juvenile delinquent'. Oldham police were informed that most of the language and action was 'necessary for the authenticity of a play which has some claims to be a serious study of what is rather euphemistically called "juvenile delinquency"'.[28]

Some plays undoubtedly trod a thin line between moral education and exploitation, and could have been accused of rather cynically tacking message onto narratives which gratuitously revelled in the criminal and vice-ridden underworld they painted. Lorraine Tier's *Reefer Girl*,† subtitled

---

* Written by Bruce Walker
† The author's name listed in the Lord Chamberlain's records is Ivor Burgoyne. Possibly Lorraine Tier was an assumed name—possibly even an assumed gender?

'The True Story of a Marijuana Addict', was submitted in the summer of 1952, and reported on, with perhaps a dash of sacrcasm, by Heriot:

> Another vice play written, I have no doubt, by a lady with high moral principles. Here is the usual mixture: the den of vice run by the harridan, whose son, a sexual maniac, is guilty of the murder for which Duke, another member of the gang, is serving a ten year sentence. The gang traps innocent young people and feeds them with 'reefers' (marijuana cigarettes) until they are addicts. One boy, who knows the real facts of the murder, is kept under control by injections of cocaine.

The manager was insistent that the play had 'great value as a warning to teen-agers', and although some cuts were imposed it was licensed without much difficulty. The play declared its moral correctness in a rather heavy-handed way right at the start, opening with the voice of one of the characters heard through a microphone before the curtain rises: 'My name is Lorraine Tier, and this is my true confession. In the hope that it will succeed in warning young girls against the horrors resulting from the smoking of marijuana, I offer my story to the public'.[29] Yet much of the play was so explicit in its depiction of vice that one might question whether the opening was more than a fairly crude attempt to pre-empt objections.

On the international front, in the aftermath of the Second World War, the need for political sensitivity was paramount. In January 1946, *Frieda*, written by a young actor-dramatist, Ronald Millar, led to considerable agonising in diplomatic circles. The play centred on a British RAF officer who escapes to Poland from a prisoner of war camp, with the help of a German girl whom he intends to marry; the wedding is subsequently cancelled when he discovers, at the last minute, that she has a brother who is 'outwardly a Polish volunteer, but inwardly a dyed-in-the-wool Nazi', and who, as a guard at a concentration camp, has been involved in committing atrocities.[30] According to reviewers, the important question raised by the play was 'How are the English to treat the Germans from now on?'.[31] Or as J.C. Trewin put in the *Observer*:

> Frieda, the German nurse who helps a British airman to escape . . . stands for the 'good Germans' as her brother for the malign spirit of the Nazis. But should an Englishman marry her? How must her race be treated? Are we—in Coward's phrase—to be beastly to the Germans, are we to be icily polite, or are we to take them back to the community?[32]

Millar's play was clearly picking up on a real and very contemporary issue. One national newspaper, for example, ran a typical news story under the headline 'Fraulein Brides', suggesting that the numbers of British soldiers falling in love with German women was causing serious difficulties:

> On the whole the Germans hate us—a hatred that burns white hot, and most of the romances are of the Montagu and Capulet kind.
>
> A girl who falls in love with an allied soldier can expect plenty of opposition from her relatives. On the other hand there are Security Officers in both the British and U.S. zones who carefully screen any marriage applications.
>
> If a girl has any Nazi background, has been a member of any of the Hitler societies, the marriage is banned. There is no appeal.[33]

Frieda was licensed without difficulty, and it was not the Anglo-German elements which caused protests but the references to Poland. The War Office Liaison Staff (Poles) wrote to the Home Office to complain that 'The whole play gives the impression that among Polish soldiers recruited from the German army (and as you know a considerable number were recruited in this way) are many Nazis'. The chief Polish press officer visited the theatre in Edinburgh where the play was to be performed, and made unsuccessful attempts to persuade the manager and author to add lines indicating that the brother was one of a very small number of Poles to have supported the Nazis. The War Office told the Home Office that

> In view of the difficulties we have already experienced in keeping public opinion favourably disposed towards Poles in the UK, and even more important in view of the increasingly large number of Poles likely to come to the UK very soon, it would seem most undesirable that this play should continue in its present form.

After an extensive provincial tour, the production was about to reach London, and that aroused particular anxiety:

> The Polish Armed Forces here are not too popular as it is, it is likely that a great many more may have to be brought here in the near future . . . and a play running in London which suggests that there are many Nazis among them will not be helpful.

The Lord Chamberlain's Office, however, recommended that the safest thing was to keep a low profile:

> Experience has shown that a good deal of publicity is caused by last minute alterations of this nature—— publicity which might well have been avoided altogether.
>
> Particularly . . . where the alterations required are in a script which has been played for some time and in a play which could be misconstrued into having some political bias.
>
> I suggest that the matter be left as it stands, but if the Poles take violent exception, and the wrong type of publicity is already being given, then necessary alterations can be examined.[34]

Another play which stimulated concern in 1947 and 1948 was *Little Holiday*,* which, in Game's words, 'Traces the fortune of a family of Roumanian Jews from the moment when, persuaded by the propaganda of the organisers of illegal immigration, they decide to go to Palestine, until their arrival ten weeks later at Famagusta, in Cyprus'.[35] Set in 1946, the play opens in an impoverished and starving household, already devastated by the Nazis, and where the survivors are reduced to begging unsuccessfully for work: 'In Rumania today there is work only for settled people. We don't buy <u>driftwood</u> . . . That's what he called us. <u>Driftwood</u> . . . When all we ask is a chance to stop drifting'. The promise of free transportation to Palestine seems to be the answer to their dreams, but subsequent scenes set in a succession of refugee camps, and in appalling conditions on board a ship which is refused permission to land, show how this turns into a nightmare. Contrasting views of who is to blame for the crisis are expressed:

> IZAK: The English! The most intransigent people in Europe . . . I think they can't see what's good for them. Look at the advantage to England in having a quiet, orderly, prosperous Palestine; yet as a result of their misrule, it's practically in a state of civil war.
> IRGA: . . . In this book it says that the English are doing all they can to settle Jews on the land in Palestine.
> IZAK: A few! A handful! A mere fifteen hundred a month . . . it's a drop in the ocean.

Izak believes that the Americans have 'made a pact with the Arabs to keep us out of our rightful place so that they can share the oil', and allies himself with the other side:

> IZAK: The Communists are realists. First you win your country—by realism, and struggle; then you develop it—by realism and hard work; then you settle down to live quietly in it—by idealism if you like, because by then the ideal will have become real . . . Nothing worth having was ever got without a struggle . . . I want to be the first of a long, long line of happy, healthy, free Palestinian citizens, owning and farming their own land, on, and on, until the end of the world . . . if we keep our eyes fixed on that we can't go wrong. The Faith, the Race, the Nation, and the Land, to become one glorious whole.

Izak's aims are clear: 'to build up a Jewish State which will be the wonder and admiration of the world . . . then, when we're strong enough, we must overthrow the British rule and clear them out of the country'. When Irga says she thinks the English will leave of their own accord, he replies:

---

* Written by E.G. Cousins

> My dear Irga, what a wrong conception you have of the English character! Haven't you ever listened to the radio? The English live by exploiting weaker nations. As soon as the weaker nations are strong enough, they turn the English out. It's happened all over the world! America, Ireland, China, Egypt—now it's happening in India. It will be our turn next.

A scene in which British naval forces are seen invading the ship to prevent it landing in Palestine is juxtaposed with others set in the British Parliament. In one of these, a Tory MP denounces the government for failing to prevent or diminish 'the flow of illegal immigration from Europe into Palestinian waters'.

> I do not say into Palestine, because by great good fortune the zeal and efficiency of the British navy remains unaffected by the degree of zeal and efficiency of the party temporarily in power. The uninvited and unwelcome guests are diverted to the island of Cyprus—where, incidentally, they are equally unwelcome and unwanted by the local populace, and where their unproductive presence has already, in nine months, cost the British taxpayer one million pounds sterling . . . among these illegal immigrants are desperate and unscrupulous characters who go to swell the ranks of thugs and terrorists guilty of the murder of so many of our young men in that distant, barren land.[36]

At a time when the problems faced by Attlee's government in relation to Palestine could hardly have been more serious, this was dangerous stuff. Having inherited a situation in which contradictory promises had been made to Jews and Arabs, and with the problem exacerbated by the post-Nazi exodus from Europe, the conflict in which the British found themselves involved has been described by historians as 'the great exception' to the 'generally untroubled start to the withdrawal from Empire'. Attlee's government was ostensibly committed to supporting an enlargement of the Jewish state, but its own Palestine Committee was concerned that massive Jewish immigration into Palestine would damage British relations with oil-rich Arab states; meanwhile the British Foreign Secretary, Ernest Bevin, pursued a policy which has been characterised as demonstrating 'insensitivity and crassness that verged on anti-Semitism'.[37] Guerrilla warfare broke out between occupying British forces and Jewish terrorist groups, and in July 1946, the blowing up of a hotel in Jersualem led to considerable loss of life and to armed British reprisals.

The events of *Little Holiday* were presumably based partly on the real-life incident in which a ship containing 4,500 Jewish immigrants, the *Exodus*, was indeed turned back by British forces. An author's note on the script insisted:

> This play is strictly factual, being based partly on personal observation and experience and partly on close interrogation of hundreds of British troops,

British and Jewish officials, and Jewish immigrants, in the course of transportation of more than seven thousand illegal Jewish immigrants from Palestine to Cyprus over a period of four and a half months.[38]

It is perhaps surprising that Game was largely positive about the play's politics, finding it 'extremely fair', and noting that 'where it does suggest condemnation it hits the right targets: the European (or Russian?) and American organisers of immigration and the terrorists in Palestine'. He approved of the fact that it drew a contrast between, on one side, 'the appalling conditions of the Immigrant Racket and the inhumanity of those who organise it' and, on the other, 'the humanity and tolerance in face of insane provocation (without making us out to be Angels) of the unfortunate Englishmen who have the misfortune to have to tackle the problem'. But inevitably, there were certain aspects which worried Game: 'these facts may be true', he commented, 'but is it a good thing to advertise them?'. He marked specific lines and speeches about which he was doubtful, but acknowledged that 'cuts in this play will look like an attempt to suppress facts'.[39] One speech, which the producer claimed was an exact copy of advertisements published in the *New York Herald Tribune*, was especially provocative:

> Letter to the Terrorists of Palestine. . . . The Jews of America are for you. You are their champion. You are the grin they wear . . . Every time you blow up a British arsenal, or wreck a British jail, or send a British railroad train sky high, or rob a British bank, or let go with your guns and bombs at the British betrayers and invaders of your homeland, the Jews of America make a little holiday in their hearts.
>
> Not all the Jews, of course. The only time the Jews present a United Front is when they lie piled by millions in the massacre pits.

This speech, admitted Game tellingly, was 'politically undesirable, though true', and the censorship insisted that it was toned down and framed in a way to ensure that it 'pins the sentiment down to a certain section of the American Jews' and did not 'generalise about Americans'. Through discreet and diplomatic discussions with the producer and the manager, the Office also persuaded them to make other amendments and to submit a revised script.[40] We can be sure that any play which had been more critical of the British role would have had real difficulty in securing a licence; *Little Holiday* was careful to absolve from blame, if not the Labour government, then at least the British navy.

As the cycle of terrorist and British army violence in Palestine continued, it became evident that there were still pockets of strong anti-Semitic sentiment in Britain. The kidnapping and hanging of two British soldiers by Jewish terrorists in July 1947 was followed by a weekend of rioting in British cities, directed against shops owned by Jews. Following this, Joan

Littlewood's Theatre Workshop had its first (but not last) serious clash with the Lord Chamberlain over additions they wished to make to Friederich Wolf's *Professor Mamlock*. Wolf's play was a pre-war anti-Nazi play, but as Game observed: 'It now seems intended as a cautionary tale for us'. The new prologue focused on the recent anti-Jewish demonstrations in Manchester, as witnessed by actors in the company; 'This seems a bit provocative', commented Game, 'though, no doubt, a salutary lesson for some hot heads'. He thought the scene could probably be licensed for the planned opening performances in Brighton, which he described as 'neutral territory'; however, it would be 'a little unwise' to perform it in Manchester, and he suggested this possibility should be taken into account:

> It seems worth considering whether we should not find out what these people's plans are about their play, as if they have any idea of carrying the war into the enemy's camp, it might be the duty of the Lord Chamberlain, under the provision of the Theatres Act, to ban the prologue as likely to promote a breach of the piece.

Clarendon questioned whether even Brighton was really 'neutral ground', and thought it 'not a good place to launch the play'. Though it is extremely doubtful whether the Office had any authority to do so, the Lord Chamberlain banned the company from stating within the programme that 'the scene is a representation of actual events witnessed by actors of Theatre Workshop in Manchester', and decreed that 'There must be no mention of Manchester or any other English town'. Meanwhile, Theatre Workshop submitted new material to be played between the prologue and the opening scene, juxtaposing recent statements made by Oswald Mosley with those of Hitler twenty-five years earlier. Game telephoned the company to tell them 'that the new prologue to *Professor Mamlock* which drags in Mosley will not do', but with the press (presumably alerted by Theatre Workshop) 'in full cry', the Office retreated. The script was licensed, though with the warning that 'Should there be any repercussion causing disturbances in the theatre it may be necessary to withdraw the prologue altogether'.[41]

One play to be completely rejected on overt political grounds was *The Baker's Daughter*,* which was refused a licence in 1950. Two years earlier, Attlee's government had found itself involved in an embarrassing and scandalous confrontation, following the controversial marriage of Seretse Khama, the chief-designate of the ruling Bamangwato tribe in the British Protectorate of Bechuanaland, and a white British woman. The mixed-race marriage caused uproar in parts of Southern Africa, especially given the prominent position the couple would occupy, and in 1950 the British

---

* Written by Michael and Peggy Walsh

government effectively tricked Khama into coming to Britain for a meeting and then forbidding him to return to Bechuanaland for five years: 'I was invited to come and now they say I am to be excluded from the territory', Khama was quoted as saying: 'I thought those things were supposed to happen only in Russia'. Khama, who would eventually become the first (and a long-ruling) president of the independent Botswana, also blamed the authorities in South Africa and Southern Rhodesia for putting pressure on Britain to prevent the founding of a mixed race dynasty on their doorsteps. In the British Parliament, Winston Churchill led the attack on the Secretary of State for Commonwealth Relations, and on the Labour government, which had tried to bribe Khama by offering him 'a suitable allowance' for himself and his wife if he would agree to remain in Britain and renounce his claim to the chieftanship. Churchill denounced this 'disreputable transaction', and accused the government of duplicity, while the Liberals called it 'a gross violation of the Declaration of Human Rights'. The British government, meanwhile, announced that as a 'temporary expedient', all power and authority in Bechuanaland would be vested in a district commissioner.[42] Although there was little sympathy in the South African press or government for the marriage itself, the Attlee government's response was described as 'a sad and sorry chapter in the distinguished history of British colonial administration', and there were predictions that the effect of such a 'deplorable blunder' would be 'disastrous on native opinion, which always had a high regard for Britain's traditional standards of justice and fair play'.[43]

The Baker's Daughter focused on the marriage of Rose Henderson, an English woman, and Gbor-Gbor (pronounced Bo-Bo), the chief-designate of the Beruba tribe in Jammatoland. It relied on a superficially fictional narrative and setting, employing imaginary names and invented and sometimes fantastic details. Yet audiences would have recognised instantly that its roots lay firmly in the real-life scandal: 'This, without any disguise, is the story of Seretse Khama's marriage', commented Heriot when the play was submitted in the summer of 1950. Although the play ostensibly focused on a domestic narrative, a fairly crude political context was also emphasised; in one scene, an official from the Department of Commonwealth Relations visits the couple before the wedding to warn them of the government's concerns and opposition to such a marriage. It was not a good play, and Heriot's description of the resolution gives a fair sense of the style and tone of what was essentially a melodrama. Gbor-Gbor has gone to England leaving his wife, Rose, in Jammatoland, where she is visited by her brother with news from England:

> Rose, now pregnant, is snubbed by the white residents and has a violent scene with Bo-Bo's uncle, the Regent, who is made into a grotesque figure

wearing a comic uniform and speaking pidgin-English. Brian suddenly appears. He has thrown up his degree and now tells Rose about the Government's offer of £1000 a year for Bo-Bo and his wife to stay out of Jammatoland. Rose rushes hysterically out into the monsoon (if they have monsoons in Africa, which I doubt) and is nearly killed by a native who mistakes her for a tiger (in spite of the fact that this is Africa). . . . There is a fear that Rose may lose her child. But it is born healthy and Bo-Bo abdicates, returning to England with his wife and child.[44]

The Lord Chamberlain sent the script to the Commonwealth Relations Office, seeking both an opinion and further information in respect of the real case which had inspired the play. After consulting with 'very high authorities indeed', the Commonwealth Relations Office declined to offer any written advice:

We feel that we ought not to attempt to convey to the Lord Chamberlain any recommendation on behalf of His Majesty's Government about the suitability of this play . . . It is entirely for him to judge and we should therefore prefer to refrain from expressing on behalf of the Secretary of State any view . . . Moreover, in respect of a case which has aroused so much public controversy we would ask also to be excused from providing information.

Doubtless aware that any sign of interference on their part would lead to damaging publicity, they insisted that

in replying to the applicant you will make it clear that a decision has been taken solely on the responsibility of the Lord Chamberlain, and that no expression of opinion has been received from any Department of His Majesty's Government.[45]

The issue of whether the play should be licensed did indeed receive press publicity, and the Lord Chamberlain was the recipient of some unpleasantly racist correspondence:

I, for one, most strongly object . . . I think it is a thoroughly disgusting play. This mixture of black and white is all wrong—look what it produces—have you ever known a half-breed who is not a thief, a liar, an adulterer and everything else objectionable. No decently bred native would dream of mixing their races . . . I do hope you will not lend yourself to the wickedness of producing a loathsome play like this.

Whether he was acting entirely on his own initiative and reading between the lines, or whether the government had signalled its views through unofficial channels, is not certain, but Nugent came up with a convenient and relatively bland justification for rejecting *The Baker's Daughter*, on the grounds that it involved 'the invidious representation on the stage of living people without their consent'. The authors subsequently informed the press that they had been advised that the licence depended on their obtaining the personal consent of Khama and his wife, but one suspects that even if they had achieved this, the Lord Chamberlain might have suddenly discovered that they needed the approval of a series of other real-life individuals on whom characters were based.[46]

Even after the onset of the Cold War, the Lord Chamberlain generally sought to avoid any denigration or burlesque of Stalin, or anything which might be seen as a direct attack on the Soviet Union. Was he unsure which way Britain would jump? In 1947, the producers of a revue in Norwich were warned that 'The impersonations of Mr. Herbert Morrison and Stalin are allowed on the understanding that they are straightforward, but not if they are offensive caricatures'.[47] In December 1948, an anti-Stalin story was cut from a show at Boscombe Hippodrome, and references to Molotov, Bevin and Eden were removed from a sketch in Nottingham.[48] In 1950, Heriot was worried by a comic reference* to someone having a pet marmoset called Joe Stalin. 'Do you think that we should ask for this to be altered?', he queried; 'It's not very important but the Slavic sense of humour is so very different from ours'. The theatre was asked to amend the script—'Had the marmoset been a bear it would have been all right'—but the producer insisted: 'The idea was to give the animal the most important name in the world—not to denigrate JS! After all, my own dog is called "'Franco'". After negotiation, the two sides settled for 'a small pet bear'.[49]

In 1949, Heriot reported on a comedy[†] which revolved around someone who imitates, and is presumed to be, the Soviet leader:

> A scion of a noble English family—of the dumb but shrewd kind found only in comedies of this type—inadvertently kidnaps from Russia, and brings back to conceal in his father's ancestral mansion, a man whom everyone, including the audience, imagines to be Stalin . . . After a great deal of amusing building up, the stranger . . . turns out to be an actor from the Moscow Arts Theatre who is normally employed as a 'double' for Stalin. He refuses to leave England, having become converted to cricket and the crazy but satisfactory ethics of the English.

Game was concerned because the audience are not in on the joke and deception:

> till the very end of the play the audience think that an impersonation of Stalin is taking place, instead as we subsequently learn of an impersonation of an impersonation. Unfriendly critics, the Russians for instance, might suggest that this is a case of conforming to the letter of our (unwritten)

---

* In *An Old Man at a Wheel*, by Falkland L. Cary
† *Red Herring*, by Dan Sutherland

rules while breaking the spirit. The Russian Embassy should be asked whether they have any objections to the impersonation, but that is a matter for the F.O. not for us.

The Lord Chamberlain sent the script to the Foreign Office: 'According to custom, I do not allow personal representation of the heads of States but in this case . . . it is only the representation of a representation and I should not require this to be deleted. Moreover, Stalin is not, in fact, head of the State'. He added, perhaps slightly dryly, 'I naturally do not wish to license any play which might in some way disgruntle our late allies'. The Foreign Office raised no objection.[50]

However, the Lord Chamberlain did insist on removing all references implicating Russia in a more seriously intended drama* about an attaché called Gourevitch, who absconds from his national embassy in London and refuses to return home when he is required to do so. The play was made worse—or, at least, more anti-Russian—by the fact that the ambassador himself secretly sympathises with Gourevitch. Although no actual country was identified by name, there was no doubt about what was intended or how it would be interpreted. Before a licence could be granted, the Lord Chamberlain therefore required that 'all references associating the play with Russia' be removed:

> It is obvious that Russia is the Foreign country whose London Embassy is the scene of the play. From a diplomatic point of view this, despite the Cold War seems undesirable.
> So we should, I think, do as we did with anti-Nazi plays, insist on the text being thoroughly ruritanianised. This will entail altering the characters' names to make them other than Slavonic, and substituting fictitious names for clue-words like 'vodka' and 'Lenin'.[51]

Similar stipulations were made in 1952 in relation to *A Muse of Fire*,† a thriller in which 'a young and handsome nuclear physicist', who is concerned about the possibility of his work being put to military purposes, is persuaded by two Soviet agents to offer his knowledge to Russia. 'This is a terribly bad play', wrote Heriot, 'but I think, even though its chances of a long run are remote, that all mention of Russia should be deleted and vague references or the name of an imaginary state substituted'. The disguise was somewhat tokenistic and transparent—the name substituted was the Union of People's Democratic States—but sufficient for the Lord Chamberlain and the British authorities to feel they had a defence against any accusations of endorsing anti-Soviet propaganda.[52]

---

* *The Hungry God*, by J. Pole
† Written by Stanley Hockman

As we have seen, some MPs were concerned that the theatre should not give a voice to pro-Soviet propaganda. But as Britain struggled to accept the changing world order and the fact that it was no longer a superpower, there was not much more enthusiasm in the Office for the coming power of America, or for the playwrights of that upstart nation. Americans were so much less refined: 'Being written in the American taste, the play needs a few cuts' (Game on Tennessee Williams's *The Long Goodbye* in 1949);[53] 'This is the sort of play, increasingly fashionable in the USA, that tries to be transcendental and only succeeds in being sentimental' (Heriot on Arthur Miller's *Death of a Salesman* in the same year).[54] The influence of Hollywood on the crime genre, and of American values on British society, were seen at St James's Palace in predominantly negative terms. Nevertheless, America still needed some protection—not least from itself and its own. In *Myself a Stranger*,* a 'rather sombre play' of 1945 which demonstrated 'the impossibility of successfully mixing racial blood', the Office ruled: 'The Lord Chamberlain does not like the references to lynchings in America . . . These may be true in fact, but reference to them might cause offence to some people'. Clarendon agreed it would be 'bad taste to refer to them'.[55] In 1946, the Office agreed to reverse the decision made in 1927 and issue a licence for Unity Theatre to perform *Chicago*†—especially since there was now a successful film version featuring Ginger Rogers. But remarkably, they specified that the stage setting must be historical and distanced from the present:

> since a revival of this play at this time by Unity might possibly be construed as a rude comment on <u>modern</u> American justice, the licence should be contingent on the play being dressed in the short skirts, low waists, bobbed hair and 'Cloche' hats of the late twenties—as a period piece in fact.[56]

The following year the censorship again intervened over a Glasgow Unity play which included 'a nightmare scene . . . wherein America is displayed not merely as anti-communist but as a potential world aggressor'. *Dragnet for Demos*‡ was licensed only after the specifically American references had been removed.[57] The censors were anxious, too, about *According to Law*,§ a drama about the unjust trial and sentence of a Negro for raping a white woman. 'I doubt whether the author has done justice to American Justice', commented Dearmer, and one of his colleagues added:

---

* Written by Hugh Burden
† Written by Maurine Watkins
‡ Written by Joe McColum
§ Written by Noel Houston

'This is a difficult subject to which Americans generally take exception—as we would at American critique of our Colonial administration'. However, since the play had already won a prize awarded by the American Civic Liberties Union, the censorship decided that this 'absolves us from any problems!'.[58]

In 1952, the Office licensed without objection a play called *The Trouble Makers*:*

> This is an indictment in dramatic form of what the author believes to be the embryonic but growing Fascist tendencies, through intolerance of the expression of any liberal opinions, in the smaller American Universities ... The play appears to be a domestic American affair not calling for English censorship.[59]

And they required only minor amendments to be made to *The Shrike*:†

> At present America is rather worried about the state of her soul, having just discovered the paradox that her intense desire to suppress Communist attacks on the American way of life may well be leading her to ... methods of suppression in themselves little short of the Communist practice.
>
> A few months ago with *The Troublemakers*, we had a dramatic exposition of this phenomenon in an Eastern University. In *The Shrike* the angle dealt with is the ease with which the American lunacy laws can be invoked improperly ... against the individual ... The implications of the denial of liberty are the same ... It is a grim and powerful play that will not, I think, prove acceptable in London ... but it rings most terrifyingly true.[60]

If anything, the Lord Chamberlain's Office seems at this period to have been more willing to license criticism of the United States of America than of its Soviet enemy. When the script for Theatre Workshop's proposed production of Ewan MacColl's *The Travellers* was submitted, Dearmer unhesitatingly described it as 'undoubtedly anti-American'; but, as he dryly added, 'that is, after all, a point of view not entirely limited to the Communists'.[61]

A few years earlier, the Office had approved a play set forty years in the future, in which 'England is a hell with plastics, poverty, atomic energy and state lotteries' and 'civilisation has split into a totalitarian America and a totalitarian Russia', and in which 'Life is controlled by inspectorates'. Someone in the Office sardonically queried: 'Why 1988? Why not 1949?'.[62]

---

* Written by George Bellak
† Written by Joseph Kramer

'Congenial Work'

In an editorial of May 1953, *The Times* drew attention to a recent increase in audiences attending theatres, and to the changing expectations of those audiences.[2] Accustomed as we still are to thinking that 1956 was the turning point when the post-war theatrical world first moved, these comments come as something of a surprise, and offer a different perspective on theatre in the early fifties. Was live performance in the process of being superseded by film and television? Not according to *The Times*, which referred instead to the 'recruits to legitimate theatre-going who, not long since, confined themselves to the cinema'; in other words, people were turning from cinema to theatre—not the other way round. Moreover, the article confidently asserted, these new audiences had 'arrived when British drama, especially in production and acting, is full of vigour and when traditional subjects for domestic treatment have lost hold'. Although we must avoid endowing one article with the weight of absolute truth, what is perhaps most striking now is the writer's emphasis on what these audiences were apparently ready to accept once they were there:

> The people who come up to town in charabancs, and who have been familiar from childhood with the cosmopolitan unrealities of Hollywood, might find some serious stage plays puzzling, shocking, or depressing. But in fact it is often the advanced and the experimental that attracts them.

In contrast to the past, 'the theatre now draws in an audience intent on concentrating on the stage', while contemporary theatre has discovered that 'the general public is . . . unafraid of trying what generations of its obedient servants were convinced it would turn its back on'. In this brave new world of the early fifties, 'Shaw's distinction between plays pleasant and unpleasant has almost ceased to have meaning', and the alteration in audience expectations is a sign of a broader, perhaps a seismic shift:

> What theme, however grave and even grim, can safely be rated as caviar to the general?
> Willingness to be absorbed in sad stories and not to demand a happy ending is a symptom of a wider change in critical values.

It was a development that 'cannot be overlooked as a cultural or social fact'. Furthermore, this 'quickening curiosity in the arts is certainly not confined to the capital'; on the contrary, 'Everywhere the minority of rebels against the unadventurous reflection of life on the stage is slowly growing'.

The Times made no specific mention of possible implications for the censorship which might follow from the changing attitudes it documented, but the question was present in the subtext. The writer noted that fifty years earlier, theatres and society had been uneasy about confronting the issues raised by Pinero's Mrs Tanqueray—issues which now seemed mild in the extreme. 'The problems set for her heirs on the stage would have made an actress of her day blush and an audience walk out in protest'. Indeed, the article's claim that 'until well within memory, the novelist enjoyed far more latitude than did the playwright in pushing forward on to once forbidden ground', seems to suggest that by 1953 this distinction no longer applied, and that the freedom afforded to the stage now matched that afforded to literature.

Coming through from some of the correspondence and memoranda of St James's Palace in the years after the Second World War is a sense of anticipation that the end is, if not hurtling towards them, then steadily and inexorably approaching—of knowing that the world in which the Lord Chamberlain controlled the stage was coming to an end. Possibly no-one realised the anachronism of the system better than those who controlled it. No doubt the reversals in British society which seemed to be heralded by Labour's landslide election victory in 1945 contributed to this sense of an approaching apocalypse. If so much of the old order was to be swept away, then surely the censorship, too, would go with it? Yet somehow it hung on. Something continued to sustain it—perhaps the difficulty the British so often seem to have in believing that any alternative to the status quo is really possible. And then as politics swung the other way in the early fifties, so one can detect the tangible return of self-belief and determination. What had seemed to be falling apart could be patched together again for a new Elizabethan age.

But still, the Censor's nemesis was looming on several fronts. Hill predicted in 1951 that the safety-valve so long provided by theatre clubs was in danger of exploding as the pressure was increased. The London County Council pulled out of an alliance intended to halt and reverse the advancing tide of stage nudity. And Paul Raymond, less biddable and gentlemanly that Vivian Van Damm, was waiting in the wings to cause maximum embarrassment: he promoted one of his shows, licensed by the Lord Chamberlain in 1953, as featuring 'the only moving nudes in Europe'. His ingenious and audacious strategy for outwitting the Lord Chamberlain's ban on such performances was to have his performers stationary but placed on a revolving turntable; when this seemed unlikely to prevent prosecution he simply announced that the performance was no longer a stage play but a music and dancing show which needed no stage licence.

As regards more serious drama, the censorship had found itself faced since the late forties by the beginnings of a new wave of European dramatists—a wave which would bring in its wake such writers as Beckett, Genet and Ionesco to disturb the final phase of the Lord Chamberlain's control of British theatre. In November 1952, Genet's *Les Bonnes* was given a private Sunday evening performance in French, and on 29 December an English version, *The Maids*, was submitted for licence; it would be turned down in January 1953, and again in February, but the Office would not find it easy to hold out against the changing cultural mood. Then there was Theatre Workshop, with whom the Office had already had some run-ins and the influence of American writers, including Tennessee Williams. There was surely only one possible end, too, to the struggle over portraying homosexual characters. As Peter Fleming advised in response to Clarendon's attempt to take the cultural and sexual temperature of the nation in 1951:

> I think that to continue to enforce the present ruling is to fight a rearguard action—which you are bound to lose in the end. ... Since the risks involved in relaxing the ban are risks which (as I see it) our society is quite certain to accept before the world is very much older—for the whole trend is towards greater frankness in these matters—I should be in favour of accepting them now.[3]

State funding represented another potential enemy for St James's Palace; could the Lord Chamberlain's Office intervene and prevent a play which enjoyed the official sanction and finance of the government? 'I do not know who or what the Arts Council of Great Britain are', wrote Game in 1946, 'but if this is the sort of thing they are going to father on the public, they will do more harm than good'.[*4] It was easy to mock the Arts Council, but it represented an alternative bastion of power, with very different values and commitments.

At the end of Volume One, I hypothesised that one reason why the system of stage censorship would eventually have its respirator turned off and be allowed to expire might be the recognition—conscious or unconscious—that what went on in theatres was no longer of prime significance, that the stage would 'no longer seem to matter'. There is little evidence of any decline in its perceived importance within the period covered by this current volume. It is true that Lord Clarendon more than

---

* He was referring to a play called *Shabby Tiger*, by Ronald Gow

once sought to persuade the Public Morality Council that their insistence that public behaviour and moral standards were crucially affected by what was shown in theatres was misplaced and exaggerated. Yet it is clear—for example from his 1951 assessment of the arguments for and against modifying the policy on portraying homosexuality—that a belief in the potential of theatre to influence society was still fundamental to his own thinking. Here is the Lord Chamberlain's secretary in 1949, writing briefing notes and pulling out all the stops to help parliamentary champions of the current system defend the censorship against those who sought to repeal the legislation and abolish it:

> 'Drama is, indeed, of all diversions the most bewitching, and the Theatre is a Magazine not to be trusted but under the official eye'. So said the old writer, and in fact the living stage is so vivid and formative that its effects cannot be disregarded.
>
> As an industry it is fashioned by commercial and competitive needs— ethical considerations, whilst not ignored, cannot be given pride of place.
>
> Thus the Censor is necessary to guard both the public and the profession from possible excesses due to these facts . . .
>
> a) It may be argued that the Common Law should be sufficient to defend the rights of the community as it is in other walks of life.
>
> b) But, consider the enormous influence for good or ill wielded by the Stage and then remember:–
>
> i) That a dramatically good and legally inoffensive play may have as its theme some extremely unpleasant subject, the dissemination of which is against the public interest. The effect may be aggravated when the purport of the play is concealed by an innocuous title . . .
>
> ii) That mere vulgarity and indecency of gesture is often not necessarily technically illegal, but much is repressed by the Censor in the lower class revue, with consequent raising of the dignity and status of the Theatre, compared with the Music Hall.
>
> iii) That there are now no Ecclesiastical Laws affecting the General Public, but the Censor has sometimes to protect Religion, and his efforts receive the approbation of the Religious communities.
>
> iv) That the police will tell you homo-sexual offences are on the increase. How much of this can be attributed to the initial awakening of interest in adolescence by 'pansy' and other effeminate characterisations on the Stage. Such stage business is not indecent enough to support a Common Law Charge. It is definately [sic] harmful and is always forbidden by the Lord Chamberlain on the legitimate stage, but it is prevalent elsewhere.[5]

As the nation entered the age of Harold Macmillan, Elizabeth II, and rebels with or without causes, whither, then, for the censorship? Although we already know the ending (at least in its most obvious manifestation), that is the question for the final volume of this study. Clarendon had retired in the autumn of 1952, to be succeeded by Lord Scarborough in time to prepare for the Coronation. Game, too, had gone, and been replaced by Sir St Vincent Wallis Troubridge, a former chairman of the Stage Society with a real enthusiasm for theatre history, who had published a brief and supportive account of the office and history of censorship in the *Stage*. According to Heriot, Troubridge was too wealthy to seek the post for financial reasons and was primarily interested in the 'honour and glory' of the position. He had written to the Comptroller to say he had time on his hands and would like to offer his services as a possible Reader, and was rewarded with a ten-year contract starting in April 1952. 'I accept with extreme satisfaction', Troubridge replied; 'It will be a great pleasure to undertake such congenial work under the direction of yourself and my old friend Tim Nugent'.[6] Little did he know what was coming.

Notes on Archive Referencing
and Authors' Names

There are two separate archives in the British Library Manuscript Collections on which I have drawn substantially; both come under the general heading: 'The Play Collections':

The texts of plays submitted for licensing between 1900 and 1968 are referenced here as 'LCP' (Lord Chamberlain's Plays) followed by a year, an oblique stroke, and a box number. This is the referencing system used within the archive and its index.

The material from the Lord Chamberlain's Correspondence Files 1900–68 is also referenced here as in the archive, using the abbreviation 'LCP CORR' to indicate the archive. Material relating to plays which were licensed is filed separately from that related to plays which were refused licences.

In the case of a *licensed play*, LCP CORR' is followed by the year under which it is filed, a file number and the title of the play.

For an *unlicensed play*, 'LCP CORR' is followed by the title of the play, then 'LR' (indicating 'Licence Refused') and a year.

There is also correspondence relating to plays which were neither licensed nor refused. These are known as 'Waiting Box Plays'. To reference these, LCP CORR' is followed by the title of the play, then 'WB' (indicating 'Waiting Box') and a year.

The other archive on which I have drawn extensively is the Lord Chamberlain's Office Files, which are part of the Royal Archive, and currently held at Windsor Castle. These files contain further general and extensive papers—letters, minutes, memoranda, cuttings etc.—from the Lord Chamberlain's Office relating to theatre licensing and censorship. This material was evidently kept separate from the material related directly to specific plays submitted for licence, which is held in the British Library collections.

All material cited from the Royal Archive is referenced as in the archive itself; namely: 'RA LC/GEN', followed by an oblique line and one of several numbers under which the material is categorised: 310, 344, 440 or 512. Although the logic for the division and location of files is not always obvious, those labelled 310 were intended to indicate that the focus was the

Advisory Board; 344, the Examiners of Plays; 440, the Theatres Act; and 512 apparently indicated Censorship. The impossibility of maintaining these as discrete categories is evidenced by the fact that 440 and 512 were effectively amalgamated after 1958. The above number is in each case followed by another oblique line and another figure which indicates the appropriate year of the file, and then the individual title which the Lord Chamberlain's Office assigned to it. It should be noted that individual files sometimes contain relevant materials drawn from years other than the one indicated by the file reference number.

I am grateful to Her Majesty Queen Elizabeth II for allowing me access to the relevant sections of the Royal Archive, and for permitting me to make use of and quote from the files.

Note on Referencing within this Book

In a departure from the practice adopted in Volume One, I have used two distinct kinds of notes and references here. Most appear, in the normal way, as endnotes, and include, as far as possible, details of when and where a play was first publicly performed (or, at least, for what venue the licence was issued). However, in order to make it less disruptive for the reader to check the names of the authors of plays discussed, on those occasions where these are not immediately identified within the text itself, they are referenced so as to appear in separate notes at the bottom of the relevant page. The only exceptions are revues or some other stage entertainments, where authors can generally not be identified.

I am confident that this use of double notes is an improvement, and I am grateful to Professor Peter Thomson for pointing out that the reader who wishes to identify authors while reading about their plays deserves not to have his or her concentration repeatedly interrupted by the necessity of flicking to endnotes:

> Such a reader will generally find that he's never heard of the author anyway—but there's always the exciting possibility that he will know the name in another connection, and undergo one of those epiphanies that socialise the lonely experience of reading a book.

I should be pleased, indeed, to think that a passing reference from me might lead someone to undergo one (or even multiple) epiphanies, while reading my book.

Finally, some caveats. All the details given in notes are correct to the best of my knowledge. However, many of the plays cited could reasonably be described as obscure, and often there is no easy way of checking elsewhere the performance details as recorded in the Lord Chamberlain's Correspondence archives. There may well be inaccuracies here, and it is possible there will be occasions when readers may have other information which reveals some of these. I would be glad to hear from them. For example, it is possible that there are occasions where a name which I have taken to indicate the author of a play in fact belongs to the manager who submitted it for licensing. It also seems extremely likely that plays were sometimes submitted under pseudonyms. Furthermore, some correspondence (and most of the titles and names as they appear on index cards) are handwritten, and I may have sometimes misinterpreted a word or a name. I have tried to indicate with a '[?]' those occasions when I am most doubtful. There are also occasions when there are discrepancies (of performance dates or venues) between information about licences issued for productions as indicated in the Lord Chamberlain's files, and the details about productions listed in J.P. Wearing's invaluable calendars of the London stage which encompass the decades on which this book is based (see Select Bibliography, below). Where there are differences which I have been unable to resolve, I have preferred the evidence of the Lord Chamberlain's archive as reliably indicating *intended* production details.

Notes

Introduction

1 See, respectively, LCP CORR: 1934/13226: *Stevedore*, and LCP CORR: *Outside Britain* WB (1938).
2 Johnston, John, *The Lord Chamberlain's Blue Pencil*, (London: Hodder & Stoughton, 1990).
3 RA LC/GEN/440/51: 'Lord Chamberlain's Representative to Lecture at the Scottish Police College'.
4 See RA LC/GEN/440/52: 'Statement of Policy for Mr Street, Senior Lecturer in Law, Manchester University'.
5 RA LC/GEN/512/51: 'Deputation Regarding Stage Play *The Children's Hour*: Theme Of Lesbianism'.
6 Minor inconsistencies of spelling and typography in the originals have been standardised, but original punctuation has generally been maintained.
7 See RA LC/GEN/310/46: 'Advisory Board. New Names Added'.
8 See RA LC/GEN/440/52: 'Statement of Policy for Mr Street, Senior Lecturer in Law, Manchester University'.
9 Jack Selford, 'Censorship', *New Theatre*, 2, September 1939, pp. 14–15.

Chapter 1

1 See LCP CORR: 1934/13372: *The Crooked Cross*.
2 Hubert Griffith, 'The Censor as Nazi Apologist', *New Statesman and Nation*, 14 April 1934, p. 545.
3 See LCP CORR: *Heroes* LR (1934). The English version was by Henrietta Leslie.
4 Griffith, 'The Censor as Nazi Apologist'.
5 George Street, Reader's Report, 3 March 1934. See LCP CORR: *Heroes* LR (1934).
6 See LCP CORR: *Take Heed* LR (1934).
7 See LCP CORR: 1933/12271: *Nine Days Wonder*. Licensed for the London Palladium, August 1933.
8 See LCP CORR: 1933/12276: *Paris Fantaisie*. Licensed for the Prince of Wales's Theatre, September 1933.
9 See LCP CORR: 1933/12365: *Revudeville No. 35*. Licensed for the Windmill Theatre, October 1935.
10 See LCP CORR: *Who Made the Iron Grow* LR (1933).
11 Cromer was writing on 26 March 1934. See LCP CORR: 1934/12916: *Whither Liberty*.
12 See LCP CORR: 1934/12916: *Whither Liberty*.
13 *News Chronicle*, 29 January 1934, p. 9; *Daily Telegraph*, 29 January 1934, p. 8.
14 *Daily Telegraph*, 29 January 1934, p. 8; *Morning Post*, 29 January 1934, p. 4.
15 *Morning Post*, 29 January 1934, p. 4.
16 Extracts taken from unpublished manuscript of *Take Heed*. See LCP 1939/48.
17 See LCP CORR: *Take Heed* LR (1934).
18 See LCP CORR: *Take Heed* LR (1934) and 1939/3106.
19 *The Times*, 7 December 1938, p. 12.
20 It was actually another four years before *Take Heed* was publicly produced at the Empire, Peterborough in March 1943.
21 See LCP CORR: 1937/834: *Going Gay*.

22 See LCP CORR: *Lucid Interval* LR (1934)
23 See LCP CORR: 1939/2282: *Juggernaut* (discussed below).
24 See LCP CORR: 1938/1770: *Everybody Cheer.* Licensed for the Peterborough Empire, September 1938.
25 See LCP CORR: 1937/861: *Green Cars Go East.*
26 RA LC/GEN/512/35: 'Particulars of Offensive "Jokes" for which "Tex" Mcleod was Convicted at Liverpool'.
27 RA LC/GEN/512/37: 'Complaint Regarding Representation of Herr Hitler in Variety Performance'.
28 See LCP CORR: 1935/14554: *Robinson Crusoe the Second.* Licensed for the People's Theatre, Newcastle, December 1935.
29 See LCP CORR: 1935/14572: *Jack and the Beanstalk.* Licensed for the Drury Lane Theatre, December 1935.
30 See LCP CORR: 1935/14571: *Dick Whittington.* Licensed for the Gateshead Empire, December 1935.
31 See LCP CORR: 1936/14693: *Out of the Dark.* Licensed for the Ambassadors Theatre, January 1936.
32 See LCP CORR: 1936/14796: *Their Majesties Pass By.* Licensed for the Cripplegate Theatre, February 1936.
33 See LCP CORR: 1936/15614: *Cinderella.* Licensed for the Theatre Royal, Eastbourne, December 1936.
34 See LCP CORR: 1936/15542: *Babes in the Wood.* Licensed for the Palace, Hull, at the end of November/early December 1936.
35 *Vicky* was licensed for the Streatham Hill Theatre in November 1935, (having been refused the previous April), before transferring to the Garrick. See LCP CORR 1935/14288: *Vicky.*
36 See LCP CORR: 1937/145: *Round About Big Ben.* Licensed for the Southampton Palace, February 1937.
37 See LCP CORR: 1936/15513: *To and Fro.* Licensed for the Comedy Theatre, November 1936.
38 See LCP CORR: 1935/14581: *Robinson Crusoe.* Licensed for the Wimbledon Theatre, December 1935.
39 See the *Daily Mirror,* 20 January 1937, p. 3.
40 See LCP CORR: 1935/14581: *Robinson Crusoe.*
41 See, for example, the *Daily Express,* 20 January 1937, p. 1.
42 See LCP CORR: 1935/13996: *Revudeville No. 59.* Licensed for the Windmill Theatre, April 1935.
43 See LCP CORR: 1937/834: *Going Gay.*
44 See LCP CORR: 1937/199: *Make a Note of It.* Licensed for the Queens Theatre, Poplar, February 1937.
45 See LCP CORR: 1938/1895: *A Perfect Gentleman,* licensed October 1938 for Hamilton. Also LCP CORR: 1938/1872: *Birmingham University Revue,* licensed for the Undergraduate Union in the same month.
46 See LCP CORR: 1939/2665: *Heaven and Charing Cross.* Licensed for St Martin's Theatre, March 1939.
47 Street's comment was made in December 1935. See LCP CORR: 1935/14554: *Robinson Crusoe the Second.* See note 28.
48 See LCP CORR: 1936/14694 : *Revudeville No. 71.* Licensed for the Windmill Theatre, January 1936.
49 See LCP CORR: 1936/14729: *Sweet Wine.* Licensed for Northwick Park Hall, Kenton, February 1936. It was a ruritanian play, set in the near future of 1940.
50 See LCP CORR: 1937/507: *All Sorts.* Licensed for Sheffield in June 1937; the Reader described it as a 'highbrow revue'. Also: LCP CORR: 1938/1622 *Rockin' The Town.* Licensed for Feldman's Theatre, Blackpool, June 1938.
51 See LCP CORR: 1938/2004: *Cinderella.* Licensed for the Tivoli in Hull, November 1938.

52 See LCP CORR: 1938/1703: *Geneva in a Dream* and also WB (1938). Licensed for the Palace Theatre, Manchester, August 1938.

53 In fact the show was abandoned and never licensed. See LCP CORR: *Geneva in a Dream* WB (1938).

54 See LCP CORR: 1938/966: *Sons of Adam*. Licensed in revised form for the Richmond Theatre, February 1938.

55 See LCP CORR: 1938/1231: *Till the Day I Die*. Licensed for York Hall at Bethnal Green in February 1938, with all direct references to Germany and the Nazis removed. The endorsement was cancelled in September 1939.

56 Anon., 'Theatre and Cinema: The Censor Holds his Hand', *Truth*, 20 January 1937, p. 95.

57 See LCP CORR: 1934/13372: *The Crooked Cross*.

58 Extracts taken from unpublished manuscript of *The Crooked Cross*. See LCP 1934/37.

59 Anon., 'Theatre and Cinema'.

60 'Big Themes Need Big Plays', *Sunday Times*, 17 January 1937, p. 6.

61 *The Times*, 14 January 1937, p. 10.

62 'Early Days of Nazi Regime: Sane and Balanced Picture', *Daily Telegraph*, 14 January 1937, p. 10.

63 See LCP CORR: 1934/13372: *The Crooked Cross*.

64 See LCP CORR: 1935/13670: *Tell England*. Licensed for the Theatre Royal, St Helen's, January 1935.

65 See LCP CORR: 1935/13792: *Official Announcement*. Licensed for the Bexhill Pavilion, February 1935.

66 Extracts taken from the unpublished manuscript of *Son of Judea*. See LCP 1935/38. Licensed for the Festival Theatre, Cambridge, May 1935. See also LCP CORR: 1935/14334: *Son of Judea*.

67 See LCP CORR: 1935/14254: *The Dog Beneath the Skin*. Licensed for the Westminster Theatre, December 1935.

68 See LCP CORR: 1935/14401: *Professor Mamlock*. Licensed for the Westminster Theatre, November 1935.

69 See LCP CORR: 1939/14401: *Professor Mamlock*. See also 1947/8627.

70 See LCP CORR: 1936/15218: *Do We Not Bleed*. Licensed for Tower Arms Hall, Iver, Midlothian, August 1936.

71 Extracts taken from the unpublished manuscript of *Do We Not Bleed*. See LCP 1936/33.

72 See LCP CORR: 1936/15218: *Do We Not Bleed*.

73 Letter of 5 May 1938. See LCP CORR: *Lorelei* WB (1938).

74 See LCP CORR: *We, the Condemned* WB (1938).

75 See LCP CORR: *Take Heed* LR (1934) and 1943/3106.

76 See LCP CORR: 1934/13514: *Judgement Day*. Licensed for the Globe Theatre, December 1934.

77 See LCP CORR: 1934/13514: *Judgement Day*.

78 *The Times*, 3 June 1937, p. 12.

79 *Tatler*, 2 June 1937, pp. 586–587.

80 Unidentified review. See Production File at the Theatre Museum: *Judgement Day*, Strand Theatre, June 1937.

81 See LCP CORR: 1934/13514: *Judgement Day*.

82 See LCP CORR: *Take Heed* LR (1934) and 1943/3106.

83 See LCP CORR: *Lorelei* WB (1938). The script was submitted by Cedric Hardwick. I discuss this particular example in more detail in Dominic Shellard, Steve Nicholson and Miriam Handley, *The Lord Chamberlain Regrets* (London: British Library Publications, 2004).

84 See LCP CORR: 1938/1637: *Spring Morning*. Licensed for the Sparrow's Nest, Lowestoft, June/July 1938.

85 See LCP CORR: 1938/1624: *Geneva*. Licensed for the Malvern Festival Theatre, June 1938.

86 Extracts taken from the unpublished manuscript of *Follow My Leader*. See LCP 1940/2.

87   See LCP CORR: 1940/3219: *Follow My Leader*. The play was eventually licensed for St James's Theatre, London, January 1940.

88   See LCP CORR: 1937/650: *Code of Honour*. Licensed for the Arts Theatre, Cambridge, September 1937.

89   See LCP CORR: 1938/1597: *Trumpeter, Play!* This version was licensed for the Garrick Theatre, London, June 1938.

90   *The Times*, 14 June 1938, p. 14.

91   'War Problems on Stage', *Daily Telegraph*, 14 June 1938, p. 14.

92   See LCP CORR: *We, the Condemned* WB (1938). Sullivan's script remained unlicensed.

93   See RA LC/GEN/512/38: 'Meeting between the Lord Chamberlain and the Three Examiners of Plays to Discuss the Licensing of Plays Containing Criticism, Veiled or Open, of Forms of Government or Political Policy of Other Countries'.

94   See LCP CORR: *Exodus* WB (1938).

95   See LCP CORR: 1939/2250: *Trial of a Judge*. Licensed for Vaughan College Theatre, Leicester, January 1939.

96   See LCP CORR: 1939/2282: *Juggernaut*. Presented privately at the Aldwych Theatre by the Repertory Players, January 1939. The script was then licensed and presented at the Saville Theatre in June 1939.

97   'Propaganda—But Good Drama, Too', *Daily Mail*, 9 January 1939, p. 13.

98   'A Word from the Authors', published in the programme for *Juggernaut* at the Saville Theatre, June 1939.

99   See LCP CORR: 1939/2895: *Professor Schelling*. Licensed for the Yiddish Arts Theatre at the Garrick Theatre, London, June 1939, to be performed in Yiddish.

100   See LCP CORR: 1939/2863: *We Need Russia*. Licensed for Unity Theatre production at St Pancras Town Hall, May 1939.

101   See LCP CORR: 1939/2928: *Unity Revue*. Licensed for the Kingsway Theatre, June/July 1939.

102   See LCP CORR: 1939/3083: *Pastor Hall*. The script was effectively refused a licence when first submitted in July 1939, as Unity refused to ruritanianise it. It was passed in its original form for Manchester Repertory Theatre in November 1939.

103   See LCP CORR: 1936/1096. Harwood's play had had difficulties over licensing because of a scene featuring Queen Victoria. It was licensed for Sheffield YMCA in January 1938. In July 1939, Harwood sought an unrestricted licence.

104   See LCP CORR: 1940/3219: *Follow My Leader*.

105   See LCP CORR: 1934/13514: *Judgement Day*. The proposed revival with the 'real' identities would have been for the Phoenix Theatre.

106   Game's observation, dated 14 September 1938, was a postscript to his report on the script of *Geneva in a Dream*. See LCP CORR: 1938/17803: *Geneva in a Dream*.

107   See LCP CORR: 1938/1231:*Till the Day I Die*.

108   See LCP CORR: 1939/2725: *East End*. Licensed for Shoreditch Town Hall, April 1939.

Chapter 2

1   Philip Godfrey, *Back-Stage: A Survey of the Contemporary English Theatre from Behind the Scenes* (London: Harrap, 1933), p. 154.

2   See 1938 Annual Report of the Public Morality Council, p. 5.

3   See 1938 Annual Report of the Public Morality Council, pp. 9–10.

4   See 1933 Annual Report of the Public Morality Council, p. 19; 1934 Annual Report, p. 14; 1935 Annual Report, p. 23; 1939 Annual Report, p. 20.

5   See 1936 Annual Report of the Public Morality Council, p. 25.

6   See 1936 Annual Report of the Public Morality Council, p.23.

7   See 1937 Annual Report of the Public Morality Council, p. 20.

8   See 1937 Annual Report of the Public Morality Council, pp. 19–20.

9   Letter sent to the Bishop of London, 17 June 1934. See LCP CORR: 1934/12904: *Men in White*.

10   See 1938 Annual Report of the Public Morality Council, p. 25.

11 See 1938 Annual Report of the Public Morality Council, p. 26.
12 See LCP CORR: 1938/1778: *Design for Living*. Licensed for the Theatre Royal, Brighton, December 1938.
13 See LCP CORR: *Happy Event* LR (1935). Major H.S. Browning's play had been refused a licence in 1925. Ten years later, a production was proposed for the Palace Pier Theatre, Brighton.
14 M. Willson Disher, 'The Throne is the Censor', *Theatre World*, February 1937, p. 56.
15 Horace Richards, 'Do We Need a Censor?', *Theatre World*, March 1932, p. 137.
16 Godfrey, *Back-Stage*, pp. 155–157.
17 RA LC/GEN/512/39: 'The Bishop of London's Further Representations Regarding Nudity on the Stage'.
18 See LCP CORR: 1938/1347: *Revudeville No. 103*. Licensed for the Windmill Theatre, March 1938.
19 See LCP CORR: 1938/1004: *Banana Ridge*. Licensed for the Garrick Theatre, Southport, April 1938. Gwatkin's letter dated 7 May 1938.
20 See LCP CORR: 1933/12340: *The Greeks Had a Word for It*. Licensed for the Shilling Theatre, Fulham, October 1933.
21 See LCP CORR: 1934/12646: *First Episode*. In fact, the Office had licensed an earlier version of the same play the previous August with only minor amendments (words such as 'pansy' were cut), even though Game had described it as 'terrible trash'.
22 Letter of 21 November 1934. See LCP CORR: 1934/13255: *Man is an Insect*. Licensed for the Q Theatre, Kew, in October 1934, the title was changed in October 1934 to *Courtship Dance*, and in November, when it opened at the Duke of York's Theatre with a rewritten last act, to *It Happened to Adam*.
23 See LCP CORR: *A New Will* LR (1934).
24 From Street's report of 26 January 1934. See LCP CORR: 1934/12711: *Squaring the Circle*. Licensed for the Ballet Club Theatre, January 1934, in a translation by N. Goold-Verschoyle.
25 Cromer's comment was made on 9 February 1934. See LCP CORR: *Sailor Beware* LR (1934). Production intended for the Palace Theatre, Shaftesbury Avenue.
26 See LCP CORR: *There's Always Tomorrow* LR (1934). Intended for the Criterion theatre, the play was renamed *A Knight in Vienna* and performed privately by the Repertory Players at the Phoenix Theatre in January 1935. Following Game's report on the performance, a licence was again refused.
27 See LCP CORR: *Fig Leaves* LR (1934), (intended for the Westminster theatre); *Laughter Outside* LR (1935), (intended for the Prince's Theatre, Manchester); *The Loving Wife* LR (1936), (intended for Croydon Repertory Theatre).
28 See LCP CORR: 1934/12710: *Don Juan*. Submitted on behalf of the New Theatre, but apparently licensed for the Globe, February 1934.
29 See LCP CORR: 1938/1427: *Elizabeth la Femme sans Homme*. Adapted by Yvette Pienne, the script had been refused a licence in November 1937 and was performed privately at the Gate Theatre before being licensed for the Haymarket in April 1938.
30 See LCP CORR: *Why Keep a Diary* LR (1935). Translated by Edith Ellis, the play was intended for the Theatre Royal, Brighton.
31 See LCP CORR: 1935/14159: *It's a Wise Child*. Licensed for the Garrick Theatre, London, July 1935. A revised version was also licensed for the Opera House, Coventry, February 1940 (See LCP CORR: 1940/3295).
32 See LCP CORR: *Flying Blind* WB (1938). A revised version was 'reluctantly' deemed acceptable, subject to further alterations; however, it appears that no licence was issued, presumably because no production or venue was ever confirmed.
33 See LCP CORR: 1937/246: *Come Out to Play*. Licensed for the Kingsway Theatre, March 1937.
34 See LCP CORR: *Stallion and Narcissus* LR (1934).
35 See LCP CORR: 1934/13113: *Let's Pretend*. Licensed for the Pleasure Gardens Theatre, Folkestone, July 1934.
36 See LCP CORR: *Hinkemann* LR (1934). A licence was again refused in 1947.

37 See LCP CORR: 1938/1535: *Sexes and Sevens*. Licensed for Newcastle Theatre Royal, June 1938.
38 See LCP CORR: 1938/1757: *Behind the Blinds*. Licensed for the Winter Garden, October 1938.
39 See LCP CORR: 1934/13005: *No Way Back*. Revised script licensed for the Whitehall Theatre, April 1934.
40 See *The Times* 27 April 1937, p. 14, reviewing Charlot's 'non-stop revue', *Red, Bright and Blue*, at the Vaudeville Theatre. Dearmer cited this reference in his report on the performance. See LCP CORR: 1937/394: *Red Bright and Blue*.
41 See LCP CORR: 1936/15685: *Revudeville No. 87*. Licensed for the Windmill Theatre, December 1936.
42 *News Review*, 14 January 1937, p. 23.
43 See LCP CORR: 1938/1615: *King Revel*. Licensed for the Blackpool Hippodrome, June 1938.
44 See LCP CORR: 1937/834 and 1938/2169: *Going Gay*. The original version was licensed for the Theatre Royal, Chatham, November 1937, and the revised version for the Empire, Shepherd's Bush, December 1938.
45 See LCP CORR: 1933/12225: *Nymph Errant*. Licensed for the Opera House, Manchester, August 1933.
46 See LCP CORR: 1933/12075: *Les Mille et Une Merveilles de Paris*. Licensed for the Prince of Wales's Theatre, April 1933.
47 See LCP CORR: 1934/13147: *West End Scandals*.
48 See LCP CORR: 1934/12904: *Men in White*.
49 See 1934 Annual Report of the Public Morality Council, p. 17 and p. 19.
50 *The Stage Plays Committee's Position in Regard to Stage Undress*, a leaflet published by the Public Morality Council (nd). See LCP CORR: 1939/3085: *Black Velvet*.
51 See, for example, 1936 Annual Report of the Public Morality Council, p. 12.
52 See LCP CORR: 1934/13521: *Folies on Parade*. Licensed in December 1934.
53 'NUDITY ON THE STAGE: Marie Tempest's Reply to the Bishop of London', *Star*, 5 January 1935, p. 3; and 'PRUDES ON THE PROWL: Flayed by Marie Tempest', *Sunday Despatch*, 6 January 1935, p. 1. For Tempest's letter itself, *The Times*, 5 January 1935, p. 6.
54 See 1936 Annual Report of the Public Morality Council, pp. 24–25.
55 See LCP CORR: 1937/394: *Red, Bright and Blue*. Licensed for the Vaudeville Theatre, April 1937.
56 See LCP CORR: 1937/289: *Stars and Strips*. Licensed for the Vaudeville Theatre, March 1937.
57 See LCP CORR: 1936/15685: *Revudeville No. 87*. Licensed for the Windmill Theatre, December 1936.
58 See LCP CORR: 1937/108: *Revudeville No. 88*. Licensed for the Windmill Theatre, January 1937.
59 See 1938 Annual Report of the Public Morality Council, p. 22.
60 Letter of 5 April 1937. See RA LC/GEN/440/37: 'Letter From Mrs. L. Cooke as to "strip-tease" Dance'.
61 See 1938 Annual Report of the Public Morality Council, p. 23. The Council reported that the Bishop's letter had been published in full in the *Daily Telegraph*, 'and in other papers in an amended form'.
62 See LCP CORR: 1938/1629: *Frivolities of France*. Licensed for the Prince of Wales's Theatre, June 1938.
63 See RA LC/GEN/512/37: 'Correspondence, Memoranda, Reports, Press Cuttings, etc. on The Subject of Nudity on the Stage, Culminating in the Meeting held by The Lord Chamberlain on the 24th June'.
64 See 1938 Annual Report of the Public Morality Council, p. 24.
65 See RA LC/GEN/512/37: 'Correspondence, Memoranda, Reports, Press Cuttings, etc. on the Subject of Nudity on the Stage . . .'.
66 See 1938 Annual Report of the Public Morality Council, p. 24.

67 See RA LC/GEN/512/38: 'Deputation from the Watch Committee of the Public Morality Council Received by The Lord Chamberlain, 26th July 1938'.
68 See 1938 Annual Report of the Public Morality Council, p. 24.
69 See 1939 Annual Report of the Public Morality Council, p. 21.
70 See tributes published after her death in February 1951, including *The Times*, 28 February 1951, p. 6.
71 See 1933 Annual Report of the Public Morality Council, p. 20.
72 *The Stage Plays Committee's Position in Regard to Stage Undress*.
73 See RA LC/GEN/512/39: 'Further Representations by the Public Morality Council re. Nudity at the Windmill Theatre, with Memorandum on the Subject of the Council, on Principles of Censorship'.
74 See LCP CORR: 1936/15022: *Bitter Harvest*.
75 See LCP CORR: *Amok* LR (1936).
76 See RA LC/GEN/310/36: 'Enquiries and Comments by Sir Ian Malcolm regarding Principles of Censorship to be Observed in Advising the Lord Chamberlain'. Malcolm's letter was written on 25 February 1936, and Cromer's reply on 13 May 1936.
77 See LCP CORR: *Moonflowers* LR (1936). The play was originally intended for the Fortune Theatre, but was performed privately at the Westminster Theatre, on Sunday 5 April 1936.
78 See LCP CORR: *The Hand of the Potter* LR (1938)
79 The memorandum was dated 5 March 1940, and followed criticism of the play in the *Tatler*. See LCP CORR: 1938/1958: *Desire Under the Elms*. The play had been refused a licence in 1925 but was licensed for the Westminster Theatre in November 1938.
80 See LCP CORR: 1938/1778: *Design for Living*.
81 See LCP CORR: *Ehe (Marriage)* LR (1938). The play was by Johanne Vaszary, translated by Lawrence Wolfe and adapted by Count T. Zichy.
82 See LCP CORR: 1935/13758: *Night Must Fall*. Licensed for the Duchess Theatre, March 1935.

Chapter 3

1 See LCP CORR: *Love of Women* LR (1934).
2 Game was writing on 13 March 1943. See LCP CORR: 1943/4864: *Baltic Passage*.
3 The first comment was made by Game in a memorandum of 17 July 1943. See LCP CORR: 1943/4989: *Mr Bolfry*. The second occurs in a Reader's report of 7 October 1945: See LCP CORR: 1945/6523: *A Man about the House*.
4 Cromer made his claim in a note of 13 January 1948. The second comment was made by Gwatkin on 31 December 1947. For both, see LCP CORR: *The Gingerbread House* WB (1948).
5 See LCP CORR: 1932/11621: *The Green Bay Tree*. Licensed for St Martin's Theatre, November 1932.
6 Michael Wilcox, 'Introduction' to *Gay Plays* (London: Methuen, 1984), p. 7.
7 See *Everyman*, 4 February 1933, p. 137.
8 See Theatre Museum Production File: *The Green Bay Tree* (St Martin's Theatre, January 1933).
9 *Observer*, 29 January 1933, p, 11.
10 *Week-End Review*, 4 February 1933, p. 121.
11 See LCP CORR: 1932/11621: *The Green Bay Tree*.
12 See LCP CORR: 1933/11840: *The Warrior's Husband*. Licensed for Birmingham Repertory Theatre, February 1933.
13 See LCP CORR: 1933/12552: *Five Aces*. Licensed for Westcliff Gardens Theatre, Clacton, December 1933.
14 See LCP CORR: 1934/12827: *Distinguished Gathering*. Licensed for the Comedy Theatre in April 1934, after a revised version was submitted in which the character was made into a drug fiend instead.

15 See LCP CORR: 1934/13124: *That Certain Something*. Licensed for the Aldwych Theatre, July 1934.

16 See LCP CORR: 1934/13156: *Josephine*. Adapted by Emlyn Williams, and licensed for His Majesty's Theatre, August 1934.

17 See LCP CORR: 1939/3009: *Spears Against Us*. Licensed for Liverpool Playhouse, August 1939.

18 See Theatre Museum Production File: *The Green Bay Tree*.

19 See LCP CORR: *Murder on the Ship* LR (1935). The play was to have been staged at the New Theatre.

20 See LCP CORR: *A Man of Fifty* LR (1938). Verneuil's script had been adapted by John Hoare. Norman Marshall, at the Gate Theatre, was the first to seek a licence.

21 See LCP CORR: 1934/13163: *Men Governing*. Licensed for the Westminster Theatre, August 1934. The title was altered to *Rose and Glove*.

22 See LCP CORR: 1934/12686: *Spring 1600*. Licensed for the Shaftesbury Theatre, January 1934.

23 See LCP CORR: 1936/14968: *Last Voyage*. Licensed for the Maddermarket Theatre, Norwich.

24 *The Times*, 26 October 1938, p. 12.

25 See LCP CORR: 1934/13225: *Never Again*. Licensed for the Embassy Theatre, September 1934.

26 See LCP CORR: 1935/13651: *Summer's Lease*. Licensed for the Embassy Theatre, January 1935.

27 See LCP CORR: 1935/13657: *Oh Edward*. Licensed for the Conservative Hall, East Molesey, January 1935.

28 Dearmer was writing on 14 December 1937. See LCP CORR: 1937/953: *Sing and Whistle*. Licensed for the Grafton Theatre, December 1937.

29 See LCP CORR: 1938/1137: *In Heaven and Earth*. Licensed for the Glasgow Athenaeum, February 1938.

30 'Fauntleroy and Some Others', *The Times*, 27 July 1937, p. 15. 'Cissy' was here spelt 'sissy'.

31 See LCP CORR: 1938/1757: *Behind the Blinds*.

32 See LCP CORR: 1939/2498: *Good Company*. Licensed for the Gateshead Empire, February 1939.

33 See LCP CORR: 1933/12058: *Splinters 1914–1933*. Licensed for the Wolverhampton Hippodrome, April 1933.

34 See LCP CORR: 1935/13817: *Cruising Around*; 1935/13953: *Off the Gold Coast*; 1937/713: *Turkish Delight*; and 1937/511: *Revudeville No. 93*.

35 Ivor Brown's review in the *Observer*, 29 January 1933, p. 11.

36 See LCP CORR: 1934/13147: *West End Scandals*. The original script was licensed for the Garrick Theatre, London, in August 1934, and two 'revised' versions were licensed for the same theatre in September and October.

37 See the *Evening News*, 11 November 1934, p. 15.

38 See RA LC/GEN/440/39: 'Press Announcement re Necessity for Giving a Complete Description of a Performance Including Acts in which there is no Spoken Dialogue, and a Clear Description of the Action, "Business", or Dress'.

39 *Evening News*, 4 October 1939, p. 4.

40 See LCP CORR: 1964/4458: *The Children's Hour*.

41 See LCP CORR: 1933/12162: *Loire*. Licensed for Wyndham's Theatre, June 1933. Also 1933/12612: *Hemlock*. Licensed for the Fortune Theatre, December 1933.

42 See LCP CORR: *Emergency Exit* WB (1934). The play was intended for amateur production by St Bride Dramatic Society at the St Bride Foundation Institute, Ludgate Circus —a building which was found to have no licence for public performance.

43 See LCP CORR: *Love of Women* LR (1934).

44 See LCP CORR: *Lady of the Sky* LR (1934).

45 See LCP CORR: *Riviera* LR (1935).

46 See LCP CORR: 1936/14705: *Children to Bless You*. Licensed for the Q Theatre in February 1936.

47 Helen Freshwater, 'Suppressed Desire: Inscriptions of Lesbianism in the British Theatre of the 1930s', *New Theatre Quarterly*, 17:4, November 2001, pp. 310–318.

48 See LCP CORR: *Dawn* WB (1936).

49 See LCP CORR: *The Gay Generation* LR (1933) and LR (1934).

50 See LCP CORR: *Lord Byron Goes out of Fashion* LR (1934).

51 See LCP CORR: *A Marriage Took Place* LR (1934). The play was to have been performed at the Temperance Hall in Kirkwall.

52 See LCP CORR: 1936/15021: *The Lord of Ferrara*. Licensed for the Century Theatre, Westbourne Grove, March 1936.

53 Ivor Brown writing in the *Observer*, 2 February 1936, p. 15.

54 'Fine Play Banned: Censorship Anomaly', *Daily Telegraph*, 6 February 1936, p. 6.

55 See LCP CORR: 1936/15040: *Deep Waters*. Licensed for the Victoria Hall, Mitford on Sea (?), April 1936.

56 See LCP CORR: *Margorie Crocker's Lover* LR (1935). The play had been intended for the Royal Artillery Theatre, Woolwich.

57 See LCP CORR: *The Chequered Board* LR (1935).

Chapter 4

1 Lord Cromer's comment was made in December 1926. See LCP CORR: 1936/15569: *The Pacifist*.

2 See LCP CORR: 1936/15569: *The Pacifist*. Licensed for the People's Theatre, Newcastle, December 1936.

3 Game writing in January 1937. The Lord Chamberlain agreed with him. See LCP CORR: 1937/129: *Who Are the English?* Licensed for the Rudolf Steiner Hall, February 1937.

4 See LCP CORR: 1938/1122: *Where's that Bomb?* A licence was refused in December 1936 but issued for York Hall, Bethnal Green, in February 1938. For further discussion of this play see Steve Nicholson, *British Theatre and the Red Peril: The Portrayal of Communism 1917-1945* (Exeter: University of Exeter Press, 1999), pp. 96–98.

5 See LCP CORR: 1937/201: *The Fall of the House of Slusher*; and 1938/1447: *The Case of the Baffled Boss*. Also, anomalously, *The Case of the Baffled Boss* LR (1938).

6 See LCP CORR: 1933/11735: *When the Crash Comes*. Licensed for Birmingham Repertory Theatre in January 1933. For further discussion of this play see Nicholson, *British Theatre and the Red Peril*, pp. 81-83.

7 See LCP CORR: 1933/11788: *Power and Poverty*. The script was described by Street as 'a propagandist play in favour of the Poor Relief being enlarged', and was licensed for the Weavers' Institute, Earley, in January 1933.

8 See LCP CORR: 1934/12683: *Mutiny*. Licensed for Birmingham Repertory Theatre, January 1934.

9 See LCP CORR: 1934/12757: *Love on the Dole*. Licensed for Manchester Repertory Theatre, February 1934.

10 Game was writing in January 1935. See LCP CORR: 1935/13636: *Harvest in the North*. Licensed for Manchester Repertory Theatre, January 1935. In May, the title was apparently changed to *God's in Heaven*.

11 See LCP CORR: 1934/13140: *The Pageant of Labour*. Licensed for Crystal Palace, July 1934.

12 See LCP CORR: 1935/14224: *Mother*. The English version was licensed for performance by the Left Theatre at the Town Hall, East Ham, in November 1935.

13 However, when a successful prosecution was brought by the Welsh police for performing unlicensed material in an unlicensed venue, Titman, who attended the court proceedings to give evidence on behalf of the Lord Chamberlain, described it in his report as 'the first case which has been brought primarily on political grounds'. See

LCP CORR: 1935/15224: *Waiting for Lefty*. The play was licensed for the Victoria Hall, Sunderland, July 1936.

14   For extracts from the script see LCP: 1939/48: *Symphony in Awakening*. For comments of the Office see LCP CORR: 1939/3107: *Symphony in Awakening*. Licensed for the Manor Social Community Centre, Sheffield, November 1939.

15   See LCP CORR: 1937/294: *Peace and Prosperity Revue*. Licensed for Morley Hall, S.E. 1, April 1937. Alan Bush was officially musical adviser to the London Labour Choral Union.

16   See LCP CORR: 1936/14841: *Peace in Our Time*. Licensed for the Festival Hall, Whitley Bay, February 1936.

17   See LCP CORR: 1936/14982: *Skyscraper*. Licensed for the Italian Club in Greek Street, London, March 1936.

18   See LCP CORR: 1936/14612: *The Everlasting Hills*. Licensed for the Vagabonds Club, Pinner, January 1936.

19   See, for example, Charles Loch Mowat, *Britain Between the Wars, 1918–1940* (London: Methuen, 1955). pp. 422–423 & 537–538.

20   See *Manchester Guardian*, 13 November 1934, p. 13.

21   See LCP CORR: 1934/13403: *Dragon's Teeth*. Licensed for Manchester Repertory Theatre, November 1934.

22   Extracts taken from the published version of the script. See Sydney Box, *Bring Me My Bow* (London: Samuel French, 1937), pp. 20 & 25.

23   See LCP CORR: 1937/633: *Bring Me My Bow*. Licensed for Welwyn Garden City Theatre, October 1937.

24   See LCP CORR: 1938/1606: *A.R.P.* Licensed for Stratford Town Hall, June 1938.

25   See LCP CORR: 1937/15334: *Idiot's Delight*. Licensed for Her Majesty's Theatre, October 1937.

26   See LCP CORR: *Living Newspaper No. 2*: *Crisis* WB (1938). The script was updated daily for its private performances.

27   See LCP CORR: 1939/2614: *Moonshine*. Licensed for Hengrove Hall, Knowle, Bristol, March 1939.

28   See LCP CORR: *Leave it to Me* LR (1939).

29   See LCP CORR: 1939/2762: *An Englishman's Home*. The adaptation of Du Maurier's original script was licensed for the Wimbledon Theatre in April 1939. The original script had been licensed for Wyndham's Theatre in December 1908. For discussion of the censorship and circumstances surrounding that production, see Steve Nicholson, *The Censorship of British Theatre 1900–1968: Volume I* (Exeter: University of Exeter Press, 2003), pp. 36–38.

30   See LCP CORR: 1934/12705: *Mountjoy*. Licensed for the Lauriston Hall, Edinburgh, January 1934.

31   See LCP CORR: 1934/12851: *Nothing in his Life*. Licensed for Feldman's Playhouse, Blackpool, March 1934.

32   See LCP CORR: 1935/14457: *Easter*. It was licensed with changes for Battersea Town Hall in December 1935. The play itself is discussed in more detail in Steve Nicholson, 'Montagu Slater and Theatre of the Thirties', in Patrick Quinn (ed.), *Re-Charting the Thirties* (London: Associated University Presses, 1996), pp. 201–220.

33   See LCP CORR: *Parnell* LR (1934). Having been already performed in Ireland, the play was to have been staged at the Shilling Theatre, Fulham.

34   *The Times*, 29 April 1936, p. 15.

35   See LCP CORR: 1936/15298: *Parnell*. The play was licensed for the New Theatre.

36   See RA LC/GEN/512/35: 'Mr St John Ervine's Letter as to Consent of Relatives in the Case of Biographical Plays'.

37   See LCP CORR: 1933/12484: *Within the Gates*. Licensed for the Royalty Theatre, December 1933.

38   See LCP CORR: 1935/13937 and 1935/14399: *Public Saviour Number One*. Licensed for the Prince of Wales's Theatre, Birmingham, in June 1935. Amendments agreed after

discussing the play with religious authorities included replacing 'The Last Supper' with 'The Final Meal'.

39 See LCP CORR: 1934/13391: *In Darkness—Light*. Licensed for the Cripplegate Theatre, December 1934.

40 See LCP CORR: *Congress in Switzerland* LR (1934). Savoir's script was adapted by Baron Henri d'Erlanger.

41 See LCP CORR: *A Strange Case Of Miss Sippy* LR (1934), and LCP CORR: *The Needle's Eye* LR (1935).

42 See LCP CORR: 1934/12718: *The Bride*. Licensed for the Strand Theatre, March 1934. The title was one of the changes made.

43 See LCP CORR: *The Faith Seller* LR (1934). The play was to have been produced at the Embassy Theatre.

44 See LCP CORR: *The Sickness of Salome* LR (1936). The play was revised and resubmitted in the same year as *Variation on a Given Theme*, but was turned down again.

45 See LCP CORR: 1937/538: *The Great Atonement*. Licensed for the Savoy Cinema, Lincoln, July 1937.

46 See LCP CORR: 1937/887: *The Birth Of Christmas*. Licensed for the Spa Rooms, Harrogate, November 1937.

47 See obituaries of Dearmer in *The Times*, 20 August 1996, p. 17a and the *Guardian* 20 August 1996, I, 16:1. Dearmer's first volume of poetry was published in 1918: Geoffrey Dearmer, *Poems* (London: William Heinemann, 1918). Most of the poems in this collection—the first of several—were to do with the war. One, 'The Turkish Trench Dog', appeared subsequently in a number of anthologies.

48 See LCP CORR: 1937/982: *Spug*. Licensed for the Century Theatre, W. 11, December 1937. An endorsement on the licence did indeed require that the Reverend Fluke 'must not be portrayed in such a manner as to give offence to the Church-going public'.

49 Dearmer was writing in September 1938. See LCP CORR: *He Himself* LR (1938).

50 See LCP CORR: 1938/1864: *The Unknown Artist*. Licensed for the Millicent Fawcett Hall, London, October 1938.

51 See LCP CORR: 1939/2479: *The Voice of Love*. Licensed for Maltby Parish Hall.

52 See LCP CORR: *He Himself* LR (1938).

53 See LCP CORR: 1938/1159: *The Love of Judas*. Licensed for the Coltismore Hall, Nottingham, February 1938.

54 See LCP CORR: *The Trial Of Father Diamond* LR (1935). The author was the founder and general secretary of the Scottish Protestant League.

55 See LCP CORR: 1939/2844: *Family Portrait*. The play was licensed for His Majesty's Theatre in September 1939, but it is not clear whether it was actually produced at this time.

56 See Mowat, *Britain Between the Wars*, pp. 532–533.

57 See LCP CORR: *Mr Gladstone* LR (1937).

58 Willson Disher, 'The Throne is the Censor', p. 56.

59 Richards, 'Do We Need a Censor?', p. 137.

60 See LCP CORR: 1933/12106: *Clear All Wires*. Licensed for the Garrick Theatre, London, May 1933.

61 See LCP CORR: *Tsar Lénine* WB (1933).

62 LCP CORR: *Queen Victoria* WB (1937).

63 See LCP CORR: 1934/13009: *Ramsgate Historical Pageant*. Licensed for Ellington Park, Ramsgate, April 1934.

64 See RA LC/GEN/512/35: 'Representation of Their Majesties in a Pageant at Wigan'.

65 See LCP CORR: *Vickie* LR (1935).

66 See RA LC/GEN/512/35: 'The Lord Chamberlain's Letter to Mr Sidney Carroll re. an Article Dealing with Impersonation of Queen Victoria on the Stage'.

67 See LCP CORR: *Four Ducks on a Pond* LR (1934).

68 See LCP CORR: 1936/15022: *Bitter Harvest*.

69 The decision was reported in *The Times*, 3 December 1936, p. 14. See also LCP CORR: 1936/15576: *Victoria Regina*. Housman's play was licensed for the Lyric Theatre, June 1937.

70 See the *Daily Herald*, 29 January 1937, p. 6.

71 Letter from Cromer to Housman, 19 August 1937. See LCP CORR: 1937/576: *Queen's Ministers*. Licensed for the Playhouse in Street, August 1937.

72 The script was submitted by St James's Theatre on 3 December 1936.

73 See LCP CORR: 1936/15576: *Victoria Regina*.

74 Letter of 3 July 1937. See LCP CORR: 1936/15576: *Victoria Regina*.

75 See LCP CORR: *Queen Victoria* WB (1937). It is not completely clear why Parker's script was not licensed and remained in the Lord Chamberlain's Waiting Box.

76 Letter of 19 August 1937. See LCP CORR: 1937/576: *Queen's Ministers*.

77 See LCP CORR: 1937/671: *Vickie*. Licensed for the Alexandra Theatre in Birmingham, September 1937. See also *Vickie* LR (1935).

78 See LCP CORR: 1937/547: *Victoria, Queen and Empress*. The play was originally submitted under the title *Empress*, and was also known as *Gentlemen, the Queen!*. Although originally intended for the Malvern Festival, the production was delayed by the requirement to obtain the permission of individuals whose relations appeared or were referred to in the script. It was licensed for performance at Birmingham Repertory Theatre in September 1937.

79 See LCP CORR: 1937/579: *Vickie and Albert*. This revised version of one of the scripts by de Reyes was licensed for the Theatre Royal, Brighton, July 1937.

80 See LCP CORR: 1936/1096: *These Mortals*. Licensed for Sheffield YMCA, January 1938.

81 See LCP CORR: 1937/802: *Holiday on Olympus*. Licensed for Streatham Hall, November 1937.

82 See LCP CORR: 1937/128: *Les Majeste*. Licensed for Birmingham Repertory Theatre, March 1937.

83 See LCP CORR: *Heart's Beloved* WB (1938). The play was to have been licensed for Richmond Theatre.

84 See LCP CORR: *This Happy Breed*. Submitted in July 1939, Coward's play was licensed for Manchester Opera House in September.

85 See LCP CORR: 1937/991: *Musical Mixture No. 3*. Licensed for the Boscombe Hippodrome, December 1937.

86 See LCP CORR: 1939/3080: *Let's Face It*. Licensed for the Chanticleer, November 1939.

87 See LCP CORR: *Babes in the Wood* LR (1939). The licence was sought for the Prince of Wales Baths, St Pancras.

88 See LCP CORR: 1939/2844: *Family Portrait*.

89 See LCP CORR: 1937/633: *Bring Me My Bow*.

Chapter 5

1 See LCP CORR: 1945/6092: *I Set a Snare*. Written by W. Grantham Parker, the script was licensed for the Queens Hall, Manchester, March 1945.

2 The ruling was officially issued by the Lord Privy Seal on 3 September 1939. See, for example, *The Times*, 4 September 1939, p. 10.

3 Letter from Gordon to Game, 18 September 1939. RA LC/GEN/344/39: 'Enquiry by Mr Game <u>re</u> employment during the War'.

4 Editorial: 'Soldiers, Plays and Players', *The Times*, 13 September 1939, p. 7.

5 *The Times*, 7 September 1939, p. 7.

6 *The Times* was quoting the words of Dean Hole, a high churchman who had died in 1904. See *The Times*, 4 September 1939, p. 6.

7 Shaw's letter to *The Times*, 5 September 1939, p. 6.

8 Letter from Basil Dean to *The Times*, 5 September 1939, p. 6.

9 Letter to *The Times*, 11 September 1939 p. 4.

10 Editorial in *The Times*, 7 September 1939, p. 7.

11 *The Times*, 18 September 1939 p. 4.

12 L.J. Collins, *Theatre at War, 1914–1918* (Basingstoke: Macmillan, 1998).

13 Basil Dean, *The Theatre at War* (London: George G. Harrap & Co. Ltd, 1956), p. 46.

14 See Angus Calder, *The People's War* (London: Jonathan Cape, 1969), p. 372.

15 See Colin Chambers, *The Story of Unity Theatre* (London: Lawrence and Wishart, 1989), p. 203. Those identified by Chambers as having strong pre-war connections to Unity and who worked with the ABCA production group were Jack Lindsay, Ted Willis and André Van Gyseghem; Living Newspapers were an important Unity influence on the group's work.

16 See John S. Harris, *Government Patronage of the Arts in Great Britain* (London and Chicago: The University of Chicago Press, 1970), p. 28, and Calder, *The People's War*, p. 372.

17 See Nicholson, *British Theatre and the Red Peri*, chapter six, pp. 118–132.

18 Editorial: 'The Exemplary Theatre', *The Times*, 2 July 1943, p. 5. The article cited revivals of Congreve, Turgenev, Ibsen and Shaw amongst a range of other plays.

19 Editorial: 'Shakespeare on the Screen', *The Times*, 1 December 1944, p. 5.

20 Cited in Harris, *Government Patronage of the Arts in Great Britain*, p. 20. See also *Parliamentary Debates (Official Report), Volume 378, House of Commons, 12 March 1942* (London: HMSO, 1942), columns 1178–1179.

21 See Chambers, *The Story of Unity Theatre*, pp. 197–203. Chambers also suggests that Unity's 'Mobile Group' received some bookings from the army groups who were 'fed up with what ENSA . . . was offering'.

22 See Nicholson, *British Theatre and the Red Peril*, pp. 128–133.

23 *The Times*, 7 September 1939, p. 7.

24 See LCP CORR: 1939/3085 and 1940/3638: *Black Velvet*. The revue was first licensed for Brighton Hippodrome in November 1939. A touring version was licensed for the Bradford Alhambra in August 1940.

25 See LCP CORR: 1939/3088 and 1940/3260: *We'll Be There*. The revue was originally licensed for the Queen's Theatre, Poplar, in November 1939, and a revised version was approved for the South London Palace in January 1940.

26 See LCP CORR: 1940/3680: *Revudeville No. 138* . Licensed for the Windmill Theatre, October 1940.

27 See LCP CORR: 1941/3954 and 1941/4007: *Fun and Games*. The original script was licensed for the Palace Theatre, Manchester in July 1941, and a revised version was approved for the Prince's Theatre, London in September of the same year.

28 See LCP CORR: 1941/4125: *Favourites of the Air*. Licensed for the Boscombe Hippodrome, December 1941.

29 See LCP CORR: 1943/4703: *Downfall*. Licensed for the King's Theatre, Edinburgh, March 1943.

30 See LCP CORR: 1940/3356: *Van Damm's Revue No. 1*. Licensed for the Garrick Theatre, London, March 1940.

31 See LCP CORR: 1940/3462: *Tres Joli*. Licensed for the Birmingham Empire, April 1940. The title was later changed to *Kiss the Girls*.

32 See LCP CORR: *Cats and Dogs* LR (1941).

33 See LCP CORR: 1941/3923: *Exeunt the Dictators*. Licensed for the Playhouse in Henley on Thames in the summer of 1941.

34 See LCP CORR: 1942/4455: *Murder Without Crime*. Licensed for the Q Theatre, Kew, July 1942. The title was changed in the same month to *To Fit the Crime*.

35 Letter written by Game, 15 March 1940. See RA LC/GEN/512/39: 'Confidential letter to the Lord Chamberlain from Sir Ian Malcolm regarding a Play entitled *Jersey Lily*'.

36 See LCP CORR: 1939/3085: *Black Velvet*.

37 See *The Times*, 20 August 1940 p. 2 and Calder, *The People's War*, p. 134.

38 See Calder, *The People's War*, p. 245.

39 See Calder, *The People's War*, pp. 246–247. The *Daily Worker* remained banned for eighteen months.

40 See LCP CORR: 1940/3231: *Children Calling*. Licensed for the Kingsway Theatre, January 1940.
41 See LCP CORR: 1940/3511: *Requiem*. Licensed for Liverpool's David Lewis Theatre, May 1940.
42 See LCP CORR: 1940/3655: *Freedom on Trial*. Licensed for Beaver Hall, Garlick Hill, September 1940. The file contains a letter from the organisation in question, outlining its history and its aims.
43 See LCP CORR: *The Star Turns Red (3rd Act)* LR (1940).
44 See LCP CORR: *Second Helping* LR (1940).
45 See LCP CORR: *The Spectre that Haunts Europe* LR (1941). The script, and its censorship, are discussed in more detail in Nicholson, *British Theatre and the Red Peril*, pp. 114–116.
46 See LCP CORR: 1942/4243: *Comrade Enemy*. Licensed for the People's Hall, Leeds, March 1942.
47 See LCP CORR: 1942/4479: *Lift the Ban*. Licensed for the Scala Theatre, August 1942.
48 See LCP CORR: 1943/4712: *We Fight On*. Licensed for the Scala Theatre, February 1943.
49 See LCP CORR: 1942/4166: *We Are The People*. Licensed for the Q Theatre, Kew, August 1942.
50 See LCP CORR: 1941/4048: *The Morning Star*. Licensed for the Globe Theatre, October 1941.
51 See LCP CORR: 1942/4500: *London West One*. Licensed for the Q Theatre, Kew, September 1942.
52 *The Times*, 20 August 1942, p. 5.
53 Angus Calder, *The Myth of the Blitz* (London: Jonathan Cape, 1991), p. 233.
54 Arthur Marwick, *The Home Front: The British and the Second World War* (London: Thames and Hudson, 1976), p. 58.
55 Cited in Calder, *The Myth of the Blitz*, p. 130.
56 See LCP CORR: 1944/5418: *The Night of the Big Blitz*. Licensed for Glasgow Unity, April 1944.
57 See LCP CORR: 1941/4048: *The Morning Star*. Licensed for the Globe Theatre, October 1941.
58 See LCP CORR: 1942/4419: *To Dream Again*. Licensed for the Prince of Wales Theatre, Cardiff, June 1942.
59 See LCP CORR: 1942/4500: *London West One*.
60 See LCP CORR: 1944/5724: *The Road That Beckons*. Licensed for the Inverness Empire, August 1944.
61 See LCP CORR: 1942/4365: *Flightpath*. Rattigan's play was originally submitted in April 1942 under the title *Next Of Kin* but was licensed under its new title for the Apollo Theatre in August.
62 See LCP CORR: 1944/5355: *Tomorrow's Eden*. Licensed for His Majesty's Theatre, Aberdeen, March 1944. The Air Ministry complained to the Lord Chamberlain's Office in June.
63 See LCP CORR: 1942/4266: *The Admiralty Regrets*. In March, the Director of Anti-Submarine Warfare at the Admiralty informed Clarendon that he was happy with another revised version, and the play could be licensed for the New Theatre, Oxford. In June, the title of the play was changed to *Escort* (see also LCP CORR: 1942/4487: *Escort*).
64 See LCP CORR: *To Stall the Grey Rat* LR (1942); also LCP CORR: 1942/4476: *Men in Shadow*. Licensed under this latter title for the Edinburgh Lyceum, August 1942.
65 See LCP CORR: 1942/4210: *This Dreamy Waste*. Licensed for Bath Assembly Rooms.
66 See LCP CORR: *Dawn* LR (1942). Intended for the Repertory Theatre, Rutherglen.
67 'Joe Corrie Play Banned', *Glasgow Herald*, 21 November 1942, p. 4.
68 See LCP CORR: *Roly-Poly* LR (1942 and 1943).
69 See LCP CORR: 1943/5119: *That Freedom*. Licensed for the Old Mill Theatre in Buckfast, November 1943.

70 See LCP CORR: 1944/5330: *The Bowl of Night*. Licensed for Hulme Hippodrome, February 1944.

71 'LIFE Breaks all the Rules of ART', *Evening Standard*, 24 March 1945, p. 6.

72 See LCP CORR: 1945/6012: *The Assassin*.

73 See LCP CORR: *Roly-Poly* LR (1942 and 1943).

74 See LCP CORR: 1944/5524: *Showtime*. The revue had been licensed for the Garrick Theatre, Southport, in April 1944, and the complaint from the Bristol clergyman came in September.

75 See LCP CORR: 1945/5998: *Beyond the Mountain*. Licensed for the Bath Pump Room, January 1945.

76 LCP CORR: 1945/6184: *Jacobowsky And The Colonel*. Licensed for the Wimbledon Theatre, April 1945.

77 See LCP CORR: *Sweet Liberty* LR (1945) and 1948/9386. The revised version was licensed for Highbury Little Theatre, Sutton Coldfield.

78 See Calder, *The People's War*, pp. 502–506.

79 Malcolm Smith, *Britain and 1940: History, Myth and Popular Memory* (London: Routledge, 2000), p. 29.

80 See Calder, *The People's War*, pp. 501–502.

81 See Imelda Whelehan and Deborah Cartmell, 'Through a Painted Curtain: Laurence Olivier's *Henry V*', in Pat Kirkham and David Thoms (eds), *War Culture: Social Change and Changing Experience in World War Two Britain* (London: Lawrence and Wishart, 1995), pp. 49–60.

82 See Calder, *The People's War*, p. 508.

Chapter 6

1 Herbert Morrison. See: RA LC/GEN/440/40: 'Minutes of Proceedings of the Lord Chamberlain's Stage Conference held at St James's Palace on Tuesday, 16th April, 1940'.

2 For all correspondence cited here, see RA LC/GEN/512/39: 'Letter from the Public Morality Council with Reports of their Stage Plays Committee, and Lord Clarendon's Reply, giving Aspects and Principles of the Censorship'.

3 Press announcement, October 1939. See RA LC/GEN/512/40: 'Correspondence with Mr Louis Casson Regarding 1) Police Action over Revues in the Provinces, 2) Inclusion of Sketches, 3) Licensing of Road Shows'.

4 Report by Game, 18 July 1940. See LCP CORR: 1940/3280: *Band Waggon*. The revue, the cast of which included Max Wall, had been licensed for the Swansea Empire in February 1940.

5 See RA LC/GEN/512/39: 'Correspondence with the Home Office (Mr. G. F. Porter) re Performances at the Prince of Wales and Windmill Theatres'.

6 See LCP CORR: 1939/3085: *Black Velvet*.

7 See LCP CORR: 1940/3245: *Revudeville No. 130*. Licensed for the Windmill Theatre, January 1940.

8 See LCP CORR: 1940/3209: *Revue des Allies*. Licensed for the Prince of Wales Theatre, January 1940.

9 See LCP CORR: 1940/3292: *Nature on Parade*. Originally licensed for the Theatre Royal, Barnsley, February 1940.

10 Mr Reginald Stamp, Chairman of the LCC Entertainments Licensing Committee, speaking at the Lord Chamberlain's Stage Conference in 1940. See RA LC/GEN/440/40: 'Minutes of Proceedings of the Lord Chamberlain's Stage Conference . . .'.

11 See RA LC/GEN/512/40: 'Correspondence from Mr George Black on Question of Interpolation, in Plays or Revues, of Gags or Business not Previously Approved by the Lord Chamberlain'.

12 See LCP CORR: 1940/3303: *Eve Takes a Bow*. Originally licensed for the Sheffield Empire, February 1940.

13 See LCP CORR: 1940/3356: *Van Damm's Revue No. 1*. Licensed for the Garrick Theatre, London, March 1940.

14 'Showgirl's [sic] Want more Clothes', *Daily Mail*, 21 February 1940, p. 7.

15 *Daily Telegraph*, 5 April 1940, p. 6.

16 Quotations from letters published in the *Daily Telegraph*, 27 March 1940, p. 6; 29 March 1940, p. 6; 1 April 1940, p. 6; 2 April 1940, p. 6; 3 April 1940, p. 6; 4 April 1940, p. 6; 13 April 1940, p. 6; 16 April 1940, p. 6.

17 See RA LC/GEN/512/40: 'Minutes at the Home Office 7th [sic] March and Conference at St James's Palace on 16th April to discuss Nudity, Bawdiness of Jokes, etc. on the Stage'.

18 *Daily Mail*, 16 April 1940, p. 7.

19 By the late 1950s, the Office had accepted 'some rather arbitrary rules' defining nudity, even though they hardly included the possibility that a man could also be nude. In answer to an enquiry, the Assistant Comptroller in 1958 would reveal that

> 'his Lordship treats as nude any female whether otherwise clothed or not,
> 1. Who exposes the nipples
> 2. Whose breasts are largely uncovered and not firmly supported
> 3. Who exposes the region at the base of the trunk'.

See RA LC/GEN/440/58: 'Mr Beament of Cambridge University asks for Definition of Term "Nude"'. However, no such working definition seems to have existed in 1940.

20 See, for example, *Daily Mail*, 17 April 1940, p. 5.

21 *Daily Mail*, 17 April 1940, p. 5

22 See LCP CORR: 1940/3453: *The Daring 1940s*. Licensed for the Birmingham Empire, April 1940.

23 See LCP CORR: 1940/3465: *International Showboat*. Licensed for the Alexandra, Stoke Newington, April 1940.

24 See LCP CORR: 1940/3468 and 1940/3591: *Nuit des Femmes*. The original version was licensed in April 1940 for the Regal in Southend and a revised version in July for the Southampton Hippodrome.

25 1940 Annual Report of the Public Morality Council, p. 7.

26 See RA LC/GEN/512/40: 'Letter from Mr. George Black re. Nudity on the Stage and the Comptroller's Reply'.

27 See LCP CORR: 1940/3280: *Band Waggon*.

28 See LCP CORR: 1940/3631: *Ladies Be Good*. Licensed for the Southampton Hippodrome, August 1940.

29 See RA LC/GEN/512/40: 'The Lord Chamberlain's Ruling Regarding Nudes'.

30 See RA LC/GEN/512/42: 'Information Given To Detective Sergeant Johnson, Hampshire County Police, re Road Shows, Nudity, etc.'.

31 See LCP CORR: 1942/4597: *Revudeville No. 159*. Licensed for the Windmill Theatre, November 1942.

32 See LCP CORR: 1944/5482: *Revudeville No. 173*. Licensed for the Windmill Theatre, April 1944.

33 See RA LC/GEN/512/42: 'Information Given To Detective Sergeant Johnson . . . '.

34 See: RA LC/GEN/440/40: 'Minutes of Proceedings of the Lord Chamberlain's Stage Conference . . . '.

35 See RA LC/GEN/512/40: 'The Lord Chamberlain's Ruling Regarding Nudes'. Game was looking at photographs for a revue: *Barnacle Bill the Sailor*.

36 See LCP CORR: 1941/3958: *Revudeville No. 146*. Licensed for the Windmill Theatre, August 1941.

37 See RA LC/GEN/512/40: 'The Lord Chamberlain's Ruling Regarding Nudes'. Again, Game was responding to *Barnacle Bill the Sailor*.

38 See LCP CORR: 1941/3958: *Revudeville No. 146*. Licensed for the Windmill Theatre, August 1941.

39   See RA LC/GEN/512/40: 'Correspondence with Home Secretary Regarding Bottle Parties. Also reporting Proceedings taken under Theatres Act'.

40   See LCP CORR: 1940/3285 and 1940/3470: *Strip Strip Hooray*. Licensed for the Theatre Royal, Castleford, February 1940, and in a revised version for the Theatre Royal, Oldham, April 1940.

41   See LCP CORR: 1940/3680: *Revudeville No. 138*. Licensed for the Windmill Theatre, October 1940.

42   See LCP CORR: 1941/3838: *Revudeville No. 143*. Licensed for the Windmill Theatre, April 1941.

43   See LCP CORR: 1941/3801: *Revudeville No. 142*. Licensed for the Windmill Theatre, March 1941.

44   See RA LC/GEN/512/40: 'The Lord Chamberlain's Ruling Regarding Nudes'.

45   See LCP CORR: 1942/4565: *Venus Comes to Town*. Originally licensed for the Whitehall Theatre, October 1942.

46   See LCP CORR: 1944/5723: *Revudeville No. 177*. Licensed for the Windmill Theatre, August 1944.

47   See RA LC/GEN/512/52: 'Meetings with London County Council on Subject of Exploitation of Nudity on the Stage'.

48   RA LC/GEN/512/52: 'Meetings with London County Council on Subject of Exploitation of Nudity on the Stage'.

49   See RA LC/GEN/440/43: 'Letter from Mr. L. Casson re "Burlesque" Strip-Tease Acts, and Reply thereto'.

50   See LCP CORR: 1943/4809: *Revudeville No. 163*. Licensed for the Windmill Theatre, April 1943.

51   See LCP CORR: 1945/6030: *Revudeville No. 181*. Licensed for the Windmill Theatre, February 1945.

52   See LCP CORR: 1945/6102: *Revudeville No. 182*. Licensed for the Windmill Theatre, March 1945.

53   *Parliamentary Debates (Official Report), Volume 378, House of Commons, 12 March 1942*, columns 1177–1778.

54   See Philip Purser and Jenny Wilkes, *The One and Only Phyllis Dixey* (London: Futura Publications, 1978), pp. 56-58.

55   Purser and Wilkes, *The One and Only Phyllis Dixey*, p. 60.

56   Purser and Wilkes, *The One and Only Phyllis Dixey*, p. 62.

57   See RA LC/GEN/512/42: 'Letter to Licensees of Theatres re. Improprieties in Stage Performances'.

58   Purser and Wilkes, *The One and Only Phyllis Dixey*, p. 65.

59   Purser and Wilkes, *The One and Only Phyllis Dixey*, p. 57.

60   See LCP CORR: 1941/3958: *Revudeville No. 146*. Licensed for the Windmill Theatre, August 1941.

61   See LCP CORR: 1943/5194: *Goodnight Ladies*. Licensed for the Whitehall Theatre, December 1943.

62   See LCP CORR: 1941/3958: *Revudeville No. 146*.

63   See LCP CORR: 1943/5194: *Goodnight Ladies*.

64   See LCP CORR: 1941/3958: *Revudeville No. 146*.

65   See LCP CORR: 1941/4089: *Revudeville No. 149*. Licensed for the Windmill Theatre, November 1941.

66   See RA LC/GEN/512/42: 'Letters from Mr. L.J. Dod, Mr. V.A. Malcolmson, Mrs. Whitting, and Public Morality Council, re (a) Nudity, and (b) Vulgarity'.

Chapter 7

1   From 'The Showing Up of Freedom of Expression', submitted as a prologue to *Genius Limited* by W.W. Blair-Fish. See LCP CORR: 1945/6120: *Genius Limited*. Licensed for Amersham Theatre, March 1945.

2   Letter from Gordon to Clarendon, 7 February 1940, and memorandum recording a meeting at the Home Office on 6 March 1940. See RA LC/GEN/512/40: 'Minutes at the Home Office 7th [sic] March and Conference at St James's Palace on 16th April to discuss Nudity, Bawdiness of Jokes, etc. on the Stage'.

3   See LCP CORR: *Queer People* LR (1940).

4   See RA LC/GEN/440/40: 'Torch Theatre, 37, Wilton Place. Visit to Test Bona Fides of Private Nature'.

5   See LCP CORR: 1940/3389: *Temporary Residence*. Licensed for the Q Theatre, Kew, March 1940. Title changed in April to *Devil's Sanctuary*.

6   See LCP CORR: 1940/3697: *A Woman of Forty*. Original version refused a licence in October 1940; revised script licensed for the Apollo Theatre, December 1940.

7   Written by Game, 23 April 1940. See RA LC/GEN/512/40: 'A request from Mr Maurice Browne for Removal of Ban on Playing *La Prisonniere* Cannot be Entertained'.

8   See LCP CORR: *Flower of Grass* LR (1941). Licence rejected in May 1941.

9   See LCP CORR: 1942/4503: *No Pansies for Mr Standish* (filed as *No . . . for Mr Standish*). Licensed for Rhyl Pavilion, September 1942. The title made implicit reference to a recent novel which had shocked many, *No Orchids for Miss Blandish*.

10   See LCP CORR: *Husbands Can't Help It* LR (1943). A revised version was eventually licensed for the Whitehall Theatre in April 1949 (see also LCP CORR: 1949/7048: *Husbands Can't Help It*).

11   See LCP CORR: 1943/4673: *Striplings*. Licensed for the Q Theatre, Kew, January 1943.

12   See LCP CORR: 1943/4864: *Baltic Passage*. The revised version was first performed at the Westminster Theatre in May 1943.

13   See LCP CORR: 1944/5770: *Judgement and the Sifers*. Licensed for the Borough Hall, Godalming, November 1944.

14   See LCP CORR: *Marry-Go-Round* LR (1940).

15   See LCP CORR: *Strange Sport* LR (1940).

16   See LCP CORR: *Lysistrata to Date* LR (1942).

17   See LCP CORR: 1943/4785: *The Infernal Machine*. Licensed for the Cambridge Arts Theatre, April 1943.

18   See LCP CORR: *The Simoun* LR (1942). Adapted by Edward Stirling, the play was to have been staged at the Playhouse Theatre.

19   Letter written by Nugent, 17 May 1939. See RA LC/GEN/512/39: 'Letter from the Office of Works re. Proposed Production of *Pericles* at the Open Air Theatre'.

20   Letters of 1 April 1940 and 4 April 1940. See RA LC/GEN/512/40: 'Correspondence with Theatrical Managers' Association re. Proposed Production, at Cambridge, of Seventeenth Century play *'Tis Pity She's A Whore*'.

21   Titman's comments of 29 January 1941, Clarendon's undated. See RA LC/GEN/512/41: 'Correspondence re. Two Special Performances of *'Tis Pity She's A Whore*'.

22   See Nicholson, *The Censorship of British Drama 1900-1968: Volume One*, pp. 117–133.

23   *The Times*, 31 July 1942, p. 6.

24   See LCP CORR: 1942/4286 and 1942/4368: *No Orchids for Miss Blandish*. The original script was licensed for the Grand Theatre, Blackpool in April 1942. A separate touring version was licensed for Brighton Hippodrome in August 1943 (see LCP CORR: 1943/5005).

25   See LCP CORR: *Early American Murder* LR (1942).

26   See LCP CORR: *Frankie and Johnnie* LR (1942). The intended production was for the Q theatre.

27   See LCP CORR: 1943/4683: *The Fifth Column*. Licensed for the Vaudeville Theatre, November 1943.

28   See LCP CORR: *Wallflowers* LR (1944).

29   See LCP CORR: 1943/5280: *Skirts*. Licensed for the Grand Theatre, Blackpool, December 1943.

30   See LCP CORR: *Seven Houses* LR (1941). The play was eventually licensed in a revised version as *Patricia's Seven Houses* for the Granville Theatre in April 1946.

31 See LCP CORR: 1943/4936: *A Soldier for Christmas*. Licensed for the Arts Theatre, Cambridge, June 1943.

32 See LCP CORR: *Felicity Jasmine* LR (1944). The script was originally licensed (1944/5645) for the Theatre Royal, Brighton in June 1944. The licence was officially withdrawn on 25 September 1944.

33 See LCP CORR: 1944/5736: *Ladies Like Them Bad*. Licensed for the Theatre Royal, Brighton, October 1944. At the start of November, the title was altered to *Gather No Moss*.

34 As discussed in Nicholson, *The Censorship of British Drama 1900–1968: Volume One*, pp. 130–131.

35 See LCP CORR: 1943/4669: *Damaged Goods*. The script was re-licensed for the Empire Theatre, Leeds, in January 1943.

36 Meanwhile, in July, following a letter of complaint from an upset parent and a threat from solicitors, Clarendon was effectively obliged to intervene and persuade the company to remove a line in which a doctor stated that a child with a harelip was evidence of syphilis in the parents.

37 See LCP CORR: *Fear* LR (1943).

38 See LCP CORR: 1943/5112: *Out of the Blitz*. Licensed for Greenwich Hippodrome, October 1943.

39 See LCP CORR: *The Great Void* WB (1943).

40 See 'Moore Raymond's Entertainment Page', *Sunday Dispatch*, 21 January 1940, p. 12.

41 Letters of 15 January 1940 and 17 January 1940. See RA LC/GEN/512/40: 'As to Use of Word "Bloody"'.

42 See 'Moore Raymond's Entertainment Page'.

43 Letter from Gordon to Clarendon, 7 February 1940. See RA LC/GEN/512/40: 'Minutes at the Home Office 7th [sic] March and Conference at St James's Palace on 16th April to discuss Nudity, Bawdiness of Jokes, etc. on the Stage'

44 See RA LC/GEN/440/40: 'Minutes of Proceedings of the Lord Chamberlain's Stage Conference held at St James's Palace, London, S.W. 1. on Tuesday, 16th April, 1940'.

45 Correspondence between Moss Empires and Gordon, March and April 1940. See RA LC/GEN/512/40: 'Correspondence from Mr George Black on Questions of Interpolation, in Plays or Revues, of Gags or Business not Previously Approved by the Lord Chamberlain'.

46 Correspondence between the Association of Touring and Producing Managers and Gordon, May to July 1940. See RA LC/GEN/512/40: 'Correspondence with Mr Louis Casson Regarding 1) Police Action over Revues in the Provinces, 2) Inclusion of Sketches, 3) Licensing of Road Shows'.

47 RA LC/GEN/512/40: 'Correspondence with Mr Louis Casson Regarding 1) Police Action over Revues in the Provinces, 2) Inclusion of Sketches, 3) Licensing of Road Shows'.

48 See LCP CORR: 1941/3762: *Nineteen Naughty One*.

49 See LCP CORR: 1941/:3907: *There'll Always Be an England*. Licensed for the New Theatre, Crewe, July 1941.

50 The lines are cited by the Public Morality Council in a letter to the Lord Chamberlain, 22 January 1942. See LCP CORR: 1941/4121: *Gangway*. The script was licensed for the London Palladium, December 1941.

51 See LCP CORR: 1943/4870: *The Air Force*. Licensed for the Chelsea Palace, June 1943.

52 See RA LC/GEN/512/44: 'Confidential Correspondence with Public Control Department, LCC, re. Appearance of Max Miller at an Entertainment at Windsor Castle'.

53 See LCP CORR: *Marry-Go-Round* LR (1940).

54 See LCP CORR: 1945/6120: *Genius Limited*.

55 LCP CORR: 1945/6120: *Genius Limited*. From 'The Showing Up of Freedom of Expression', submitted as prologue to *Genius Limited* by W.W. Blair-Fish.

Chapter 8

1 *Parliamentary Debates (Official Report), Volume 463, House of Commons, 25 March 1949* (London: HMSO, 1949), columns 775–776.
2 See RA LC/GEN/344/48: 'Examiner of Plays. As to Mr. H.C. Game's retirement'.
3 See RA LC/GEN/310/46: 'Advisory Board. New Names Added'.
4 See the report and the leader column in *The Times*, 9 February 1948 pp. 2 & 5.
5 *Stage*, 19 February 1948 p. 4.
6 See Chapter Seven of this volume for discussion of *Felicity Jasmine* and Chapter Eleven for *Mr Lincoln Meets a Lady.*
7 RA LC/GEN/512/45: 'Issues Raised in the House of Commons about the Censorship'.
8 Letter from Smith to Morrison dated 8 January 1945. RA LC/GEN/512/45: 'Issues Raised in the House of Commons about the Censorship'.
9 RA LC/GEN/440/48: 'Attorney General Enquires Regarding Miss Dixey's Act and who in the House of Commons is Responsible for Answering Questions Concerning the Stage'.
10 On 4 March 1948. See RA LC/GEN/440/48: 'Powers of Local Authorities to require alterations in stage plays licensed by the Lord Chamberlain'.
11 See RA LC/GEN/440/48: 'Powers of Local Authorities to require alterations in stage plays licensed by the Lord Chamberlain'.
12 See RA LC/GEN/49: 'Parliamentary Bill proposing the abolition of Stage Censorship'.
13 Letter from the Home Office to Titman, 12 February 1949. RA LC/GEN/49: 'Parliamentary Bill proposing the abolition of Stage Censorship'.
14 Letter from Nugent to Captain Malcolm Bullock, 3 March 1949. RA LC/GEN/49: 'Parliamentary Bill proposing the abolition of Stage Censorship'.
15 Undated and unsigned document, probably written by Hill to Titman. RA LC/GEN/49: 'Parliamentary Bill proposing the abolition of Stage Censorship'.
16 Letter from Hill to the Assistant Comptroller, 21 February 1949. RA LC/GEN/49: 'Parliamentary Bill proposing the abolition of Stage Censorship'.
17 RA LC/GEN/49: 'Parliamentary Bill proposing the abolition of Stage Censorship'.
18 RA LC/GEN/49: 'Parliamentary Bill proposing the abolition of Stage Censorship'.
19 Letter from Warren Chetham-Strode to *The Times*, published 5 April 1949, p. 5.
20 *Stage*, 3 March 1949, p. 5.
21 See Smith's speech proposing the Censorship of Plays (Repeal) Bill. *Parliamentary Debates (Official Report), Volume 463, House of Commons, 25 March 1949*, column 717, and for all subsequent quotations here, see columns 713–796.
22 See letter from Clarendon to the Home Secretary, 3 March 1949. RA LC/GEN/49: 'Parliamentary Bill Proposing the Abolition of Stage Censorship'.
23 *Parliamentary Debates (Official Report), Volume 463*.
24 See the *People*, 3 April 1949, p. 2; *Daily Mirror*, 26 March 1949, p. 3; *Tribune*, 1 April 1949, p. 4.
25 Charles Graves, 'Earl with a Blue Pencil', *John Bull*, 7 May 1949, pp. 9 & 14.
26 Letters published in *The Times*, 28 March 1949, p. 5; 31 March 1949, p. 5; 1 April 1949, p. 5; 5 April 1949, p. 5.
27 *Stage*, 19 May 1949, p. 8.
28 Letter sent by the Theatres National Committee to the Home Office and the Lord Chamberlain's Office, 9 March 1949. See RA LC/GEN/49: 'Parliamentary Bill proposing the Abolition of Stage Censorship'.
29 Letter from Gwatkin, 2 February 1949. See RA LC/GEN/440/48: 'Experimental Theatre Manchester informed regarding private performances'.
30 Anon., 'Theatre Clubs and the Law', *New Statesman and Nation*, 3 November 1951, p. 484.
31 Memorandum by Hill, 15 November 1951. See RA LC/GEN/440/51: 'An Article and Comments on the Current Standing of The Private Theatre—Especially as Regards the Practice of "Affiliated Membership"'.

Chapter 9

1 Letter from Gwatkin, 13 November 1950, responding to one of several complaint from members of the public about a bedroom scene and a reference to 'handsome tits' in Anouilh's *Points of Departure*. See LCP CORR: 1950/1992: *Points of Departure*. The play had been licensed for the Theatre Royal, Brighton, in October 1950.

2 See LCP CORR: 1945/6565: *The Celibate*. Licensed for the Granville Theatre, Walham Green, October 1945.

3 Extracts from the manuscript of *The Celibate* by Frederick Witney. See LCP 1945/31.

4 See LCP CORR: 1945/6565: *The Celibate*.

5 See LCP CORR: 1946/7013: *Patricia's Seven Houses*. Licensed for the Granville Theatre in April 1946, in a version revised by L.B. Pierson. An earlier version under the title *Seven Houses* had been refused a licence in 1941. See above, Chapter Seven.

6 See the review of the production in *The Times*, 12 April 1946, p. 12.

7 See LCP CORR: *Maya* LR (1929).

8 See LCP CORR: *Maya* WB (1946).

9 See LCP CORR: 1947/ 7906: *The Respectable Prostitute*. Licensed for the County Theatre, Bangor, May 1947.

10 See LCP CORR: 1947/8011: *Heloise*. Licensed for the Welfare Hall, Blackwood, April 1947.

11 See LCP CORR: *Le Petit Hutte*. WB (1948). The plan was apparently for the text to be adapted from the French by Emlyn Williams .

12 See LCP CORR: *Modernity* LR (1949).

13 See LCP CORR: *The House of Shame* LR (1950). Another revised version was eventually licensed for the Palace Court at Bournemouth in February 1953 (see LCP CORR: 1953/5240: *The House of Shame*). The play seems to have gone through a series of title changes, including *Lady of the House*, *Women of Sin*, *The Call Girl Racket* and *Women of the Streets*.

14 See LCP CORR: *Sex for Sale* LR (1950).

15 See LCP CORR: *Woman of the Streets* LR (1950) . A revised version was licensed for the Dolphin, Brighton, in May 1951, under the title *This Way But Once*. See LCP CORR: 1951/2873. In June, the title was altered to *City of Sin*.

16 See LCP CORR: *Street Girl* LR (1950).

17 See LCP CORR: *Naked Lady* LR (1950).

18 Memorandum written by Hill, 8 June 1951. See RA LC/GEN/440/51: 'Letter from Home Office and Other Notes on Unsavoury Theatre Advertising'.

19 See LCP CORR: 1946/7032: *Revudeville No. 193*. Licensed for the Windmill Theatre, April 1946.

20 1948 Annual Report of the Public Morality Council, pp. 7–8 & 13. Also quoted in newspaper reports, e.g. *Evening News*, 29 April 1949, p. 5.

21 See LCP CORR: 1949/397: *Revudeville No. 221*. Licensed for the Windmill Theatre, April 1949.

22 See RA LC/GEN/440/51: 'Letter from Home Office and Other Notes on Unsavoury Theatre Advertising'.

23 Paper dated 4 June 1951. See RA LC/GEN/512/52: 'Meetings with London County Council on Subject of Exploitation of Nudity on the Stage'.

24 Undated paper by Hill. RA LC/GEN/512/52: 'Meetings with London County Council on Subject of Exploitation of Nudity on the Stage'.

25 Titman's paper dated 9 August 1951. RA LC/GEN/512/52: 'Meetings with London County Council on Subject of Exploitation of Nudity on the Stage'.

26 RA LC/GEN/512/52: 'Meetings with London County Council on Subject of Exploitation of Nudity on the Stage'.

27 Reported by Nugent, 17 July 1952. RA LC/GEN/512/52: 'Meetings with London County Council on Subject of Exploitation of Nudity on the Stage'.

28 See LCP CORR: 1952/4074: *Revudeville No. 248*. Licensed for the Windmill Theatre, April 1952.

29   See RA LC/GEN/440/52: 'Mr Pollard a Solicitor Advised as to Rules Governing Nude
      Representations on the Stage'.
30   Letter dated 7 February 1951. See RA LC/GEN/512/51: 'Deputation Regarding Stage
      Play *The Children's Hour*. Theme of Lesbianism. See also 512/46'.
31   See LCP CORR: 1949/273 and 1951/2624: *Folies Bergère*. First licensed for Birmingham
      Hippodrome, March 1949. In March 1952, the title was changed to *C'est la Folie*.
32   Memorandum written by Hill on the subject of 'unsavoury advertising', 8 June 1951.
      See RA LC/GEN/440/51: 'Letter from Home Office and Other Notes on Unsavoury
      Theatre Advertising'.
33   The original letter was sent out by Gwatkin on 3 July 1951, and the subsequent
      comment comparing the responses of the two theatres is dated 20 July 1951. See RA
      LC/GEN/440/51: 'More Complaints Against the Advertising of the London
      Hippodrome and London Casino'.
34   Gwatkin's letter dated 27 January 1950. See RA LC/GEN/512/50: 'Miss Penwarden
      Complains of Oaths in Plays'.

Chapter 10

1   RA LC/GEN/512/51: 'Deputation Regarding Stage Play *The Children's Hour*: Theme of
      Lesbianism. See also 512/46'.
2   LCP CORR: 1945/6276: *Boys Will Be Girls*. Licensed for the Oldham Empire, May
      1945. At various times the show went under the title of *Meet the Boys* and *Soldiers in
      Skirts*, and a revised version was licensed for the Grand, Blackpool, in January 1946 (See
      LCP CORR: 1946/6791).
3   LCP CORR: 1947/7870: *Get In for Laughter*. Also known as *Get In*, the script was
      licensed for the Bolton Grand in March 1947.
4   Correspondence of November 1953. See RA LC/GEN/440/53: 'Complaint that Actors
      in All Male Shows are Perverts, Captain Gray'.
5   LCP CORR: 1945/6512: *Girls Out of Uniform*. Licensed for the Metropolitan Theatre,
      October 1945.
6   See RA LC/GEN/440/46: 'Legal Opinion as to the Lord Chamberlain's Powers to Issue
      a Stage Play Licence to a Particular Theatre for a Specified Period Only'.
7   LCP CORR: *Outrageous Fortune* LR (1945).
8   LCP CORR: *Surface* LR (1945).
9   LCP CORR: 1945/6523: *A Man About the House*. Licensed for the Grand Theatre,
      Derby, October 1945.
10   See RA LC/GEN/440/46: 'Legal Opinion as to the Lord Chamberlain's Powers to Issue
      a Stage Play Licence . . .'.
11   Letter from Beaumont to Gwatkin, 11 March 1946. See LCP CORR: 1964/4458: *The
      Children's Hour*. Hellman's play was eventually licensed in 1964 for performance at the
      Guildhall School of Music and Drama.
12   Letter dated 27 February 1946. See RA LC/GEN/512/51: 'Deputation Regarding Stage
      Play *The Children's Hour* . . .'.
13   RA LC/GEN/512/51: 'Deputation Regarding Stage Play *The Children's Hour* . . .'.
14   See RA LC/GEN/440/46: 'Legal Opinion as to the Lord Chamberlain's Powers to Issue
      a Stage Play Licence . . .'.
15   See RA LC/GEN/512/51: 'Deputation Regarding Stage Play *The Children's Hour* . . .'.
16   See RA LC/GEN/440/46: 'Legal Opinion as to the Lord Chamberlain's Powers to Issue
      a Stage Play Licence . . .'.
17   See RA LC/GEN/440/46: 'Legal Opinion as to the Lord Chamberlain's Powers to Issue
      a Stage Play Licence . . .'.
18   All correspondence March to May 1946. See LCP CORR: 1964/4458: *The Children's
      Hour*.
19   Game's report of December 1945. See LCP CORR: *Huis Close* LR (1945). The play was
      licensed as *In Camera* in 1959 (LCP CORR: 1959/1888), and also as *Huis Clos*: 1959/522.
20   Heriot's report of 4 August 1946. LCP CORR: *Huis Clos* 1959/522.

21 Letter from Gwatkin, 3 July 1947. LCP CORR: *Huis Clos* 1959/522.
22 See LCP CORR: 1946/7206: *But For The Grace Of God*. Licensed for the Edinburgh Lyceum, June 1946.
23 See LCP CORR: 1950/2022: *Atalanta*. Licensed for the Lowestoft Playhouse, October 1950.
24 See LCP CORR: *Oscar Wilde* LR (1946).
25 See LCP CORR: 1947/7860: '*Now Barabbas . . .*'. Licensed for the Vaudeville Theatre, March 1947.
26 See *Sunday Times*, 18 May 1947, p. 2, and *Evening Standard*, 21 March 1947, p. 9.
27 See LCP CORR: 1947/8274: *Baffled Spring*. Licensed for Northampton Repertory Theatre, July 1947.
28 See LCP CORR: 1947/8511: *The Shadow of Our Night*. Licensed for the Theatre Royal, Aldershot, December 1947.
29 See *Sunday Times*, 1 February 1948, p. 2, and *Evening Standard*, 9 April 1948, p. 6. The play was licensed in December 1947 and produced by the Mask Theatre. It opened at the Bolton's Theatre before transferring to the Fortune. The playwright was himself a teacher in a boys' school.
30 See LCP CORR: 1947/8738: *The Hidden Years*.
31 See LCP CORR: *The Gingerbread House* WB (1948). The play was first submitted for licence in December 1947.
32 See LCP CORR: 1948/9686: *The Miraculous Miss Mann*. Licensed for the Q Theatre, Kew, December 1948.
33 Extract taken from unpublished manuscript. See LCP 1949/56 *Seagulls over Sorrento*.
34 See LCP CORR: 1949/929 and 1950/1388: *Seagulls over Sorrento*. The play was first licensed for the Globe Theatre in December 1949, and in its revised version for the same theatre in April 1950.
35 See LCP CORR: 1949/388 and 1950/2044: *A Streetcar Named Desire*. Licensed for the Globe Theatre in April 1949, and again in October 1950.
36 See LCP CORR: *Hiatus* LR (1950).
37 See LCP CORR: *Ostrich Eggs* LR (1951).
38 See LCP CORR: *Third Person* LR (1951), and LCP CORR: 1951/ 3375: *Third Person*. Licensed for the Criterion Theatre, January 1952.
39 See LCP CORR: *The Lonely Heart* LR (1951).
40 See LCP CORR: *White Terror* LR (1952), and LCP CORR: *Two Loves I Have* LR (1952).
41 See *Daily Telegraph*, 6 November 1950, p. 6, and *News Chronicle*, 10 November 1950, p. 4. Presumably the book referred to by the *Telegraph* was Peter Cotes's *No Star Nonsense*, which had been published in 1949.
42 See *Daily Mail*, 22 November 1950 p. 5, and *Evening Standard*, 24 November 1950 p. 9.
43 See LCP CORR: 1964/4458: *The Children's Hour*.
44 See, for example, Freshwater, 'Suppressed Desire', pp. 310–318, citing Lynda Hart, 'Canonizing Lesbians', in June Schlueter (ed.), *Modern American Drama: The Female Canon* (Toronto: Associated University Presses, 1990).
45 Quotations from minutes of meeting held at St James's Palace, 2 February 1951. See RA LC/GEN/512/51: 'Deputation Regarding Stage Play *The Children's Hour . . .*'.
46 Letter sent out on 6 February 1951. RA LC/GEN/512/51: 'Deputation Regarding Stage Play *The Children's Hour . . .*'.
47 See Kenneth Walker, *Sex and a Changing Civilisation* (London: John Lane, the Bodley Head, 1935); and *Sex Difficulties in the Male* (London: Jonathan Cape, 1934), both in *passim*. An earlier version of the latter book was originally published in 1930 as *Male Disorders of Sex*.
48 See RA LC/GEN/512/51: 'Deputation Regarding Stage Play *The Children's Hour . . .*'.
49 Letter to Carroll dated 16 February 1951. RA LC/GEN/512/51: 'Deputation Regarding Stage Play *The Children's Hour . . .*'.
50 Letter from Nugent, 11 January 1952. See RA LC/GEN/440/52: 'Statement of Policy for Mr Street, Senior Lecturer in Law, Manchester University'.

51 Letter from Gwatkin, 9 July 1952. See RA LC/GEN/512/52: 'A Film Involving a Theme of Lesbianism Passed by the BBFC'.

Chapter 11

1 Mr K. Lindsay, MP, speaking in the parliamentary debate on the Repeal of Theatre Censorship bill, 25 March 1949. See *Parliamentary Debates (Official Report), Volume 463, House of Commons* (London: HMSO, 1949), 25 March 1949, column 772.

2 House of Commons Debate, 'Censorship of Plays (Repeal) Bill'. See *Parliamentary Debates (Official Report), Volume 463, House of Commons, 25 March 1949*, columns 771–772.

3 See LCP CORR: 1945/6304: *Blimpton Won't Budge*. Licensed for the Playhouse, Amersham, June 1945.

4 See LCP CORR: *The Star Turns Red (3rd Act)* LR (1940).

5 See LCP CORR: 1946/7144 and 1948/8957: *The Gorbals Story*. Licensed for Glasgow Athenaeum in May/June 1946, and in a revised version for the Garrick Theatre in February 1948.

6 See LCP CORR: 1949/637: *The Jolly George*. Licensed for Unity Theatre and the Congregational Church Hall, Harrow, July/August 1949. (Author misidentified in Lord Chamberlain's files as Tod Willis.)

7 See RA LC/GEN/512/45: 'Issues Raised in the House of Commons about the Censorship'.

8 See the Reader's report. LCP CORR: *Mr Lincoln Meets a Lady* LR (1944). Also, RA LC/GEN/512/45: 'Issues Raised in the House of Commons about the Censorship'.

9 See LCP CORR: *Birthday Bouquet* LR (1951).

10 See LCP CORR: *My Good Brown* LR (1951).

11 Writing on 17 April 1951. See LCP CORR: *Birthday Bouquet* LR (1951).

12 See LCP CORR: 1952/4436: *The Glorious Days*. Licensed for the Palace Theatre, Manchester, July 1952.

13 See LCP CORR: 1953/6045: *At the Lyric*. Licensed for the Cambridge Arts Theatre, November 1953. In May 1954, the title was changed to *Going to Town*.

14 Letters of 22 April 1948. See RA LC/GEN/440/48: 'Presentation of T.M. in a Tableau Forbidden'.

15 Letter from Gwatkin, 10 June 1952. See RA LC/GEN/440/52: 'Mr Tebbs as to his Daughter Representing the Queen at a Gymnkhana'.

16 Speech made in Newcastle on Tyne and reported in newspapers, for example *News Chronicle*, 29 April 1946, p. 3.

17 The play opened at the New Lindsey Theatre Club, under the direction of Peter Cotes, in May 1946.

18 Quotations taken from the manuscript of Elsa Shelley's *The Pick-Up Girl*. See LCP 1946/20.

19 See programme in the production file for *The Pick-Up Girl* at the Theatre Museum.

20 *Evening Standard*, 18 May 1946, p. 6.

21 See LCP CORR: 1946/7417: *The Pick-Up Girl*. The play was licensed for the Prince of Wales's Theatre.

22 See, for example, *The Times*, 27 May 1946, p. 6.

23 See *Daily Mail*, 24 July 1946, p. 3; *Daily Telegraph*, 24 July 1946, p. 5; *Sunday Express*, 28 July 1946, p. 7; *The Times*, 24 July 1946, p. 6; *Picture Post*, 10 August 1946, pp. 18–19; *Tatler and Bystander*, 14 August 1946, p. 198.

24 See House of Commons Debate, 'Censorship of Plays (Repeal) Bill'. *Parliamentary Debates (Official Report), Volume 463, House of Commons, 25 March 1949*, column 729.

25 See LCP CORR: 1946/7383: *Away From It All*. Licensed for the Embassy Theatre, September 1946.

26 See LCP CORR: 1948/9073: *Symphony in Violence*. The play was also called *Red Sky*. It was licensed for the Embassy Theatre, March 1948.

27 See LCP CORR: 1948/9174: *No Trees in the Street*. Licensed for the Liverpool Playhouse, April/May 1948.

28 See LCP CORR: 1951/2740: *Cosh Boy*. Licensed for the Embassy Theatre, April 1951; In October 1951 the title was changed to *Master Crook*. The complaint from the Oldham police was sent in April 1952.

29 See LCP CORR: 1952/4362: *Reefer Girl*. Licensed for the Theatre Royal, Oldham, June 1952. A revised version was licensed for Cleethorpes Empire in January 1953. See also the manuscripts of the script: LCP 1952/3 and 1953/1.

30 Game's report of January 1946. See LCP CORR: 1946/6835: *Frieda*. Written by Ronald Millar, the script was licensed for the Savoy Theatre in February 1946. A film version was released in the summer of 1947.

31 See Lionel Hale, 'Pint-Size Parable', *Daily Mail*, 3 May 1946, p. 3.

32 See *Observer*, 6 May 1946, p. 2.

33 See *Star*, 7 November 1946, p. 6.

34 See LCP CORR: 1946/6835: *Frieda*.

35 See LCP CORR: 1947/8392: *Little Holiday* and 1948//8911. Licensed for Windsor Theatre, October 1947. A revised version was licensed for the King's Theatre, Glasgow, February 1948.

36 Extracts taken from the manuscript of *Little Holiday*: LCP 1947/33 and 1948/7.

37 See Kenneth O. Morgan, *The People's Peace: British History 1945–1990* (Oxford: Oxford University Press, 1990), pp. 49–50.

38 See manuscript versions of *Little Holiday*: LCP 1947/33 and 1948/7

39 See LCP CORR: 1947/8392: *Little Holiday* and 1948//8911.

40 Unfortunately, the files contain no copy of the original script to allow a close examination of alterations which were made. All quotations here, other than where specified, are taken from the revised and licensed script.

41 See LCP CORR: 1947/8627: *Professor Mamlock*. The licence was issued for the Dolphin Theatre, Brighton, in December 1947. The submitted script credited the adaptation to Joan Littlewood.

42 See, for example, *The Times*, 7 March 1950, p. 6; 9 March 1950, p. 6; and 13 March 1950, p. 4.

43 From a leader in *Natal Mercury*, quoted in *The Times*, 9 March 1950, p. 6.

44 See LCP CORR: *The Baker's Daughter* LR (1951). Application for licence submitted on behalf of the Spa Theatre, Bridlington.

45 Letter sent from the Commonwealth Relations Office on 4 September 1950. LCP CORR: *The Baker's Daughter* LR (1951).

46 Reported in several newspapers, including *Daily Mail* and *Daily Herald* on 9 September 1950.

47 LCP CORR: 1947/7798: *Follow Me Around*. Licensed for the Bedford Theatre, Camden Town, February 1947.

48 See LCP CORR: 1948/9816: *What's Jane Doing Today*. Licensed for the Boscombe Hippodrome, December 1948.

49 See LCP CORR: 1950/1264: *An Old Man at a Wheel*. Licensed for the Institute, Fleet, February 1950.

50 See LCP CORR: 1952/4099: *Red Herring*. Licensed for the Civic Theatre, Bedford, September 1952. Although first submitted in 1949, it was not until 1952 that a theatre was found in which to stage the play.

51 See LCP CORR: 1952/3752: *The Hungry God*. Licensed for the Q Theatre, Kew, January 1952.

52 See LCP CORR: 1952/4019: *A Muse of Fire*. Licensed for the Swindon Playhouse, March 1952.

53 See LCP CORR: 1949/9971: *The Long Goodbye*. Licensed for the Lyric, Glasgow, January 1949.

54 See LCP CORR: 1949/473: *Death of a Salesman*. Licensed for the Phoenix Theatre, July 1949.

55 See LCP CORR: 1945/6349: *Myself a Stranger*. Licensed for the Embassy Theatre, July 1945.

56 See LCP CORR: 1946/7460: *Chicago*. Licensed for the Hartley Hall, Mill Hill, October 1946.

57 See LCP CORR: 1947/8234: *Dragnet for Demos*. Licensed for the Glasgow Athenaeum, December 1947.

58 See LCP CORR: 1947/8443: *According to Law*. Licensed for Edmonton Town Hall, October 1947.

59 See LCP CORR: 1952/4488: *The Trouble Makers*. Licensed for the Theatre Royal, Brighton, August 1952.

60 See LCP CORR: 1952/4396: *The Shrike*. Licensed for the Theatre Royal, Brighton, December 1952.

61 See LCP CORR: 1952/4462: *The Travellers*. Licensed for the Oddfellows Hall, Edinburgh, July 1952.

62 See LCP CORR: 1948/9091: *The Van Winkles*. Licensed for the De La Ware Pavilion, Bexhill on Sea, March 1948.

Afterword

1 From a letter sent by the Assistant Comptroller. See RA LC/GEN/512/52: 'A Film Involving a Theme of Lesbianism Passed by the BBFC'.

2 'Mrs Tanqueray's New Look', *The Times*, 9 May 1953, p. 7.

3 See RA LC/GEN/512/51: 'Deputation regarding stage play *The Children's Hour*: Theme of Lesbianism. See also 512/46'.

4 See LCP CORR: 1946/7281: *Shabby Tiger*. Licensed for the Theatre Royal, Halifax, July 1946.

5 See RA LC/GEN/49: 'Parliamentary Bill Proposing the Abolition of Stage Censorship'.

6 Letter from Troubridge, 11 August 1951. See RA LC/GEN/344/52: 'Mr Game to retire as from 12th March 1952. Appointment of Sir St Vincent Troubridge 1/4/52'.

Select Bibliography

Archival Material

The Lord Chamberlain's Correspondence Files (Manuscript Room, British Library).

Lord Chamberlain's Office Files (Royal Archive, Windsor).

The Lord Chamberlain's Collection of Licensed Plays 1900–1968 (Manuscript Room, British Library).

The Lord Chamberlain's Daybooks (Manuscript Room, British Library).

Annual Reports of the Public Morality Council.

Production Files (Theatre Museum).

Government And Parliamentary Reports

Hansard's Parliamentary Debates.

Parliamentary Debates (Official Report), Volume 378, House of Commons, 12 March 1942 (London: HMSO, 1942), columns 1177–1778.

Parliamentary Debates (Official Report), Volume 463, House of Commons, Session 1948–1949, 5th series, 21 March 1949–14 April 1949 (London: HMSO, 1949), columns 713–796.

Books, Articles and Unpublished Dissertations

N.B. Playscripts which are referred to in the text, even when these were published are *not* included in this list.

Anonymous, 'Theatre and Cinema: The Censor Holds his Hand', *Truth*, 20 January 1937, p.95.

Anonymous, 'Theatre Clubs and the Law', *New Statesman and Nation*, 3 November 1951, p. 484.

Barker, Clive, and Gale, Maggie, (eds), *British Theatre Between the Wars, 1918–1939* (Cambridge: Cambridge University Press, 2000).

Calder, Angus, *The Myth of the Blitz* (London: Jonathan Cape, 1991).

Calder, Angus, *The People's War* (London: Jonathan Cape, 1969).

Chambers, Colin, *The Story of Unity Theatre* (London: Lawrence and Wishart, 1989).

Chandos, John, pseud. [John Lithgow Chandos MacConnell], *To Deprave and Corrupt: Original Studies in the Nature and Definition of Obscenity* (London: Souvenir Press, 1962).

Childs, David, *Britain Since 1945: A Political History* (London: Routledge, 1997).

Chothia, Jean, *English Drama of the Early Modern Period, 1890–1940* (London: Longman, 1996)

Collins, L.J., *Theatre at War, 1914–1918* (Basingstoke: Macmillan, 1998).

Conolly, L.W., *The Censorship of English Drama 1737–1824* (San Marino, California: Huntington Library, 1976).

Cotes, Peter [Sydney Boulting], *No Star Nonsense* (London: Rockliff Publishing Corporation, 1949).

Curtin, Kaier, *'We Can Always Call them Bulgarians': The Emergence of Lesbians and Gay Men on the American Stage* (Boston: Alyson Publications, 1987).

Davies, Andrew, *Other Theatres: The Development of Alternative and Experimental Theatre in Britain* (London: Macmillan, 1987).

Dean, Basil *The Theatre at War* (London: George G. Harrap & Co., 1956).

Dearmer, Geoffrey, *Poems* (London: William Heinemann, 1918).

de Jongh, Nicholas, *Not in Front of the Audience: Homosexuality on Stage* (London: Routledge, 1992).

de Jongh, Nicholas, *Politics, Prudery and Perversions: The Censoring of the English Stage 1901–1968* (London: Methuen, 2000).

Etienne, Anne, 'Les Coulisses de Lord Chamberlain: La Censure Théâtrale de 1900 à 1968', unpublished Ph.D. dissertation, L'Université d'Orleans, 1999.

Findlater, Richard, *Banned!: A Review of Theatrical Censorship in Britain* (London: MacGibbon & Kee, 1967).

Florance, John Allan, 'Theatrical Censorship in Britain 1901–1968', Unpublished Ph.D. dissertation, University of Wales, 1980.

Freshwater, Helen, 'Suppressed Desire: Inscriptions of Lesbianism in the British Theatre of the 1930s', *New Theatre Quarterly*, 17:4, November 2001, pp. 310–318.

Godfrey, Philip, *Back-Stage: A Survey of the Contemporary English Theatre from Behind the Scenes* (London: Harrap, 1933).

Graves, Charles, 'Earl with a Blue Pencil', *John Bull*, 7 May 1949, pp. 9 & 14.

Griffith, Hubert, 'The Censor as Nazi Apologist', *New Statesman and Nation*, 14 April 1934, p. 545.

Harris, John S., *Government Patronage of the Arts in Great Britain* (London and Chicago: The University of Chicago Press, 1970).

Houchin, John, *Censorship of the American Theatre in the Twentieth Century* (Cambridge: Cambridge University Press, 2003).

Housman, Laurence, *The Unexpected Years* (London: Jonathan Cape, 1937).

Johnston, John, *The Lord Chamberlain's Blue Pencil* (London: Hodder & Stoughton, 1990).

Kirkham, Pat, and Thoms, David, *War Culture: Social Change and Changing Experience in World War Two Britain* (London: Lawrence and Wishart, 1995).

Knowles Dorothy, *The Censor, the Drama and the Film* (London: Allen & Unwin, 1934).

Lawrence, D.H., *Sex, Literature and Censorship*, edited by Harry T. Moore (London: Heinemann, 1955).

Marwick, Arthur, *The Home Front: The British and the Second World War* (London: Thames and Hudson, 1976).

Morgan, Kenneth O., *The People's Peace: British History 1945–1990*. (London: Oxford University Press, 1990).

Mowat, Charles Loch, *Britain Between the Wars, 1918–1940* (London: Methuen, 1955).

Nicholson, Steve, *British Theatre and the Red Peril: The Portrayal of Communism 1917–1945* (Exeter: University of Exeter Press, 1999).

Nicholson, Steve, *The Censorship of British Drama 1900–1968: Volume One: 1900–1932* (Exeter: University of Exeter Press, 2000).

Nicholson, Steve, '"Irritating Tricks": Aesthetic Experimentation and Political Theatre', in Keith Williams and Steven Matthews (ed.), *Rewriting the Thirties: Modernism and After* (London: Longman, 1997), pp. 147–162.

Nicholson, Steve, 'Montagu Slater and Theatre of the Thirties', in Patrick Quinn (ed.), *Re-Charting the Thirties*. (London: Associated University Presses, 1996), pp. 201–220.

O'Higgins, Paul, *Censorship in Britain*. (London: Nelson, 1972).

Purser, Philip, and Wilkes, Jenny, *The One and Only Phyllis Dixey* (London: Futura Publications, 1978).

Richards, Horace, 'Do We Need a Censor?', *Theatre World*, March 1932, p. 137.

Selford, Jack, 'Censorship', *New Theatre*, 2, September 1939, pp. 14–15.

Shellard, Dominic, (ed.), *British Theatre in the 1950s* (Sheffield: Sheffield Academic Press, 2000).

Shellard, Dominic, *British Theatre since the War* (New Haven: Yale University Press, 2000).

Shellard, Dominic, Nicholson, Steve, and Handley, Miriam, *The Lord Chamberlain Regrets* (London: British Library Publications, 2004).

Smith, Malcolm, *Britain and 1940: History, Myth and Popular Memory* (London: Routledge, 2000).

Stephens, John Russell, *The Censorship of English Drama 1824–1901* (Cambridge: Cambridge University Press, 1980).

Swaffer, Hannen, 'Open Letter to the Bishop of London', *John Bull*, 22 December 1934, p. 10.

Travis, Allen, *Bound and Gagged: A Secret History of Obscenity in Britain* (London: Profile Books Ltd., 2000).

Van Damm, Vivian, *Tonight and Every Night: The Windmill Story* (London: Stanley Paul and Co., 1952).

Van Druten, John, 'Sex and Censorship in the Theatre', in Norman Haine (ed.), *World League for Sexual Reform: Proceedings of the Third Congress* (London: Kegan Paul, Trench, Trubener & Co. Ltd., 1930), pp. 317–322.

Walker, Kenneth, *Sex Difficulties in the Male*, (London: Jonathan Cape, 1934).

Walker, Kenneth, *Sex and a Changing Civilisation* (London: John Lane, The Bodley Head, 1935).

Wearing, J.P., *The London Stage 1930–1939: A Calendar of Plays and Players*, 3 volumes (London: Scarecrow Press, 1990).

Wearing, J.P., *The London Stage 1940–1949: A Calendar of Plays and Players*, 2 volumes (London: Scarecrow Press, 1991).

Wearing, J.P., *The London Stage 1950–1959: A Calendar of Plays and Players*, 2 volumes (London: Scarecrow Press, 1993).

Willson Disher, M. 'The Throne is the Censor', *Theatre World*, 27:145, February 1937, p. 56.

Young, Eugene J., *Looking Behind the Censorship* (London: Lovat Dickson, 1938).

Newspapers

The following have been particularly and frequently valuable sources:

Daily Mail.
Daily Telegraph.
New Statesman.
Stage.
The Times.

Index